shakespeare
and his sources

shakespeare
and his sources

JOSEPH SATIN

Midwestern University, Wichita Falls, Texas

HOUGHTON MIFFLIN COMPANY · BOSTON

New York · Atlanta
Geneva, Ill. · Dallas · Palo Alto

for SELMA,

a sourcey wench

Acknowledgments

My grateful thanks to my colleagues Bettye and David Smith for help with texts and to Laurence McNamee for tips on arcanal sources; to Paul Vagt and Millie Richards for opening many library doors; to Pam Amrhein, Judy Watts, and Krispen Young for tireless typing; to Midwestern University for a summer research grant that speeded progress; and to Thomas D. Wittenberg of Houghton Mifflin Company for genially showing me how all's well that ends well.

Copyright © 1966 by Joseph Satin.

CONTENTS

Othello

King Lear

Macbeth

Antony and Cleopatra

PREFACE

The aim of this book is to bring together the sources for thirteen of Shakespeare's plays, with modernized texts of the English sources and fresh translations of the foreign language ones. The versions of the sources used here are directed at the Shakespeare student, beginning or advanced, as well as at the general reader receptive to the excitements of finding landmarks on a clearly marked terrain. The modernized texts should yield fresh enjoyment of the sources' genuine merit, rather than becloud the pleasure of reading them with the archaisms of labored spelling and syntax. The Holinshed-More account, for example, of the death of Anne, wife of Richard III; Plutarch's account of the characters of Brutus and Cassius; and the Countess of Pembroke's version of Cleopatra's farewell to Antony, when presented in language easily understood, are rich in intrinsic value.

The uses which Shakespeare makes of his sources are as varied as the facets of his plays, although the most obvious use — plot — overrides all others. Of Shakespeare's thirty-seven plays only two, *Love's Labor's Lost* and *The Merry Wives of Windsor,* can boast original plots, although ever-widening studies of Shakespeare sources indicate that even these two owe much to subordinate sources, perhaps even derive from central ones yet undiscovered. Of the thirty-five other plays, the plots of at least twenty-seven derive from central sources, *i.e.,* sources which supply the general outlines of Shakespeare's main plot; and all of them owe something to subordinate sources, *i.e.,* sources which contribute shards of plot, situation, character, or statement. Of the thirteen plays dealt with in this book, the plots of twelve derive from central sources. This is in part deliberate choosing, because central sources give the student more substance to work with, and because the plays selected for study are among Shakespeare's major works — in itself pregnant commentary on the role that central sources play in Shakespeare's art.

While Shakespeare, like most playwrights of his day, almost always turns to central sources for the main plots of his greater plays, his handling of those sources is never routine; it is as various as the turns of plot itself. Sometimes Shakespeare follows right in the tracks of his central source, as in *Richard III* and *Henry IV, Part One.* More often he selects and compresses, as in his handling of Holinshed in *Richard II* and *Henry IV, Part Two* and of North's *Plutarch* in *Antony and*

Cleopatra. Sometimes he follows his source faithfully up to a point where, by veering away, plot becomes illumination, as in *Othello* and *King Lear*, in which the original endings have been neatly trimmed and reversed respectively. In *Macbeth* he fits disparate segments of Holinshed together into a seamless unit, while in *Hamlet* he offers perhaps the best example of shaping a fragment into a whole.

Often Shakespeare complicates the plot line of his central source by graftings from subordinate sources: the ending of *Thomas of Woodstock*, for example, enriches Shakespeare's motivation for the overthrow of Richard II; and Appian's *History* suggests Antony's "Friends, Romans, countrymen" speech and its focal position in Shakespeare's plot. Sometimes subordinate sources provide Shakespeare with a subplot, or at least with the gist of it: *The Famous Victories of Henry V* suggests the Falstaff subplot of *Henry IV, Part One*, and to a lesser extent of *Part Two*; *Gl'Ingannati* foreshadows several incidents as well as the tone and mood of *Twelfth Night*; the Gloucester subplot of *King Lear* is taken almost intact from Sidney's *Arcadia*. Thus with central and subordinate sources Shakespeare develops variety in techniques of plotting. He shapes his sources with increasing skill, as seen by his handling of Holinshed for *Richard III* and *Richard II*; his imaginative handling of Holinshed for *Macbeth*; and the ways he uses Plutarch to maximum advantage in plotting *Antony and Cleopatra.*

But Shakespeare also depends on his sources for characterization, and the transformation of characters is one of the miracles in his work. His favorite sources, Holinshed and Plutarch, offer him his most consistently vivid models. Holinshed's kings and Plutarch's illustrious men have a life of their own, and several of them rival Shakespeare's creations: Holinshed-More's Richard III, for example, and Holinshed's Henry IV and Henry V; and Plutarch's Julius Caesar, Brutus, and Antony, and his Cleopatra, Cassius, and Octavius. Some of the characters in other sources are drawn well enough to offer challenge: Clemenzia and Gherardo in *Gl'Ingannati*, the lovers in Masuccio's novella, Macbeth in the *Rerum Scoticarum Historia* of Buchanan, Gonorill and Ragan in *The True Chronicle History of King Leir*. Other of the characters in the sources are refashioned in such a way so that only a trait or two will be carried over in the adaptation: the ensign in Cinthio's novella, Lancaster in *Thomas of Woodstock*, Giannetto in Fiorentino's novella, the Thief in *The Famous Victories of Henry V.*

To be sure, Shakespeare's general sensibility — what he knew and encountered and read — contributed more to his language and ideas than did any central or subordinate sources. Still, Shakespeare sometimes paraphrases whole passages from his sources and at other times uses language parallel, tangential, or contrasting to the original. Footnote references in the text help to connect the gaps between Shakespeare's language and that of his sources, but naturally not all the nuances of Shakespeare-source correspondences can be footnoted. But all the major derivations and enough of the minor shadings are pointed out to give the reader a fair sense of where Shakespeare's indebtedness to his sources begins and ends. The line references are based on those of the Globe edition. In cases where comparable Shakespeare passages run to the end of a scene, ff. is used to so indicate: *i.e.*, I.ii. 41ff. means that Shakespeare's borrowing from this particular source passage runs from line 41 to the end of scene ii.

Shakespeare's most frequently consulted sources for seminal ideas are Holinshed and Plutarch. Holinshed's concept of kingship — the king as God's vicar on earth, not to be deposed by mortal man — reflected a standard Renaissance view understandably dear to the Tudor monarchs, and to Queen Elizabeth especially. Shakespeare's use of this idea in *Richard II* and in *Henry IV, Parts One and Two*, owed reinforcement, if not its origin, to Holinshed. Plutarch's handling of omens parallels Shakespeare's in *Julius Caesar*; and his discussion of *Amimetobion*, "incomparable, unmatchable love," becomes one of the informing forces of *Antony and Cleopatra*. Less seminal are the ideas of melancholy in de Belleforest's "Amleth" and of appearance determining character in Cinthio's novella.

While the creative spirit instinctively opposes mechanical aids, this book *is* a mechanical aid arranged, paradoxically, to stimulate creative insights. The ultimate purpose of modernizing these sources is to make them accessible to the reader. Shakespeare valued his sources enough to adapt them, and the versions here reflect much of their original attractiveness. North's *Plutarch*, the central source of all his Roman history plays, is a serene literary translation of a profound work. Holinshed's *Chronicles*, while full of inaccuracies that lure Shakespeare into error, is consistently vivid and often charged with dramatic excitement that rivals Shakespeare, as in Hastings' intimations of his betrayal by Richard III, the final quarrel and reconciliation between Henry IV and Prince Hal, and the Battle of Agincourt. The Italian novelle that form the basis of several Shakespearean plays are rooted in the rich tradition of Boccaccio, whose own stories engender *All's Well That Ends Well* and *Cymbeline*. The Christian connotations in Cinthio's story of the Moor may well have sparked the Christian overtones of *Othello*; and the stylistic elegance of Masuccio's Fourteenth Novella invites the last act dialogue between Jessica and Lorenzo in *The Merchant of Venice*. The list could be extended to include the cloudy moralizing of de Belleforest's "Amleth," the psychological thrust of Buchanan's account of Macbeth, the pathos of the Countess of Pembroke's *Antonie,* and the ingenuity of Riche's plotting.

With the exception of *Gl'Ingannati,* the plays Shakespeare depended on were distinctly inferior as literature to his other sources. English drama was young in Shakespeare's day, still crude and fumbling. As a result, the source plays he turned to, — *The True Tragedy of Richard III, Thomas of Woodstock, The True Chronicle History of King Leir,* and *The Famous Victories of Henry the Fifth* — are slapdash and unpolished. Yet for the discerning reader even these have nuggets of value: *The True Tragedy of Richard III* compresses incidents so tightly that it communicates a sense of energy and movement caught up by Shakespeare's play; *Thomas of Woodstock* conveys, however slightly, the sense of national guilt characteristic of Richard's reign; *The True Chronicle History of King Leir,* though wordy and diffuse, does well with character types and character conflicts and at times lights up its drab and gloomy canvas with a flash of wit; and *The Famous Victories of Henry V* nurtures the seed of Falstaff.

Whatever their merits, however, the chief function of these sources is to illuminate the genius of Shakespeare. They show us how Shakespeare framed his plots, how he copied, compressed, omitted, expanded, altered, and reversed. They frequently supply prototypes for Shakespearean characters ranging from three dimensional human beings to flat stereotypes, their graded levels of achievement paralleling Shakespeare's own. And they sometimes provide passages good enough for Shakespeare to adapt in close paraphrase.

Besides those comparisons, the sources taken as a whole offer a nearly endless range of questions on the creative process. For instance, what kind of incidents does Shakespeare delete from his sources? What kinds does he add or expand? What happens when Shakespeare follows his sources in strict chronology — or when he does not? How does he use Holinshed differently from Plutarch? From Italian novelle? From earlier plays? Can one find patterns in his use of secondary sources? Does his characterization gain or lose when source characterizations are good, fair, poor? Do certain kinds of sources stimulate him to greater heights? And if we append to each of these queries the prime question "why," we begin to comprehend the genius that is Shakespeare's alone.

The headnotes to the sources sketch specific ways in which Shakespeare uses these sources for plot, characterization, and idea. By themselves they cover some basics and offer guidelines, but at the same time they leave the reader free to pursue favorite areas of comparison and analysis. Some of their exploratory suggestions, particularly about Shakespearean ideas, are calculated to challenge and to stimulate thinking about Shakespeare-source relationships in fresh and different ways. Yet, being exploratory, these headnotes do not offer detailed analyses of Shakespeare's indebtedness. For this the impressively thorough treatment of the comedies and tragedies by Kenneth Muir, *Shakespeare's Sources* (London: Methuen & Co., 1961) may profitably be consulted. Further reading in Shakespearean sources is recommended in "Some Sources for Further Study" found after each group in the text; this list is suggestive, not exhaustive, and intended for the reader interested in more probing inquiry than the limited scope of this book. For a rich collection of sources the reader would do well to consult first the monumental series by Geoffrey Bullough, *Narrative and Dramatic Sources of Shakespeare* (New York: Columbia University Press, 1957–1964, five volumes completed, the remainder in preparation).

Shakespeare's sources open up a range of possibilities that extend the uses of this book almost beyond perception, for every approach to them penetrates the special world of creativity from a new angle. The more varied the use of this book the more stimulating the challenge, because each ascent toward an understanding of how Shakespeare adapted his sources demands heightened insight on the part of the reader. Modernized texts and translations permit all of the labor with less of the drudgery. They let us view towering creative achievements across a leveled plain of common language.

Wichita Falls, Texas   Joseph Satin

• A NOTE ON THE MODERNIZED TEXTS

The texts in this volume are modernized to achieve a readable mean somewhere between the archaic spelling, syntax, and punctuation of the original and the glossy smoothness of modern writing. In the case of plays, the original punctuation is largely kept so as to retain a sense of the phrasing used in the original production. In the case of the masterful Elizabethan translation of Plutarch by Sir Thomas North, the modernization by W. W. Skeat has been used almost without alteration, since it brings the North classic forward to readability with the barest minimum of tampering with phrasing and diction.

RICHARD III

The main source of this play is Raphael Holinshed, *The Chronicles of England, Scotland, and Ireland* (the 1587 edition), the general source for all of Shakespeare's English history plays. For his history of Richard III, Holinshed varied his usual practice of adapting from several sources and instead copied almost verbatim from two successive sources. The English version of Sir Thomas More's *History of King Richard III*, 1513, provided all of his material up to Richard's coronation; the coronation was adapted from the histories of Edward Hall and Richard Grafton (see p. 71); then More's unfinished manuscript was used up to the falling out between Richard and Buckingham (p. 40); after that Holinshed relied mainly on Hall, who in turn had taken the remainder of Richard's history from the *Historia Anglica* of Polydore Vergil, 1534.

There are stylistic differences between Holinshed's usual sources, such as Hall, and Sir Thomas More that require a caveat to the modern reader. More's sentences tend to get tangled up in their own length, and he uses words in ways that glance off the periphery of modern meanings. In the present reprint spelling, punctuation, and, in some cases, syntax have been modernized as far as is consistent with fairness to the original, but many of More's passages still require a special effort for comprehension. The more characteristic Holinshed — from p. 40 on — reads easily and one can understand why he became one of Shakespeare's favorite sources. In More's defense it should be said that the style grows easier with practice, and his anecdotes and reminiscences give his biography an unrivaled sense of immediacy and life.

Richard III belonged to the House of York, in Tudor eyes the powder keg that set off the Wars of the Roses, and the accounts of him that a Tudor historian like Holinshed would favor are anti-Yorkist accounts. The most partisan and slanderous of them all was More's *History*, the basis of which was the eyewitness testimony of More's erstwhile master and tutor, Cardinal John Morton (perhaps sole or part author of the *History*), whom Richard III imprisoned and who escaped to join the revolt led by Henry VII. To cite only a couple of More's inaccuracies, his description of Richard's monstrous physical deformities appears to be largely untrue. (John Rous, who says he saw Richard, reports only that "He was of low stature, having a short face, unequal shoulders, the right being higher than the left"); and the suggestion that Richard was in any way responsible for the death of his wife, Queen Anne, is found nowhere but in More and seems to have no basis in fact. That Holinshed and Shakespeare record both of those items without blinking reflects the view that Tudor historian and Tudor dramatist may be expected to take toward Richard III.

The time covered in Shakespeare's play runs from 1471, three months after the Battle of Tewksbury, to the death of Richard in 1485, but only Act I deals with anything before 1483, and its two chief scenes, Richard's wooing of Anne and the curse of Margaret, are not in Holinshed and seem to be Shakespeare's own invention. Acts II–V trace the events of 1483–1485 in detail and closely follow historical chronology. Shakespeare includes almost everything from Holinshed's account of those years — trifles, gossip, rumors, orations, even jingles. In his later plays he will use Holinshed more selectively and deviate more freely from chronology, but here he relies so minutely on his central source that Holinshed becomes a kind of program needed to follow the play.

Another basic source for *Richard III* is *The True Tragedy of Richard III*, an anonymous play first published in 1594 in the wake of the success of *Richard III* but certainly written much earlier, as its dramatic crudeness attests. *The True Tragedy* at once supplies Shakespeare with a dramatic example to work from and jam-packs incidents from Holinshed even more tightly than Shakespeare will. The excerpts reprinted below include the Prologue, which telescopes past history into a single passage and leaves the playwright free to begin near the death of Edward IV; scene x, a tour de force of compression which contains the material of four of Shakespeare's scenes and covers in all the execution of the queen's faction at Pomfret Castle, the harangue of Dr. Shaw, Buckingham's plea at the Guild Hall for Richard to be chosen king, Hastings' arrest and execution, Richard's arrangement with Tyrrel to kill the princes, and — a bonus not in Shakespeare — the punishments decreed for Shore's wife; and scene xix, the final battle scene, whose "A horse, a horse, a fresh horse" foreshadows *Richard III* (V.iv. 7). The bare, compressed quality of *The True Tragedy* points up Shakespeare's skill even at this early stage of his career.

Richard III belongs to its namesake, who dominates the other characters like a puppet master. He is a Marlovian megalomaniac with all the one-sided intensity of the heroes of *Tamburlaine the Great, The Jew of Malta,* and *Dr. Faustus.* More calls him "a deep dissembler . . . arrogant of heart . . . despiteous and cruel," and these broad strokes of character in general comprise Shakespeare's analysis of him. Richard's victims pretty much retain the flat characterizations of their sources, except Queen Margaret, widow of Henry VI, whom Shakespeare introduces contrary to history (the real life Margaret left England in November, 1475, and died August 25, 1482). Shakespeare makes of her a Senecan prophetess of doom, and her threats and lamentations blend history with a Renaissance belief in omens. Dead before the avalanche of 1483 begins, she may represent a kind of symbol threading together the past and the world beyond.

Apart from the cloudy symbolism for Queen Margaret, there is little in the sources or in the Shakespeare play that can be termed idea. *Richard III* is at heart a melodrama which reaffirms the Tudor view that the Yorks were villains and which at most asserts such melodramatic views as Murder Will Out and Defy the Foul Fiend. Shakespeare and his sources will do better for one another in future plays.

☙ RAPHAEL HOLINSHED

The Chronicles of England, Scotland, and Ireland,* 1587

The History of King Edward the Fifth and King Richard the Third, Unfinished,

Written by Master Thomas More then one of the under sheriffs of London, about the year of our Lord 1513, according to a copy of his own hand, printed among his other works.

[1483]¹ King Edward the Fourth of that name, after that he had lived fifty and three years, seven months, and six days, and thereof reigned two and twenty years, one month, and eight days, died at Westminster the ninth day of April, the year of our Redemption, a thousand four hundred fourscore and three, leaving much fair issue: that is, to wit, Edward the prince, at thirteen years of age; Richard, Duke of York, two years younger; Elizabeth, whose fortune and grace was after to be queen wife unto King Henry the Seventh, and mother unto the Eighth; Cecily, not so fortunate as fair; Bridgit, which repre-

---

* text modernized.

¹ While Act II of Shakespeare's play begins in 1483, with Edward IV at the point of death, Act I combines events of 1483 with events of twelve previous years to form one continuous and swift-paced unit. Richard tells us in I.ii. 241–242 that he stabbed Edward, Prince of Wales and son of Henry VI, "some three months since . . . at Tewksbury," an event of the year 1471. Clarence is confined to the Tower quite early in Shakespeare's play (I.i. 42–45) though he was actually sent there in February, 1478. Despite this twelve-year span and juggling of chronology, the basis of Act I rests upon Holinshed's history of Edward V, which begins in 1483. The only noteworthy exception is the reference (I.ii 55–56) to the corpse of Henry VI bleeding afresh, a couplet probably suggested by two earlier sentences from Holinshed which read: "The dead corpse was conveyed from the Tower to the Church of St. Paul and there laid on a bier or coffin bare-faced; the same in presence of beholders did bleed. From thence he was carried to the Blackfriars and bled there likewise."

4

senting the virtue of her, whose name she bore, professed and observed a religious life in Dertford, an house of close nuns; Anne, that was after honorably married unto Thomas, then Lord Howard, and after Earl of Surrey; and Katherine, which long time tossed in either fortune, sometime in wealth, oft in adversity, at the last, if this be the last (for yet she lives) is by the benignity of her nephew, King Henry the Eighth, in very prosperous estate, and worthy her birth and virtue.

This noble prince deceased at his palace of Westminster, and with great funeral honor and heaviness of his people from thence conveyed, was interred at Windsor. A king of such governance and behavior, in time of peace (for in war each part must needs be other's enemy) that there was never any prince of this land, attaining the crown by battle, so heartily beloved with the substance of the people: nor he himself so specially in any part of his life as at the time of his death. Which favor and affection, yet after his decease, by the cruelty, mischief, and trouble of the tempestuous world that followed, highly toward him more increased. At such time as he died, the displeasure of those that bore him grudge for King Henry's sake the Sixth, whom he deposed, was well assuaged, and in effect quenched, in that many of them were dead in more than twenty years of his reign, a great part of a long life: and many of them in the mean season grown into his favor, of which he was never strange.[2]

He was a goodly personage and princely to behold, of heart courageous, politic in counsel, in adversity nothing abashed, in prosperity rather joyful than proud, in peace just and merciful, in war sharp and fierce, in the field bold and hardy, and nevertheless no further (than wisdom would) adventurous, whose wars whoso well considered, he shall no less commend his wisdom where he voided than his manhood where he vanquished. He was of visage lovely, of body mighty, strong, and clean made, howbeit, in his latter days with over liberal diet some what corpulent and boorish, and nevertheless not uncomely. He was of youth greatly given to fleshly wantoness: from which health of body, in great prosperity and fortune, without a special grace hardly refrains. . . .

[During the last part of his reign Edward IV won the people to him in a "willing and loving obedience." To understand the problems that arose after his death it must be remembered that his father Richard, Duke of York, was slain at Wakefield in revolt against Henry VI and that Richard, Duke of York, had three sons.]

---

[2] grudging, distant.

Edward [IV], revenging his father's death, deprived King Henry [VI] and attained the crown. George, Duke of Clarence, was a goodly noble prince and at all times fortunate, if either his own ambition had not set him against his brother, or the envy of his enemies his brother against him.[3] For were it by the queen and lords of her blood, which highly maligned the king's kindred (as women commonly not of malice, but of nature hate them whom their husbands love) or were a proud appetite of the duke himself, intending to be king; at the leastwise, heinous treason was there laid to his charge. [4]And finally, were he faulty, were he faultless, attainted[5] was he by Parliament, and judged to the death, and thereupon hastily drowned in a butt of malmsey. Whose death King Edward (albeit he commanded it) when he wist it was done, pitiously bewailed, and sorrowfully repented.

Richard, the third son, of whom we now intreat, was in wit and courage equal with either of them, in body and prowess far under them both;[6] little of stature, ill featured of limbs, crookbacked, his left shoulder much higher than his right, hard favored of visage, and such as is in states called warly,[7] in other men otherwise; he was malicious, wrathful, envious, and from afore his birth ever froward. [8]It is for truth reported, that the duchess his mother had so much ado in her travail, that she could not be delivered of him uncut; and that he came into the world with the feet forward, as men be born outward; and (as the fame runs also) not untoothed, whether men of hatred report above the truth, or else that nature changed her course in his beginning, which in the course of his life many things unnaturally committed. So that the full confluence of these qualities, with the defects of favor and amiable proportion, gave proof to this rule of physiognomy:

Distortum vultum sequitur distorsio morum.[9]

[10]No evil captain was he in the war, as to which his disposition was more meet than for peace. Sundry victories had he, and sometimes overthrows, but never on default as for his own person, either of hardiness or politic order. Free was he called of dispense, and some-

---

[3] A suggested cause of the breach between Clarence and Edward was that Clarence wanted to marry Mary, daughter and heir of the Duke of Burgundy, but Edward opposed this match, hoping to obtain Mary for his brother-in-law, Lord Rivers.

[4] I.iv. 276–277.

[5] convicted.

[6] I.i. 14–23; I.iii. 228–246.

[7] bellicose.

[8] IV.iv. 162–174.

[9] A distortion of nature follows a distorted countenance.

[10] I.i. 5–15.

what above his power liberal. With large gifts he got him unsteadfast friendship, for which he was fain to pill and spoil in other places, and got him steadfast hatred. He was close and secret, a deep dissembler, lowly of countenance, arrogant of heart, outwardly companiable where he inwardly hated, not letting[11] to kiss whom he thought to kill: despiteous and cruel, not for evil will always, but oftener for ambition, and either for the surety or increase of his estate.[12]

Friend and foe was muchwhat indifferent, where his advantage grew; he spared no man's death whose life withstood his purpose. He slew with his own hands King Henry the Sixth, being prisoner in the Tower, as men constantly said, and that without commandment or knowledge of the king, which would undoubtedly (if he had intended that thing) have appointed that butcherly office to some other than his own born brother. [13]Some wise men also ween[14] that his drift covertly conveyed lacked not in helping forth his brother of Clarence to his death: which he resisted openly, howbeit somewhat (as men deemed) more faintly than he that were heartily minded to his wealth.

And they that thus deem think that he long time in King Edward's life forethought to be king, in case that the king his brother [15](whose life he looked that evil diet should shorten) should happen to decease (as indeed he did) while his children were young. And they deem that for this intent he was glad of his brother's death, the Duke of Clarence, whose life must needs have hindered him so intending, whether the same Duke of Clarence had kept him true to his nephew, the young king, or enterprised to be king himself. But of all this

---

[11] refraining.

[12] Reinforcing, and enriching, More's analysis of Richard is the one Holinshed (after Hall) places after his account of Richard's death, which reads: "As he was small and little of stature, so was he of body greatly deformed, the one shoulder higher than the other; his face was small, but his countenance cruel, and such that at the first aspect a man would judge it to savor and smell of malice, fraud, and deceit. When he stood musing, he would bite and chew busily his lower lip, as who said that his fierce nature in his cruel body always chafed, stirred and was ever unquiet. Besides that, the dagger which he wore he would (when he studied) with his hand pluck up and down in the sheath to the midst, never drawing it fully out. He was of a ready, pregnant, and quick wit, wily to feign and apt to dissemble. He had a proud mind and an arrogant stomach, the which accompanied him even to his death, rather choosing to suffer the same by dint of sword than, being forsaken and left helpless of his unfaithful companions, to preserve by cowardly flight such a frail and uncertain life which by malice, sickness, or condign punishment was like shortly to come to confusion."

[13] I.iii. 339ff; I.iv. 232–255. Shakespeare accuses Richard of the murder of Clarence far more openly than do Holinshed or More.

[14] conjecture.

[15] I.i. 139–140.

point is there no certainty, and whoso divines upon conjectures may as well shoot too far as too short.

Howbeit this have I by credible information learned, that the self night in which King Edward died, one Mistlebrook, long ere morning, came in great haste to the house of one Pottier dwelling in Red Cross Street, without Cripplegate. And when he was with hasty rapping quickly let in, he shewed unto Pottier that King Edward was departed. "By my troth, man," quoth Pottier, "then will my master the Duke of Gloucester be king." What cause he had so to think, hard it is to say; whether he being toward him, anything knew that he such thing proposed, or otherwise had any inkling thereof. For he was not likely to speak it of naught.

But now to return to the course of this history. Were it that the Duke of Gloucester had of old foreminded this conclusion, or was now at first there-unto moved, and put in hope by the occasion of the tender age of the young princes, his nephews (as opportunity and likelihood of speed puts a man in courage of that he never intended) certain it is that he contrived their destruction, with the usurpation of the regal dignity upon himself. [16]And forsomuch as he well wist and helped to maintain a long continued grudge and heartburning between the queen's kindred and the king's blood, either party envying other's authority, he now thought that their division should be (as it was indeed) a further beginning to the pursuit of his intent.

Nay he was resolved that the same was a sure ground for the foundation of all his building, if he might first (under the pretext of revenging of old displeasure) abuse the anger and ignorance of the one party to the destruction of the other, and then win to his purpose as many as he could; and those that could not be won might be lost ere they looked therefore.[17] For of one thing was he certain, that if his intent was perceived, he should soon have made peace between both the parties with his own blood. [18]King Edward, in his life, albeit that this dissension between his friends somewhat irked him, yet in his good health he somewhat the less regarded it; because he thought whatsoever business should fall between them, himself should always be able to rule both the parties.

But in his last sickness, when he perceived his natural strength so sore enfeebled that he despaired all recovery, then he, considering the youth of his children — albeit he nothing less mistrusted than that that happened — yet well foreseeing that many harms might grow by their debate, while the youth of his children should lack discretion

---

[16] II.i. 134ff.
[17] for that (loss).
[18] II.i. 1–133.

of themselves, and good counsel of their friends, of which either party should counsel for their own commodity, and rather by pleasant advice to win themselves favor, than by profitable advertisement to do the children good, he called some of them before him that were at variance, and in especially the Lord Marquis Dorset, the queen's son by her first husband.

So did he also William, Lord Hastings, a nobleman, then Lord Chamberlain, against whom the queen specially grudged for the great favor the king bore him: and also for that she thought him secretly familiar with the king in wanton company. Her kindred also bore him sore, as well for that the king had made him Captain of Calais, which office the Lord Rivers, brother to the queen, claimed of the king's former promise, as for divers other great gifts which he received that they looked for. When these lords, with divers others of both the parties, were come in presence, the king lifting up himself, and under-set with pillows, as it is reported, on this wise said unto them:

The oration of the King on his death-bed.

"My lords, my dear kinsmen and allies, in what plight I lie you see, and I feel. By which the less while I look to live with you, the more deeply am I moved to care in what case I leave you, for such as I leave you, such be my children like to find you. Which if they should (as God forbid) find you at variance, might hap to fall themselves at war, ere their discretion would serve to set you at peace. You see their youth, of which I reckon the only surety to rest in your concord. For it suffices not that all you love them, if each of you hate [the] other. If they were men, your faithfulness haply would suffice. But childhood must be maintained by men's authority, and slippery youth underpropped with elder counsel, which neither they can have but ye give it, nor ye give it if ye agree not. . . .

But this shall I desire you to remember, that the one part of you is of my blood, the other of mine allies, and each of you with other either of kindred or affinity — which spiritual kindred of affinity (if the sacraments of Christ's church bear that weight with us that would God they did) should no less move us to charity than the respect of fleshly consanguinity. Our Lord forbid that you love together the worse for the self cause that you ought to love the better. And yet that happens, and nowhere find we so deadly debate as among them which by nature and law most ought to agree together. Such a pestilent serpent is ambition and desire of vainglory and sovereignty, which among states where she once enters, creeps forth so far, till with division and variance she turns all to mischief: first longing to be next unto the best, afterward equal with the best, and at last chief and above the best. . . .

But if you among yourselves in a child's reign fall at debate, many a good man shall perish, and haply he too, and ye too, ere this land find peace again. Wherefore in these last words that ever I look to speak with you, I exhort you and require you all, for the love that you have ever borne to me, for the love that I have ever borne unto you; for the love that our Lord bears to us all: from this time forward (all griefs forgotten) each of you love other. Which I verily trust you will, if ye anything earthly regard, either God or your king, affinity or kindred, this realm, your own country, or your own surety." And therewithal the king no longer enduring to sit up, laid him down on his right side, his face towards them. And none was there present that could refrain from weeping.

But the lords recomforting him with as good words as they could, and answering for the time, as they thought to stand with his pleasure, there in his presence, as by their words appeared, each forgave other and joined their hands together, when (as it after appeared by their deeds) their hearts were far asunder. As soon as the King was departed, the noble prince,[19] his son, drew toward London, which at the time of his decease kept his household at Ludlow in Wales, which country being far off from the law and recourse to justice was begun to be far out of good rule, and waxen[20] wild robbers and reavers,[21] walking at liberty uncorrected. And for this occasion the prince was in the life of his father sent thither, to the end that the authority of his presence should refrain evil disposed persons from the boldness of their former outrages.

[22]To the governance and ordering of this young prince at his sending thither was there appointed Sir Anthony Woodville, Lord Rivers, and brother unto the queen, a right honorable man, as valiant of hand as politic in council. Adjoined were there unto him other of the same party; and in effect every one as he was nearest of kin unto the queen, so was he planted next about the prince. That drift, by the queen not unwisely devised, whereby her blood might of youth be rooted into the prince's favor, the Duke of Gloucester turned unto their destruction, and upon that ground set the foundation of all his unhappy building. For whomsoever he perceived either at variance with them, or bearing himself their favor, he brake unto them, some by mouth, and some by writing.

Nay, he sent secret messengers saying that it neither was reason, nor in any wise to be suffered, that the young king, their master and kinsman, should be in the hands and custody of his mother's kindred, sequestered in manner from their company and attendance, of which

---

[19] Edward, Prince of Wales, afterward Edward V.
[20] to breed.
[21] thieves.
[22] II.ii. 96–145.

every one owed him as faithful service as they, and many of them far more honorable part of kin than his mother's side. "Whose blood" (quoth he) "saving the king's pleasure, was full unmeetly to be matched with his. Which now to be, as they say, removed from the king, and the less noble to be left about him, is," (quoth he), "neither honorable to his majesty nor to us, and also to his grace no surety to have the mightiest of his friends from him; and unto us no little jeopardy, to suffer our well-proved evil willers to grow in overgreat authority with the prince in youth; namely, which is light of belief and soon persuaded. . . . Nor none of us (I believe) is so unwise over soon to trust a new friend made of an old foe; or to think that an hourly kindness, suddenly contracted in one hour, continued yet scant a fortnight, should be deeper settled in their stomachs, than a long accustomed malice many years rooted." With these words and writings, and such other, the Duke of Gloucester soon set on fire them that were of themselves easy to kindle, and in specially twain: Edward, Duke of Buckingham, and William, Lord Hastings, then Chamberlain, both men of honor and of great power, the one by long succession from his ancestry, the other by his office and the king's favor. These two, not bearing each to other so much love as hatred both unto the queen's part, in this point accorded together with the Duke of Gloucester, that they would utterly remove from the king's company all his mother's friends, under the name of their enemies.

Upon this concluded the Duke of Gloucester, understanding that the lords, which at that time were about the king, intended to bring him up to his coronation accompanied with such power of their friends, that it should be hard for him to bring his purpose to pass, without the gathering and great assembly of people and in manner of open war, whereof the end (he wist) was doubtful, and in which the king being on their side, his part should have the face and name of rebellion. [23]He secretly therefore by divers means caused the queen to be persuaded and brought in the mind, that it neither were need, and also should be jeopardous, the king to come up strong. . . .

[24]Now was the king in his way to London gone from Northampton, when these Dukes of Gloucester and Buckingham came thither, where remained behind the Lord Rivers, the king's uncle, intending on the morrow to follow the king, and to be with him at Stony-Stratford [certain] miles thence early ere he departed. So was there made that night much friendly cheer between these dukes and the Lord Rivers a great while, but incontinent. After that they were openly with great courtesy departed, and the Lord Rivers lodged, the dukes secretly with

---

[23] II.ii. 146–150. Shakespeare has Buckingham propose this scheme.
[24] II.iv. 1–54. Compare More's expanded and dramatic telling of the taking of Grey and Rivers with Shakespeare's oblique reference to it.

a few of their most privy friends set them down in council, wherein they spent a great part of the night.

And at their rising in the dawning of the day, they sent about privily to their servants in their inns and lodgings about, giving them commandment to make themselves shortly ready, for their lords were to horse backward.[25] Upon which messages, many of their folk were attendant, when many of the Lord Rivers' servants were unready. Now had these dukes taken also into their custody the keys of the inn, that none should pass forth without their license. And over this, in the highway toward Stony-Stratford, where the king lay, they had bestowed certain of their folk, that should send back again and compel to return any man that were gotten out of Northampton, toward Stony-Stratford, till they should give other license. Forasmuch as the dukes themselves intended for the show of their diligence to be the first that should that day attend upon the king's highness out of that town. Thus bore they folk in hand.[26]

But when the Lord Rivers understood the gates closed, and the ways on every side beset, neither his servants nor himself suffered to go on out, perceiving well so great a thing without his knowledge not begun for naught, comparing this manner present with this last night's cheer, in so few hours so great a change, marvelously misliked. Howbeit, since he could not get away, and keep himself close he would not, lest he should seem to hide himself for some secret fear of his own fault, whereof he saw no such cause in himself; he determined upon the surety of his own conscience to go boldly to them and inquire what this matter might mean. Whom as soon as they saw, they began to quarrel with him and say that he intended to set distance between the king and them, and to bring them to confusion, but it should not lie in his power.

And when he began (as he was a very well spoken man) in goodly wise to excuse himself, they tarried not the end of his answer, but shortly took him, and put him in ward, and that done, forthwith went to horseback, and took the way to Stony-Stratford, where they found the king with his company, ready to leap on horseback and depart forward to leave that lodging for them, because it was too strait for both companies. And as soon as they came in his presence, they light adown with all their company about them. To whom the Duke of Buckingham said: "Go afore, gentlemen, and yeomen keep your rooms." And thus in a goodly array they came to the king, and on their knees in very humble wise saluted his grace, which received them in very joyous and amiable manner, nothing earthly knowing nor mistrusting as yet.

---

[25] return.
[26] Kept the people under control.

But even by and by in his presence they picked a quarrel to the Lord Richard Grey, the king's other brother by his mother, saying that he with the Lord Marquis, his brother, and the Lord Rivers, his uncle, had compassed to rule the king and the realm, and to set variance among the states, and to subdue and destroy the noble blood of the realm. Toward the accomplishing whereof they said that the Lord Marquis had entered into the Tower of London, and thence taken out the king's treasure, and sent men to the sea. All which things these dukes wist well were done for good purposes and necessary, by the whole council at London, saving that somewhat they must say.

Unto which words the king answered: "What my brother Marquis has done I cannot say, but in good faith I dare well answer for mine Uncle Rivers and my brother here, that they be innocent of any such matter. "Yea, my liege" (quoth the Duke of Buckingham) "they have kept their dealing in these matters far from the knowledge of your good grace." And forthwith they arrested the Lord Richard and Sir Thomas Vaughan, Knight, in the king's presence, and brought the king and all back unto Northampton, where they took again further council. And there they sent away from the king whom it pleased them, and set new servants about him, such as liked better them than him. At which dealing he wept, and was nothing content; but it booted not.

And at dinner, the Duke of Gloucester sent a dish from his own table unto the Lord Rivers, praying him to be of good cheer: all should be well enough. And he thanked the Duke, and prayed the messenger to bear it to his nephew the Lord Richard, with the same message for his comfort, who he thought had more need of comfort, as one to whom such adversity was strange. But himself had been all his days in use therewith, and therefore could bear it the better. But for all this comfortable courtesy of the Duke of Gloucester, he sent the Lord Rivers, and the Lord Richard, with Sir Thomas Vaughan into the north country, into divers places to prison, and afterward all to Pomfret, where they were in conclusion beheaded.

In this wise the Duke of Gloucester took upon himself the order and governance of the young king, whom with much honor and humble reverence he conveyed upward towards the city. [27]But anon, the tidings of this matter came hastily to the queen a little before the midnight following, and that in the sorest wise: that the king her son was taken, her brother, her son, and her other friends arrested, and sent no man wist whither, to be done with God wot what. With which tidings the queen in great flight and heaviness, bewailing her child's

---

[27] II.iv. 66ff.

reign, her friends' mischance, and her own misfortune, damning the time that ever she dissuaded the gathering of power about the king, got herself in all the haste possible with her younger son and her daughters out of the palace of Westminster, in which she then lay, into the sanctuary, lodging herself and her company there in the abbot's place.

Now came there one in likewise not long after midnight from the Lord Chamberlain, to Doctor Rotheram, the Archbishop of York, then Chancellor of England, to his place not far from Westminster. ... And thereupon, by and by after the messenger departed, he caused in all the haste all his servants to be called up, and so with his own household about him, and every man weaponed, he took the great seal with him, and came yet before day unto the queen. ...

The queen herself sat alone low on the rushes all desolate and dismayed, whom the archbishop comforted in best manner he could, showing her that he trusted the matter was nothing so sore as she took it for and that he was put in good hope and out of fear by the message sent him from the Lord Chamberlain. "Ah, woe worth[28] him," (quoth she) "for he is one of them that labors to destroy me and my blood." "Madame," (quoth he) "be ye of good cheer, for I assure you, if they crown any other king than your son, whom they now have with them, we shall on the morrow crown his brother, whom you have here with you. And here is the great seal, which in likewise as that noble prince your husband delivered it unto me, so here I deliver it unto you, to the use and behoof of your son." And therewith he betook her the great seal, and departed home again, yet in the dawning of the day. ...

[29]When the king approached near to the city, Edmund Shaw, goldsmith, then mayor, with William White and John Matthew, sheriffs, and all the other aldermen in scarlet, with five hundred horse of the citizens, in violet, received him reverently at Harnesy; and riding from thence accompanied him into the city, which he entered the fourth day of May, the first and last year of his reign. But the Duke of Gloucester bore him in open sight so reverently to the prince, with all semblance of lowliness, that from the great obloquy in which he was so late before, he was suddenly fallen in so great trust that at the council next assembled he was made the only man chosen, and thought most meet, to be protector of the king and his realm, so that (were it destiny or were it folly) the lamb was betaken to the wolf to keep.

At which council also, the Archbishop of York, Chancellor of England, which had delivered up the great seal to the queen, was thereof

---

28 for, toward.
29 III.i. 17–19.

greatly reproved, and the seal taken from him, and delivered to Doctor Russell, Bishop of Lincoln, a wise man and a good, and of much experience, and one of the best learned men undoubtedly that England had in his time. Divers lords and knights were appointed unto divers rooms. The Lord Chamberlain and some others kept still their offices that they had before. Now all were it so that the protector so sore thirsted for the finishing of that he had begun, that [he] thought every day a year till it were achieved; yet durst he no further attempt, as long as he had but half his prey in his hand.

And why? Well did he weet that if he deposed the one brother all the realm would fall to the other, if he either remained in sanctuary or should happily be shortly conveyed to his father's liberty. [30]Wherefore incontinent at the next meeting of the lords at the council, he proposed to them, that[31] it was a heinous deed of the queen, and proceeding of great malice toward the king's counselors, that she should keep in sanctuary the king's brother from him, whose special pleasure and comfort were to have his brother with him. And that [was] by her done to none other intent but to bring all the lords in obloquy and murmur of the people. . . .

. . . [32]"Wherefore methinks it were not worst to send unto the queen, for the redress of this matter, some honorable trusty man, such as both tenders the king's weal and the honor of his council, and is also in favor and credence with her. For all which considerations, none seems more meet than our reverend father here present, my Lord Cardinal, who may in this matter do most good of any man, if it please him to take the pain; which I doubt not of his goodness he will not refuse for the king's sake and ours, and weal of the young duke himself, the king's most honorable brother, and (after my sovereign lord himself) my most dear nephew, considered that thereby shall be ceased the slanderous rumor and obloquy now going, and the hurts avoided that thereof might ensue, and much rest and quiet grow to all the realm. . . ."

Which thing the Archbishop of York, whom they all agreed also to be thereto most convenient, took upon him to move her, and therein to do his uttermost devoir. [33]Howbeit, if she could be in no wise entreated with her good will to deliver him, then, thought he, and such others as were of the spirituality present, that it were not in any wise to be attempted to take him out against her will. . . .

---

[30] III.i. 25–36. Note how Shakespeare contracts these several days' events into a single scene.

[31] Holinshed does not indicate precisely where this speech of Richard's begins.

[32] III.i. 31–43.

[33] III.i. 37–43.

"And I trust" (quoth he) "with God's grace, we shall not need it. But for any manner [of] need, I would not we should do it. I trust that she shall be with reason contented, and all things in good manner obtained. And if it happen that I bring it not so to pass, yet shall I toward it so far forth do my best, that ye shall all well perceive that no lack of my devoir, but the mother's dread and womanish fear shall be the let."

"Womanish fear, nay, womanish frowardness" (quoth the Duke of Buckingham). For I dare take it upon my soul, she well knows she needs no such thing to fear, either for her son or for herself. . . .

[34]"A sanctuary serves always to defend the body of that man that stands in danger abroad, not of great hurt only, but also of lawful hurt: for against unlawful harms, never pope nor king intended to privilege any one place, for that privilege hath every place. Knows any man any place wherein it is lawful one man to do another wrong? That no man unlawfully take hurt, that liberty, the king, the law, and very nature forbids in every place, and makes (to that regard) for every man every place a sanctuary. But where a man is by lawful means in peril, there needs he the tuition of some special privilege, which is the only ground and cause of all sanctuaries.

"From which necessity, this noble prince is far, whose love to his king, nature and kindred proveth; whose innocency to all the world, his tender youth proves; and so sanctuary, as for him, neither none he needs, nor also none can have. Men come not to sanctuary as they come to baptism, to require it by their godfathers. He must ask it himself that must have it, and reason: since no man has cause to have it but whose conscience of his own fault makes him fain[35] need to require it. . . .

"And if no body may be taken out of sanctuary, that says he will bide there, then if a child will take sanctuary because he fears to go to school, his master must let him alone. And as simple as that sample is, yet is there less reason in our case than in that; for therein, though it be a childish fear, yet is there at the leastwise some fear, and herein is there none at all. And verily, I have often heard of sanctuary men, but I never heard erst of sanctuary children.

"And therefore, as for the conclusion of my mind, whoso may have deserved to need it, if they think it for their surety, let them keep it. But he can be no sanctuary man that neither has wisdom to desire it nor malice to deserve it; whose life or liberty can by no lawful process stand in jeopardy. And he that takes one out of sanctuary to do him good, I say plainly, that he breaks no sanctuary." When the duke had done, the temporal men whole, and a good part of the spiritual also,

---

[34] III.i. 44–56.
[35] obliged.

thinking no hurt earthly meant toward the young babe, condescended in effect, that if he were not delivered, he should be fetched. Howbeit they thought it all best in the avoiding of all manner of rumor, that the Lord Cardinal should first assay to get him with her good will. . . .

[*The Lord Cardinal went into the sanctuary of the queen, and after lengthy persuasions secured custody of her two young sons.*]

[36]When the Lord Cardinal, and these other lords with him, had received this young duke, they brought him into the Star Chamber, where the protector took him in his arms and kissed him with these words: "Now welcome, my lord, even with all my very heart." And he said in that, of likelihood, as he thought. Thereupon forthwith they brought him unto the king his brother into the bishop's palace at Paul's, and from thence through the city honorably into the Tower, out of the which after that day they never came abroad. [37]When the protector had both the children in his hands, he opened himself more boldly both to certain other men, and also chiefly to the Duke of Buckingham — although I know that many thought that this duke was privy to all the protector's council, even from the beginning. And some of the protector's friends said that the duke was the first mover of the protector to this matter, sending a privy messenger unto him, straight after King Edward's death.

But others again, which knew better the subtle wit of the protector, deny that he ever opened his enterprise to the duke until he had brought to pass the things before rehearsed. But when he had imprisoned the queen's kinfolks, and gotten both her sons into his own hands, then he opened the rest of his purpose with less fear to them whom he thought meet for the matter, and specially to the Duke, who being won to his purpose, he thought his strength more than half increased. . . . Then it was agreed, that the protector should have the duke's aid to make him king, and that the protector's only lawful son should marry the duke's daughter, and that the protector should grant him the quiet possession of the earldom of Hereford, which he claimed as his inheritance, and could never obtain it in King Edward's time.

Besides these requests of the duke, the protector, of his own mind, promised him a great qauntity of the king's treasure and of his household stuff. And when they were thus at a point between themselves, they went about to prepare for the coronation of the young king, as they would have it seem. And that they might turn both the eyes and minds of men from perceiving of their drifts otherwhere, the lords

---

[36] III.i. 95–150.
[37] III.i. 151ff.

being sent for from all parts of the realm came thick to that solemnity. But the protector and the duke, after that they had sent the Lord Cardinal, the Archbishop of York, then Lord Chancellor, the Bishop of Ely, the Lord Stanley, and the Lord Hastings, then Lord Chamberlain, with many other noblemen to common and devise about the coronation in one place, as fast were they in another place, contriving the contrary, and to make the protector king.

To which council albeit there were adhibited[38] very few, and they were secret. Yet began there here and thereabouts some manner of muttering among the people, as though all should not long be well, though they neither wist what they feared, nor wherefore. Were it that before such great things, men's hearts of a secret instinct of nature misgave them, as the sea without wind swells of himself sometime before a tempest; or were it that some one man, haply somewhat perceiving, filled many men with suspicion, though he showed few men what he knew. Howbeit somewhat the dealing itself made men to muse on the matter, though the council were close. For by little and little all folk withdrew from the Tower, and drew unto Crosbys in Bishop's Gates Street, where the protector kept his household. The protector had the resort; the king in manor desolate.

While some for their business made suit to them that had the doing, some were by their friends secretly warned, that it might haply turn them to no good to be too much attendant about the king without the protector's appointment, which removed also divers of the prince's old servants from him and set new about him. Thus many things coming together, partly by chance, partly of purpose, caused at length not common people only, that wound with the wind, but wise men also, and some lords eke to mark the matter and muse thereon; [39]so far forth that the Lord Stanley that was after Earl of Derby, wisely mistrusted it, and said unto the Lord Hastings, that he much misliked these two several councils. "For while we" (quoth he) "talk of one matter in the one place, little wot we whereof they talk in the other place."

"My lord" (quoth the Lord Hastings) "on my life, never doubt you. For while one man is there, which is never thence, never can there be thing once moved, that should sound amiss toward me, but it should be in mine ears ere it were well out of their mouths." This meant he by Catesby, which was of his near secret counsel, and whom he very familiarly used, and in his most weighty matters put no man in so special trust, reckoning himself to no man so lief, since he well wist there was no man so much to him beholden as was this Catesby, which

---

[38] let in.
[39] III.ii. 19–33; 74–96.

was a man well learned in the laws of this land, and by the special favor of the Lord Chamberlain in good authority, and much rule bore in all the county of Leicester, where the Lord Chamberlain's power chiefly lay.

But surely great pity was it, that he had not had either more truth, or less wit. For his dissimulation only kept all that mischief up. In whom if the Lord Hastings had not put so special trust, the Lord Stanley and he had departed with divers other lords, and broken all the dance. For many ill signs that he saw, which he now construes all to the best. So surely thought he that there could be no harm toward him in that council intended, where Catesby was. And of truth the protector and Duke of Buckingham made very good semblance unto the Lord Hastings, and kept him much in company. And undoubtedly the protector loved him well, and loth was to have lost him, saving[40] for fear lest his life should have quelled their purpose.

[41]For which cause he moved Catesby to prove with some words cast out afar off, whether he could think it possible to win the Lord Hastings unto their part. [42]But Catesby, whether he assayed him, or assayed him not, reported unto them that he found him so fast, and heard him speak so terrible words, that he durst no further break. And of truth, the Lord Chamberlain of very trust showed unto Catesby the distrust that others began to have in the matter. And therefore he, fearing lest their motion might with the Lord Hastings minish his credence — whereunto only all the matter leaned — procured the protector hastily to rid him. And much the rather, for that he trusted by his death to obtain much of the rule that the Lord Hastings bore in his country: the only desire whereof was the allective[43] that induced him to be partner, and one special contriver, of all this horrible treason.

[44]Whereupon soon after, that is to wit, on the Friday (being the thirteenth of June) many lords assembled in the Tower, and there sat in council, devising the honorable solemnity of the king's coronation, of which the time appointed then so near approached, that the pageants and subtleties were in making day and night at Westminster and much vittles[45] killed therefore that afterward was cast away. These lords so sitting together communing of this matter, the protector came in amongst them, first about nine of the clock, saluting them courteously, and excusing himself that he had been from them so long, saying merrily that he had been a sleeper that day.

---

[40] except.
[41] III.i. 167–193.
[42] III.ii. 35–70.
[43] allurement.
[44] III.iv. 1–32.
[45] victuals, ground produce.

[46]After a little talking with them, he said unto the Bishop Ely, "My lord, you have very good strawberries at your garden in Holborne. I require you let us have a mess of them." "Gladly, my lord," (quoth he) "would God I had some better thing as ready to your pleasure as that!" And therewithal in all the haste he sent his servant for a mess of strawberries. The protector set the lords fast in communing, and thereupon praying them to spare him for a little while, departed thence. And soon after one hour, between ten and eleven he returned into the chamber amongst them all, changed with a wonderful sour angry countenance, knitting the brows, frowning and fretting, and gnawing on his lips, and so sat him down in his place.

All the lords were much dismayed and sore marveled at this manner of sudden change, and what thing should him ail. Then, when he had sat still a while, thus he began. "What were they worthy to have, that compass and imagine the destruction of me, being so near of blood unto the king, and protector of his royal person and his realm?" At this question, all the lords sat sore astonished, musing much by whom this question should be meant, of which every man wist himself clear. Then the Lord Chamberlain (as he that for the love between them thought he might be boldest with him) answered and said, that they were worthy to be punished as heinous traitors, whatsoever they were. And all the others affirmed the same. "That is," (quoth he) "yonder sorceress, my brother's wife, and others with her." (meaning the queen).

At these words many of the other lords were greatly abashed, that favored her. But the Lord Hastings was in his mind better content, that it was moved by her, than by any other whom he loved better. Albeit his heart somewhat grudged that he was not afore made of counsel in this matter, as he was of the taking of her kindred, and of their putting to death, which were by his assent before devised to be beheaded at Pomfret this selfsame day — in which he was not aware that it was by others devised that he himself should be beheaded the same day at London. Then said the protector, "Ye shall all see in what wise that sorceress, and that other witch of her counsel, Shore's wife, with their affinity, have by their sorcery and witchcraft wasted my body." And therewith he plucked up his doublet sleeve to his elbow upon his left arm, where he showed a weerish[47] withered arm, and small, as it was never other.

Hereupon every man's mind sore misgave them, well perceiving that this matter was but a quarrel. For they well wist that the queen was too wise to go about any such folly. And also if she would, yet

---

[46] III.iv. 32–81.
[47] shrivelled.

would she of all folk least, make Shore's wife of her counsel, whom of all women she most hated, as that concubine whom the king her husband had most loved. And also, no man was there present, but well knew that his arm was ever such since his birth. Nevertheless, the Lord Chamberlain (which from the death of King Edward kept Shore's wife, on whom he somewhat doted in the king's life, saving [as it is said] he that while forbear her [out] of reverence toward the king, or else of a certain kind of fidelity to his friend) answered and said: "Certainly, my lord, if they have so heinously done, they be worthy heinous punishment."

"What!" (quoth the protector) "Thou servest me I ween with if's and with and's. I tell thee they have so done, and that I will make good on thy body, traitor." And therewith as in a great anger, he clapped his fist upon the board a great rap. At which token one cried, "Treason!" without the chamber. Therewith a door clapped, and in came there rushing men in harness, as many as the chamber might hold. And anon the protector said to the Lord Hastings: "I arrest thee, traitor." "What me, my lord?" (quoth he). "Yea, thee, traitor," quoth the protector. And another let fly at the Lord Stanley, which shrunk at the stroke and fell under the table, or else his head had been cleft to the teeth. For as shortly as he shrank, yet ran the blood about his ears.

Then were they all quickly bestowed in divers chambers, except the Lord Chamberlain, whom the protector bade speed and shrive him apace. "For by Saint Paul," (quoth he) "I will not to dinner till I see thy head off." It booted him not to ask why, but heavily took a priest at adventure, and made a short shrift. For a longer would not be suffered, the protector made so much haste to dinner — which he might not go to, until this were done for saving of his oath. So was he brought forth to the green beside the chapel within the Tower, and his head laid down upon a long log of timber, and there stricken off, and afterward his body with the head interred at Windsor beside the body of King Edward, both whose souls Our Lord pardon. (Thus began he to establish his kingdom in blood, growing thereby in hatred of the nobles, and also abridging both the line of his life, and the time of his regimen. For God will not have bloodthirsty tyrants' days prolonged, but will cut them off in their ruff;[48] according to David's words:

> Impio, fallaci, avidoque caedis
> Fila mors rumpet viridi in iuventa.)[49]

---

[48] Peak. This sentence, then, expresses the standard Medieval-Renaissance concept of the Wheel of Fortune.

[49] Murderous death breaks the thread of an irreverent, deceitful, and greedy man in vigorous youth.

A marvelous case is it to hear either the warnings of that he should have avoided, or the tokens of that he could not avoid. [50]For the self night next before his death, the Lord Stanley sent a trusty messenger unto him at midnight in all the haste, requiring him to rise and ride away with him, for he was disposed utterly no longer to bide. He had so fearful a dream in which he thought that a boar with his tusks so razed[51] them both by the heads that the blood ran about both their shoulders. And forsomuch as the protector gave the boar for his cognisance,[52] this dream made so fearful an impression in his heart, that he was thoroughly determined no longer to tarry, but had his horse ready, if the Lord Hastings would go with him, to ride yet so far the same night that they should be out of danger ere day.

"Ha, good lord," (quoth the Lord Hastings to this messenger), "leans my lord thy master so much to such trifles, and has such faith in dreams, which either his own fear fantasies or do rise in the night's rest by reason of his day's thought? Tell him it is plain witchcraft to believe in such dreams, which if they were tokens of things to come, why thinks he not that we might be as likely to make them true by our going, if we were caught and brought back, as friends fail fleers. For then had the boar a cause likely to raze us with his tusks, as folk that fled for some falsehood. Wherefore, either is there peril, or none there is indeed. Or if any be, it is rather in going than biding. And in case we should needs fall in peril one way or other, yet had I rather that men should see that it were by other men's falsehood, than think it were either by our own fault, or faint heart. And therefore go to thy master, man, and commend me to him, and pray him be merry and have no fear. For I insure him I am as sure of the man that he wots of as I am of mine own hand." "God send grace, sir," (quoth the messenger) and went his way.

[53] Certain is it also, that in riding towards the Tower, the same morning in which he was beheaded, his horse twice or thrice stumbled with him, almost to the falling. Which thing, albeit each man wot well daily happens to them to whom no such mischance is toward, yet has it been of an old rite and custom observed, as a token oftentimes notably foregoing some great misfortune. Now this that follows was no warning, but an envious scorn. [54]The same morning ere he was up, came a knight unto him, as it were of courtesy, to accompany him to the council; but of truth sent by the protector to haste him thither-

---

[50] III.iv. 84–85.

[51] To raze (rase), or rash is an old hunting term used specifically to describe the violence of the boar.

[52] i.e., Richard's crest was adorned with the figure of a boar.

[53] III.iv. 86–88.

[54] III.ii. 110–116.

wards, with whom he was of secret confederacy in that purpose; a mean man at that time and now of great authority.

This knight (I say) when it happened the Lord Chamberlain by the way to stay his horse and commune a while with a priest whom he met in the Tower street, brake his tale, and said merrily to him: "What, my lord, I pray you come on. Whereto talk you so long with that priest? You have no need of a priest yet." And therewith he laughed upon him, as though he would say, ye shall have soon. But so little wist the other what he meant, and so little mistrusted, that he was never merrier, nor never so full of good hope in his life, which self thing is oft seen a sign of change. . . .

[55]Upon the very Tower wharf, so near the place where his head was off soon after, there met he with one Hastings, a pursuivant of his own name. And at their meeting in that place, he was put in remembrance of another time, in which it had happened them before to meet in like manner together in the same place. At which other time the Lord Chamberlain had been accused unto King Edward by the Lord Rivers, the queen's brother, in such wise as he was for the while (but it lasted not long) far fallen into the king's indignation and stood in great fear of himself. And forsomuch as he now met this pursuivant in the same place, that jeopardy so well passed, it gave him great pleasure to talk with him thereof, with whom he had before talked thereof in the same place while he was therein.

And therefore he said: "Ha, Hastings, art thou remembered when I met thee here once with an heavy heart?" "Yea, my lord," (quoth he) "that remember I well. And thanked be God they got no good, nor you no harm thereby." "Thou wouldst say so," (quoth he) "if thou knewest as much as I know, which few know else as yet, and more shall shortly." That meant he by the lords of the queen's kindred that were taken before, and should that day be beheaded at Pomfret: which he well wist, but nothing ware that the ax hung over his own head. "In faith, man" (quoth he) "I was never so sorry, nor never stood in so great dread in my life, as I did when thou and I met here. And lo how the world is turned. Now stand mine enemies in the danger (as thou mayest hap to hear more hereafter) and I never in my life so merry, nor never in so great surety."

O good God, the blindness of our mortal nature. When he most feared, he was in good surety; when he reckoned himself surest, he lost his life, and that within two hours after. Thus ended this honorable man, a good knight and a gentle, of great authority with his prince, of living somewhat dissolute, plain and open to his enemy, and secret to his friend, easy to beguile, as he that of good heart and

---

[55] III.ii. 97–109; 117ff.

courage forestudied no perils; a loving man, and passing well beloved; very faithful, and trusty enough, trusting too much. Now flew the fame of this lord's death swiftly through the city, and so forth further about like a wind in every man's ear. But the protector, immediately after dinner, intending to set some color upon the matter, sent in all the haste for many substantial men out of the city into the Tower.

[56]Now at their coming, himself with the Duke of Buckingham stood harnassed in old ill faring briganders,[57] such as no man should ween that they would vouchsafe to have put upon their backs, except that some sudden necessity had constrained them. And then the protector showed them that the Lord Chamberlain, and others of his conspiracy, had contrived to have suddenly destroyed him and the Duke, there the same day in the council. And what they intended further was as yet not well known. Of which their treason he never had knowledge before ten of the clock the same forenoon, which sudden fear drove them to put on for their defense such harness as came next to hand. And so had God helped them, that the mischief turned upon them that would have done it. And this he required them to report.

Every man answered him fair, as though no man mistrusted the matter, which of truth no man believed. Yet for the further appeasing of the people's minds, he sent immediately after dinner in all the haste one herald of arms with a proclamation to be made through the city in the king's name, containing that the Lord Hastings, with divers others of his traitorous purpose, had before conspired the same day to have slain the Lord Protector and the Duke of Buckingham sitting in the council; and after to have taken upon them to rule the king and the realm at their pleasure, and thereby to pill and spoil whom they list uncontrolled. And much matter there was in that proclamation, devised to the slander of the Lord Chamberlain, as that he was an ill councilor to the king's father, enticing him to many things highly redounding to the minishing of his honor, and to the universal hurt of the realm.

The means whereby: namely, his evil company, sinister procuring, and ungratious example, as well in many other things as in the vicious living and inordinate abuse of his body with many others, and also specially with Shore's wife — which was one also of his most secret council in this most heinous treason, with whom he lay nightly, and namely the night last past next before his death. So that it was the less marvel if ungracious living brought him to an unhappy ending,

---

[56] III.v. 1–71.
[57] Body armor for foot soldiers. The stage direction tells of Gloucester and Buckingham entering in "rotten armor."

which he was now put unto by the most dread commandment of the king's highness and of his honorable and faithful council, both for his demerits, being so openly taken in his falsely conceived treason, and also lest the delaying of his execution might have encouraged other mischievous persons, partners of his conspiracy, to gather and assemble themselves together, in making some great commotion for his deliverance — whose hope being now by his well deserved death politically repressed, all the realm should (by God's grace) rest in good quiet and peace.

[58]Now was this proclamation made within two hours after that he was beheaded, and it was so curiously indicted, and so fair written in parchment, in so well a set hand, and therewith of itself so long a process, that every child might well perceive that it was prepared before. For all the time, between his death and the proclaiming, could scant have sufficed unto the bare writing alone all had it been but in paper and scribbled forth in haste at adventure. So that upon the proclaiming thereof, one that was schoolmaster of Paul's of chance standing by, and comparing the shortness of the time with the length of the matter, said unto them that stood about him, "Here is a gay goodly cast full cast away for haste." And a merchant answered him that it was written by prophesy.

[59]Now then by and by, as it were for anger, not for coveting, the protector sent into the house of Shore's wife (for her husband dwelled not with her) and spoiled her of all that ever she had above the value of two or three thousand marks, and sent her body to prison. And when he had a while laid unto her (for the manner's sake) that she went about to bewitch him, and that she was of council with the Lord Chamberlain to destroy him. In conclusion, when that no color could fasten upon these matters, then he laid heinously to her charge that thing that herself could not deny, and that all the world wist was true, and that nevertheless every man laughed at, to hear it then so suddenly so highly taken, that she was naught of her body.

And for this cause (as a goodly continent prince, clean and faultless of himself, sent out of heaven into this vicious world for the amendment of men's manners) he caused the Bishop of London to put her to open penance, going before the cross in procession upon a Sunday with a taper in her hand. In which she went in countenance and

---

[58] III.vi. 1ff.

[59] III.v. 29–51. While Shakespeare does not directly use the material in the following passage describing the fortunes of Shore's wife, he mentions her frequently and uses her in lines like these to develop plot. More's account of her, therefore, is included for its value to an understanding of the play as well as of history. See also her treatment in *The True Tragedy of Richard III*, p. 67ff.

pace demure so womanly; that albeit she were out of all array, save her kirtle only, yet went she so fair and lovely, namely while the wondering of the people cast a comely red in her cheeks (of which she before had most missed) that her great shame won her much praise among those that were more amorous of her body than curious of her soul. And many good folks also that hated her living, and glad were to see sin corrected, yet pitied they more her penance than rejoiced therein, when they considerd that the protector procured it more of a corrupt intent than any virtuous affection.

This woman was born in London, worshipfully friended, honestly brought up, and very well married, saving somewhat too soon, her husband an honest citizen, young and godly, and of good substance. But forsomuch as they were coupled ere she were well ripe, she not very fervently loved him for whom she never longed — which was haply the thing that the more easily made her incline unto the king's appetite, when he required her. Howbeit the respect of his royalty, the hope of gay apparel, ease, and other wanton wealth, was able soon to pierce a soft tender heart, so that she became flexible and pliant to the king's appetite and will. . . .

When the king died, the Lord Chamberlain took her, which in the king's days, albeit he was sore enamored upon her, yet he forbare her, either for reverence, or for a certain friendly faithfulness. Proper she was and fair; nothing in her body that you would have changed, but if ye would have wished her somewhat higher. Thus say they that knew her in her youth. . . .

For now is she old, lean, withered, and dried up, nothing left but shriveled skin and hard bone. And yet being even such, who so well advise her visage might guess and devise which parts how filled would make it a fair face. Yet delighted not men so much in her beauty, as in her pleasant behavior. For a proper wit had she, and could both read well and write, merry in company, ready and quick of answer, neither mute not full of babble, sometime taunting without displeasure, and not without disport. . . .

[60]Now was it so devised by the protector and his council that the self day in which the Lord Chamberlain was beheaded in the Tower of London, and about the self same hour, was there (not without his assent) beheaded at Pomfret the fore-remembered lords and knights that were taken from the king at Northampton and Stony-Stratford. Which thing was done in the presence and by the order of Sir Richard Ratcliff, knight, whose service the protector specially used in that council, and in the execution of such lawless enterprises as a man that had been long secret with him, having experience of the

---

[60] III.iii 1ff.

world, and a shrewd wit, short and rude in speech, rough and boisterous of behavior, bold in mischief, as far from pity as from all fear
of God.

This knight bringing them out of the prison to the scaffold, and
showing to the people about that they were traitors (not suffering
them to declare and speak their innocency, lest their words might
have inclined men to pity them, and to hate the protector and his
part) caused them hastily, without judgment, process, or manner of
order to be beheaded, and without other earthly guilt but only that
they were good men, too true to the king, and too nigh to the queen.
Now when the Lord Chamberlain and these other lords and knights
were thus beheaded, and rid out of the way, then thought the protector: that when men mused what the matter meant, while the lords
of the realm were about him out of their own strengths, while no
man wist what to think nor whom to trust, ere ever they should have
space to dispute and digest the matter and make parties, it were
best hastily to pursue his purpose and put himself in possession of the
crown, ere men could have time to devise any way to resist.

But now was all the study by what means this matter, being of itself
so heinous, might be first broken to the people in such wise that it
might be well taken. To this council they took divers, such as they
thought meetly[61] to be trusted, likely to be induced to that part, and
able to stand them instead, either by power or policy. Among whom
they made of council Edmund Shaw, knight, then Mayor of London,
which upon trust of his own advancement, whereof he was of a
proud heart highly desirous, should frame the city to their appetite.
Of spiritual men they took such as had wit, and were in authority
among the people for opinion of their learning, and had no scrupulous
conscience. Among these had they [62]John Shaw, clerk, brother to the
mayor, and Friar Penker, provincial of the Augustine friars, both
doctors of divinity, both great preachers, both of more learning than
virtue, of more fame than learning. For they were before greatly
esteemed among the people. But after that never.

Of these two the one had a sermon in praise of the protector before the coronation, the other after, both so full of tedious flattery
that no man's ears could abide them. Penker in his sermon so lost
his voice that he was fain to leave off and come down in the midst.
Doctor Shaw by his sermon lost his honesty, and soon after his
life, for very shame of the world, into which he durst never after come
abroad. But the friar forced for no shame, and so it harmed him the
less. Howbeit some doubt, and many think, that Penker was not

---

[61] fit.

[62] III.v. 103–104.

of council in the matter before the coronation, but after the common manner fell to flattery after: namely, since his sermon was not incontinently upon it, but at Saint Mary Hospital at the Easter after.

But certain it is that Doctor Shaw was of council in the beginning, so far forth that they determined that he should first break the matter in a sermon at Paul's Cross, in which he should (by the authority of his preaching) incline the people to the protector's ghostly[63] purpose. But now was all the labor and study in the device of some convenient pretext for which the people should be content to depose the prince, and accept the protector for king. In which divers things they devised. [64]But the chief thing and the weightiest of all that invention rested in this, that they should allege bastardy, either in King Edward himself, or in his children, or both. So that he should seem disabled to inherit the crown by the Duke of York, and the prince by him.

To lay bastardy in King Edward sounded openly to the rebuke of the protector's own mother, which was mother to them both; for in that point could be no other color. But to pretend that his own mother was an adultress, which notwithstanding to further this purpose, he letted not. But nevertheless he would that point should be less, and more favorably, handled: not even fully plain and directly, but that the matter should be touched aslope craftily, as though men spared in that point to speak all the truth for fear of his displeasure. But the other point concerning the bastardy that they devised to surmise in King Edward's children, that would he should be openly declared and enforced to the uttermost. . . .

Now then (as I began to show you) it was by the protector and his council concluded that this Doctor Shaw should in a sermon at Paul's Cross signify to the people that neither King Edward himself nor the Duke of Clarence were lawfully begotten, nor were not the very children of the Duke of York, but gotten unlawfully by other persons, in adultery, of the duchess, their mother. [65]And that also Dame Elizabeth Lucy was verily the wife of King Edward, and so the prince and all his children bastards, that were begotten upon the queen. According to this device Doctor Shaw the Sunday after, at

---

63 devilish.

64 III.v. 72–94.

65 Elizabeth Lucy had been the concubine of Edward before his marriage, and some rumors had arisen that they were affianced; but a brief court trial proved otherwise (III.vii 4–6). Another aspersion launched against Edward, which Shakespeare mentions (III.v. 76–79) and which appears in Hall and Grafton, but not Holinshed, is that a wealthy London grocer named Walker boasted of possibly being the father of one of Edward's sons, for which Edward had Walker put to death.

Paul's Cross in a great audience (as always assembled great number to his preaching) he took for his theme: *Spuria vitilamina non agent radices altas,* that is to say: bastard slips shall never take deep root. . . .

Then on the Tuesday following this sermon, there came to the Guildhall in London the Duke of Buckingham, accompanied with divers lords and knights more than haply knew the message that they brought. And there in the east end of the hall, where the mayor keeps the hustings,[66] the mayor, and all the aldermen being assembled about him, all the commons of the city gathered before them. After silence commanded upon great pain in the protector's name, the duke stood up, and (as he was neither unlearned, and of nature marvelously well spoken) he said unto the people with a clear and loud voice in this manner of wise:

The Duke of Buckingham's oration to the assembly of the mayor, aldermen, and commoners.

[67]"Friends, for the zeal and hearty favor that we bear you, we be come to break unto you of a matter right great and weighty, and no less weighty than pleasing to God, and profitable to all the realm. Nor to no part of the realm more profitable than to you the citizens of this noble city. For why? That thing that we wote well ye have long time lacked, and sore longed for, that ye would have given great good for, that ye would have gone far to fetch. That thing we be come hither to bring you without your labor, pain, cost, adventure or jeopardy. What thing is that? Certes, the surety of your own bodies, the quiet of your wives and your daughters, the safeguard of your goods: of all which things in times past ye stood evermore in doubt. For who was there of you all that would reckon himself lord of his own goods among so many grens[68] and traps as was set therefore; among so much pilling and polling; among so many taxes and tallages, of which there was never end, and oftentimes no need? . . .

"What manner of folk he most favored we shall for his honor spare to speak of. Howbeit, this wote you well all, that whoso was best bore always least rule; and more suit was in his days to Shore's wife, a vile and an abominable strumpet, than to all the lords in England — except unto those that made her their proctor.[69] Which simple woman was well named and honest, till the king for his wanton lust and sinful affection bereft her from her husband, a right honest substantial young man among you. And in that point, which in good faith I am sorry to speak of, saving that it is in vain to keep in council

---

66 special councils.
67 III.vii. 1–22.
68 snares.
69 deputy.

that thing that all men know, the king's greedy appetite was insatiable, and everywhere over all the realm intolerable.

"For no woman was there anywhere, young or old, rich or poor, whom he set his eye upon, in whom he anything liked, either person or favor, speech, pace or countenance, but without any fear of God, or respect of his honor, murmur or grudge of the world, he would importunately pursue his appetite, and have her, to the great destruction of many a good woman, and great dolor to their husbands, and their other friends — which being honest people of themselves, so much regard the cleanness of their house, the chastity of their wives, and their children, that them were liefer to lose all that they had beside than to have such a villainy done them....

"I am not so proud to look therefore that ye should reckon my words of as great authority as the preacher's of the word of God, namely a man so cunning and so wise that no man better wot what he should say, and thereto so good and virtuous that he would not say the thing which he wist he should not say in the pulpit, namely, into the which no honest man comes to lie. Which honorable preacher, ye well remember, substantially declared unto you at Paul's Cross, on Sunday last passed, the right and title that the most excellent Prince Richard, Duke of Gloucester, now protector of this realm, has unto the crown and kingdom of the same. For as the worshipful man groundly made open unto you, the children of King Edward the Fourth were never lawfully begotten, forsomuch as the king (leaving his very wife, Dame Elizabeth Lucy) was never lawfully married unto the queen their mother, whose blood, saving that he set his voluptuous pleasure before his honor, was full unmeetly to be matched with his. And the mingling of whose bloods together has been the effusion of a great part of the noble blood of this realm.

"Whereby it may well seem the marriage not well made, of which there is so much mischief grown. For lack of which lawful coupling, and also of other things which the said worshipful doctor rather signified than fully explained — and which things shall not be spoken for me — as the thing wherein every man forbears to say that he knows, in avoiding displeasure of my noble Lord Protector, bearing (as nature requires) a filial reverence to the duchess, his mother. For these causes (I say) before remembered, that is, to wit: for lack of other issue lawfully of the late noble prince, Richard, Duke of York, to whose royal blood the crown of England and of France is by the high authority of Parliament entailed, the right and title of the same is by the just course of inheritance (according to the common laws of the land) devolved and come unto the most excellent prince, the Lord Protector, as to the very lawfully begotten son of the foreremembered noble Duke of York.

"Which thing well considered, and the great knightly prowess pondered, with manifold virtues which in his noble person singularly abound, the nobles and commons also of this realm, and specially in the north part, not willing any bastard blood to have the rule of the land, nor the abuses before in the same used any longer to continue, have condescended and fully determined to make humble petition to the most puissant prince, the Lord Protector, that it may like his grace (at our humble request) to take upon him the guiding and governance of this realm, to the wealth and increase of the same, according to his very right and just title. . . .

"Yet shall he to our petition in that behalf more graciously incline, if ye the worshipful citizens of this the chief city of this realm, join with us the nobles in our said request. Which for your own weal (we doubt not) but ye will. And nevertheless I heartily pray you so to do, whereby you shall do great profit to all this realm beside in choosing them so good a king, and unto yourselves special commodity, to whom his majesty shall ever after bear so much the more tender favor, in how much he shall perceive you the more prone and benevolently minded toward his election. Wherein, dear friends, what mind you have, we require you plainly to show us."

[70]When the duke had said, and looked that the people, whom he hoped that the mayor had framed before should after this proposition made have cried: "King Richard, King Richard!" all was hushed and mute, and not one word answered thereunto. Wherewith the duke was marvelously abashed, and taking the mayor nearer to him, with others that were about him privy to that matter, said unto them softly, "What means this, that the people be so still?" "Sir," (quoth the mayor) "percase they perceive you not well." "That shall we mend," (quoth he) "if that will help." And by and by somewhat louder he rehearsed to them the same matter again in other order, and other words, so well and ornately, and nevertheless so evidently and plain, with voice, gesture and countenance so comely and so convenient, that every man much marveled that heard him, and thought that they never had in their lives heard so evil a tale so well told (insomuch that he seemed as cunning an orator, as he of whom the poet spake to his high praise and commendation, saying:

Quaelibet eloquio causa fit apta suo.)[71]

But were it for wonder or fear, or that each looked that other should speak first, not one word was there answered of all the people that stood before. But all was as still as the midnight, not so much

---

[70] III.vii. 24–41.

[71] Everywhere the cause becomes suited to his eloquence.

as rouning[72] amongst them, by which they might seem to commune what was best to do. When the mayor saw this, he with other partners of that council drew about the duke and said that the people had not been accustomed there to be spoken unto but by the recorder, which is the mouth of the city, and haply to him they will answer. With that the recorder, called Fitzwilliam, a sad[73] man, and an honest, which was so new come into that office that he never had spoken to the people before, and loth was with that matter to begin, notwithstanding thereunto commanded by the mayor made rehearsal to the commons of that the duke had twice rehearsed to them himself.

But the recorder so tempered his tale, that he showed everything as the duke's words, and no part his own. But all this noting[74] no change made in the people . . . till at the last in the nether end of the hall an ambushment of the duke's servants, and Nashfield's, and others belonging to the protector, with some 'prentices and lads that thrust into the hall amongst the press, began suddenly at men's backs to cry out as loud as their throats would give: "King Richard, King Richard!" and threw up their caps in token of joy. And they that stood before cast back their heads marveling thereof, but nothing they said. Now when the duke and the mayor saw this manner, they wisely turned it to their purpose and said it was a goodly cry, and a joyful, to hear every man with one voice, no man saying nay.

"Wherefore, friends," (quoth the duke) "since we perceive it is all your whole mind to have this nobleman for your king (whereof we shall make his grace so effectual report, that we doubt not but it shall redound unto your great weal and commodity) we require ye that ye tomorrow go with us and we with you unto his noble grace, to make our humble request unto him in manner before remembered." And therewith the lords came down, and the company dissolved and departed, the more part all sad: some with glad semblance that were not very merry, and some of those that came thither with the duke not able to dissemble their sorrow, were fain at his back to turn their face to the wall while the dolor of their hearts burst out of their eyes.

[75]Then on the morrow after, the mayor with all the aldermen and chief commoners of the city, in their best manner apparelled, assembling themselves together, resorted unto Baynard's Castle, where the protector lay. To which place repaired also (according to their appointment) the Duke of Buckingham and divers noblemen with him,

---

[72] whispering.
[73] valiant.
[74] remarking, talking.
[75] III.vii. 44ff. In this scene Shakespeare follows closely the next several incidents in More, but he eliminates the time lapses so as to knit them into a single episode.

beside many knights and other gentlemen. And thereupon the duke sent word unto the Lord Protector of the being there of a great and honorable company to move a great matter unto his grace. Whereupon the protector made difficulty to come out unto them, but if he first knew some part of their errand, as though he doubted and partly mistrusted the coming of such a number unto him so suddenly, without any warning or knowledge, whether they came for good or harm.

Then the duke, when he had showed this to the mayor and others, that they might thereby see how little the protector looked for this matter, they sent unto him by the messenger such loving message again, and therewith so humbly besought him to vouchsafe that they might resort to his presence to propose their intent — of which they would unto none other person any part disclose — that at the last he came forth of his chamber, and yet not down unto them, but stood above in a gallery over them where they might see him and speak to him, as though he would not yet come too near them till he wist what they meant. And thereupon the Duke of Buckingham first made humble petition unto him on the behalf of them all, that his grace would pardon them and license them to propose unto his grace the intent of their coming, without his displeasure, without which pardon obtained they durst not be bold to move him of that matter.

In which, albeit they meant as much honor to his grace as wealth to all the realm beside, yet were they not sure how his grace would take it, whom they would in no wise offend. Then the protector (as he was very gentle of himself, and also longed sore to wit what they meant) gave him leave to propose what him liked, verily trusting (for the good mind that he bare them all) none of them anything would intend unto him word wherewith he ought to be grieved. When the duke had this leave and pardon to speak, then waxed he bold to show him their intent and purpose, with all the causes moving them thereunto (as ye before have heard) and finally to beseech his grace that it would like him, of his accustomed goodness and zeal unto the realm, now with his eye of pity to behold the long continued distress and decay of the same, and to set his gracious hands to redress and amendment thereof.

All which he might well do by taking upon him the crown and governance of this realm, according to his right and title lawfully descended unto him, and to the laud of God, profit of the land, and unto his noble grace so much the more honor, and less pain, in that, that never prince reigned upon any people that were so glad to live under his obeisance as the people of this realm under his. When the protector had heard the proposition, he looked very strangely thereat, and answered: that all were it that he partly knew the things by them alleged to be true, yet such entire love he bare unto King

Edward and his children; that so much more regarded his honor in other realms about than the crown of any one of which he was never desirous; that he could not find in his heart in this point to incline to their desire. For in all other nations, where the truth were not well known, it should peradventure be thought that it were his own ambitious mind and device to depose the prince and take himself the crown.

With which infamy he would not have his honor stained for any crown, in which he had ever perceived much more labor and pain than pleasure to him that so would use it — as he that would not were not worthy to have it. Notwithstanding, he not only pardoned them the motion that they made him, but also thanked them for the love and hearty favor they bare him, praying them for his sake to give and bear the same to the prince, under whom he was and would be content to live; and with his labor and council (as far as should like the king to use him) he would do his uttermost devoir to set the realm in good state, which was already in this little while of his protectorship (the praise given to God) well begun — in that the malice of such as were before occasion of the contrary, and of new intended to be, were now, partly by good policy and partly more by God's special providence than man's provision, repressed.

Upon this answer given, the duke, by the protector's license, a little rowned[76] as well with other noblemen about him as with the mayor and recorder of London. And after that (upon like pardon desired and obtained) he showed aloud unto the protector that for a final conclusion that the realm was appointed[77] King Edward's line should not any longer reign upon them, both for that they had so far gone that it was now no surety to retreat. As for that, they thought it for the weal universal to take that way, although they had not yet begun it. Wherefore, if it would like his grace to take the crown upon him, they would humbly beseech him thereunto. If he would give them a resolute answer to the contrary, which they would be loth to hear, then must they needs seek and should not fail to find some other nobleman that would. These words much moved the protector, which else (as every man may weet) would never of likelihood have inclined thereunto.

But when he saw there was none other way but that either he must take it, or else he and his both go from it, he said unto the lords and commons: "Since we perceive well that all the realm is so set, whereof we be very sorry that they will not suffer in any wise King Edward's line to govern them, whom no man earthly can govern against their

---

[76] whispered privately.
[77] determined.

wills; and we well also perceive that no man is there to whom the crown can by just title appertain as to ourselves, as very right heir lawfully begotten of the body of our most dear father Richard, late Duke of York; to which title is now joined your election, the nobles and commons of this realm, which we of all titles possible take for the most effectual: we be content and agree favorably to incline to your petition and request, and (according to the same) here we take upon us the royal estate, preeminence and kingdom of the two noble realms, England and France: the one from this day forward by us and our heirs to rule, govern, and defend; the other, by God's grace and your good help, to get again and subdue and establish forever in due obedience unto this realm of England, the advancement whereof we never ask of God longer to live than we intend to procure."

With this there was a great shout, crying: "King Richard, King Richard!" And then the lords went up to the king (for so was he from that time called) and the people departed, talking diversely of the matter, every man as his fantasy gave him. But much they talked and marveled of the manner of this dealing, that the matter was on both parts made so strange, as though neither had ever communed with other thereof before, when that themselves wist there was no man so dull that heard them but he perceived well enough that all the matter was made between them. Howbeit some excused that again, and said all must be done in good order, though. And men must sometime for the manner's sake not be knowing what they know. . . . [78]The next day the protector with a great train went to Westminster Hall, and there when he had placed himself in the court of the King's Bench declared to the audience that he would take upon him the crown in that place there, where the king himself sits and ministers the law, because he considered that it was the chiefest duty of a king to minister the laws. Then with as pleasant an oration as he could, he went about to win unto him the nobles, the merchants, the artificers, and in conclusion all kind of men, but especially the lawyers of this realm. And finally to the intent that no man should hate him for fear, and that his deceitful clemency might get him the good will of the people, when he had declared the discommodities of discord, and the commodities of concord and unity, he made an open proclamation that he did put out of his mind all enmities, and that he there did openly pardon all offenses committed against him. . . .

On the morrow, being the sixth day of July, the king with Queen Anne, his wife, came down out of the White hall into the great hall

---

[78] Understandably Shakespeare omits all of the coronation ceremony, which would take place somewhere between scene i and scene ii of Act IV of his play. In IV.ii. Richard enters "in pomp, crowned."

at Westminster and went directly into the King's Bench. And from thence the king and the queen going upon ray cloth, barefooted, went unto Saint Edward's shrine, and all his nobility going with him, every lord in his degree. . . .

They passed through the palace and entered the abbey at the west end, and so came to their seats of estate. And after divers songs solemnly sung, they both ascended to the high altar, and were shifted from their robes, and had divers places open from the middle upward, in which places they were anointed. Then both the king and the queen changed them into cloth of gold, and ascended to their seats, where the Cardinal of Canterbury and other bishops them crowned according to the custom of the realm, giving him the scepter in the left hand and the ball with the cross in the right hand; and the queen had the scepter in her right hand and the rod with the dove in her left hand. . . .

And so in order as they came, they departed to Westminster Hall. . . . When all persons were set, the Duke of Norfolk, Earl Marshal, the Earl of Surrey, Constable for that day, the Lord Stanley, Lord Steward, Sir William Hopton, Treasurer, and Sir Thomas Percy, Comptroller, came in and served the king solemnly, with one dish of gold and another of silver, and the queen all in gilt vessel, and the bishop all in silver.

At the second course came into the hall Sir Robert Dimmock, the king's champion, making proclamation that whosoever would say that King Richard was not lawful king, he would fight with him at the utterance, and threw down his gauntlet, and then all the hall cried: "King Richard!" And so he did in three parts of the hall, and then one brought him a cup of wine covered, and when he had drunk he cast out the drink and departed with the cup. After that, the heralds cried a largess thrice in the hall, and so went up to their stage. At the end of dinner the Mayor of London served the king and queen with sweet wine, and had of each of them a cup of gold with a cover of gold. And by that time that all was done, it was dark night. And so the king returned to his chamber, and every man to his lodging.

When this feast was thus finished, the king sent home all the lords into their countries that would depart, except the Lord Stanley, whom he retained till he heard what his son the Lord Strange went about.[79] And to such as went home, he gave straight charge and commandment to see their countries well ordered and that no wrong nor extortion should be done to his subjects. And thus he taught others to execute justice and equity, the contrary whereof he daily exercised. He also

---

[79] Later Richard will hold Lord Strange as hostage (see below, p. 49 and also Shakespeare: IV.iv. 488–499).

with great rewards given to the Northern men, which he sent for to his coronation, sent them home to their country with great thanks: whereof divers of them (as they be all of nature very greedy of authority, and specially when they think to have any comfort of favor) took on them so highly,[80] and wrought such masteries, that the king was fain to ride thither in his first year and to put some in execution, and stay the country, or else no small mischief had ensued. . . .

King Richard after his coronation, taking his way to Gloucester to visit (in his new honor) the town of which he bare the name of his old, devised (as he rode) to fulfill the thing which he before had intended. And forsomuch as his mind gave him, that his nephews living, men would not reckon that he could have right to the realm, he thought therefore without delay to rid them, as though the killing of his kinsmen could amend his cause and make him a kindly king. Whereupon he sent one John Green (whom he specially trusted) unto Sir Robert Brakenbury, Constable of the Tower, with a letter and credence also, that the same Sir Robert should in any wise put the two children to death.

This John Green did his errand unto Brakenbury, kneeling before Our Lady in the Tower. [81]Who plainly answered that he would never put them to death to die therefore. With which answer John Green returning recounted the same to King Richard at Warwick yet in his way. [82]Wherewith he took such displeasure and thought, that the same night he said unto a secret page of his: "Ah! whom shall a man trust? Those that I have brought up myself, those that I had weened would most surely serve me, even those fail me, and at my commandment will do nothing for me." "Sir," (quoth his page) "there lies one on your pallet without, that I dare well say, to do your grace pleasure the thing were right hard that he would refuse." Meaning this by Sir James Tyrrel, which was a man of right goodly personage, and for nature's gifts worthy to have served a much better prince, if he had well served God, and by grace obtained as much truth and good will as he had strength and wit.

The man had an high heart, and sore longed upward, not rising yet so fast as he had hoped, being hindered and kept under by the means of Sir Richard Ratcliff and Sir William Catesby, which longing for no more partners of the prince's favor — and namely, not for him, whose pride they wist would bear no peer — kept him by secret drifts out of all secret trust, which thing this page well had marked and known. Wherefore this occasion offered, of very special friendship

---

[80] acted so haughtily.
[81] IV.ii. 1–25. In Shakespeare this refusal is made by Buckingham.
[82] IV.ii. 32–41.

he took his time to put him forward, and by such wise do him good, that all the enemies he had (except the devil) could never have done him so much hurt. [83]For upon this page's words King Richard arose (for this communication had he sitting at the draught,[84] a convenient carpet for such a council) and came out into the pallet chamber on which he found in bed Sir James and Sir Thomas Tyrrel, of person like and brethren of blood, but nothing of kin in conditions.

Then said the king merrily to them: "What sirs, be ye in bed so soon?" And calling up Sir James, broke to him secretly his mind in this mischievous matter, in which he found him nothing strange. [85]Wherefore on the morrow he sent him to Brakenbury with a letter, by which he was commanded to deliver Sir James all the keys of the Tower for one night, to the end he might there accomplish the king's pleasure in such things as he had given him commandment. After which letter delivered, and the keys received, Sir James appointed the night next ensuing to destroy them, devising before and preparing the means. The prince (as soon as the protector left that name, and took himself as king) had it showed unto him that he should not reign, but his uncle should have the crown. At which word the prince sore abashed began to sigh, and said: "Alas, I would my uncle would let me have my life yet, though I lose my kingdom."

Then he that told him the tale used him with good words, and put him in the best comfort he could. But forthwith was the prince and his brother both shut up, and all others removed from them, only one (called Black Will, or William Slaughter) excepted, set to serve them and see them sure. After which time the prince never tied his points, nor ought wrought of himself, but with that young babe, his brother, lingered with thought and heaviness until this traitorous death delivered them of that wretchedness. For Sir James Tyrrel devised that they should be murdered in their beds. To the execution whereof, he appointed Miles Forrest, one of the four that kept them, a fellow fleshed in murder before time. To him he joined one John Dighton, his own horsekeeper, a big, broad, square, and strong knave.

Then all the others being removed from them, this Miles Forrest and John Dighton, about midnight (the silly[86] children lying in their beds) came into the chamber, and suddenly lapping them up among the clothes so too bewrapped them and entangled them, keeping down by force the feather-bed and pillows hard unto their mouths, that within a while, smothered and stifled, their breath failing, they gave

---

[83] IV.ii. 67–85.
[84] privy.
[85] IV.iii. 1–35.
[86] innocent.

up to God their innocent souls into the joys of heaven, leaving to the tormentors their bodies dead in the bed. Which after that the wretches perceived, first by the struggling with the pains of death and after long lying still, to be thoroughly dead, they laid their bodies naked out upon the bed and fetched Sir James to see them; which upon the sight of them, caused those murderers to bury them at the stair foot, meetly deep in the ground, under a great heap of stones.

Then rode Sir James in great haste to King Richard, and showed him all the manner of the murder; who gave him great thanks, and (as some say) there made him knight. But he allowed not (as I have heard) the burying in so vile a corner, saying that he would have them buried in a better place, because they were a king's sons. Lo, the honorable courage of a king. Whereupon they say that a priest of Sir Robert Brakenbury's took up the bodies again and secretly interred them in such a place, as by the occasion of his death which only knew it, could never since come to light. Very truth is it, and well known, that at such time as Sir James Tyrrel was in the Tower, for treason committed against the most famous prince King Henry the Seventh, both Dighton and he were examined, and confessed the murder in manner above written. But whither the bodies were removed, they could nothing tell. . . .

I have heard by credible report of such as were secret with his chamberlain, that after this abominable deed done, he [King Richard] never had a quiet mind. . . . He never thought himself sure. Where he went abroad, his eyes whirled about, his body privily fenced, his hand ever upon his dagger, his countenance and manner like one always ready to strike again. [87]He took ill rest at nights, lay long waking and musing, sore wearied with care and watch, rather slumbered than slept, troubled with fearful dreams, suddenly sometimes started up, leapt out of his bed and ran about the chamber. So was his restless heart continually tossed and tumbled with the tedious impression and stormy remembrance of his abominable deed. Now had he outward no long time in rest. For hereupon soon after began the conspiracy, or rather good confederation, between the Duke of Buckingham and many other gentlemen against him. The occasion whereupon the king and the duke fell out is of divers folk in divers wise pretended. . . .

[88]Some have I heard say that the duke, a little before his coronation, among other things required of the protector the Duke of Hereford's lands, to the which he pretended himself just inheritor. And forsomuch as the title, which he claimed by inheritance, was somewhat interlaced with the title to the crown by the line of King

---

[87] IV.i. 83–85.
[88] IV.ii. 86ff.

Henry before deprived,[89] the protector conceived such indignation that he rejected the duke's request with many spiteful and minatory words. Which so wounded his heart with hatred and mistrust, that he never after could endure to look aright on King Richard, but ever feared his own life; so far forth that when the protector rode through London toward his coronation, he feigned himself sick, because he would not ride with him. And the other also taking it in evil part, sent him word to rise, and come ride, or he would make him to be carried. Whereupon he rode on with evil will, and that notwithstanding on the morrow rose from the feast feigning himself sick, and King Richard said it was done in hatred and despite of him. . . .

[From then on Richard and Buckingham lived in "hatred and distrust" of one another. Buckingham, returning home to his estate, had there in his custody Doctor Morton, Bishop of Ely — whom Sir Thomas More served as page and who is described here as "a man of great natural wit, very well learned and honorable in behavior." In an extended series of conversations lasting several days Morton and Buckingham come to agree that Richard III is too evil a king to be endured.[90] Morton then tells Buckingham how he was inspired by the following idea for the succession to the throne.]

"For (as I told you before) the Countess of Richmond in my return from the new-named king, meeting me in the highway, prayed me first for kindred sake, secondly for the love that I bare to my grandfather, Duke Humphrey, which was sworn brother to her father, to move the king to be good to her son Henry, Earl of Richmond, and to license him with his favor to return again into England.[91] And if it were his pleasure so to do, she promised that the earl her son should marry one of King Edward's daughters, at the appointment of the king, without anything to be taken or demanded for the said espousals, but

---

[89] Buckingham was Henry Stafford, who was descended on his father's side from Thomas of Woodstock, the sixth son of Edward III.

[90] Near the beginning of these conversations Sir Thomas More's manuscript ends and the remainder of Holinshed's account is taken from Polydore Vergil via Edward Hall. (See headnote.)

[91] Margaret, Countess of Richmond, was the mother of the Earl of Richmond, future Henry VII. Being the great-granddaughter to John of Gaunt by Catherine Swynford made her son the first surviving male representative of the House of Lancaster. Her first husband, the father of Henry, was Edmund, Earl of Richmond, son of Owen Tudor and Katherine, widow of Henry V. Her third husband was Lord Stanley, from whom she had no more children.

Henry, Earl of Richmond, took refuge in France after the battle of Tewksbury (1371) with Francois II, Duke of Brittany.

only the king's favor: which request I soon overpassed,[92] and gave her fair words, and so departed.

"But after in my lodging, when I called to memory with a deliberate study and did circumspectly ponder them, I fully adjudged that the Holy Ghost caused her to move a thing (the end whereof she could not consider) both for the security of the realm, as also for the preferment of her child and the destruction and final confusion of the common enemy, King Richard. Which thing, she neither then thought (I am sure) as I by her words could make conjecture, nor I myself cast not, her desire to be so profitable to the realm as I now do perceive. But such a Lord is God, that with a little sparkle he kindles a great fire, and (to the admiration of the world) of impossibilities he makes possibilities, of small beginnings mighty increasings, of drops great floods.

"And so finally to declare to you the very conclusion to which I am both bent and set, my mind is, and my power and purse shall help, that the Earl of Richmond, very heir of the House of Lancaster (in the quarrel of the which lineage, both my father and grandfath[er] lost their lives in battle) shall take to wife Lady Elizabeth, elde[st] daughter to King Edward, by the which marriage both the Houses o[f] York and Lancaster may be joined and united in one, to the clear establishment of the title to the crown of this noble realm. . . ."

[*Buckingham declares himself pleased by this arrangement and begins to assemble an army to support the Earl of Richmond. Morton journeys to Flanders where Richmond is and "where he did the Earl of Richmond good service." Arrangements go on in secret to wed Elizabeth of York to the Earl of Richmond and the armies opposed to Richard III continue to assemble. Richard, hearing rumors of these developments, summons the Duke of Buckingham to his royal presence.*]

The duke made to the messenger a determinate answer, that he would not come to his mortal enemy, whom he neither loved nor favored, and immediately prepared open war against him, and persuaded all his complices and partakers, that every man in his quarter with all diligence should raise up people and make a commotion. [93]And by this means almost in one moment Thomas, Marquis Dorset, came out of sanctuary, where since the beginning of King Richard's days he had continued — whose life by the only help of Sir Thomas

---

[92] rejected.
[93] IV.ii. 47–49.

Lovell was preserved from all danger and peril in this troublous world — gathered together a great band of men in Yorkshire.

[94] Sir Edward Courtney, and Peter his brother, Bishop of Exeter, raised another army in Devonshire and Cornwall. In Kent, Richard Guildford and other gentlemen collected a great company of soldiers and openly began war. But King Richard, who in the meantime had gotten together a great strength and puissance, thinking it not most for his part beneficial to disperse and divide his great army into small branches, and particularly to persecute any one of the conjuration by himself, determined (all other things being set aside) with his whole puissance to set on the chief head, which was the Duke of Buckingham. And so removing from London, he took his journey towards Salisbury, to the intent that in his journey he might set on the duke's army, if he might know him in any place encamped or in order of battle arrayed.

[95] The king was scarce two days' journey from Salisbury when the Duke of Buckingham, accompanied with a great power of wild Welshmen, whom he (being a man of great courage and sharp speech) in manner against their wills had rather thereto enforced and compelled by lordly and strict commandment, than by liberal wages and gentle demeanor — which thing was the very occasion why they left him desolate, and cowardly forsook him. The duke with all his power marched through the forest of Dean, intending to have passed the River Severn at Gloucester, and there to have joined his army with the Courtneys and other Western men of his confederacy and affinity. Which if he [had] done, no doubt but King Richard had been in great jeopardy, either of privation of his realm, or loss of his life, or both.

[96]But see the chance. Before he could attain to Severn side, by force of continual rain and moisture the river rose so high that it overflowed all the country adjoining, insomuch that men were drowned in their beds and houses with the extreme violence were overturned, children were carried about the fields swimming in cradles, beasts were drowned on hills. Which rage of water lasted continually ten days, insomuch that in the country adjoining they call it to this day, The Great Water, or The Duke of Buckingham's Great Water. By this flood the passages were so closed that neither the duke could come over Severn to his adherents, nor they to him. During the which time, the Welshmen lingering idly and without money, victuals, or wages, suddenly scattered and departed, and for all the duke's fair

[94] IV.iv. 500–507.
[95] IV.iii. 50.
[96] IV.iv. 508–515.

promises, threatenings, and enforcement, would in no wise either go further nor abide.

The duke (being thus left almost post alone) was of necessity compelled to fly, and in flight was with this sudden fortune marvelously dismayed. And being unpurveyed[97] what council he should take and what way he should follow, like a man in despair, not knowing what to do, of very trust and confidence conveyed himself into the house of Humphrey Bannister, his servant, beside Shrewsbury, whom he had tenderly brought up and whom he above all men loved, favored, and trusted — now not doubting but that in his extreme necessity he should find him faithful, secret, and trusty, intending there covertly to lurk till either he might raise again a new army or else shortly to sail into Brittany, to the Earl of Richmond. (But, alas, good duke, the means (by occasion of God's providence, shaking men out of their shifts of supposed safety) failed him, and he fell unfortunately into the hands of the foaming boar that tore him in pieces with his tusks.) . . .

[98]Humphrey Bannister (were it more for fear of life and loss of goods, or allured and provoked by the avaricious desire of the thousand pounds) he bewrayed his guest and master to John Mitton, then Sheriff of Shropshire, which suddenly with a strong power of men in harness apprehended the duke in a little grove adjoining to the mansion of Humphrey Bannister, and in great haste and evil speed conveyed him apparelled in a piled black cloak to the town of Shrewsbury [Salisbury]? where King Richard then kept his household. . . .

[99]The duke being by certain of the king's council diligently upon interrogatories examined, what things he knew prejudicial unto the king's person, opened and declared frankly and freely all the conjuration, without dissembling or glozing; trusting, because he had truly and plainly revealed and confessed all things that were of him required, that he should have license to speak to the king: which (whether it were to sue for pardon and grace, or whether he being brought to his presence would have sticked him with a dagger as men then judged) he sore desired and required. But when he had confessed the whole fact and conspiracy, upon All Souls' day, without arraignment or judgment he was at Salisbury in the open marketplace on a new scaffold beheaded and put to death.

This death (as a reward) the Duke of Buckingham received at the hands of King Richard, whom he before in his affairs, purposes, and

---

[97] Unprovided, ignorant.
[98] IV.v. 533ff.
[99] V.i. 1ff.

enterprises had holpen, sustained, and set forward, above all God forbode. By this all men may easily perceive that he not only loses both his labor, travail, and industry (and further stains and spots his line with a perpetual ignominy and reproach) which in evil and mischief assists and aids an evil disposed person — considering for the most part that he for his friendly favor should receive some great displeasure or importunate chance. Besides that, God of His justice in conclusion appointed him a condign pain and affliction for his merits and deserts. . . .

[100]While these things were thus handled and ordered in England, Henry, Earl of Richmond, prepared an army of five thousand manly Bretons and forty well furnished ships. When all things were prepared in a readiness and the day of departing and setting forward was appointed, which was the twelfth day of the month of October, the whole army went on shipboard and hauled up their sails and with a prosperous wind took the sea. But toward night the wind changed, and the weather turned, and so huge and terrible a tempest so suddenly arose that with the very power and strength of the storm the ships were disparkled, severed and separated asunder: some by force were driven into Normandy, some were compelled to return again into Brittany. The ship wherein the Earl of Richmond was, associate only with one other bark, was all night tossed and turmoiled.

In the morning after, when the rage of the furious tempest was assauged and the ire of blustering wind was some deal appeased, about the hour of noon the same day the earl approached to the south part of the realm of England, even at the mouth of the haven of Pole, in the county of Dorset, where he might plainly perceive all the sea banks and shores garnished and furnished with men of war and soldiers, appointed and deputed there to defend his arrival and landing (as before is mentioned). Wherefore he gave strict charge and sore commandment that no person should presume to take land and go to shore until such time as the whole navy were assembled and come together. And while he tarried and lingered, he sent out a shipboat toward the land side to know whether they, which stood there in such a number and so well furnished in apparel defensive, were his foes and enemies, or else his friends and comforters.

They that were sent to inquire were instantly desired of the men of war keeping the coast (which thereof were before instructed and admonished) to descend and take land, affirming that they were appointed by the Duke of Buckingham there to await and tarry for

---

[100] IV.iv. 522–529.

the arrival and landing of the Earl of Richmond, and to conduct him safely into the camp, where the duke not far off lay incamped with a mighty army, and an host of great strength and power, to the intent that the duke and the earl, joining in puissances and forces together, might prosecute and chase King Richard, being destitute of men and in manner desperate, and so by that means, and their own labors, to obtain the end of their enterprise which they had before begun.

The Earl of Richmond suspecting their flattering request to be but a fraud (as it was indeed) after he perceived none of his ships to appear in sight, he weighed up his anchors, hauled up his sails, and having a prosperous and strainable wind and a fresh gale sent even by God to deliver him from that peril and jeopardy, arrived safe and in all security in the Duchy of Normandy. . . .

[*Richmond was determined to return to England safe and widely accepted, and to that end he got leave from King Charles VIII of France to pass through Normandy. He made a solemn vow on Christmas day to wed the Lady Elizabeth, daughter of King Edward IV. In the meantime King Richard did "tyrannically persecute and execute" his enemies, real and imagined, throughout the kingdom.*]

[1484] In this troublous season, nothing was more marvelled at than that the Lord Stanley had not been taken and reputed as an enemy to the king, considering the working of the Lady Margaret, his wife, mother to the Earl of Richmond. But forsomuch as the enterprise of a woman was of him reputed of no regard or estimation — and that the Lord Thomas, her husband, had purged himself sufficiently to be innocent of all doings and attempts by her perpetrated and committed — it was given him in charge to keep her in some secret place at home, without having any servant or company. So that from thenceforth she should never send letter or messenger unto her son, nor any of his friends or confederates, by the which the king might be molested or troubled, or any hurt or prejudice might be attempted against his realm and communalty. Which commandment was a while put in execution and accomplished, according to his dreadful commandment.

Yet the wild worm of vengeance wavering in his head could not be content with the death of divers gentlemen suspected of treason; but also he must extend his bloody fury against a poor gentleman called Collingborn for making a small rhyme of three of his unfortunate counsellors, which were the Lord Lovell, Sir Richard Ratcliff, his mischievous minion, and Sir William Catesby, his secret seducer, which meter or rhyme was thus framed:

> The cat, the rat, and Lovell our dog,
> Rule all England under an hog.[101]

Meaning by the hog, the dreadful wild boar, which was the king's cognisance. But because the first line ended in dog, the metrician could not (observing the regimens of meter) end the second verse in boar, but called the boar an hog. This poetical schoolmaster, corrector of briefs and longs, caused Collingborn to be abbreviated shorter by the head, and to be divided into four quarters. . . .

[*Alarmed by the growing popular unrest Richard made a three year truce with Scotland so as to be free to concentrate on the problem of the Earl of Richmond. He attempted to get the Duke of Brittany to turn Richmond over to him, but Richmond escaped from Brittany and found refuge in the court of France. While Richmond sojourned in Paris a large number of English noblemen came to him to pledge allegiance to his cause.*]

In the mean season, King Richard was credibly advertised what promises and oaths the earl and his confederates had made and sworn together at Reims, and how by the earl's means all the Englishmen were passed out of Brittany into France. [102]Wherefore being sore dismayed, and in a manner desperate, because his crafty chievance[103] took no effect in Britain, he imagined and devised how to infringe and disturb the earl's purpose by another means — so that by the marriage of Lady Elizabeth, his niece, he should pretend no claim nor title to the crown. For he thought if that marriage failed, the earl's chief comb had been clearly cut. And because that he being blinded with the ambitious desire of rule before this time in obtaining the kingdom had committed and done many cursed acts and detestable tyrannies, yet according to the old proverb, "Let him take the bull that stole away the calf" he thought all acts by him committed in times past to be but of small moment, and not to be regarded in comparison of that mischievous imagination which he now newly began and attempted.

[104]There came into his ungracious mind a thing not only detestable to be spoken of in the remembrance of man, but much more cruel and

---

[101] Shakespeare does not use this rhyme and "cognisance" directly, but does have Queen Margaret refer to it glancingly: I.iii. 228.

[102] IV.ii. 61–66.

[103] achievement.

[104] IV.iv. 203–431; IV.ii. 50–60. More is the only contemporary historian or biographer who suggests that Richard was in any way guilty of the death of Queen Anne.

abominable to be put in execution. For when he revolved in his wavering mind how great a fountain of mischief toward him should spring, if the Earl of Richmond should be advanced to the marriage of his niece — which thing he heard say by the rumor of the people that no small number of wise and witty personages enterprised to compass and bring to conclusion — he clearly determined to reconcile to his favor his brother's wife, Queen Elizabeth, either by fair words or liberal promises; firmly believing, her favor once obtained, that she would not stick to commit (and lovingly credit) to him the rule and governance both of her and her daughters; and so by that means the Earl of Richmond of the affinity of his niece should be utterly defrauded and beguiled.

And if no ingenious remedy could be otherwise invented to save the innumerable mischiefs which were even at hand, and like to fall, if it should happen Queen Anne, his wife, to depart out of this present life, then he himself would rather take to wife his cousin and niece the Lady Elizabeth. [Better that] than for lack of that affinity the whole realm should run to ruin. As who said that if he once fell from his estate and dignity, the ruin of the realm must needs shortly ensue and follow. Wherefore he sent to the queen (being in sanctuary) divers and often messengers, which first should excuse and purge him of all things before against her attempted or procured, and after should so largely promise promotions innumerable, and benefits, not only to her, but also to her son, Lord Thomas, Marquis Dorset, that they should bring her (if it were possible) into some wan hope, or (as men say) into a fool's paradise.

The messengers, being men both of wit and gravity, so persuaded the queen with great and pregnant reasons, and what with fair and large promises, that she began somewhat to relent and to give to them no deaf ear; insomuch that she faithfully promised to submit and yield herself fully and frankly to the king's will and pleasure. And so she, putting in oblivion the murder of her innocent children, the infamy and dishonor spoken by the king her husband, the living in adultery laid to her charge, the bastarding of her daughters; forgetting also the faithful promise and open oath made to the Countess of Richmond, mother to the Earl Henry, blinded by avaricious affection and seduced by flattering words, first delivered into King Richard's hands her five daughters, as lambs once again committed to the custody of the ravenous wolf.

After, she sent letters to the marquis, her son, being then at Paris with the Earl of Richmond, willing him in any wise to leave the earl and without delay to repair into England where for him were provided great honors and honorable promotions; ascertaining him further that all offenses on both parts were forgotten and forgiven, and both he and she highly incorporated in the king's heart. Surely the inconstancy of this woman were much to be marvelled at, if all women had been found constant; but let men speak, yet women of the very bond of nature will follow their own sex. But it was no small allurement that King Richard used to overcome her (for we know by experience that women are of a proud disposition, and that the way to win them is by promises of preferment) and therefore it is the less marvel that he by his wily wit had made conquest of her wavering will. Besides that, it is to be presumed that she stood in fear to impugn his demands by denials, lest he in his malicious mood might take occasion to deal roughly with her, being a weak woman and of timorous spirit.

Now when King Richard had thus with glorious promises, and flattering words, pleased and appeased the mutable mind of Queen Elizabeth, which knew nothing less than that he most intended, he caused all his brother's daughters to be conveyed into his palace with solemn receiving: as though with his new familiar and loving entertainment they should forget and in their minds blot out the old committed injury and late executed tyranny. Now nothing was contrary and against his devilish purpose but that his mansion was not void of his wife, which thing he in any wise adjudged necessary to be done. But there was one thing that so much feared and stayed him from committing this abominable murder, because (as you have heard before) he began to counterfeit the image of a good and well disposed person. And therefore he was afeared lest the sudden death of his wife once openly known, he should lose the good and credible opinion which the people had of him, without any desert, conceived and reported.

[105]But in conclusion, evil council prevailed in a wit lately minded to mischief and turned from all goodness, so that his ungracious desire overcame his honest fear. And first, to enter into the gates of his imagined enterprise, he abstained both from the bed and company of his wife. Then he complained to divers noblemen of the realm of the unfortunate sterility and barrenness of his wife, because she brought forth no fruit and generation of her body. And in especial he recounted to Thomas Rotheram, Archbishop of York (whom lately he had delivered out of ward and captivity) these impediments of his queen, and divers others, thinking that he would reveal to her all these things, trusting the sequel hereof to take due effect, that she hearing this grudge of her husband and taking therefore an inward thought would not long live in this world.

---

[105] IV.iii. 39. A rare instance of a source scene richer and more psychologically probing than Shakespeare's adaptation of it.

Of this the bishop gathered (which well knew the complexion and usage of the king) that the queen's days were short, and that he declared to certain of his secret friends. After this he procured a common rumor (but he would not have the author known) to be published and spread abroad among the common people, that the queen was dead; to the intent that she taking some conceit of this strange fame should fall into some sudden sickness or grievous malady. And to prove, if afterwards she should fortune by that or any other ways to lease her life, whether the people would impute her death to the thought or sickness, or thereof would lay the blame to him. Now when the queen heard tell that so horrible a rumor of her death was sprung amongst the communalty, she sore suspected and judged the world to be almost at an end with her. And in that sorrowful agony, she with lamentable countenance and sorrowful cheer repaired to the presence of the king her husband, demanding of him what it should mean that he had judged her worthy to die.

The king answered her with fair words, and with smiling and flattering leasings comforted her, and bade her be of good cheer, for (to his knowledge) she should have no other cause. But howsoever that it fortuned, either by inward thought and pensiveness of heart, or by infection of poison (which is affirmed to be most likely) within few days after, the queen departed out of this transitory life and was with due solemnity buried in the Church of Saint Peter at Westminster. . . .

Amongst the noblemen whom he [Richard III] most mistrusted, these were the principal: Thomas, Lord Stanley, Sir William Stanley, his brother, Gilbert Talbot, and six hundred others of whose purposes although King Richard were not ignorant, yet he gave neither confidence nor credence to any one of them; and least of all to the Lord Stanley, because he was joined in matrimony with the Lady Margaret, mother to the Earl of Richmond, as afterward apparently ye may perceive. [106]For when the said Lord Stanley would have departed into his country to visit his family, and to recreate and refresh his spirits (as he openly said, but the truth was, to the intent to be in a perfect readiness to receive the Earl of Richmond at his first arrival in England) the king in no wise would suffer him to depart before he had left as an hostage in the court George Stanley, Lord Strange, his first begotten son and heir.

[1485] While King Richard was thus troubled and vexed with imaginations of the troublous time that was like to come, lo, even suddenly he heard news: that fire was sprung out of the smoke and the war freshly begun; and that the castle of Hammes was delivered

---

[106] IV.iv. 488–499.

into the hands of the Earl of Richmond by the means of the Earl of Oxford; and that not only he but also James Blunt, captain of the castle, were fled into France to aid the Earl Henry....

[Richard ordered some skirmishes set in motion in France, but these proved indecisive and he recalled his ships of war. Shortly after, the Earl of Richmond learned that Richard intended to marry Lady Elizabeth and that news spurred Richmond into attempting once again to invade England.]

[107]After that all things were in readiness, the earl being accompanied only with two thousand men and a small number of ships, weighed up his anchors and hauled up his sails in the month of August, and sailed from Harfleur with so prosperous a wind that the seventh day after his departure he arrived in Wales in the evening, at a place called Milford Haven; and incontinent took land and came to a place called Dalle, where he heard say that a certain company of his adversaries were laid in garrison to defend his arrival all the last winter. And the earl at the sun rising removed to Hereford west, being distant from Dalle not full ten miles, where he was joyfully received of the people, and he arrived there so suddenly that he was come and entered the town at the same time when the citizens had but knowledge of his coming....

Then the earl advanced forward in good haste, making no repose or abode in any one place.... But to the intent his friends should know in what readiness he was, and how he proceeded forward, he sent of his most secret and faithful servants with letters and instructions to the Lady Margaret, his mother, to the Lord Stanley and his brother, to Sir Gilbert Talbot, and to other his trusty friends: declaring to them that he being succored and helped with the aid and relief of his friends intended to pass over the river of Severn at Shrewsbury, and so to pass directly to the city of London.... And in his passing there met and saluted him Rice ap Thomas with a goodly band of Welshmen, which making an oath and promise to the earl, submitted himself wholly to his order and commandment. For the Earl of Richmond two days before made to him promise that if he would swear to take his part and be obedient to him he would make him chief governor of Wales: which part as he faithfully promised and granted, so (after that he had obtained and possessed the realm and diadem) he liberally performed and accomplished the same.... In the evening the same day came to him Sir Gilbert Talbot, with the whole power of the young Earl of Shrewsbury, then being in ward, which

---

[107] IV.v. 6–16.

were accounted to the number of two thousand men. And thus his power increasing, he arrived at the town of Stafford and there paused.

There also came Sir William Stanley accompanied with a few persons. And after that the earl and he had communed no long time together, he reverted to his soldiers whom he had assembled together to serve the earl: which from thence departed to Lichfield and lay without the walls in his camp all the night. The next morning he entered into the town and was with all honor like a prince received. A day or two before, the Lord Stanley, having in his band almost five thousand men, lodged in the same town. But hearing that the Earl of Richmond was marching thitherward gave to him place, dislodging him and his, and repaired to a town called Atherstone, there abiding the coming of the earl. And this wily fox did this act to avoid all suspicion on King Richard's part.

[108]For the Lord Stanley was afraid lest if he should seem openly to be a fautor[109] or aider to the earl, his son-in-law, before the day of the battle, that King Richard, which yet utterly did not put in him diffidence and mistrust would put to some cruel death his son and heir apparent George, Lord Strange, whom King Richard (as you have heard before) kept with him as a pledge or hostage to the intent that the Lord Stanley his father should attempt nothing prejudicial to him. King Richard at this season keeping his house in the Castle of Nottingham was informed that the Earl of Richmond, with such banished men as were fled out of England to him, were now arrived in Wales, and that all things necessary to his enterprise were unprovided, unpurveyed and very weak, nothing meet to withstand the power of such as the king had appointed to meet him. . . .

Wherefore he sent to John, Duke of Norfolk, Henry, Earl of Northumberland, Thomas, Earl of Surrey, and to other of his especial and trusty friends of the nobility, which he judged more to prefer and esteem his wealth and honor than their own riches and private commodity; willing them to muster and view all their servants and tenants and to elect and choose the most courageous and active persons of the whole number, and with them to repair to his presence with all speed and diligence. Also he wrote to Robert Brakenbury, Lieutenant of the Tower, commanding him with his power to come to his army and to bring with him (as fellows in arms) Sir Thomas Bourchier and Sir Walter Hungerford and divers other knights and squires, in whom he cast no small suspicion. . . .

The Earl of Richmond raised his camp and departed from Lichfield to the town of Tamworth thereto near adjoining, and in the mid way

---

[108] IV.v. 1–5.
[109] partisan.

passing, there saluted him Sir Walter Hungerford and Sir Thomas Bourchier, knights, and divers others which yielded and submitted themselves to his pleasure. For they, being advertised that King Richard had them in suspicion and jealousy, a little beyond Stony-Stratford left and forsook privily their Captain Robert Brakenbury; and wandering by night, and in manner by unknown paths, and uncertain ways searching, at the last came at Earl Henry. Divers other noble personages, which inwardly hated King Richard worse than a toad or a serpent did likewise resort to him with all their power and strength, wishing and working his destruction, who otherwise would have been the instrument of their casting away. . . .

In the mean season, King Richard which was appointed now to finish his last labor by the very divine justice and providence of God (which called him to condign punishment for his mischievous deserts) marched to a place meet for two battles to encounter by a village called Bosworth, not far from Leicester. And there he pitched his field on a hill called Ann Beam [Anne of Bohemia] refreshed his soldiers, and took his rest.

[110]The fame went that he had the same night a dreadful and terrible dream. For it seemed to him being asleep that he did see divers images like terrible devils which pulled and haled him, not suffering him to take any quiet or rest. The which strange vision not so suddenly struck his heart with a sudden fear, but it stuffed his head and troubled his mind with many busy and dreadful imaginations. For incontinent after, his heart being almost damped, he prognosticated before[111] the doubtful chance of the battle to come, not using the alacrity and mirth of mind and countenance as he was accustomed to do before he came toward the battle. And lest that it might be suspected that he was abashed for fear of his enemies, and for that cause looked so pitiously, he recited and declared to his familiar friends in the morning his wonderful vision and fearful dream.

But I think this was no dream, but a punction[112] and prick of his sinful conscience. For the conscience is so much more charged and aggrieved as the offense is greater and more heinous in degree. (So that King Richard, by this reckoning, must needs have a wonderful troubled mind, because the deeds that he had done, as they were heinous and unnatural, so did they excite and stir up extraordinary motions of trouble and vexations in his conscience.) Which sting of conscience, although it strike not always, yet at the last day of

---

[110] V.iii. 118–178.
[111] in advance.
[112] dagger, dagger thrust.

extreme life it is wont to show and represent to us our faults and offenses, and the pains and punishments which hang over our heads for the committing of the same, to the intent that at that instant, we for our deserts being penitent and repentant, may be compelled (lamenting and bewailing our sins like forsakers of this world) jocund to depart out of this mischief life.

[113]Now to return again to our purpose. The next day after, King Richard being furnished with men and all habiliments of war, bringing all his men out of their camp into the plain, ordered his forward in a marvelous length, in which he appointed both horsemen and footmen, to the intent to imprint in the hearts of them that looked afar off a sudden terror and deadly fear for the great multitude of the armed soldiers. And in the forefront he placed the archers like a strong fortified trench or bulwark. Over this battle was captain John, Duke of Norfolk, with whom was Thomas, Earl of Surrey, his son. After this long vanguard followed King Richard himself with a strong company of chosen and approved men of war, having horsemen for wings on both sides of his battle.

[114]After that the Earl of Richmond was departed from the communication of his friends (as you have heard before) he began to be of a better stomach and of a more valiant courage, and with all diligence pitched his field just by the camp of his enemies, and there he lodged that night. In the morning betimes he caused his men to put on their armor, and apparel themselves ready to fight and give battle. . . .

He made his forward somewhat single and slender, according to the small number of his people. In the front he placed the archers, of whom he made captain John, Earl of Oxford. To the right wing of the battle he appointed Sir Gilbert Talbot to be the leader. To the left wing he assigned Sir John Savage who had brought thither with him a crew of right able personages, clad in white coats and hoods, which mustered[115] in the eyes of their adversaries right brimly.[116] The Earl of Richmond himself, with aid of the Lord Stanley, governed the battle, accompanied with the Earl of Pembroke, having a good company of horsemen and a small number of footmen. For all his whole number exceeded not five thousand men, beside the power of the Stanleys whereof three thousand were in the field under the standard of Sir William Stanley. The king's number was double

---

[113] V.iii. 291–300.
[114] V.iii. 227–233.
[115] shone.
[116] brilliantly.

so much and more.[117] When both these armies were thus ordered, and all men ready to set forward, King Richard called his chieftains together and to them said as follows:

The oration of King Richard the Third to the chieftains of his army.

[118]"My most faithful and assured fellows, most trusty and well beloved friends, and elected captains, by whose wisdom and policy I have obtained the crown . . . I doubt not but you know how the devil (continual enemy to human nature, disturber of concord, and sower of sedition) has entered into the heart of an unknown Welshman (whose father I never knew, nor him personally saw) exciting him to aspire and covet our realm, crown, and dignity, and thereof clearly to deprive and spoil us and our posterity. Ye see further how a company of traitors, thieves, outlaws, and renegades of our own nation be aiders and partakers of his feat and enterprise, ready at hand to overcome and oppress us.

"You see also what a number of beggerly Bretons and fainthearted Frenchmen be with him arrived to destroy us, our wives and children. Which imminent mischiefs and apparent inconveniences, if we will withstand and repel, we must live together as brethren, fight together like lions, and fear not to die together like men. And observing and keeping this rule and precept, believe me, the fearful hare never fled faster before the greedy greyhound, nor the silly lark before the sparrowhawk, nor yet the simple sheep before the ravenous wolf than your proud bragging adversaries, astonished and amazed with the only sight of your manly visages, will flee, run, and skirr out of the field. For if you consider and wisely ponder all things in your mind, you shall perceive that we have manifest causes and apparent tokens of triumph and victory.

"And to begin with the Earl of Richmond, captain of this rebellion, he is a Welsh milksop, a man of small courage and of less experience in martial acts and feats of war, brought up by my mother's means, and mine, like a captive in a close cage in the court of Francis, Duke of Brittany; and never saw army, nor was exercised in martial affairs. . . .

"And as for the Frenchmen and Bretons, their valiantness is such that our noble progenitors and your valiant parts have them oftener vanquished and overcome in one month than they in the be-

---

[117] Richard's forces totaled about 12,000 men, Richmond's about 5,000; Stanley lay nearby with some 3,000 men whom Richard also counted upon, though events proved otherwise.

[118] V.iii. 314–341.

ginning imagined possible to compass and finish in a whole year. What will you make of them? Braggers without audacity, drunkards without discretion, ribalds without reason, cowards without resisting, and in conclusion the most effeminate and lascivious people that ever showed themselves in front of battle; ten times more courageous to flee and escape than once to assault the breast of our strong and populous army. Wherefore considering all these advantages, expel out of your thoughts all doubts, avoid out of your minds all fear, and like valiant champions advance forth your standards and assay whether your enemies can decide and try the title of battle by dint of sword. Advance (I say again) forward my captains, in whom lacks neither policy, wisdom, nor yet puissance. Everyone give but one sure stripe, and surely the journey is ours. What prevails a handful to a whole realm?

"Desiring you for the love that you bear to me and the affection that you have to your native and natural country, and to the safeguard of your prince and yourselves, that you will this day take to you your accustomed courage and courageous spirits, for the defense and safeguard of us all. And as for me, I assure you this day I will triumph by glorious victory or suffer death for immortal fame. For they be maimed and out of the palace of fame disgraded, dying without renown, which do not as much prefer and exalt the perpetual honor of their native country as their own mortal and transitory life. [119]Now, Saint George to borrow, let us set forward and remember well that I am he which shall with high advancements reward and prefer the valiant and hardy champions and punish and torment the shameful cowards and dreadful dastards." ...

When the earl of Richmond knew by his foreriders that the king was so near embattled, he rode about his army from rank to rank and from wing to wing, giving comfortable words to all men; and that finished (being armed at all pieces saving his helmet) mounted on a little hill so that all his people might see and behold him perfectly, to their great rejoicing. For he was a man of no great stature, but so formed and decorated with all gifts and lineaments of nature that he seemed more an angelical creature, than a terrestrial personage. His countenance and aspect was cheerful and courageous, his hair yellow like the burnished gold, his eyes gray, shining and quick; prompt and ready in answering, but of such sobriety that it could never be judged whether he were more dull than quick in speaking (such was his temperance). Now when he had overlooked his army over every

---

[119] V.iii. 301.

side, he paused a while, and after with a loud voice and bold spirit spoke to his companions these or the like words following:

The oration of King Henry the Seventh to his army.

[120]"If ever God gave victory to men fighting in a just quarrel, or if He ever aided such as made war for the wealth and tuition of their own natural and nutritive country, or if He ever succored them which adventured their lives for the relief of innocents, suppressing of malefactors and apparent offenders, no doubt my fellows and friends but He of His bountiful goodness will this day send us triumphant victory and a lucky journey over our proud enemies and arrogant adversaries. For if you remember and consider the very cause of our just quarrel, you shall apparently perceive the same to be true, godly, and virtuous. In the which I doubt not but God will rather aid us (yea, and fight for us) than see us vanquished and overthrown by such as neither fear Him nor His laws, nor yet regard justice or honesty.

"Our cause is so just that no enterprise can be of more virtue, both by the laws divine and civil. For what can be a more honest, goodly, or godly quarrel than to fight against a captain being a homicide and murderer of his own blood or progeny, an extreme destroyer of his nobility, and to his and our country and the poor subjects of the same a deadly mallet, a fiery brand, and a burden intolerable? Besides him, consider who be of his band and company: such as by murder and untruth committed against their own kin and lineage — yea, against their prince and sovereign lord — have disinherited me and you and wrongfully detain and usurp our lawful patrimony and lineal inheritance. For he that calls himself king keeps from me the crown and regimen of this noble realm and country, contrary to all justice and equity.

"Likewise his mates and friends occupy your lands, cut down your woods, and destroy your manors, letting your wives and children range abroad for their living: which persons for their penance and punishment I doubt not but God of His goodness will either deliver into our hands as a great gain and booty, or cause them (being grieved and compuncted with the prick of their corrupt consciences) cowardly to fly and not abide the battle. Besides this I assure you that there be yonder in the great battle men brought thither for fear and not for love; soldiers by force compelled and not with good will assembled; persons which desire rather the destruction than salvation of their master and captain; and finally a multitude whereof the most part will be our friends and the least part our enemies. . . . .

---

[120] V.iii. 237–270.

"If we had come to conquer Wales and had achieved it, our praise had been great and our gain more. But if we win this battle the whole rich realm of England, with the lords and rulers of the same, shall be ours; the profit shall be ours and the honor shall be ours. Therefore labor for your gain and sweat for your right. While we were in Brittany, we had small livings and little plenty of wealth or welfare. Now is the time come to get abundance of riches and copious of profit, which is the reward of your service and merit of your pains. And this remember with yourselves, that before us be our enemies; and on either side of us be such as I neither surely trust nor greatly believe; backward we cannot flee; so that here we stand like sheep in a fold, circumvented and compassed between our enemies and our doubtful friends.

"Wherefore let all fear be set aside, and like sworn brethren let us join in one; for this day shall be the end of our travail and the gain of our labor, either by honorable death or famous victory. And as I trust, the battle shall not be so sour as the profit shall be sweet. Remember that victory is not gotten with the multitudes of men but with the courage of hearts and valiantness of minds. The smaller that our number is the more glory is to us if we vanquish. If we be overcome, yet no laud is to be attributed to the victors, considering that ten men fought against one. And if we die so glorious a death in so good a quarrel, neither fretting time, nor cancarding[121] oblivion shall be able to darken or raise out of the book of fame either our names or our godly attempt. And this one thing I assure you, that in so just and good a cause and so notable a quarrel you shall find me this day rather a dead carrion upon the cold ground than a free prisoner on a carpet in a lady's chamber.

"Let us therefore fight like invincible giants, and set on our enemies like un-timorous tigers, and banish all fear like ramping lions. And now advance forward true men against traitors, pitiful[122] persons against murderers, true inheritors against usurpers, the scourges of God against tyrants. Display by banner with a good courage, march forth like strong and robustious champions, and begin the battle like hardy conquerors. The battle is at hand and the victory approaches; and if we shamefully recoil, or cowardly flee, we and all our sequel be destroyed and dishonored forever. This is the day of gain and this is the time of loss; get this day victory, and be conquerors: and lose this day's battle, and be villains. And therefore in the name of God and Saint George, let every man courageously advance forth his standard."

---

121 tarnishing.
122 piteous.

These cheerful words he set forth with such gestures of his body, and smiling countenance, as though already he had vanquished his enemies and gotten the spoil. He had scant finished his saying but the one army spied the other. Lord, how hastily the soldiers buckled their helms, how quickly the archers bent their bows and frushed[123] their feathers, how readily the billmen shook their bills and proved their staves, ready to approach and join when the terrible trumpet should sound the bloody blast to victory or death! Between both armies there was a great marsh then (but at this present, by reason of ditches cast, it is grown to be firm ground) which the Earl of Richmond left on his right hand for this intent: that it should be on that side a defense for his part. And in so doing he had the sun at his back and in the faces of his enemies. When King Richard saw the earl's company was past the marsh he did command with all haste to set upon them. Then the trumpets sounded and the soldiers shouted and the king's archers courageously let fly their arrows. The earl's bowmen stood not still, but paid them home again.

The terrible shot once passed, the armies joined and came to hand-strokes, where neither sword nor bill was spared, at which encounter the Lord Stanley joined with the earl. The Earl of Oxford, in the mean season, fearing lest while his company was fighting they should be compassed and circumvented with the multitude of the enemies, gave commandment in every rank that no man should be so hardy as to go above ten foot from the standard. Which commandment once known, they knit themselves together and ceased a little from fighting. The adversaries suddenly abashed at the matter, and mistrusting some fraud and deceit, began also to pause and left striking — and not against the wills of many, which had rather had the king destroyed than saved, and therefore they fought very faintly, or stood still.

The Earl of Oxford, bringing all his band together on the one part, set on his enemies freshly again. The adversaries perceiving that, placed their men slender and thin before, but thick and broad behind, beginning again hardily the battle. [124]While the two forwards thus mortally fought, each intending to vanquish and convince the other, King Richard was admonished by his explorators and espials that the Earl of Richmond (accompanied with a small number of men of arms) was not far off. And as he approached and marched toward him he perfectly knew his personage by certain demonstrations and tokens which he had learned and known of others that were able to give him full information. Now being inflamed with ire and vexed

---

123 spread.
124 V.iv,v, *passim.*

with outrageous malice, he put his spurs to his horse and rode out of the side of the range of his battle, leaving the vanguard fighting, and like a hungry lion ran with spear in rest toward him. The Earl of Richmond perceived well the king furiously coming toward him, and because the whole hope of his wealth and purpose was to be determined by battle, he gladly proffered to encounter with him body to body and man to man.

King Richard set on so sharply at the first brunt that he overthrew the earl's standard and slew Sir William Brandon,[125] his standard-bearer, (which was father to Sir Charles Brandon by King Henry the Eighth, created Duke of Suffolk) and matched hand to hand with Sir John Cheney, a man of great force and strength, which would have resisted him. But the said John was by him manfully overthrown. And so he making open passage by dint of sword, as he went forward, the Earl of Richmond withstood his violence and kept him at the sword's point without advantage longer than his companions either thought or judged — which being almost in despair of victory were suddenly recomforted by Sir William Stanley, which came to his succor with three thousand tall men. [126]At which very instant, King Richard's men were driven back and fled and he himself, manfully fighting in the middle of his enemies, was slain, and (as he worthily had deserved) came to a bloody death, as he had led a bloody life.

In the mean season, the Earl of Oxford with the aid of the Lord Stanley, after no long fight, discomfited the forward of King Richard, whereof a great number were slain in the chase and fight. But the greatest number which (compelled by fear of the king, and not of their mere voluntary motion) came to the field, gave never a stroke, and having no harm nor damage, safely departed, which came not thither in hope to see the king prosper and prevail but to hear that he should be shamefully confounded and brought to ruin. In this battle died few above the number of a thousand persons. [127]And of the nobility were slain John, Duke of Norfolk, which was warned by divers to refrain from the field, insomuch that the night before he should set forward toward the king, one wrote this rhyme upon his gate:

> Jack of Norfolk be not too bold,
> For Dickon thy master is bought and sold.

---

[125] Shakespeare copies Holinshed's error in saying that Sir William Brandon was slain at Bosworth; in reality he was merely unhorsed. In November, 1485 he presented — very much alive — a petition at the first Parliament of Henry VII.

[126] V.v. Stage directions.

[127] V.iii. 302–306; V.v. 12–13.

Yet all this notwithstanding, he regarded more his oath, his honor, and promise made to King Richard like a gentleman; and as a faithful subject to his prince, absented not himself from his master; but as he faithfully lived under him, so he manfully died with him, to his great fame and laud. . . .

[128]There were slain besides him Walter, Lord Ferrers of Chartley, Sir Richard Ratcliff, and Robert Brakenbury, Lieutenant of the Tower, and not many gentlemen more. . . . On the Earl of Richmond's part were slain scarce one hundred persons, among whom the principal was Sir William Brandon, his standard-bearer. This battle was fought at Bosworth in Leicestershire, the two and twentieth day of August, in the year of Our Redemption, 1485. The whole conflict endured little above two hours. . . .

[129]When the earl had thus obtained victory, and slain his mortal enemy, he kneeled down and rendered to almighty God his hearty thanks, with devout and godly orisons, beseeching His goodness to send him grace to advance and defend the Catholic faith and to maintain justice and concord amongst his subjects and people, by God now to his governance committed and assigned. Which prayer finished he, replenished with incomparable gladness, ascended up to the top of a little mountain where he not only praised and lauded his valiant soldiers but also gave unto them his hearty thanks, with promise of condign recompense for their fidelity and valiant acts, willing and commanding all the hurt and wounded persons to be cured, and the dead carcasses to be delivered to the sepulture. Then the people rejoiced and clapped their hands, crying up to heaven, "King Henry, King Henry!"

When the Lord Stanley saw the good will and gladness of the people, he took the crown of King Richard, which was found amongst the spoil in the field, and set it on the earl's head as though he had been elected king by the voice of the people, as in ancient times past in divers realms it has been accustomed. And this was the first sign and token of his good luck and felicity.

[130]I must put you here in remembrance how that King Richard (putting some diffidence in the Lord Stanley) had with him as an hostage the Lord Strange, his eldest son, which Lord Stanley (as ye have heard before) joined not at the first with his son-in-law's army, for fear the king would have slain the Lord Strange, his heir.

[131]When King Richard was come to Bosworth, he sent a pursuivant to the Lord Stanley commanding him to advance forward with his

---

[128] V.v. 12–14.
[129] V.v. 18ff.
[130] IV.iv. 487–499; V.iii. 91–96.
[131] V.iii. 342–346.

company and to come to his presence; which thing if he refused to do, he swore by Christ's passion that he would strike off his son's head before he dined. The Lord Stanley answered the pursuivant that if the king did so, he had more sons alive; and as to come to him, he was not then so determined. When King Richard heard this answer he commanded the Lord Strange incontinent to be beheaded — which was at that very same season when both the armies had sight each of other. But the counsellors of King Richard pondered the time and cause, knowing also the Lord Strange to be innocent of his father's offense, and persuaded the king that it was now time to fight, and no time to execute.

Besides that, they advised him to keep the Lord Strange as prisoner till the battle were ended, and then at leisure his pleasure might be accomplished. So (as God would) King Richard broke his holy oath, and the lord was delivered to the keepers of the king's tents to be kept as prisoner. Which, when the field was done and their master slain and proclamation made to know where the child was, they submitted themselves as prisoners to the Lord Strange; [132]and he gently received them and brought them to the new proclaimed king where, of him and of his father, he was received with great joy. After this the whole camp removed with bag and baggage.

The same night in the evening, King Henry with great pomp came to the town of Leicester, where as well for the refreshing of his people and soldiers as for preparing all things necessary for his journey toward London, he rested and reposed himself two days. In the mean season the dead corpse of King Richard was as shamefully carried to the town of Leicester as he gorgeously (the day before) with pomp and pride departed out of the same town. For his body was naked and despoiled to the skin, and nothing left about him, not so much as a clout to cover his privy members.

---

[132] V.v. 9–11.

company and to come to his presence; which thing if he refused to do,
he swore by Christ's passion that he would strike off his son's head
before he dined. The Lord Stanley answered the pursuivant that if
the king did so, he had more sons alive; and as to come to him, was
not then so determined. Which message done to King Richard, he
commanded the ⸻ — which
was at that very same season when both the armies had sight each of
other. But the councellors of King Richard pondered the time and
cause, knowing also the Lord Strange to be innocent of his father's
offence, and persuaded the king that it was now time to fight, and no
time to execute.

Besides that, they advised him to keep the Lord Strange as prisoner

⚜ ANONYMOUS, C. 1594
The True Tragedy of Richard III*

[*The True Tragedy* owes most of its scenes and situations to Holinshed and roughly parallels Acts II–V of Shakespeare's play. It begins
with Edward IV at the brink of death, and the 1594 title page, repro-
duced below, provides all the plot summary needed to place the following excerpts in proper context.]

"The True Tragedy of Richard the Third: Wherein is shown the
death of Edward the Fourth, with the smothering of the two young
princes in the Tower. With a lamentable end of Shore's wife, an example for all wicked women. And lastly, the conjunction and joining
of the two noble Houses, Lancaster and York."

PROLOGUE[1]

Enter TRUTH *and* POETRY. *To them the* GHOST *of George,*
Duke of Clarence.

GHOST. *Cresce, cruor: sanguis satietur sanguine: cresce, quod spero*
citò. O citò. citò, vendicta.[2]

POETRY. Truth, well met.

TRUTH. Thanks, Poetry. What makest thou upon a stage?

POETRY. Shadows.

TRUTH.   Then will I add bodies to the shadows.
Therefore depart and give Truth leave
To show her pageant.

POETRY.   Why? Will Truth be a Player?

TRUTH. No, but Tragedia likes for to present
A tragedy in England, done but late,
That will revive the hearts of drooping minds.   10

---

* text modernized.
[1] Compare this Prologue with Shakespeare: I.iv.; II.i.; I.i. 14–30.
[2] Gore, increase: let blood be satiated by blood: rise up, that which I hope
for, quickly. Oh quickly, quickly, vengeance!

POETRY. Whereof?

TRUTH. Marry, thus:

Richard Plantagenet of the House of York,[3]
Claiming the crown by wars, not by descent,
Had, as the chronicles make manifest,
In the two and twentieth year of Henry the Sixth
By act of Parliament, entailed to him
The crown and titles to that dignity
And to his offspring lawfully begotten
After the decease of that forenamed king.   20
Yet not contented for to stay the time,
Made wars upon King Henry then the Sixth,
And by outrage suppressed that virtuous king
And won the Crown of England to himself.
But since,[4] at Wakefield in a battle pitched
Outrageous Richard breathed his latest breath,
Leaving behind three branches of that line,
Three sons: the first was Edward[5] now the king;
George of Clarence; and Richard, Gloucester's duke.
Then Henry claiming after his [Plantagenet's] decease   30
His stile,[6] his crown and former dignity,
Was quite suppressed till this Edward the Fourth.

POETRY. But tell me, Truth, of Henry what ensued?

TRUTH. Imprisoned he, in the Tower of London lies
By strict command from Edward, England's king.
Since cruelly murdered by Richard, Gloucester's duke.

POETRY. Whose ghost was that did appear to us?

TRUTH. It was the ghost of George, Duke of Clarence,
Who was attected[7] in King Edward's reign
Falsely of treason to his royalty,   40
Imprisoned in the Tower was most unnaturally
By his own brother, shame to parents' stock,
By Gloucester's duke drowned in a butt of wine.

POETRY. What shield was that he let fall?

TRUTH. A shield containing this, in full effect:

---

[3] Richard Plantagenet, third Duke of York, during the War of the Roses
made peace with Henry VI on the king's assurance that he would succeed
Henry as king. Impatient, he again went to war and was killed by the Lan-
castrians at Wakefield in 1460.

[4] afterward.

[5] Edward IV.

[6] advancement.

[7] accused.

"Blood sprinkled, springs: blood spilt craves due revenge:"
Whereupon he writes, "*Cresce, cruor:*
Sanguis satietur sanguine: cresce,
Quod spero citò. O citò, citò, vendicta!"

POETRY. What manner of man was this Richard, Duke of Gloucester?

TRUTH. A man ill-shaped, crooked backed, lame armed, withal   51
Valiantly minded, but tyrannous in authority.
So during the minority of the young prince,[8]
He is made Lord Protector over the realm.
Gentles, suppose that Edward[9] now has reigned
Full two and twenty years, and now like to die
Hath summoned all his nobles to the court,
To swear allegiance with the duke, his brother,
For troth unto his son, the tender prince,
Whose father's soul is now near flight to God,   60
Leaving behind two sons of tender age,
Five daughters to comfort the hapless queen.
All under the protection of the Duke of Gloucester.
Thus, gentles, excuse the length by the matter;
And here begins Truth's pageant: Poetry,
Wend with me.

(*Exeunt.*)

Scene X.[10]

Enter four watchmen. Enter Richard's PAGE.

PAGE. Why, thus by keeping company am I become like unto
those with whom I keep company. As my lord hopes to wear the
crown, so I hope by that means to have preferment. But instead
of the crown, the blood of the headless light upon his head! He   70
hath made but a wrong match, for blood is a threatener and will
have revenge. He makes havoc of all to bring his purpose to pass.
All those of the queen's kindred that were committed to Pomfret
Castle he hath caused them to be secretly put to death without
judgment. The like was never seen in England. He spares none.
Whom he but mistrusts to be a hinderer to his proceedings, he is
straight chopped up in prison. The valiant Earl of Oxford being
but mistrusted is kept close prisoner in Hammes Castle. Again,
how well Doctor Shaw has pleased my lord, that preached at Paul's

---

[8] Edward V.
[9] Edward IV.
[10] Compare this scene with Shakespeare: III.iii–v; IV.ii.

Cross yesterday, that proved the two princes to be bastards. 80
Whereupon in the afternoon came down my Lord Mayor and
the aldermen to Baynard's Castle and offered my lord the whole
estate upon him, and offered to make him king, which he refused
so faintly that if it had been offered once more I know he would
have taken it. The Duke of Buckingham is gone about it and is
now in the Guild Hall making his oration. But here comes my lord.

(*Enter* RICHARD *and* CATESBY.)

RICHARD. Catesby, content thee, I have warned the Lord
Hastings to this court, and since he is so hard to be won 'tis
better to cut him off then suffer him. He has been all this while
partaker to our secrets, and if he should but by some mislike 90
utter it, then were we all cast away.

CATESBY. Nay, my lord, do as you will. Yet I have spoken what
I can in my friend's cause.

RICHARD. Go to, no more ado, Catesby. They say I have been a
long sleeper today, but I'll be awake anon to some of their costs.
(*to the page.*) But sirrah, are those men in readiness that I appointed you to get?

PAGE. Aye, my Lord, and give diligent attendance upon your
grace.

RICHARD. Go to, look to it then, Catesby. Get thee thy 100
weapons ready, for I will enter the court.

CATESBY. I will, my lord.

(*Exit* RICHARD *and* CATESBY.)

PAGE. Does my lord say he has been a long sleeper today?
There are those of the court that are of another opinion, that
think his grace lies never long enough abed. Now there is court
held today by divers of the Council, which I fear me will cost
the Lord Hastings and Lord Stanley their best caps. For my lord
has willed me to get half a dozen ruffians in readiness, and when
he knocks with his fist upon the board, they to rush in and to cry,
"Treason, treason!" and to lay hands upon the Lord Hastings and 110
the Lord Stanley: which for fear I should let slip I will give my
diligent attendance.

(*Enter* RICHARD, CATESBY, [SIR THOMAS LOVEL] *and others,*
pulling LORD HASTINGS.)

RICHARD. Come, bring him away. Let this suffice: thou and
that accursed sorceress, the mother queen, hast bewitched me with
assistance of that famous strumpet of my brother's, Shore's wife.
My withered arm is sufficient testimony; deny it if thou canst.
Lay not Shore's wife with thee last night?

HASTINGS. That she was in my house, my lord, I cannot deny,
but not for any such matter. If —

RICHARD. If, villain? Feedst thou me with ifs and ands? Go 120
fetch me a priest, make a short shrift and dispatch him quickly.
For by the blessed St. Paul [I] swear I will not dine till I see the
traitor's head. [*To Lovel.*] Away, Sir Thomas, suffer him not to
speak.[11] See him executed straight and let his co-partner the Lord
Stanley be carried to prison also. 'Tis not his broken head I have
given him shall excuse him.

(*Exit* [LOVEL] *with* HASTINGS.)

Catesby, go you and see it presently proclaimed throughout the
city of London by a Herald of Arms that the cause of his death
and the rest were for conspiring by witchcraft the death of me
and the Duke of Buckingham, that so they might govern the king 130
and rule the realm. I think the proclamation be almost done.

CATESBY. Aye, my good Lord, and finished too.

RICHARD. Well then, about it. But hearest thou, Catesby:
meanwhile I will listen after success of the Duke of Buckingham,
who is laboring all this while with the citizens of London to make
me king, which I hope will be shortly. For thou seest our foes
now are fewer, and we nearer the mark than before. And when I
have it, look thou for the place of thy friend, the Lord Hastings.
Meanwhile about thy business.

CATESBY. I thank your grace. (*Exit* CATESBY.) 140

RICHARD. Now sirrah, to thee. There is one thing more undone
which grieves me more than all the rest. And to say the truth it
is of more importance than all the rest.

PAGE. Ah, that my lord would utter it to his page. Then should
I count myself a happy man if I could ease my lord of that great
doubt.

RICHARD. I commend thy willingness, but it is too mighty and
reaches the stars.

PAGE. The more weighty it is, the sooner shall I by doing it
increase your honor's good liking toward me. 150

RICHARD. Be assured of that. But the matter is of weight and
great importance and does concern the state.

PAGE. Why, my lord, I will choke them with gifts that shall
perform it. Therefore, good my lord, trust me in this cause.

RICHARD. Indeed, thy trust I know to be so true that I care[12]
not to utter it unto thee. Come hither — and yet the matter is too
weighty for so mean a man.

---

[11] In Holinshed, Stanley who was present during the seizure of Hastings was
also attacked and wounded (p. 21). Shakespeare, digressing from the source,
has Hastings apprehended alone.

[12] fear.

PAGE. Yet good my lord, utter it.

RICHARD. Why, thus it is: I would have my two nephews, the young prince and his brother, secretly murdered. Zounds, villain, 160 'tis out! Wilt thou do it, or wilt thou betray me?

PAGE. My lord, you shall see my forwardness herein. I am acquainted with one James Tyrrel that lodges hard by your honor's chamber. With him, my lord, will I so work that soon at night you shall speak with him.

RICHARD. Of what reputation or calling is that Tyrrel? May we trust him with that which, once known, were the utter confusion of me and my friends forever?

PAGE. For his trust, my lord, I dare be bound only [by] this: a poor gentleman he is, hoping for preferment by your grace. And 170 upon my credit, my lord, he will see it done.

RICHARD. Well, in this be very circumspect and sure with thy diligence; be liberal[13] and look for a day to make thee bless thyself wherein thou servedst so good a lord. [14]And now that Shore's wife's goods be confiscate, go from me to the Bishop of London and see that she receive her open penance. Let her be turned out of prison, but so bare as a wretch that worthily hath deserved that plague. And let there be straight proclamation made by my lord the Mayor that none shall relieve her nor pity her, and privy spies set in every corner of the city, that they may take notice of them that relieve 180 her. For as her beginning was most famous above all, so will I have her end most infamous above all. Have care now, my boy, and win thy master's heart forever.

SCENE XVIII.[15]

Enter the KING *and the* LORD LOVEL.

KING. The hell of life that hangs upon the crown,
The daily cares, the nightly dreams,
The wretched crews,[16] the treason of the foe,
And horror of my bloody practise past
Strikes such a terror to my wounded conscience
That sleep I, wake I, or whatsoever I do
Methinks their ghosts come gaping for revenge 190
Whom I have slain in reaching for a crown.

---

[13] unrestrained in action.

[14] This judgment upon Shore's wife comes straight from Holinshed, pp. 25–26. Perhaps Shakespeare's bypassing of it makes it seem so irrelevant in this play.

[15] Compare these two scenes with Shakespeare: V.iii.iv.

[16] mobs, people.

Clarence complains, and crieth for revenge.
My nephews' blood, "Revenge, revenge!" doth cry.
The headless peers come preasing[17] for revenge,
And everyone cries let the tyrant die.
The sun by day shines hotly for revenge.
The moon by night eclipses for revenge.
The stars are turned to comets for revenge.
The planets change their courses for revenge.
The birds sing not, but sorrow for revenge.   200
The silly lambs sit bleating for revenge.
The shrieking raven sits croaking for revenge.
Whole herds of beasts come bellowing for revenge.
And all, yea all the world, I think,
Cries for revenge and nothing but revenge.
But to conclude, I have deserved revenge.
In company I dare not trust my friend;
Being alone, I dread the secret foe.
I doubt my food, lest poison lurk therein.
My bed is uncouth,[18] rest refrains my head.   210
Then such a life I count far worse to be
Than thousand deaths unto a damned death.
How wast death? I said. Who dare attempt death?
Nay, who dare so much as once to think my death?
Though enemies there be that would my body kill,
Yet shall they leave a never dying mind.
But you, villains, rebels, traitors as you are,
How came the foe in, preasing so near?
Where, where slept the garrison that should a' beat them back?
Where were our friends to intercept the foe?   220
All gone, quite fled, their loyalty quite laid abed?
Then vengeance, mischief, horror with mischance,
Wild-fire with whirlwinds, light upon your heads
That thus betrayed your prince by your untruth.
                    [*Pause, then more calmly.*]
Frantic man, what meanst thou by this mood?
Now he is come, more need to beat him back.

    LOVEL. Sour is his sweet that savors thy delight; great is his
power that threats thy overthrow.

    KING. The bad rebellion of my foe is not so much as for to see
my friends do flee in flocks from me.   230

---

[17] pressing.
[18] uncomfortable.

LOVEL. May it please your grace to rest yourself content, for you have power enough to defend your land.

KING. Dares Richmond set his foot on land with such a small power of straggling fugitives?

LOVEL. May it please your grace to participate[19] the cause that thus doth trouble you?

KING. The cause, buzzard? What cause should I participate to thee? My friends are gone away and fled from me. Keep silence, villain, lest I by post do send thy soul to hell. Not one word more, if thou dost love thy life.   240

(*Enter* CATESBY.)

CATESBY. My lord.

KING. Yet again, villain? O Catesby, is it thou? What? Comes the Lord Stanley or no?

CATESBY. My lord, he answers no.

KING. Why, didst not tell him then I would send his son George Stanley's head to him?

CATESBY. My lord, I did so, and he answered he had another son left to make Lord Stanley.

KING. O villain vile and breaker of his oath, the bastard's ghost shall haunt him at the heels and cry revenge for his vile father's   250 wrongs. Go, Lovel, Catesby, fetch George Stanley forth. Him with these hands will I butcher for the deed and send his headless body to his sire.

CATESBY. Leave off executions now. The foe is here that threatens us most cruelly of our lives.

KING. Zounds, foe me no foes! The father's fact[20] condemns the son to die.

LOVEL. But guiltless blood will for revengement cry.

KING. Why was not he left for father's loyalty?

LOVEL. Therein his father greatly injured him.   260

KING. Did not yourselves in presence see the bonds sealed and assigned?

LOVEL. What though my lord the vardit[21] own, the titles doth resign.

KING. The bond is broke and I will sue the fine, except you will hinder me. What will you have so?

LOVEL. In doing true justice, else we answer no.

---

[19] communicate.
[20] deed.
[21] verdict. The sense of this line is: Suppose, though the verdict is yours you do not claim the forfeit.

KING. His treacherous father hath neglected his word and done impartial waste by dint of sword. Therefore, sirrah, go fetch him. Zounds, draw you cuts who shall go. I bid you go, Catesby. 270 (*aside.*) Ah, Richard, now mayst thou see thy end at hand. (*aloud.*) Why sirs, why fear you thus? Why, we are ten to one! If you seek promotion, I am king already in possession, better able to perform than he. Lovel, Catesby, let's join lovingly and devoutly together and I will divide my whole kingdom amongst you.

BOTH. We will, my lord.

KING. We will, my lord. Ah, Catesby, thou lookst like a dog, and thou Lovel too.[22] But you will run away with them that be gone, and the devil go with you all! God, I hope — God? What talk I of God that have served the devil all this while? No. For- 280 tune and courage for me. And join England against me, with England. Join Europe, with Europe come Christendom, and with Christendom the whole world, and yet I will never yield but by death only. By death. No, [do not] die. Part not childishly from thy crown. But come the devil to claim it, strike him down, and though that Fortune has decreed to set revenge with triumphs on my wretched head, yet death, sweet death, my latest friend has sworn to make a bargain for my lasting fame. And this, aye, this very day, I hope with this lame hand of mine to rake out that hateful heart of Richmond, and when I have it to eat it panting 290 hot with salt and drink his blood lukewarm — though I be sure 'twill poison me. Sirs, you that be resolute follow me. The rest go hang yourselves!

(*Exit.*)

Scene XIX.

The battle. Enter RICHARD *wounded, with his* PAGE.

KING. A horse, a horse, a fresh horse.[23]

PAGE. Ah, fly, my lord, and save your life.

KING. Fly, villain? Look I as though I would fly? No, first shall this dull and senseless ball of earth receive my body cold and void of sense. You watery heavens roll[24] on my gloomy day and dark- some clouds close up my cheerful sound. Down is thy sun, Rich- ard, never to shine again. The birds whose feathers should adorn 300 my head hover aloft and dare not come in sight. Yet faint not,

---

[22] A reference to the current jingle about Lovel, Catesby, Ratcliff, and Richard. See Holinshed, p. 46.

[23] V.iv. 7.

[24] pour.

man, for this day, if Fortune will, shall make thee king possessed with quiet crown; if Fates deny, this ground must be my grave. Yet golden thoughts that reach for a crown, daunted before by Fortune's cruel spite, are come as comforts to my drooping heart and bid me keep my crown and die a king. These are my last. What more I have to say I'll make report among the damned souls.

(*Exit.*)

Enter RICHMOND *to battle again, and kills* RICHARD.

□ *Some Sources for Further Study*

1. SENECA (c. 1 B.C.–65 A.D.) — *Medea.* Medea is a melodramatic revenge character suggestive of Queen Margaret.
    Agamemnon. Cassandra, like Queen Margaret, is a prophetess of doom.
2. NICCOLO MACHIAVELLI — *The Prince* (c. 1514). In *Henry VI, Part Three* Richard announces his intention to "set the murderous Machiavel to school" (III.ii. 193). *The Prince* sets the pattern for Richard's conduct in a number of ways: Richard acquires his kingdom by his own ability; he counterfeits piety; he prefers to be feared rather than loved.
3. POLYDORE VERGIL — *Historia Anglica* (1534).
4. EDWARD HALL — *The Union of the Two Noble and Illustrious Families of Lancaster and York* (1548).
5. RICHARD GRAFTON — *A Chronicle at Large and Mere History of the Affairs of England and Kings of the Same* (1569).
6. *A Mirror for Magistrates* (1559, 1563).
    "George, Duke of Clarence"
    "Edward IV"
    "Sir Anthony Woodvile, Lord Rivers"
    "Lord Hastings"
    "The Complaint of Henry, Duke of Buckingham"
    "Shore's Wife"
7. THOMAS LEGGE — *Richardus Tertius* (1579). A drama written in Latin, a Senecan version of the life of Richard.
8. CHRISTOPHER MARLOWE — *Tamburlaine the Great, Parts One and Two* (1587–1588). *The Jew of Malta* (1588). *Dr. Faustus* (1588–1589).
9. "The Song of Lady Bessy," in James Orchard Halliwell-Phillips, *Palatine Anthology.* A long ballad, first transcribed in 1600, which offers a popular and less partisan view of the affairs that led up to the marriage of Elizabeth of York and the Earl of Richmond.

RICHARD II

The main source is again Holinshed, and as in *Richard III* Shakespeare compresses a decade of previous events — in this case the nobles' rebellion of 1387 and Richard's belated revenge in 1397 when he, abetted by Thomas Mowbray, had Thomas of Woodstock, Duke of Gloucester, killed — into motivation for a brief, climactic period in history. The time covered in *Richard II* begins with Bolingbroke's challenge in 1398 and ends shortly after his coronation in 1400, although the Holinshed selection in the text begins with some earlier incidents that help to clarify the conflicts at the start of the play.

Shakespeare builds his play around several key situations, all of them in Holinshed though not all of them as weighty in Holinshed as in Shakespeare. These include the conflict between Bolingbroke and Mowbray; the death of John of Gaunt; Bolingbroke's return from exile; the deposition of Richard; the death of Richard. He follows chronology in his placement of these events and of most of the other details borrowed from Holinshed, but occasionally varies it as in the death of the Duchess of Gloucester, which he brings in earlier for dramatic effect. Despite the brief time span covered Shakespeare deletes several major historical episodes — Richard's preventing the marriage of Bolingbroke to the daughter of the Duke of Berry, uncle of the French king; Richard's severe tax laws whereby Bushy, Bagot, and Green "farm" England; and Richard's Irish invasion — thereby simplifying plot line. At the same time he enriches it by adding embellishments of his own: the death-bed scene of Gaunt; Richard's conduct during the deposition; Richard's tender farewell to Queen Isabelle (V.i), who was in actual fact twelve years old at that time; and the plea of the Duchess of York for her son's life (V.iii), although in fact she had died six years before.

Comparisons beckon between Shakespeare's handling of Holinshed in *Richard III* and in *Richard II*, and to start with the obvious conclusion, Shakespeare makes more plastic use of his material in *Richard*

73

II. In *Richard II* he condenses motivation from past events into scene i, where in *Richard III* he needed an entire act. In *Richard II* he focuses on a few key incidents instead of many. In *Richard II* he pares major events from history in the interests of clarity and power, and his own additions are more numerous and various — curiously, in *Richard III* the additions are all centered around women.

Like *Richard III*, *Richard II* also has a source play behind it, although *Thomas of Woodstock*, c. 1591, is not nearly so direct an influence as *The True Tragedy*. *Woodstock* deals with events of Richard's reign up through 1397, is in a sense *Richard II, Part One* — and it has sometimes been so named — but the impact of *Woodstock's* death does carry over into the early acts of Shakespeare's play. Scenes ii-v of Act V of *Woodstock*, presented in the text, correspond most closely to *Richard II*. The most notable parallels they offer are Lancaster's lamentation over the death of Woodstock; Lancaster's scoring Richard's corruption; and Richard's lament over the corpse of Green. *Woodstock* also contains seeds of character and idea for *Richard II*, as will be seen.

Richard II, like *Richard III*, mainly revolves around a central character, but where *Richard III* is a stark cartoon, *Richard II* takes on the colors and shadows of humanity. A second-rate king, a second-rate human being, and (perhaps worst of all) a second-rate poet, he rants and writhes against constricting events when in reality he is confined by his own near-greatness. Since Shakespeare's sources for *Richard II* and *Richard III* are almost constants, the difference between his protagonists would be due in major part to his development as a dramatist, and it is revealing to assess that development by comparing sources and achievement. The minor characters in *Richard II* and *Richard III* also offer basis for comparison: Bolingbroke, like Buckingham, acts as foil to the main character, but note how Shakespeare humanizes Bolingbroke by showing his grief over the body of the dead king (V.vi. 45ff.); John of Gaunt, as symbol of the integrity of England, points the way toward the profound symbolic use Shakespeare will make of character in later plays like *Henry IV, Part One*; and no relationships between minor characters in *Richard III* are as intricate and real as those between the Duke and Duchess of York.

The central political idea in *Richard II* is the Tudor belief, implicit in Holinshed, that a king is, in Gaunt's words,

> God's substitute,
> His deputy anointed in His sight. (I.ii. 37–38)

and that therefore a subject

> may never lift
> An angry arm against His minister. (I.ii. 40–41)

Bolingbroke does, of course, and successfully, but his sense of guilt is keen and immediate, darkens his entire career as Holinshed (pp. 103, 154, and 179) and Shakespeare in his *Henry IV* plays make clear. While the plot of *Thomas of Woodstock* refutes this idea — Gloucester is noble, Richard frivolous — Richard's reference to himself as

The highest God's anointed deputy

may well be the direct source of Gaunt's similar statement.

Richard II contains at least two more notable ideas which, while not in the direct sources, belong to that body of general Renaissance thought that a writer of Shakespeare's sensibility would have absorbed through the skin. One is the linking, *in the garden*, of Richards' abdication with the fall of man (III.iv), a standard Renaissance custom of finding Christian connotations in worldly events. The other concerns the Renaissance view of this world as a microcosm of God's universe, an idea which Richard tries to build upon in a last-ditch grasp at greatness but which, on Richard's lips, characteristically trails off into self-pity (V.v).

汇 RAPHAEL HOLINSHED

The Chronicles of England, Scotland, and Ireland, * 1587

[*The opening scene of Shakespeare's play (1398) stems from events of the end of June, 1397 when the Duke of Gloucester formulated a plot to murder King Richard. The duke was Thomas of Woodstock, youngest son of Edward III, uncle to Richard II, a man noted for bloodthirsty cruelty even in that violent age. With him in the plot were Henry Bolingbroke,[1] Thomas Mowbray, the Earls of Warwick and Arundel, and others who met at Arundel Castle that June and planned to seize the king and his uncles, the Dukes of Lancaster and York, and to execute the rest of the King's council. Mowbray revealed this plot[2] to Richard, and afterwards by the king's order he arrested the Duke of Gloucester.*]

[1397] Immediately upon his [the Duke of Gloucester's] apprehension, the Earl Marshal [Thomas Mowbray] conveyed him unto the Thames, and there being set aboard in a ship prepared of purpose, he was brought to Calais where he was at length dispatched out of life, either strangled or smothered with pillows (as some do write)....

When the time came that the Parliament should be held at Westminster . . . the cause of assembling that Parliament was showed, as that the king had called it for reformation of divers transgressions and oppressions committed against the peace of his land by the Duke of Gloucester, the Earls of Arundel, Warwick, and others. . . .

On the feast day of Saint Matthew, Richard Fitzallen, Earl of Arundel, was brought forth to swear before the king and whole Parlia-

---

* text modernized.

[1] Henry Plantagenet, eldest son of John of Gaunt, was surnamed Bolingbroke because he was born in the town of Bolingbroke in Lincolnshire.

[2] Which betrayal of conspirators sets the opening scene in Shakespeare's play (Bolingbroke's accusation against Mowbray of treachery to King Richard) in proper perspective.

76

ment to such articles as he was to be charged with. And as he stood at the bar, the Lord Neville was commanded by the Duke of Lancaster, which sat that day as High Steward of England, to take the hood from his neck and the girdle from his waist. . . . when the earl had nothing more to say for himself, the duke pronounced judgment against him as in cases of treason is used.

But after he had made an end, and paused a little, he said: "The king, our sovereign lord, of his mercy and grace because thou art of his blood and one of the peers of the realm, has remitted all the other pains saving the last, that is to say, the beheading. And so thou shalt only lose thy head." And forthwith he was had away and led through London unto the Tower Hill. . . .

But now to return to the Parliament. After the death of this earl, the lord Thomas Beauchamp, Earl of Warwick, was brought forth to abide his trial by Parliament. And when his accusers charged him in like points of treason, such as before were imposed to the Earl of Arundel, he answered that he never meant evil to the king's person nor thought that those roads[3] and assemblies that were made in company of the Duke of Gloucester, the Earl of Arundel, and others, might not be accounted treason. But when the judges showed him that they could not be otherwise taken than for treason, he humbly besought the king of mercy and grace. The king then asked of him whether he had ridden with the Duke of Gloucester and the Earl of Arundel, as had been alleged. He answered that he could not deny it, and wished that he had never seen them. Then said the king, "Do ye not know that you are guilty of treason?" He answered again, "I acknowledge it," and with sobbing tears besought all them that were present to make intercession to the king's majesty for him.

Then the king and the Duke of Lancaster communed, and after the king had awhile with silence considered of the matter, he said to the earl, "By Saint John Baptist, Thomas of Warwick, this confession that thou hast made is unto me more available than all the Duke of Gloucester's and the Earl of Warwick's lands." Herewith the earl making still intercession for pardon, the lords humbly besought the king to grant it. Finally the king pardoned him of life, but banished him into the Isle of Man. . . .

[1398] The king then came down to Lichfield, and there held a royal Christmas, which being ended, he took his journey towards Shrewsbury, where the Parliament was appointed to begin in the quindene[4] of Saint Hilary, as before you have heard. In which Parliament there held upon prorogation, for the love that the king bore to

---

[3] raids.
[4] the fifteenth day after a church festival.

the gentlemen and commons of the Shire of Chester he caused it to be ordained that from thenceforth it should be called and known by the name of the Principality of Chester: and herewith he entitled himself Prince of Chester. He held also a royal feast, keeping open household for all honest comers, during which feast he created five dukes and a duchess, a marquis, and four earls. The Earl of Derby was created Duke of Hereford; the Earl of Nottingham, that was also Earl Marshal, Duke of Norfolk; the Earl of Rutland, Duke of Aumerle; the Earl of Kent, Duke of Surrey; and the Earl of Huntington, Duke of Exeter; the Lady Margaret Marshall, Countess of Norfolk, was created Duchess of Norfolk; the Earl of Somerset, Marquis Dorset; the Lord Spenser, Earl of Gloucester; the Lord Neville, surnamed Dauraby, Earl of Westmoreland; the Lord William Scroop, Lord Chamberlain, Earl of Wiltshire; and the Lord Thomas Percy, Lord Steward of the King's House, Earl of Worcester.

And for the better maintenance of the estate of these noblemen, whom he had thus advanced to higher degrees of honor, he gave unto them a great part of those lands that belonged to the Duke of Gloucester, the Earls of Warwick and Arundel. And now he was in good hope that he had rooted up all plants of treason, and therefore cared less who might be his friend or his foe than before he had done, esteeming himself higher in degree than any prince living, and so presumed further than ever his grandfather did and took upon him to bear the arms of Saint Edward, joining them unto his own arms. To conclude, whatsoever he then did, none durst speak a word contrary thereunto. And yet such as were chief of his council were esteemed of the commons to be the worst creatures that might be, as the Dukes of Aumerle, Norfolk and Exeter, the Earl of Wiltshire, Sir John Bushy, Sir William Bagot, and Sir Thomas Green: which three last remembered were knights of the Bath, against whom the commons undoubtedly bore great and privy hatred. . . .

Many other things were done in this Parliament, to the displeasure of no small number of people; namely, for that divers rightful heirs were disinherited of their lands and livings, by authority of the same Parliament: with which wrongful doings the people were much offended, so that the king and those that were about him and chief in council came into great infamy and slander. Indeed the king after he had dispatched the Duke of Gloucester, and the other noblemen, was not a little glad, for that he knew them still ready to disappoint him in all his purposes; and therefore being now as it were careless, did not behave himself (as some have written) in such discreet order as many wished. But rather (as in time of prosperity it often happens) he forgot himself and began to rule by will more than by reason, threatening death to each one that obeyed not his inordinate desires.

By means whereof the lords of the realm began to fear their own estates, being in danger of his furious outrage, whom they took for a man destitute of sobriety and wisdom, and therefore could not like of him, that so abused his authority.

Hereupon there were sundry of the nobles that lamented these mischiefs, and especially showed their griefs unto such by whose naughty council they understood the king to be misled; and this they did, to the end that they being about him might either turn their copies, and give him better council; or else he having knowledge what evil report went of him, might mend his manners misliked of his nobles. [5]But all was in vain, for so it fell out that in this Parliament held at Shrewsbury, Henry, Duke of Hereford, accused Thomas Mowbray, Duke of Norfolk, of certain words which he should utter in talk had betwixt them, as they rode together lately before betwixt London and Brainford, sounding highly to the king's dishonor. And for further proof thereof, he presented a supplication to the king wherein he appealed[6] the Duke of Norfolk, in field of battle, for a traitor, false and disloyal to the king, and enemy unto the realm. This supplication was read before both the dukes, in presence of the king: which done, the Duke of Norfolk took upon him to answer it, declaring that whatsoever the Duke of Hereford had said against him other than well, he lied falsely like an untrue knight as he was. And when the king asked of the Duke of Hereford what he said to it, he taking his hood off his head said: "My sovereign lord, even as the supplication which I took you imports, right so I say for truth that Thomas Mowbray, Duke of Norfolk, is a traitor, false and disloyal to your royal majesty, your crown, and to all states of your realm."

Then the Duke of Norfolk being asked what he said to this, he answered: "Right dear lord, with your favor that I make answer unto your cousin here, I say (your reverence saved) that Henry of Lancaster, Duke of Hereford, like a false and disloyal traitor as he is, does lie in that he has or shall say of me otherwise than well." "No more," said the king, "We have heard enough." And herewith commanded the Duke of Surrey, for that term Marshal of England, to arrest in his name the two dukes: the Duke of Lancaster, father to the Duke of Hereford; the Duke of York, the Duke of Aumerle, Constable of England. And the Duke of Surrey, Marshal of the realm, undertook as pledges body for body for the Duke of Hereford. But the Duke of Norfolk was not suffered to put in pledges, and so under arrest was led unto Windsor Castle and there guarded with keepers that were appointed to see him safely kept.

---

[5] I.i. 1ff.
[6] accused.

⁷ Now after the dissolving of the Parliament at Shrewsbury, there was a day appointed about six weeks after for the king to come unto Windsor to hear and to take some order betwixt the two dukes, which had thus appealed each other. There was a great scaffold erected within the Castle of Windsor for the king to sit with the lords and prelates of his realm. And so at the day appointed, he with the said lords and prelates being come thither and set in their places, the Duke of Hereford appellant, and the Duke of Norfolk defendant, were sent for to come and appear before the king sitting there in his seat of justice. And then began Sir John Bushy to speak for the king, declaring to the lords how they should understand that where the Duke of Hereford had presented a supplication to the king, who was there set to minister justice to all men that would demand the same as appertained to his royal majesty, he therefore would now hear what the parties could say one against another; and withal the king commanded the Dukes of Aumerle and Surrey, the one being Constable and the other Marshal, to go unto the two dukes, appellant and defendant, requiring them on his behalf, to grow to some agreement. And for his part, he would be ready to pardon all that had been said or done amiss betwixt them, touching any harm or dishonor to him or his realm. But they answered both assuredly that it was not possible to have any peace or agreement made betwixt them.

When he heard what they had answered, he commanded that they should be brought forthwith before his presence to hear what they would say. Herewith an herald in the king's name with loud voice commanded the dukes to come before the king, either of them to show his reason, or else to make peace together without more delay. When they were come before the king and lords, the king spoke himself to them, willing them to agree, and make peace together. "For it is" (said he) "the best way you can take." The Duke of Norfolk with due reverence hereunto answered it could not be so brought to pass, his honor saved. Then the king asked of the Duke of Hereford what it was that he demanded of the Duke of Norfolk, and what is the matter that you can not make peace together and become friends?

Then stood forth a knight, who asking and obtaining license to speak for the Duke of Hereford, said: "Right dear and sovereign lord, here is Henry of Lancaster, Duke of Hereford and Earl of Derby, who says, and I for him likewise say, that Thomas Mowbray, Duke of Norfolk, is a false and disloyal traitor to you and your royal majesty, and

---

⁷ I.iii. 1ff. This scene is substantially the subject of the next thirteen paragraphs in Holinshed, although Shakespeare makes some use of those paragraphs in other parts of his play as well.

to your whole realm. [8]And likewise the Duke of Hereford says and I for him, that Thomas Mowbray, Duke of Norfolk, has received eight thousand nobles to pay the soldiers that keep your town of Calais, which he has not done as he ought. And furthermore the said Duke of Norfolk has been the occasion of all the treason that has been contrived in your realm for the space of these eighteen years, and by his false suggestions and malicious council he has caused to die and to be murdered your right dear uncle, the Duke of Gloucester, son to King Edward. Moreover, the Duke of Hereford says, and I for him, that he will prove this with his body against the body of the said Duke of Norfolk within lists." The king herewith waxed angry, and asked the Duke of Hereford if these were his words, who answered: "Right dear lord, they are my words; and hereof I require right, and the battle against him."

There was a knight also that asked license to speak for the Duke of Norfolk, and obtaining it began to answer thus: "Right dear sovereign lord, here is Thomas Mowbray, Duke of Norfolk, who answers and says, and I for him, that all which Henry of Lancaster has said and declared (saving the reverence due to the king and his council) is a lie; and the said Henry of Lancaster has falsely and wickedly lied as a false and disloyal knight, and both has been and is a traitor against you, your crown, royal majesty, and realm. This will I prove and defend as becomes a loyal knight to do with my body against his. Right dear lord, I beseech you therefore and your council that it may please you in your royal discretion to consider and mark what Henry of Lancaster, Duke of Hereford, such a one as he is, has said."

The king then demanded of the Duke of Norfolk, if these were his words, and whether he had any more to say. The Duke of Norfolk then answered for himself: [9]"Right dear sir, true it is that I have received so much gold to pay your people of the town of Calais, which I have done; and I do avouch that your town of Calais is as well kept at your commandment as ever it was at any time before, and that there never has been by any of Calais any complaint made unto you of me. Right dear and my sovereign lord, for the voyage that I made into France about your marriage I never received either gold or silver of you, nor yet for the voyage that the Duke of Aumerle and I made into Almany,[10] where we spent great treasure. Marry, true it is that once I laid an ambush to have slain the Duke of Lancaster, that there sits. But nevertheless he has pardoned me thereof, and there was good peace

---

[8] I.i. 88–103.
[9] I.i. 124–151.
[10] Germany.

made betwixt us, for the which I yield him hearty thanks. This is that which I have to answer, and I am ready to defend myself against mine adversary; I beseech you therefore of right, and to have the battle against him in upright judgement."

After this, when the king had communed with his council a little, he commanded the two dukes to stand forth that their answers might be heard. [11]The king then caused them once again to be asked if they would agree and make peace together, but they both flatly answered that they would not. And withal the Duke of Hereford cast down his gage, and the Duke of Norfolk took it up. The king perceiving this demeanor betwixt them swore by St. John Baptist that he would never seek to make peace betwixt them again. And therefore Sir John Bushy in name of the king and his council declared that the king and his council had commanded and ordained that they should have a day of battle appointed them at Coventry.

Here writers disagree about the day that was appointed. For some say it was upon a Monday in August; other upon St. Lambert's Day, being the seventeenth of September; other on the eleventh of September. But true it is that the king assigned them not only the day but also appointed them lists and place for the combat, and thereupon great preparation was made as to such a matter appertained.

At the time appointed the king came to Coventry, where the two dukes were ready, according to the order prescribed therein, coming thither in great array, accompanied with the lords and gentlemen of their lineages. The king caused a sumptuous scaffold or theater and royal lists there to be erected and prepared. The Sunday before they should fight, after dinner the Duke of Hereford came to the king (being lodged about a quarter of a mile without the town in a tower that belonged to Sir William Bagot) to take his leave of him. The morrow after, being the day appointed for the combat, about the spring of the day, came the Duke of Norfolk to the court to take leave likewise of the king. The Duke of Hereford armed him in his tent, that was set up near to the lists, and the Duke of Norfolk put on his armor betwixt the gate and the barrier of the town, in a beautiful house having a fair perclose[12] of wood towards the gate, that none might see what was done within the house.

The Duke of Aumerle that day being High Constable of England, and the Duke of Surrey, Marshal, placed themselves betwixt them, well armed and appointed; and when they saw their time they first entered into the lists with a great company of men apparelled in silk

---

[11] I.i. 152–173.
[12] parclose: enclosure, screen.

sendal,[13] embroidered with silver both richly and curiously, every man having a tipped staff to keep the field in order. About the hour of prime came to the barriers of the lists the Duke of Hereford, mounted on a white courser barded[14] with green and blue velvet embroidered sumptuously with swans and antelopes of goldsmiths' work, armed at all points. The constable and marshal came to the barriers, demanding of him what he was. He answered, "I am Henry of Lancaster, Duke of Hereford, which am come hither to do mine endeavor against Thomas Mowbray, Duke of Norfolk, as a traitor untrue to God, the king, his realm, and me." Then incontinently he swore upon the holy evangelists that his quarrel was true and just, and upon that point he required to enter the lists. Then he put up his sword, which before he held naked in his hand, and putting down his visor, made a cross on his horse, and with spear in hand entered into the lists and descended from his horse and set him down in a chair of green velvet at the one end of the lists, and there reposed himself, abiding the coming of his adversary.

Soon after him entered into the field with great triumph King Richard accompanied with all the peers of the realm, and in his company was the Earl of St. Pol, which was come out of France in post to see this challenge performed. The king had there above ten thousand men in armor, lest some fray or tumult might arise amongst his nobles by quarreling or partaking. When the king was set in his seat, which was richly hanged and adorned, a k[night] at arms made open proclamation prohibiting all men in the name of the king, and of the high constable and marshal, to enterprise or attempt to approach or touch any part of the lists upon pain of death, except such as were appointed to order or marshal the field. The proclamation ended, another herald cried, "Behold here Henry Lancaster, Duke of Hereford appellant, which is entered into the lists royal to do his devoir against Thomas Mowbray, Duke of Norfolk defendant, upon pain to be found false and recreant."

The Duke of Norfolk hovered on horseback at the entry of the lists, his horse being barded with crimson velvet embroidered richly with lions of silver and mulberry trees; and when he had made his oath before the constable and marshal that his quarrel was just and true, he entered the field manfully, saying aloud: "God aid him that has the right." And then he departed from his horse and sat him down in his chair which was of crimson velvet curtained about with white and red damask. The Lord Marshal viewed their spears to see that

---

[13] fine cloth.
[14] its breast and flanks armored.

they were of equal length, and delivered the one spear himself to the Duke of Hereford, and sent the other unto the Duke of Norfolk by a knight. Then the herald proclaimed that the traverses and chairs of the champions should be removed, commanding them on the king's behalf to mount on horseback and address themselves to the battle and combat.

The Duke of Hereford was quickly horsed and closed his bavier[15] and cast his spear into the rest, and when the trumpet sounded set forward courageously towards his enemy six or seven paces. The Duke of Norfolk was not fully set forward when the king cast down his warder, and the heralds cried, "Ho! Ho!" Then the king caused their spears to be taken from them and commanded them to repair again to their chairs, where they remained two long hours while the king and his council deliberately consulted what order was best to be had in so weighty a cause. Finally, after they had devised and fully determined what should be done therein, the heralds cried silence; and Sir John Bushy, the king's secretary, read the sentence and determination of the king and his council in a long roll, the effect whereof was that Henry, Duke of Hereford, should within fifteen days depart out of the realm, and not to return before the term of ten years were expired except by the king he should be repealed again, and this upon pain of death; and that Thomas Mowbray, Duke of Norfolk, because he had sown sedition in the realm by his words, should likewise avoid the realm and never to return again into England nor approach the borders or confines thereof upon pain of death; and that the king would stay the profits of his lands till he had levied thereof such sums of money as the duke had taken up of the king's treasurer for the wages of the garrison of Calais, which were still unpaid.

When these judgments were once read, the king called before him both the parties and made them to swear that the one should never come in place where the other was, willingly, nor keep any company together in any foreign region: which oath they both received humbly, and so went their ways.[16] The Duke of Norfolk departed sorrowfully out of the realm into Almany, and at the last came to Venice, where he for thought and melancholy deceased. For he was in hope (as writers record) that he should have been borne out in the matter by the king, which when it fell out otherwise it grieved him not a little. The Duke of Hereford took his leave of the king at Eltham, who there released four years of his banishment. So he took his journey over into Calais, and from thence went into France where he remained.

---

[15] visor.

[16] Here ends the material of I.iii. The final reference to the Duke of Norfolk appears in IV.i. 91–100.

[17]A wonder it was to see what number of people ran after him in every town and street where he came, before he took the sea, lamenting and bewailing his departure, as who would say that when he departed the only shield, defense and comfort of the commonwealth was faded and gone. . . .

[*Bolingbroke was cordially received by the King of France, while in England "great grudge and murmuring arose among the people" because of Richard's unjust taxation methods.*]

[1399][18] In this meantime, the Duke of Lancaster departed out of this life at the Bishop of Ely's Palace in Holborn,[19] and lies buried in the cathedral church of St. Paul in London, on the northside of the high altar, by the Lady Blanche, his first wife. The death of this duke gave occasion of increasing more hatred in the people of this realm toward the king, for he seized into his hands all the goods that belonged to him, and also received all the rents and revenues of his lands which ought to have descended unto the Duke of Hereford by lawful inheritance in revoking his letters patents[20] which he had granted to him before — by virtue whereof he might make his attorneys-general to sue livery[21] for him of any manner of inheritances or possessions that might from thenceforth fall unto him; and that his homage might be respited, with making reasonable fine. Whereby it was evident that the king meant his utter undoing.

This hard dealing was much misliked of all the nobility and cried out against of the meaner sort. But namely the Duke of York was therewith sore moved, who before this time had borne things with so patient a mind as he could, though the same touched him very near, as the death of his brother, the Duke of Gloucester; the banishment of his nephew, the said Duke of Hereford; and other more injuries in great number, which for the slippery youth of the king he passed over for the time and did forget as well as he might. But now perceiving that neither law, justice, nor equity could take place where the king's willful will was bent upon any wrongful purpose, he considered that the glory of the public wealth of his country must needs decay, by reason of the king's lack of wit and want of such as would (without flattery) admonish him of his duty; and therefore he thought it the part of a wise man to get him in time to a resting place and to leave

---

[17] I.iv. 23–36.
[18] I.iv. 54–64; II.i. 147–214. Note how closely ll.201–204 follow Holinshed's language.
[19] Shakespeare refers to it as Ely House (I.iv. 58).
[20] royal grants.
[21] delivery.

the following of such an unadvised captain as with a leaden sword would cut his own throat.

Hereupon he with the Duke of Aumerle his son went to his house at Langley,[22] rejoicing that nothing had mishappened in the commonwealth through his device or consent. The common bruit ran that the king had set to farm the realm of England unto Sir William Scroop, Earl of Wiltshire and then Treasurer of England, to Sir John Bushy, Sir John Bagot, and Sir Henry Green, knights. . . .

[King Richard "being destitute of treasure" borrowed great sums of money from his nobles and from the church and fined seventeen shires for having aided the Duke of Gloucester during the rebellion of 1387.]

[23]In this year in a manner throughout all the realm of England, old bay trees withered, and afterwards, contrary to all men's thinking, grew green again, a strange sight and supposed to import some unknown event.

In this meantime the king being advertised that the wild Irish daily wasted and destroyed the towns and villages within the English pale, and had slain many of the soldiers which lay there in garrison for defense of that country, determined to make eftsoons a voyage thither and prepared all things necessary for his passage now against the spring. A little before his setting forth, he caused a joust to be held at Windsor of forty knights and forty squires, against all comers, and they to be apparelled in green, with a white falcon, and the queen to be there well accompanied with ladies and damsels. When these jousts were finished, the king departed toward Bristol, from thence to pass into Ireland, leaving the queen with her train still at Windsor. [24]He appointed for his lieutenant general in his absence his uncle, the Duke of York. And so in the month of April, as divers authors write, he set forward from Windsor and finally took shipping at Milford, and from thence with two hundred ships and a puissant power of men of arms and archers he sailed into Ireland. The Friday next after his arrival, there were slain two hundred Irishmen at Fourd in Kenlis within the county of Kildare by that valiant gentleman, Jenico Dartois and such Englishmen as he had there with him. And on the morrow next ensuing, the citizens of Dublin invaded the country of Obrin and slew thirty and three Irishmen. . . .

---

[22] Edmund, Duke of York, fifth son of Edward III, was born at Langley near St. Albans, for which reason he acquired the surname of St. Albans.

[23] II.iv. 8–15.

[24] II.i. 219–221.

[*For several months Richard pursued a campaign against Art Mac-Murrough of Leinster, "the principal rebel in that season within Ireland," won several decisive battles and finally quartered his army in Dublin while making preparations for further engagements.*]

[25]Now while he was thus occupied in devising how to reduce them into subjection and taking orders for the good stay and quiet government of the country, divers of the nobility, as well prelates as other, and likewise many of the magistrates and rulers of the cities, towns, and communalty here in England, perceiving daily how the realm drew to utter ruin, not like to be recovered to the former state of wealth whilst King Richard lived and reigned (as they took it), devised with great deliberation and considered advice to send and signify by letters unto Duke Henry — whom they now called (as he was indeed) Duke of Lancaster and Hereford — requiring him with all convenient speed to convey himself into England, promising him all their aid, power and assistance, if he, expelling King Richard as a man not meet for the office he bore, would take upon him the scepter, rule, and diadem of his native land and region.

He therefore being thus called upon by messengers and letters from his friends, and chiefly through the earnest persuasion of Thomas Arundel, late Archbishop of Canterbury, who (as before you have heard) had been removed from his see and banished the realm by King Richard's means, got him down to Brittany, together with the said archbishop, where he was joyfully received of the duke and duchess and found such friendship at the duke's hands, that there were certain ships rigged and made ready for him at a place in base Brittany called Le Port Blanc, as we find in the Chronicles of Brittany. And when all his provision was made ready, he took the sea together with the said Archbishop of Canterbury and his nephew, Thomas Arundel, son and heir to the late Earl of Arundel, beheaded at the Tower Hill, as you have heard. There were also with him Reginald, Lord Cobham, Sir Thomas Erpingham, and Sir Thomas Ramston, knights, John Norbury, Robert Waterton, and Francis Coint, esquires. Few else were there, for (as some write) he had not past fifteen lances, as they termed them in those days: that is to say, men of arms furnished and appointed as the use then was.

[26]Yet others write that the Duke of Brittany delivered unto him three thousand men of war to attend him, and that he had eight ships well furnished for the war, where Froissart yet speaks but of three.

---

[25] II.i. 228ff. Shakespeare follows these next two paragraphs in Holinshed quite closely.

[26] II.i. 285–286.

Moreover, where Froissart and also the Chronicles of Brittany vouch that he should land at Plymouth, by our English writers it seems otherwise. For it appears by their assured report that he approaching to the shore did not straight take land, but lay hovering aloof and showed himself now in this place, and now in that, to see what countenance was made by the people, whether they meant enviously to resist him, or friendly to receive him.

[27]When the Lord Governor, Edmund, Duke of York was advertised that the Duke of Lancaster kept still the sea and was ready to arrive (but where he meant first to set foot on land there was not any that understood the certainty) he sent for the Lord Chancellor, Edmund Stafford, Bishop of Exeter, and for the Lord Treasurer, William Scroop, Earl of Wiltshire, and others of the king's Privy Council, as John Bushy, William Bagot, Henry Green, and John Russell, knights. Of these he required to know what they thought good to be done in this matter, concerning the Duke of Lancaster being on the seas. Their advice was to depart from London unto St. Albans, and there to gather an army to resist the duke in his landing; but to how small purpose their council served the conclusion thereof plainly declared, for the most part that were called, when they came thither, boldly protested that they would not fight against the Duke of Lancaster, whom they knew to be evilly dealt withal.

[28]The Lord Treasurer, Bushy, Bagot, and Green, perceiving that the commons would cleave unto and take part with the duke, slipped away, leaving the Lord Governor of the realm, and the Lord Chancellor to make what shift they could for themselves. Bagot got him to Chester, and so escaped into Ireland; the others fled to the castle of Bristol, in hope there to be in safety. [29]The Duke of Lancaster, after that he had coasted along the shore a certain time and had got some intelligence how the people's minds were affected towards him, landed about the beginning of July in Yorkshire at a place sometime called Ravenspurgh betwixt Hull and Bridlington — and with him not past threescore persons, as some write. But he was so joyfully received of the lords, knights, and gentlemen of those parts that he found means (by their help) forthwith to assemble a great number of people that were willing to take his part. The first that came to him were the lords of Lincolnshire and other counties adjoining, as the Lords Willoughby, Ross, Darcy, and Beaumont.

At his coming unto Doncaster, the Earl of Northumberland and his son, Sir Henry Percy, wardens of the marches against Scotland,

---

[27] II.ii. 73–89.
[28] II.ii. 123ff.
[29] II.iii. 1–80.

with the Earl of Westmoreland came unto him, where he swore unto those lords that he would demand no more but the lands that were to him descended by inheritance from his father and in right of his wife. Moreover, he undertook to cause the payment of taxes and tallages to be laid down, and to bring the king to good government, and to remove from him the Cheshire men which were envied of many: for that the king esteemed of them more than of any other, haply because they were more faithful to him than other, ready in all respects to obey his commandments and pleasure. From Doncaster having now got a mighty army about him, he marched forth with all speed through the countries, coming by Evesham unto Berkeley. Within the space of three days, all the king's castles in those parts were surrendered unto him.

The Duke of York, whom King Richard had left as governor of the realm in his absence, hearing that his nephew the Duke of Lancaster was thus arrived and had gathered an army, he also assembled a puissant power of men of arms and archers (as before you have heard). But all was in vain, for there was not a man that willingly would thrust out one arrow against the Duke of Lancaster or his partakers, or in any wise offend him or his friends. [30]The Duke of York therefore passing forth towards Wales to meet the king, at his coming forth of Ireland, was received into the Castle of Berkeley, and there remained till the coming thither of the Duke of Lancaster (whom when he perceived that he was not able to resist). On the Sunday after the feast of St. James, which as that year came about fell upon the Friday, he came forth into the church that stood without the castle and there communed with the Duke of Lancaster. With the Duke of York were the Bishop of Norwich, the Lord Berkeley, the Lord Seymour, and others. With the Duke of Lancaster were these: Thomas Arundel, Archbishop of Canterbury that had been banished, the Abbot of Leicester, the Earls of Northumberland and Westmoreland, Thomas Arundel, son to Richard, late Earl of Arundel, the Baron of Greystoke, the Lords Willoughby and Ross with divers other lords, knights, and other people which daily came to him from every part of the realm. Those that came not were spoiled of all they had so as they were never able to recover themselves again, for their goods being taken away were never restored. And thus what for love, and what for fear of loss, they came flocking unto him from every part.

At the same present there was arrested and committed to safe custody the Bishop of Norwich, Sir William Elmham and Sir Walter Burley, knights, Laurence Drew and John Golofer, esquires. [31]On

---

[30] II.iii. 76–83.
[31] II.iii. 163ff.

the morrow after, the foresaid dukes with their power went towards Bristol where (at their coming) they showed themselves before the town and castle, being an huge multitude of people. There were enclosed within the castle the Lord William Scroop, Earl of Wiltshire and Treasurer of England, Sir Henry Green and Sir John Bushy, knights, who prepared to make resistance. [32]But when it would not prevail they were taken and brought forth bound as prisoners into the camp, before the Duke of Lancaster. On the morrow next ensuing, they were arraigned before the constable and marshal and found guilty of treason, for misgoverning the king and realm, and forthwith had their heads smit off. Sir John Russell was also taken there, who feigning himself to be out of his wits escaped their hands for a time.

In this meantime, King Richard advertised how the Duke of Lancaster was landed in England and that the lords, gentlemen, and commons assembled themselves to take his part, he forthwith caused the Lord Henry, son to the said Duke of Lancaster, and the Lord Humphrey, son to the Duke of Gloucester, to be shut up fast in the castle of Trimme, and with all speed made haste to return into England in hope with an army to encounter the duke before he should have time to assemble his friends together. But here you shall note that it fortuned at the same time in which the Duke of Hereford or Lancaster, whether you list to call him, arrived thus in England the seas were so troubled by tempests and the winds blew so contrary for any passage (to come over forth of England) to the king remaining still in Ireland, that for the space of six weeks he received no advertisements from thence. Yet at length, when the seas became calm and the wind once turned any thing favorable, there came over a ship, whereby the king understood the manner of the duke's arrival and all his proceedings till that day in which the ship departed from the coast of England; whereupon he meant forthwith to have returned over into England to make resistance against the duke. But through persuasion of the Duke of Aumerle (as was thought) he stayed till he might have all his ships, and other provision, fully ready for his passage.

[33] In the meantime, he sent the Earl of Salisbury over into England to gather a power together, by help of the king's friends in Wales and Cheshire, with all speed possible that they might be ready to assist him against the duke upon his arrival; for he meant himself to follow the earl within six days after. The earl passing over into Wales landed at Conway and sent forth letters to the king's friends, both in Wales and Cheshire, to levy their people and to come with all

---

[32] III.i. 1–35.
[33] II.iv. 1ff.

speed to assist the king — whose request with great desire and very willing minds they fulfilled, hoping to have found the king himself at Conway, insomuch that within four days' space there were to the number of forty thousand men assembled, ready to march with the king against his enemies, if he had been there himself in person.

But when they missed the king, there was a bruit spread amongst them that the king was surely dead, which wrought such an impression and evil disposition in the minds of the Welshmen and others, that for any persuasion which the Earl of Salisbury might use, they would not go forth with him till they saw the king. Only they were contented to stay fourteen days to see if he should come or not; but when he came not within that term, they would no longer abide, but scaled[34] and departed away; whereas if the king had come before their breaking up, no doubt but they would have put the Duke of Hereford in adventure of a field. So that the king's lingering of time before his coming over gave opportunity to the duke to bring things to pass as he could have wished, and took from the king all occasion to recover afterwards any forces sufficient to resist him.

At length, about eighteen days after that the king had sent from him the Earl of Salisbury, he took the sea together with the Dukes of Aumerle, Exeter, Surrey, and divers others of the nobility, with the Bishops of London, Lincoln, and Carlyle. [35]They landed near the Castle of Barkloughly[36] in Wales, about the feast of St. James the apostle, and stayed a while in the same castle, being advertised of the great forces which the Duke of Lancaster had got together against him; wherewith he was marvellously amazed, knowing certainly that those which were thus in arms with the Duke of Lancaster against him would rather die than give place, as well for the hatred as fear which they had conceived at him. Nevertheless he departing from Barkloughly hasted with all speed towards Conway, where he understood the Earl of Salisbury to be still remaining.

He therefore taking with him such Cheshire men as he had with him at that present (in whom all his trust was reposed) he doubted not to revenge himself of his adversaries; and so at the first he passed with a good courage. But when he understood as he went thus forward that all the castles, even from the borders of Scotland unto Bristol, were delivered unto the Duke of Lancaster, and that likewise the nobles and commons as well of the south parts as the north were fully bent to take part with the same duke against him — and further,

---

[34] mounted.

[35] III.ii. 1ff.

[36] Barkloughly is probably a printer's error for Hertlowli (i.e., Harlech, in Wales). Shakespeare, following Holinshed, calls the castle Barkloughly (III.ii. 1).

hearing how his trusty councellors had lost their heads at Bristol — he became so greatly discomforted that sorrowfully lamenting his miserable state he utterly despaired of his own safety, and calling his army together, which was not small, licensed every man to depart to his home.

The soldiers being well bent to fight in his defense besought him to be of good cheer, promising with an oath to stand with him against the duke and all his partakers unto death. But this could not encourage him at all; so that in the night next ensuing he stole from his army, and with the Dukes of Exeter and Surrey, the Bishop of Carlyle, and Sir Stephan Scroop and about half a score others, he got him to the Castle of Conway where he found the Earl of Salisbury determining there to hold himself till he might see the world at some better stay. For what council to take to remedy the mischief thus pressing upon him he wist not. On the one part he knew his title just, true, and infallible, and his conscience clean, pure, and without spot of envy or malice. He had also no small affiance in the Welshmen and Cheshire men. On the other side, he saw the puissance of his adversaries, the sudden departing of them whom he most trusted, and all things turned upside down. He evidently saw, and manifestly perceived, that he was forsaken of them by whom in time he might have been aided and relieved, where now it was too late and too far overpassed. . . .

[Here follows a long list of nobles who went over to the side of Henry Bolingbroke.]

[37]After this, the duke, with advice of his council, sent the Earl of Northumberland unto the king accompanied with four hundred lances and a thousand archers, who coming to the castle of Flint had it delivered unto him; and from thence he hasted forth towards Conway.[38] But before he approached near the place, he left his power behind him, hid closely in two ambushes behind a craggy mountain beside the highway that leads from Flint to Conway.

This done, taking not past four or five with him, he passed forth till he came before the town, and then sending an herald to the king requested a safe conduct from the king that he might come and talk with him, which the king granted. And so the Earl of Northumberland, passing the water, entered the castle, and coming to the king declared to him that if it might please his grace to undertake that

---

[37] III.iii. 20ff. Shakespeare compresses the actions of these next eight paragraphs into a single dramatic scene.

[38] Shakespeare has Richard lodged in Flint Castle, not Conway.

there should be a Parliament assembled, in the which justice might be had against such as were enemies to the commonwealth and had procured the destruction of the Duke of Gloucester and other noblemen. And [if Richard would] herewith pardon the Duke of Hereford of all things wherein he had offended him, the duke would be ready to come to him on his knees, to crave of him forgiveness, and as an humble subject to obey him in all dutiful services. The king taking advice[39] upon these offers, and others made by the Earl of Northumberland on the behalf of the Duke of Hereford — upon the earl's oath for assurance that the same should be performed in each condition — agreed to go with the earl to meet the duke. And hereupon taking their horses they rode forth, but the earl rode before, as it were to prepare dinner for the king at Rutland; but coming to the place where he had left his people he stayed there with them.

The king keeping on his way had not ridden past four miles when he came to the place where the ambushes were lodged, and being entered within danger of them before he was aware, showed himself to be sore abashed. But now there was no remedy. For the earl being there with his men would not suffer him to return, as he gladly would have done if he might; but being enclosed with the sea on the one side and the rocks on the other, having his adversaries so near at hand before him, he could not shift away by any means. For if he should have fled back they might easily have overtaken him ere he could have got out of their danger. And thus of force he was then constrained to go with the earl, who brought him to Rutland where they dined, and from thence they rode unto Flint to bed. The king had very few about him of his friends, except only the Earl of Salisbury, the Bishop of Carlyle, the Lord Stephan Scroop, Sir Nicholas Fereby, a son also of the Countess of Salisbury, and Jenico Dartois, a Gascoigne that still wore the cognizance or device of his master, King Richard, that is to say, a white hart, and would not put it from him neither for persuasions nor threats: by reason whereof when the Duke of Hereford understood it he caused him to be committed to prison within the Castle of Chester. This man was the last (as says mine author) which wore that device, and showed well thereby his constant "hart" toward his master, for the which it was thought he should have lost his life, but yet he was pardoned and at length reconciled to the duke's favor, after he was king.

But now to our purpose. King Richard being thus come unto the castle of Flint on the Monday, the eighteenth of August, and the Duke of Hereford being still advertised from hour to hour by posts how the Earl of Northumberland sped, the morrow following being

---

[39] considering.

Tuesday and the nineteenth of August, he came thither and mustered his army before the king's presence — which undoubtedly made a passing fair show, being very well ordered by the Lord Henry Percy that was appointed general or rather (as we may call him) master of the camp, under the duke, of the whole army. There were come already to the castle before the approaching of the main army the Archbishop of Canterbury, the Duke of Aumerle, the Earl of Worcester, and divers others. The archbishop entered first and then followed the others, coming into the first ward.

The king that was walking aloft on the braes of the walls to behold the coming of the duke afar off, might see that the archbishop and the others were come, and (as he took it) to talk with him. Whereupon he forthwith came down unto them, and beholding that they did their due reverence to him on their knees he took them up and drawing the archbishop aside from the residue talked with him a good while; and as it was reported the archbishop willed him to be of good comfort, for he should be assured not to have any hurt, as touching his person; but he prophecied not as a prelate, but as a Pilate. For was it no hurt (think you) to his person to be spoiled of his royalty, to be deposed from his crown, to be translated from principality to prison, and to fall from honor into horror? All which befell him to his extreme heart grief (no doubt), which to increase, means alas there were many; but to diminish, helps (God wot) but a few.[40] So that he might have said with the forlorn man in the merciless seas of his miseries:

> Ut fera nimboso tumuerunt aequora vento,
> In mediis lacera nave relinquor aquis.[41]

Some write (as before in a marginal note I have quoted) that the Archbishop of Canterbury went with the Earl of Northumberland unto Conway and there talked with him. And further that even then the king offered, in consideration of his insufficiency to govern, freely to resign the crown and his kingly title to the same unto the Duke of Hereford. But forsomuch as those that were continually attendant about the king during the whole time of his abode at Conway and till his coming to Flint do plainly affirm that the archbishop came not to him till this Tuesday before his removing from Flint unto Chester, it may be thought (the circumstances well considered) that he rather made that promise here at Flint than at Conway — although by the

---

[40] i.e., there were many means to increase his grief, but few helps to diminish it.

[41] Just as the savage seas begin to swell with fierce wind, In the midst of the waves I am deserted by my battered ship.

tenor of an instrument containing the declaration of the Archbishop of York and other commissioners sent from the estates assembled in the next Parliament unto the said king, it is recorded to be at Conway, as after ye may read. But there may be some default in the copy, as taking the one place for the other.

But wheresoever this offer was made, after that the archbishop had now here at Flint communed with the king, he departed, and taking his horse again rode back to meet the duke, who began at that present to approach the castle and compassed it round about, even down to the sea, with his people ranged in good and seemly order at the foot of the mountains. And then the Earl of Northumberland passing forth of the castle to the duke talked with him a while in sight of the king, being again got up to the walls to take better view of the army being now advanced within two bow shots of the castle, to the small rejoicing (you may be sure) of the sorrowful king. The Earl of Northumberland, returning to the castle, appointed the king to be set to dinner (for he was fasting till then), and after he had dined the duke came down to the castle himself and entered the same all armed, his basinet only excepted; and being within the first gate he stayed there till the king came forth of the inner part of the castle unto him.

The king accompanied with the Bishop of Carlyle, the Earl of Salisbury, and Sir Stephan Scroop, knight, who bore the sword before him, and a few others, came forth into the outer ward and sat down in a place prepared for him. Forthwith as the duke got sight of the king, he showed a reverend duty as became him, in bowing his knee, and coming forward did so likewise the second and third time, till the king took him by the hand and lift him up, saying, "Dear cousin, you are welcome." The duke, humbly thanking him said, "My sovereign lord and king, the cause of my coming at this present is (your honor saved) to have again restitution of my person, my lands and heritage through your favorable license." The king hereunto answered, "Dear cousin, I am ready to accomplish your will, so that you may enjoy all that is yours without exception."

[42]Meeting thus together, they came forth of the castle, and the king there called for wine, and after they had drunk they mounted on horseback and rode that night to Flint, and the next day unto Chester, the third unto Nantwich, the fourth to Newcastle. Here, with glad countenance, the Lord Thomas Beauchamp, Earl of Warwick, met them, that had been confined into the Isle of Man, as before you have heard, but now was revoked home by the Duke of Lancaster. From Newcastle they rode to Stafford, and the sixth day unto Lichfield, and

---

[42] Note how Shakespeare turns this situation into parable: III.iv. 1ff.

there rested Sunday all day. After this they rode forth and lodged at these places ensuing: Coventry, Dantry, Northampton, Dunstable, St. Albans, and so came to London. Neither was the king permitted all this while to change his apparel, but rode still through all these towns simply clothed in one suit of raiment; and yet he was in his time exceeding sumptuous in apparel insomuch as he had one coat, which he caused to be made for him of gold and stone, valued at 30,000 marks. And so he was brought the next way to Westminster.

[43]As for the duke, he was received with all the joy and pomp that might be of the Londoners and was lodged in the bishop's palace by Paul's Church. It was a wonder to see what great concourse of people and what number of horses came to him on the way as he thus passed the countries, till his coming to London where (upon his approach to the city) the mayor rode forth to receive him, and a great number of other citizens. Also the clergy met him with procession, and such joy appeared in the countenances of the people, uttering the same also with words, as the like not lightly[44] been seen. For in every town and village where he passed, children rejoiced, women clapped their hands, and men cried out for joy. But to speak of the great numbers of people that flocked together in the fields and streets of London at his coming, I here omit; neither will I speak of the presents, welcomings, lauds, and gratifications made to him by the citizens and communality.

But now to the purpose. The next day after his coming to London, the king from Westminster was had to the Tower and there committed to safe custody. Many evil disposed persons, assembling themselves together in great numbers, intended to have met with him and to have taken him from such as had the conveying of him, that they might have slain him. But the mayor and aldermen gathered to them the worshipful commoners and grave citizens, by whose policy and not without much ado, the others were revoked from their evil purpose. Albeit before they might be pacified they coming to Westminster took Master John Slake, dean of the king's chapel, and from thence brought him to Newgate and there laid him fast in irons.

[45]After this was a Parliament called by the Duke of Lancaster using the name of King Richard in the writs directed forth to the lords and other estates for their summons. This Parliament[46] began the

---

[43] V.ii. 4–21.
[44] usually.
[45] IV.i. 162–318.
[46] This Parliament met in Westminster Hall, which was being rebuilt by Richard since 1397 for the purpose of making it the new parliamentary seat. It is ironic that the first meeting of Parliament in its new building was for the purpose of deposing the builder.

thirteenth day of September, in which the many heinous points of misgovernance and injurious dealings in the administration of his kingly office were laid to the charge of this noble prince, King Richard, the which (to the end the commons might be persuaded that he was an unprofitable prince to the commonwealth and worthy to be deposed) were engrossed up in 33 solemn articles, heinous to the ears of all men, and to some almost incredible. . . .

[Holinshed presents an abridgement of them, copied from Hall, which generally summarize the accusations against and crimes of Richard as already described in this narrative.]

Thus was King Richard deprived of all kingly honor and princely dignity, by reason he was so given to follow evil council and used such inconvenient ways and means, through insolent misgovernance and youthful outrage, though otherwise a right noble and worthy prince. He reigned two and twenty years, three months and eight days. He delivered to King Henry now that he was thus deposed all the goods that he had, to the sum of three hundred thousand pounds in coin, besides plate and jewels, as a pledge and satisfaction of the injuries by him committed and done, in hope to be in more surety of life for the delivery thereof.[47] But whatsoever was promised, he was deceived therein. For shortly after his resignation he was conveyed to the castle of Leeds in Kent, and from thence to Pomfret, where he departed out of this miserable life (as after you shall hear). . . .

[48]Thus much ado there was in this Parliament, specially about them that were thought to be guilty of the Duke of Gloucester's death, and of the condemning of the other lords that were adjudged traitors in the foresaid late Parliament held in the said one and twentieth year of King Richard's reign. Sir John Bagot, knight, then prisoner in the Tower,[49] disclosed many secrets unto the which he was privy; and being brought on a day to the bar, a bill was read in English which he had made containing certain evil practises of King Richard; and further what great affection the same king bore to the Duke of Aumerle, insomuch that he heard him say that if he should renounce the government of the kingdom he wished to leave it to the said duke, as to the most able man (for wisdom and manhood) of all other. For though he could like better of the Duke of Hereford, yet he said

---

[47] V.i. 51-52.
[48] IV.i. 1-90.
[49] Bagot had fled to Ireland, as Holinshed tells us earlier, but had been captured there by Bolingbroke's soldiers and brought back to the Tower in chains. This questioning took place on Thursday, October 16, 1399.

that he knew if he were once king, he would prove an extreme enemy and cruel tyrant to the church.

It was further contained in that bill that as the same Bagot rode on a day behind the Duke of Norfolk in the Savoy Street toward Westminster, the duke asked him what he knew of the manner of the Duke of Gloucester his death, and he answered that he knew nothing at all. But the people (quoth he) do say that you have murdered him. Whereunto the duke swore great oaths that it was untrue, and that he had saved his life contrary to the will of the king and certain other lords, by the space of three weeks and more; affirming withal, that he was never in all his lifetime more afraid of death than he was at his coming home again from Calais at that time to the king's presence, by reason he had not put the duke to death. And then (said he) the king appointed one of his own servants and certain others that were servants to other lords to go with him to see the said Duke of Gloucester put to death, swearing that as he should answer afore God, it was never his mind that he should have died in the fort, but only for fear of the king and saving of his own life. Nevertheless, there was no man in the realm to whom King Richard was so much beholden as to the Duke of Aumerle. For he was the man that to fulfill his mind had set him in hand with all that was done against the said duke and the other lords. There was also contained in that bill what secret malice King Richard had conceived against the Duke of Hereford being in exile, whereof the same Bagot had sent intelligence unto the duke into France, by one Roger Smart, who certified it to him by Pierce Buckton and others to the intent he should the better have regard to himself. There was also contained in the said bill that Bagot had heard the Duke of Aumerle say that he had rather than twenty thousand pounds that the Duke of Hereford were dead, not for any fear he had of him, but for the trouble and mischief that he was like to procure within the realm. . . .

The Lord Fitzwater herewith rose up and said to the king that where the Duke of Aumerle excuses himself of the Duke of Gloucester's death, "I say" (quoth he) "that he was the very cause of his death." And so he appealed him of treason, offering by throwing down his hood as a gage to prove it with his body. There were twenty other lords also that threw down their hoods as pledges to prove the like matter against the Duke of Aumerle. The Duke of Aumerle threw down his hood to try it against the Lord Fitzwater, as against him that lied falsely in that he had charged him with by that his appeal. These gages were delivered to the Constable and Marshal of England and the parties put under arrest.

The Duke of Surrey stood up also against the Lord Fitzwater,

avouching that where he had said that the appellants were causers of
the Duke of Gloucester's death, it was false, for they were constrained
to sue the same appeal in like manner as the said Lord Fitzwater was
compelled to give judgment against the Duke of Gloucester and the
Earl of Arundel; so that the suing of the appeal was done by con-
straint, and if he said contrary he lied. And therewith he threw
down his hood. The Lord Fitzwater answered hereunto that he was
not present in the Parliament house when judgement was given against
them, and all the lords bore witness thereof. Moreover, where it was
alleged that the Duke of Aumerle should send two of his servants to
Calais to murder the Duke of Gloucester, the said Duke of Aumerle
said that if the Duke of Norfolk affirm it, he lied falsely, and that he
would prove with his body — throwing down another hood which he
had borrowed. The same was likewise delivered to the Constable and
Marshal of England, and the king licensed the Duke of Norfolk to
return, that he might arraign his appeal. . . .

[50][1400] This year Thomas Mowbray, Duke of Norfolk, died in
exile at Venice, whose death might have been worthily bewailed of
all the realm if he had not been consenting to the death of the Duke
of Gloucester. [51]The same year deceased the Duchess of Gloucester,
through sorrow (as was thought) which she conceived for the loss of
her son and heir, the Lord Humphrey, who being sent for forth of
Ireland (as before you have heard) was taken with the pestilence and
died by the way.

[52]But now to speak of the conspiracy, which was contrived by the
Abbot of Westminster as chief instrument thereof. You shall understand that this abbot (as it is reported) upon a time heard King Henry
say, when he was but Earl of Derby and young of years, that princes
had too little and religious men too much. He, therefore, doubting
now lest if the king continued long in the estate he would remove
the great beam that then grieved his eyes and pricked his conscience,
became an instrument to search out the minds of the nobility and
to bring them to an assembly and council where they might consult
and common together, how to bring that to effect which they earnestly
wished and desired: that was, the destruction of King Henry, and
the restoring of King Richard. For there were divers lords that
showed themselves outwardly to favor King Henry, where they secretly
wished and sought his confusion. The abbot, after he had felt the
minds of sundry of them, called to his house on a day in the term[53]

[50] IV.i. 92–100.
[51] II.ii. 90–97.
[52] IV.i. 321ff.
[53] while Parliament was meeting (?).

time all such lords and other persons which he either knew or thought to be as affectioned to King Richard, so envious to the prosperity of King Henry: whose names were, John Holland, Earl of Huntington, late Duke of Exeter; Thomas Holland, Earl of Kent, late Duke of Surrey; Edward, Earl of Rutland, late Duke of Aumerle, son to the Duke of York; John Montagu, Earl of Salisbury; Hugh, Lord Spenser, late Earl of Gloucester; John, the Bishop of Carlyle; Sir Thomas Blunt; and Maudeleyn, a priest, one of King Richard's chapel, a man as like him in stature and proportion in all lineaments of body as unlike in birth, dignity, and conditions.

The abbot highly feasted these lords, his special friends, and when they had well dined they withdrew into a secret chamber where they sat down in council; and after much talk and conference had about the bringing of their purpose to pass concerning the destruction of King Henry, at length by the advice of the Earl of Huntington it was devised that they should take upon them a solemn joust to be enterprised between him and twenty on his part, and the Earl of Salisbury and twenty with him at Oxford — to the which triumph King Henry should be desired, and when he should be most busily marking the martial pastime he suddenly should be slain and destroyed; and so by that means King Richard, who as yet lived, might be restored to liberty and have his former estate and dignity. It was further appointed who should assemble the people, the number and persons which should accomplish and put in execution their devised enterprise. Hereupon was an indenture sexpartite made, sealed with their seals and signed with their hands, in the which each stood bound to other to do their whole endeavor for the accomplishing of their purposed exploit. Moreover, they swore on the holy evangelists to be true and secret each to other, even to the hour and point of death.

When all things were thus appointed, the Earl of Huntington came to the king unto Windsor, earnestly requiring him that he would vouchsafe to be at Brentford on the day appointed of their jousts, both to behold the same and to be the discoverer and indifferent judge (if any ambiguity should rise) of their courageous acts and doings. The king being thus, insistently required of his brother-in-law, and nothing less imagining than that which was pretended, gently granted to fulfill his request. Which thing obtained, all the lords of the conspiracy departed home to their houses, as they noised it, to set armorers on work about the trimming of their armor against the joust, and to prepare all other furniture and things ready as to such a high and solemn triumph appertained. The Earl of Huntington came to his house and raised men on every side, and prepared horse and harness for his compassed purpose. And when he had all things ready he departed towards Brentford, and at his coming thither he found all his mates and confederates there well appointed for their purpose — except the Earl of Rutland by whose folly their practiced conspiracy was brought to light and disclosed to King Henry. [54]For this Earl of Rutland departing before from Westminster to see his father, the Duke of York, as he sat at dinner had his counterpane of the indenture of the confederacy in his bosom.

The father espying it would needs see what it was. And though the son humbly denied to show it, the father being more earnest to see it by force took it out of his bosom; and perceiving the contents thereof, in a great rage caused his horses to be saddled out of hand. And spitefully reproving his son of treason, for whom he was become surety and mainpernor[55] for his good bearing in open Parliament, he incontinently mounted on horseback to ride towards Windsor to the king to declare unto him the malicious intent of his complices. [56]The Earl of Rutland, seeing in what danger he stood, took his horse and rode another way to Windsor in post, so that he got thither before his father and, when he was alighted at the castle gate, he caused the gates to be shut, saying that he must needs deliver the keys to the king. When he came before the king's presence, he kneeled down on his knees beseeching him of mercy and forgiveness and, declaring the whole matter unto him in order as everything had passed, obtained pardon. Therewith came his father, and being let in delivered the indenture which he had taken from his son unto the king, who thereby perceiving his son's words to be true, changed his purpose for his going to Brentford, and dispatched messengers forth to signify unto the Earl of Northumberland, his High Constable, and to the Earl of Westmoreland, his High Marshal, and to other his assured friends of all the doubtful danger and perilous jeopardy.

The conspirators being at Brentford at length perceived by the lack of the Earl of Rutland that their enterprise was revealed to the king, and thereupon determined now openly with spear and shield to bring that to pass which before they covertly attempted. And so they adorned Maudeleyn, a man most resembling King Richard, in royal and princely vesture, and named him to be King Richard, affirming that by favour of his keepers he was escaped out of prison. And so they came forwards in order of war, to the intent to destroy King

---

[54] V.ii. 41ff.

[55] one who stands surety for a prisoner's appearance in court.

[56] V.iii. 23ff. However the plea of the duchess for her son, ll.76–136, is wholly Shakespeare's invention and is anachronistic, Aumerle's mother having died in 1394.

Henry. Whilst the confederators with their new published idol accompanied with a strong army of men took the direct way towards Windsor, King Henry, admonished thereof, with a few horsemen in the night came to the Tower of London about twelve of the clock, where in the morning he caused the mayor of the city to apparel in armor the best and most courageous persons of the city — which brought to him three thousand archers, and three thousand billmen, besides them that were appointed to keep and defend the city.

[57]The conspirators coming to Windsor entered the castle and understanding that the king was gone from thence to London determined with all speed to make towards the city. But changing that determination as they were on their way, they turned to Colbroke and there stayed. King Henry, issuing out of London with twenty thousand men, came straight to Hunslow Heath and there pitched his camp to abide the coming of his enemies. But when they were advertised of the king's puissance, amazed with fear, and forthinking[58] their begun enterprise, as men mistrusting their own company, departed from thence to Berkhamsteed and so to Cicester, and there the lords took their lodging: the Earl of Kent and the Earl of Salisbury in one inn, and the Earl of Huntington and Lord Spenser in another. And all the host lay in the fields, whereupon in the night season the bailiff of the town with fourscore archers set on the house where the Earl of Kent and the others lay, which house was manfully assaulted and strongly defended a great space. The Earl of Huntington, being in another inn with the Lord Spenser, set fire on divers houses in the town, thinking that the assailants would leave the assault and rescue their goods, which thing they nothing regarded. The host lying without, hearing noise, and seeing this fire in the town, thought verily that King Henry had been come thither with his puissance, and thereupon fled without measure, every man making shift to save himself. And so that which the lords devised for their help wrought their destruction; for if the army that lay without the town had not mistaken the matter, when they saw the houses on fire they might easily have succored their chieftains in the town that were assailed but with a few of the townsmen, in comparison of the great multitude that lay abroad in the fields. But such was the ordinance of the mighty Lord of Hosts, who disposeth all things at His pleasure.

The Earl of Huntington and his company, seeing the force of the townsmen to increase, fled out on the backside, intending to repair to the army which they found dispersed and gone. Then the earl, seeing

---

[57] V.vi. 1–16.

[58] regretting.

no hope of comfort, fled into Essex. The other lords which were left fighting in the town of Cicester were wounded to death and taken and their heads stricken off and sent to London. . . .

Many others that were privy to this conspiracy were taken and put to death; some at Oxford as Sir Thomas Blunt, Sir Bennet Seely, knight, and Thomas Wintercel, esquire; but Sir Leonard Brocas and Sir John Shelly, knights, John Maudeleyn and William Fereby, chaplains, were drawn, hanged, and beheaded at London. There were nineteen in all executed in one place and other, and the heads of the chief conspirators were set on poles over London Bridge to the terror of others. [59]Shortly after, the Abbot of Westminster, in whose house the conspiracy was begun (as is said) going between his monastery and mansion, for thought fell into a sudden palsy and shortly after, without speech, ended his life. [60]The Bishop of Carlyle was impeached and condemned of the same conspiracy; but the king of his merciful clemency pardoned him of that offense, although he died shortly after, more through fear than force of sickness, as some have written. Thus all the associates of this unhappy conspiracy tasted the painful penance of their pleasant pastime. . . .

And immediately after, King Henry, to rid himself of any such like danger to be attempted against him thereafter, caused King Richard to die of a violent death, that no man should afterward feign himself to represent his person — though some have said he was not privy to that wicked offense. The common fame is that he was every day served at the table with costly meat, like a king, to the intent that no creature should suspect anything done contrary to the order taken in the Parliament; and when the meat was set before him, he was forbidden once to touch it; yea, he was not permitted so much as to smell it, and so he died of forced famine. . . .

[61]One writer, which seems to have great knowledge of King Richard's doings, says that King Henry, sitting on a day at his table, sore sighing, said, "Have I no faithful friend which will deliver me of him, whose life will be my death, and whose death will be the preservation of my life?" This saying was much noted of them which were present, and especially of one called Sir Pierce of Exton. This knight incontinently departed from the court with eight strong persons in his com-

---

[59] V.vi. 19–21.
[60] V.vi. 22–29.
[61] V.iv. 1ff; V.v. 95ff; V.vi. 30–44. The oldest authority for this account of Richard's death is Caxton's additions to *Hygden's Polychronicon*. The story was pretty much discredited by Holinshed's time — though Shakespeare uses it — and the forced famine theory was generally accepted.

pany and came to Pomfret, commanding the squire that was accustomed to sew and take the assay[62] before King Richard to do so no more, saying: "Let him eat now, for he shall not long eat." King Richard sat down to dinner and was served without courtesy or assay, whereupon much marveling at the sudden change he demanded of the squire why he did not his duty: "Sir" (said he) "I am otherwise commanded by Sir Pierce of Exton, which is newly come from King Henry." When King Richard heard that word, he took the carving knife in his hand and struck the squire on the head, saying, "The devil take Henry of Lancaster and thee together!" And with that word Sir Pierce entered the chamber, well armed, with eight tall men likewise armed, every of them having a bill in his hand.

King Richard perceiving this put the table from him and, stepping to the foremost man, wrung the bill out of his hands and so valiantly defended himself that he slew four of those that thus came to assail him. Sir Pierce, being half dismayed herewith, leapt into the chair where King Richard was wont to sit, while the other four persons fought with him and chased him about the chamber. And in conclusion as King Richard traversed his ground from one side of the chamber to another, and coming by the chair where Sir Pierce stood, he was felled with a stroke of a poleaxe which Sir Pierce gave him upon the head and therewith rid him out of life without giving him respite once to call to God for mercy of his past offenses. It is said that Sir Pierce of Exton, after he had thus slain him, wept right bitterly as one stricken with the prick of a guilty conscience for murdering him whom he had so long time obeyed as king. After he was thus dead, his body was embalmed and seared and covered with lead, all save the face, to the intent that all men might see him and perceive that he was departed this life. For as the corpse was conveyed from Pomfret to London, in all the towns and places where those that had the conveyance of it did stay with it all night, they caused dirges to be sung in the evening and mass of requiem in the morning; and as well after the one service as the other, his face discovered was showed to all that courted to behold it.

Thus was the corpse first brought to the Tower, and after through the city to the cathedral church of St. Paul, barefaced, where it lay three days together that all men might behold it. There was a solemn obsequy done for him both at Paul's and after at Westminster, at which time both at dirge over night and in the morning at the mass of requiem the king and the citizens of London were present. When the same was ended, the corpse was commanded to be had unto

---

62 taste food.

Langley, there to be buried in the church of the friar preachers. The Bishop of Chester, the Abbots of St. Albans and Waltham, celebrated the exequies for the burial, none of the nobles nor any of the commons (to accompt of) being present. Neither was there any to bid them to dinner after they had laid him in the ground and finished the funeral service.[63]

---

[63] Holinshed goes on to say: "He was after by King Henry the Fifth removed to Westminster, and there honorably entombed with Queen Anne, his wife, although the Scots untruly write, that he escaped out of prison, and led a virtuous and a solitary life in Scotland, and there died, and is buried (as they hold) in the Blackfriars at Sterling."

ANONYMOUS, C. 1591

The First Part of the Reign of King Richard II, or *Thomas of Woodstock*[*]

The action of this play covers a span of sixteen years, from the marriage of Richard and Anne of Bohemia in 1382 to the rebellion of the nobles against him in 1397. Thomas of Woodstock, Duke of Gloucester and uncle of Richard, is here portrayed as a benevolent and patriotic man, the victim of his nephew's unwarranted suspicions. At the end of Act IV Richard, stricken with conscience pangs, sends word to Calais where he holds his uncle prisoner countermanding his earlier order to murder "good uncle Woodstock." He is too late, however, and Woodstock's murder (V.i) is the tragic climax of the drama. It precipitates the revolt of the nobles against Richard, and V.ii. opens with Richard's loyal follower, Tresilian, discussing counter measures with his shrewdly comic servant, Nimble.

ACT V

SCENE II.

(*Drums. March within.*)[1]

Enter TRESILIAN *and* NIMBLE *with armor.*

TRESILIAN. These proclamations we have sent abroad,
Wherein we have accused the dukes of treason,
Will dent their pride and make the people leave them.
I hope no less at least. Where art thou, Nimble?

NIMBLE. So laden with armor I cannot stir, my lord.

TRESILIAN. Whose drums were those that beat even now?

NIMBLE. King Richard's drums, my lord; the young lords are pressing soldiers.

TRESILIAN. Oh, and do they take their press with willingness?

---

[*] text modernized.
[1] offstage.

NIMBLE. As willing as a punk[2] that's pressed on a feather bed; 10
they take there a piece with great patience. Marry, the lords no
sooner turn their backs but they run away like sheep, sir.

TRESILIAN. They shall be hanged like dogs for it.
What? Dare the slaves refuse their sovereign?

NIMBLE. They say the proclamation's false, my lord,
And they'll not fight against the king's friends.[3]

TRESILIAN. So I feared as much, and since 'tis come to this
I must provide betimes and seek for safety.
For now the king and our audacious peers
Are grown to such a height of burning rage 20
As nothing now can quench their kindled ire
But open trial by the sword and lance,
And then I fear King Richard's part will fail.
Nimble, our soldiers run, thou sayest?

NIMBLE. Aye, by my troth, my lord. And I think 'tis our best
course to run after them. For if they run now, what will they do
when the battle begins? If we tarry here and the king's uncles
catch us, we are sure to be hanged. My lord, have you no trick of
law to defend us, no demurrer or writ of error to remove us?

TRESILIAN. Nimble, we must be wise. 30

NIMBLE. Then let's not stay to have more wit beaten into our
heads. I like not that, my lord.

TRESILIAN. I am a man for peace and not for war.

NIMBLE. And yet they say you have made more wrangling in
the land than all the wars have done this seven years.

TRESILIAN. This battle will revenge their base exclaims.
But hearest thou, Nimble, I'll not be there today.
One man amongst so many is no maim;[4]
Therefore I'll keep aloof till all be done.
If good, I stay; if bad, away I run. 40
Nimble, it shall be so! I'll neither fight nor die,
But thus resolved disguise myself and fly — (*Exit* TRESILIAN.)

NIMBLE. 'Tis the wisest course, my lord,
And I'll go put off mine armor that I may run lustily too. (*Exit* NIMBLE.)

(*Enter with drum and colors,* YORK, LANCASTER, ARUNDEL, SURREY,
with the DUCHESS OF GLOUCESTER, *soldiers, and* CHENEY.)

LANCASTER. [5]Go to our tents, dear sister, cease your sorrows,
We will revenge our noble brother's wrongs

---

[2] prostitute.
[3] See Bolingbroke's protestation of friendship: I.i. 20–21.
[4] loss.
[5] Compare with I.ii. 1–36; II.i. 128–131.

And force that wanton tyrant to reveal
The death of his dear uncle, harmless Woodstock,
So traitorously betrayed.

    YORK. Alack, good man,   50
It was an easy task to work on him.
His plainness was too open to their view.
He feared no wrong, because his heart was true.
Good sister, cease your weeping, there is none here
But are as full of woe and touched as near.
Conduct and guard her, Cheney, to the tent.
Expect to hear severest punishment
On all their heads, that have procured his harms,
Struck from the terror of our threatening arms.

    DUCHESS. May all the powers of heaven assist your hands,   60
And may their sins sit heavy on their souls,
That they in death this day may perish all
That traitorously conspired good Woodstock's fall.

                (*Exit* CHENEY *and the* DUCHESS.)

    LANCASTER. If he be dead, by good King Edward's soul
[6]We'll call King Richard to a strict account
For that, and for all his realm's misgovernment.
You peers of England, raised in righteous arms   (*drums.*)
Here to re-edify[7] our country's reign,
Join all your hearts and hands never to cease
Till with our swords we work fair England's peace.   70

    ARUNDEL. Most princely Lancaster, our lands and lives
Are to these just proceedings ever vowed.

    SURREY. Those flattering minions that overturn the state
This day in death shall meet their endless fate.

    ARUNDEL. Never such vipers were endured so long
To grip and eat the hearts of all the kingdom.   (*drums.*)

    LANCASTER. This day shall here de-terminate[8] all wrongs.
The meanest man, taxed by their foul oppressions,
Shall be permitted freely to accuse,
And right they shall have to regain their own,   80
Or all shall sink to dark confusion.   (*drum sounds within.*)
How now, what drums are these?

               (*Enter* CHENEY.)

    CHENEY. To arms, my lords! The minions of the king
Are swiftly marching on to give you battle.

---

[6] Compare with II.i. 77–115; 238–258.
[7] reconstruct.
[8] terminate.

LANCASTER. They march to death then, Cheney. Dare the traitors
Presume to brave the field with English princes?

YORK. Where is King Richard? He was resolved but lately
To take some hold of strength[9] and so secure him.

CHENEY. Knowing their states were all so desperate   90
It seems they have persuaded him otherwise,
For now he comes with full resolve to fight.
La Pole this morning is arrived at court
With the Calais soldiers and some French supplies
To back this now intended enterprise.

LANCASTER. Those new supplies have spurred their forward hopes
And thrust their resolutions boldly on
To meet with death and sad destruction.

YORK. Their drums are near. Just heaven, direct this deed,   100
And as our cause deserves our fortunes speed.   (*march about.*)

(*Enter with drum and colors: The* KING, GREEN, BUSHY, BAGOT,
      SCROOP, LA POLE, *and soldiers. They march about.*)

KING. Although we could have easily surprised,
Dispersed, and overthrown your rebel troops
That draw your swords against our sacred person,
[10]The highest God's anointed deputy,
Breaking your holy oaths to heaven and us,
Yet of our mild and princely clemency
We have foreborne. That by this Parliament
We might be made partaker of the cause
That moved you rise in this rebellious sort.   110

LANCASTER. [11]Hast thou, King Richard, made us infamous
By proclamations false and impudent?
Hast thou condemned us in our absence too
As most notorious traitors to the crown,
Betrayed our brother Woodstock's harmless life,
And sought base means to put us all to death?
And dost thou now plead doltish ignorance
Why we are banded thus in our defense?

GREEN. Methinks your treasons to his majesty,
Raising his subjects against his royal life,   120
Should make you beg for mercy at his feet.

KING. You have forgotten, Uncle Lancaster,

---

[9] strongly fortified place.
[10] I.ii. 37–41.
[11] II.i. 73–138; 163–185.

How you in prison murdered cruelly
A friar Carmelite, because he was
To bring in evidence against your grace
Of most ungracious deeds and practices.

LANCASTER. And you, my lord, remember not so well
That by that Carmelite at London once,
When at a supper, you'd have poisoned us.

YORK. For shame, King Richard, leave this company 130
That like dark clouds obscure the sparkling stars
Of thy great birth and true nobility.

ARUNDEL. Yield to your uncles. Who but they should have
The guidance of your sacred state and counsel?

BAGOT. Yield first your heads, and so he shall be sure
To keep his person and his state secure.

KING. And by my crown, if still you thus persist
Your heads and hearts ere long shall answer it.

ARUNDEL. Not till you send for more supplies from France,
For England will not yield you strength to do it. 140

YORK. Thou well mayst doubt their loves that lost their heart.[12]
Ungracious prince, cannot thy native country
Find men to back this desperate enterprise?

LANCASTER. His native country? Why, that is France, my lords,
At Bordeaux was he born, which place allures
And ties his deep affections still to France.
Richard is English blood, not English born.
Thy mother travailed in unhappy hours
When she at Bordeaux left her heavy load;
The soil is fat for wines, not fit for men. 150
And England now laments that heavy time;
Her royalties are lost, her state made base,
And thou no king but landlord now become
To this great state that terrored Christendom.

KING. I cannot brook these braves.[13] Let drums sound death,
And strike at once to stop this traitor's breath.

BAGOT. Stay, my dear lord, and once more hear me, princes:
The king was minded ere this brawl began
To come to terms of composition.

LANCASTER. Let him revoke the proclamations, 160
Clear us of all supposed crimes of treason,
Reveal where our good brother Gloucester keeps,
And grant that these pernicious flatterers

---

[12] i.e. Woodstock.
[13] bravos, assassins.

May by the law be tried to quit themselves
Of all such heinous crimes alleged against them.
And we'll lay down our weapons at thy feet.

MINIONS.[14] Presumptuous traitors!

ALL. Traitors!

KING. Again we double it, rebellious traitors!

Traitors to heaven and us. Draw all your swords,   **170**
And fling defiance to those traitorous lords.

(*Enter [fighting]* BAGOT *and* CHENEY.)

ALL. Let our drums thunder and begin the fight.

(*Enter [fighting]* BUSHY *and* SURREY.)

Just heaven protect us and defend the right.

(*Exeunt omnes.*)

SCENE III.

(*Alarum. Enter* GREEN *and* CHENEY; *[they] meet armed.*)

CHENEY. Stand, traitor, for thou cannot escape my sword.

GREEN. What villain confronts me with the name of traitor?
Was it thou, false Cheney? Now by King Richard's love
I'll tilt thy soul out for that base reproach.
I would thy master and the late protector,
With both his treacherous brothers, Gaunt and York,
Were all opposed with thee to try these arms.   **180**
I'd seal it on all your hearts.

CHENEY. This shall suffice
To free the kingdom from thy villainies. (*They fight.*)

(*Enter* ARUNDEL.)

ARUNDEL. Thou huntst a noble game, right warlike Cheney.
Cut but this ulcer off, thou healst the kingdom.
Yield thee, false traitor, most detested man,
That sets King Richard 'gainst his reverent uncles
To shed the royal bloods and make the realm
Weep for their timeless desolation.
Cast down thy weapons, for by this my sword   **190**
We'll bear thee from this place, alive or dead.

GREEN. Come both then. I'll stand firm and dare your worst.
He that flies from it, be his soul accursed.

[GREEN *is slain.*][15]

---

[14] Bushy, Bagot, Green.

[15] In Shakespeare Green is captured by Bolingbroke and executed at his command. III.i. 1ff.

ARUNDEL. So may the foes of England fall in blood,
Most dissolute traitor. Up with his body, Cheney,
And haul it to the tent of Lancaster.

                (*[Enter]* BAGOT, BUSHY, SCROOP, *and soldiers.*)

CHENEY. Stand firm, my lord, here's rescue.

ARUNDEL. Courage then, we'll bear his body hence in spite of
them.

  (*They fight. To them enter* LANCASTER, YORK, *and* SURREY *and beat*
    them all away. Enter the KING [*who sees the body of* GREEN.])

KING. [16]Oh princely youth, King Richard's dearest friend.
What heavy star this day had dominance   200
To cut off all thy flowering youthful hopes.
Prosper proud rebels as you dealt by him,
Hard-hearted uncles, unrelenting churls,
That here have murdered all my earthly joys.
Oh my dear Green, wert thou alive to see
How I'll revenge thy timeless tragedy
On all their heads, that did but lift a hand
To hurt this body that I held so dear.
Even by this kiss, and by my crown, I swear.   (*Alarum.*)

      (*Enter* BAGOT, BUSHY, *and* SCROOP *to the king.*)

BAGOT. Away, my lord, stand not to wail his death.   210
The field is lost, our soldiers shrink and fly.
La Pole is taken prisoner by the lords.
Hie to the Tower. There is no help in swords.

SCROOP. Still to continue war were childishness.
Their odds, a mountain; ours a molehill is.

BUSHY. Let's fly to London and make strong the Tower.
Loud proclamations post throughout the camp
With promise of reward to all that take us.
Get safety for our lives, my princely lord.
If here we stay we shall be all betrayed.   220

KING. [17]Oh my dear friends, the fearful wrath of heaven
Sits heavy on our heads for Woodstock's death.
Blood cries for blood, and that almighty hand
Permits not murder unrevenged to stand. Come, come,
We may yet hide ourselves from worldly strength,
But heaven will find us out and strike at length.
Each lend a hand to bear this load of woe,
That erst King Richard loved and tendered so.

                             (*Exeunt omnes.*)

---

[16] Compare with III.ii. 144–177.
[17] Compare with I.ii. 1–8.

Scene IV.

Enter TRESILIAN *disguised, and* NIMBLE.

TRESILIAN. Where art thou, Nimble?

NIMBLE. As light as a feather, my lord. I have put off my shoes   230
that I might run lustily. The battle's lost and all are prisoners.
What shall we do, my lord? Yonder's a ditch. We may run along
that and never be seen, I warrant.

TRESILIAN. I did suspect no less. And so 'tis fallen.
The day is lost, and dashed are all our hopes.
King Richard's taken prisoner by the peers.
Oh, that I were upon some steep rock
Where I might tumble headlong to the sea,
Before those cruel lords do seize on me.

NIMBLE. Oh, that I were transformed into a mouse, that I   240
might run into any hole in the house, and I cared not.

TRESILIAN. Come, Nimble, 'tis no time to use delay.
I'll keep me in this poor disguise awhile,
And so unknown prolong my weary life
In hope King Richard shall conclude my peace.   (*Sound retreat.*)
Hark, hark, the trumpets call the soldiers back.
Retreat is sounded. Now the time serves fit,
And we may steal from hence. Away, good Nimble.

NIMBLE. Nay, stay my lord. Slain and you go that way. But
and you'll be ruled by me, I have thought of a trick that you shall   250
escape them all most bravely.

TRESILIAN. Bethink thyself, good Nimble, quickly man.

NIMBLE. I'll meditate, my lord, and then I'm for you. Now,
Nimble, show thyself a man of valor, think of thy fortunes. 'Tis
a hanging matter if thou conceal him; besides, there's a thousand
marks for him that takes him, with the duke's favor and free
pardon; besides, he's but a coward — he would ne'er have run from
the battle else. St. Anthony assist me, I'll set upon him presently.
My lord, I have thought upon this trick. I must take you prisoner.

TRESILIAN. How, prisoner?   260

NIMBLE. There's no way to escape else. Then must I carry you
to the king's uncles, who presently condemn you for a traitor, send
you away to hanging, and then God bless my Lord Tresilian.

TRESILIAN. Wilt thou betray thy master, villain?

NIMBLE. Aye, if my master be a villain. You think 'tis nothing
for a man to be hanged for his master? You hear not the proclamations?

TRESILIAN. What proclamations?

NIMBLE. Oh sir, all the country is full of them: that whosoever
sees you [and] does not presently take you and bring you to the 270
lords shall be hanged for his labor. Therefore no more words, lest
I raise the whole camp upon you. You see one of your own swords
of justice drawn over you. Therefore go quietly, lest I cut your head
off and save the hangman a labor.

TRESILIAN. O villain!

NIMBLE. No more words. Away, sir.

(*Exeunt.*)

Scene V.

Sound a retreat, then a flourish. Drum, colors. Enter with victory
LANCASTER, YORK, CHENEY, ARUNDEL, SURREY, *and soldiers with* LA
POLE, BUSHY, *and* SCROOP, *prisoners.*

LANCASTER. Thus princely Edward's sons, in tender care
Of wanton Richard and their father's realm,
[18]Have toiled to purge fair England's pleasant field
Of all those rancorous weeds that choked the grounds 280
And left her pleasant meads like barren hills.
Who is it can tell us which way Bagot fled?

ARUNDEL. Some say to Bristol to make strong the castle.

LANCASTER. See that the ports be laid.[19] He'll fly the land
For England has no hold[20] can keep him from us.
Had we Tresilian hanged, then all were sure.

CHENEY. Where slept our scouts that he escaped the field?
He fled they say before the fight began.

LANCASTER. Our proclamations soon shall find him forth,
The root and ground of all these vile abuses. 290

(*Enter* NIMBLE *with* TRESILIAN, *bound and guarded.*)

LANCASTER. How now, what guard is that, what traitor is there?

NIMBLE. The traitor now is taken. I here present the villain.
And if you needs will know his name,
God bless my Lord Tresilian.

CHENEY. Tresilian, my lord, attached[21] and apprehended by this
man.

NIMBLE. Yes, and it please ye, my lord, 'twas I that took him.
I was once a trampler in the law after him, and I thank him he
taught me this trick to save myself from hanging.

---

[18] Compare with III.iv. 43–47.
[19] guarded, i.e., by laying up, or docking all ships.
[20] stronghold, defense.
[21] arrested.

LANCASTER. Thou art a good lawyer, and hast removed the 300
cause from thyself fairly.

NIMBLE. I have removed it with a *habis*[22] *corpus*, and then I
took him with a *surseraris*[23] and bound him in this bond to answer
it. Nay, I have studied for my learning, I can tell ye, my lord.
There was not a stone between Westminster Hall and Temple
Bar but I have told them every morning.

ARUNDEL. What moved thee, being his man, to apprehend him?

NIMBLE. Partly for these causes: first, the fear of the proclamation, for I have plodded in Plowden[24] and can find no law . . .[25] 309

□ *Some Sources for Further Study*

Holinshed based his *Chronicles* on a number of earlier sources, and
according to the authoritative survey by Geoffrey Bullough[26] Shakespeare most likely knew the four following ones. For anyone wishing to
supplement Holinshed with more intense investigation, these would be
the most probable subsidiary sources.

1. ROBERT FABYAN — *The New Chronicles of England and France*
   (1516).
2. EDWARD HALL — *The Union of the Two Noble and Illustrious
   Families of Lancaster and York* (1548).
3. RICHARD GRAFTON — *A Chronicle at Large and Mere History of
   the Affairs of England and Kings of the Same* (1569).
4. JOHN STOW — *Annals, or a General Chronicle of England* (1580).
   Of special importance for one detail of *Richard II*, the Annals seem
   to be the source for Mowbray's sojourn to Palestine (IV.i 92–95).

Other *Richard II* sources include:

5. *A Mirror for Magistrates* (1559).
   "Lord Mowbray and King Richard II": flaccid and moralizing, un-
   like Shakespeare's play except perhaps in the sense that his
   Richard II sometimes poetized weakly.

---

22 Corrupt form of *habeas*.

23 Probably a garbled form of the Latin *certiorari*. The legal writ of *certiorari*
was an ancillary process to the writ of *habeas corpus* in criminal cases.

24 The text gives "ployden" but this is almost certainly a reference to
Plowden's *Commentaries*, a black-letter law book written in French. *Surseraris*
adds weight to this assumption.

25 Here the text ends.

26 Geoffrey Bullough, *Narrative and Dramatic Sources of Shakespeare*, Vol.
III (London: Routledge and Kegan Paul, 1960), pp. 1–15; 227.

6. Christopher Marlowe — *Edward II* (1591). For strong similarities of character and situation to *Richard II*.
7. Samuel Daniel — *The First Four Books of the Civil Wars between the Houses of Lancaster and York* (1595). See Book One.

the merchant of venice

While all of the other plays in this volume mostly depend upon a central source or sources, The Merchant of Venice is built upon several peer sources each contributing a key block of material to the total structure. In this sense it compares with *Love's Labor's Lost*, *A Midsummer Night's Dream*, *Cymbeline*, and *The Tempest*, but *The Merchant of Venice* sources dovetail more smoothly and completely than any of those others and permit us to account for just about every element of plot. It is worth noting that the Shakespeare plays built upon multiple sources are all comedies, which may offer a special insight into Shakespeare's comic method and perhaps into the general make-up of comedy as well.

The most productive source for this play is a novella by Giovanni Fiorentino (i.e., the Florentine, clearly a pseudonym) which appeared in a collection of his entitled *Il Pecorone* (The Big Sheep, or, colloquially, The Big Fool) in 1378. *Il Pecorone* consists of fifty novellas divided into "Days," groups of ten stories, like its model the *Decameron*, but unlike Boccaccio's masterpiece its stories have no profound core and are awkwardly written. The "merchant of Venice" story is the first story of the fourth day, and no translation of it existed in Shakespeare's day. We may assume that Shakespeare read it in the original, surely not too difficult a feat for a man who knew medieval Latin, who included Italian dialogue in *The Taming of the Shrew*, and who had a certain verbal dexterity. The last half of Fiorentino's story matches up with many parts of Shakespeare's play, especially with Acts III–V. The pound of flesh story, the lady-judge resolving the merchant's dilemma at the expense of the Jew, and the ring demanded as a fee all appear in Fiorentino. On the other hand Fiorentino's Anselmo is Giannetto's godfather, where Antonio is Bassanio's friend; Giannetto's lady has a streak of larceny alien to Portia; and Anselmo's trial is held at the judge's inn instead of at the Ducal Court. But these differences, all of them settled in Shakespeare's favor, are minor.

The *Gesta Romanorum*, that collection of Latin *exempla* derived from older European and Oriental sources and compiled in England around 1300, contains the story of the caskets which motivates the plot of Shakespeare's play, which slants across Acts I–III, and which is a vehicle for character and idea as well as plot. The story of "Ancelmus the Emperor" contains the caskets episode, and the anonymous translation of it used here stems from the earliest known one in English and is the one generally preferred in connection with Shakespeare. Like Fiorentino's novella only the latter part of the *Gesta* story pertains to *The Merchant of Venice*, and that part concerns three caskets, of gold, silver, and lead, the lead casket in both story and play concealing the prize. In the *Gesta* story the princess must choose correctly to prove herself worthy of a husband, while in Shakespeare Bassanio chooses to prove himself worthy of Portia.

Alexandre Sylvain ("Englished" as Silvayn) published *Epitomes de Cent Histoires* in 1581, a series of debates on questions of moral conduct stimulated by stories by older writers, the idea probably taken from the *dubbii* (debates on conduct) in Boccaccio's Filocopo. This book was translated into English by L. P. [Lazarus Piot] and published in 1596 as The Orator, and one of its debates dealt with the merchant of Venice story of Giovanni Fiorentino. The debate starts *after* the judge's decision against the Jew, and while it adds nothing to the plot of Shakespeare's play it provides bases for many of Shylock's attitudes and arguments during the trial scene and for those of Antonio earlier.

The Jessica-Lorenzo subplot derives from another Italian novella, this one by Masuccio Salernitano, an elegant and skillful writer whose *Novellino*, 1476, a collection of fifty stories, nearly rivals the Decameron. *Il Novellino*, like *Il Pecorone*, was not available in English during Shakespeare's day. Novella the Fourteenth contains the following elements in common with Shakespeare's play: a young girl is closely guarded by her father, a wealthy miser (not a Jew); a young man uses his female servant (faintly reminiscent of Launcelot Gobbo) to persuade the girl to run off with him; she does so, first stealing a hoard of her father's jewels and money; they go off to Ischia where they are hospitably received by the lord of that place, a friend of the young man's — a situation similar to that in *The Merchant of Venice* where Jessica and Lorenzo are received by Portia, and which may have suggested the link between Shakespeare's plot and subplot. The character of the miser and his outcries at the loss of his money, jewels, and daughter also serve to bind this source to the main plot.

Mention should be made of a lost play, *The Jew*, cited by Stephen Gosson in his *School of Abuse*, 1579. Gosson, himself a writer of plays, attacks the stage in this book but lists four plays that are above rebuke, one of them, *The Jew*, acted at the Bull, a morally improving work "representing the greediness of worldly choosers, and bloody minds of usurers." While this comment may seem to nominate *The Jew* as another source for Shakespeare's play, that play may well have been as lost to Shakespeare as it is to us, or of minor relevance to *The Merchant of Venice*. Certainly in view of the strong ties between *The Merchant of Venice* and the four sources just discussed, *The Jew* can make little claim to be another Ur-Hamlet.

The most frequently discussed character in this play is, of course, Shylock, and Shakespeare in contrast to his sources has humanized him considerably. But the roots of prejudice lie deep in those sources, and in reinforcing ones like Marlowe's *The Jew of Malta*, and Shylock for all of his rasping and bitter truths and the gallant efforts of Edmund Kean and Sir Henry Irving still partakes of caricature. Richer and more natural are the noblest characters of the play, Portia and Antonio, who derive in large part from Shakespeare's own world of Juliet and Friar Laurence. Notably the first words each utters deal with melancholy, touched off perhaps by Timothy Bright's *Treatise of Melancholy*, 1586, and serving among other things to set off the radiant freshness and language of Jessica and Lorenzo. Despite his many points of contact with his sources, Shakespeare managed to introduce two new characters, perhaps three, into his play: Gratiano, an echo of Mercutio, and certainly a more plausible husband for Nerissa than Anselmo was for the Lady of Belmont's maid; and Launcelot Gobbo and his father, who owe far more to Will Kempe, the slapstick comedian in Shakespeare's company, than to Masuccio.

Contrast between Shylock and the other characters leads easily to the central idea of the play, that love and loyalty outweigh gold. The idea is implicit in Fiorentino, and in Silvayn, and is even reflected in the choice of caskets. But if Shakespeare is in part bound by his sources' caricature view of the Jew, he also retains their view of the Jew's inflexibility and perhaps uses it to express another, deeper idea. In *The Merchant of Venice* Shylock alone does not change and is thereby destroyed. In a changing era when the Renaissance was dissolving into seventeenth century scientism, one had to adapt or perish, which is perhaps why Portia who will lose her independence and Antonio who will lose his first friend have premonition pangs of melancholy — they will be, after all, the two who destroy Shylock.

IL PECORONE,[1] *1378*

Giovanni Fiorentino

*The Fourth Day, First Story**

There was in Florence in the house of the Scali[2] a merchant named Bindo who had been to Tana and Alexandria several times and on all the great trading voyages. This Bindo was very rich and had three grown sons, and when he was nearing death he called his oldest and middle sons to him and made his will in their presence, leaving them heirs to all his worldly goods. And he left nothing to his youngest son.

After the will his youngest son, Giannetto, went to his bedside and said: "Father, I am much amazed by what you have done, not remembering me in your will." "Giannetto my son," his father answered, "there is no one in the world whom I love more than you. For this reason I do not want you to stay in this city after my death. I want you to go instead to Venice, to Ansaldo your godfather, who has no children and has written me many times to send you to him. He is, let me tell you, the richest merchant in Christendom today. I want you to go to him after my death and take this letter to him. And if you use your judgement you will become a rich man." "Father," said the young man, "I am ready to do what you want me to," whereupon his father gave him his blessing. A few days afterward he died, and all his sons grieved greatly and buried him with fitting ceremony. Then Giannetto's brothers sent for him and said: "Brother, while our father left us his heirs and made no provision for you in his will, nevertheless you are still our brother and will share in our fortune." "My brothers," Giannetto replied, "I thank you for your offer, but I intend to seek my fortune elsewhere. I have made up my mind. Your holy and blessed inheritance is yours to keep." And his brothers, seeing his determination, gave him a horse and a sum of money.

---

* translated by Joseph Satin.
[1] The Big Sheep, or, colloquially, The Big Fool.
[2] a wealthy Florentine family.

Giannetto took leave of them and went to Venice. He came to the market place of Ansaldo and handed him the letter which his father had given him. Ansaldo read it and learned that here was the son of his dearest friend Bindo,[3] and he embraced the boy saying: "Welcome, my son whom I have long desired to see." He asked about Bindo and when Giannetto told him that Bindo was dead he embraced the youth again and kissed him tearfully, saying: "Now, although I mourn the death of Bindo, since he helped me to earn a large part of what I have, my happiness in having you is so great that it diminishes my sorrow." He took the youth home and ordered his stewards, attendants, grooms, servants — everyone in his household — to serve and obey Giannetto more than himself. He gave him the keys to all of his coffers and said: "My son, whatever is here is yours. Spend it now on clothing and clubs as you wish, give dinners for the local people and make yourself known. As far as I am concerned, the better you are liked the more I shall like it."

Giannetto began to enter Venetian society, giving dinners and suppers, owning liveried servants, buying fine steeds, jousting, giving gay parties — a gentleman expert and masterful and generous and courteous in everything. He knew well how to show honor and courtesy wherever he should, and he always honored Ansaldo more than if he were a hundred times his father. He comported himself so wisely with every class of people that almost the whole of Venice loved him and judged him wise, courteous, extraordinary, delightful. He was the light of Ansaldo's eye, and all the ladies, and gentlemen too, loved him, so pleasing were his manners and behavior. There was almost no festivity in Venice to which Giannetto was not invited, so well liked was he by everybody.

Now it happened that two of his dear friends wanted to voyage to Alexandria with their merchant ships, as was their custom every year. They asked Gianneto whether he would care to amuse himself by going with them to see the world, especially Damascus and that part of the world. Giannetto answered: "In truth I would be very glad to go if my father Ansaldo gives permission." "We will see to it," they said, "that he gives it to you willingly." Shortly after they went to Ansaldo and told him: "We hope that you will give Giannetto permission to go with us to Alexandria this spring and will furnish him with a ship so that he may see a little of the world." "I am willing," said Ansaldo, "if he wishes." "Sir, he is willing," they told him.

In a short time Ansaldo had a most magnificent ship fitted out for him, laden with merchandise, and bedecked with flags and carrying as much armament as necessary. When that was done Ansaldo ordered

---

[3] In Shakespeare Bassanio and Antonio are kinsmen: I.i. 57.

the captain and the others of the crew to do whatever Giannetto commanded them. "For I am not sending him," he said, "for the profit he might earn, but that he may have the pleasure of seeing the world."

When Giannetto was about to leave all Venice came down to watch him, for so magnificent and well furnished a ship as this one had not sailed from Venice for a long time. Everyone grieved at his parting, and thus he took leave of Ansaldo and all his friends. The ships moved out to sea and the crews hoisted sail and got underway for Alexandria in the name of God and of good fortune.

After the three friends had been sailing day after day, very early one morning Giannetto saw a most beautiful harbor in the gulf of a sea and asked the captain the name of it. The captain replied: "Sir, this harbor belongs to a gentle lady, a widow, who has brought many gentlemen to peril." "How so?" asked Giannetto. "Sir," he was answered, "this lovely and beautiful lady has proclaimed this law: that whoever arrives here must spend the entire first night awake; if he stays awake until morning he wins the lady for his wife and is lord of this whole country; but if he falls asleep, he loses everything he has." After a moment's thought Giannetto said: "Use any method you wish but land in that harbor." "Sir," said the captain, "beware of what I told you, for many gentlemen have gone there and been ruined there and died." "Do what I tell you," said Giannetto, "and don't worry."

And it was done. The ship veered and landed in the harbor without a word to those on the other ships. And that morning the news ran throughout the city of this magnificent ship which had arrived in port, and all the people hurried to see it. The lady was soon informed. She sent for Giannetto who went to her straightway and greeted her with great respect. She took him by the hand and asked him who he was and from where and whether he knew the custom of the country. Giannetto replied that he did and that he had come here for no other purpose. "You are a hundred times welcome," she told him. All that day she paid him the highest honors and invited a number of her barons, counts and gentlemen to keep him company. All of these lords were pleased by the manners of this youth, so easy, pleasant and amiable was he, and almost everyone fell in love with him. All that day there was dancing, singing and revelry at the court out of love for him, and everyone would have been glad to have had him as ruler.

When evening came the lady took him by the hand and led him into a chamber. Two young damsels entered bearing wine and sweetmeats. "I know that you are thirsty," the lady said, "and therefore drink." Giannetto took some sweetmeats and drank the wine which, although he did not know it, was drugged to make him sleepy. It tasted delicious and he drank half a glass of it. Soon he undressed and lay down to rest, and as soon as his head touched the pillow he fell asleep, not waking up until around nine o'clock the next morning. With the coming of day the lady ordered the unloading of his ship, which she found filled with the richest and finest merchandise.

At nine o'clock one of the lady's servants came to his bed, woke him and told him to go with God, since he had lost his ship and its contents. He was ashamed, knowing he had done a foolish thing. The lady ordered him to be given a horse and some expense money, whereupon, sad and gloomy, he mounted the horse and rode toward Venice.

When he arrived in Venice he stayed away from Ansaldo's house for shame and spent the night at the house of a friend.

His friend was surprised to see him and said: "Giannetto, what is the matter?" "My ship," he answered, "crashed against a rock one night and was destroyed, and everything went helter-skelter into the sea. I held onto a timber which carried me to shore and made my way here."

He stayed concealed in his friend's house for several days until one day his friend visited Ansaldo and finding him quite melancholy, asked: "What is wrong?" Ansaldo said: "I am so terribly afraid that my son might be dead or injured at sea I cannot stop worrying. So great is the love I bear him that any day I do not see him is an evil day." "Sir," the young man said, "I do not quite know how to tell you this: he has had a shipwreck and has lost everything, except himself." "God be praised!" said Ansaldo. "Since he is saved I am happy and care nothing about what is lost." And the young man led Ansaldo to Giannetto, and when Ansaldo saw him he ran to him and embraced him, saying: "My son, do not be ashamed. Ships are often lost at sea, which is nothing to worry about. As long as you have come to no harm I am truly happy." Thus comforting him he took him home. The news spread over all of Venice, and everyone sympathized with Giannetto's misfortune.

A short while later his friends returned from Alexandria quite rich. When they arrived they asked about Giannetto and were told what had befallen him. They ran to embrace him saying: "How did you happen to leave us and where did you go? We turned back and looked for you all that day, but could never find a trace of you. We were grief stricken and our entire journey was miserable because we thought you were dead." Giannetto answered: "A wind came up out of the gulf and pushed my ship straight into a rock near the shore. I barely escaped and lost everything in the confusion." (This was the excuse Giannetto gave them in order to cover his guilt.) The young men held a great party to give thanks that he had escaped, and they told him: "Next Spring, with the grace of God, we will gain back your losses. In the meantime let us enjoy ourselves." — which they did with revels and gaiety as in times past.

But Giannetto thought only about how he could return to the lady, dreaming about it and saying to himself: "I must have her as my wife, or I shall die." He was rarely contented, and Ansaldo said to him over and over: "My son, do not be sad, for we have goods enough to keep us rich forever." "My lord," Giannetto finally replied, "I will never be happy unless I make that sea voyage one more time." Seeing how strong was his desire, Ansaldo furnished him with another ship of even greater value and with even more merchandise, which cost him the greater part of his fortune.

When Giannetto's friends had loaded their ships with cargo they all set sail again and began their journey. Day after day Giannetto kept watch for the lady's harbor (called the Harbor of the Lady of Belmonte[4]). One night he reached the mouth of this harbor, recognized it immediately, veered sail and rudder and landed there.

[5]That morning when the lady awoke and looked down at the harbor she saw the flags of a ship flying. She called one of her maids and asked: "Do you know those flags?" "My lady," said her servant, "they seem to belong to that youth who arrived a year ago and left us so rich a prize." "You are absolutely right," said the lady. "And he must surely be in love with me, for never has anyone come here more than once." Her maid added: "Never have I seen a more courteous or gracious man than he."

The lady sent many damsels and squires in search of him. They greeted him with great festivity and he them with many signs of joy. Thus he came into the presence of the lady. When she saw him she embraced him with utmost gaiety and happiness, and he embraced her with great reverence. All that day was spent in revelry and pleasure, for the lady invited many nobles and ladies to come to court for festivities in honor of Giannetto. Nearly all the nobles sympathized with the young man' and gladly would have had him as their ruler, impressed by his amiable courtesy. Nearly all the ladies fell in love with him, so perfectly did he lead the dancing and so alert and lively was his manner. All were convinced that he was the son of some great nobleman.

---

4 Portia too is from Belmont: I.i. 161.
5 II.i. 85ff.

When it came time for bed Giannetto and the lady went to the chamber, and after they had sat down two damsels came in with wine and sweetmeats. As soon as Giannetto drank the wine he fell asleep and — to be brief — slept through the entire night. When morning came the lady had the ship unloaded. After nine o'clock Giannetto awoke. He raised his head, and saw that it was full morning, and arose heavy with shame. He was given a horse and some expense money and quickly departed, sad and grieving, journeying without stopping to Venice. At night he went to his friend's house who, when he saw him, was the most amazed man in the world and exclaimed: "What's this?" "A misfortune for me," Giannetto answered. "Cursed be the fate that ever brought me to this country!" "You do well to curse," said his friend, "since you have deserted Ansaldo, the finest and richest merchant in Christendom, and the shame you have brought to him is worse than the hurt."

Giannetto remained hidden in his friend's house for several days, not knowing what to do or say. He had almost decided to return to Florence without a word to Ansaldo, but in the end decided to face him, which he did. When Ansaldo saw him he jumped up and ran to embrace him saying: "Welcome, son!" Giannetto embraced him weeping and Ansaldo said: "Look here, Giannetto, not a bit of grief. As long as I have you back I am content. We still have enough money to live with ease."

The news of this went all over Venice and everyone said of Ansaldo: "Good for him." But it fell out that he had to sell many of his possessions to pay the creditors who had given him the lost merchandise.

Giannetto's friends returned to Venice rich, and when they arrived were told how Giannetto had lost and destroyed everything. They were amazed and said it was the strangest thing imaginable. They once before I die, I can die willingly." Giannetto promised, Ansaldo "Sir, do not be worried, for we plan to go out next year and earn money for you, since we have been more or less the reason for your losses; for it was we who induced Giannetto to come with us in the first place. But never fear; as long as we have merchandise consider it yours." Ansaldo thanked them weeping and told them that he still had enough to support him and Giannetto rather well.

[6]Morning and night, however, Giannetto kept thinking about what had happened and could not be at ease. Ansaldo asked him many times what was the matter with him, and Giannetto finally answered: "I will never be happy if I do not gain back what I have lost." "My son," said Ansaldo, "I do not want you to go out there again, for it is better

---

[6] I.i. 122–152.

that we hold on to this little we have than to risk it further." But Giannetto said: "I am determined to do it. I would hold myself in utter contempt if I just went along like this."

[7]Seeing that that was what he wanted, Ansaldo set about selling everything he had in the world so as to outfit another ship for him. To do so he sold everything he had to outfit a most magnificent merchant ship — except that he still needed ten thousand ducats.[8] [9]He went to a Jew at Mestri and got it from him under the following agreements and conditions: that if he did not return the money by the Feast of St. John next June, the Jew could take a pound of flesh from any part of his body. Ansaldo agreed to this and the Jew had a formal agreement drawn up with witnesses and with all the necessary formalities. Then he counted out ten thousand golden ducats. With that money, Ansaldo completed equipping the ship and though the other two ships had been beautiful this third one was even richer and better appointed.

Giannetto's two friends accompanied him on the voyage, with the intention of giving him whatever they earned. When the moment of departure came Ansaldo said to Giannetto: "My son, you are going away while I remain behind. One grace I beg of you: even if things go badly for you, may it please you to return to me. If I can see you once before I die, I can die willingly." Giannetto promised, Ansaldo gave him his blessing, and thus they took leave of one another and the voyage began.

Giannetto's friends kept constant watch over his ship, unaware that Giannetto had every intention of leaving them and dropping off into the harbor of Belmonte. One night, with the aid of one of his helmsmen, he did so and landed his boat at the harbor of his lady. The next morning his friends in the other ships looked all around for him, and not seeing his boat anywhere said: "This is indeed evil fortune!" and they marvelling greatly continued on their route.

Meanwhile the whole city ran to see this new ship in the harbor realizing that Giannetto had returned. They marvelled greatly over this, saying: "He must certainly be the son of some very important man, seeing how he comes to us every year with such merchandise in such magnificent ships. Please God that he become our ruler." Thus he was visited by all the dignitaries, nobles, and gentlemen of that city. The lady was informed that Giannetto had arrived and she went to the window and saw this magnificent ship and the flags it

[7] I.i. 177ff.
[8] in Shakespeare, three thousand.
[9] I.iii. 1–154.

flew, and she crossed herself saying: "It must surely be he who has brought such great abundance to this land." And she sent for him.

Giannetto went to her and they greeted one another with many embraces and courtesies. The entire day was spent amid joy and revelry, and for the love of Giannetto a fine tournament was held and many noblemen and gentlemen jousted that day. Giannetto too turned to jousting, and performed many miraculous feats, so skillful was he with arms and horsemanship. His conduct so pleased all the nobles that they longed for him to be their ruler. When night came and it was time for bed the lady took Giannetto by the hand and said: "Let us go and rest."

[10]But one of the lady's chambermaids, feeling sorry for Giannetto whispered to him in a low voice: "Pretend to drink, but do not drink tonight." Giannetto heard these words and then entered the chamber. "I know you are thirsty," said the lady, "and therefore wish to drink something before going to sleep." Two damsels, who looked like two angels entered with the customary wine and sweetmeats and solicitously offered him the wine. "Who could refuse wine from two damsels as lovely as these?" Giannetto said, and the lady laughed. Giannetto took the cup and pretended to drink but poured it inside his shirt. The lady thinking that he had drunk said to herself: "You will bring us another ship, for now you have lost this one." Giannetto went to the bed feeling wide awake and in fine spirits, though it seemed to him that the morning was a thousand years away. "I have surely won!" he said to himself, "she is caught in her own trap!" In short he who had slept soundly the other times did not close his eyes all that night.

Therefore when morning came the lady sent for all her lords and gentlemen and many other citizens and announced: "Prepare to celebrate, for Giannetto is your ruler." "Long live our ruler!" the roar went up, and bells rang and bands played and the nobles sent word to those outside the city to come and behold their ruler. A grand, magnificent court was assembled, and when Giannetto left his chamber he was made a knight and placed on a sceptered throne. Amid great pomp, he was joyously proclaimed ruler for the remainder of his lifetime. After all of the nobles and ladies of the court arrived he married his gentle lady amid joy and revelry beyond imagining. All the lords and nobles from the surrounding countryside came to celebrate with jousting, tourneying, dancing, singing, music, and so forth. Giannetto,

---

[10] Shakespeare too provides extralegal help for his suitor. The song, "Tell Me Where Is Fancy Bred" (III.ii. 63–72) begins with three lines that rhyme with lead, the third rhyme so forced as to call especial attention to itself.

generous as ever, began to give away the bolts of silk and other rich stuffs that he had brought and also to show himself manly enough to command respect and to maintain law and justice for all classes of people. [11]Thus he continued to live amid this triumph and revelry without heeding or remembering the ruined Ansaldo, who remained liable to the Jew for ten thousand ducats.

One day when Giannetto was standing at the window with his lady he saw a group of men with torches proceeding through the city square on the way to a certain church. "What is that all about?" Giannetto asked, and his lady answered: "They are a group of craftsmen going to give offerings at the Church of St. John, because today is his feast day." Thereupon Giannetto remembered Ansaldo, and he backed away from the window sighing bitterly. His expression changed entirely and he paced up and down the room. His lady asked what was the matter with him and Giannetto told her nothing, but she began to worry and said: "Surely it is something, but you will not tell me." And she kept asking him so insistently that Giannetto told her the whole story — how Ansaldo had remained liable for ten thousand ducats which were due that day and for which he would now have to lose a pound of flesh from his back. "Mount a horse quickly," his lady told him, "take what companions you wish and a hundred thousand ducats and do not rest until you reach Venice. And if you can save Ansaldo, bring him here with you." Straightway he sounded a call to arms, and with more than a hundred companions on horseback and with much money he galloped rapidly toward Venice. [12]Meanwhile, the note being due, the Jew had Ansaldo arrested and wanted to cut off his pound of flesh. Ansaldo begged him to delay that death for several days so that, should his Giannetto come, at least he might be able to see him. The Jew said: "I am content to do as you wish as far as the delay is concerned, but if he comes a hundred times over I still intend to take a pound of flesh from your body, according to my bond." Ansaldo replied that he was content.

Everyone in Venice was talking about this affair and everyone sympathized with Ansaldo. A number of merchants contributed enough money to pay his debt. But the Jew would not budge, preferring to commit murder so as to say he had killed the greatest merchant in Christendom.

[13]After Giannetto's departure his lady acted swiftly, disguised herself as a judge and followed Giannetto with two of her servants.

---

[11] III.ii. 234ff. An example of how Shakespeare knits several incidents into a single scene.

[12] III.iii. 1–17.

[13] III.iv. 57ff.

[14]Giannetto, arriving in Venice went straight to the house of the Jew where he embraced Ansaldò with great joy. Then he told the Jew that he wanted to pay him his money and as much more as he might desire. The Jew replied that he did not want the money, since he had not gotten it in time, but rather that he wanted to cut off his pound of flesh. His answer set off a vigorous debate. Everybody blamed the Jew, but since Venice was the seat of reason and the Jew's reasons were backed by law, nobody could find reasons to prevent him except by pleading with him. All of the merchants of Venice went to the Jew's counting house to plead for Ansaldo, but he became more stubborn than ever.

Giannetto offered him twenty thousand ducats but he would not budge; he went to thirty thousand, then forty thousand, then fifty thousand and on up to one hundred thousand. But the Jew told him: "Do you know what? If you were to offer me more than the value of this whole city I would not take it so as to enjoy this pleasure. I just want to act according to my bond."

While the debate was raging throughout the city the lady, disguised as a judge, arrived in Venice and dismounted at an inn. "Who is this gentleman?" the innkeeper inquired, and her servant, already instructed by the lady, replied: "This gentleman is a judge who comes from Bologna where he has studied and is returning home." The innkeeper received them with much respect, and at dinner the judge asked him: "How is this country governed?" "Sir," the host replied, "they observe the letter of the law too strictly here." "How so?" asked the judge. "Sir," replied the host, "I will tell you. A young man named Giannetto came here from Florence to live with his godfather, whose name is Ansaldo. He was so gifted and delightful that everybody loved him. His godfather outfitted him with three ships of the highest value, and each time misfortune struck. Ansaldo did not have enough money for the last ship and borrowed ten thousand ducats from a Jew under these terms: that if he did not return the money by the Feast of St. John the Jew could take a pound of flesh from whatever part of his body he wished. Now the youth has returned and wants to give one hundred thousand ducats for those ten thousand, but the evil Jew will not agree. All the good men of the city have pleaded with him, with no success."

"This question is actionable and easy to resolve," said the judge. "If you could stay here and see to it that this good man does not die," said the host, "you would gain the grace and love of the finest youth that was ever born and of all the people of this city." Accordingly the judge sent a proclamation throughout the land that anyone with a question to decide might come to him.

---

[14] IV.i. 63–103.

[15]Giannetto was informed that a judge had come from Bologna who could settle any question. Thereupon he said to the Jew: "Let us go to this judge to hear his decision." "Let us," said the Jew. When they arrived in the judge's presence and paid their respects the judge recognized Giannetto right away. Giannetto, however, did not know him since the lady had disguised herself with certain dyes. Giannetto and the Jew discussed the question step by step before the judge, and the judge took the Jew's bond, read it and then told him: "It is my wish that you take one hundred thousand ducats and free that good man. That way these two will always remain in your debt." "That is not my wish at all," answered the Jew. "It is in your best interest," urged the judge, but the Jew absolutely refused and the judge said: "Then bring him here and take a pound of flesh from anywhere you wish."

The Jew sent for Ansaldo and when he had arrived the judge told the Jew: "Do what you must." The Jew had Ansaldo stripped naked and took in his hand a razor which he had prepared for this. Giannetto turned to the judge and protested: "Sir, this is not what I had hoped of you." "Do not worry," the judge replied. "Leave things to me." And seeing the Jew approaching Ansaldo he said: "Take care what you do. For if you take more or less than one pound I shall have your head cut off. More, if one single drop of blood is spilled I will have you killed, since your bond makes no mention of the shedding of blood. It states that you take a pound of flesh, nothing more or less. If you are sensible you had better find a way to do it." And he quickly called for the executioner who set up his block and axe. "As soon as I see a drop of blood spilled," went on the judge, "I will have your head cut off." The Jew began to grow frightened and Giannetto to rejoice. After many discussions the Jew said: "Your Honor, you have been wiser than I. Give me the hundred thousand ducats and I am content." But the judge said: "I wish you to take a pound of flesh according to your bond and I will not give you a single coin. You should have taken the ducats when I wanted to give them to you." He went down to ninety thousand, then eighty thousand, but the judge held firm. Giannetto said to the judge: "Let us give him what he wants as long as he releases Ansaldo to us." "Leave this to me," the judge told him. "Let me have fifty thousand," said the Jew, but the judge replied, "I would not give you the shabbiest coin that you ever had." "At least give me my ten thousand," said the Jew, "and a curse on this land." "Perhaps you do not understand me," said the judge. "I do not intend to give you anything. If you want to

---

[15] IV.i. 119–400. Again several incidents are combined into a single Shakespearean scene.

take his flesh, take it. If not, I will declare the bond forfeit." Everyone there was overjoyed at this and they all made fun of the Jew,
telling him: "The bird hunter is a dead bird!" The Jew, seeing that
he was helpless, took his bond and tore it up in a rage. Thus Ansaldo
was freed and Giannetto led him home with the greatest joy.

[16] Then Giannetto took the hundred thousand ducats and went
to the judge. He found him in his chamber getting ready to depart.
"Sir," Giannetto told him, "you have done me the greatest service ever,
and I want you to take this money, for you have surely earned it."
The judge said: "My deepest thanks, my dear Giannetto, but I don't
need it. You keep it lest your lady say you have misused it." "By my
father," Giannetto answered, "she is so generous and gracious and
good that if I spent four times as much as this she would be pleased.
Indeed, she wanted me to take a lot more money than this." "How
happy are you with her?" the judge asked him, and Giannetto replied:
"There is no Christian in the world happier than I or who loves his
lady more, for she is as wise and as beautiful as nature could make her.
It would give me great pleasure if you could come and visit her. You
would marvel at her courtesy and would see all that I have told you
or more." "Do this for me," said the judge, "when you return to her
send her my greetings." Giannetto said: "It will be done, but I do
wish you would take this money." While he was talking the judge saw
a ring on his finger and said: "I should like this ring and no other
reward." "Granted," Giannetto said, "but I do so reluctantly. For
my lady gave this ring to me and told me to wear it always for love
of her. If she sees I do not have it she will think I have given it to
some woman and will be angry at me thinking I love another, though
I love her better than myself." The judge replied: "I am sure that she
loves you enough to believe you when you tell her that you gave it to
me. But perhaps you wanted to give it to one of your former sweethearts here." "I love and trust her so much," Giannetto replied, "that
I would not exchange her for any other woman in the world. She is so
perfect in everything." He took the ring from his finger and gave it
to the judge. Then they embraced, bowed to one another and prepared to take their leaves when the judge said: "Do me one favor."
"Ask it," replied Giannetto. "Do not delay here but return immediately to your lady," said the judge, and Giannetto agreed saying: "It
seems a thousand years since I saw her last." They parted and the
judge went toward the sea. Giannetto organized banquets and parties,
gave horses and money to his friends, held more celebrations and then,
taking Ansaldo with him, took leave of all of Venice. Many of his
former companions left with him, and most of the ladies and gentle-

[16] IV.i. 408–454.

men wept at his departure, so delightful had he been to everyone during the time he had lived in Venice. Thus he departed and returned to Belmonte.

His lady had arrived a while before, and dressed in her own clothes again pretended to have been at a spa.[17] She made great preparations for festivities, lined all the streets with silk and costumed many companies of jousters. When Giannetto and Ansaldo arrived all the nobles of the court went to meet them crying out: "Long live our ruler!" When they came into the city the lady hurried to embrace Ansaldo, but seemed a little angry at Giannetto, although she really loved him better than herself. During the great festival wherein all the lords and ladies were enjoying the jousting, tourneying, dancing, and singing Giannetto noticed that his wife did not look as fondly on him as usual. Alone in their chamber he asked her what was the matter and tried to embrace her, but his lady said: "You do not have to show me this affection. I know well that you were with your former sweethearts in Venice." Giannetto began to make denials but his lady said: [18]"Where is the ring I gave you?" Giannetto said: "Something unexpected happened. I knew you would think ill of me because of it. But I swear to you by my faith in God and you that I gave your ring to the judge who won my suit for me." His lady said: "And I swear to you by my faith in God and you that you gave it to a lady, whom I know. Aren't you ashamed denying it?" "May God strike me dead," Giannetto told her, "if I am not telling you the truth. I even warned him of this when he asked me for it." The lady said: "You should have stayed there and just sent Ansaldo here while you enjoyed yourself with all those sweethearts of yours, for I am told that all the ladies wept when you departed."

Giannetto began to weep and to worry greatly, saying: "What you have sworn to is not and cannot be true."

Seeing him weep, the lady knew she had cut him to the quick and ran quickly to embrace him and gave him the most beautiful smile in the world.[19] She showed him the ring and told him everything,

---

[17] in Shakespeare, a monastery. III.iv. 26–32.

[18] V.i. 166–270.

[19] It may be that the Lady of Belmont only smiles and nothing more (see also p. 127) because of the primitive simplicity of this story. On the other hand her smile may partake of a deeper Renaissance tradition. In the *Divine Comedy* the high point of the poet's meeting with Beatrice in the Garden of Eden (Purgatory, xxxi) is the moment when she smiles upon him — which symbolizes his perception of her love for him. Dante was using the current truism that of all God's creatures only human beings were capable of smiling to reveal, through her smile, the wonderful *humanity* of Beatrice. Perhaps Fiorentino had the same intention.

about how she was the judge and the things that he had told the judge. Giannetto was beside himself with amazement, and when he realized it was all true he was overjoyed. Leaving the chamber he told the story to several of his lords and companions, and because of this deed the love between those two grew and multiplied. Then Giannetto summoned the maid who had warned him not to drink that trial evening and gave her to Ansaldo as a wife.[20] And thus all their days were spent in joy and revelry and they lived happily ever after.

---

[20] Compare with Shakespeare's pairing of Gratiano and Nerissa.

Gesta Romanorum[1]

"Ancelmus the Emperor"*

Ancelmus reigned emperor in the city of Rome, and he wedded to wife the king's daughter of Jerusalem, the which was a fair woman and long dwelt in his company; but she never conceived nor brought forth fruit, and thereof were [his] lords greatly heavied and sorry. Happening in a certain evening, as he walked after his supper in a fair green and thought of all the world, and especially that he had no heir, and how that the king of Naples strongly therefore annoyed[2] him each year; and so, when it was night, he went to bed and took a sleep and dreamed this. He saw the firmament in its most clearness, and more clear than it was wont to be, and the moon was more pale; and on a part of the moon was a fair colored bird, and beside her stood two beasts the which nourished the bird with their heat and breath. After this came divers beasts and birds flying, and they sang so sweetly that the emperor was with the song awakened. Then on the morrow the emperor had great marvel of this sweven,[3] and called to him diviners and lords of all the empire and said to them, "Dear friends, tell me what is the interpretation of my sweven, and I shall well reward you; and but if[4] you do you shall be dead." And then they said, "Lord, show to us thy dream and we shall tell thee the interpretation of it." And then the emperor told them as is said before, from beginning to ending. And then they were glad, and with a great gladness spoke to him and said, "Sir, this was a good sweven; for the firmament that thou saw so clear is the empire, the which henceforward shall be

---

* text modernized.
[1] An English version was first printed by Wynkyn de Worde, 1510–1515. The version here presented is based upon the edition of 1838 made by S. J. H. Herrtage for the *Early English Text Society* series.
[2] by warring against the emperor (see below).
[3] dream, vision.
[4] unless.

in prosperity; the pale moon is the empress, the which hath conceived, and for her conceiving is the more discolored;[5] the little bird is the fair son whom the empress shall bring forth when the time comes; and the two beasts are rich men and wise men that shall be obedient to thy child; the other beasts are other folk that never made homage and now shall be subject to thy son; the bird that sang so sweetly is the empire of Rome that shall joy of thy child's birth; and, sir, this is the interpretation of your dream." When the empress heard this she was glad enough; and soon she bore a fair son, and thereof was made much joy.[6] And when the King of Naples heard that, he thought to himself, "I have long time held war against the emperor, and it may not be but [7]that it will be told to his son, when that he comes to his full age, how that I have fought all my life against his father. "Yea," thought he, "he is now a child, and it is good that I procure for peace that I may have rest of him when he is in his best and I in my worst." So he wrote letters to the emperor for peace to be had; and the emperor seeing that he did that more for cause of dread than of love, he sent him word again and said that he would make him surety of peace with condition that he would be in his servitude and yield him homage all his life each year. Then the king called his council, and asked of them what was best to do; and the lords of his kingdom said that it was good to follow the emperor in his will. "In the first [letter] you asked of him surety of peace; to that we say thus: thou hast a daughter and he hath a son; let matrimony be made between them, and so there shall be good security; also it is good to make him homage and yield him rents." Then the king sent word to the emperor and said that he would fulfill his will in all points and give his daughter to his son in wife, if that it were pleasing to him. This answer liked well the emperor, but he sent word again that he would not assent to matrimony, but if[8] that his daughter had been a virgin from her nativity. The king was herewith highly glad, for his daughter was such, a clean virgin. So letters were made of this covenant; and he made a ship to be ordained to lead his daughter with a certain[9] of knights and ladies to the emperor to be married with his son. And when they were in the ship and had far passed from the land there rose up a great horrible tempest and drowned all that were in the ship

---

[5] It is highly conjectural, but there might be some connection between the paleness of the moon (symbolizing, we are told, the successful wife and mother) and the paleness of lead, in contrast to gold and silver, in the three vessels incident below.

[6] Much joy was made thereof.

[7] It will surely be.

[8] unless.

[9] company.

except the maid. Then the maid set all her hope strongly in God; and at last the tempest ceased; but there followed strongly a great whale to devour this maid. And when she saw that she much dreaded; and when the night came the maid dreading that the whale would have swallowed the ship, smote fire at[10] a stone and had great plenty of fire; and as long as the fire lasted the whale durst come no nearer; but about cock's crow the maid for great vexation that she had with the tempest fell on sleep, and in her sleep the fire went out; and when it was out the whale came nigh and swallowed both the ship and the maid. And when the maid felt that she was in the womb of a whale, she smote and made great fire and grievously wounded the whale with a little knife insomuch that he drew to the land and died; for that [whale] is the kind to draw to the land when he shall die. And in this time there was an earl named Pirius, and he walked in his disport[11] by the sea; and afore him he saw the whale come toward the land. He gathered great help and strength of men; with divers instruments they smote the whale in every part of him. And when the damsel heard the great strokes she cried with an high voice and said, "Gentle sirs, have pity of me, for I am the daughter of a king, and a maid have I been since I was born." When the earl heard this, he marvelled greatly and opened the whale and took out the damsel. Then the maid told by order how that she was a king's daughter and how she lost her goods in the sea and how she should be married to the son of the emperor. And when the earl heard these words he was glad and held the maid with him a great while, till time that she was well comforted; and then he sent her solemnly to the emperor. And when he saw her coming and heard that she had tribulations in the sea he had great compassion for her in his heart and said to her, "Good damsel, thou hast suffered much anguish for the love of my son; nevertheless, if that thou be worthy to have him I shall soon prove." [12]The emperor lately made three vessels. And the first was of clean gold and full of precious stones outward, and within full of dead bones; and it had a superscription in these words: They that choose me shall find in me that they deserved. The second vessel was all of clean silver and full of precious stones; and outward it had this superscription: They that choose me shall find in me that nature and kind desire. And the third vessel was of lead and within was full of precious stones; and without was set[13] this scripture: They that choose me shall find

---

[10] from.

[11] for his amusement.

[12] I.ii 30–36; II.vii; II.ix; III.ii 1–139.

[13] During Shakespeare's lifetime Richard Robinson brought out six editions of the *Gesta Romanorum* in which he tinkered somewhat with the translations.

[in] me that God hath disposed. These three vessels took the emperor and showed the maid, saying, "Lo, dear damsel, here be three worthy vessels; and thou choose [the] one of these wherein is profit, and oweth[14] to be chosen, then thou shalt have my son to husband; and if thou choose that that is not profitable to thee nor to none other, forsooth then thou shalt not have him." When the daughter heard this and saw the three vessels she lifted up her eyes to God and said, "Thou, Lord, that knowest all things, grant me Thy grace now in the need of this time, scil.,[15] that I may choose at this time wherethrough [16]I may enjoy the son of the emperor and have him to husband." Then she beheld the first vessel, that was subtly made, and read the superscription; and then she thought: what have I deserved for to have so precious a vessel, and though it be never so gay without, I [know] not how foul it is within; so she told the emperor that she would by no way choose that. Then she looked to the second, that was of silver, and read the superscription; and then she said: "My nature and kind ask but delectations of the flesh. Forsooth sir," quoth she, "and I refuse this." Then she looked to the third, that was of lead, and read the superscription; and then she said, "Sooth, God disposed never evil; forsooth, that which God hath disposed will I take and choose." And when the emperor saw that he said, "Good damsel, open now that vessel and see what thou hast found." And when it was opened it was full of gold and precious stones. And then the emperor said unto her again, "Damsel, thou hast wisely chosen and won my son to thine husband." So the day was set of her bridal and great joy was made; and the son reigned after the decease of the father, the which made fair end. *Ad quod nos perducat!*[17] Amen.

J. R. Brown in his New Arden edition of *The Merchant of Venice* points out that in Robinson's 1595 edition he substituted "insculpt" for "set" here and that the only time Shakespeare used "insculped" was in this play where the Prince of Morocco debates which casket to choose: II.vii. 57.

[14] deserves.
[15] *scilicet*: to wit.
[16] whereby.
[17] May we be led to the same!

ALEXANDER SILVAYN

The Orator

"Englished by L.P." [Lazarus Piot] 1596

Of a Jew, who would for his debt have a pound of the flesh of a Christian*

A Jew unto whom a Christian merchant owed nine hundred crowns would have summoned him for the same in Turkey. [1]The merchant because he would not be discredited promised to pay the said sum within the term of three months, and if he paid it not he was bound to give him a pound of the flesh of his body. The term being past some fifteen days, the Jew refused to take his money and demanded the pound of flesh. The ordinary judge of that place appointed him to cut a just pound of the Christian's flesh, and if he cut either more or less, then his own head should be smitten off. The Jew appealed from this sentence unto the chief judge, saying:

Impossible is it to break the credit of traffic amongst men without great detriment unto the commonwealth. Wherefore no man ought to bind himself unto such covenants which he cannot or will not accomplish; for by that means should no man fear to be deceived; and credit being maintained, every man might be assured of his own. But since deceit has taken place, never wonder if obligations are made more rigorous and strict than they were wont, seeing that although the bonds are made never so strong, yet can no man be very certain that he shall not be a loser. [2]It seems at the first sight that it is a thing no less strange than cruel to bind a man to pay a pound of the flesh of his body for want of money. Surely, in that it is a thing not usual, it appears to be somewhat the more admirable.[3] But there are divers

---

* text modernized.
[1] I.iii; IV.i.
[2] IV.i. 40–61.
[3] strange.

others that are more cruel, which because they are in use seem nothing terrible at all: as to bind all the body unto a most loathsome prison or unto an intolerable slavery, where not only the whole body but also all the senses and spirits are tormented, the which is commonly practised not only betwixt those which are either in sect or nation contrary, but also even amongst those that are all of one sect and nation — yea, amongst neighbors and kindred and even amongst Christians it has been seen, that the son has imprisoned the father for money. [4]Likewise in the Roman Commonwealth, so famous for laws and arms, it was lawful for debt to imprison, beat, and afflict with torments the free citizens. How many of them (do you think) would have thought themselves happy if for a small debt they might have been excused with the payment of a pound of their flesh? Who ought then to marvel if a Jew require so small a thing of a Christian, to discharge him of a good round sum? A man may ask why I would not rather take silver of this man than his flesh. I might allege many reasons. For I might say that none but myself can tell what the breach of his promise has cost me and what I have thereby paid for want of money to my creditors [5]of that which I have lost in my credit. For the misery of those men which esteem their reputation is so great that oftentimes they had rather endure anything secretly than to have their discredit blazed abroad, because they would not be both shamed and harmed. Nevertheless I do freely confess that I had rather lose a pound of my flesh than my credit should be in any sort cracked. I might also say that I have need of this flesh to cure a friend of mine of a certain malady, which is otherwise incurable, or that I would have it to terrify thereby the Christians from abusing the Jews any more hereafter. But I will only say that by his obligation he owes it me. It is lawful to kill a soldier if he come unto the wars but an hour too late, and also to hang a thief though he steal never so little. Is it then such a great matter to cause such a one to pay a pound of his flesh that has broken his promise many times, or that puts another in danger to lose both credit and reputation — yea and it may be life and all — for grief? Were it not better for him to lose that which I demand than his soul, already bound by his faith? Neither am I to take that which he owes me, but he is to deliver it me. And especially because no man knows better than he where the same may be spared to the least hurt of his person. For I might take it in such a place as he might thereby happen to lose his life. What a matter were it, then, if I should cut off his privy members, supposing that the same would altogether weigh a just pound? Or else his head, should I be suffered to cut it off, al-

---

[4] IV.i. 90–103.
[5] because of.

though it were with the danger of mine own life? I believe I should not.[6] Because there were as little reason therein as there could be in the amends whereunto I should be bound. Or else if I would cut off his nose, his lips, his ears, and pull out his eyes, to make them altogether a pound, should I be suffered?[7] Surely I think not, because the obligation does not specify that I ought either to choose, cut, or take the same, but that he ought to give me a pound of his flesh. Of everything that is sold, he which delivers the same is to make weight, and he which receives takes heed that it be just. Seeing then that neither the obligation, custom, nor law does bind me to cut, or weigh, much less unto the abovementioned satisfaction,[8] I refuse it all and require that the same which is due should be delivered unto me.

The Christian's Answer.

[9]It is no strange matter to hear those dispute of equity which are themselves most unjust; and such as have no faith at all desirous that others should observe the same inviolable, the which were yet the more tolerable if such men would be contented with reasonable things, or at the least not altogether unreasonable. But what reason is there that one man should unto his own prejudice desire the hurt of another? As this Jew is content to lose nine hundred crowns to have a pound of my flesh, whereby is manifestly seen the ancient and cruel hate which he bears not only unto Christians but unto all others which are not of his sect — yea, even unto the Turks, who overkindly do suffer such vermin to dwell amongst them. Seeing that this presumptuous wretch dare not only doubt but appeal from the judgment of a good and just judge, and afterwards he would by sophistical reasons prove that his abomination is equity. Truly I confess that I have suffered fifteen days of the term to pass. Yet who can tell whether he or I is the cause thereof. As for me I think that by secret means he has caused the money to be delayed, which from sundry places ought to have come unto me before the term which I promised unto him. Otherwise, I would never have been so rash as to bind myself so strictly. But although he were not the cause of the fault, is it therefore said[10] that he ought to be so impudent as to go about to prove it no strange matter that he should be willing to be paid with man's flesh, which is a thing more natural for tigers than men (the which also was never heard of). [11]But this devil in shape of a man, seeing me oppressed

---

6 Cut off the flesh myself.

7 permitted.

8 And the bond makes it even less mandatory.

9 IV.i. 70–80.

10 Should it be said.

11 A suggestion of I.iii. 98–103.

with necessity, propounded this accursed obligation unto me. Whereas he alleges the Romans for an example, why does he not as well tell on how for that cruelty in afflicting debtors over-grievously the commonwealth was almost overthrown, and that shortly after it was forbidden to imprison men any more for debt? To break promise, when a man swears or promises a thing the which he has no desire to perform which yet [he does] upon an extreme necessity, is somewhat excusable. As for me I have promised and accomplished my promise, yet not so soon as I would. And although I knew the danger wherein I was to satisfy the cruelty of this mischievous man with the price of my flesh and blood, yet did I not fly away, but submitted myself unto the discretion of the judge who has justly repressed his beastliness. Wherein then have I falsified my promise? Is it in that I would not (like him) disobey the judgment of the judge? Behold, I will present a part of my body unto him that he may pay himself according to the contents of the judgment. Where is then my promise broken? [12]But it is no marvel if this race be so obstinate and cruel against us, for they do it of set purpose to offend our God whom they have crucified. And wherefore? Because He was holy, as He is yet so reputed of this worthy Turkish nation. But what shall I say? Their own Bible is full of rebellion against God, against their priests, judges, and leaders. What did not the very patriarchs themselves [do], from whom they have their beginning? They sold their brother, and had it not been for one amongst them they had slain him even for very envy. How many adulteries and abominations were committed amongst them? How many murders? Absalom, did not he cause his brother to be murdered? Did he not persecute his father? Is it not for their iniquity that God has dispersed them without leaving them one only foot of ground? If then, when they had newly received their law from God, when they saw His wondrous works with their eyes and had yet their judges amongst them they were so wicked, what may one hope of them now when they have neither faith nor law but their rapines and usuries? And [is it] that they believe they do a charitable work when they do some great wrong unto any that is not a Jew? It may please you then, most righteous judge, to consider all these circumstances, having pity of him who does wholly submit himself unto your just clemency, hoping thereby to be delivered from this monster's cruelty.

---

[12] I.iii. 106–114.

⚜ MASUCCIO SALERNITANO

Il Novellino[1] 1476

translated by W. G. Waters, 1895

Novella the Fourteenth

ARGUMENT

A cavalier of Messina falls in love with a young Neapolitan girl.
He learns that her father is very avaricious, wherefore he contrives
to become acquainted with him, and puts him in way of making
vast gain in traffic. After a time he pretends that he must needs return
home, and offers to leave behind him in pawn a slave, the said slave
being one well instructed as to the deed he had in view. This slave,
a woman, beguiles the young girl, and the two plunder the old father
and take to flight in company with the lover. Finally the cavalier marries the damsel; they return to Naples, and are happy in their love.

Messer Tommaso Mariconda, my grandfather and a kinsman of your
own, was, as no doubt you know well, a very notable and elegant cavalier, and one who in his time was held in no small repute and esteem
in this our city. Now this gentleman, when he was aged and full of
years, took vast delight, as is the habit of old men, in telling to his
listeners great numbers of very remarkable stories, all of which he
would set forth with the most distinguished eloquence, and with the
most marvellous memory. And amongst others I well remember to
have heard him tell, when I was a very young child, as a real and undoubted fact, how, after the death of King Charles III,[2] there arose in
our kingdom grave and prolonged warfare provoked by the habitual
tyranny of the house of Anjou. At this time there chanced to be in

---

[1] (The Collection of Novellas) There are fifty in all, and they are models
of style and plot development. This translation captures Masuccio's style quite
well, conveying a sense of what Shakespeare would have experienced, assuming
he read the work in the original.

[2] 1386.

Naples a certain cavalier of the city of Messina, called by name Giuffredi Saccano, a man who was a vehement partisan of the house of
Durazzo; and one day when, according to his habit, he was making a
round of the city on horseback, he happened to espy at a window a very
lovely young damsel, the daughter of an old man, a merchant, whose
name at this moment I cannot rightly call to mind. Now, as he was
beyond all measure delighted with her appearance, he found himself
straightway inflamed with a violent passion for her, and, as the kindly
fortune of both of them willed it, the young girl, whose name was
Carmosina, perceived in her heart that she had found favour in the
eyes of this gentleman. Although she had never before known what
manner of thing love might be, and had scarcely ever set eyes on a man,
the affair now came to a strange issue, and one almost unheard of
before, inasmuch as one flame set those two hearts ablaze at one and
the same moment. Indeed, they were both stricken therewith in such
fashion that neither one nor the other could move from the spot.
Nevertheless, after a certain time had passed, being drawn away by
modesty and bashfulness, they parted one from another, though not
without sorrow and regret on either side.

Whereupon Messer Giuffredi, being well assured how love had all
on a sudden levelled two mortals to the earth with a single blow, and
that nothing but the advent of some favourable opportunity was
needed to allow them to satisfy their sympathetic desires, gave himself up entirely, as is the habit of lovers, to the task of searching out
who the maiden might be, and what was her parentage. At last he
discovered who her father was, and learned besides that he was an
old man inordinately jealous and avaricious, inasmuch as he was
possessed by these vices even beyond the common measure of old
age. Furthermore he ascertained that the miser, in order to escape
the prayers of suitors to bestow his only daughter in marriage, was
accustomed to keep her always closely shut up in the house, treating
her the while worse than the meanest servant.[3]

Now the cavalier, having thoroughly informed himself concerning
the things written above, began to feign to be enamoured, now with
one and now with another of the young women who dwelt near to
the damsel's abode, so that he might be able to advance some colour-
able reason for betaking himself into that quarter, and at least glad-
dening his eyes with the sight of the walls which contained her, if he
might not see her in person. When this became known he was set
down by many of his friends as nothing better than one who fills
himself with wind, and his cunning sagacity was made a mock of by
all the fools of the place. But he, caring naught for all this, and

[3] A slight suggestion of II.iii. 1–3.

following resolutely the purpose he had framed, contrived to contract a close and intimate friendship with the damsel's father, who was engaged in the traffic of merchandise, purchasing very often from the old man divers wares at a monstrous price, for which things he had no need whatever; and over and beyond this, in order to inveigle the miser still more, he would not fail to bring other clients every day into the warehouse, so that the old man made fresh profits without ceasing.

Seeing that the old merchant drew very great advantage from his traffic with the cavalier and his friends, he let grow up between himself and the young man so close a friendship and intimacy that all those who knew him were mightily astonished thereat. However, after a time the cavalier, being seized with the desire to bring his scheme to the end he had designed, found opportunity one day to shut himself up with the old merchant in the warehouse, whereupon he began to address him in the following words: "For the reason that I stand in need of counsel and help in my affairs, I feel that I cannot do better than have recourse to you, whom, on account of your goodness, I love and reverence as my own father. Wherefore I will not hold back from laying bare all my secrets to you, and I will first let you know that, at a season now many years past, I left my father's house, and since that time I have been detained in this city on account of the love I bear to your king and of the circumstances of the war. And things have fared with me in such wise that, up to this present time, no chance has been offered to me of going back to my country. But now for several days past I have been urged by my father, who has sent many letters and messengers to me concerning this matter, that I should forthwith betake myself to see him once again before the season of his old age shall be sped. As I cannot refuse to hearken to these commands of his or to the voice of filial love, I have made up my mind to go to him straightway, and, after having tarried with him some short period, I intend at once to return hither, and to take up again my service under my lord the king. Now as I know of no one to whom I can more conveniently entrust my confidence on such an occasion than to you, I come to ask you whether you would be willing to take under your charge certain possessions of mine, and to keep the same for me till the time of my return. [4]And above all this, the chief concern I feel is on account of a certain female slave of mine, one whom I am most unwilling and aggrieved to sell by reason of her worth and goodness. But, on the other hand, finding myself sorely beset by the lack of

---

[4] The slave girl may have offered suggestions for Launcelot Gobbo.

thirty ducats, and being kept back by my honour from requesting any friend of mine to make me a loan so trifling, I have determined, finding myself placed in this doubtful position, rather to take security of you alone in this business, and to give you the trouble to advance me the sum aforesaid, leaving in your hands the slave as a pledge for the same. If at any time before I shall return you may find an opportunity of selling her for the price of seventy ducats, which is the sum I gave for her, I will beg you to deal with her as if she were your own."

The old man, who in sooth was far more of a miser than of a sage, began to busy his brains in canvassing and considering what possible profit might come to him if he should consent to do the cavalier the service that was demanded, and, without detecting aught therein of the nature of fraud or debating the affair further with himself, made answer in these words: "See here, Messer Giuffredi, the love which I bear towards you is so great, that I assuredly could never bring myself to answer no to any request you might make of me, supposing that the thing demanded lay within my power to perform, and for this reason I am strongly disposed to accommodate you with whatever sum of money you may want for your purposes. And besides this, I will keep the slave on your behalf, in order that you may not suffer ill through having to sell her. Then, when you shall have come back here safe and sound — supposing always that the slave should have done what was needed of her — I will settle my account with you in such fashion that you will find you could not have been better treated even if you had been my own son."

The cavalier, rejoicing greatly at the answer he received from the old man, then replied to him saying, "In sooth I did not expect any other answer from you, and it seems to me that to render you thanks therefor would be superfluous, but may our Lord God grant that I may be able to lay before you clearly the product of this our friendship to our common profit and advantage." And after he had thus brought his discourse to an end he took leave of the old man, and having mounted his horse according to his wont, he made his way along the street in which was the lodging of his lady-love; and, as he passed along, by the working of the fate which ruled the lives of the one and the other, he espied by chance the form of the damsel partially revealed at the casement of her chamber — a boon granted perchance for the satisfaction of both of them. Then drawing herself back from the window like one bewildered, she cast down upon him a sweet and piteous glance; whereupon he, looking cautiously around him and observing no one in the neighbourhood, and conscious that he had no time to spare for the making of long speeches, said to her, "My Carmosina, be comforted, forasmuch as I have at last found a means by which I shall be able to deliver you from your prison." And having thus spoken he went his way, God speeding him.

Meantime the young damsel, who had understood quite clearly the purport of her lover's words, was in no small measure comforted therewith, and although it did not enter her head to hope that from such a speech could ensue any working which might make for her advantage, nevertheless the bare hope roused in her breast thereby gave her heart, though she knew not wherefore. The cavalier, when he had returned to his house, called his slave into his presence and said, "My good Anna, the business which we discussed and arranged is already set in order, wherefore see that you prove wary and prudent in the affair which you will have to bring to pass." And although the slave was already well instructed in all the arts and methods she would be called upon to employ, nevertheless the cavalier caused her to rehearse several times afresh the concerted plan of their subtle stratagem.

When a few days had elapsed, and when he had set everything duly in order, the cavalier went once more to the old merchant and addressed him in the following words: "Alas! how irksome it is to me to withdraw myself for ever so limited a time from your friendship, which has been so precious and so profitable to me. Of this he who truly knows all our secrets will be a witness. Nevertheless, as it is convenient for my purpose that I should take my departure this very night, for the reason that all preparations for my passage are now complete, I have come hither to take my leave of you, and besides this to fetch the money which I begged you to advance me as a loan. Also I am come to bid you send for the chattel you wot of." The old man, who could have prayed God for nothing better, was overjoyed at this news, seeing that he had begun to feel some apprehension lest the cavalier might have repented him of his proposal. Whereupon, without further delay he counted out the thirty ducats, and, having done this, he sent to fetch the slave, who forthwith went to his house, taking with her certain small and delicate things which were the property of the cavalier.

Now when the evening was at last come, Messer Giuffredi, accompanied by the old merchant and certain others of his friends, betook himself to the seashore, and then, having embraced them all and bidden them farewell, he embarked on board a light galley which was about to set sail for Messina. But when the aforesaid ship had fared a short distance from the port of Naples, he made the shipmen place at his service a small boat (which matter in sooth he had already arranged with the captain), and in this he had himself conveyed to Procida.[5] Having come there, he found lodging in the house of a certain friend of his and there he tarried until three days had passed. On the night of the third day, when the hour had come which he had appointed with the slave and with other associates of his, Sicilian fellows keen to act and well set towards any deed of dangerous adventure, he returned to Naples and made his way into the city in very cautious wise. Having come there, he took secret lodging, together with his associates, in a certain house hard by that of the old merchant — a dwelling which, through the ill times brought about by the wars, was at that period quite void of occupants, and there they all abode hidden and silent until the following day came.

In the meantime the cunning and quick-witted slave had gone to the merchant's house, and had there met with most friendly and joyful reception from Carmosina. The last-named, knowing full well from whom the woman had come, in a brief space of time became on very intimate terms with her; whereupon the slave, spurred on by remembering how short was the time in which her purpose would have to be accomplished, laid bare to the damsel point by point the reasons for which she had come thither, using the while the most consummate arts and the most skilful discourse, and furthermore telling her exactly what her master had settled with her concerning the matter in question, and heartening the damsel little by little by the arguments she brought forward to carry out in daring fashion the enterprise to its issue, so as to secure for herself and her lover a lasting time of peace and happiness. The young girl, who for many reasons was even more strongly minded than the cavalier towards this end, did not suffer the slave to waste more time in adding one lengthy argument to another, but told her straightway that she was fully prepared to consent to every one of the proposals just made by her, and likewise to follow all the directions laid down by the cavalier, whom she herself loved as she loved her own life.

[6]To these words the slave replied: "My daughter, if it should happen that you have a few little things of your own which you would like to carry away with you, I would counsel you to get the same in order at once, seeing that our plan will have to be put in execution this very night. You must know also that my master and his servant and certain other companions of his are now concealed in the house next door to us. This fact I have learnt from a signal which I have this day seen displayed from the house in question, and, as you well know, it would be an easy task to get into it from our paved courtyard." When the young girl heard how short was the time before her flight,

[5] An island lying between Ischia and the mainland. (trans.)
[6] II.iii. 1ff.

she gave the slave a hundred kisses, and told her that she possessed nothing of her own, either great or small, which she could take away with her, but that she had made up her mind to abstract from the store of her avaricious old father a much greater sum of money than anyone could have reckoned sufficient for her dowry.

[7]When they had brought the matter to this conclusion, and when the midnight hour had come, and the old man and everyone else in the house were fast asleep, Carmosina and the slave broke open a chest and took out therefrom jewels and money of a value exceeding one thousand five hundred ducats, and, having bestowed these safely away, they silently crossed over the courtyard and came to the spot where the cavalier was awaiting them. He, with the greatest joy, took the young girl in his arms and covered her lips with ardent kisses. Further pleasure they did not enjoy, seeing how precarious was their present abiding-place; wherefore the whole company set out on their way, and took the road which led to the seashore. Having cautiously issued from the city through a breach in the wall behind the slaughter-houses, they found their bark ready armed and fully equipped for a swift passage, and ready to cast off at a moment's notice. Whereupon they all went on board the same, and, having dipped their oars in the water, they found themselves at Ischia before many hours had elapsed. [8]Then the cavalier and all those accompanying him presented themselves before the lord of that place, who chanced to be a particular friend of Messer Giuffredi, and one indeed who had been made privy to the whole affair. From this gentleman they all received most kindly and hospitable reception, and while they were abiding there the lovers, deeming that they were now upon safe ground, partook of the first and sweetest delights of their reciprocal love, and rejoiced the one as well as the other with no less joy over the circumstances of their flight.

[9]In the meantime the old father, when the daylight came, first found that neither his daughter nor the slave whom he had taken in pledge were in the house, and then became aware that he had been robbed of his money and of his jewels to boot, and for the last-named loss he felt no less grief than for the first; indeed, how sore were his tears and lamentations each one may judge for himself. Moreover, no one need wonder to hear that he found his affliction so sharp and cruel that he was over and over again fain to hang himself by the neck therefor. And thus, overcome by his losses and the shame that

---

[7] II.vi. 1–59.

[8] III.ii. 223–228; V.i. 1–88. The creative power of Shakespeare in reshaping his sources is nowhere more evident than in this latter passage.

[9] II.viii. 12–22.

had been put upon him, he spent his days in continual weeping shut up in his house.

Meantime the enamoured couple in Ischia lived their lives in the greatest delight, and by reason of their constant intercourse it came to pass that the fair damsel became with child. Which thing, when the cavalier came to know it, caused him the greatest delight, and he forthwith made a resolve to treat her with a worthy spirit of generosity, and at the same time to give full satisfaction to God, to the world, and to himself. Wherefore, having despatched a message through the intervention of the lord of Ischia to the father of Carmosina and to divers of his own kinsfolk, these aforesaid all came to Ischia, and, when they were all there assembled, and after certain contracts had been duly signed, the cavalier, by the favour of the king and with the universal approval and general rejoicing of the people of Naples, took Carmosina for his lawful wife. Thus, having exchanged the secret sport of Venus for the career of married folk, they went back to their Neapolitan home and passed their days in great happiness as long as they both lived. In this manner it may be seen how the jealous, miserly, and foolish old man atoned for the deed after all the damage had been done.

□ *Some Sources for Further Study*

1. GIOVANNI BOCCACCIO — *The Decameron* (c. 1354). The Tenth Day, First Story is the caskets story in a different context.
2. ANTHONY MUNDAY — *Zeauto* (1580). A novel about a usurer and a bloody bond, a grim variation on Fiorentino's novella.
3. CHRISTOPHER MARLOWE — *The Jew of Malta* (1588). Some few situations in common with Shakespeare's play; reinforces attitudes already available in the non-dramatic sources.
4. "Gernutus, the Jew of Venice," available in Thomas Percy, *Reliques of Ancient English Poetry*. A ballad containing the bond and pound of flesh situations, but may have been written after *The Merchant of Venice*.

henry IV—part one

The chief source of the main plot is Holinshed, in this case the segment dealing with the attempted revolt led by Northumberland, Hotspur, and Glendower against Henry IV. The time span covered is a brief one, from the birth of the nobles' rebellion in 1401 to the Battle of Shrewsbury on July 21, 1403. Shakespeare follows Holinshed in this play in as close chronological sequence as he ever will, as a check of the footnote references will bear out, and the many references to Acts I and V reflect how much his exposition and resolution depend upon the Chronicles. The only major and conspicuous tampering with chronology occurs in the mutual confession scene between Henry IV and Prince Hal (III.ii. 1–161) which actually took place in 1413 and which appears in the Holinshed source for Henry IV, Part Two, pp. 176–177. Otherwise Holinshed uncut provides almost the entire plot skeleton, leaving Shakespeare free to build upon it. Since this is by common consent Shakespeare's greatest history play, one possible inference might be that Shakespeare, having a ready made plot at hand, was left freer than usual to invest it with what R. P. Blackmur calls "the riches of direct sensibility." Certainly the existence of ready made plots for Hamlet, Othello, Lear, and Antony and Cleopatra lends support to this conjecture.

Falstaff properly speaking belongs to the subplot — though his blazing humanity frequently overshadows the rest of the play — and is not to be found in Holinshed. Holinshed later mentions that Prince Hal "had chosen him companions agreeable to his age, with whom he spent the time in such recreations, exercises, and delights as he fancied." (p. 177) and he supplies an account of Sir John Oldcastle (pp. 181–182), in part Falstaff's archetype. But what Shakespeare owes to sources for Falstaff is due mainly to The Famous Victories of Henry V. The first half of that play revolves around the "recreations, exercises, and delights" of Prince Hal, and here Sir John Oldcastle (Falstaff) makes his comic debut. Those comic incidents which Shakespeare borrows from The Famous Victories all find their way

151

into *Henry IV, Part One*: Hal's use of Ned (Poins?) as confidant; the Gadshill robbery; the roistering at Eastcheap Tavern; and Hal's summons, while carousing, from the king. The Falstaff sequel in *Henry IV, Part Two* relies mostly on Shakespeare's own invention.

It is Holinshed who provides most of the source suggestions for characterization in Shakespeare's play. From what Henry IV does and from Holinshed's character analysis of him (pp. 179–180) he emerges the mixture of integrity, sternness and guile characteristic of every successful ruler. Holinshed's portrait of Henry V as hero-king (pp. 212–213) presents the standard Tudor view of him that Shakespeare followed. The youthful intensity of Hotspur, however, owes nothing to Holinshed and is historically inaccurate besides, and the Sir John Oldcastle of *The Famous Victories* is a *buffo* character with only a few surface mannerisms in common with Falstaff. His flowering into Falstaff assesses and illuminates Shakespeare's developing creative genius.

The chief political idea of this play once again reflects the thinking of a Tudor playwright and his Tudor historian source: monarchy, no matter how acquired, is preferable to divisive rebellion. By this stage of Shakespeare's development, however, his plays spark off ideas in all directions, and no source or commentary can do more than point out an obvious few. One obvious emphasis in *Henry IV, Part One* is its use of character to represent broad concepts. Hal, for example, represents the ideal Renaissance Prince perfectly balanced between the physical and social graces of this world and the ethical and spiritual ones of the next. Hotspur, whose common, concrete images reflect his absorption in the sensible world around him, represents those scientific and Puritan pragmatisms which the High Renaissance saw growing at so rapid and alarming a rate and which Shakespeare had already touched upon in the characters of Richard III and Shylock. And while Shakespeare created and then broke the mold for the character of Falstaff, all that the fat knight symbolizes is universal. In its most comprehensive outlines, if we may skirt partisan views, the character of Falstaff summarizes all common humanity, its appeal, its sinfulness, and its illusions most of all.

☙ RAPHAEL HOLINSHED

The Chronicles of England, Scotland, and Ireland,[*] *1587*

[*Following the deposition of Richard II, Henry IV was "conse-crated, annointed, and crowned king" on the thirteenth of October, 1399 by the Archbishop of Canterbury. Parliament designated the king's eldest son, Lord Henry, Prince of Wales, bypassing the young Earl of March, whom Richard II had appointed to be his heir. Counter to the general rejoicing, "Edmund Mortimer, Earl of March, which was cousin and heir to Lionel, Duke of Clarence, the third begotten son of King Edward," was "neither pleased nor contented."*

Shortly after the coronation of Henry IV, the House of Commons investigated the recent murder of the Duke of Gloucester. Sir John Bagot implicated many former supporters of Richard II and disclosed the complicity of the Duke of Aumerle, a close friend of Henry IV. After the execution of one John Hall, who helped with the actual murder — he was "hanged, bowelled, headed, and quartered: his head being sent to Calais there to be set up, where the duke was murdered" — Henry imprisoned a few, pardoned many, and in general put an end to the affair.

During the Parliament of 1400–1, the king had an act passed de-claring his lawfully begotten heirs true successors to the crown.[1] The Archbishop of Canterbury "declared how that the king that now is had granted King Richard his life; but in such wise as he should remain in perpetual prison, so safely kept that neither the king nor realm should be troubled with him."

During 1400–1, Archibald, Earl of Douglas, leader of the Scottish insurgents against England, invaded the English borders and rode

---

[*] text modernized.

[1] Of historical note, it was the Parliament of 1401 that first accepted the statute of *De heretico comburendo*, with the consent of the king, Parliament, and Commons, which empowered the clergy to suppress Lollardy "by force" — i.e., by faggot and flame.

into Northumberland and burned several towns in the shire of Bamborough. "In the king's absence, whilst he was forth of the realm in Scotland against his enemies, the Welshmen took occasion to rebel under the conduct of their captain, Owen Glendower."

The king entered Wales with an army, but the Welsh withdrew into the mountains of Snowdon. "The king therefore did much hurt in the countries with fire and sword. . . . and so with a great booty of beasts and cattle he returned.]

[1401] About the same time, Owen Glendower and his Welshmen did much hurt to the king's subjects. [2]One night as the king was going to bed, he was in danger to have been destroyed; for some naughty traitorous persons had conveyed into his bed a certain iron made with smith's craft, like a caltrop,[3] with three long pricks, sharp and small, standing upright in such sort that when he had laid him down, and that the weight of his body should come upon the bed, he should have been thrust in with those pricks and peradventure slain. But as God would, the king not thinking of any such thing chanced yet to feel and perceive the instrument before he laid him down, and so escaped the danger.

Howbeit he was not so soon delivered from fear; for he might well have his life in suspicion,[4] and [have to] provide for the preservation of the same, since perils of death crept into his secret chamber and lay lurking in the bed of down where his body was to be reposed and to take rest. Oh, what a suspected state therefore is that of a king holding his regimen with the hatred of his people, the hard grudgings of his courtiers, and the peremptory practices of both together! Could he confidently compose or settle himself to sleep for fear of strangling? Durst he boldly eat and drink without dread of poisoning? Might he adventure to show himself in great meetings or solemn assemblies without mistrust of mischief against his person intended? What pleasure or what felicity could he take in his princely pomp, which he knew by manifest and fearful experience to be envied and maligned to the very death? The state of such a king is noted by the poet Dionysius, as in a mirror, concerning whom it is said,

Districtus ensis cui super impia
Cervice pendet, non Siculae Dapes

---

[2] I.i. 34ff.
[3] a snare.
[4] jeopardy.

> Dulcem elaborabunt saporem,
> Non avium cytharaeq. cantus.[5]

[1402] This year, the eighth day of April deceased the lord Thomas Beauchamp Earl of Warwick. [6]In the month of March appeared a blazing star, first between the east part of the firmament and the north, flashing forth fiery beams towards the north, foreshowing (as was thought) the great effusion of blood that followed, about the parts of Wales and Northumberland. For much about the same time, Owen Glendower (with his Welshmen) fought with the Lord Grey of Ruthen, coming forth to defend his possessions, which the same Owen wasted and destroyed and as the fortune of that day's work fell out, the Lord Grey was taken prisoner, and many of his men were slain. This hap lifted the Welshmen into high pride, and increased marvelously their wicked and presumptuous attempts.

About Whitsuntide a conspiracy was devised by certain persons, that wished the king's death, maintaining and bruiting abroad, that King Richard was alive, and therefore exhorted men to stand with him, for shortly he would come to light, and reward such as took his part with just recompense. . . .

[7]Owen Glendower, according to his accustomed manner, robbing and spoiling within the English borders, caused all the forces of the shire of Hereford to assemble together against them [Glendower's troops] under the conduct of Edmund Mortimer, Earl of March.[8] But coming to try the matter by battle, whether by treason or otherwise, so it fortuned that the English power was discomfited, the earl taken prisoner, and above a thousand of his people slain in the place. The shameful villainy used by the Welshwomen towards the dead carcasses was such as honest ears would be ashamed to hear and continent tongues to speak thereof. The dead bodies might not be buried without great sums of money given for liberty to convey them away.

[9]The king was not hasty to purchase the deliverance of the Earl of March, because his title to the crown was well enough known, and

---

[5] For him over whose irreverent neck there dangles a hesitating, two-edged sword, neither the Feasts of the Little Dagger [love affairs] nor the melody of birds or of a lyre will produce sweet savor.

[6] III.i. 13–17.

[7] I.i. 34–46.

[8] The Edmund Mortimer whose "title to the crown was well enough known" was the *fifth* Earl of March and, in 1402, a minor and Henry's ward. Glendower's prisoner was the Sir Edmund Mortimer who was brother to Roger Mortimer, fourth Earl of March and uncle to the fifth earl. Holinshed's error is perpetuated by Shakespeare. I.iii. 156.

[9] I.iii. 154–159.

therefore suffered him to remain in miserable prison, wishing both the said earl and all others of his lineage out of his life with God and his saints in heaven — so they had been out of the way, for then all had been well enough, as he thought. But to let these things pass, the king this year sent his eldest daughter Blanche, accompanied with the Earl of Somerset, the Bishop of Worcester, the Lord Clifford, and others, into Almany,[10] which brought her to Cologne, and there with great triumph she was married to William, Duke of Bavaria, son and heir to Lewis the Emperor. [11]About mid of August, the king to chastise the presumptuous attempts of the Welshmen went with a great power of men into Wales, to pursue the captain of the Welsh rebels Owen Glendower, but in effect he lost his labor; for Owen conveyed himself out of the way into his known lurking places, and (as was thought) through art magic he caused such foul weather of winds, tempest, rain, snow, and hail to be raised, for the annoyance of the king's army, that the like had not been heard of; in such sort that the king was constrained to return home, having caused his people yet to spoil and burn first a great part of the country. The same time the Lord Edmund of Langley, Duke of York, departed this life, and was buried at Langley with his brethren. The Scots under the leading of Patrick Hepburn, of the Hales the younger, entering into England, were overthrown at Nesbit, in the marches, as in the *Scottish Chronicle* you may find more at large. This battle was fought the two and twentieth of June, in this year of Our Lord, 1402.

[12]Archibald, Earl Douglas, sore displeased in his mind for this overthrow, procured a commission to invade England, and that to his cost, as you may likewise read in the Scottish histories. For at a place called Homildon[13] they were so fiercely assailed by the Englishmen under the leading of the Lord Percy, surnamed Henry Hotspur, and George, Earl of March, that with violence of the English shot they were quite vanquished and put to flight on the Rood Day in harvest, with a great slaughter made by the Englishmen.

We know that the Scottish writers note this battle to have chanced in the year 1403. But we, following Thomas Walsingham in this place and other English writers for the accompt of times, have thought good to place it in this year 1402, as in the same writers we find it. There were slain of men of estimation, Sir John Swinton, Sir Adam Gordon, Sir John Lewiston, Sir Alexander Ramsay of Dalhousie, and three and

---

[10] Germany.
[11] I.iii. 93–117.
[12] I.i. 62ff.
[13] Present name: Humbleton (in Northumberland).

twenty knights, besides ten thousand of the commons. And of prisoners among others were these: Mordrake,[14] Earl of Fife, son to the governor[,][15] Archibald, Earl of Douglas, which in the fight lost one of his eyes, Thomas, Earl of Murray, Robert, Earl of Angus, and (as some writers have) the Earls of Athol and Menteith,[16] with five hundred other of meaner degrees. After this, the Lord Percy, having bestowed the prisoners in sure keeping, entered Teviotdale, wasting and destroying the whole country, and then besieged the castle of Cocklawes, whereof was captain one Sir John Grenlow, who compounded with the Englishmen that if the castle were not succored within three months, then he would deliver it into their hands.

[17]The first two months passed, and no likelihood of rescue appeared; but ere the third month was expired the Englishmen being sent for to go with the king into Wales raised their seige and departed, leaving the noblemen prisoners with the Earl of Northumberland, and with his son the Lord Percy, to keep them to the king's use. In this meanwhile. . . . [18]Edmund Mortimer, Earl of March, prisoner with Owen Glendower, whether for irksomeness of cruel captivity, or fear of death, or for what other cause it is uncertain, agreed to take part with Owen against the King of England, and took to wife the daughter of the said Owen.

[19]Strange wonders happened (as men reported) at the nativity of this man, for the same night he was born all his father's horses in the stable were found to stand in blood up to their bellies. [20]The morrow after the feast of Saint Michael, a Parliament began at Westminster which continued the space of seven weeks; in the same was a tenth

---

[14] Modern spelling is Murdoch, but Shakespeare like Holinshed uses Mordrake.

[15] A most important comma is missing here. Mordrake was eldest son to the governor, who was Robert Steward, Duke of Albany. He was not related to Archibald, Earl of Douglas. However, Holinshed's punctuation leads Shakespeare to declare:

> Of prisoners, Hotspur took
> Mordrake the Earl of Fife, and eldest son
> To beaten Douglas. (I.i. 70–72).

[16] Menteith was another title of Mordrake, Earl of Fife, not another prisoner taken by Percy. Here too Holinshed misleads Shakespeare. (I.i. 73).

[17] I.iii. 22–29.

[18] I.iii. 80–85; III.i. 192–228.

[19] III.i. 13–40.

[20] While the events in these next three paragraphs are not used by Shakespeare, they offer a more fully dimensional picture than Shakespeare does of the busy and often harassed king and help to explain his outbursts (in Shakespeare) against Prince Hal.

and a half granted by the clergy and a fifteenth by the communalty. Moreover, the commons in this Parliament besought the king to have the person of George, Earl of March, a Scotsman, recommended to His Majesty for that the same earl showed himself faithful to the king and his realm.

[1403] There was also a statute made that the friars beggars should not receive any into their order under the age of fourteen years. In this fourth year of King Henry's reign, ambassadors were sent over into Brittany to bring from thence the Duchess of Brittany, the Lady Jane de Navarre, the widow of John de Montfort, late Duke of Brittany, surnamed the conquerer, with whom by procurators the king had contracted matrimony. In the beginning of February those that were sent returned with her in safety, but not without tasting the bitter storms of the wind and weather that tossed them sore to and fro before they could get to land. The king met her at Winchester, where the seventh of February the marriage was solemnized betwixt them.

Whilst these things were thus in doing in England, Waleran, Earl of St. Pol,[21] bearing still a deadly and malicious hatred toward King Henry, having assembled sixteen or seventeen hundred men of war, embarked them at Harfleur and taking the sea landed in the Isle of Wight, in the which he burned two villages and four simple cottages, and for a triumph of so noble an act made four knights. But when he heard that the people of the isle were assembled and approached to fight with him, he hasted to his ships and returned home: wherewith the noble men of his company were displeased, considering his provision to be great and his gain small. In the same very season, John, Earl of Clermont, son to the Duke of Bourbon, won in Gascoigne out of the Englishmen's possession the castles of St. Peter, St. Marie, and the New Castle; and the Lord Delabreth won the castle of Carlassin, which was no small loss to the English nation.

[[22]Henry, Earl of Northumberland, with his brother Thomas, Earl of Worcester, and his son the Lord Henry Percy, surnamed Hotspur, which were to King Henry in the beginning of his reign both faithful friends and earnest aiders, began now to envy his wealth and felicity; and especially they were grieved because the king demanded of the earl and his son such Scottish prisoners as were taken at Homildon and Nesbit. For of all the captives which were taken in the conflicts fought in those two places,[23] there was delivered to the king's possession only Mordrake, Earl of Fife, the Duke of Albany's son, though the king did divers and sundry times require deliverance of the residue,

---

[21] In actuality a count.
[22] I.iii. 1–124.
[23] I.i. 95.

and that with great threatenings.[24] [25]Wherewith the Percys being sore offended, for that they claimed them as their own proper prisoners and the[ir] peculiar prize, by the counsel of the Lord Thomas Percy, Earl of Worcester, whose study was ever (as some write) to procure malice and set things in a broil, came to the king unto Windsor (upon a purpose to prove him) and there required of him that either by ransom or otherwise, he would cause to be delivered out of prison Edmund Mortimer, Earl of March, their cousin germane, whom (as they reported) Owen Glendower kept in filthy prison, shackled with irons, only for that he took his part and was to him faithful and true.

The king began not a little to muse at this request, and not without cause. For indeed it touched him somewhat near, since this Edmund was son to Roger, Earl of March, son to the Lady Philippa, daughter of Lionel, Duke of Clarence, the third son of King Edward the Third; which Edmund at King Richard's going into Ireland was proclaimed heir apparent to the crown and realm, whose aunt called Elinor, the Lord Henry Percy had married; and therefore King Henry could not well hear, that any man should be in earnest about the advancement of that lineage. The king when he had studied on the matter made answer that the Earl of March was not taken prisoner for his cause, nor in his service, but willingly suffered himself to be taken because he would not withstand the attempts of Owen Glendower and his complices, and therefore he would neither ransom him nor relieve him.

[26]The Percys with this answer and fraudulent excuse were not a little fumed, insomuch that Henry Hotspur said openly, "Behold, the heir of the realm is robbed of his right, and yet the robber with his own will not redeem him." So in this fury the Percys departed, minding nothing more than to depose King Henry from the high type of his royalty, and to place in his seat their cousin Edmund, Earl of March, whom they did not only deliver out of capitivity but also (to the high displeasure of King Henry) entered in league with the foresaid Owen Glendower. [27]Herewith, they by their deputies in the house of the Archdeacon of Bangor, divided the realm amongst them, causing a tripartite indenture to be made and sealed with their seals, by the covenants whereof all England from Severn and Trent, south and eastward was assigned to the Earl of March: all Wales, and the lands

---

[24] However, the king had no legitimate right to those prisoners. By the law of arms every man had a right to keep any captives he had taken except those whose ransom exceeded ten thousand crowns. Of Percy's prisoners only the Earl of Fife would so qualify, he being a prince of the royal blood.

[25] I.iii. 77–159.

[26] I.iii. 219ff.

[27] III.i. 70–82.

beyond Severn westward, were appointed to Owen Glendower: and all the remnant from Trent northward, to the Lord Percy.]

[28]This was done (as some have said) through a foolish credit given to a vain prophecy, as though King Henry was the moldwarp,[29] cursed of God's own mouth, and they three were the dragon, the lion, and the wolf, which should divide this realm between them. Such is the deviation (says Hall) and not divination of those blind and fantastical dreams of the Welsh propheciers. King Henry not knowing of this new confederacy, and nothing less minding than that which after happened, gathered a great army to go again into Wales;[30] whereof the Earl of Northumberland and his son were advertised by the Earl of Worcester, and with all diligence raised all the power they could make, and sent to the Scots which before were taken prisoners at Homildon, for aid of men, promising to the Earl of Douglas the town of Berwick and a part of Northumberland, and to other Scottish lords great lordships and seigniories if they obtained the upper hand. The Scots in hope of gain, and desirous to be revenged of their old griefs, came to the earl with a great company well appointed.

The Percys to make their part seem good, devised certain articles by the advice of Richard Scroop, Archbishop of York, brother to the Lord Scroop, whom King Henry had caused to be beheaded at Bristol. These articles being showed to divers noblemen and other estates of the realm, moved them to favor their purpose insomuch that many of them did not only promise to the Percys aid and succour by words, but also by their writings and scales[31] confirmed the same. [32]Howbeit when the matter came to trial, the most part of the confederates abandoned them and at the day of the conflict left them alone. Thus after that the conspirators had discovered[33] themselves, the Lord Henry Percy desirous to proceed in the enterprise, upon trust to be assisted by Owen Glendower, the Earl of March and others, assembled an army of men of arms and archers forth of Cheshire and Wales. Incontinently his uncle Thomas Percy, Earl of Worcester, that had the government of the Prince of Wales, who as then lay at London in secret manner,[34] conveyed himself out of the prince's house; and coming to Stafford (where he met his nephew) they increased their power by all ways and means they could devise. [35]The Earl of Northumber-

---

[28] III.i. 148–169.
[29] mole.
[30] IV.i. 1–12.
[31] weighing the issues in the balance.
[32] II.iii. 1–14.
[33] revealed.
[34] in hiding.
[35] IV.i. 13–38.

land himself was not with them, but being sick had promised upon his amendment to repair unto them (as some write) with all convenient speed.

These noblemen, to make their conspiracy to seem excusable, besides the articles abovementioned sent letters abroad wherein was contained that their gathering of an army tended to none other end but only for the safeguard of their own persons, and to put some better government in the commonwealth. For whereas taxes and tallages[36] were daily levied, under pretense to be employed in defence of the realm, the same were vainly wasted and unprofitably consumed. And where through the slanderous reports of their enemies the king had taken a grievous displeasure with them, they durst not appear personally in the king's presence until the prelates and barons of the realm had obtained of the king license for them to come and purge themselves before him, by lawful trial of their peers, whose judgement (as they pretended) they would in no wise refuse. Many that saw and heard these letters did commend their diligence and highly praised their assured fidelity and trustiness towards the commonwealth.

[37]But the king understanding their cloaked drift, devised (by what means he might) to quiet and appease the commons and deface their contrived forgeries; and therefore he wrote an answer to their libels that he marvelled much, since the Earl of Northumberland and the Lord Henry Percy, his son, had received the most part of the sums of money granted to him by the clergy and communalty for defence of the marches, as he could evidently prove, what should move them to complain and raise such manifest slanders. And whereas he understood that the Earls of Northumberland and Worcester and the Lord Percy had by their letters signified to their friends abroad that by reason of the slanderous reports of their enemies they durst not appear in his presence without the mediation of the prelates and nobles of the realm — so as they required pledges whereby they might safely come afore him to declare and allege what they had to say in proof of their innocence — he protested by letters sent forth under his seal that they might safely come and go without all danger or any manner of endamagement to be offered to their persons.

[38]But this could not satisfy those men, but that, resolved to go forward with their enterprise, they marched towards Shrewsbury upon hope to be aided (as men thought) by Owen Glendower and his Welshmen; publishing abroad throughout the countries on each side that King Richard was alive, whom if they wished to see, they willed

---

[36] arbitrary levies, especially municipal taxes or customs duties.
[37] IV.i. 40–41.
[38] IV.i. 124.

them to repair in armor unto the castle of Chester where (without all doubt) he was at that present and ready to come forward. This tale being raised, though it were most untrue, yet it bred variable motions in men's minds, causing them to waver, so as they knew not to which part they should stick; and verily, divers were well affected towards King Richard, specially such as had tasted of his princely bountifulness, of which there was no small number. [39]And to speak a truth, no marvel it was if many envied the prosperous state of King Henry, since it was evident enough to the world that he had with wrong usurped the crown, and not only violently deposed King Richard but also cruelly procured his death; for the which undoubtedly both he and his posterity tasted such troubles as put them still in danger of their states, till their direct succeeding line was quite rooted out by the contrary faction, as in Henry the Sixth and Edward the Fourth it may appear.

But now to return where we left. [40]King Henry, advertised of the proceedings of the Percys, forthwith gathered about him such power as he might make, and being earnestly called upon by the Scot, the Earl of March, to make haste and give battle to his enemies before their power by delaying of time should still too much increase, he passed forward with such speed that he was in sight of his enemies lying in camp near to Shrewsbury before they were in doubt of any such thing. For the Percys thought that he would have stayed at Burton upon Trent till his council had come thither to him to give their advice what he were best to do. But herein the enemy was deceived of his expectation, since the king had great regard of expedition and making speed for the safety of his own person — whereunto the Earl of March incited him — considering that in delay is danger and loss in lingering, as the poet in the like case says:

Tolle moras, nocuit semper differre paratis,
Dum trepidant nullo firmatae robore partes[41]

By reason of the king's sudden coming in this sort they stayed from assaulting the town of Shrewsbury, which enterprise they were ready at that instant to have taken in hand;[42] and forthwith the Lord Percy (as a captain of high courage) began to exhort the captains and soldiers to prepare themselves to battle, since the matter was grown to that point that by no means it could be avoided; so that (said he)

[39] IV.iii. 90–105.
[40] IV.iv. 1ff.
[41] Remove delays, (for) it always does harm to postpone preparations so long that men waver, fortified by no enduring strength.
[42] V.ii. 82–89.

"this day shall either bring us all to advancement and honor, or else if it shall chance us to be overcome, shall deliver us from the king's spiteful malice and cruel disdain. For playing the men (as we ought to do) better it is to die in battle for the commonwealth's cause, than through cowardlike fear to prolong life, which after shall be taken from us by sentence of the enemy."

Hereupon the whole army being in number about fourteen thousand chosen men promised to stand with him so long as life lasted. There were with the Percys as chieftains of this army the Earl of Douglas, a Scottish man, the Baron of Kinderton, Sir Hugh Browne and Sir Richard Vernon, knights, with divers other stout and right valiant captains. [43]Now when the two armies were encamped, the one against the other, the Earl of Worcester and the Lord Percy with their complices sent the articles (whereof I spoke before) by Thomas Caiton and Thomas Salvain, squires to King Henry, under their hands and seals: which articles in effect charged him with manifest perjury in that (contrary to his oath received upon the evangelists at Doncaster, when he first entered the realm after his exile) he had taken upon him the crown and royal dignity, imprisoned King Richard, caused him to resign his title and finally to be murdered. Divers other matters they laid to his charge, as levying of taxes and tallages contrary to his promise, infringing of laws and customs of the realm, and suffering the Earl of March to remain in prison without travailing to have him delivered. All which things they as procurors and protectors of the commonwealth took upon them to prove against him, as they protested unto the whole world.

King Henry after he had read their articles, with the defiance which they annexed to the same, answered the squires that he was ready with dint of sword and fierce battle to prove their quarrel false, and nothing else than a forged matter, not doubting but that God would aid and assist him in his righteous cause against the disloyal and false foresworn traitors. The next day in the morning early, being the eve[44] of Mary Magdalen, they set their battles in order on both sides. And now whilst the warriors looked when the token of battle should be given, the Abbot of Shrewsbury and one of the clerks of the Privy Seal were sent from the king unto the Percys to offer them pardon, if they would come to any reasonable agreement.[45] By their persuasions the Lord Henry Percy began to give ear unto the king's offers,

---

[43] V.i. 30–71; see also IV.iii. 52ff.

[44] day.

[45] As Holinshed offers no explanation here for Worcester's conduct, Shakespeare's explanation (ll.1–25) provides an insight into the creative process: V.ii. 1–41.

and so sent with them his uncle, the Earl of Worcester, to declare unto the king the causes of those troubles and to require some effectual reformation in the same.

It was reported for a truth that now when the king had condescended unto all that was reasonable at his hands to be required, and seemed to humble himself more than was meet for his estate, the Earl of Worcester (upon his return to his nephew) made relation clean contrary to that the king had said, in such sort that he set his nephew's heart more in displeasure towards the king than ever it was before, driving him by that means to fight whether he would or not;[46] then suddenly blew the trumpets, the king's part crying "St. George!" upon them; the adversaries cried "Esperance Percy!" and so the two armies furiously joined. The archers on both sides shot for the best game, laying on such load with arrows that many died and were driven down that never rose again.

The Scots (as some write) which had the forward on the Percys' side, intending to be revenged of their old displeasures done to them by the English nation, set so fiercely on the king's forward, led by the Earl of Stafford, that they made the same draw back and had almost broken their adversaries' array. The Welshmen also which before had lain lurking in the woods, mountains, and marshes, hearing of this battle toward, came to the aid of the Percys and refreshed the wearied people with new succors. The king perceiving that his men were thus put to distress, what with the violent impression of the Scots and the tempestuous storms of arrows that his adversaries discharged freely against him and his people, it was no need to will him to stir. For suddenly with his fresh battle he approached and relieved his men, so that the battle began more fierce than before. [47]Here the Lord Henry Percy and the Earl Douglas, a right stout and hardy captain, not regarding the shot of the king's battle nor the close order of the ranks, pressing forward together bent their whole forces towards the king's person, coming upon him with spears and swords so fiercely that the Earl of March, the Scot, perceiving their purpose, withdrew the king from that side of the field (as some write) for his great benefit and safeguard (as it appeared). For they gave such a violent onset upon them that stood about the king's standard, that slaying his standard-bearer, Sir Walter Blunt, and overthrowing the standard, they made slaughter of all those that stood about it, as the Earl of Stafford, that day made by the king constable of the realm, and divers others.

[48]The prince that day helped his father like a lusty young gentle-

---

46 V.ii. 43ff.
47 V.iii. 1–13; V.iv. 25–38.
48 V.iv. 1–24.

man. For although he was hurt in the face with an arrow, so that divers noblemen that were about him would have conveyed him forth of the field, yet he would not suffer them so to do lest his departure from amongst his men might haply have stricken some fear into their hearts. And so without regard of his hurt, he continued with his men and never ceased either to fight where the battle was most hot or to encourage his men where it seemed most need. [49]This battle lasted three long hours, with indifferent fortune on both parts, till at length the king crying, "St. George, victory!" broke the array of his enemies and adventured so far, that (as some write) the Earl Douglas struck him down and at that instant slew Sir Walter Blunt and three others apparelled in the king's suit and clothing, saying:[50] "I marvel to see so many kings thus suddenly arise one in the neck of another." The king indeed was raised, and did that day many a noble feat of arms; for as it is written he slew that day with his own hands six and thirty persons of his enemies. [51]The others on his part, encouraged by his doings, fought valiantly and slew the Lord Percy, called Sir Henry Hotspur. [52]To conclude, the king's enemies were vanquished and put to flight, in which flight the Earl of Douglas, for haste, falling from the crag of an high mountain, broke one of his cullions[53] and was taken, and for his valiantness of the king frankly and freely delivered.

[54] There was also taken the Earl of Worcester, the procurer and setter forth of all this mischief, Sir Richard Vernon and the Baron of Kinderton, with divers others. There were slain upon the king's part, besides the Earl of Stafford, to the number of ten knights, Sir Hugh Shorley, Sir John Clifton, Sir John Cokaine, Sir Nicholas Gausell, Sir Walter Blunt, Sir John Calverley, Sir John Massey of Podington, Sir Hugh Mortimer, and Sir Robert Gausell, all the which received the same morning the order of knighthood. Sir Thomas Wendesley was wounded to death, and so passed out of this life shortly after. There died in all upon the king's side sixteen hundred, and four thousand were grievously wounded. On the contrary side were slain, besides the Lord Percy, the most part of the knights and squires of the county of Chester, to the number of two hundred, besides yeo-

---

49 V.iii. 1–13.

50 V.iv. 25–28.

51 V.iv. 59–101. Shakespeare makes profound use of Hal's killing Hotspur, which in actuality he did not. In actuality, too, Hotspur was some twenty years older than Hal — and older than Henry IV — although Shakespeare represents them as being about the same age.

52 V.v. 17–31.

53 testicles.

54 V.v. 1–14.

men and footmen; in all there died of those that fought on the Percys' side about five thousand. This battle was fought on Mary Magdalen eve, being Saturday. Upon the Monday following, the Earl of Worcester, the Baron of Kinderton and Sir Richard Vernon, knights, were condemned and beheaded. The earl's head was sent to London, there to be set on the bridge.

□ Some Sources for Further Study

1–4. For supplements to Holinshead see p. 115, sources 1–4.

   5. *A Mirror for Magistrates* (1559).

      "Henry Percy, Earl of Northumberland": contains some slight character study of Hotspur, but mainly portrays him as treacherous and the victim of Fortune.

   6. The *Commedia dell'arte*. The stock situations and figures of this genre offer some similarities to the subplot and to some of the minor subplot characters in *Henry IV, Parts One and Two*. Kathleen M. Lea, *Italian Popular Comedy*, 1934, 2 volumes, provides a good survey of this genre.

henry iv—part two

The central source is once again Holinshed's Chronicles, this time the material covered from 1405 to 1413. The historical highlights of this play are Archbishop Scroop's rebellion (1405), the defeat of Northumberland (1408), and the death of Henry IV and coronation of Henry V (1413), and Shakespeare fuses these wide-spread events into a dramatic unity that seemingly occupies a brief stretch of time. He does so by telescoping time spans — for example, he has the defeat of Northumberland and the death of Henry IV follow in close succession — and by juggling chronology, as witness this sequence of Act references which footnote Holinshed: I,I,I,IV,IV, IV,IV,IV,II,IV,IV,III,IV,IV,IV,V,V.

Shakespeare seems to have read Holinshed this time with an eye out for Falstaff, for he inserts Falstaff into an event proper to the main plot, the capture of Lord Coleville (IV.iii). Conversely The Famous Victories, which contributed only to the subplot of Henry IV, Part One, sketches two episodes of the main plot of Part Two: Hal's taking up the crown while his father is sleeping (IV.v) and Hal's final judgment on the Lord Chief Justice (V.ii). Of the incidents involving Falstaff, The Famous Victories supplies only the final one, the banishment of Falstaff-Oldcastle and — more important, as far as the source play is concerned — of Ned. The remainder of the Falstaff scenes seem to be Shakespeare's own invention, and note how these, the king's press scene, for instance (III.ii), slope over from universal humor into satire.

With Falstaff thus involved in social issues and headed as he is toward tragedy, his character in this play is a shade more constricted and cruel than in Part One. A hint of this may be found in scene vi of The Famous Victories where Oldcastle savors the prospect of Henry IV dying. Too, a hint of Ancient Pistol may be found in the character of the Thief. Hotspur is gone, of course, and Hal involved in the intricacies of a more complicated plot has little opportunity to expand. A ripe situation for character development in Holinshed, the mutual confession scene between Henry IV and Hal, was excerpted and used in *Part One*. Whatever the reasons, the more interesting new characters in *Part Two*, Shallow and Silence and Doll Tearsheet, owe far less to sources than to Shakespeare's London and to his earlier canon. Vicentio of *The Taming of the Shrew* and Holofernes of *Love's Labor's Lost* foreshadow Shallow (as does Sir Thomas Lucy from real life?); Sir Nathaniel from *Love's Labor's Lost* and Old Gobbo from *The Merchant of Venice* smack of Silence; for Doll Tearsheet, perhaps the nurse in *Romeo and Juliet* and Jaquenetta in *Love's Labor's Lost*.

The political theme of the play is a reprise of the Tudor and Renaissance concept that a king is God's substitute here on earth and is not to be deposed. There is no opposition in *Part Two* as strong or as attractive as Hotspur or Owen Glendower and therefore that theme comes through with unimpeded force and clarity — especially since Henry IV, here shown at the end of life, is presented in a more mellow light. On the other hand, characterization in general being somewhat thinner in *Part Two*, the play lends itself less to characters representing ideas or universal predicaments.

If the sources of *Henry IV*, *Part One* and *Part Two* are examined side by side several conclusions about the effects of sources on Shakespeare's plays suggest themselves, at least as possibilities. Certainly *Part One* is the greater play, and in it Shakespeare is able to work within a briefer, more tidy chronological span; in it he follows more closely the sequence of his central source; in it he has more prefabricated incidents to build upon — all of which would seem to leave him freer to concentrate on life and its meanings.

✺ RAPHAEL HOLINSHED

The Chronicles of England, Scotland, and Ireland,* 1587

[1405] Whilst such doings were in hand betwixt the English and French, as the besieging of Marck Castle by the Earl of St. Pol and the sending forth of the English fleet under the governance of the Lord Thomas of Lancaster and the Earl of Kent, the king was minded to have gone into Wales against the Welsh rebels, that under their chieftain, Owen Glendower, ceased not to do much mischief still against the English subjects.[1]

[2]But at the same time, to his further disquieting, there was a conspiracy put in practice against him at home by the Earl of Northumberland, who had conspired with Richard Scroop, Archbishop of York, Thomas Mowbray, Earl Marshal, son to Thomas, Duke of Norfolk, who for the quarrel betwixt him and King Henry had been banished (as you have heard), the Lord Hastings, Fauconberg, Bardolph, and divers others. It was appointed that they should meet altogether with their whole power, upon Yorkswold, at a day assigned, and that the Earl of Northumberland should be chieftain, promising to bring with him a great number of Scots. The archbishop, accompanied with the Earl Marshal, devised certain articles of such matters as it was supposed that not only the commonality of the realm but also the nobility found themselves grieved with: which articles they showed first unto such of their adherents as were near about them, and after sent them abroad to their friends further off, assuring them

---

* text modernized.

[1] The Second Part of *Henry IV* is separated from Part One by an interval of nearly two years, between the battle of Shrewsbury (July 21, 1403) and Archbishop Scroop's rebellion (May, June 1405). I.i. 1–185: summarize the events of Shrewsbury and provide transition to the Scroop-Northumberland conspiracy. The events covered in Part Two extend to the coronation of Henry V on April 9, 1413.

[2] I.i. 186ff.

that for redress of such oppressions they would shed the last drop of blood in their bodies, if need were.

[3]The archbishop, not meaning to stay, after he saw himself accompanied with a great number of men that came flocking to York to take his part in this quarrel, forthwith discovered his enterprise, causing the articles aforesaid to be set up in the public streets of the city of York, and upon the gates of the monasteries, that each man might understand the cause that moved him to rise in arms against the king, the reforming whereof did not yet appertain unto him. Hereupon knights, squires, gentlemen, yeomen, and others of the commons as well [as] of the city, towns and countries about, being allured either for desire of change or else for desire to see a reformation in such things as were mentioned in the articles, assembled together in great numbers; and the archbishop coming forth amongst them clad in armor encouraged, exhorted, and (by all means he could) pricked them forth to take the enterprise in hand and manfully to continue in their begun purpose, promising forgiveness of sins to all them whose hap it was to die in the quarrel. And thus not only all the citizens of York, but all others in the countries about that were able to bear weapons came to the archbishop and the Earl Marshal. Indeed the respect that men had to the archbishop caused them to like the better of the cause, since the gravity of his age, his integrity of life, and incomparable learning, with the reverent aspect of his amiable personage, moved all men to have him in no small estimation.

The king advertised of these matters, meaning to prevent them, left his journey into Wales and marched with all speed towards the north parts. Also Ralph Nevill, Earl of Westmoreland, that was not far off, together with the Lord John of Lancaster, the king's son,[4] being informed of this rebellious attempt, assembled together such power as they might make, and together with those which were appointed to attend on the said Lord John to defend the borders against the Scots, as the Lord Henry Fitzhugh, the Lord Ralph Evers, the Lord Robert Umfrevile, and others, made forward against the rebels; [5]and coming into a plain within the forest of Gaultree caused their standards to be pitched down in like sort as the archbishop had pitched his over against them, being far stronger in number of people than the others, for (as some write) there were of the rebels at the least twenty thousand men.

---

[3] I.iii. 85ff.

[4] whom Holinshed correctly identifies as the Duke of Bedford (see p. 180) but whom Shakespeare, probably because of this passage, calls the Duke of Lancaster (I.iii. 82), a title belonging to Henry, Prince of Wales.

[5] IV.i. 1ff.

[6] When the Earl of Westmoreland perceived the force of the adversaries, and that they lay still and attempted not to come forward upon him, he subtly devised how to quell their purpose, and forthwith dispatched messengers unto the archbishop to understand the cause as it were of that great assembly, and for what cause (contrary to the king's peace) they came so in armor. The archbishop answered that he took nothing in hand against the king's peace, but that whatsoever he did tended rather to advance the peace and quiet of the commonwealth than otherwise; and where he and his company were in arms, it was for fear of the king, to whom he could have no free access by reason of such a multitude of flatterers as were about him; and therefore he maintained that his purpose to be good and profitable, as well for the king himself as for the realm, if men were willing to understand a truth: and herewith he showed forth a scroll in which the articles were written whereof before you have heard.

The messengers returning to the Earl of Westmoreland showed him what they had heard and brought from the archbishop. When he had read the articles, he showed in word and countenance outwardly that he liked of the archbishop's holy and virtuous intent and purpose, promising that he and his would prosecute the same in assisting the archbishop; who rejoicing hereat, gave credit to the earl and persuaded the Earl Marshal (against his will as it were) to go with him to a place appointed for them to commune together. Here when they were met with like number on either part, the articles were read over and without any more ado the Earl of Westmoreland and those that were with him agreed to do their best to see that a reformation might be had according to the same.

The Earl of Westmoreland using more policy than the rest: "Well" (said he) "then our travail is come to the wished end. And where our peoples have been long in armor, let them depart home to their wonted trades and occupations. In the meantime let us drink together in sign of agreement, that the people on both sides may see it, and know that it is true that we be light at a point."[7] They had no sooner shaken hands together but that a knight was sent straightways from the archbishop to bring word to the people that there was peace concluded, commanding each man to lay aside his arms and to resort home to their houses. The people beholding such tokens of peace, as shaking of hands and drinking together of the lords in loving manner, they being already wearied with the unaccustomed travail of war, broke up their field and returned homewards. But in the meantime, whilst the people of the archbishop's side withdrew away, the number of the contrary

---

[6] IV.ii. 1ff.
[7] in accord.

part[y] increased, according to order given by the Earl of Westmoreland; and yet the archbishop perceived not that he was deceived until the Earl of Westmoreland arrested both him and the Earl Marshal with divers others. Thus says Walsingham.

[8]But others write somewhat otherwise of this matter, affirming that the Earl of Westmoreland indeed and the Lord Ralph Evers procured the archbishop and the Earl Marshal to come to a communication with them upon a ground just in the midway betwixt both the armies, where the Earl of Westmoreland in talk declared to them how perilous an enterprise they had taken in hand, so to raise the people and to move war against the king; advising them therefore to submit themselves without further delay unto the king's mercy and his son, the Lord John, who was present there in the field with banners spread, ready to try the matter by dint of sword if they refused this counsel. And therefore he willed them to remember themselves well.[9] And if they would not yield and crave the king's pardon, he bade them do their best to defend themselves.

Hereupon as well the archbishop as the Earl Marshal submitted themselves unto the king and to his son the Lord John that was there present, and returned not to their army. Whereupon their troops scaled[10] and fled their ways. But being pursued many were taken, many slain, and many spoiled of that that they had about them, and so permitted to go their ways. Howsoever the matter was handled, true it is that the archbishop and the Earl Marshal were brought to Pomfret to the king, who in this meanwhile was advanced thither with his power, and from thence he went to York, whither the prisoners were also brought, and there beheaded the morrow after Whitsunday in a place without the city, that is to understand, the archbishop himself, the Earl Marshal, Sir John Lampley, and Sir Robert Plumpton.

Unto all which persons though indemnity were promised, yet was the same to none of them at any hand performed. By the issue hereof, I mean the death of the aforesaid — but especially of the archbishop — the prophecy of a sickly canon of Bridlington in Yorkshire fell out to be true, who darkly enough foretold this matter and the unfortunate event thereof in these words hereafter following, saying:

> Pacem tractabunt, sed fraudem subter arabunt,
> Pro nulla marca, saluabitur ille hierarcha.[11]

---

[8] IV.i. 225–228; IV.ii. 1ff. Shakespeare follows this version more closely than the first one.

[9] remind themselves, consider.

[10] scambled(?) (meaning scattered).

[11] They will discuss peace, but underneath they will cultivate fraud, he will be in touch with the hierarchy without a (perceptible) trace.

The archbishop suffered death very constantly, insomuch as the common people took it he died a martyr, affirming that certain miracles were wrought as well in the field where he was executed, as also in the place where he was buried. And immediately upon such bruits both men and women began to worship his dead carcass, whom they loved so much when he was alive, till they were forbidden by the king's friends, and for fear gave over to visit the place of his sepulture. The Earl Marshal's body by the king's leave was buried in the cathedral church, many lamenting his destiny; but his head was set on a pole aloft on the walls for a certain space, till by the king's permission (after the same had suffered many a hot sunny day and many a wet shower of rain) it was taken down and buried together with the body.

After the king, accordingly as seemed to him good, had ransomed and punished by grievous fines the citizens of York (which had borne armor on their archbishop's side against him) he departed from York with an army of thirty and seven thousand fighting men, furnished with all provision necessary, marching northwards against the Earl of Northumberland. [12]At his coming to Durham, the Lord Hastings, the Lord Fauconberg, Sir John Colevile of the Dale, and Sir John Griffith, being convicted of the conspiracy, were there beheaded. The Earl of Northumberland, hearing that his counsel was betrayed and his confederates brought to confusion through too much haste of the Archbishop of York, with three hundred horses got him to Berwick. The king coming forward quickly won the castle of Warkeworth. [13]Whereupon the Earl of Northumberland, not thinking himself in surety at Berwick, fled with the Lord Bardolph into Scotland where they were received of David Lord Fleming. . . .

[*Henry IV pursued the rebels for a while, successfully in Scotland and less so in Wales. The French then entered the conflict on the side of Owen Glendower, and after protracted and indecisive battles they returned to Brittany. The next few years passed amid rumors that Richard II was still alive, a plague that forced the king out of London for a time, and a growth in the power of the conspiracy against him.*]

[1408][14] The Earl of Northumberland and the Lord Bardolph, after they had been in Wales, in France, and Flanders to purchase aid against King Henry, were returned back into Scotland and had re-

---

[12] IV.iii. 1–81. Note how Shakespeare turns this incident into a display piece for Falstaff.

[13] II.iii. 62ff.

[14] Contrast this detailed account with Shakespeare's brief mention of Northumberland's overthrow: IV.iv. 97–99.

mained there now for the space of a whole year. And as their evil fortune would, whilst the king held a council of the nobility at London, the said Earl of Northumberland and Lord Bardolph, in a dismal hour, with a great power of Scots returned into England, recovering divers of the earl's castles and seigniories, for the people in great numbers resorted unto them. Hereupon encouraged with hope of good success, they entered into Yorkshire and there began to destroy the country. At their coming to Thirsk, they published a proclamation signifying that they were come in comfort of the English nation, as to relieve the commonwealth, willing all such as loved the liberty of their country, to repair unto them, with their armor on their backs, and in defensible wise to assist them.

The king advertised hereof, caused a great army to be assembled, and came forward with the same towards his enemies. But ere the king came to Nottingham, Sir Thomas, or (as other copies have) Ralph Rokeby, sheriff of Yorkshire, assembled the forces of the country to resist the earl and his power, coming to Grimbaut brigs, beside Knaresborough, there to stop them the passage; but they returning aside, got to Weatherby, and so to Tadcaster, and finally came forward unto Bramham Moor, near Hazelwood, where they chose their ground meet to fight upon. The sheriff was as ready to give battle as the earl to receive it, and so with a standard of St. George spread set fiercely upon the earl, who under a standard of his own arms encountered his adversaries with great manhood. There was a sore encounter and cruel conflict betwixt the parties, but in the end the victory fell to the sheriff. The Lord Bardolph was taken, but sore wounded so that he shortly after died of the hurts.

As for the Earl of Northumberland, he was slain outright.[15] So that now the prophecy was fulfilled, which gave an inkling of this his heavy hap long before; namely,

Stirps Persitina periet confusa ruina.[16]

For this earl was the stock and main root of all that were left alive called by the name of Percy, and of many more [Percys] by divers slaughters dispatched. For whose misfortune the people were not a little sorry, making report of the gentleman's valiantness, renown, and honour, and applying unto him certain lamentable verses out of Lucan, saying:

---

[15] Immediately preceding this account (IV.iv. 97–99) Shakespeare has Westmoreland describe Archbishop Scroop's surrender to Prince John (ll.81–90) — an event of the year 1405 — typical of how Shakespeare juggles events and chronology in this play.

[16] The line of Percys will perish in disordered ruin.

> Sed nos nec sanguis, nec tantum vulnera nostri
> Affecere senis; quantum gestata per urbem
> Ora ducis, quae transfixo deformia pilo
> Vidimus.[17]

For his head, full of silver hoary hairs, being put upon a stake was openly carried through London and set upon the bridge of the same city. In like manner was the Lord Bardolph's. The Bishop of Bangor was taken and pardoned by the king, for that when he was apprehended he had no armor on his back. This battle was fought the nineteenth day of February.

The king to purge the North parts of all rebellion and to take order for the punishment of those that were accused to have succoured and assisted the Earl of Northumberland, went to York where when many were condemned and divers put to great fines and the country brought to quietness, he caused the Abbot of Hailes to be hanged, who had been in armor against him with the aforesaid earl. . . .

[1409][18] The Welsh rebel Owen Glendower made an end of his wretched life in this tenth year of King Henry his reign; being driven now in his latter time (as we find recorded) to such misery that, in manner despairing of all comfort, he fled into desert places and solitary caves, where, being destitute of all relief and succour, dreading to show his face to any creature, and finally lacking meat to sustain nature, for mere hunger and lack of food miserably pined away and died. . . .

[1413] The Lord Henry Prince of Wales, eldest son to King Henry, got knowledge that certain of his father's servants were busy to give informations against him whereby discord might arise betwixt him and his father. For they put into the king's head not only what evil rule (according to the course of youth) the prince kept to the offense of many, but also what great resort of people came to his house, so that the court was nothing furnished with such a train as daily followed the prince. These tales brought no small suspicion into the king's head, lest his son would presume to usurp the crown, he being yet alive, through which suspicious jealousy it was perceived that he favored not his son, as in times past he had done.

The prince sore offended with such persons as by slanderous reports sought not only to spot his good name abroad in the realm but to sow

---

[17] But neither the blood nor the wounds of our old man affected us as much as the mutilated head of the general which we saw fixed on a pike carried through the city.

[18] III.i. 102–103. Shakespeare is here repeating Holinshed's error, for Glendower did not die until Henry V had been on the throne for several years. Records of him go on at least until February 24, 1416.

discord also betwixt him and his father, wrote his letters into every part of the realm to reprove all such slanderous devices of those that sought his discredit. [19]And to clear himself the better, that the world might understand what wrong he had to be slandered in such wise, about the feast of Peter and Paul, to wit, the nine and twentieth day of June, he came to the court with such a number of noblemen, and others his friends that wished him well, as the like train had been seldom seen repairing to the court at any one time in those days. He was apparelled in a gown of blue satin, full of small oilet[20] holes, at every hole the needle hanging by a silk thread with which it was sewed. About his arm he wore an hound's collar set full of S's of gold, and the tirets[21] likewise being of the same metal.

The court was then at Westminster, where he being entered into the hall, not one of his company durst once advance himself further than the fire in the same hall, notwithstanding they were earnestly requested by the lords to come higher. But they regarding what they had in commandment of the prince, would not presume to do anything contrary thereunto. He himself only accompanied with those of the king's house was straight admitted to the presence of the king, his father, who being at that time grievously diseased, yet caused himself in his chair to be borne into his privy chamber, where in the presence of three or four persons in whom he had most confidence, he commanded the prince to show what he had to say concerning the cause of his coming.

The prince kneeling down before his father said: "Most redoubted and sovereign lord and father, I am at this time come to your presence as your liege man, and as your natural son, in all things to be at your commandment. And where I understand you have in suspicion my demeanor against Your Grace, you know very well that if I knew any man within this realm of whom you should stand in fear, my duty were to punish that person, thereby to remove that grief from your heart. Then how much more ought I to suffer death, to ease Your Grace of that grief which you have of me, being your natural son and liege man. And to that end I have this day made myself ready by confession and receiving of the sacrament. And therefore I beseech you most redoubted Lord and dear Father, for the honour of God, to ease your heart of all such suspicion as you have of me and to dispatch me here before your knees with this same dagger," (and withal he delivered unto the king his dagger, in all humble reverence; adding further that his life was not so dear to him that he wished to live one day with his

---

[19] *H. IV*. Part One, III.ii. 1–161.
[20] round holes worked in cloth for the purpose of fastening.
[21] terrets, loops used in fastening.

[father's] displeasure). "And therefore in thus ridding me out of life, and yourself from all suspicion, here in presence of these lords, and before God at the day of the general judgement, I faithfully protest clearly to forgive you."

The king moved herewith, cast from him the dagger and embracing the prince kissed him, and with shedding tears confessed that indeed he had him partly in suspicion, though now (as he perceived) not with just cause; and therefore from thenceforth no misreport should cause him to have him in mistrust, and this he promised of his honor. So by his great wisdom was the wrongful <u>suspicion</u> which his father had conceived against him removed, and he restored to his favor. And further, where he could not but grievously complain of them that had slandered him so greatly, to the defacing not only of his honor but also putting him in danger of his life, he humbly besought the king that they might answer their unjust accusation; and in case they were found to have forged such matters upon a malicious purpose, that then they might suffer some punishment for their faults, though not to the full of that they had deserved. The king seeming to grant his reasonable desire, yet told him that he must tarry a Parliament, that such offenders might be punished by judgement of their peers. And so for that time he was dismissed, with great love and signs of fatherly affection.

Thus were the father and the son reconciled betwixt whom the said pickthanks[22] had sown division, insomuch that the son upon a vehement conceit of unkindness sprung in the father was in the way to be worn out[23] of favor. Which was the more likely to come to pass by their informations that privily charged him with riot and other uncivil demeanor unseemly for a prince. Indeed he was youthfully [thus] given, grown to audacity, and had chosen him companions agreeable to his age, with whom he spent the time in such recreations, exercises, and delights as he fancied.[24] But yet (it should seem by the report of some writers) that his behaviour was not offensive or at least tending to the damage of anybody — since he had a care to avoid doing of wrong and to tender his affections within the tract of virtue, whereby he opened unto himself a ready passage of good liking among the prudent sort and was beloved of such as could discern his disposition, which was in no degree so excessive as that he deserved in such vehement manner to be suspected.[25]

---

[22] talebearing flatterers.
[23] threatened with loss of.
[24] In this sentence there is a hint at least of Hal's carryings on with Falstaff and the others.
[25] A hint here of *H. IV*. Part One, I.ii. 219ff.

[*An English army under the Duke of Clarence, son of Henry IV, invaded France ostensibly to aid the Duke of Orleans, but it did little more than pillage the countryside. Richard Whittington was elected Mayor of London — he served three terms in all — a most worthy, philanthropic, "notable minded gentleman."*]

In this fourteenth and last year of King Henry's reign, a council was held in the White Friars in London, at the which, among other things, order was taken for ships and galleys to be builded and made ready, and all other things necessary to be provided for a voyage which he meant to make into the Holy Land, there to recover the city of Jerusalem from the infidels. For it grieved him to consider the great malice of Christian princes that were bent upon a mischievous purpose to destroy one another, to the peril of their own souls, rather than to make war against the enemies of the Christian faith, as in conscience (it seemed to him) they were bound. [26]He held his Christmas this year at Eltham, being sore vexed with sickness, so that it was thought sometimes that he had been dead; notwithstanding, it pleased God that he somewhat recovered his strength again, and so passed that Christmas with as much joy as he might.

The morrow after Candlemas Day began a Parliament, which he had called at London, but he departed this life before the same Parliament was ended. For now that his provisions were ready and that he was furnished with sufficient treasure, soldiers, captains, victuals, munitions, tall ships, strong galleys, and all things necessary for such a royal journey as he pretended[27] to take into the Holy Land, he was eftsoons taken with a sore sickness, which was not a leprosy — stricken by the hand of God (says Master Hall) as foolish friars imagined — but a very apoplexy, of the which he languished till his appointed hour, and had none other grief nor malady. So that what man ordains God alters at His good will and pleasure, not giving place more to the prince than to the poorest creature living, when He sees His time to dispose of him this way or that, as to His omnipotent power and divine providence seems expedient. [28]During this his last sickness, he caused his crown (as some write) to be set on a pillow at his bed's head, and suddenly his pangs so sore troubled him that he lay as though all his vital spirits had been from him departed. Such as were about him,

---

[26] IV.iv. 102ff. Note how Shakespeare ties this illness (1413) together with the defeats of Scroop and Northumberland (1405 and 1408) — ll.80–101 — to form a single incident.

[27] intended.

[28] IV.v. 5–225.

thinking verily that he had been departed, covered his face with a linen cloth.

The prince his son being hereof advertised, entered into the chamber, took away the crown, and departed. The father being suddenly revived out of that trance, quickly perceived the lack of his crown; and having knowledge that the prince his son had taken it away, caused him to come before his presence, requiring of him what he meant so to misuse himself. The prince with a good audacity answered: "Sir, to mine and all men's judgements you seemed dead in this world, wherefore I as your next heir apparent took that as mine own, and not as yours." "Well, fair son," (said the king with a great sigh) "what right I had to it, God knows." "Well" (said the prince) "if you die king, I will have the garland, and trust to keep it with the sword against all mine enemies as you have done." Then said the king, "I commit all to God, and remember[29] you to do well." With that he turned himself in his bed and shortly after departed to God in a chamber of the Abbey of Westminster called Jerusalem, the twentieth day of March, in the year 1413, and in the year of his age 46, when he had reigned thirteen years, five months and odd days, in great perplexity and little pleasure. . . .

We find that he was taken with his last sickness while he was making his prayers at St. Edward's shrine, there as it were to take his leave, and so to proceed forth on his journey. He was so suddenly and grievously taken that such as were about him feared lest he would have died presently; wherefore to relieve him (if it were possible) they bore him into a chamber that was next at hand, belonging to the Abbot of Westminster, where they laid him on a pallet before the fire and used all remedies to revive him. [30]At length he recovered his speech, and understanding and perceiving himself in a strange place which he knew not, he willed to know if the chamber had any particular name, whereunto answer was made that it was called Jerusalem. Then said the king: "Lauds be given to the Father of Heaven, for now I know that I shall die here in this chamber, according to the prophecy of me declared, that I should depart this life in Jerusalem."[31]

Whether this was true that so he spoke, as one that gave too much credit to foolish prophecies and vain tales, or whether it was feigned, as in such cases it commonly happens, we leave it to the advised reader to judge. His body with all funeral pomp was conveyed unto Canter-

---

[29] remind.

[30] IV.v. 233ff.

[31] Henry Bolingbroke probably did make a pilgrimage to Jerusalem *before* ascending the throne. Venetian documents exist mentioning his leaving Venice for the Holy Land (November 30, 1392) and his returning from the Holy Land to Venice (March 31, 1393).

bury, and there solemnly buried, leaving behind him by the Lady Marie daughter to the Lord Humphrey Bohun, Earl of Hereford and North-ampton: Henry, Prince of Wales; Thomas, Duke of Clarence; John, Duke of Bedford; Humphrey, Duke of Gloucester; Blanche, Duchess of Bavaria; and Philippa, Queen of Denmark. By his last wife Jane he had no children. This king was of a mean[32] stature, well-proportioned, and formally compact,[33] quick and lively, and of a stout courage. In his latter days he showed himself so gentle that he got more love amongst the nobles and people of this realm than he had purchased malice and evil will in the beginning.

But yet to speak a truth, by his proceedings, after he had attained to the crown, what with such taxes, tallages, subsidies, and exactions as he was constrained to charge the people with, and what by punishing such as moved with disdain to see him usurp the crown (contrary to the oath taken at his entering into this land, upon his return from exile) did at sundry times rebel against him, he won himself more hatred than in all his lifetime (if it had been longer by many years than it was) had been possible for him to have weeded out and re-moved. And yet, doubtless, worthy were his subjects to taste of that bitter cup, since they were so ready to join and clap hands with him for the deposing of their rightful and natural prince, King Richard, whose chief fault rested only in that: that he was too bountiful to his friends and too merciful to his foes; especially if he had not been drawn by others to seek revenge of those that abused his good and courteous nature. . . .

[Whereupon (1413) Henry the Fifth was proclaimed king.] Such great hope and good expectation was had of this man's fortunate suc-cess to follow, that within three days after his father's decease divers noblemen and honorable personages did him homage and swore to him due obedience, which had not been seen done to any of his predecessor kings of this realm till they had been possessed of the crown. He was crowned the ninth of April, being Passion Sunday, which was a sore, rugged, and tempestuous day, with wind, snow and sleet, that men greatly marvelled thereat, making divers interpreta-tions what the same might signify. But this king even at first appoint-ing with himself to show that in his person princely honors should change public manners, he determined to put on him the shape of a new man. [34]For whereas aforetime he had made himself a companion unto misruly mates of dissolute order and life, he now banished them

---

[32] medium.
[33] well-proportioned.
[34] V.v. 44–75.

all from his presence (but not unrewarded, or else unpreferred) inhibiting them upon a great pain not once to approach, lodge, or sojourn within ten miles of his court or presence. [35]And in their places he chose men of gravity, wit, and high policy, by whose wise counsel he might at all times rule to his honor and dignity; calling to mind how once to high offence of the king his father, he had with his fist stricken the Chief Justice for sending one of his minions (upon desert) to prison, when the justice stoutly commanded himself also straight to ward,[36] and he (then prince) obeyed. . . .

[1414] Also in this first year of this king's reign, Sir John Oldcastle,[37] which by his wife was called Lord Cobham,[38] a valiant captain and a hardy gentleman, was accused to the Archbishop of Canterbury of certain points of heresy, who knowing him to be highly in the king's favor declared to His Highness the whole accusation. The king first having compassion of the nobleman required the prelates, that if he were a strayed sheep, rather by gentleness than by rigor to reduce him to the fold. And after this, he himself sent for him, and right earnestly exhorted him and lovingly admonished him to reconcile himself to God and to His laws. The Lord Cobham not only thanked him for his most favorable clemency, but also declared first to him by mouth, and afterwards by writing, the foundation of his myth and the ground of his belief, affirming his grace to be his supreme head and competent judge, and none other person, offering an hundred knights and squires to come to his purgation or else to fight in open lists in defense of his just cause.

The king, understanding and persuaded by his counsel that by order of the laws of his realm, such accusations touching matters of faith ought to be tried by his spiritual prelates, sent him to the Tower of London, there to abide the determination of the clergy, according to the statutes in that case provided: after which time a solemn session was appointed in the cathedral church of St. Paul, upon the three and twentieth day of September, and another the five and twentieth day of the same month in the hall of the Blackfriars at London, in which places the said lord was examined, apposed,[39] and fully heard; and in

---

[35] V.ii. 63ff.
[36] prison.
[37] In *The Famous Victories of Henry the Fifth*, reprinted below, one of Prince Hal's boon companions is Sir John Oldcastle, presumably the source of Shakespeare's Falstaff. In *H. IV. Part One*, I.ii. 47–48, Hal calls Falstaff "my old lad of the castle," clearly a reference to Falstaff's earlier self. This passage from Holinshed shows us the defiance and elusiveness characteristic of Oldcastle and, in part, of Falstaff.
[38] That is, by marriage to Lady Cobham.
[39] interrogated.

conclusion by the Archbishop of Canterbury denounced a heretic and remitted again to the Tower of London, from which place either by help of friends or favor of keepers he privily escaped and came into Wales, where he remained for a season.[40]

□ *Some Sources for Further Study*

See the supplementary sources after *Henry IV, Part One.*

---

[40] After which this rugged and outspoken Protestant martyr evaded the king's forces until 1417. For a long while he lay hid among the hills of his native Herefordshire, close to where the aged Owen Glendower hid with his only surviving son. There is a good possibility, but no evidence either way, that the two outlaws met from time to time.

henry v

The main source of material is still Holinshed, and this play, like Henry IV, Part Two, covers a wide span of events, beginning during the Lenten season of 1414 with the legendary shipment of tennis balls from the Dauphin to Henry V, and ending on May 21, 1420 with the betrothal of Henry to Katherine of Valois. As in Henry IV, Part Two Shakespeare fits together an eclectic pattern of episodes, and while he follows Holinshed in close chronological order — see the progression of Shakespeare footnote references in the text — he bypasses long stretches of history. For example, he merges Henry's two campaigns in France (1415–1420) into one, using a few lines of the Prologue to Act V (ll. 39–43) to bridge the interval from October 29, 1415, when Henry embarks from Calais after Agincourt, to 1420, the year of the close of his second campaign. Henry V courses from tennis balls to the siege of Harfleur to Agincourt to the wooing of Katherine with an economy that makes Holinshed seem fussy — except for the Battle of Agincourt. There history rivals imagination, and although Shakespeare skillfully inserts tense suggestions of the battle, Holinshed's vivid descriptions capture more firmly its real excitement.

In the use of Holinshed Henry V falls about midway between Henry IV, Part One and Part Two. Like Part One it follows Holinshed chronologically, which Part Two does not; like Part Two it lacks the taut time span of Part One. Comparisons like these tempt one to weigh the merit of Shakespeare's plays alongside the use he makes of central sources, and in line with speculation this most dramatic of the plays dealing with Prince Hal (Henry V) has a ready made drama as a second main source. The Famous Victories rings with childish gusto, and its dialogue is repetitive and always ready to further plot at the expense of character, in contrast to the many-sided rhetoric of Shakespeare's play. Yet starting from the middle of scene ix — about the midpoint of the play — its plot manipulates Holinshed essentially the same way Shakespeare will. The two invasions into France are fused into one, and the plot moves in a single sweep from tennis balls to the wooing of Katherine. Moreover, although scenes ix–xx differ almost entirely in theme and focus from what has gone before, they retain enough of the earlier comic thrusts to reach out at times and touch the subplot of Shakespeare's play; scene x involving the Thief, John Cobbler, and his wife suggest Shakespeare's scene (II.i) involving Bardolph, Nym, Pistol and the Hostess; and scene xvii, Derick's comic business with the French soldier, looks forward to Pistol's capture of one in *Henry V*, IV.iv.

Subplot, however, is comparatively minor in a play so dominated by the deeds and character of one man. Shakespeare's Henry V is less a symbol of complete Renaissance man than in the earlier plays and more akin to Holinshed's "prince whom all men loved . . . a lodestar in honor, and mirror of magnificence." The "Character of Henry V" which concludes the Holinshed selection below paints the Tudor portrait of hero-king, and Shakespeare's Henry V is drawn in its image — the play is, after all, essentially a jingoistic celebration.

The returning subplot characters are developed out of *The Famous Victories* much as they were in the *Henry IV* plays, but the sharply typical British types — Gower, Fluellen, Macmorris, Jamy, Williams — appear in neither central source and are evidently Shakespeare's own creations derived from the world around him.

By its nature *Henry V* is far more concerned with events than with ideas, and most of the statements it makes are not so much ideas as attitudes — Tudor attitudes of approval of everything that Henry V represents. Similar attitudes are reflected in Holinshed and, with zest, in *The Famous Victories*. The full measure of difference that is Shakespeare lies mainly in language and dramatic craftsmanship.

RAPHAEL HOLINSHED

The Chronicles of England, Scotland, and Ireland,* 1587

[1414] ¹Whilst in the Lent season the king lay at Killingworth, there came to him from Charles, Dauphin of France, certain ambassadors that brought with them a barrel of Paris balls,² which from their master they presented to him for a token that was taken in very ill part, as sent in scorn to signify that it was more meet for the king to pass the time with such childish exercise than to attempt any worthy exploit. Wherefore the king wrote to him that ere aught long he would toss him some London balls that perchance should shake the walls of the best court in France.

This year, Thomas Arundel, Archbishop of Canterbury, departed this life, a stout prelate and an earnest maintainer of the Romish religion. Henry Chichele, Bishop of St. David, succeeded the same Arundel in the see of Canterbury; and the king's confessor, Stephen Patrington, a Carmelite friar, was made Bishop of St. David. Henry Percy, then but a child, son to the Lord Henry Percy surnamed Hotspur, after his father's decease that was slain at Shrewsbury Field was conveyed into Scotland and there left by his grandfather, where ever since he had remained. The king therefore pitied his case, and so procured for him that he came home and was restored to all his lands and earldom of Northumberland, which lands before had been given to the Lord John, the king's brother. . . .

In the second year of his reign King Henry called his high court of Parliament, the last day of April in the town of Leicester, in which Parliament many profitable laws were concluded, and many petitions

---

* text modernized.
¹ I.ii. 234–297. Note how by changing Henry's letter to a ringing speech Shakespeare heightens the drama of this passage.
² tennis balls. This incident, used with such dramatic effectiveness by Shakespeare and in *The Famous Victories,* is of doubtful authenticity. The Dauphin was not quite nineteen at this time, while "childish" Henry was twenty-five.

moved were for that time deferred. Amongst which, one was that a bill exhibited in the Parliament held at Westminster in the eleventh year of King Henry the Fourth (which by reason the king was then troubled with evil discord, came to none effect) might now with good deliberation be pondered, and brought to some good conclusion. [3]The effect of which supplication was that the temporal lands devoutly given, and disordinately spent by religious and other spiritual persons, should be seized into the king's hands; since the same might suffice to maintain, to the honor of the king and defense of the realm, fifteen earls, fifteen hundred knights, six thousand and two hundred squires, and a hundred almshouses for relief only of the poor, impotent, and needy persons; and the king to have clearly to his coffers twenty thousand pounds, with many other provisions and values of religious houses, which I pass over.

[4]This bill was much noted and more feared among the religious sort, whom surely it touched very near, and therefore to find remedy against it they determined to assay all ways to put by and overthrow this bill. [5]Wherein they thought best to try if they might move the king's mood with some sharp invention, that he should not regard the importunate petitions of the commons. Whereupon on a day in the Parliament Henry Chichele, Archbishop of Canterbury, made a pithy oration wherein he declared how not only the duchies of Normandy and Aquitaine, with the counties of Anjou and Maine and the country of Gascony, were by undoubted title appertaining to the king, as to the lawful and only heir of the same; but also the whole realm of France, as heir to his great grandfather, King Edward the Third.

[6]Herein did he much inveigh against the surmised and false feigned law Salic,[7] which the Frenchmen allege ever against the kings of England in bar of their just title to the crown of France. The very words of that supposed law are these, *In terram Salicam mulieres ne succedant,* that is to say, "Into the Salic land let not women succeed." Which the French glossers expound to be the realm of France and that this law was made by King Pharamond; whereas yet their own authors affirm that the land Salic is in Germany, between the rivers of Elbe and Sala; and that when Charles the Great had overcome the Saxons, he placed there certain Frenchmen, which having in disdain the dishonest manners of the German women made a law that the

---

[3] I.i. 1–20.

[4] I.i. 69–71.

[5] I.i. 75ff.

[6] I.ii. 33–102. Shakespeare follows the next two paragraphs of Holinshed quite closely.

[7] Or Salique, but Salic is the spelling used in most modern texts.

females should not succeed to any inheritance within that land, which at this day is called Meisen. So that if this be true, this law was not made for the realm of France nor the Frenchmen possessed the land Salic, till four hundred and one and twenty years after the death of Pharamond, the supposed maker of this Salic law; for this Pharamond deceased in the year 426, and Charles the Great subdued the Saxons and placed the Frenchmen in those parts beyond the river of Sala in the year 805.

Moreover, it appears by their own writers that King Pepin, which deposed Childeric, claimed the crown of France as heir general for that he was descended of Blithild, daughter to King Clothair the First. Hugh Capet also, who usurped the crown upon Charles, Duke of Lorraine, the sole heir male of the line and stock of Charles the Great, to make his title seem true and appear good — though indeed it was stark naught — conveyed himself as heir to the Lady Lingard, daughter to King Charlemagne, son to Lewis[8] the emperor that was son to Charles the Great. King Lewis, also the Tenth,[9] otherwise called St. Lewis, being very heir to the said usurper Hugh Capet, could never be satisfied in his conscience how he might justly keep and possess the crown of France till he was persuaded and fully instructed that Queen Isabel his grandmother was lineally descended of the Lady Ermengard, daughter and heir to the above named Charles, Duke of Lorraine; by the which marriage the blood and line of Charles the Great was again united and restored to the crown and scepter of France, so that more clear than the sun it openly appears that the title of King Pepin, the claim of Hugh Capet, the possession of Lewis, yea, and the French kings to this day are derived and conveyed from the heir female — though they would under the color of such a feigned law bar the kings and princes of this realm of England of their right and lawful inheritance.

The archbishop further alleged out of the Book of Numbers this saying: "When a man dieth without a son, let the inheritance descend to his daughter."[10] [11]At length, having said sufficiently for the proof of the king's just and lawful title to the crown of France, he exhorted him to advance forth his banner to fight for his right, to conquer his inheritance, to spare neither blood, sword, nor fire, since his war was just, his cause good, and his claim true. And to the in-

---

[8] In French, Louis, but Holinshed and Shakespeare both use this spelling.

[9] Historically, Lewis the Ninth. Holinshed is in error and Shakespeare (I.ii. 77) repeats this error.

[10] *Numbers* XXVII. 8.

[11] I.ii. 103–135. The archbishop's reminiscence of Edward III "on a hill" (l.108.) will also be remembered later on by Charles VI (II.iv. 56–58).

tent his loving chaplains and obedient subjects of the spirituality might show themselves willing and desirous to aid his majesty for the recovery of his ancient right and true inheritance, the archbishop declared that in their spiritual convocation they had granted to his highness such a sum of money as never by no spiritual persons was to any prince before those days given or advanced.

[12]When the archbishop had ended his prepared tale, Ralph Nevill, Earl of Westmoreland, and as then Lord Warden of the marches against Scotland, understanding that the king upon a courageous desire to recover his right in France would surely take the wars in hand, thought good to move the king to begin first with Scotland and thereupon declared how easy a matter it should be to make a conquest there and how greatly the same should further his wished purpose for the subduing of the Frenchmen, concluding the sum of his tale with this old saying: "that whoso will France win, must with Scotland first begin." Many matters he touched, as well to show how necessary the conquest of Scotland should be as also to prove how just a cause the king had to attempt it, trusting to persuade the king and all others to be of his opinion.

But after he had made an end, the Duke of Exeter, uncle to the king, a man well learned and wise (who had been sent into Italy by his father intending that he should have been a priest) replied against the Earl of Westmoreland's oration, affirming rather that he which would Scotland win, he with France must first begin. For if the king might once compass the conquest of France, Scotland could not long resist; so that conquer France, and Scotland would soon obey. For where should the Scots learn policy and skill to defend themselves, if they had not their bringing up and training in France? If the French pensions maintained not the Scottish nobility, in what case should they be? Then take away France, and the Scots will soon be tamed; France being to Scotland the same that the sap is to the tree, which being taken away, the tree must needs die and wither.

To be brief, the Duke of Exeter used such earnest and pithy persuasions to induce the king and the whole assembly of the Parliament to credit his words, that immediately after he had made an end all the company began to cry: "War, war! France, France!" Hereby the bill for dissolving of religious houses was clearly set aside, and nothing thought on but only the recovering of France, according as the archbishop had moved. And upon this point, after a few acts besides for the wealth of the realm established, the Parliament was prorogued unto Westminster.

---

[12] I.ii. 136–183.

[13]Some write that in this Parliament it was enacted that Lollards and heretics with their maintainers and favorers should be *ipso facto* adjudged guilty of high treason. But in the statute made in the same Parliament against Lollards we find no such words. Albeit by force of that statute it was ordained that persons so convicted and executed should lose their lands held in fee simple and all others their goods and chattels, as in cases of felony.

During this Parliament there came to the king ambassadors, as well from the French king that was then in the hands of the Orleans faction as also from the Duke of Burgundy, for aid against that faction, promising more (as was said) than lay well in his power to perform. The king shortly after sent ambassadors to them both, as the Bishop of Durham, and Norwich, with others. Moreover at this Parliament, John, the king's brother, was created Duke of Bedford, and his brother Humphrey, Duke of Gloucester. Also, Thomas Beaufort, Marquis Dorset, was created Duke of Exeter. Immediately after, the king sent over into France his uncle, the Duke of Exeter, the Lord Grey, Admiral of England, the Archbishop of Dublin, and the Bishop of Norwich, ambassadors unto the French king, with five hundred horses which were lodged in the temple house in Paris, keeping such triumphant cheer in their lodging and such a solemn estate in their riding through the city that the Parisians and all the Frenchmen had no small marvel at their honorable port.

The French king received them very honorably and banqueted them right sumptuously, showing to them jousts and martial pastimes by the space of three days together, in the which jousts the king himself, to show his courage and activity to the Englishmen, manfully broke spears and lustily tourneyed. When the triumph was ended, the English ambassadors, having a time appointed them to declare their message, admitted to the French king's presence, required of him to deliver unto the King of England the realm and crown of France with the entire duchies of Aquitaine, Normandy and Anjou, with the countries of Ponthieu and Maine. Many other requests they made, and this offered withal: that if the French king would without war and effusion of Christian blood render to the king their master his very right and lawful inheritance, that he would be content to take in marriage the Lady Katherine, daughter to the French king, and to endow her with all the duchies and countries before rehearsed; and if he would not so do, then the King of England did express and signify to

---

[13] The next three paragraphs, containing irrelevant and at most tangential material, have been included in order to give the reader a fuller picture of this source. Subsequent lengthy irrelevant passages will be deleted.

him that with the aid of God and help of his people he would recover his right and inheritance wrongfully withheld from him, with mortal war and dint of sword. . . .

The Frenchmen being not a little abashed at these demands thought not to make any absolute answer in so weighty a cause till they had further breathed; and therefore prayed the English ambassadors to say to the king their master that they now having no opportunity to conclude in so high a matter would shortly send ambassadors into England, which should certify and declare to the king their whole mind, purpose, and intent. The English ambassadors returned with this answer, making relation of everything that was said or done. [14]King Henry, after the return of his ambassadors, determined fully to make war in France, conceiving a good and perfect hope to have fortunate success, since victory for the most part follows where right leads, being advanced forward by justice and set forth by equity. . . .

[Early in 1415 Henry V called a council to tighten security at home and to make other military preparations for the invasion of France.]

[1415] The Frenchmen having knowledge hereof, the Dauphin, who had the governance of the realm because his father was fallen into his old disease of frenzy,[15] sent for the Dukes of Berry and Alençon and all the other lords of the council of France; by whose advice it was determined that they should not only prepare a sufficient army to resist the King of England, whensoever he arrived to invade France, but also to stuff and furnish the towns on the frontiers and sea coasts with convenient garrisons of men; [16]and further to send to the King of England a solemn embassage to make to him some offers according to the demands before rehearsed. The charge of this embassage was committed to the Earl of Vendôme, to Master William Bouratier, Archbishop of Bourges, and to Master Peter Fremel, Bishop of Lisieux, to the Lords of Yvry and Braquemont, and to Master Gaultier Cole, the king's secretary, and divers others.

These ambassadors accompanied with 350 horses passed the sea at Calais and landed at Dover, before whose arrival the king was departed from Windsor to Winchester, intending to have gone to Hampton there to have surveyed his navy; but hearing of the ambassadors approaching, he tarried still at Winchester, where the said French lords showed themselves very honorably before the king and his nobility.

---

[14] I.ii. 299ff.
[15] recurrent insanity.
[16] II.Prologue. 12–15.

[17]At time prefixed, before the king's presence sitting in his throne imperial, the Archbishop of Bourges made an eloquent and a long oration, dissuading war and praising peace, offering to the King of England a great sum of money with divers countries — being in very deed but base and poor — as a dowry with the Lady Katherine in marriage so that he would dissolve his army and dismiss his soldiers, which he had gathered and put in a readiness.

When his oration was ended, the king caused the ambassadors to be highly feasted and set them at his own table. And after a day assigned in the aforesaid hall, the Archbishop of Canterbury to their oration made a notable answer, the effect whereof was that if the French king would not give with his daughter in marriage the duchies of Aquitaine, Anjou and all other seigniories and dominions sometimes appertaining to the noble progenitors of the King of England, he would in no wise retire his army nor break his journey; but would with all diligence enter into France and destroy the people, waste the country, and subvert the towns with blood, sword, and fire, and never cease till he had recovered his ancient right and lawful patrimony. The king avowed the archbishop's saying, and in the word of a prince promised to perform it to the uttermost.

The Archbishop of Bourges, much grieved that his embassage was no more regarded, after certain brags blustered out with impatience, as more presuming upon his prelacy than respecting his duty of considerance to whom he spoke and what became him to say, he prayed safe conduct to depart. Which the king gently granted and added withal to this effect: "I little esteem your French brags, and less set by your power and strength; I know perfectly my right to my region, which you usurp; and except you deny the apparent truth, so do your selves also; if you neither do nor will know it, yet God and the world knows it. The power of your master you see, but my puissance you have not yet tasted. If he have loving subjects, I am (I thank God) not unstored of the same. And I say this unto you, that before one year passes I trust to make the highest crown of your country to stoop, and the proudest mitre to learn his *humiliatedo*. In the meantime tell this to the usurper, your master: that within three months I will enter into France, as into mine own true and lawful patrimony, appointing to acquire the same not with brag of words but with deeds of men and dint of sword, by the aid of God in whom is my whole trust and confidence. Further matter at this present I impart not unto you, saving that with warrant you may depart surely and safely into your country, where I trust sooner to visit you, than you shall have cause

---

[17] III.Prologue. 28–32.

to bid me welcome." With this answer the ambassadors, sore displeased in their minds (although they were highly entertained and
liberally rewarded) departed into their country, reporting to the
dauphin how they had sped.

After the French ambassadors were departed, the king like a provident prince thought good to take order for the resisting of the Scots
— if (according to their manner) they should attempt anything
against his subjects in his absence. For that point appointed he the
Earl of Westmoreland, the Lord Scroop, the Baron of Greystoke. Sir
Robert Umfrevile, and divers other valiant captains to keep the frontiers and marches of Scotland (which Sir Robert Umfrevile on the
day of Mary Magdalen fought with the Scots at the town of Gedering,
having in his company only three hundred archers and seven score
spears, where he [after long conflict] slew of his enemies sixty and odd,
took three hundred and sixty prisoners, discomfited and put to flight
one thousand and more whom he followed in chase above twelve
miles, but their hands full of preys and prisoners retired homeward [not
unhurt] to the castle of Rockesborough, of the which he was captain).

When the king had all provisions ready and ordered all things for
the defense of his realm, he leaving behind him for governor of the
realm the queen, his mother-in-law [i.e., the queen dowager], departed
to Southampton to take ship into France. [18]And first princely appointing to advertise the French king of his coming, therefore dispatched Antelope his pursuivant[19] at arms with letters to him for restitution of that which he wrongfully withheld contrary to the laws of God
and man. The king further declaring how sorry he was that he should
be thus compelled, for repeating of his right and just title of inheritance, to make war to the destruction of Christian people — but since
he had offered peace which could not be received, now for fault of
justice he was forced to take arms — nevertheless exhorted the French
king in the bowels of Jesus Christ to render him that which was his
own, whereby effusion of Christian blood might be avoided. These
letters chiefly to this effect and purpose were written and dated from
Hampton the fifth of August. When the same were presented to the
French king, and by his council well perused, answer was made that
he would take advice[20] and provide therein as time and place should
be convenient, so the messenger licensed to depart at his pleasure.

[21]When King Henry had fully furnished his navy with men, muni-

---

[18] II.iv. 76–95.
[19] pursuivant, a king's messenger.
[20] consider the matter.
[21] II.ii. 12ff. Another very close parallel between Shakespeare and his
source.

tion, and other provisions, perceiving that his captains misliked nothing so much as delay, determined his soldiers to go a shipboard and away. But see the hap, the night before the day appointed for their departure he was credibly informed that Richard, Earl of Cambridge, brother to Edward, Duke of York, and Henry, Lord Scroop, of Masham Lord Treasurer, with Thomas Gray, a knight of Northumberland, being confederate together had conspired his death. Wherefore he caused them to be apprehended. The said Lord Scroop was in such favor with the king that he admitted him sometime to be his bedfellow, in whose fidelity the king reposed such trust that when any private or public council was in hand this lord had much in the determination of it. For he represented so great gravity in his countenance, such modesty in behaviour, and so virtuous zeal to all godliness in his talk, that whatsoever he said was thought for the most part necessary to be done and followed. Also the said Sir Thomas Gray (as some write) was of the king's Privy Council.

These prisoners, upon their examination, confessed that for a great sum of money which they had received of the French king they intended verily either to have delivered the king alive into the hands of his enemies, or else to have murdered him before he should arrive in the duchy of Normandy. When King Henry had heard all things opened, which he desired to know, he caused all his nobility to come before his presence, before whom he caused to be brought the offenders also, and to them said: "Having thus conspired the death and destruction of me, which am the head of the realm and governor of the people, it may be (no doubt) but that you likewise have sworn the confusion of all that are here with me, and also the desolation of your own country. To what horror (O Lord) for any true English heart to consider: that such an execrable iniquity should ever so betray you, as for pleasing of a foreign enemy to imbrue your hands in your blood and to ruin your own native soil. [22]Revenge herein touching my person, though I seek not, yet for the safeguard of you, my dear friends, and for due preservation of all sorts, I am by office to cause example to be showed. Get you hence therefore you poor miserable wretches to the receiving of your just reward, wherein God's majesty give you grace of His mercy and repentence of your heinous offenses." And so immediately they were had to execution.

This done, the king calling his lords again afore him, said in words few and with good grace. Of his enterprises he recounted the honor and glory, whereof they with him were to be partakers, the great confidence he had in their noble minds, which could not but remember them of the famous feats that their ancestors aforetime in France had

---

[22] II.ii. 174–178.

achieved, whereof the due report forever recorded remained yet in register. The great mercy of God that had so graciously revealed unto him the treason at hand, whereby the true hearts of those afore him made so eminent and apparent in his eye as they might be right sure he would never forget it. The doubt of danger to be nothing in respect of the certainty of honor that they should acquire, wherein himself (as they saw) in person would be lord and leader through God's grace. To whose majesty as chiefly was known the equity of his demand. Even so to His mercy did he only recommend the success of his travails. When the king had said, all the noblemen kneeled down and promised faithfully to serve him, duly to obey him, and rather to die than to suffer him to fall into the hands of his enemies.

This done, the king thought that surely all treason and conspiracy had been utterly extinct — not suspecting the fire which was newly kindled and ceased not to increase, till at length it burst out into such a flame that, catching the beams of his house and family, his line and stock was clean consumed to ashes.[23] . . .

[Holinshed pauses here for a time to report on the conspirators' earlier schemes and preparations.]

But now to proceed with King Henry's doings. After this, when the wind came about prosperous to his purpose, he caused the mariners to weigh up anchors and hoist up sails and to set forward with a thousand ships, on the vigil of Our Lady's Day, the Assumption, and took land at Caux, commonly called Chef de Caux, where the river of Seine runs into the sea, without resistance.[24] At his first coming on land he caused proclamation to be made that no person should be so hardy on pain of death either to take anything out of any church that belonged to the same or to hurt or do any violence either to priests, women, or any such as should be found without weapon or armor and not ready to make resistance. Also that no man should renew any quarrel or strife whereby any fray might arise to the disquieting of the army.

The next day after his landing, he marched toward the town of Harfleur, standing on the river of Seine between two hills; he besieged it on every side, raising bulwarks and a bastel,[25] in which the two Earls of Kent and Huntington were placed with Cornwall, Gray,

---

[23] A reference to the Wars of the Roses.

[24] III.vi. 41–47. Compare with Holinshed's more specific sources for these lines, p. 199.

[25] fortified garrison.

Steward, and Porter. On that side towards the sea the king lodged with his field, and the Duke of Clarence on the further side towards Roven. There were within the town the Lords de Touteville and Gaucourt, with divers others that valiantly defended the siege, doing what damage they could to their adversaries; and damming up the river that has his course through the town, the water rose so high betwixt the king's camp and the Duke of Clarence's camp (divided by the same river) that the Englishmen were constrained to withdraw their artillery from one side, where they had planted the same.

[26]The French king being advertised that King Henry was arrived on that coast sent in all haste the Lord Delabreth,[27] Constable of France; the seneschal of France; the Lord Bouciqualt, Marshal of France; the seneschal of Hainault; the Lord Ligny with others, which fortified towns with men, victuals, and artillery on all those frontiers towards the sea. And hearing that Harfleur was besieged, they came to the castle of Caudebecke, being not far from Harfleur, to the intent they might succor their friends which were besieged, by some policy or means. But the Englishmen, notwithstanding all the damage that the Frenchmen could work against them, forayed the country, spoiled the villages, bringing many a rich prey to the camp before Harfleur. [28]And daily was the town assaulted. For the Duke of Gloucester, to whom the order of the siege was committed, made three mines under the ground, and approaching to the walls with his engines and ordinance, would not suffer them within to take any rest.

For although they with their countermining somewhat disappointed the Englishmen and came to fight with them hand to hand within the mines, so that they went no further forward with that work, yet they were so enclosed on each side, as well by water as land, that succor they saw could none come to them. For the king [was] lying with his battle on the hillside on the one part, and the Duke of Clarence beyond the river that passes by the town and runs into Seine on the other part, besides other lords and captains that were lodged with their retinues for their most advantage. None could be suffered to go in or come forth without their license; insomuch that such powder as was sent to have been conveyed into the town by water was taken by the English ships that watched the river.

[29]The captains within the town, perceiving that they were not able long to resist the continual assaults of the Englishmen, knowing that

---

26 II.iv. 1–14.
27 His name was really D'Albret; Shakespeare follows Holinshed's variant very possibly because it was more metrical.
28 III.ii. 58ff.
29 III.iii. 1–50.

their walls were undermined and like to be overthrown (as one of their bulwarks was already, where the Earls of Huntington and Kent had set up their banners) sent an officer at arms forth about midnight after the feast day of St. Lambert, which fell that year upon the Tuesday, to beseech the King of England to appoint some certain persons as commissioners from him, with whom they within might treat about some agreement. The Duke of Clarence, to whom this messenger first declared his errand, advertised the king of their request, who granting thereto, appointed the Duke of Exeter with the Lord Fitzhugh and Sir Thomas Erpingham to understand their minds, who at the first requested a truce until Sunday next following the feast of St. Michael, in which meantime if no succor came to remove the siege, they would undertake to deliver the town into the king's hands, their lives and goods saved.

The king advertised hereof, sent them word that except they would surrender the town to him the morrow next ensuing, without any condition, they should spend no more time in talk about the matter. But yet at length through the earnest suit of the French lords, the king was contented to grant them truce until nine of the clock the next Sunday, being the two and twentieth of September; with condition, that if in the meantime no rescue came they should yield the town at that hour, with their bodies and goods to stand at the king's pleasure. And for assurance thereof, they delivered into the king's hands thirty of their best captains and merchants within that town as pledges. But others write that it was covenanted that they should deliver only twelve pledges, and that if the siege were not raised by the French king's power within six days next following, then should they deliver the town into the King of England's hands, and thirty of the chiefest personages within the same to stand for life or death at his will and pleasure. And as for the residue of the men of war and townsmen, they should depart whither they would, without carrying forth either armor, weapon, or goods.

The king nevertheless was after[ward] content to grant a respite upon certain conditions: that the captains within might have time[30] to send to the French king for succor (as before you have heard) lest he, intending greater exploits, might lose time in such small matters. When this composition was agreed upon, the Lord Baqueville was sent unto the French king to declare in what point the town stood. To whom the Dauphin answered that the king's power was not yet assembled in such number as was convenient to raise so great a siege. This answer being brought unto the captains within the town, they rendered it up to the King of England, after that the third day was

---

[30] i.e., a fixed, limited time.

expired, which was on the day of St. Maurice, being the seven and thirtieth day after the siege was first laid. [31]The soldiers were ransomed and the town sacked, to the great gain of the Englishmen.

Some writing of this yielding up of Harfleur do in like sort make mention of the distress whereto the people, then expelled out of their habitations, were driven: insomuch as parents with their children, young maids and old folk went out of the town gates with heavy hearts (God wot) as put to their present shifts to seek them a new abode. Besides that, King Henry caused proclamation to be made within his own dominions of England, that whosoever (either handicraftsman, merchantman, gentleman, or plowman) would inhabit in Harfleur, should have his dwelling given him *gratis*, and his heirs after him also enjoy the like grace and favor. Insomuch that great multitudes flocked to the sea coasts, waiting wind and weather for their transportage into Harfleur, where being arrived wonderful it is to tell within how short a time the town was peopled. . . .

[32]All this done, the king ordained captain to the town his uncle the Duke of Exeter, who established his lieutenant there, one Sir John Fastolf, with fifteen hundred men, or (as some have) two thousand and thirty six knights, whereof the Baron of Carew and Sir Hugh Lutterell were two councillors. And because many of his nobles whilst this siege lay before Harfleur fell sick of the flix[33] and other diseases — divers also died, amongst whom the Earl of Stafford, the Bishop of Norwich, the Lords Molins and Burnell were four (beside others) — the king licensed his brother, the Duke of Clarence, John, Earl Marshal, and John, Earl of Arundel, being infected with that disease, to return into England.

King Henry, after the winning of Harfleur, determined to have proceeded further in the winning of other towns and fortresses; but because the dead time of the winter approached it was determined by advice of his council that he should in all convenient speed set forward and march through the country towards Calais by land, lest his return as then homewards should of slanderous tongues be named a running away. And yet that journey was adjudged perilous by reason that the number of his people was much minished by the flix and other fevers, which sore vexed and brought to death above fifteen hundred persons of the army. And this was the cause that his return was the sooner appointed and concluded.

But before his departing thence he entered into the town of Harfleur and went to the church of St. Martin and there offered. All the men

---

[31] I.Prologue. 6–8.
[32] III.iii. 51ff.
[33] obs. flux: dysentery.

of war which had not paid their ransoms, he swore them on the holy evangelists to yield themselves prisoners at Calais by the feast of St. Martin in November next. There were two strong towers standing on the haven side at Harfleur, which looking for aid did not yield till ten days after the town was rendered. When the king had repaired the walls, bulwarks and rampiers[34] about the town and furnished it with victuals and artillery, he removed from Harfleur toward Pontoise, intending to pass the river of Somme with his army before the bridges were either withdrawn or broken. Such victuals and other necessaries as were to be carried with the army he appointed to be laid on horses, leaving the carts and wagons behind for less incombre.[35]

The French king, hearing that the town of Harfleur was gotten, and that the King of England was marching forward into the bowels of the realm of France, sent out proclamations and assembled people on every side, committing the whole charge of his army to his son, the Dauphin, and Duke of Aquitaine, who incontinently[36] caused the bridges to be broken and the passages to be kept. Also they caused all the corn and victuals to be conveyed away, or destroyed in all places where it was conjectured that the Englishmen would pass. The King of England nothing dismayed herewith, kept his journey in spite of his enemies, constraining them within divers towns and holds to furnish him with victuals. . . .

[*King Henry and his army then approached the Somme River, but for a while determined French resistance prevented their crossing. Finally after a series of fierce and bloody battles the English army*]

found a shallow, between Corbie and Péronne, which never was espied before, at which he with his army and carriages the night ensuing passed the water of Somme without let or danger; and therewith determined to make haste toward Calais and not to seek for battle except he were thereto constrained, because that his army by sickness was sore diminished, insomuch that he had but only two thousand horsemen and thirteen thousand archers, billmen,[37] and of all sorts of other footmen.

The Englishmen were brought into some distress in this journey, by reason of their victuals in manner spent and no hope to get more. For the enemies had destroyed all the corn before they came. Rest could they none take, for their enemies with alarms did ever so infest

---

[34] barricades, ramparts.
[35] encumbrance.
[36] immediately.
[37] bill: halberd, pike.

them. Daily it rained and nightly it froze. Of fuel there was great scarcity, of fluxes[38] plenty. Money enough, but wares for their relief to bestow it on had they none. [39]Yet in this great necessity the poor people of the country were not spoiled, nor anything taken of them without payment, nor any outrage or offense done by the Englishmen except one, which was that a soldier took a pyx out of a church, for which he was apprehended; and the king not once removed[40] till the box was restored and the offender strangled. The people of the counties thereabout, hearing of such zeal in him to the maintenance of justice, ministered to his army victuals and other necessaries, although by open proclamation so to do they were prohibited.

[41]The French king being at Roven, and hearing that King Henry was passed the river of Somme, was much displeased therewith, and assembling his council to the number of five and thirty asked their advice what was to be done. There was amongst these five and thirty his son, the Dauphin, calling himself King of Sicily, the Dukes of Berry and Brittany, the Earl of Ponthieu, the king's youngest son, and other high estates. At length thirty of them agreed that the Englishmen should not depart unfought withal, and five were of a contrary opinion, but the greater number ruled the matter. And so Montjoy, King at Arms, was sent to the King of England to defy him as the enemy of France and to tell him that he should shortly have battle. [42]King Henry advisedly answered: "Mine intent is to do as it pleases God. I will not seek your master at this time; but if he or his seek me, I will meet with them, God willing. If any of your nation attempt once to stop me in my journey now towards Calais, at their jeopardy be it; and yet I wish not any of you so unadvised as to be the occasion that I dye your tawny ground with your red blood."

When he had thus answered the herald he gave him a princely reward and license to depart. Upon whose return with this answer, it was incontinently on the French side proclaimed that all men of war should resort to the constable to fight with the King of England. Whereupon all men apt for armor and desirous of honor drew them toward the field. [43]The Dauphin sore desired to have been at the battle, but he was prohibited by his father. Likewise Philip, Earl of Charolais, would gladly have been there, if his father the Duke of Burgundy would have suffered him. Many of his men stole away and

[38] dysentery.
[39] III.vi. 41–47.
[40] did not move on.
[41] III.v. 1ff; III.vi. 121–145.
[42] III.vi. 148–176.
[43] III.v. 64–66.

went to the Frenchmen. [44]The King of England hearing that the Frenchmen approached and that there was another river for him to pass with his army by a bridge, and doubting lest if the same bridge should be broken it would be greatly to his hindrance, appointed certain captains with their bands to go thither with all speed before him and to take possession thereof, and so to keep it till his coming thither.

[45]Those that were sent, finding the Frenchmen busy to break down their bridge, assailed them so vigorously that they discomfited them, and took and slew them; and so the bridge was preserved till the king came and passed the river by the same with his whole army. This was on the two and twentieth day of October. The Duke of York that led the vanguard (after the army was passed the river) mounted up to the height of an hill with his people and sent out scouts to discover the country, the which upon their return advertised him that a great army of Frenchmen was at hand, approaching towards them. The duke declared to the king what he had heard, and the king thereupon without all fear or trouble of mind caused the battle, which he led himself, to stay, and incontinently rode forth to view his adversaries; and that done returned to his people, and with cheerful countenance caused them to be put in order of battle, assigning to every captain such room and place as he thought convenient; and so kept them still in that order till night was come, and then determined to seek a place to encamp and lodge his army in for that night.

There was not one amongst them that knew any certain place whither to go in that unknown country. But by chance they happened upon a beaten way, white in sight; by the which they were brought unto a little village where they were refreshed with meat and drink somewhat more plenteously than they had been divers days before. [46]Order was taken by commandment from the king, after the army was first set in battle array, that no noise or clamor should be made in the host; so that in marching forth to this village every man kept himself quiet. But at their coming into the village fires were made to give light on every side, as there likewise were in the French host which was encamped not past two hundred and fifty paces distant from the English. The chief leaders of the French host were these: the Constable of France, the Marshal, the Admiral, the Lord Rambures, Master of the Crossbows, and others of the French nobility which came and pitched down their standards and banners in the county of St. Pol, within the territory of Agincourt, having in their

[44] III.vi. 1–15.
[45] III.vi. 86–101.
[46] IV.i. 64–84.

army (as some write) to the number of three-score thousand horsemen,[47] besides footmen, wagoners and others.

[48]They were lodged even in the way by which the Englishmen must needs pass towards Calais, and all that night after their coming thither made great cheer, and were very merry, pleasant, and full of game. [49]The Englishmen also for their parts were of good comfort, and nothing abashed of the matter, and yet they were both hungry, weary, sore travelled, and vexed with many cold diseases. Howbeit reconciling themselves with God by housel[50] and shrift, requiring assistance at His hands that is the only giver of victory, they determined rather to die than to yield or flee. [51]The day following was the five and twentieth of October in the year 1415, being then Friday, and the feast of Crispin and Crispianus, a day fair and fortunate to the English, but most sorrowful and unlucky to the French.

In the morning the French captains made three battles.[52] In the vaward[53] were eight thousand helms of knights and squires, four thousand archers, and fifteen hundred crossbows which were guided by the Lord Delabreth, Constable of France, having with him the Dukes of Orleans and Bourbon, the Earls of Eu and Richemont, the Marshal Bouciqualt, and the Master of the Crossbows, the Lord Dampier, Admiral of France, and other captains. The Earl of Vendôme with sixteen hundred men of arms were ordered for a wing to that battle. And the other wing was guided by Sir Guichard Dauphine, Sir Clugnet of Brabant, and Sir Lewis Bourdon, with eight hundred men of arms, of elect chosen persons. And to break the shot of the Englishmen, were appointed Sir Guillaume de Saveuses, with Hector and Philip, his brethren, Ferry de Maillie and Allen de Gaspanes with other eight hundred of arms.

In the middle ward were assigned as many persons, or more, as were in the foremost battle, and the charge thereof was committed to the Dukes of Bar and Alençon, the Earls of Nevers, Vaudemont, Blamont, Salinges, Grandpré, and of Roussi. And in the rearward were all the other men of arms, guided by the Earls of Marle, Dammartin, Fauconberg, and the Lord of Lourri, Captain of Arde, who had with him the men of the frontiers of Boulonnais. Thus the Frenchmen, being ordered under their standards and banners, made a great

---

[47] IV.iii. 3.

[48] III.vii. 1ff.

[49] Contrast the simplicity of these two sentences with Shakespeare's vaulting lines: IV.i. 1–322.

[50] communion.

[51] IV.iii. 40–48.

[52] battle formations.

[53] forward echelon, vanguard.

show. For surely they were esteemed in number six times as many or more than was the whole company of the Englishmen, with wagoners, pages and all. They rested themselves, waiting for the bloody blast of the terrible trumpet, till the hour between nine and ten of the clock of the same day, during which season the constable made unto the captains and other men of war a pithy oration, exhorting and encouraging them to do valiantly, with many comfortable words and sensible reasons. King Henry also like a leader and not as one led, like a sovereign and not an inferior, perceiving a plot of ground very strong and meet for his purpose, which on the back half was fenced with the village wherein he had lodged the night before, and on both sides defended with hedges and bushes, thought good there to embattle his host; and so ordered his men in the same place, as he saw occasion and as stood for his most advantage.

First he sent privily two hundred archers into a low meadow, which was near to the vanguard of his enemies — but separated with a great ditch — commanding them there to keep themselves close till they had a token to them given to let drive at their adversaries: besides this, he appointed a vaward, of the which he made captain Edward, Duke of York, who of an haughty courage had desired that office; and with him were the Lords Beaumont, Willoughby, and Fanhope; and this battle was all of archers. The middle ward was governed by the king himself, with his brother the Duke of Gloucester, and the Earls of Marshal, Oxford and Suffolk, in the which were all the strong billmen. The Duke of Exeter, uncle to the king, led the rearward, which was mixed both with billmen and archers. The horsemen like wings went on every side of the battle.

Thus the king, having ordered his battles, feared not the puissance of his enemies, but yet to provide[54] that they should not with the multitude of horsemen break the order of his archers in whom the force of his army consisted.

For in those days the yeomen had their limbs at liberty, since their hose were then fastened with one point and their jackets long and easy to shoot in; so that they might draw bows of great strength and shoot arrows of a yard long; beside the head he caused stakes bound with iron, sharp at both ends, of the length of five or six foot, to be pitched before the archers and of each side the footmen, like an hedge, to the intent that if the barded[55] horses ran rashly upon them they might shortly be gored and destroyed. Certain persons also were appointed to remove the stakes, as by the moving of the archers occasion and time should require, so that the footmen were hedged about with

---

[54] made provision.
[55] armored, their breasts and flanks covered with metal or leather.

stakes and the horsemen stood like a bulwark between them and their enemies, without the stakes. This device of fortifying an army was at this time first invented. But since that time they have devised cal-trops,[56] harrows, and other new engines against the force of horsemen; so that if the enemies run hastily upon the same, either are their horses wounded with the stakes or their feet hurt with the other engines, so as thereby the beasts are gored or else made unable to maintain their course.

King Henry, by reason of his small number of people to fill up his battles, placed his vanguard so on the right hand of the main battle, which himself led, that the distance betwixt them might scarce be perceived; and so in like case was the rearward joined on the left hand, that the one might the more readily succor another in time of need. When he had thus ordered his battles he left a small company to keep his camp and carriage, which remained still in the village. And then calling his captains and soldiers about him he made to them a right grave oration, moving them to play the men, whereby to obtain a glorious victory, as there was hope certain they should, the rather if they would but remember the just cause for which they fought and whom they should encounter, such faint-hearted people as their an-cestors had so often overcome. To conclude, many words of courage he uttered to stir them to do manfully, assuring them that England should never be charged with his ransom, nor any Frenchman triumph over him as a captive; for either by famous death or glorious victory would he (by God's grace) win honor and fame.

[57]It is said that as he heard one of [his] host utter his wish to another thus: "I would to God there were with us now so many good soldiers as are at this hour within England!" The king answered: "I would not wish a man more here than I have. We are indeed in comparison to the enemy's but a few, but, if God of His clemency do favor us and our just cause (as I trust He will) we shall speed well enough. But let no man ascribe victory to our own strength and might, but only to God's assistance, to whom I have no doubt we shall worthily have cause to give thanks therefore. And if so be that for our offenses' sakes we shall be delivered into the hands of our enemies, the less number we be, the less damage shall the realm of England sustain. But if we should fight in trust of multitude of men and so get the victory (our minds being prone to pride) we should thereupon peradventure ascribe the victory not so much to the gift of God as to our own puissance, and thereby provoke His high indignation and displeasure against us. And if the enemy get the upper hand, then should our realm and

---

[56] snares.
[57] IV.iii. 16–78.

country suffer more damage and stand in further danger. But be you of good comfort and show yourselves valiant. God and our just quarrel shall defend us and deliver these our proud adversaries with all the multitude of them which you see (or at the least the most of them) into our hands." Whilst the king was yet thus in speech, either army so maligned the other, being as then in open sight, that every man cried, "Forward, forward!" The Dukes of Clarence, Gloucester, and York were of the same opinion, yet the king stayed a while, lest any jeopardy were not foreseen or any hazard not prevented. [58]The Frenchmen in the meanwhile, as though they had been sure of victory, made great triumph; for the captains had determined before how to divide the spoil, and the soldiers the night before had played the Englishmen at dice. The noblemen had devised a chariot, wherein they might triumphantly convey the king captive to the city of Paris, crying to their soldiers, "Haste you to the spoil! Glory and honor!" Little weening (God wot) how soon their brags should be blown away.

[59]Here we may not forget how the French thus in their jollity sent an herald to King Henry to inquire what ransom he would offer. Whereunto he answered that within two or three hours he hoped it would so happen that the Frenchmen should be glad to common[60] rather with the Englishmen for their ransoms than the English to take thought for their deliverance; promising for his own part that his dead carcass should rather be a prize to the Frenchmen than that his living body should pay any ransom. When the messenger was come back to the French host, the men of war put on their helmets and caused their trumpets to blow to the battle. They thought themselves so sure of victory that divers of the noblemen made such haste towards the battle that they left many of their servants and men of war behind them, and some of them would not once stay for their standards: [61]as amongst others, the Duke of Brabant, when his standard was not come, caused a banner to be taken from a trumpet and fastened to a spear, the which he commanded to be borne before him instead of his standard.

[62]But when both these armies coming within danger either of other set in full order of battle on both sides, they stood still at the first, beholding either other's demeanor, being not distant in sunder[63] past three bow shots. And when they had on both parts thus stayed

---

[58] IV.ii. 1ff; IV.Prologue. 18–20.

[59] III.vi. 133–137; IV.iii. 79–125.

[60] confer.

[61] IV.ii. 60–62.

[62] The next four paragraphs, describing the Battle of Agincourt, form one of the most vivid and exciting passages in Holinshed.

[63] separated from one another.

a good while without doing anything (except that certain of the French horsemen advancing forwards, betwixt both the hosts, were by the English archers constrained to return back) advice was taken amongst the Englishmen what was best for them to do. Thereupon, all things considered, it was determined that since the Frenchmen would not come forward, the king with his army embattled (as you have heard) should march towards them, and so leaving their truss and baggage in the village where they lodged the night before, only with their weapons, armor, and stakes prepared for the purpose, as you have heard.

These made somewhat forward, before whom there went an old knight, Sir Thomas Erpingham (a man of great experience in the war) with a warder in his hand; and when he cast up his warder all the army shouted; but that was a sign to the archers in the meadow which therewith shot wholly altogether at the vaward of the Frenchmen; who when they perceived the archers in the meadow and saw they could not come at them for a ditch that was betwixt them, with all haste set upon the forward of King Henry; but ere they could join, the archers in the forefront and the archers on that side which stood in the meadow so wounded the footmen, galled the horses, and cumbered[64] the men of arms, that the footmen[65] durst not go forward; the horsemen ran together upon thumps without order; some overthrew such as were next to them, and the horses overthrew their masters. And so at the first joining the Frenchmen were foully discomforted, and the Englishmen highly encouraged.

When the French vaward was thus brought to confusion, the English archers cast away their bows and took into their hands axes, malls, swords, bills, and other hand-weapons, and with the same slew the Frenchmen until they came to the middleward. Then approached the king, and so encouraged his people that shortly the second battle of the Frenchmen was overthrown and dispersed, not without great slaughter of men. Howbeit, divers were relieved by their valets and conveyed out of the field. The Englishmen were so busied in fighting and taking of the prisoners at hand that they followed not in chase of their enemies, nor would once break out of their array of battle. Yet sundry of the Frenchmen strongly withstood the fierceness of the English, when they came to hand strokes, so that the fight sometime was doubtful and perilous. Yet as part of the French horsemen set their course to have entered upon the king's battle, with the stakes overthrown they were either taken or slain. Thus this battle continued three long hours.

---

[64] overwhelmed.
[65] foot troops.

[66]The king that day showed himself a valiant knight, albeit almost felled by the Duke of Alençon; yet with plain strength he slew two of the duke's company and felled the duke himself, whom, when he would have yielded, the king's guard (contrary to his mind) slew out of hand. In conclusion, the king minding to make an end of that day's journey caused his horsemen to fetch a compass[67] about and to join with him against the rearward of the Frenchmen, in the which was the greatest number of people. When the Frenchmen perceived his intent they were suddenly amazed and ran away like sheep, without order or array. Which when the king perceived, he encouraged his men and followed so quickly upon the enemies that they ran hither and thither, casting away their armor. Many on their knees desired to have their lives saved.

[68]In the mean season, while the battle thus continued and that the Englishmen had taken a great number of prisoners, certain Frenchmen on horseback, whereof were Captains Robinet of Borneville, Rifflart of Clamas, Isambard of Agincourt, and other men of arms to the number of six hundred horsemen, which were the first that fled, hearing that the English tents and pavilions were a good way distant from the army without any sufficient guard to defend the same, either upon a covetous meaning to gain by the spoil, or upon a desire to be revenged, entered upon the king's camp and there spoiled the hails,[69] robbed the tents, broke up chests and carried away caskets, and slew such servants as they found to make any resistance. For which treason and haskardy[70] in thus leaving their camp at the very point of fight, for winning of spoil where [were] none to defend it, very many were after committed to prison and had lost their lives if the Dauphin had longer lived.

[71]But when the outcry of the lackies and boys, which ran away for fear of the Frenchmen thus spoiling the camp, came to the king's ears, he doubting lest his enemies should gather together again and begin a new field — and mistrusting further that the prisoners would be an aid to his enemies or the very enemies to their takers in deed if they were suffered to live — contrary to his accustomed gentleness, commanded by sound of trumpet that every man (upon pain of death) should incontinently slay his prisoner. When this dolorous decree

---

66 IV.vii. 160–166. A situation which Shakespeare ties skillfully to the Fluellen-Williams subplot.
67 turn.
68 IV.vii. 1–8.
69 variant spelling of hales: pavilions.
70 baseness.
71 IV.vi. 35ff; IV.vii. 8–10.

and pitiful proclamation was pronounced, pity it was to see how some Frenchmen were suddenly sticked with daggers, some were brained with poleaxes, some slain with malls, others had their throats cut and some their bellies panched,[72] so that in effect, having respect to their great number, few prisoners were saved.

[73]When this lamentable slaughter was ended, the Englishmen disposed themselves in order of battle, ready to abide a new field and also to invade and newly set on their enemies; with great force they assailed the Earls of Marle and Faulconberg and the Lords of Lourri and Thine, with six hundred men of arms who had all that day kept together, but [were] now slain and beaten down out of hand.

[74]Some write that the king perceiving his enemies in one part to assemble together, as though they meant to give a new battle for preservation of the prisoners, sent to them an herald commanding them either to depart out of his sight or else to come forward at once and give battle: promising herewith that if they did offer to fight again, not only those prisoners which his people already had taken, but also so many of them as in this new conflict which they thus attempted should fall into his hands, should die the death without redemption.[75]

The Frenchmen fearing the sentence of so terrible a decree, without further delay parted out of the field. [76]And so about four of the clock in the afternoon, the king when he saw no appearance of enemies caused the retreat to be blown; and gathering his army together gave thanks to almighty God for so happy a victory, causing his prelates and chaplains to sing this psalm: "*In exitu Israel de Aegypto;*[77] and commanded every man to kneel down on the ground at this verse: *Non nobis Domine, non nobis, sed nomini tuo da gloriam.*[78] Which done, he caused *Te Deum* with certain anthems to be sung, giving laud and praise to God, without boasting of his own force or any human power. That night he and his people took rest and refreshed themselves with such victuals as they found in the French camp, but lodged in the same village where he lay the night before.

---

[72] stabbed.

[73] Apparently the suggestion for IV.vi. 35–36, in which case it typifies Shakespeare's custom of presenting battle scenes in unchronological fragments.

[74] IV.vii. 58–68.

[75] Shakespeare omits this glimpse into the brutality of Henry.

[76] IV.viii. 111–129.

[77] Psalm cxiv. In the Purgatory section of Dante's *Divine Comedy*, the joyous souls en route to the mountain of purification are chanting this same psalm.

[78] Not for us, O Lord, not for us, but for the glory of Thy name.

[79]In the morning Montjoy, King at Arms, and four other French heralds came to the king to know the number of prisoners and to desire burial for the dead. Before he made them answer (to understand what they would say) he demanded of them why they made to him that request, considering that he knew not whether the victory was his or theirs. When Montjoy by true and just confession had cleared that doubt to the high praise of the king, he desired of Montjoy to understand the name of the castle near adjoining. When they had told him that it was called Agincourt, he said, "Then shall this conflict be called the battle of Agincourt." He feasted the French officers of arms that day and granted them their request, which busily sought through the field for such as were slain. But the Englishmen suffered them not to go alone, for they searched with them and found many hurt but not in jeopardy of their lives, whom they took prisoners and brought them to their tents. When the King of England had well refreshed himself and his soldiers, that had taken the spoil of such as were slain, [80]he with his prisoners in good order returned to his town of Calais.

When tidings of this great victory was blown into England, solemn processions and other praisings to almighty God with bonfires and joyful triumphs were ordained in every town, city, and borough; and the mayor and citizens of London went the morrow after the day of St. Simon and Jude from the church of St. Paul to the church of St. Peter at Westminster in devout manner, rendering to God hearty thanks for such fortunate luck sent to the king and his army. The same Sunday that the king removed from the camp at Agincourt towards Calais, divers Frenchmen came to the field to view again the dead bodies; and the peasants of the country spoiled the carcasses of all such apparel and other things as the Englishmen had left — who took nothing but gold and silver, jewels, rich apparel and costly armor. But the plowmen and peasants left nothing behind, neither shirt nor clout, so that the bodies lay stark naked until Wednesday. On the which day divers of the noblemen were conveyed into their countries, and the remnants were by Philip, Earl Charolois (sore lamenting the chance, and moved with pity) at his costs and charges buried in a square plot of ground of fifteen hundred yards; in the which he caused to be made three pits, wherein were buried by account five thousand and eight hundred persons, besides them that were carried away by their friends and servants, and others which being wounded died in hospitals and other places.

---

[79] IV.vii. 69–123.
[80] IV.viii. 130.

After this their dolorous journey and pitiful slaughter, divers clerks of Paris made many a lamentable verse, complaining that the king reigned by will, and that councillors were partial; affirming that the noblemen fled against nature and that the commons were destroyed by their prodigality; declaring also that the clergy were dumb and durst not say the truth; and that the humble commons duly obeyed and yet ever suffered punishment — for which cause by divine persecution the less number vanquished the greater. Wherefore they concluded that all things went out of order, and yet was there no man that studied to bring the unruly to frame. It was no marvel, though, this battle was lamentable to the French nation, for in it were taken and slain the flower of all the nobility of France.

[81]There were taken prisoners Charles, Duke of Orleans, nephew to the French king, John, Duke of Bourbon, the Lord Bouciqualt, one of the Marshals of France (he after died in England), with a number of other lords, knights, and squires, at the least fifteen hundred, besides the common people. There were slain in all of the French part to the number of ten thousand men, whereof were princes and noblemen bearing banners one hundred twenty and six; to these of knights, squires, and gentlemen so many as made up the number of eight thousand and four hundred (of the which five hundred were dubbed knights the night before the battle); so as of the meaner sort, not past sixteen hundred. Amongst those of the nobility that were slain, these were the chiefest: Charles, Lord Delabreth, High Constable of France, Jacques of Chatillon, Lord of Dampier, Admiral of France, the Lord Rambures, Master of the Crossbows, Sir Guichard Dauphin, Great Master of France, John, Duke of Alençon, Anthony, Duke of Brabant, brother to the Duke of Burgundy, Edward, Duke of Bar, the Earl of Nevers, another brother to the Duke of Burgundy, with the Earls of Marle, Vaudemont, Beaumont, Grandpré, Roussi, Fauconberg, Foix, and Lestrale, besides a great number of lords and barons of name.

Of Englishmen there died at this battle Edward, Duke of York, the Earl of Suffolk, Sir Richard Ketly, and Davy Gam, esquire, and of all others not above five and twenty persons, as some do report; but other writers of greater credit affirm that there were slain above five or six hundred persons. Titus Livius says that there were slain of Englishmen, besides the Duke of York and the Earl of Suffolk, an hundred persons at the first encounter. The Duke of Gloucester, the king's brother, was sore wounded about the hips and borne down to the ground, so that he fell backwards, with his feet towards his enemies — whom the king bestrid and like a brother valiantly rescued

---

[81] IV.viii. 78–111. Another passage closely paralled by Shakespeare.

from his enemies, and so saving his life caused him to be conveyed out of the fight into a place of more safety. . . .

[82]After that the King of England had refreshed himself and his people at Calais, and that such prisoners as he had left at Harfleur (as you have heard) were come to Calais unto him, the sixth day of November he with all his prisoners took shipping and the same day landed at Dover, having with him the dead bodies of the Duke of York and the Earl of Suffolk; and caused the duke to be buried at his college of Fodringhey and the earl at New Elm. In this passage the seas were so rough and troublous that two ships belonging to Sir John Cornwall, Lord Fanhope, were driven into Zealand; howbeit, nothing was lost, nor any person perished.

[83]The mayor of London and the aldermen, apparelled in orient grained scarlet, and four hundred commoners clad in beautiful murry, well mounted and trimly horsed, with rich collars and great chains, met the king on Blackheath, rejoicing at his return. And the clergy of London with rich crosses, sumptuous copes, and massy censers received him at St. Thomas of Waterings with solemn procession. . . .

[*Henry V bore his triumph with becoming modesty and settled down once more in England. Scottish invasions and Sir John Oldcastle troubled the peace of the kingdom somewhat, but affairs were stable enough in 1417 for Henry to return to France with another army. This second campaign lasted for almost four years and was a decisive victory. In 1420 the French expressed willingness to sign a peace treaty at Troyes.*]

[1420] Now was the French king and the queen with their daughter Katherine at Troyes in Champagne governed and ordered by them, which so much favored the Duke of Burgundy[84] that they would not for any earthly good once hinder or pull back one jot of such articles as the same duke should seek to prefer. And therefore, what needs many words: a truce tripartite was accorded between the two kings and the duke and their countries, and order taken that the King of England should send in the company of the Duke of Burgundy his ambassadors unto Troyes in Champagne, sufficiently authorized to treat and conclude of so great matter. The King of England, being in good hope that all his affairs should take [as] good success as he could wish or desire, sent to the Duke of Burgundy his uncle, the Duke of Exeter,

---

[82] V.Prologue. 6–14.

[83] V.Prologue. 24–28.

[84] This duke was Philip the Good, who at the time of Agincourt (1415) was Count of Charolois and was cited (III.v. 45) by Charles VI.

the Earl of Salisbury, the Bishop of Ely, the Lord Fanhope, the Lord Fitzhugh, Sir John Robsert, and Sir Philip Hall, with divers doctors, to the number of five hundred horse, which in the company of the Duke of Burgundy came to the city of Troyes the eleventh of March. The king, the queen and the Lady Katherine them received and heartily welcomed, showing great signs and tokens of love and amity.

After a few days they fell to council, in which at length it was concluded that King Henry of England should come to Troyes and marry the Lady Katherine; and the king her father after his death should make him heir of his realm, crown and dignity. It was also agreed that King Henry during his father-in-law's life should in his stead have the whole government of the realm of France, as regent thereof, with many other covenants and articles, as after shall appear. To the performance whereof, it was accorded that all the nobles and estates of the realm of France, as well spiritual as temporal, and also the cities and commonalties, citizens and burgesses of towns, that were obeisant at that time to the French king should take a corporal oath. These articles were not at the first in all points brought to a perfect conclusion. But after the effect and meaning of them was agreed upon by the commissioners, the Englishmen departed towards the king their master and left Sir John Robsert behind to give his attendance on the Lady Katherine.

King Henry being informed by them of that which they had done was well content with the agreement, and with all diligence prepared to go unto Troyes; and thereupon having all things in readiness, he being accompanied with his brethren the Dukes of Clarence and Gloucester, the Earls of Warwick, Salisbury, Huntington, Eu, Tankervile and Longvile, and fifteen thousand men of war, went from Rhone to Pontoise; and departing from thence the eighth day of May came to Saint Denis, two leagues from Paris, and after to Pontcharenton where he left a strong garrison of men with Sir William Gascoigne to keep the passage;[85] and so then entering into Brie he took by the way a castle which was kept against him, causing them that so kept it some to be hanged and the residue to be led forth with him as prisoners. And after this, keeping on his journey by Provins and Nogent, at length he came to Troyes.

The Duke of Burgundy, accompanied with many noblemen, received him two leagues without the town and conveyed him to his lodging. All his army was lodged in small villages thereabout. [86]And after that he had reposed himself a little he went to visit the French king, the queen, and the Lady Katherine, whom he found in St. Peter's church,

---

[85] A view of Henry V somewhat different from Shakespeare's.
[86] V.ii. 1–356.

where was a very joyous meeting betwixt them (and this was on the twentieth day of May); and there the King of England and the Lady Katherine were affianced. After this, the two kings and their Councils assembled together divers days, wherein the first concluded agreement was in divers points altered and brought to a certainty, according to the effect abovementioned. [87]When this great matter was finished, the kings swore for their parts to observe all the covenants of this league and agreement[88]. . . .

[*Character of Henry* V]

Holinshed

This Henry was a king of life without spot, a prince whom all men loved, and of none disdained; a captain against whom fortune never frowned nor mischance once spurned; whose people him so severe a justicer both loved and obeyed (and so humane withal) that he left no offense unpunished nor friendship unrewarded; a terror to rebels and suppressor of sedition, his virtues notable, his qualities most praiseworthy.

In strength and nimbleness of body from his youth few to him comparable, for in wrestling, leaping, and running no man well able to compare. In casting of great iron bars and heavy stones he excelled commonly all men, never shrinking at cold nor slothful for heat; and when he most labored, his head commonly uncovered; [he wore] no more weary of harness than a light cloak, very valiantly abiding at needs both hunger and thirst; so manful of mind as never seen to quench at a wound or to smart at the pain; nor to turn his nose from evil savour, nor close his eyes from smoke or dust; no man more moderate in eating and drinking, with diet not delicate but rather more meet for men of war than for princes or tender stomachs. Every honest person was permitted to come to him, sitting at meal, where either secretly or openly to declare his mind. High and weighty causes as well between men of war and others he would gladly hear, and either determined them himself or else for end committed them to others. He slept very little, but that very soundly, insomuch that when his soldiers sang at nights or minstrels played he then slept

---

[87] V.ii. 357–384.

[88] Of particular interest among the thirty-three "articles and appointments of peace between the realms of England and France" is the twenty-fifth, which requires Charles VI to do as follows: "Also that our said father, during his life shall name, call, and write us in French in this manner: *Notre très cher fils Henri, Roi d'Angleterre, Héritier de France.* And in Latin in this manner: *Praeclarissimus filius noster Henricus, Rex Angliae et Haeres Franciae.*" See V.ii. 363–370.

ҳstest; of courage invincible, of purpose immutable, so wisehardy
ays as fear was banished from him; at every alarum he first in armor
foremost in ordering. In time of war such was his providence,
ity and hap, as he had true intelligence not only what his enemies
it what they said and intended; of his devices and purposes, few
the thing was at the point to be done should be made privy.

ιe had such knowledge in ordering and guiding an army, with such
ҳ gift to encourage his people, that the Frenchmen had constant
opinion he could never be vanquished in battle. Such wit, such prudence, and such policy withal, that he never enterprised any thing
before he had fully debated and forecast all the main chances that
might happen, which done with all diligence and courage he set his
purpose forward. What policy he had in finding present remedies for
sudden mischiefs, and what engines in saving himself and his people
in sharp distresses! Were it not that by his acts they did plainly appear, hard were it by words to make them credible. Wantonness of
life and thirst in avarice had he quite quenched in him; virtues in
deed in such an estate of sovereignty, youth, and power, as very rare,
so right commendable in the highest degree. So staid of mind and
countenance beside, that [he was] never jolly or triumphant for victory
nor sad or damped for loss or misfortune. For bountifulness and
liberality no man more free, gentle, and frank, in bestowing rewards
to all persons, according to their deserts. For his saying was that he
never desired money to keep but to give and spend.

Although that story [history] properly serves not for theme of praise
or dispraise, yet what in brevity may well be remembered in truth
would not be forgotten by sloth — were it but only to remain as a
spectable for magnanimity to have always in eye and for encouragement to nobles in honorable enterprises. Known be it therefore, of
person and form was this prince rightly representing his heroical effects:
of stature and proportion tall and manly, rather lean than gross, somewhat long necked and black haired, of countenance amiable; eloquent
and grave was his speech and of great grace and power to persuade.
For conclusion, a majesty was he that both lived and died, a pattern
in princehood, a lodestar in honor, and mirror of magnificence. The
more highly exalted in his life, the more deeply lamented at his death,
and famous to the world always.[89]

---

[89] Note the many similarities between Holinshed's character of Henry V and
Shakespeare's. Holinshed's assessment, it must be noted, is copied almost
verbatim from Hall.

ANONYMOUS, 1598

The Famous Victories of Henry the Fifth*

<hr>

CHARACTERS

English

KING HENRY IV
HENRY V, THE YOUNG PRINCE
LORD CHIEF JUSTICE
ARCHBISHOP OF CANTERBURY
EARL OF EXETER
LORD OF OXFORD
DUKE OF YORK
LORD MAYOR OF LONDON
JOCKEY (SIR JOHN OLDCASTLE)
DERICK
THIEF
NED
TOM
JOHN COBBLER
ROBIN PEWTERER
LAWRENCE COSTERMONGER
JOHN COBBLER'S WIFE
TWO RECEIVERS, CLERK,
  SECRETARY, CAPTAIN, SOLDIER,
  JAILER, PORTER, VINTNER'S BOY.

French

KING
PRINCE DAUPHIN
DUKE OF BURGUNDY
ARCHBISHOP OF BOURGES
LORD HIGH CONSTABLE
LADY KATHERINE
SECRETARY, CAPTAIN, SOLDIERS,
  DRUMMER, MESSENGER,
  HERALD.

Scene I.

Enter the young prince, Ned, and Tom.

HENRY. ¹Come away, Ned and Tom.

<hr>

* text modernized. *Ye* and *ay*, while modernized throughout the Holinshed
selections as *you* and *aye*, are retained as *ye* and *ay* here to help connote the
earthier diction of this play.
¹ H.IV. One, I.ii. 101–217; II.i,ii.

BOTH.   Here, my lord.

HENRY.   Come away, my lads.

Tell me, sirs, how much gold have you got?

NED.   Faith, my lord, I have got five hundred pound.

HENRY.   But tell me, Tom, how much hast thou got?

TOM.   Faith, my lord, some four hundred pound.

HENRY.   Four hundred pounds, bravely spoken, lads.

But tell me, sirs, think you not that it was a villainous part of
    me to rob my father's receivers?   10

NED.   Why no, my lord, it was but a trick of youth.

HENRY.   Faith, Ned, thou sayest true.

But tell me, sirs, whereabouts are we?

TOM.   My lord, we are now about a mile off London.

HENRY.   But sirs, I marvel that Sir John Oldcastle

Comes not away: zounds, see where he comes.   (*Enter Jockey.*)[2]

How now, Jockey, what news with thee?

JOCKEY.   Faith, my lord such news as passes,

For the town of Detfort is risen

With hue and cry after your man,   20

Which parted from us the last night

And has set upon, and has robbed a poor carrier.

HENRY.   Zounds, the villain that was wont to spy

Out our booties?

JOCKEY.   Ay, my lord, even the very same.

HENRY.   Now, base minded rascal to rob a poor carrier,

Well, it skills not, I'll save the base villain's life.

Ay, I may. But tell me, Jockey, whereabout be the receivers?

JOCKEY.   Faith, my lord, they are hard by,

But the best is, we are a horseback and they be afoot,   30

So we may escape them.

HENRY.   Well, if the villains come, let me alone with them.

But tell me, Jockey, how much gotst thou from the knaves?

For I am sure I got something, for one of the villains

So belamed me about the shoulders

As I shall feel it this month.

JOCKEY.   Faith, my lord, I have got a hundred pound.

HENRY.   A hundred pound, now bravely spoken, Jockey.

---

[2] Jockey: John. Here is the early version of Falstaff. Although Shakespeare changes the name in deference to the memory of the real Sir John Oldcastle, he makes a clear allusion to the link between the source character and his own: *H.IV.* Part One, I.ii. 47–48.

As an example of creative development, compare the subordinate role of Oldcastle throughout this play with the role of Shakespeare's Falstaff.

But come, sirs, lay all your money before me.
Now by heaven here is a brave show: 40
But as I am true gentleman, I will have the half
Of this spent tonight; but sirs take up your bags,
[3]Here come the receivers; let me alone.   (*Enter two receivers.*)
    1ST RECEIVER. Alas, good fellow, what shall we do?
I dare never go home to the Court, for I shall be hanged.
But look, here is the young prince, what shall we do?
    HENRY. How now, you villains, what are you?
    1ST RECEIVER. Speak you to him.
    2ND RECEIVER. No, I pray, speak you to him.
    HENRY. Why how now you rascals, why speak you not?   50
    1ST RECEIVER. Forsooth we bepray speak you to him.
    HENRY. Zounds, villains speak, or I'll cut off your heads.
    2ND RECEIVER. Forsooth he can tell the tale better than I.
    1ST RECEIVER. Forsooth we be your father's receivers.
    HENRY. Are you my father's receivers?
Then I hope ye have brought me some money.
    1ST RECEIVER. Money? [4]Alas, sir, we be robbed.
    HENRY. Robbed, how many were there of them?
    1ST RECEIVER. Marry, sir, there were four of them.
And one of them had Sir John Oldcastle's bay, Hobbie,   60
And your black nag.
    HENRY. Gog's wounds, how like you this, Jockey?
Blood, you villains! My father robbed of his money abroad,
And we robbed in our stables!
But tell me, how many were of them?
    1ST RECEIVER. If it please you, there were four of them,
And there was one about the bigness of you:
But I am sure I so belamed him about the shoulders,
That he will feel it this month.
    HENRY. Gog's wounds, you lamed them fairly,   70
So that they have carried away your money.
But come, sirs, what shall we do with the villains?
    BOTH RECEIVERS. I beseech your grace, be good to us.
    NED. I pray you, my lord, forgive them this once.
    HENRY. Well, stand up and get you gone,
And look that you speak not a word of it,
For if there be, zounds, I'll hang you and all your kin.
                                   (*Exeunt receivers.*)

---

   [3] H.IV. One. II.iv. 536–574. The contrast in characterization here between
Shakespeare and his source is illuminating.
   [4] H.IV. One, II.iv. 126–292. Noteworthy again is the contrast between
Shakespeare and his source.

HENRY. Now sirs, how like you this?
Was not this bravely done?
For now the villains dare not speak a word of it,   80
I have so feared them with words.
Now, whither shall we go?
ALL. Why, my lord, you know our old hostess
At Feversham?
HENRY. Our hostess at Feversham, blood, what shall we do there?
We have a thousand pound about us,
And we shall go to a petty alehouse?
No, no. ⁵You know the old tavern in Eastcheap,
There is good wine. Besides, there is a pretty wench
That can talk well, for I delight as much in their tongues   90
As any part about them.
ALL. We are ready to wait upon your grace.
HENRY. ⁶Gog's wounds, wait, we will go all together,
We are all fellows. I tell you, sirs, and the king
My father were dead, we would be all kings,
Therefore come away.
NED. Gog's wounds, bravely spoken, Harry.

SCENE II.

Enter John Cobbler, Robin Pewterer, Lawrence Costermonger.
JOHN. All is well here, all is well, masters.
LAWRENCE. How say you, neighbor John Cobbler?
I think it best that my neighbor   100
Robin Pewterer went to Pudding Lane end,
And we will watch here at Billingsgate ward.
How say you, neighbor Robin, how like you this?
ROBIN. Marry, well neighbors.
I care not much if I go to Pudding Lane's end.
But neighbors, and you hear any ado about me,
Make haste. And if I hear any ado about you,
I will come to you.   (*Exit Robin.*)
LAWRENCE. Neighbor, what news hear you of the young prince?
JOHN. Marry neighbor, I hear say he is a toward young prince,   110
For if he met any by the highway,

---

⁵ *H.IV.* One, I.ii. 143–144. Too, Eastcheap was near Prince Hal's own
residence, a mansion called Cold Harbour, near All-Hallows Church, Upper
Thames Street. Shakespeare (*H.IV.* One, II.iv) gives the tavern the specific
name of Boar's Head, which was a real tavern close to Blackfriars' Playhouse.
⁶ Contrast with *H.IV.* One, I.ii. 218ff.

He will not let to talk with him.
I dare not call him thief, but sure he is one of these taking fellows.

LAWRENCE. Indeed neighbor, I hear say he is as lively
A young prince as ever was.

JOHN. Ay, and I hear say if he use it long,[7]
His father will cut him off from the crown.
But neighbor, say nothing of that.

LAWRENCE. No, no, neighbor, I warrant you.

JOHN. Neighbor, methinks you begin to sleep.   120
If you will, we will sit down,
For I think it is about midnight.

LAWRENCE. Marry content, neighbor, let us sleep.

(Enter Derick roving.)

DERICK. Who, who there, who there?   *(Exit Derick.)*

(Enter Robin.)

ROBIN. O neighbors, what mean you to sleep,
And such ado in the streets?

JOHN AND LAWRENCE. How now, neighbor, what's the matter?

(Enter Derick again.)

DERICK. Who there, who there, who there?

JOHN. Why, what ails thou? Here is no horses.

DERICK. O alas, man, I am robbed, who there, who there?   130

ROBIN. Hold him, neighbor Cobbler.

JOHN. Why I see thou art a plain clown.

DERICK. Am I a clown? Zounds, masters,
Do clowns go in silk apparel?
I am sure all we gentlemen clowns in Kent scant go so
Well. Zounds, you know clowns very well.
Hear you, are you master Constable? And you be, speak,
For I will not take it at his hands.

JOHN. Faith I am not master Constable,
But I am one of his bade[8] officers, for he is not here.   140

DERICK. Is not master Constable here?
Well, it is no matter, I'll have the law at his hands.

JOHN. Nay, I pray you do not take the law of us.

DERICK. Well, you are one of his beastly officers.

JOHN. I am one of his bade officers.

DERICK. Why then I charge thee look to him.   *(Draws sword.)*

JOHN. Nay but hear ye, sir, you seem to be an honest
Fellow, and we are poor men, and now 'tis night.

---

[7] Continue this way of life long.
[8] deputy.

And we would be loth to have anything ado,
Therefore I pray thee put it up. 150

DERICK. First, thou sayest true, I am an honest fellow.
And a proper handsome fellow too.
And you seem to be poor men, therefore I care not greatly,
Nay, I am quickly pacified.
But and you chance to spy the thief,
I pray you lay hold on him.

ROBIN. Yes, that we will, I warrant you.

DERICK. 'Tis a wonderful thing to see how glad the knave
Is, now I have forgiven him.

JOHN. Neighbors, do ye look about you. 160
How now, who's there? (*Enter the thief.*)

THIEF. Here is a good fellow, I pray you which is the
Way to the old tavern in Eastcheap?

DERICK. Whoop, hallo, now Gadshill, knowest thou me?

THIEF. I know thee for an ass.

DERICK. And I know thee for a taking fellow,
Upon Gadshill in Kent.
A bots[9] light upon ye.

THIEF. The whoreson villain would be knocked.

DERICK. Masters, villain, and ye be men stand to him, 170
And take his weapon from him, let him not pass you.

JOHN. My friend, what make you abroad now?
It is too late to walk now.

THIEF. It is not too late for true men to walk.

LAWRENCE. We know thee not to be a true man.

THIEF. Why, what do you mean to do with me?
Zounds, I am one of the king's liege people.

DERICK. Hear you sir, are you one of the king's liege people?

THIEF. Ay, marry am I, sir, what say you to it?

DERICK. Marry sir, I say you are one of the king's filching people.

JOHN. Come, come, let's have him away. 181

THIEF. Why, what have I done?

ROBIN. Thou hast robbed a poor fellow,
And taken away his goods from him.

THIEF. I never saw him before.

DERICK. Masters, who comes here? (*Enter the vintner's boy.*)

BOY. How now, good man Cobbler?

JOHN. How now, Robin, what makest thou abroad
At this time of night?

---

[9] pox.

BOY. Marry I have been at the Counter,[10]   190
I can tell such news as never you have heard the like.

JOHN. What is that, Robin, what is the matter?

BOY. [11]Why, this night about two hours ago, there came the
young prince, and three or four more of his companions, and called
for wine good store, and then they sent for a noise of musicians,
and were very merry for the space of an hour; then whether
their music like them not, or whether they had drunk too much
wine or no, I cannot tell, but our pots flew against the walls;
and then they drew their swords, and went into the street
and fought, and some took one part, and some took another, but   200
for the space of half an hour there was such a bloody fray as passes,
and none could part them until such time as the mayor and
sheriff were sent for; and then at the last with much ado they took
them, and so the young prince was carried to the Counter; and
then about one hour after, there came a messenger from the court
in all haste from the king, for my lord mayor and the sheriff, but
for what cause I know not.

JOHN. Here is news indeed, Robert.

LAWRENCE. Marry, neighbor, this news is strange indeed. I
think it best, neighbor, to rid our hands of this fellow first.   210

THIEF. What mean you to do with me?

JOHN. We mean to carry you to the prison, and there to remain
till the sessions day.

THIEF. Then I pray you let me go to the prison where my master
is.

JOHN. Nay, thou must go to the country prison, to Newgate,
therefore come away.

THIEF. I pray thee be good to me honest fellow.

DERICK. Ay, marry will I, I'll be very charitable to thee,
For I will never leave thee, till I see thee on the gallows.   220

SCENE III.

*Enter Henry the Fourth, with the Earl of Exeter, and the
Lord of Oxford.*

OXFORD. And please your majesty, here is my Lord Mayor and
the Sheriff of London, to speak with your majesty.

KING HENRY IV. Admit them to our presence.

----

[10] debtors prison.
[11] *H.IV.* One, II.iv. 1–574.

(*Enter the mayor and the sheriff.*)

Now my good Lord Mayor of London, the cause of my sending
for you at this time is to tell you of a matter which I have learned
of my Council: herein I understand that you have committed my
son to prison without our leave and license. What although he be
a rude youth, and likely to give occasion, yet you might have considered that he is a prince, and my son, and not to be hauled to
prison by every subject.   230

MAYOR. May it please your majesty to give us leave to tell our
tale?

KING HENRY IV. Or else, God forbid, otherwise you might think
me an unequal judge, having more affection to my son than to any
rightful judgment.

MAYOR. Then I do not doubt but we shall rather deserve commendations at your majesty's hands than any anger.

KING HENRY IV. Go to, say on.

MAYOR. Then if it please your majesty, this night betwixt two
and three of the clock in the morning, my lord the young prince   240
with a very disordered company came to the old tavern in Eastcheap, and whether it was that their music like them not, or
whether they were overcome with wine, I know not; but they drew
their swords, and into the street they went, and some took my
lord the young prince's part, and some took the other; but betwixt
them there was such a bloody fray for the space of half an hour
that neither watchmen nor any other could stay them, till my
brother the Sheriff of London and I were sent for;[12] and at the
last with much ado we stayed them, but it was long first, which
was a great disquieting to all your loving subjects thereabouts. And   250
then, my good lord, we knew not whether your grace had sent
them to try us, whether we would do justice, or whether it were
of their own voluntary will or not, we cannot tell. And therefore
in such a case we knew not what to do, but for our own safeguard
we sent him to ward, where he wants nothing that is fit for his
grace, and your majesty's son. And thus most humbly beseeching
your majesty to think of our answer.

KING HENRY IV. Stand aside until we have further deliberated
on your answer.   (*Exit mayor.*)

Ah Harry, Harry, now thrice accursed Harry,   260
That hath gotten a son, which with grief
Will end his father's days.
Oh my son, a prince thou art, ay, a prince indeed,
And to deserve imprisonment!

---

[12] Contrast this violence with the playfulness of *H.IV.* One, II.iv. 1–574.

And well have they done, and like faithful subjects:
Discharge them and let them go.

EXETER. I beseech your grace, be good to my lord the young
prince.

KING HENRY IV. Nay, nay, 'tis no matter, let him alone.

OXFORD. Perchance the mayor and the sheriff have been too 270
precise in this matter.

KING HENRY IV. No, they have done like faithful subjects.
I will go myself to discharge them, and let them go.   (*Exit omnes.*)

SCENE IV.

Enter Lord Chief Justice, Clerk of the Office, jailer,
John Cobbler, Derick, and the thief.

JUDGE. Jailer, bring the prisoner to the bar.

DERICK. Hear you, my lord, I pray you bring the bar to the
prisoner.

JUDGE. Hold thy hand up at the bar.

THIEF. Here it is, my lord.

JUDGE. Clerk of the Office, read his indictment.

CLERK. What is thy name?   280

THIEF. My name was known before I came here,
And shall be when I am gone, I warrant you.

JUDGE. Ay, I think so, but we will know it better before thou
go.

DERICK. Zounds, and you do but send to the next jail,
We are sure to know his name. For this is not the first prison he
has been in, I'll warrant you.

CLERK. What is thy name?

THIEF. What need you to ask, and have it in writing.

CLERK. Is not thy name Cuthbert Cutter?   290

THIEF. What the devil need you ask, and know it so well.

CLERK. Why then, Cuthbert Cutter, I indict thee by the name
of Cuthbert Cutter, for robbing a poor carrier the 20 day of May
last past, in the fourteenth year of the reign of our sovereign lord
King Henry the Fourth, for setting upon a poor carrier upon
Gadshill in Kent, and having beaten and wounded the said carrier
and taken his goods from him.

DERICK. Oh masters stay there, nay, let's never belie the man, for
he has not beaten and wounded me also, but he has beaten and
wounded my pack, and has taken the great root of ginger that 300
bouncing Bess with the jolly buttocks should have had; that grieves
me most.

JUDGE. Well, what sayest thou, art thou guilty, or not guilty?

THIEF. Not guilty, my lord.

JUDGE. By whom wilt thou be tried?

THIEF. By my lord the young prince, or by myself, whether you will.

(Enter the young prince, with Ned and Tom.)

HENRY. Come away my lads, Gog's wounds ye villain, what make you here? I must go about my business myself, and you must stand loitering here.   310

THIEF. Why, my lord, they have bound me, and will not let me go.

HENRY. Have they bound thee, villain? Why, how now my lord?

JUDGE. I am glad to see your grace in good health.

HENRY. Why, my lord, this is my man,
'Tis marvel you knew him not long before this,
I tell you he is a man of his hands.

THIEF. Ay, Gog's wounds that I am, try me who dare.

JUDGE. Your grace shall find small credit by acknowledging him to be your man.   320

HENRY. Why, my lord, what hath he done?

JUDGE. And it please your majesty, he hath robbed a poor carrier.

DERICK. Hear you, sir, marry it was one Derick,
Goodman Hobbling's man of Kent.

HENRY. What, was it you, button breech?
Of my word, my lord, he did it but in jest.

DERICK. Hear you, sir, is it your man's quality to rob folks in jest? In faith, he shall be hanged in earnest.

HENRY. Well, my lord, what do you mean to do with my man?   330

JUDGE. And please your grace, the law must pass on him,
According to justice, then he must be executed.

DERICK. Hear you sir, I pray you, is it your man's quality to rob folks in jest? In faith he shall be hanged in jest.

HENRY. Well, my lord, what mean you to do with my man?

JUDGE. And please your grace, the law must pass on him,
According to justice, then he must be executed.

HENRY. Why then belike you mean to hang my man?

JUDGE. I am sorry that it falls out so.

HENRY. Why, my lord, I pray ye, who am I?   340

JUDGE. And please your grace, you are my lord the young prince,
our king that shall be after the decease of our sovereign lord, King
Henry the Fourth, whom God grant long to reign.

HENRY. You say true, my lord:
And you will hang my man?

JUDGE. And like your grace, I must needs do justice.

HENRY. [13]Tell me, my lord, shall I have my man?

JUDGE. I cannot, my lord.

HENRY. But will you not let him go?

JUDGE. I am sorry that his case is so ill. 350

HENRY. Tush, case me no casings; shall I have my man?

JUDGE. I cannot, nor I may not, my lord.

HENRY. Nay, and I shall not say, and then I am answered?

JUDGE. No.

HENRY. No? Then I will have him. (*He gives him a box on the ear.*)

NED. Gog's wounds, my lord, shall I cut off his head?

HENRY. No, I charge you draw not your swords,
But get you hence, provide a noise of musicians,
Away, be gone. (*Exeunt Ned and Tom.*)

JUDGE. Well, my lord, I am content to take it at your hands. 360

HENRY. Nay and you be not, you shall have more.

JUDGE. Why, I pray you, my lord, who am I?

HENRY. You, who knows not you?
Why man, you are Lord Chief Justice of England.

JUDGE. Your grace has said truth, therefore in striking me in this place you greatly abuse me, and not me only, but also your father, whose lively person here in this place I do represent. And therefore to teach you what prerogatives mean, I commit you to the Fleet until we have spoken with your father.

HENRY. Why then belike you mean to send me to the Fleet? 370

JUDGE. Ay, indeed, and therefore carry him away.

(*Exeunt Henry with the officers.*)

JUDGE. Jailer, carry the prisoner to Newgate again, until the next 'sizes.

JAILER. At your commandment, my lord, it shall be done.

(*Exeunt Jailer and thief.*)

Scene V.

Enter Derick and John Cobbler.

DERICK. Zounds, masters, here's ado,
When princes must go to prison.
Why, John, didst ever see the like?

JOHN. O Derick, trust me, I never saw the like.

DERICK. Why, John, thou mayest see what princes be in collar.
A judge a box on the ear, I'll tell thee, John, O John, 380
I would not have done it for twenty shillings.

---

[13] *H.IV.* Two, V.ii. 1–80.

JOHN. No more I. There had been no way but one with us,
We should have been hanged.

DERICK. [14]Faith, John, I'll tell thee what, thou shalt be my
Lord Chief Justice, and thou shalt sit in the chair,
And I'll be the young prince, and hit thee a box on the ear,
And then thou shalt say, to teach you what prerogatives
Mean, I commit you to the Fleet.

JOHN. Come on, I'll be your judge,
But thou shalt not hit me hard.   390

DERICK. No, no.

JOHN. What hath he done?

DERICK. Marry, he hath robbed Derick.

JOHN. Why then I cannot let him go.

DERICK. I must needs have my man.

JOHN. You shall not have him.

DERICK. Shall I not have my man, say no and you dare!
How say you, shall I not have my man?

JOHN. No, marry shall you not.

DERICK. Shall I not, John?   400

JOHN. No, Derick.

DERICK. Why then, take you that till more come,
Zounds, shall I not have him?

JOHN. Well, I am content to take this at your hand,
But I pray you, who am I?

DERICK. Who art thou, zounds, do you not know thyself?

JOHN. No.

DERICK. Now away, simple fellow,
Why man, thou art John the Cobbler.

JOHN. No, I am my Lord Chief Justice of England.   410

DERICK. Oh John, Mass,[15] thou sayst true, thou art indeed.

JOHN. Why, then to teach you what prerogatives mean
I commit you to the Fleet.

DERICK. Well, I will go, but in faith, you graybeard knave, I'll
course you. (*Exit, and straight enters again.*) Oh John, come,
come out of thy chair, why what a clown were thou, to let me hit
thee a box on the ear, and now thou seest they will not take me to
the Fleet. I think that thou art one of these workaday clowns.

JOHN. But I marvel what will become of thee?

DERICK. Faith, I'll be no more a carrier.   420

---

[14] *H.IV.* One, II.iv. 413–526. In Shakespeare it is Falstaff with Hal, and
Henry IV is imitated; and during that scene of shifting realities are made
some of the most profound statements of the play.

[15] by the Mass.

JOHN. What wilt thou do then?

DERICK. I'll dwell with thee and be a cobbler.

JOHN. With me? Alas, I am not able to keep thee,
Why, thou wilt eat me out of doors.

DERICK. O John, no John, I am none of these great slouching
fellows that devour these great pieces of beef and broth; alas, a
trifle serves me, a woodcock, a chicken, or a capon's leg, or any
such little thing serves me.

JOHN. A capon, why man, I cannot get a capon once a year, ex-   430
cept it be at Christmas, at some other man's house, for we cobblers
be glad of a dish of roots.

DERICK. Roots, why, are you so good at rooting?
Nay, Cobbler, we'll have you ringed.[16]

JOHN. But Derick, though we be so poor,
Yet will we have in store a crab in the fire,
With nut brown ale, that is full stale,[17]
Which will a man quail and lay in the mire.

DERICK. A bots on you, and be—; but for your ale
I'll dwell with you; come, let's away as fast as we can.   (*Exeunt.*)

Scene VI.

Enter the young prince, with Ned and Tom.

HENRY. Come away, sirs, Gog's wounds, Ned,   440
Didst thou not see what a box on the ear
I took my Lord Chief Justice?

TOM. By gog's blood it did me good to see it,
It made his teeth jar in his head.

(*Enter Sir John Oldcastle.*)

HENRY. How now, Sir John Oldcastle,
What news with you?

JOCKEY. I am glad to see your grace at liberty,
I was come, ay, to visit you in prison.

HENRY. To visit me? Didst thou not know that I am a prince's
son? Why, 'tis enough for me to look into a prison, though I come   450
not in my self. But here's such ado nowadays, here's prisoning,
here's hanging, whipping, and the devil and all. But I tell you,
sirs, when I am king, we will have no such things; but, my lads, if
the old king my father were dead, we would be all kings.

---

[16] Perhaps Derick's bawdy jest is also a botanical pun, *rings* being the
elevated bands on the *roots* of plants.

[17] aged.

JOCKEY. He is a good old man, God take him to his mercy the
sooner.[18]

HENRY. [19]But Ned, so soon as I am king, the first thing
I will do shall be to put my Lord Chief Justice out of office,
And thou shalt be my Lord Chief Justice of England.

NED. Shall I be Lord Chief Justice?   460
By gog's wounds, I'll be the bravest Lord Chief Justice
That ever was in England.

HENRY. Then, Ned, I'll turn all these prisons into fence schools,
and I will endow thee with them, with lands to maintain them
withal. Then I will have a bout with my Lord Chief Justice. Thou
shalt hang none but pickpurses and horse stealers, and such base
minded villains, but that fellow that will stand by the highway
side courageously with his sword and buckler and take a purse, that
fellow give him commendations; besides that, send him to me and
I will give him an annual pension out of my exchequer, to main-   470
tain him all the days of his life.

JOCKEY. Nobly spoken, Harry, we shall never have a merry
world till the old king be dead.

NED. But whither are ye going now?

HENRY. To the court, for I hear say my father lies very sick.

TOM. But I doubt he will not die.

HENRY. Yet will I go thither, for the breath shall be no sooner
out of his mouth, but I will clap the crown on my head.

JOCKEY. Will you go to the court with that cloak so full of
needles?   480

HENRY. Cloak, eyelet-holes, needles, and all was of mine own
devising, and therefore I will wear it.

TOM. I pray you, my lord, what may be the meaning thereof?

HENRY. Why man, 'tis a sign that I stand upon thorns, till
the crown be on my head.

JOCKEY. Or that every needle might be a prick to their hearts
that repine at your doings.

HENRY. Thou sayst true, Jockey, but there's some will say, the
young prince will be a well toward young man and all this gear,
that I had as lief they would break my head with a pot, as to say   490
any such thing. But we stand prating here too long. I must needs
speak with my father, therefore come away.

PORTER. What a rapping keep you at the king's court gate?

HENRY. Here's one that must speak with the king.

---

[18] This selfish cruelty contains suggestions of the Falstaff of H.IV. Two.
[19] H.IV. Two, V.iii. 143–145.

PORTER. The king is very sick, and none must speak with him.

HENRY. No, you rascal, do you not know me?

PORTER. You are my lord the young prince.

HENRY. Then go and tell my father that I must and will speak with him.

NED. Shall I cut off his head?   500

HENRY. No, no, though I would help you in other places, yet I have nothing to do here, for you are in my father's court.

NED. I will write him in my tables, for so soon as I am made Lord Chief Justice I will put him out of his office.

(*The trumpet sounds.*)

HENRY. Gog's wounds, sirs, the king comes,
Let's all stand aside.

(*Enter the king, with the Lord Earl of Exeter.*)

KING HENRY IV. And is it true, my lord, that my son is already sent to the Fleet? Now truly that man is more fitter to rule the realm than I, for by no means could I rule my son, and he by one word has caused him to be ruled. Oh my son, my son, no sooner 510 out of one prison, but into another. I had thought once, while I had lived, to have seen this noble realm of England flourish by thee, my son, but now I see it goes to ruin and decay. (*He weeps.*)

(*Enter Lord of Oxford.*)

OXFORD. And please your grace, here is my lord your son,
That comes to speak with you,
He saith, he must and will speak with you.

KING HENRY IV. Who? My son Harry?

OXFORD. Ay, and please your majesty.

KING HENRY IV. I know wherefore he comes,
But look that none come with him.   520

OXFORD. A very disordered company, and such as make
Very ill rule in your majesty's house.

KING HENRY IV. [20]Well, let him come,
But look that none come with him.   (*He goes.*)

OXFORD. And please your grace,
My lord the king sends for you.

HENRY. Come away sirs, let's go all together.

OXFORD. And please your grace, none must go with you.

HENRY. Why, I must needs have them with me,
Otherwise I can do my father no countenance,   530
Therefore come away.

OXFORD. The king your father commands
There should none come.

---

[20] *H.IV.* One, III.ii. 1–3.

HENRY. Well sirs, then be gone,
And provide me three noise of musicians.   (*Exeunt knights.*)
          (*Enter the prince with a dagger in his hand.*)[21]

KING HENRY IV. [22]Come my son, come on, a God's name,
I know wherefore thy coming is.
Oh my son, my son, what cause has ever been,
That thou shouldst forsake me, and follow this wild and
Reprobate company, which abuses youth so manifestly: 540
Oh my son, thou knowest that these thy doings
Will end thy father's days.   (*He weeps.*)
Ay so, so, my son, thou fearest not to approach the presence of
thy sick father in that disguised sort. I tell thee, my son, that
there is never a needle in thy cloak, but is a prick to my heart,
and never an eyelet-hole, but it is a hole to my soul. And wherefore thou bringest that dagger in thy hand I know not, but by
conjecture.   (*He weeps.*)
HENRY. My conscience accuses me, most sovereign lord, and
well beloved father, to answer first to the last point: that is,   550
whereas you conjecture that this hand and this dagger shall be
armed against your life — no. Know, my beloved father, far be the
thoughts of your son — son said I, an unworthy son for so good a
father — but far be the thoughts of any such pretended mischief;
and I most humbly render it to your majesty's hand. And live,
my lord and sovereign, forever. And with your dagger arm show
like vengeance upon the body of — your son, I was about say, and
dare not; ah, woe is me therefore — that your wild slave. 'Tis not
the crown that I come for, sweet father, because I am unworthy.
And those vile and reprobate company I abandon, and utterly   560
abolish their company forever. Pardon, sweet father, pardon: the
least thing and most desired. And this ruffianly cloak, I here tear
from my back, and sacrifice it to the devil, which is master of all
mischief. Pardon me, sweet father, pardon me. Good my Lord of
Exeter, speak for me. Pardon me, pardon, good father. Not a word?
Ah, he will not speak one word! Ah, Harry, now thrice unhappy
Harry! But what shall I do? I will go take me into some solitary
place, and there lament my sinful life, and when I have done I
will lay me down and die.   (*Exit.*)
KING HENRY IV. Call him again, call my son again.   570
          (*The prince returns.*)
HENRY. And does my father call me again? Now, Harry,
Happy be the time that thy father calls thee again.

---

[21] This glimpse into the relations between Prince Hal and his father is
closer to Holinshed than to Shakespeare.
[22] *H.IV.* One, III.ii. 1–169.

KING HENRY IV. Stand up, my son, and do not think thy father
But at the request of thee, my son, will [not] pardon thee,
And God bless thee, and make thee His servant.

HENRY. Thanks, good my lord, and no doubt but this day,
Even this day, I am born new again.

KING HENRY IV. Come, my son and lords, take me by the hands.

(*Exeunt omnes.*)

SCENE VII.

Enter Derick.

DERICK. Thou art a stinking whore, and a whoreson stinking
whore,   580
Dost think I'll take it at thy hands?

(*Enter John Cobbler running.*)

JOHN. Derick, Derick, Derick, hearest thou,
Do, Derick, never while thou livest use that.
Why, what will my neighbors say, and thou go away so?

DERICK. She's an arrant whore, and I'll have the law on you,
John.

JOHN. Why, what has she done?

DERICK. Marry, mark thou John,
I will prove it, that I will.

JOHN. What wilt thou prove?   590

DERICK. That she called me in to dinner.
John, mark the tale well, John, and when I was set,
She brought me a dish of roots, and a piece of barrel butter
Therein: and she is a very knave,
And thou a drab if thou take her part.

JOHN. Hearest thou, Derick, is this the matter?
Nay, and it be no worse, we will go home again,
And all shall be amended.

DERICK. Oh John, hearest thou John, is all well?

JOHN. Ay, all is well.   600

DERICK. Then I'll go home before, and break all the glass
windows.

SCENE VIII.

Enter the king with his [two] lords.

KING HENRY IV. [23]Come, my lords, I see it boots me not to take
any physic, for all the physicians in the world cannot cure me, no

---

[23] *H.IV.* Two, IV.v. 1–225. Shakespeare follows this scene about as closely
as he does anything in this source play.

not one. But, good my lords, remember my last will and testament
concerning my son, for truly my lords, I do not think but he will
prove as valiant and victorious a king as ever reigned in England.

BOTH LORDS. Let heaven and earth be witness between us, if we
accomplish not thy will to the uttermost.

KING HENRY IV. I give you most unfeigned thanks, good my lords, 610
Draw the curtains and depart my chamber a while,
And cause some music to rock me asleep.   (*Exeunt lords.*)
            (*He sleeps. Enter the prince.*)

HENRY. Ah Harry, thrice unhappy, that hath neglected so long
from visiting of thy sick father. I will go. Nay, but why do
I not go to the chamber of my sick father, to comfort the melancholy soul of his body. His soul, said I; here is his body indeed,
but his soul is whereas it needs no body. Now thrice accursed
Harry, that has offended thy father so much and could not aye
crave pardon for all. Oh my dying father, cursed be the day
wherein I was born, and accursed be the hour wherein I was 620
begotten. But what shall I do? If weeping tears which come too
late may suffice the negligence neglected too soon, I will weep
day and night until the fountain be dry with weeping.   (*Exit.*)
            (*Enter Lords of Exeter and Oxford.*)

EXETER. Come easily, my lord, for waking of the king.

KING HENRY IV. Now, my lords.

OXFORD. How does your grace feel yourself?

KING HENRY IV. Somewhat better after my sleep,
But, good my lords, take off my crown,
Remove my chair a little back, and set me right.

BOTH. And please your grace, the crown is taken away.   630

KING HENRY IV. The crown taken away?
Good my Lord of Oxford, go see who has done this deed.
No doubt 'tis some vile traitor that has done it,
To deprive my son; they that would do it now,
Would seek to scrape and scrawl[24] for it after my death.
            (*Enter Lord of Oxford with the prince.*)

OXFORD. Here and please your grace,
Is my lord the young prince with the crown.

KING HENRY IV. Why, how now my son?
I had thought the last time I had you in schooling,
I had given you a lesson for all,   640
And do you now begin again?
Why, tell me, my son,

---

24 claw.

Dost thou think the time so long,
That thou wouldst have it before the
Breath be out of my mouth?

HENRY. Most sovereign lord, and well beloved father,
I came into your chamber to comfort the melancholy
Soul of your body, and finding you at that time
Past all recovery, and dead, to my thinking —
God is my witness — and what should I do,   650
But with weeping tears lament the death of you, my father,
And after that, seeing the crown, I took it.
And tell me my father, who might better take it than I
After your death? But seeing you live,
I most humbly render it into your majesty's hands,
And the happiest man alive, that my father lives.
And live, my lord and father, forever.

KING HENRY IV. Stand up, my son,
Thine answer has sounded well in mine ears,
For I must need confess that I was in a very sound sleep,   660
And altogether unmindful of thy coming:
But come near, my son,
And let me put thee in possession whilst I live,
That none deprive thee of it after my death.

HENRY. Well may I take it at your majesty's hands,
But it shall never touch my head, so long as my father lives.

                                        (He takes the crown.)

KING HENRY IV. God give thee joy, my son,
God bless thee and make thee His servant,
And send thee a prosperous reign.
For God knows, my son, how hardly I came by it,   670
And how hardly I have maintained it.

HENRY. Howsoever you came by it, I know not.
But now I have it from you, and from you I will keep it.
And he that seeks to take the crown from my head,
Let him look that his armour be thicker than mine,
Or I will pierce him to the heart,
Were it harder than brass or bullion.

KING HENRY IV. Nobly spoken, and like a king.
Now trust me, my lords, I fear not but my son
Will be as warlike and victorious a prince   680
As ever reigned in England.

BOTH. His former life shows no less.

KING HENRY IV. Well, my lords, I know not whether it be for
sleep,

Or drawing near of drowsy summer of death,
But I am very much given to sleep.   (*Exeunt omnes.*)
                              (*The king dies.*)

SCENE IX.

Enter the thief.

THIEF. [25]Ah God, I am now much like to a bird
Which has escaped out of the cage,
For so soon as my Lord Chief Justice heard
That the old king was dead, he was glad to let me go,   690
For fear of my lord, the young prince.
But here comes some of his companions,
I will see and I can get anything of them,
For old acquaintance.
                    (*Enter Tom, Ned, Jockey.*)
TOM. Gog's wounds, the king is dead.
JOCKEY. Dead, then gog's blood, we shall be all kings.
NED. Gog's wounds, I shall be Lord Chief Justice of England.
                                          (*Sees thief.*)
TOM. Why, how are you broken out of prison?
NED. Gog's wounds, how the villain stinks.
JOCKEY. Why, what will become of thee now?   700
Fie upon him, how the rascal stinks.
THIEF. Marry, I will go and serve my master again.
TOM. Gog's blood, dost think that he will have any such
Scabb'd knave as thou art? What man, he is a king now.
NED. Hold thee, here's a couple of angels for thee,
And get thee gone, for the king will not be long
Before he come this way:
And hereafter I will tell the king of thee.   (*Exit thief.*)
JOCKEY. Oh, how it did me good to see the king
When he was crowned: 710
Methought his seat was like the figure of heaven,
And his person like unto a god.
NED. But who would have thought,
That the king would have changed his countenance so?
JOCKEY. Did you not see with what grace
He sent his embassage into France? To tell the French king

---

[25] H.IV. Two, V.iii. 84ff. This scene in the old play suggests that there
may be points of comparison between the thief and Shakespeare's Pistol.

That Harry of England has sent for the crown,
And Harry of England will have it.

TOM.   But 'twas but a little to make the people believe
That he was sorry for his father's death.   720

(*The trumpet sounds.*)

NED.   Gog's wounds, the king comes,
Let's all stand aside.

(*Enter the king with the archbishop and the Lord of Oxford.*)

JOCKEY.   [26]How do you, my lord?

NED.   How now, Harry?
Tut, my lord, put away these dumps,
You are a king, and all the realm is yours.
What, man, do you not remember the old sayings?
You know I must be Lord Chief Justice of England.
Trust me, my lord, methinks you are very much changed,
And 'tis but with a little sorrowing, to make folks believe   730
The death of your father grieves you,
And 'tis nothing so.

HENRY.   I pray thee, Ned, mend thy manners,
And be more modest in thy terms,
For my unfeigned grief is not to be ruled by thy flattering
And dissembling talk. Thou sayest I am changed,
So I am indeed, and so must thou be, and that quickly,
Or else I must cause thee to be changed.

JOCKEY.   Gog's wounds, how like you this?
Zounds, 'tis not so sweet as music.   740

TOM.   I trust we have not offended your grace no way.

HENRY.   Ah Tom, your former life grieves me,
And makes me to abandon and abolish your company forever
And therefore not upon pain of death to approach my presence
By ten miles space; then if I hear well of you,
It may be I will do somewhat for you,
Otherwise look for no more favor at my hands,
Than at any other man's. And therefore be gone,
We have other matters to talk on.   (*Exeunt knights.*)
Now,[27] my good Lord Archbishop of Canterbury,   750
What say you to our embassage[28] into France?

ARCHBISHOP.   Your right to the French crown of France
Came by your great grandmother Isabel,
Wife to King Edward the Third,

---

[26] H.IV. Two, V.v. 43–76.
[27] H.V. I.ii. 33–114.
[28] embassy. The same word is used by Holinshed.

And sister to Charles the French king.
Now if the French king deny it, as likely enough he will,
Then must you take your sword in hand,
And conquer the right.
Let the usurped Frenchman know,
Although your predecessors have let it pass, you will not.   760
²⁹For your countrymen are willing with purse and men
To aid you.
³⁰Then, my good lord, as it has been always known,
That Scotland has been in league with France,
By a sort of pensions which yearly come from thence,
I think it therefore best to conquer Scotland,
And then I think that you may go more easily into France.
And this is all I can say, my good lord.

    HENRY. I thank you, my good Lord Archbishop of Canterbury.
What say you, my good Lord of Oxford.   770
    OXFORD. And please your majesty,
I agree to my Lord Archbishop, saving in this.
He that will Scotland win, must first with France begin,
According to the old saying.
Therefore, my good lord, I think it best first to invade France,
For in conquering Scotland you conquer but one,
And conquer France, and conquer both.

                (Enter Lord of Exeter.)

    EXETER. And please your majesty,
My lord ambassador is come out of France.
    HENRY. Now trust me, my lord,   780
He was the last man that we talked of.
I am glad that he is come to resolve us of our answer,
Commit him to our presence.

                (Enter Duke of York.)

    YORK. God save the life of my sovereign lord the king.
    HENRY. Now, my good lord the Duke of York,
What news from our brother the French king?
    YORK. And please your majesty,
I delivered him my embassage,

---

²⁹ H.V. I.i. 75–81.
³⁰ H.V. I.ii. 136–183. However the last four lines of the Shakespeare passage are strongly reminiscent of the passages in Book IV of Plato's Republic that read: "It is not wisdom and strength alone that make a state wise and strong; but order, like the harmony called the diapason, runs through the whole state, making the weakest and the strongest and the middling people move in one consent. . . . The harmonic power of political justice is the same as that musical consent which connects the three chords, the octave, the bass, and the fifth."

Whereof I took some deliberation,
But for the answer he has sent,   790
My Lord Archbishop of Bourges, the Duke of Burgundy,
Monsieur le Cole, with two hundred and fifty horsemen,
To bring the embassage.
    HENRY. ³¹Commit my Lord Archbishop of Bourges
Into our presence.
                (*Enter Archbishop of Bourges.*)
Now my Lord Archbishop of Bourges,
We do learn by our lord ambassador,
That you have our message to do
From our brother the French king.
Here, my good lord, according to our accustomed order,   800
We give you free liberty and license to speak,
With good audience.
    BOURGES. God save the mighty King of England!
My lord and master, the most Christian king,
Charles the Seventh, the great and mighty King of France,
As a most noble and Christian king,
Not minding to shed innocent blood, is rather content
To yield somewhat to your unreasonable demands:
That of fifty thousand crowns a year with his daughter
The said Lady Katherine, in marriage,   810
And some crowns which he may well spare,
Not hurting of his kingdom,
He is content to yield so far to your unreasonable desire.
    HENRY. Why then, belike your lord and master,
Thinks to puff me up with fifty thousand crowns a year!
No, tell thy lord and master
That all the crowns in France shall not serve me,
Except the crown and kingdom itself.
And perchance hereafter I will have his daughter.
    BOURGES. ³²And it please your majesty,   820
My Lord Prince Dauphin greets you well,
With this present. (*He delivers a tun of tennis balls.*)
    HENRY. What a gilded tun!
I pray you, my Lord of York, look what is in it?
    YORK. And it please your grace,
Here is a carpet and a tun of tennis balls.

---

³¹ *H.V.* III.Prologue. 28–32.
³² *H.V.* I.ii. 233–297.

HENRY. A tun of tennis balls?
I pray you, good my Lord Archbishop,
What might the meaning thereof be?
  BOURGES. And it please you, my lord,   830
A messenger, you know, ought to keep close his message,
And specially an ambassador.
  HENRY. But I know that you may declare your message
To a king: the law of arms allows no less.
  BOURGES. My lord, hearing of your wildness before your
Father's death, sent you this, my good lord,
Meaning that you are more fitter for a carpet than the camp.
  HENRY. My lord Prince Dauphin is very pleasant with me.
But tell him, that instead of balls of leather,
We will toss him balls of brass and iron,   840
Yea, such balls as never were tossed in France.
The proudest tennis court shall rue it,
Ay, and thou priest of Bourges shall rue it.
Therefore get thee hence, and tell him thy message quickly,
Lest I be there before thee. Away, priest, be gone.
  BOURGES. I beseech your grace, to deliver me your safe
Conduct under your broad seal manual.
  HENRY. Priest of Bourges, know
That the hand and seal of a king and his word is all one,
And instead of my hand and seal,   850
I will bring him my hand and sword.
And tell thy lord and master, that I, Harry of England, said it,
And I, Harry of England, will perform it.
My Lord of York, deliver him our safe conduct,
Under our broad seal manual.

                  (*Exeunt archbishop and the Duke of York.*)

Now, my lords, to arms, to arms,
For I vow by heaven and earth, that the proudest
Frenchman in all France shall rue the time that ever
These tennis balls were sent into England.
[33]My lord, I will that there be provided a great navy of ships, 860
With all speed, at Southhampton,
For there I mean to ship my men,
For I would be there before him, if it were possible,
Therefore come. But stay,
I had almost forgot the chiefest thing of all, with chafing

---

[33] *H.V.* II.Prologue. 34–42.

With this French ambassador.
Call in my Lord Chief Justice of England.

(Enter Lord Chief Justice of England.)

EXETER. Here is the king, my lord.

JUDGE. God preserve your majesty.

HENRY. Why, how now, my lord, what is the matter?   870

JUDGE. I would it were unknown to your majesty.

HENRY. Why, what ails you?

JUDGE. Your majesty knows my grief well.

HENRY. Oh, my lord, you remember you sent me to the Fleet,
did you not?

JUDGE. I trust your grace have forgotten that.

HENRY. Ay, truly, my lord, and for revengement
I have chosen you to be my protector over my realm,
Until it shall please God to give me speedy return
Out of France.   880

JUDGE. And if it please your majesty, I am far unworthy
Of so high a dignity.

HENRY. Tut, my lord, you are not unworthy,
Because I think you worthy.
For you that would not spare me,
I think will not spare another,
It must needs be so. And therefore come,
Let us be gone, and get our men in readiness.   *(Exeunt omnes.)*

SCENE X.

Enter a captain, John Cobbler and his wife.

CAPTAIN. [34]Come, come, there's no remedy,
Thou must needs serve the king.   890

JOHN. Good master captain, let me go,
I am not able to go so far.

WIFE. I pray you, good master captain,
Be good to my husband.

CAPTAIN. Why, I am sure he is not too good to serve the king.

JOHN. Alas, no, but a great deal too bad,
Therefore I pray you let me go.

CAPTAIN. No, no, thou shalt go.

JOHN. Oh sir, I have a great many shoes at home to cobble.

WIFE. I pray you, let him go home again.   900

CAPTAIN. Tush, I care not, thou shalt go.

JOHN. Oh wife, and you had been a loving wife to me,

---

[34] H.V. II.i. 1ff. This entire scene and Shakespeare's are roughly parallel.

This had not been, for I have said many times
That I would go away, and now I must go
Against my will. (*He weeps.*)

(*Enter Derick.*)

DERICK. How now, ho, *bacillus manus*,[35] for an old codpiece.
Master, captain, shall we away?
Zounds, how now, John, what, a crying?
What make you and my dame there?
I marvel whose head you will throw the stools at,   910
Now we are gone.

WIFE. I'll tell you, come ye cloghead,
What do you with my pot lid? Hear you,
Will you have it rapped about your pate?
(*She beats him with her pot lid.*)

DERICK. Oh, good dame, (*Here he shakes her.*)
And I had my dagger here, I would worry you all to pieces.
That I would.

WIFE. Would you so, I'll try that. (*She beats him.*)

DERICK. Master captain will ye suffer her?
Go to, dame, I will go back as far as I can,   920
But and you come again,
I'll clap the law on your back, that's flat.
I'll tell you, master captain, what you shall do:
Press her for a soldier. I warrant you,
She will do as much good as her husband and I too. (*Enter the thief.*)
Zounds, who comes yonder?

CAPTAIN. How now, good fellow, dost thou want a master?

THIEF. Ay, truly sir.

CAPTAIN. Hold thee then, I press thee for a soldier,
To serve the king in France.   930

DERICK. How now, gads, what, dost know us, thinkest?

THIEF. Ay, I knew thee long ago.

DERICK. Hear you, master captain?

CAPTAIN. What sayest thou?

DERICK. I pray you, let me go home again.

CAPTAIN. Why, what wouldst thou do at home?

DERICK. Marry, I have brought two shirts with me,
And I would carry one of them home again,
For I am sure he'll steal it from me,
He is such a filching fellow.   940

CAPTAIN. I warrant thee he will not steal it from thee,
Come, let's away.

---

[35] hand kisser, in punning, corrupt Latin.

DERICK. Come, master captain, let's away,
Come, follow me.

JOHN. Come, wife, let's part lovingly.

WIFE. Farewell, good husband.

DERICK. Fie, what a kissing and crying is here?
Zounds, do ye think he will never come again?
Why John, come away, dost think that we are so base
Minded to die among Frenchmen?   950
Zounds, we know not whether they will lay
Us in the church or no. Come, master captain, let's away.

CAPTAIN. I cannot stay no longer, therefore come away.

(Exeunt omnes.)

Scene XI.

Enter the king, Prince Dauphin, and Lord High Constable of France.

KING. [36]Now my Lord High Constable
What say you to our embassage into England?

CONSTABLE. And it please your majesty, I can say nothing
Until my lord's ambassadors be come home,
But yet methinks your grace has done well,
To get your men in so good a readiness,
For fear of the worst.   960

KING. Ay, my lord, we have some in a readiness,
But if the King of England make against us,
We must have thrice so many more.

DAUPHIN. Tut, my lord, although the King of England
Be young and wild headed, yet never think he will be so
Unwise to make battle against the mighty King of France.

KING. Oh my son, although the King of England be
Young and wild headed, yet never think but he is ruled
By his wise councillors.

(Enter Archbishop of Bourges.)

BOURGES. God save the life of my sovereign lord the king.   970

KING. Now my good Lord Archbishop of Bourges,
What news from our brother the English king?

BOURGES. And please your majesty,
He is so far from your expectation
That nothing will serve him but the crown
And kingdom itself; besides, he bade me haste quickly,
Lest he be there before me, and so far as I hear,

---

[36] H.V. II.iv. 1–74.

He has kept promise, for, they say, he is already landed
At Chef de Caux in Normandy, upon the River of Seine,
And laid his siege to the garrison town of Harfleur.   980
    KING. You have made great haste in the meantime,
Have you not?
    DAUPHIN. I pray you, my lord, how did the King of England
take my presents?
    BOURGES. Truly, my lord, in very ill part,
For these your balls of leather
He will toss you balls of brass and iron.
Trust me, my lord, I was very afraid of him,
He is such a haughty and high minded prince,
He is as fierce as a lion.   990
    CONSTABLE. Tush, We will make him as tame as a lamb, I
warrant you.
                  (*Enter a messenger.*)
    MESSENGER. God save the mighty King of France.
    KING. Now, messenger, what news?
    MESSENGER. [37]And it please your majesty,
I come from your poor distressed town of Harfleur,
Which is so beset on every side,
If your majesty do not send present aid,
The town will be yielded to the English king.
    KING. Come my lords, come, shall we stand still   1000
Till our country be spoiled under our noses?
My lords, let the Normans, Brabants, Picards,
And Danes be sent for with all speed.
And you, my Lord High Constable, I make general
Over all my whole army.
Monsieur le Cole, Master of the Bows,
Signor Devens, and all the rest, at your appointment.
    DAUPHIN. I trust your majesty will bestow
Some part of the battle on me,
I hope not to present any otherwise than well.   1010
    KING. I tell thee, my son,
Although I should get the victory, and thou lose thy life,
I should think myself quite conquered,
And the Englishmen to have the victory.
    DAUPHIN. Why my lord and father,
I would have the petty king of England to know
That I dare encounter him in any ground of the world.

---

[37] H.V. III.i. 1ff; III.v. 48–66.

KING. I know well, my son,
But at this time I will have it thus.
Therefore come away.   1020

(*Exeunt omnes.*)

Scene XII.

Enter Henry the Fifth, with his lords.

HENRY. Come my lords of England,
No doubt this good luck of winning this town
Is a sign of an honorable victory to come.
But, good my lord, go and speak to the captains
With all speed, to number the host of the Frenchmen,
And by that means we may the better know
How to appoint the battle.

YORK. [38]And it please your majesty,
There are many of your men sick and diseased,
And many of them die for want of victuals.   1030

HENRY. And why did you not tell me of it before?
If we cannot have it for money,
We will have it by dint of sword,
The law of arms allows no less.

OXFORD. I beseech your grace to grant me a boon.

HENRY. What is that, my good lord?

OXFORD. That your grace would give me the
Vanguard in the battle.

HENRY. Trust me, my Lord of Oxford, I cannot.
For I have already given it to my uncle the Duke of York,   1040
Yet I thank you for your good will.   (*a trumpet sounds.*)
How now, what is that?

YORK. [39]I think it be some Herald of Arms.

(*Enter a herald.*)

HERALD. King of England, my Lord High Constable,
And others of the noblemen of France,
Send me to defy thee, as open enemy to God,
Our country, and us, and hereupon,
They presently bid thee battle.

HENRY. Herald, tell them that I defy them
As open enemies to God, my country, and me,   1050
And as wrongful usurpers of my right.
And whereas thou sayest they presently bid me battle,

---

[38] H.V. III.iii. 55–56.
[39] H.V. IV.iii. 79–125.

Tell them that I think they know how to please me.
But I pray thee what place has my lord Prince Dauphin
Here in battle?

HERALD. And it please your grace,
My lord and king, his father,
Will not let him come into the field.

HENRY. Why then he does me great injury.
I thought that he and I should have played at tennis together,   1060
Therefore I have brought tennis balls for him,
But other manner of ones than he sent me.
And herald, tell my lord Prince Dauphin
That I have injured my hands with other kind of weapons
Than tennis balls, ere this time of day,
And that he shall find out ere it be long,
And so adieu, my friend.
And tell my lord that I am ready when he will.   (*Exit herald.*)
Come my lords, I care[40] not, and I go to our captains,
And I'll see the number of the French army myself.   1070
Strike up the drum.   (*Exit omnes.*)

SCENE XIII.

Enter French soldiers.

1ST SOLDIER. [41]Come away, Jack Drummer, come away all,
And me will tell you what me will do,
Me will tro' one chance on the dice,
Who shall have the King of England and his lords.

2ND SOLDIER. Come away, Jack Drummer,
And tro' your chance, and lay down your drum.   (*Enter drummer.*)

DRUMMER. Oh the brave apparel that the Englishmans
Ha' bro't over, I will tell you what
Me ha' done, me ha' provided a hundret trunks,   1080
And all to put the fine 'parel of the Englishmans in.

1ST SOLDIER. What do thou mean by trunks?

2ND SOLDIER. A shest, man, a hundred shests.

1ST SOLDIER. Ah oui, ah oui, ah oui, me will tell you what,
Me ha' put five shildren out of my house,
And all too little to put the fine apparel of the
Englishmans in.

---

40 fear, worry.
41 Essentially this scene derives from Holinshed's report that the French
"soldiers the night before had played the Englishmen at dice." (*H.V.* IV.Pro-
logue. 18–20). Shakespeare does construct a similar scene, however, but using
noblemen instead of soldiers: *H.V.* III.vii. 74ff.

DRUMMER. Oh the brave, the brave apparel that we shall
Have anon, but come, and you shall see what me will tro'
At the king's drummer and fife.   1090
Ha, me ha' no good luck. Tro' you.

3RD SOLDIER. Faith me will tro' at the Earl of Northumberland
And my Lord a Willoughby, with his great horse,
Snorting, farting, oh brave horse.

1ST SOLDIER. Ha, but laddie, you ha' reasonable good luck,
Now I will tro' at the king himself.
Ha, me have no good luck.

(*Enter a captain.*)

CAPTAIN. How now, what make you here,
So far from the camp?

2ND SOLDIER. Shall me tell our captain what we have done here? 1100
DRUMMER. Ah oui, ah oui.   (*Exeunt drummer, and one soldier.*)
2ND SOLDIER. I will tell you what we have doone,
We have been tro'ing our shance on the dice,
But none can win the king.

CAPTAIN. I think so. Why, he is left behind for me,
And I have set three or four chair-makers to work,
To make a new disguised chair to set that womanly
King of England in, that all the people may laugh
And scoff at him.

2ND SOLDIER. Oh brave captain.   1110
CAPTAIN. I am glad, and yet with the kind of pity,
To see the poor king.
Why, whoever saw a more flourishing army in France
In one day, than here is? Are not here all the peers of
France? Are not here the Normans with their fiery hand
Guns, and slaunching[42] cutlasses?
Are not here the barbarians with their hard horses,
And launching spears?
Are not here Picards with their crossbows and piercing
Darts?   1120
The Aisneux with their cutting glaives and sharp carbuncles?[43]
Are not here the lance knights of Burgundy?
And on the other side, a sight of poor English scabs?
Why, take an Englishman out of his warm bed
And his stale drink but one month,
And alas what will become of him?

---

[42] slashing.
[43] Shields faced with carbuncles, a common practise in those days.

But give the Frenchman a radish root,
And he will live with it all the days of his life.

2ND SOLDIER. Oh, the brave apparel that we shall have of the
Englishmans.   1130

Scene XIV.

Enter the King of England and his lords.

HENRY. [44]Come, my lords and fellows of arms,
What company is there of the Frenchmen?

OXFORD. And it please your majesty,
Our captains have numbered them,
And so near as they can judge,
They are about threescore thousand horsemen,
And forty thousand footmen.

HENRY. They threescore thousand,
And we but two thousand.
They twoscore thousand footmen,   1140
And we twelve thousand.
They are a hundred thousand,
And we forty thousand, ten to one.
[45]My lords and loving countrymen,
Though we be few and they many,
Fear not, your quarrel is good, and God will defend you.
Pluck up your hearts, for this day we shall either have
A valiant victory, or an honorable death.
Now my lords, I will that my uncle the Duke of York,
Have the vanguard in the battle.   1150
The Earl of Derby, the Earl of Oxford,
The Earl of Kent, the Earl of Nottingham,
The Earl of Huntington, I will have beside the army,
That they may come fresh upon them.
And I myself with the Duke of Bedford,
The Duke of Clarence and the Duke of Gloucester,
Will be in the midst of the battle.
Furthermore, I will that my Lord of Willoughby,
And the Earl of Northumberland,
With their troops of horsemen, be continually running like   1160
Wings on both sides of the army;

---

[44] H.V. IV.iii. 1–5. In this play the odds are ten to one, in Shakespeare
five to one.
[45] H.V. IV.iii. 20–67.

My Lord of Northumberland, on the left wing.
Then I will, that every archer provide him a stake of
A tree, and sharp it at both ends,
And at the first encounter of the horsemen,
To pitch their stakes down into the ground before them,
That they may gore themselves upon them,
And then to recoil back, and shoot wholly altogether,
And so discomfort them.

OXFORD. And it please your majesty,   1170
I will take that in charge, if your grace be therewith content.

HENRY. With all my heart, my good Lord of Oxford.
And go and provide quickly.

OXFORD. I thank your highness.

HENRY. Well, my lords, our battles are ordained,
And the French making of bonfires, and at their banquets.
But let them look, for I mean to set upon them.

(*The trumpet sounds.*)

Soft, here comes some other French message.

(*Enter herald.*)

HERALD. [46]King of England, my Lord High Constable
And other of my lords, considering the poor state of thee   1180
And thy poor countrymen,
Sends me to know what thou wilt give for thy ransom?
Perhaps thou mayest agree better cheap now,
Than when thou art conquered.

HENRY. Why then belike your high constable
Sends to know what I will give for my ransom?
Now trust me, herald, not so much as a tun of tennis balls,
No, not so much as one poor tennis ball;
Rather shall my body lie dead in the field, to feed crows,
Than ever England shall pay one penny ransom   1190
For my body.

HERALD. A kingly resolution.

HENRY. Know, herald, 'tis a kingly resolution,
And the resolution of a king.
Here, take this for thy pains.   (*Exit herald.*)
But stay, my lords, what time is it?

ALL. Prime, my lord.

HENRY. Then is it good time no doubt,
For all England prays for us.
What, my lords, methinks you look cheerfully upon me.   1200
Why then with one voice and like true English hearts,

_____

[46] H.V. IV.iii. 79–125.

With me throw up your caps, and for England,
Cry St. George, and God and St. George help us.

(*Strike drummer. Exeunt omnes.*)
(*The Frenchmen cry within,*
"St. Denis, St. Denis, Montjoy, St. Denis.")
(*The Battle.*[47])

SCENE XV.

Enter King of England, and his lords.

HENRY. Come my lords, come, by this time our
Swords are almost drunk with French blood,
[48]But my lords, which of you can tell me how many of our
Army be slain in the battle?

OXFORD. And it please your majesty,
There are of the French army slain,
Above ten thousand, twenty six hundred   1210
Whereof are princes and nobles bearing banners.
Besides, all the nobility of France are taken prisoners.
Of your majesty's army, are slain none but the good
Duke of York, and not above five or six and twenty
Common soldiers.

HENRY. For the good Duke of York, my uncle,
I am heartily sorry, and greatly lament his misfortune,
Yet the honorable victory which the Lord hath given us
Doth make me much rejoice.[49] But stay,
Here comes another French message.   1220

(*Sound trumpet.*)
(*Enter a herald and kneels.*)

HERALD. God save the life of the most mighty conquerer,
The honorable King of England.

HENRY. Now herald, methinks the world is changed
With you now. What I am sure, it is a great disgrace for a
Herald to kneel to the King of England.
What is thy message?

HERALD. My lord and master, the conquered King of France,
Sends thee long health, with hearty greeting.

HENRY. Herald, his greetings are welcome,
But I thank God for my health.   1230
Well, herald, say on.

---

[47] Contrast these simple stage directions with all that Shakespeare manages
to do with the battle. *H.V.* IV.iv,v,vi,vii.

[48] *H.V.* IV.viii. 77–117.

[49] *H.V.* IV.vii. 69–123.

HERALD. He has sent me to desire your majesty
To give him leave to go into the field to view his poor
Countrymen, that they may all be honorably buried.

HENRY. Why, herald, doth thy lord and master
Send to me to bury the dead?
Let him bury them, a God's name.
But I pray thee, herald, where is my Lord High Constable,
And those that would have had my ransom?

HERALD. And it please your majesty,   1240
He was slain in the battle.

HENRY. Why you may see you will make yourselves
Sure before the victory be won. But herald,
What castle is this so near adjoining to our camp?

HERALD. And it please your majesty,
'Tis called the Castle of Agincourt.

HENRY. Well then, my lords of England,
For the more honor of our English men,
I will that this be forever called the Battle of Agincourt.

HERALD. And it please your majesty,   1250
I have a further message to deliver to your majesty.

HENRY. What is that, herald? Say on.

HERALD. And it please your majesty, my lord and master
Craves to parley with your majesty.

HENRY. With a good will, so some of my nobles
View the place for fear of treachery and treason.

HERALD. Your grace needs not to doubt that.

HENRY. Well, tell him then, I will come.
Now my lords, I will go into the field myself,
To view my countrymen, and to have them honorably   1260
Buried, for the French king shall never surpass me in
Courtesy whiles I am Harry, King of England.
Come on, my lords.   (*Exeunt omnes.*)

Scene XVI.

Enter John Cobbler, and Robin Pewterer.

ROBIN. Now, John Cobbler,
Didst thou see how the king did behave himself?

JOHN. But Robin, didst thou see what a policy
The king had, to see how the French men were killed
With the stakes of the trees?

ROBIN. Ay, John, there was a brave policy.

(*Enter an English soldier, roaming.*)

SOLDIER. [50]What are you, my masters?   1270
BOTH. Why, we be Englishmen.
SOLDIER. Are you Englishmen? Then change your language,
For the king's tents are set afire,
And all they that speak English will be killed.
JOHN. What shall we do, Robin? Faith, I'll shift,
For I can speak broken French.
ROBIN. Faith, so can I, let's hear how thou canst speak?
JOHN. *Commondevales,*[51] *Monsieur.*
ROBIN. That's well, come, let's be gone.

(*Drum and trumpet sound.*)

Scene XVII.

Enter Derick roaming,
after him a Frenchman and takes him prisoner.
DERICK. [52]O good monsieur.   1280
FRENCHMAN. Come, come, you villeaco.[53]
DERICK. Oh I will, sir, I will.
FRENCHMAN. Come quickly, you peasant.
DERICK. I will, sir, what shall I give you?
FRENCHMAN. Marry, thou shalt give me,
One, two, three, four hundred crowns.
DERICK. Nay, sir, I will give you more.
I will give you as many crowns as will lie on your sword.
FRENCHMAN. Wilt thou give me as many crowns
As will lie on my sword?   1290
DERICK. Ay, marry will I, ay, but you must lay down your
Sword, or else they will not lie on your sword.

(*Here the Frenchman lays down his sword, and*
the clown takes it up, and hurls him down.)

DERICK. Thou villain, darest thou look up?
FRENCHMAN. O good monsieur, *compassion!*
Monsieur, pardon me.
DERICK. Oh you villain, now you lie at my mercy,
Dost thou remember since thou lamest me in thy short el?[54]
O villain, now I will strike off thy head.

(*Here while he turns his back, the Frenchman runs away.*)

---

[50] H.V. IV.vii. 1–8.
[51] Corrupt form of *Comment allez-vous.*
[52] H.V. IV.iv. 1ff.
[53] Corrupt form of *vigliaccaccio,* villain.
[54] L-shaped axe.

What, is he gone? Mass, I am glad of it,
For if he had stayed, I was afraid he would have stirred again,   1300
And then I should have been split.
But I will away, to kill more Frenchmen.

Scene XVIII.

(Enter King of France, King of England, and attendants.)
HENRY. Now my good brother of France,
My coming into this land was not to shed blood,
But for the right of my country, which if you can deny,
I am content peaceably to leave my siege,
And to depart out of your land.[55]
KING. [56]What is it you demand,
My loving brother of England?
HENRY. My secretary has it written; read it.   1310
SECRETARY. Item, that immediately Henry of England
Be crowned King of France.
KING. A very hard sentence,
My good brother of England.
HENRY. No more but right, my good brother of France.
KING. Well, read on.
SECRETARY. Item, that after the death of the said Henry,
The crown remain to him and his heirs forever.
KING. Why, then you do not only mean to
Dispossess me, but also my son.   1320
HENRY. Why, my good brother of France,
You have had it long enough.
And as for Prince Dauphin,
It skills not though he sit beside the saddle.
Thus I have set it down, and thus it shall be.
KING. You are very peremptory
My good brother of England.
HENRY. And you as perverse, my good brother of France.
KING. Why then, belike, all that I have here is yours.
HENRY. Ay, even as far as the kingdom of France reaches.   1330
KING. Ay, for by this hot beginning,
We shall scarce bring it to a calm ending.
HENRY. It is as you please, here is my resolution.

---

[55] This play, like Shakespeare's, telescopes the two invasions into a single one.
[56] H.V. V.ii. 64–90. Unlike Shakespeare and Holinshed, the author of this play does not use Burgundy as a mediator.

KING. Well, my brother of England,
If you will give me a copy,
We will meet you again tomorrow.

HENRY. With a good will, my good brother of France.
Secretary, deliver him a copy.

> (*Exit King of France, and all his attendants.*)

My lords of England, go before,
And I will follow you.   1340

> (*Exeunt lords.*)

> (*Speaks to himself.*)

Ah, Harry, thrice unhappy Harry,
Hast thou now conquered the French king,
And begins a fresh supply with his daughter.
But with what face canst thou seek to gain her love,
Which has sought to win her father's crown?
Her father's crown, said I. No, it is mine own.
Ay, but I love her, and must crave her.
Nay, I love her and will have her.

> (*Enter Lady Katherine and her ladies.*)

[57]But here she comes.
How now, fair Lady Katherine of France,   1350
What news?

KATHERINE. And it please your majesty,
My father sent me to know if you will debate any of these
Unreasonable demands which you require.

HENRY. Now trust me, Kate,
I commend thy father's wit greatly in this,
For none in the world could sooner have made me debate it
If it were possible.
But tell me, sweet Kate, canst thou tell how to love?

KATHERINE. I cannot hate, my good lord,   1360
Therefore far unfit were it for me to love.

HENRY. Tush, Kate, but tell me in plain terms,
    Canst thou love the King of England?
I cannot do as these countries do,
That spend half their time in wooing.
Tush, wench, I am none such.
But wilt thou go over to England?

KATHERINE. I would to God that I had your majesty
As fast in love as you have my father in wars.
I would not vouchsafe so much as one look,   1370
Until you had restated all these unreasonable demands.

---

[57] H.V. V.ii. 90–306.

HENRY. Tush, Kate, I know thou wouldst not use me so
Hardly. But tell me, canst thou love the King of England?

KATHERINE. How should I love him, that has dealt so hardly
With my father.

HENRY. But I'll deal as easily with thee
As thy heart can imagine, or tongue can require.
How sayest thou, what will it be?

KATHERINE. If I were of my own direction,
I could give you answer.   1380
But seeing I stand at my father's direction,
I must first know his will.

HENRY. But shall I have thy good will in the mean season?

KATHERINE. Whereas I can put your grace in no assurance,
I would be loth to put you in any despair.

HENRY. Now before God, it is a sweet wench.
            (*She goes aside, and speaks as follows.*)

KATHERINE. I may think myself the happiest in the world,
That is beloved of the mighty King of England.

HENRY. Well, Kate, are you at home with me?
Sweet Kate, tell thy father from me,   1390
That none in the world could sooner have persuaded me to
It than thou, and so tell thy father from me.

KATHERINE. God keep your majesty in good health.   (*Exit Kate.*)

HENRY. Farewell, sweet Kate. In faith, it is a sweet wench,
But if I knew I could not have her father's good will,
I would so rouse the towers over his ears,
That I would make him be glad to bring her me,
Upon his hands and knees.   (*Exit Henry.*)

SCENE XIX.

Enter Derick, with his girdle full of shoes.

DERICK. How now? Zounds, it did me good to see how
I did triumph over the Frenchmen.   1400
      (*Enter John Cobbler, roving, with a pack full of apparel.*)

JOHN. Whoop, Derick, how dost thou?

DERICK. What, John, Comedevales? Alive yet?

JOHN. I promise thee, Derick, I escaped hardly,
For I was within half a mile when one was killed.

DERICK. Were you so?

JOHN. Ay, trust me, I had like been slain.

DERICK. But once killed, why it is nothing.
I was four or five times slain.

JOHN. Four or five times slain?
Why, how couldst thou have been alive now?   1410
    DERICK. O John, never say so,
For I was called the bloody soldier amongst them all.
    JOHN. Why, what didst thou?
    DERICK. Why, I will tell thee, John.
Every day when I went into the field,
[58]I would take a straw and thrust it into my nose,
And make my nose bleed, and then I would go into the field,
And when the captain saw me, he would say,
Peace! a bloody soldier, and bid me stand aside,
Whereof I was glad.   1420
But mark the chance, John.
I went and stood behind a tree, but mark then, John.
I thought I had been safe, but on a sudden,
There steps to me a lusty tall Frenchman,
Now he drew, and I drew,
Now I lay here, and he lay there,
Now I set this leg before, and turned this backward,
And skipped quite over a hedge,
And he saw me no more there that day.
And was not this well done, John?   1430
    JOHN. Mass, Derick, thou hast a witty head.
    DERICK. Ay, John, thou mayest see, if thou hadst taken my
counsel,
But what hast thou there?
I think thou hast been robbing the Frenchmen.
    JOHN. I' faith, Derick, I have gotten some apparel
To carry home to my wife.
    DERICK. And I have got some shoes,
For I'll tell thee what I did. When they were dead,
I would go take off all their shoes.   1400
    JOHN. Ay, but Derick, how shall we get home?
    DERICK. Nay, zounds, and they take thee,
They will hang thee.
O John, never do so. If it be thy fortune to be hanged,
Be hanged in thy own language, whatsoever thou dost.
    JOHN. Why Derick, the wars is done,
We may go home now.
    DERICK. Ay, but you may not go before you ask the king leave.
[59]But I know a way to go home, and ask the king no leave.

---

[58] *H.IV.* One, II.iv. 340-343.
[59] *H.V.* V.i. 85ff.

JOHN. How is that, Derick?   1450

DERICK. Why, John, thou knowest the Duke of York's
Funeral must be carried into England, dost thou not?

JOHN. Ay, that I do.

DERICK. Why, then thou knowest we'll go with it.

JOHN. Ay, but Derick, how shall we do for to meet them?

DERICK. Zounds, if I make not shift to meet them, hang me.
Sirra, thou knowest that in every town there will
Be ringing, and there will be cakes and drink.
Now I will go to the clerk and sexton
And keep a talking, and say, oh, this fellow rings well,   1460
And thou shalt go and take a piece of cake, then I'll ring,
And thou shalt say, oh this fellow keeps a good stint,
And then I will go drink to thee all the way.
But I marvel what my dame will say when we come home,
Because we have not a French word to cast at a dog
By the way.

JOHN. Why, what shall we do, Derick?

DERICK. Why John, I'll go before and call my dame whore,
And thou shalt come after and set fire on the house,
We may do it, John, for I'll prove it,   1470
Because we be soldiers.   (*The trumpets sound.*)

JOHN. Derick, help me to carry my shoes' and boots.   (*Exeunt.*)

SCENE XX.

*Enter King of England, Lords of Oxford and Exeter, then the King of
France, Prince Dauphin, and the Duke of Burgundy, and attendants.*

HENRY. [60]Now my good brothers of France,
I hope by this time you have deliberated of your answer?

KING. Ay, my well-beloved brother of England,
We have viewed it over with our learned Council,
But cannot find that you should be crowned
King of France.

HENRY. What, not King of France? Then nothing.
I must be King. But my loving brother of France,   1480
I can hardly forget the late injuries offered me
When I came last to parley.
The Frenchmen had better a raked
The bowels out of their fathers' carcasses

---

[60] H.V. V.ii. 357ff. In Shakespeare, the final agreement between Henry V
and Charles VI is contrastingly quick and easy.

Than to have fired my tents,
And if I knew thy son Prince Dauphin for one,
I would so rouse him, as he was never so roused.

KING. I dare swear for my son's innocence
In this matter.
But if this please you: that immediately you be   1490
Proclaimed and crowned heir and regent of France,
Not king, because I myself was once crowned king.

HENRY. Heir and regent of France, that is well,
But that is not all that I must have.

KING. The rest my secretary has in writing.

FRENCH SECRETARY. Item, that Henry, King of England,
Be crowned heir and regent of France,
During the life of King Charles, and after his death,
The crown with all rights to remain to King Henry
of England, and to his heirs forever.   1500

HENRY. Well, my good brother of France,
There is one thing I must needs desire.

KING. What is that, my good brother of England?

HENRY. That all your nobles must be sworn to be true to me.

KING. Whereas they have not stuck with greater
Matters, I know they will not stick with such a trifle.
Begin you, my Lord Duke of Burgundy.

HENRY. Come, my Lord of Burgundy,
Take your oath upon my sword.

BURGUNDY. I, Philip, Duke of Burgundy,   1510
Swear to Henry, King of England,
To be true to him, and to become his liege man,
And that if I, Philip, hear of any foreign power
Coming to invade the said Henry or his heirs,
Then I, the said Philip, to send him word,
And aid him with all the power I can make,
And thereunto I take my oath.

(*He kisses the sword.*)

HENRY. Come, Prince Dauphin, you must swear too.

(*He kisses the sword.*)

HENRY. Well, my brother of France,
There is one thing more I must needs require of you.   1520

KING. Wherein is it that we may satisfy your majesty?

HENRY. A trifle, my good brother of France.
I mean to make your daughter Queen of England,
If she be willing, and you therewith content.
How sayest thou, Kate, canst thou love the King of England?

KATHERINE. How should I love thee, which is my father's enemy?

HENRY. Tut, stand not upon these points,
'Tis you must make us friends.
I know, Kate, thou art not a little proud that I love thee.
What, wench, the King of England?   1530 .

KING. Daughter, let nothing stand betwixt the
King of England and thee, agree to it.

KATHERINE. I had best whilst he is willing,
Lest when I would, he will not.
I rest at your majesty's command.

HENRY. Welcome, sweet Kate. But my brother of France,
What say you to it?

KING. With all my heart I like it,
But when shall be your wedding day?

HENRY. The first Sunday of the next month,   1540
God willing.

(Sound trumpets.)

(Exeunt omnes.)

Finis.

□ *Some Sources for Further Study*

1–4. For supplements to Holinshed see p. 115, sources 1–4.

5. JEAN LE FEVRE DE SAINT-REMY — *Memoires,* 1408–1435. The
French view of the invasions of Henry V presented by the official
chronicler of the court of Burgundy during those years.

6. SAMUEL DANIEL — *The First Four Books of the Civil Wars between the Houses of Lancaster and York* (1595). See Book Four.

Julius Caesar

The central source for this play is the monumental translation of Plutarch's *Parallel Lives* by Shakespeare's near contemporary, Sir Thomas North, whose work appeared in 1578. North's
Plutarch was translated from the French of Jacques Amyot, Bishop
of Auxerre, who brushed a light glaze of moralizing onto the original,
and the resultant blend of classical nobility and pat sixteenth century
morality has a special appeal for Shakespeare. He keeps at least as
close — in most cases closer — to North as to any source.[1] For this
play, Shakespeare uses segments of three of the *Lives*, *Julius Caesar*,
Marcus Brutus, and *Marcus Antonius*, and these supply him with
every incident large and small and also with seeds of character, idea,
and even dialogue.

The last part of the *Life of Caesar*, brackets all of the material of
Shakespeare's play. Its starting point as Shakespeare source is Caesar's
triumphant return to Rome in 45 B.C., when the people chose him
"perpetual dictator" and he declined. Shakespeare fuses that incident
with the Festival of Lupercal, which happened six months later, in
44 B.C., around a month before Caesar's death, the hub and climax
of this *Life* and Act III of Shakespeare's play. Acts IV and V, the
civil war between the conspirators and the triumvirate, are covered in
quick summary in this *Life*, occupying only about a page.

The *Life of Brutus* yields the richest storehouse of *Julius Caesar*
materials, not only the main outlines of all five Acts but also minor incidents such as the discontent of Caius Ligarius, Porcia's [Portia's]
self-inflicted wound, and the symbolic appearance of eagles before
Philippi (V.i. 80–84). *Brutus* also furnishes language — impressive
lines for Caesar (pp. 262 and 265) and a hint for Antonius's eloquence (p. 283) — but its chief value lies in its treatment of the co-
conspirators, Brutus and Cassius. The *Life of Brutus* revolves around
two hubs, the Brutus-Cassius conspiracy and their fate at the Battle

---

[1] Casca is Shakespeare's only significant interpolation in this play.

of Philippi, and the emphasis on these events in Shakespeare's play reflects the importance of this source. Like all Shakespeare's sources, however, even this one is reshaped to serve dramatic needs. The extended power struggle between Antonius and Octavius Caesar is ignored as is the twenty day hiatus between the first and second battles of Philippi, prunings which help to fit the story into one vast arc.

The chief value of the Life of Antonius here is its two-sided view of him, first from the conspirators' viewpoint as they plot the assassination of his friend and leader, then from a third person omniscient view of him as one "that revels long a-nights." The swift movement in this Life from Caesar's return to Rome to the Festival of Lupercal might have suggested the fusion Shakespeare makes of those incidents, and its insight into the Triumvirate deepens our perception of that group. It deals even more briefly than the Life of Caesar with Acts IV and V, gives them only a single paragraph, so that the Life of Brutus alone remains the main source for the final development and resolution of Shakespeare's play.

The most famous scene in Julius Caesar, Antony's speech to the Roman citizens (III.ii), may owe a debt to an anonymous translation published in 1578 of The Ancient History and Exquisite Chronicle of the Roman Wars, Both Civil and Foreign of Appian, a second century Alexandrian who wrote in Greek. Ernest Schanzer, whose work on Shakespeare and Appian is authoritative,[2] finds similarities of content and hints for Shakespeare's characterization of a crafty and manipulating Antony in the speeches of Antonius and Lepidus to the citizens after the assassination of Caesar. These are presented in the text with special attention called to the touches of character in and around them.

Plutarch pauses for character analyses somewhere in each of his Lives, and those on Caesar, Brutus, Cassius, and Antonius are placed at the end of each appropriate Life in this volume, a method paralleling Holinshed's. They may have furnished Shakespeare with broad character suggestions — Caesar had "noble courage," Brutus was "framed unto virtue," and so forth — but those assessments, even with Appian's complicating hints of Antonius's duplicity, hardly account for the probing psychological depth of this play. Antony's funeral oration is a classic exercise in psychological manipulation. Just as valid, and digging deeper, are Cassius's assurance to Antony that

> Your voice shall be as strong as any man's
> In the disposing of new dignities. (III.i. 177–178),

---

[2] Ernest Schanzer, Shakespeare's Appian (Liverpool: Liverpool University Press, 1956).

whereby he projects his own true motive for the assassination; the conspirators' ensnaring Brutus by luring him into making decisions as to who will be killed (II.i. 141–191); and Brutus's quarrel with Cassius over money while suppressing the real reason for his self-destructive anger, the death of Portia (IV.iii. 1–57). A possible cause of these searching, unconscious motivations might be the three separate angles of vision supplied by Plutarch which, like the cubist's technique of simultaneous multiple vision, might well have offered views of greater depth and dimensionality.

The chief political idea of this play, to beware the opponents of monarchy, is implicit in the events surrounding Caesar's death and would gain the moral approval of Plutarch's French translator and his Tudor counterpart. Plutarch also advances another idea in these Lives that Shakespeare responds to with deep sympathy: that omens convey truth and are to be believed. The soothsayer and Calpurnia correctly foresee Caesar's death; the "monstrous spirit" at Philippi signifies, and truly, the coming death of Brutus. Cassius, who affects the pragmatic doctrines of Epicurus — the Lives of Caesar and Brutus both tell us this — changes his mind at the brink of death and turns, as Hotspur did, to prophecy. The Renaissance with its strong sense of being a microcosm of God's universe would tend to accept omens as intimations of that universe. Shakespeare not only reflects this idea in his deaths of Brutus and Cassius but also in previous plays — the ghosts that visit Richard III and the dreams and visions of Romeo and Juliet are likewise harbingers of truth. With seventeenth century scientism encroaching, along with pragmatic middle class and Puritan values, the Renaissance, and Shakespeare, sought comfort in the significance and serenity of a more ancient and traditional world.

PLUTARCH (C. 46–120 A.D.)
Parallel Lives

translated by Sir Thomas North, 1579[3]

THE LIFE OF JULIUS CAESAR

[Julius Caesar (100–44 B.C.) embarked upon a life of intrigue and incident from the time he had, as Plutarch writes, "scant any hair on his face." Married as a youth to Cornelia, daughter of an enemy of Sulla, then dictator of Rome, he was forced to flee Rome and journeyed to Asia. En route he was captured by pirates, ransomed, then as he had promised his captors, returned to capture and crucify the majority of them. At Rhodes he studied under the masterful rhetoritician Apollonius, who was also the teacher of Cicero. Upon the death of Sulla, Caesar returned to Rome where his eloquence swayed the people to choose him tribune — i.e., colonel of one thousand footmen — and shortly after, in 63 B.C., Pontifex Maximus (chief bishop) thanks largely to "the poor needy persons, which were they that put all their hope in Caesar."

At that juncture Publius Clodius, a young nobleman, paid suit to Pompeia, Caesar's second wife, and during a festival was discovered in the chamber of Pompeia's maid disguised as a woman. Caesar at once "put his wife away" with the explanation that: "I will not that my wife be so much as suspected."

Shortly afterwards, in 61 B.C., he was made praetor (governor) of Spain where he enjoyed his first major triumph both as general and as political leader. He returned to Rome where he reconciled the two

---

[3] The title of North's translation reads: The Lives of the Noble Grecians and Romans, Compared Together By That Grave Learned Philosopher and Historiographer, Plutarch of Chaironeia. The modernized version of North used here (with slight emendations by the present editor) is by the Rev. Walter W. Skeat, Shakespeare's Plutarch (London: Macmillan and Co., 1875). Skeat's version retains virtually all of the original punctuation so that the phrasing is just about the same as Shakespeare saw and adapted.

major, and then hostile, leaders — Pompey, the chief politician, and Crassus, "the richest man of all Rome," — and joined with them to form the first triumvirate. To strengthen the alliance, Pompey married Caesar's daughter Julia, and Caesar married Pompey's daughter Calp[h]urnia. Caesar and his armies then marched upon Gaul, and for the next nine years Caesar enjoyed an unbroken string of victories, repelling the invading Helvetii, taking possession of all Gaul, conquering the Belgae, twice bridging the Rhine and conquering the tribes beyond it, twice sailing over to Britain and conquering its natives.

During this time the armies of Pompey fought in Spain, those of Crassus in the Middle East, but two events — the death of Julia, Pompey's wife, and the death of Crassus during a campaign against the Parthians — drove a wedge between Pompey and Caesar that opened up a deep and bitter rivalry. Pompey, who was then in Rome, used his influence with the common people to be made dictator, but Cato, renowned judge, prevented that and Pompey had to settle for the consulship instead. Even so, Pompey was able to frustrate and abuse Caesar, who was then in Gaul, and influenced the senate to order Caesar's resignation and to proclaim him, Pompey, general of the Roman army. Caesar, however, in 49 B.C. gathered his army and crossed "the little river of Rubicon, which divided Gaul on this side of the Alps from Italy."

He entered Rome and conquered it almost without striking a blow, and Pompey fled to Greece. The senate made Caesar dictator, a rank which he relinquished after eleven days to accept a co-consulship instead. He then pursued Pompey into Greece and after a see-saw battle overcame Pompey's army at Pharsalia — as prophecied by his soothsayer. Pompey's captured officers included one Marcus Junius Brutus, whom Caesar pardoned. Pompey himself escaped to Egypt, but there he was assassinated by Pothinus, a eunuch who had driven Cleopatra from her court. Caesar, on a journey of conquest into Egypt, sent for Cleopatra to come secretly to him, whereupon [4]"she laid herself down upon a mattress or flockbed, which Apollodorus her friend tied and bound up together like a bundle with a great leather thong, and so took her upon his back and brought her thus hampered in this fardle[5] unto Caesar in at the castle gate." Her "sweet conversation and pleasant entertainment" made Caesar fall in love with her, and he made her his "sister queen of Egypt." Cleopatra had a son by Caesar named Caesarion.

From Egypt Caesar journeyed to Syria where he conquered King

---

[4] *Antony and Cleopatra*: II.vi. 65–71.
[5] bundle.

*Pharnaces so swiftly that he described the victory in a letter to a
friend in Rome by three words only: veni, vidi, vici (I came, I saw,
I conquered). He returned to Rome soon after, was made dictator
for a year, and in 46 B.C. crossed to Africa where he defeated Cato and
Scipio. He was made consul for the fourth time, campaigned in Spain
against Pompey's sons, and early in 44 B.C. the Romans]*

chose him perpetual dictator. This was a plain tyranny; for to this absolute power of Dictator, they added this, never to be afraid to be deposed.
Cicero pronounced before the Senate, that they should give him
such honours as were meet for a man: howbeit others afterwards
added too honours beyond all reason. For men striving who should
most honour him, they made him hateful and troublesome to themselves that most favoured him, by reason of the unmeasurable greatness
and honours which they gave him. Thereupon it is reported, that
even they that most hated him were no less favourers and furtherers
of his honours than they that most flattered him, because they might
have greater occasions to rise, and that it might appear they had just
cause and colour to attempt that they did against him. And now for
himself, after he had ended his civil wars, he did so honourably behave
himself, that there was no fault to be found in him: and therefore
methinks, amongst other honours they gave him, he rightly deserved
this, that they should build him a temple of Clemency, to thank him
for his courtesy he had used unto them in his victory. For he pardoned
many of them that had borne arms against him, and furthermore, did
prefer some of them to honour and office in the commonwealth: as,
amongst others, Cassius and Brutus, both the which were made Praetors. And, where Pompey's images had been thrown down, he caused
them to be set up again: whereupon Cicero said then, that, Caesar
setting up Pompey's images again, he made his own to stand the surer.
And when some of his friends did counsel him to have a guard for
the safety of his person, and some also did offer themselves to serve
him, he would never consent to it, but said: [6]"It was better to die once,
than always to be afraid of death." But to win himself the love and
goodwill of the people, as the honourablest guard and best safety he
could have, he made common feasts again and general distributions of
corn. . . .

*[To further gratify the Romans he rebuilt and replenished the cities
of Carthage and Corinth. He made preparations for another world-
wide tour of conquest, and at the same time set in motion a wide variety
of civil improvements as well as the reform of the calendar. Upon re-*

[6] II.ii. 32–33.

turning from a journey to Alba, the senate and the people planned a series of celebrations in his honor, but he shrugged them off. Afterwards]

he imputed it [his rudeness] to his disease saying, that their wits are not perfect which have this disease of the falling evil,[7] when standing on their feet they speak to the common people, but are soon troubled with a trembling of their body, and a sudden dimness and giddiness. [8]At that time the feast *Lupercalia* was celebrated, the which in old time men say was the feast of shepherds or herdmen, and is much like unto the feast of the Lycaeans in Arcadia. [9]But howsoever it is, that day there are divers noblemen's sons, young men, (and some of them magistrates themselves that govern then), which run naked through the city, striking in sport them they meet in their way with leather thongs, hair and all on, to make them give place. And many noblewomen and gentlewomen also go of purpose to stand in their way, and do put forth their hands to be stricken, as scholars hold them out to their schoolmaster to be stricken with the ferule: persuading themselves that, being with child, they shall have good delivery; and so, being barren, that it will make them to conceive with child. Caesar sat to behold that sport upon the pulpit for orations, in a chain of gold, apparelled in triumphant manner. Antonius, who was Consul at that time, was one of them that ran this holy course.[10] So when he came into the market-place, the people made a lane for him to run at liberty, and he came to Caesar, and presented him a diadem wreathed about with laurel. Whereupon there rose a certain cry of rejoicing, not very great, done only by a few appointed for the purpose. But when Caesar refused the diadem, then all the people together made an outcry of joy. Then Antonius offering it him again, there was a second shout of joy, but yet of a few. But when Caesar refused it again the second time, then all the whole people shouted. Caesar having made this proof, found that the people did not like of it, and thereupon rose out of his chair, and commanded the crown to be carried unto Jupiter in the Capitol. [11]After that, there were set up images of Caesar in the city, with diadems upon their heads like kings. Those the two tribunes, Flavius and Marullus, went and pulled down, and furthermore, meeting with them that first saluted Caesar as king, they committed them to prison. The people followed them rejoicing at it, and called them

---

[7] epilepsy.
[8] I.i. 72.
[9] I.ii. 1–10. Calpurnia's participation in this ceremony is Shakespeare's own invention.
[10] I.ii. 220–248.
[11] I.i. 1–65; I.ii. 288–289.

Brutes, because of Brutus, who had in old time driven the kings out of Rome, and that brought the kingdom of one person unto the government of the Senate and people. Caesar was so offended withal, that he deprived Marullus and Flavius of their tribuneships, and accusing them, he spake also against the people, and called them Bruti and Cumani, to wit, beasts and fools.

Hereupon the people went straight unto Marcus Brutus, who from his father came of the first Brutus, and by his mother of the house of the Servilians, a noble house as any was in Rome, and was also nephew and son-in-law of Marcus Cato. Notwithstanding, the great honours and favour Caesar shewed unto him kept him back that of himself alone he did not conspire nor consent to depose him of his kingdom. For Caesar did not only save his life after the battle of Pharsalia, when Pompey fled, and did at his request also save many more of his friends besides: but furthermore, he put a marvellous confidence in him. For he had already preferred him to the Praetorship for that year, and furthermore was appointed to be Consul the fourth year after that, having through Caesar's friendship obtained it before Cassius, who likewise made suit for the same: [12]and Caesar also, as it is reported, said in this contention, "indeed Cassius hath alleged best reason, but yet shall he not be chosen before Brutus." Some one day accusing Brutus while he practised this conspiracy, Caesar would not hear of it, but, clapping his hand on his body, told them, "Brutus will look for this skin:" meaning thereby, that Brutus for his virtue deserved to rule after him, but yet that, for ambition's sake, he would not shew himself unthankful or dishonourable.[13] Now they that desired change, and wished Brutus only their prince and governor above all other, they durst not come to him themselves to tell him what they would have him to do, but in the night did cast sundry papers into the Praetor's seat, where he gave audience, and the most of them to this effect: "Thou sleepest, Brutus, and art not Brutus indeed."[14] Cassius, finding Brutus' ambition stirred up the more by these seditious bills did prick him forward and egg him on the more, for a private quarrel he had conceived against Caesar: the circumstance whereof we have set down more at large in Brutus' life. Caesar also had Cassius in great jealousy, and suspected him much: whereupon he said on a time to his friends, "what will Cassius do, think ye? I like not his pale looks." [15]Another time when Caesar's friends complained unto him of Antonius and Dolabella, that they pretended[16] some mischief

---

[12] I.ii. 312–319.
[13] I.ii. 319ff.
[14] I.ii. 25–297.
[15] I.ii. 190–210.
[16] plotted.

towards him: he answered them again, "As for those fat men and smooth-combed heads," quoth he, "I never reckon of them; but these pale-visaged and carrion-lean people, I fear them most," meaning Brutus and Cassius.

[17]Certainly destiny may easier be foreseen than avoided, considering the strange and wonderful signs that were said to be seen before Caesar's death. For, touching the fires in the element, and spirits running up and down in the night, and also the solitary birds to be seen at noondays sitting in the great market-place, are not all these signs perhaps worth the noting, in such a wonderful chance as happened? But Strabo the philosopher writeth, that divers men were seen going up and down in fire: and furthermore, that there was a slave of the soldiers that did cast a marvellous burning flame out of his hand, insomuch as they that saw it thought he had been burnt; but when the fire was out, it was found he had no hurt. Caesar self also doing sacrifice unto the gods, found that one of the beasts which was sacrificed had no heart: and that was a strange thing in nature, how a beast could live without a heart. [18]Furthermore there was a certain soothsayer that had given Caesar warning long time afore, to take heed of the day of the Ides of March, (which is the fifteenth of the month), for on that day he should be in great danger. [19]That day being come, Caesar going unto the Senate-house, and speaking merrily unto the soothsayer, told him, "the Ides of March be come:" "so they be," softly answered the soothsayer, "but yet are they not past." And the very day before, Caesar, supping with Marcus Lepidus, sealed certain letters, as he was wont to do, at the board: so, talk falling out amongst them, reasoning what death was best, he, preventing[20] their opinions, cried out aloud, "death unlooked for." [21]Then going to bed the same night, as his manner was, and lying with his wife Calpurnia, all the windows and doors of his chamber flying open, the noise awoke him, and made him afraid when he saw such light: but more, when he heard his wife Calpurnia, being fast asleep, weep and sigh, and put forth many fumbling lamentable speeches: for she dreamed that Caesar was slain, and that she had him in her arms. Others also do deny that she had any such dream, as, amongst other, Titus Livius writeth that it was in this sort: the Senate having set upon the top of Caesar's house, for an ornament and setting forth of the same, a certain pinnacle, Calpurnia dreamed that she saw it broken down, and that she thought she lamented and wept for it. Insomuch that,

---

[17] I.iii. 1–78.
[18] I.ii. 12–24.
[19] III.i. 1–2.
[20] anticipating.
[21] II.ii. 1–56.

Caesar rising in the morning, she prayed him, if it were possible, not to go out of the doors that day, but to adjourn the session of the Senate until another day. And if that he made no reckoning of her dream, yet that he would search further of the soothsayers by their sacrifices, to know what should happen him that day. Thereby it seemed that Caesar likewise did fear or suspect somewhat, because his wife Calpurnia until that time was never given to any fear and superstition: and that then he saw her so troubled in mind with this dream she had. But much more afterwards, when the soothsayers having sacrificed many beasts one after another, told him that none did like them: then he determined to send Antonius to adjourn the session of the Senate.

[22]But in the mean time came Decius Brutus,[23] surnamed Albinus, in whom Caesar put such confidence, that in his last will and testament he had appointed him to be his next heir, and yet was of the conspiracy with Cassius and Brutus: he, fearing that if Caesar did adjourn the session that day, the conspiracy would be betrayed, laughed at the soothsayers, and reproved Caesar, saying, "that he gave the Senate occasion to mislike with him, and that they might think he mocked them, considering that by his commandment they were assembled, and that they were ready willingly to grant him all things, and to proclaim him king of all his provinces of the Empire of Rome out of Italy, and that he should wear his diadem in all other places both by sea and land. And furthermore, that if any man should tell them from him they should depart for that present time, and return again when Calpurnia should have better dreams, what would his enemies and ill-willers say, and how could they like of his friends' words? And who could persuade them otherwise, but that they would think his dominion a slavery unto them and tyrannical in himself? And yet if it be so," said he, "that you utterly mislike of this day, it is better that you go yourself in person, and, saluting the Senate, to dismiss them till another time." Therewithal he took Caesar by the hand, and brought him out of his house. Caesar was not gone far from his house, but a bond-man, a stranger, did what he could to speak with him: and when he saw he was put back by the great press and multitude of people that followed him, he went straight into his house, and put himself into Calpurnia's hands, to be kept till Caesar came back again, telling her that he had greater matters to impart unto him. [24]And one Artemidorus also, born in the isle of Gnidos, a

---

[22] II.ii. 57–107.
[23] Not Decius but Decimus: this is North's error, repeated in the opening stage direction of I.ii.
[24] II.iii. 1ff.

doctor of rhetoric in the Greek tongue, who by means of his profession was very familiar with certain of Brutus' confederates, and therefore knew the most part of all their practices against Caesar, came
and brought him a little bill, written with his own hand, of all that
he meant to tell him. [25]He, marking how Caesar received all the
supplications that were offered him, and that he gave them straight
to his men that were about him, pressed nearer to him, and said:
"Caesar, read this memorial to yourself, and that quickly, for they be
matters of great weight, and touch you nearly." Caesar took it of
him, but could never read it, though he many times attempted it, for
the number of people that did salute him: but holding it still in his
hand, keeping it to himself, went on withal into the Senate-house.
Howbeit others are of opinion, that it was some man else that gave
him that memorial, and not Artemidorus, who did what he could all
the way as he went to give it Caesar, but he was always repulsed by the
people. For these things, they may seem to come by chance; but the
place where the murder was prepared, and where the Senate were
assembled, and where also there stood up an image of Pompey dedi-
cated by himself amongst other ornaments which he gave unto the
theatre, all these were manifest proofs, that it was the ordinance of
some god that made this treason to be executed, specially in that very
place. It is also reported, that Cassius (though otherwise he did favour
the doctrine of Epicurus[26] beholding the image of Pompey, before
they entered into the action of their traitorous enterprise, he did
softly call upon it to aid him: but the instant danger of the present
time, taking away his former reason, did suddenly put him into a
furious passion, and made him like a man half beside himself. [27]Now
Antonius, that was a faithful friend to Caesar, and a valiant man besides of his hands, him Decius Brutus Albinus entertained out of the
Senate-house, having begun a long tale of set purpose. So Caesar coming into the house,[28] all the Senate stood up on their feet to do him

---

[25] III.i. 3–12.

[26] I.ii. 140–141; V.i. 77–79. Note how significant is this parenthetical remark and its qualification to the central ideas of this drama.

[27] III.i. 25–26. In Shakespeare Trebonius, not Decius, draws Antony aside.

[28] The *Curia Pompeiana*, where Caesar was actually killed. Shakespeare
alters the site of the murder to the Capitol, but not without a prior source.
Chaucer, in "The Monk's Tale" wrote:
>In the Capitol anon him hente (seized)
>This false Brutus, and his other foon,
>And stikked him with bodekins anoon
>With many a wound, and thus they let him lie.

And later Shakespeare in *Hamlet* has Polonius recall that in his student days:
>I did enact Julius Caesar. I was killed i' the
>Capitol. Brutus killed me. (III.ii. 108–109.)

honour. [29]Then part of Brutus' company and confederates stood round about Caesar's chair, and part of them also came towards him, as though they made suit with Metellus Cimber, to call home his brother again from banishment: and thus prosecuting still their suit, they followed Caesar till he was set in his chair. Who denying their petitions, and being offended with them one after another, because the more they were denied the more they pressed upon him and were the earnester with him, Metellus at length, taking his gown with both his hands, pulled it over his neck, which was the sign given the confederates to set upon him. Then Casca, behind him, struck him in the neck with his sword; howbeit the wound was not great nor mortal, because it seemed the fear of such a devilish attempt did amaze him and take his strength from him, that he killed him not at the first blow. But Caesar, turning straight unto him, caught hold of his sword and held it hard; and they both cried out, Caesar in Latin: "O vile traitor Casca, what doest thou?" and Casca, in Greek, to his brother: "Brother, help me." At the beginning of this stir, they that were present, not knowing of the conspiracy, were so amazed with the horrible sight they saw, they had no power to fly, neither to help him, nor so much as once to make an outcry. They on the other side that had conspired his death compassed him in on every side with their swords drawn in their hands, that Caesar turned him no where but he was stricken at by some, and still had naked swords in his face, and was hacked and mangled among them, as a wild beast taken of hunters. For it was agreed among them that every man should give him a wound, because all their parts should be in this murder: and then Brutus himself gave him one wound about his privities. Men report also, that Caesar did still defend himself against the rest, running every way with his body [30]but when he saw Brutus with his sword drawn in his hand, then he pulled his gown over his head, and made no more resistance, and was driven either casually or purposely, by the counsel of the conspirators, against the base whereupon Pompey's image stood, which ran all of a gore-blood till he was slain. [31]Thus it seemed that the image took just revenge of Pompey's enemy, being thrown down on the ground at his feet, and yielding up the ghost there, for the number of wounds he had upon him. For it is reported, that he had three and twenty wounds upon his body[32] and divers of the conspirators did hurt themselves, striking one body with so many blows.

---

[29] III.i. 27–77. For the source of Shakespeare's *"Et tu, Brute?"* see footnote 28, p. 281.

[30] III.ii. 180–193.

[31] III.i. 114–116.

[32] Compare in Shakespeare "Caesar's three-and-thirty wounds" (V.i. 53).

³³When Caesar was slain, the Senate (though Brutus stood in the midst amongst them, as though he would have said something touching this fact) presently ran out of the house, and flying, filled all the city with marvellous fear and tumult. Insomuch as some did shut to the doors, others forsook their shops and warehouses, and others ran to the place to see what the matter was: and others also that had seen it ran home to their houses again. But Antonius and Lepidus, which were two of Caesar's chiefest friends, secretly conveying themselves away, fled into other men's houses and forsook their own. ³⁴Brutus and his confederates on the other side, being yet hot with this murder they had committed, having their swords drawn in their hands, came all in a troop together out of the Senate and went into the market-place, not as men that made countenance to fly, but otherwise boldly holding up their heads like men of courage, and called to the people to defend their liberty, and stayed to speak with every great personage whom they met in their way. Of them, some followed this troup and went amongst them, as if they had been of the conspiracy, and falsely challenged part of the honour with them: amongst them was Caius Octavius and Lentulus Spinther. But both of them were afterwards put to death for their vain covetousness of honour, by Antonius and Octavius Caesar the younger; and yet had no part of that honour for the which they were both put to death, neither did any man believe that they were any of the confederates or of counsel with them. For they that did put them to death took revenge rather of the will they had to offend than of any act they had committed. ³⁵The next morning, Brutus and his confederates came into the market-place to speak unto the people, who gave them such audience, that it seemed they neither greatly reproved nor allowed the act for by their great silence they shewed that they were sorry for Caesar's death, and also that they did reverence Brutus. Now the Senate granted general pardon for all that was past; and, to pacify every man, ordained besides, that Caesar's funerals should be honoured as a god, and established all things that he had done, and gave certain provinces also and convenient honours unto Brutus and his confederates, whereby every man thought all things were brought to good peace and quietness again. ³⁶But when they had opened Caesar's testament, and found a liberal legacy of money bequeathed unto every citizen of Rome, and that they saw his body (which was brought into the market-place) all bemangled with gashes of swords, then there

---

³³ III.i. 96–98.
³⁴ III.i. 103–121.
³⁵ III.ii. 1–58.
³⁶ III.ii. 78–264.

was no order to keep the multitude and common people quiet, but they plucked up forms, tables, and stools, and laid them all about the body; and setting them afire, burnt the corse. Then when the fire was well kindled, they took the fire-brands, and went unto their houses that had slain Caesar, to set them afire. Others also ran up and down the city to see if they could meet with any of them, to cut them in pieces: howbeit they could meet with never a man of them, because they had locked themselves up safely in their houses. [37]There was one of Caesar's friends called Cinna, that had a marvellous strange and terrible dream the night before. He dreamed that Caesar bade him to supper, and that he refused and would not go: then that Caesar took him by the hand, and led him against his will. Now Cinna, hearing at that time that they burnt Caesar's body in the market-place, notwithstanding that he feared his dream, and had an ague on him besides, he went into the market-place to honour his funerals. When he came thither, one of the mean sort asked him what his name was? He was straight called by his name. The first man told it to another, and that other unto another, so that it ran straight through them all, that he was one of them that murdered Caesar: (for indeed one of the traitors to Caesar was also called Cinna as himself) wherefore taking him for Cinna the murderer, they fell upon him with such fury that they presently dispatched him in the market-place. This stir and fury made Brutus and Cassius more afraid than of all that was past, and therefore within few days after they departed out of Rome: and touching their doings afterwards, and what calamity they suffered till their deaths, we have written it at large in the life of Brutus. Caesar died at six and fifty years of age, and Pompey also lived not passing four years more than he. So he reaped no other fruit of all his reign and dominion, which he had so vehemently desired all his life and pursued with such extreme danger, but a vain name only and a superficial glory, that procured him the envy and hatred of his country.

But his great prosperity and good fortune that favoured him all his lifetime, did continue afterwards in the revenge of his death, pursuing the murderers both by sea and land, till they had not left a man more to be executed, of all them that were actors or counsellers in the conspiracy of his death. [38]Furthermore, of all the chances that happen unto men upon the earth, that which came to Cassius above all other, is most to be wondered at: for he, being overcome in battle at the journey of Philippi, slew himself with the same sword with the which he struck Caesar. Again, of signs in the element, the great comet, which seven nights together was seen very bright after Caesar's

---

[37] III.iii. 1ff.
[38] V.iii. 1–90.

death, the eighth night after was never seen more. Also the brightness of the sun was darkened, the which all that year through rose very pale and shined not out, whereby it gave but small heat: therefore the air being very cloudy and dark, by the weakness of the heat that could not come forth, did cause the earth to bring forth but raw and unripe fruit, which rotted before it could ripe. [39]But above all, the ghost that appeared unto Brutus shewed plainly, that the gods were offended with the murder of Caesar. The vision was thus: Brutus being ready to pass over his army from the city of Abydos to the other coast lying directly against it, slept every night (as his manner was) in his tent; and being yet awake, thinking of his affairs (for by report he was as careful a captain and lived with as little sleep as ever man did) he thought he heard a noise at his tent-door, and looking towards the light of the lamp that waxed very dim, he saw a horrible vision of a man, of a wonderful greatness and dreadful look, which at the first made him marvellously afraid. But when he saw that it did him no hurt, but stood by his bed-side and said nothing; at length he asked him what he was. The image answered him: "I am thy ill angel, Brutus, and thou shalt see me by the city of Philippi." Then Brutus replied again, and said, "Well, I shall see thee then." Therewithal the spirit presently vanished from him. [40]After that time Brutus, being in battle near unto the city of Philippi against Antonius and Octavius Caesar, at the first battle he won the victory, and overthrowing all them that withstood him, he drove them into young Caesar's camp, which he took. The second battle being at hand, this spirit appeared again unto him, but spake never a word. Thereupon Brutus, knowing that he should die, did put himself to all hazard in battle, but yet fighting could not be slain. So seeing his men put to flight and overthrown, he ran unto a little rock not far off, and there setting his sword's point to his breast, fell upon it and slew himself; but yet, as it is reported, with the help of his friend that despatched him.

[The Character of Caesar]

. . . he was so entirely beloved of his soldiers, that to do him service (where otherwise they were no more than other men in any private quarrel) if Caesar's honour were touched, they were invincible, and would so desperately venture themselves and with such fury, that no man was able to abide them. . . .

Now Caesar's self did breed this noble courage and life in them. First, for that he gave them bountifully, and did honour them also,

---

[39] IV.iii. 275–286.
[40] V.iii. 6–8; V.v. 1–51.

shewing thereby, that he did not heap up riches in the wars to maintain his life afterwards in wantonness and pleasure, but that he did keep it in store, honourably to reward their valiant service: and that by so much he thought himself rich, by how much he was liberal in rewarding of them that had deserved it. Furthermore, they did not wonder so much at his valiantness in putting himself at every instant in such manifest danger, and in taking so extreme pains as he did, knowing that it was his greedy desire of honour that set him on fire, and pricked him forward to do it: but that he always continued all labour and hardness, more than his body could bear, that filled them all with admiration. For, concerning the constitution of his body, he was lean, white, and soft-skinned, and often subject to headache, and otherwhile to the falling sickness (the which took him the first time, as it is reported, in Corduba, a city of Spain:) but yet therefore yielded not, to the disease of his body, to make it a cloak to cherish him withal, but contrarily, took the pains of war as a medicine to cure his sick body, fighting always with his disease, travelling continually, living soberly, and commonly lying abroad in the field. For the most nights he slept in his coach or litter, and thereby bestowed his rest, to make him always able to do something: and in the day-time he would travel up and down the country to see towns, castles, and strong places. He had always a secretary with him in the coach, who did still write as he went by the way, and a soldier behind him that carried his sword. He made such speed the first time he came from Rome, when he had his office, that in eight days he came to the River of Rhone. He was so excellent a rider of horse from his youth, that holding his hands behind him, he would gallop his horse upon the spur.

THE LIFE OF MARCUS BRUTUS

[Marcus Junius Brutus (85–42 B.C.) as a youth favored Pompey over Caesar because he considered Pompey's the juster cause — this although Pompey had put Brutus's father to death. In the battle of Pharsalia Brutus surrendered to Caesar, who pardoned him — perhaps, hints Plutarch, because when Caesar "was a young man he had been acquainted with Servilia (Brutus's mother), who was extremely in love with him. And because Brutus was born in that time when their love was hottest, he persuaded himself that he begat him." Brutus used Caesar's affection to obtain pardon for Cassius, who had also fought for Pompey, and as a further sign of Caesar's trust and friendship obtained the governorship of Cisalpine Gaul when Caesar left to invade Africa. Brutus governed so admirably that, upon Caesar's return to Rome, Brutus was named first praetor of Rome. He had competed for this honor against Cassius, which caused a rift between *them, even though Cassius had married Junia, Brutus's sister. Despite Caesar's fondness for Brutus, however, he]*

did not trust him overmuch, nor was without tales brought unto him against him: howbeit he feared his great mind, authority, and friends. Yet, on the other side also, he trusted his good nature and fair conditions. [1]For, intelligence being brought him one day, that Antonius and Dolabella did conspire against him: he answered "That these fat long-haired men made him not afraid, but the lean and whitely-faced fellows," meaning that by Brutus and Cassius. At another time also when one accused Brutus unto him, and bade him beware of him: "What," said he again, clapping his hands on his breast, "think ye that Brutus will not tarry till this body die?" meaning that none but Brutus after him was meet to have such power as he had. And surely, (in my opinion) I am persuaded that Brutus might indeed have come to have been the chiefest man of Rome, if he could have contented himself for a time to have been next unto Caesar, and to have suffered his glory and authority, which he had gotten by his great victories, to consume with time. [2]But Cassius, being a choleric man, and hating Caesar privately more than he did the tyranny openly, he incensed Brutus against him. It is also reported, that Brutus could evil away with[3] the tyranny, and that Cassius hated the tyrant: making many complaints for the injuries he had done him; and amongst others, for that he had taken away his lions from him. Cassius had provided them for his sports when he should be Aedilis; and they were found in the city of Megara, when it was won by Calenus: and Caesar kept them. The rumour went, that these lions did marvellous great hurt to the Megarians: for when the city was taken, they brake their cages where they were tied up and turned them loose, thinking they would have done great mischief to the enemies, and have kept them from setting upon them: but the lions (contrary to expectation) turned upon themselves that fled unarmed, and did so cruelly tear some in pieces, that it pitied their enemies to see them. And this was the cause (as some do report) that made Cassius conspire against Caesar. But this holds no water:[4] for Cassius, even from his cradle, could not abide any manner of tyrants; as it appeared when he was but a boy, and went unto the same school that Faustus the son of Sylla did. And Faustus, bragging among other boys, highly boasted of his father's kingdom: Cassius rose up on his feet, and gave him two good wirts[5] on

---

[1] I.ii. 190–210.
[2] I.ii; I.iii; II.i.
[3] ill put up with.
[4] And Shakespeare wisely omits it.
[5] blows.

the ear. Faustus' governors would have put this matter in suit against Cassius: but Pompey would not suffer them, but caused the two boys to be brought before him, and asked them how the matter came to pass. Then Cassius (as it is written of him) said unto the other: "Go to, Faustus, speak again, and thou darest, before this nobleman here, the same words that made me angry with thee, that my fists may walk once again about thine ears." Such was Cassius' hot stirring nature. 6But for Brutus, his friends and countrymen, both by divers procurements and sundry rumours of the city, and by many bills also, did openly call and procure him to do that he did. For under the image of his ancestor Junius Brutus, (that drove the kings out of Rome) they wrote: "O, that it pleased the gods thou wert now alive, Brutus!" and again, "that thou wert here among us now!" His tribunal or chair, where he gave audience during the time he was Praetor, was full of such bills: "Brutus, thou art asleep, and art not Brutus indeed." And of all this Caesar's flatterers were the cause: who, beside many other exceeding and unspeakable honours they daily devised for him, in the night-time they put diadems upon the heads of his images, supposing thereby to allure the common people to call him King, instead of Dictator. Howbeit it turned to the contrary, as we have written more at large in Julius Caesar's life.

7Now when Cassius felt his friends, and did stir them up against Caesar: they all agreed, and promised to take part with him, so Brutus were the chief of their conspiracy. For they told him that so high an enterprise and attempt as that, did not so much require men of manhood and courage to draw their swords, as it stood them upon to have a man of such estimation as Brutus, to make every man boldly think, that by his only presence the fact were holy and just. If he took not this course, then that they should go to it with fainter hearts; and when they had done it, they should be more fearful: because every man would think that Brutus would not have refused to have made one with them, if the cause had been good and honest. 8Therefore Cassius, considering this matter with himself, did first of all speak to Brutus, since they grew strange together for the suit they had for the praetorship. So when he was reconciled to him again, and that they had embraced one another, Cassius asked him if he were determined to be in the Senate-house the first day of the month of March, because he heard say that Caesar's friends should move the council that day, that Caesar should be called king by the Senate. Brutus answered

---

6 I.ii; I.iii; II.i.

7 I.iii. 140ff.

8 I.ii. 25–177.

him, he would not be there. "But if we be sent for," said Cassius, "how then?" "For myself then," said Brutus, "I mean not to hold my peace, but to withstand it, and rather die than lose my liberty." Cassius being bold, and taking hold of this word: "Why," quoth he, "what Roman is he alive that will suffer thee to die for thy liberty? What? knowest thou not that thou art Brutus? [9]Thinkest thou that they be cobblers, tapsters, or suchlike base mechanical people, that write these bills and scrolls which are found daily in thy praetor's chair, and not the noblest men and best citizens that do it? No; be thou well assured that of other praetors they look for gifts, common distributions amongst the people, and for common plays, and to see fencers fight at the sharp, to shew the people pastime: but at thy hands they specially require (as a due debt unto them) the taking away of the tyranny, being fully bent to suffer any extremity for thy sake, so that thou wilt shew thyself to be the man thou art taken for, and that they hope thou art." Thereupon he kissed Brutus and embraced him: and so each taking leave of other, they went both to speak with their friends about it. [10]Now amongst Pompey's friends, there was one called Caius Ligarius,[11] who had been accused unto Caesar for taking part with Pompey, and Caesar discharged him. But Ligarius thanked not Caesar so much for his discharge, as he was offended with him for that he was brought in danger by his tyrannical power; and therefore in his heart he was always his mortal enemy, and was besides very familiar with Brutus, who went to see him being sick in his bed, and said unto him: "Ligarius, in what a time art thou sick?" Ligarius rising up in his bed, and taking him by the right hand, said unto him: "Brutus," said he, "if thou hast any great enterprise in hand worthy of thyself, I am whole."

[12]After that time they began to feel all their acquaintance whom they trusted, and laid their heads together, consulting upon it, and did not only pick out their friends, but all those also whom they thought stout enough to attempt any desperate matter, and that were not afraid to lose their lives. For this cause they durst not acquaint Cicero with their conspiracy, although he was a man whom they loved dearly, and trusted best: for they were afraid that he being a coward by nature, and age also having increased his fear, he would quite turn and

---

[9] I.i. 1–30. Note how Shakespeare excerpts this sentence from the Cassius-Brutus scene and uses it directly in connection with the "base mechanicals."

[10] II.i. 310ff.

[11] His actual name was Quintus Ligarius, and Plutarch names him accurately in his Life of Octavius Caesar Augustus. Shakespeare, following the Life of Brutus, misnames him Caius (II.i. 215).

[12] II.i. 86–220.

alter all their purpose, and quench the heat of their enterprise, (the which specially required hot and earnest execution), seeking by persuasion to bring all things to such safety, as there should be no peril. Brutus also did let other of his friends alone, as Statilius Epicurian, and Faonius, that made profession to follow Marcus Cato: because that, having cast out words afar off, disputing together in philosophy to feel their minds, Faonius answered, 'that civil war was worse than tyrannical government usurped against the law.' And Statilius told him also, 'that it were an unwise part for him to put his life in danger, for a sort of ignorant fools and asses.' Labeo was present at this talk, and maintained the contrary against them both. But Brutus held his peace, as though it had been a doubtful matter, and a hard thing to have been decided. But afterwards, being out of their company, he made Labeo privy to his intent; who very readily offered himself to make one. And they thought good also to bring in another Brutus to join with him, surnamed Albinus: who was no man of his hands himself, but because he was able to bring good force of a great number of slaves, and fencers at the sharp, whom he kept to shew the people pastime with their fighting, besides also that Caesar had some trust in him. Cassius and Labeo told Brutus Albinus of it at the first, but he made them no answer. But when he had spoken with Brutus himself alone, and that Brutus had told him he was the chief ringleader of all this conspiracy, then he willingly promised him the best aid he could. Furthermore, the only name and great calling of Brutus did bring on the most of them to give consent to this conspiracy: who having never taken oaths together, nor taken or given any caution or assurance, nor binding themselves one to another by any religious oaths, they all kept the matter so secret to themselves, and could so cunningly handle it, that notwithstanding the gods did reveal it by manifest signs and tokens from above, and by predictions of sacrifices, yet all this would not be believed. [13]Now Brutus, who knew very well that for his sake all the noblest, valiantest, and most courageous men of Rome did venture their lives, weighing with himself the greatness of the danger: when he was out of his house, he did so frame and fashion his countenance and looks that no man could discern he had anything to trouble his mind. But when night came that he was in his own house, then he was clean changed: for either care did wake him against his will when he would have slept, or else oftentimes of himself he fell into such deep thoughts of this enterprise, casting in his mind all the dangers that might happen:[14] that his wife, lying by

---

[13] II.i. 224–233.
[14] II.i. 233–308. Shakespeare follows this passage closely.

him, found that there was some marvellous great matter that troubled his mind, not being wont to be in that taking,[15] and that he could not well determine with himself.

His wife Porcia (as we have told you before) was the daughter of Cato, whom Brutus married being his cousin, not a maiden, but a young widow after the death of her first husband Bibulus, by whom she had also a young son called Bibulus, who afterwards wrote a book of the acts and gests of Brutus, extant at this present day. This young lady, being excellently well seen in philosophy, loving her husband well, and being of a noble courage, as she was also wise: because she would not ask her husband what he ailed before she had made some proof by her self: she took a little razor, such as barbers occupy to pare men's nails, and, causing her maids and women to go out of her chamber, gave herself a great gash withal in her thigh, that she was straight all of a gore blood: and incontinently after a vehement fever took her, by reason of the pain of her wound. Then perceiving her husband was marvellously out of quiet, and that he could take no rest, even in her greatest pain of all she spake in this sort unto him: "I being, O Brutus," said she "the daughter of Cato, was married unto thee; not to be thy bed-fellow and companion in bed and at board only, like a harlot, but to be partaker also with thee of thy good and evil fortune. Now for thyself, I can find no cause of fault in thee touching our match: but for my part, how may I shew my duty towards thee and how much I would do for thy sake, if I cannot constantly bear a secret mischief or grief with thee, which requireth secrecy and fidelity? I confess that a woman's wit commonly is too weak to keep a secret safely: but yet, Brutus, good education and the company of virtuous men have some power to reform the defect of nature. And for myself, I have this benefit moreover, that I am the daughter of Cato, and wife of Brutus. This notwithstanding, I did not trust to any of these things before, until that now I have found by experience that no pain or grief whatsoever can overcome me." With those words she shewed him her wound on her thigh, and told him what she had done to prove herself. Brutus was amazed to hear what she said unto him, and lifting up his hands to heaven, he besought the gods to give him the grace he might bring his enterprise to so good pass, that he might be found a husband worthy of so noble a wife as Porcia: so he then did comfort her the best he could.

Now a day being appointed for the meeting of the Senate, at what time they hoped Caesar would not fail to come, the conspirators determined then to put their enterprise in execution, because they might

---

[15] state.

meet safely at that time without suspicion; and the rather, for that all the noblest and chiefest men of the city would be there: who, when they should see such a great matter executed, would every man set to their hands, for the defence of their liberty. Furthermore they thought also, that the appointment of the place where the council should be kept was chosen of purpose by divine providence, and made all for them. [16]For it was one of the porches about the theatre, in the which there was a certain place full of seats for men to sit in; where also was set up the image of Pompey, which the city had made and consecrated in honour of him, when he did beautify that part of the city with the theatre he built, with divers porches about it. [17]In this place was the assembly of the Senate appointed to be, just on the fifteenth day of the month March, which the Romans call *Idus Martias*: so that it seemed some god of purpose had brought Caesar thither to be slain, for revenge of Pompey's death. So when the day was come, Brutus went out of his house with a dagger by his side under his long gown, that nobody saw nor knew but his wife only. The other conspirators were all assembled at Cassius' house, to bring his son into the market-place, who on that day did put on the man's gown, called *toga virilis*; and from thence they came all in a troop together unto Pompey's porch, looking that Caesar would straight come thither. But here is to be noted the wonderful assured constancy of these conspirators, in so dangerous and weighty an enterprise as they had undertaken. For many of them being praetors, by reason of their office (whose duty is to minister justice to everybody) did not only with great quietness and courtesy hear them that spake unto them, or that pleaded matters before them, and gave them attentive ear as if they had no other matter in their heads: but moreover they gave just sentence, and carefully despatched the causes before them. So there was one among them, who, being condemned in a certain sum of money, refused to pay it, and cried out that he did appeal unto Caesar. Then Brutus, casting his eyes upon the conspirators, said: "Caesar shall not let[18] me to see the law executed." Notwithstanding this, by chance there fell out many misfortunes unto them, which was enough to have marred the enterprise.[19] The first and chiefest was Caesar's long tarrying, who came very late to the Senate: for, because the signs of the sacrifices appeared unlucky, his wife Calpurnia kept him at home,

---

[16] While Shakespeare uses Pompey's porch (the *Curia Pompeiana*) as an earlier meeting place for the conspirators (I.iii. 147) he has Caesar assassinated in the Capitol instead of in Pompey's porch, where Plutarch, following history had placed it. See footnote 28, p. 267.

[17] III.i. 1–2.

[18] prevent.

[19] II.ii. 1–56.

and the soothsayers bade him beware he went not abroad. The second cause was, when one came unto Casca being a conspirator, and taking him by the hand, said unto him: "O Casca, thou keptest it close from me, but Brutus hath told me all." Casca being amazed at it, the other went on with his tale, and said: "Why, how now, how cometh it to pass thou art thus rich, that thou dost sue to be Aedilis?" Thus Casca being deceived by the other's doubtful words, he told them it was a thousand to one, he blabbed not out all the conspiracy. [20]Another Senator, called Popilius Laena, after he had saluted Brutus and Cassius more friendly than he was wont to do, he rounded[21] softly in their ears, and told them: "I pray the gods you may go through with that you have taken in hand; but withal, despatch, I read[22] you, for your enterprise is betrayed." When he had said, he presently departed from them, and left them both afraid that their conspiracy would out.

[23]Now in the meantime, there came one of Brutus' men post-haste unto him, and told him his wife was a-dying. For Porcia, being very careful and pensive for that which was to come, and being too weak to away with so great and inward grief of mind, she could hardly keep within, but was frighted with every little noise and cry she heard, as those that are taken and possessed with the fury of the Bacchantes; asking every man that came from the market-place what Brutus did, and still sent messenger after messenger, to know what news. At length Caesar's coming being prolonged (as you have heard), Porcia's weakness was not able to hold out any longer, and thereupon she suddenly swooned, that she had no leisure to go to her chamber, but was taken in the midst of her house, where her speech and senses failed her. Howbeit she soon came to herself again, and so was laid in her bed, and attended by her women. When Brutus heard these news, it grieved him, as it is to be presupposed: yet he left not off the care of his country and commonwealth, neither went home to his house for any news he heard.

Now it was reported that Caesar was coming in his litter: for he determined not to stay in the Senate all that day (because he was afraid of the unlucky signs of the sacrifices) but to adjourn matters of importance unto the next session and council holden, feigning himself not to be well at ease. [24]When Caesar came out of his litter, Popilius Laena (that had talked before with Brutus and Cassius, and

---

[20] III.i. 13–17.
[21] whispered.
[22] advise.
[23] II.iv. 1ff.
[24] III.i. 18–24.

had prayed the gods they might bring this enterprise to pass) went unto Caesar, and kept him a long time with a talk. Caesar gave good ear unto him: wherefore the conspirators (if so they should be called) not hearing what he said to Caesar, but conjecturing by that he had told them a little before that his talk was none other but the very discovery of their conspiracy, they were afraid every man of them; and, one looking in another's face, it was easy to see that they all were of a mind, that it was no tarrying for them till they were apprehended, but rather that they should kill themselves with their own hands. And when Cassius and certain others clapped their hands on their swords under their gowns to draw them, Brutus, marking the countenance and gesture of Laena, and considering that he did use himself rather like an humble and earnest suitor than like an accuser, he said nothing to his companion (because there were many amongst them that were not of the conspiracy), but with a pleasant countenance encouraged Cassius. And immediately after Laena went from Caesar, and kissed his hand; which shewed plainly that it was for some matter concerning himself that he had held him so long in talk. Now all the Senators being entered first into this place or chapter-house where the council should be kept, all the other conspirators straight stood about Caesar's chair, as if they had had something to say unto him. And some say that Cassius, casting his eyes upon Pompey's image, made his prayer unto it, as if it had been alive.[25] Trebonius[26] on the other side drew Antonius aside, as he came into the house where the Senate sat, and held him with a long talk without. When Caesar was come into the house, all the Senate rose to honour him at his coming in. [27]So when he was set, the conspirators flocked about him, and amongst them they presented one Tullius Cimber,[28] who made humble suit for the calling home again of his brother that was banished. They all made as though they were intercessors for him, and took Caesar by the hands, and kissed his head and breast. Caesar at the first simply refused their kindness and entreaties; but afterwards, perceiving they still pressed on him, he violently thrust them from him. Then Cimber with both his hands plucked Caesar's gown over his shoulders, and Casca, that stood behind him, drew his dagger first and strake Caesar upon the shoulder, but gave him no great wound. Caesar, feeling himself hurt, took him straight by the hand he held his dagger in, and cried out in Latin: "O traitor Casca, what dost thou?" Casca on the other side cried in Greek,

---

[25] III.i. 25–26.
[26] In Caesar's life it is said, it was Decius Brutus Albinus that kept Antonius by a talk without. (W.W.S.)
[27] III.i. 27–77.
[28] In Caesar's life he is called Metellus Cimber. (W.W.S.)

and called his brother to help him. So divers running on a heap together to fly upon Caesar, he, looking about him to have fled, saw Brutus with a sword drawn in his hand ready to strike at him: then he let Casca's hand go, and casting his gown over his face, suffered every man to strike at him that would.[29] Then the conspirators thronging one upon another, because every man was desirous to have a cut at him, so many swords and daggers lighting upon one body, one of them hurt another, and among them Brutus caught a blow on his hand, because he would make one in murdering of him, and all the rest also were every man of them bloodied.

[30]Caesar being slain in this manner, Brutus, standing in the midst of the house, would have spoken, and stayed the other Senators that were not of the conspiracy, to have told them the reason why they had done this fact. But they, as men both afraid and amazed, fled one upon another's neck in haste to get out at the door, and no man followed them. For it was set down and agreed between them, that they should kill no man but Caesar only, and should entreat all the rest to look to defend their liberty. [31]All the conspirators, but Brutus, determining upon this matter, thought it good also to kill Antonius, because he was a wicked man, and that in nature favoured tyranny: besides also, for that he was in great estimation with soldiers, having been conversant of long time amongst them: and especially having a mind bent to great enterprises, he was also of great authority at that time, being Consul with Caesar. But Brutus would not agree to it. First, for that he said it was not honest: secondly, because he told them there was hope of change in him. For he did not mistrust but that Antonius, being a noble-minded and courageous man, (when he should know that Caesar was dead), would willingly help his country to recover her liberty, having them an example unto him to follow their courage and virtue. So Brutus by this means saved Antonius' life, who at that present time disguised himself and stole away; [32]but Brutus and his consorts, having their swords bloody in their hands, went straight to the Capitol, persuading the Romans as they went to take their liberty

---

[29] Here, as in his life of Caesar, Plutarch has Caesar suffer Brutus's betrayal in silence. Shakespeare's famous *Et tu, Brute?*, however, is not without a source. Suetonius in *The Twelve Caesars* states that the dying Caesar said to Brutus in Greek: and thou, my son. These words became proverbial in Elizabethan England, appearing among many other places in *Mirror for Magistrates*, where Caesar is made to say:

"O this, quoth I, is violence: then Cassius pierced my breast;
And Brutus thou, my son, quoth I, whom erst I loved best."

[30] III.i. 96–98.
[31] II.i. 154–190.
[32] III.i. 105–110.

again. Now at the first time, when the murder was newly done, there were sudden outcries of people that ran up and down the city, the which indeed did the more increase the fear and tumult. But when they saw they slew no man, neither did spoil or make havoc of anything, then certain of the Senators and many of the people, emboldening themselves, went to the Capitol unto them.

[33]There, a great number of men being assembled together one after another, Brutus made an oration unto them, to win the favour of the people, and to justify that they had done. All those that were by said they had done well, and cried unto them that they should boldly come down from the Capitol: whereupon Brutus and his companions came boldly down into the market-place. The rest followed in troop, but Brutus went foremost, very honourably compassed in round about with the noblest men of the city, which brought him from the Capitol, through the market-place, to the pulpit for orations. When the people saw him in the pulpit, although they were a multitude of rakehells of all sorts, and had a good will to make some stir; yet, being ashamed to do it, for the reverence they bare unto Brutus, they kept silence to hear what he would say. When Brutus began to speak, they gave him quiet audience: howbeit, immediately after, they shewed that they were not all contented with the murder. For when another, called Cinna, would have spoken, and began to accuse Caesar, they fell into a great uproar among them, and marvellously reviled him; insomuch that the conspirators returned again into the Capitol. There Brutus, being afraid to be besieged, sent back again the noblemen that came thither with him, thinking it no reason that they, which were no partakers of the murder, should be partakers of the danger. Then the next morning, the Senate being assembled, and holden within the temple of the goddess Tellus, to wit, the Earth: and Antonius, Plancus, and Cicero, having made a motion to the Senate in that assembly that they should take an order to pardon and forget all that was past, and to establish friendship and peace again: it was decreed, that they should not only be pardoned, but also that the Consuls should refer it to the Senate, what honours should be appointed unto them. This being agreed upon, the Senate brake up; and Antonius the Consul, to put them in heart that were in the Capitol, sent them his son for a pledge. Upon this assurance, Brutus and his companions came down from the Capitol, where every man saluted and embraced each other; among the which Antonius himself did bid Cassius to supper to him, and Lepidus also bade Brutus; and so one bade another, as they had friendship and acquaintance together.

---

[33] III.ii. 1–58. Shakespeare's account of the mob's reaction to Brutus after the death of Caesar contrasts sharply with Plutarch's.

The next day following, the Senate, being called again to council, did first of all commend Antonius, for that he had wisely stayed and quenched the beginning of a civil war: then they also gave Brutus and his consorts great praises; and lastly they appointed them several governments of Provinces. For unto Brutus they appointed Creta; Africa unto Cassius; Asia unto Trebonius; Bithynia unto Cimber; and unto the other, Decius Brutus Albinus, Gaul on this side of the Alps. When this was done, they came to talk of Caesar's will and testament and of his funerals and tomb. [34]Then Antonius, thinking good his testament should be read openly, and also that his body should be honourably buried, and not in hugger-mugger, lest the people might thereby take occasion to be worse offended if they did otherwise: Cassius stoutly spake against it. But Brutus went with the motion, and agreed unto it; wherein it seemeth he committed a second fault. For the first fault he did, was when he would not consent to his fellow-conspirators, that Antonius should be slain; and therefore he was justly accused, that thereby he had saved and strengthened a strong and grievous enemy of their conspiracy. The second fault was, when he agreed that Caesar's funerals should be as Antonius would have them, the which indeed marred all. [35]For first of all, when Caesar's testament was openly read among them, whereby it appeared that he bequeathed unto every citizen of Rome 75 drachmas a man; and that he left his gardens and arbours unto the people, which he had on this side of the river Tiber, in the place where now the temple of Fortune is built: the people then loved him, and were marvellous sorry for him. Afterwards, when Caesar's body was brought into the market-place, Antonius making his funeral oration in praise of the dead, according to the ancient custom of Rome, and perceiving that his words moved the common people to compassion, he framed his eloquence to make their hearts yearn the more;[36] and taking Caesar's gown all bloody in his hand, he laid it open to the sight of them all, shewing what a number of cuts and holes it had upon it. Therewithal the people fell presently into such a rage and mutiny, that there was no more order kept amongst the common people. For some of them cried out, "Kill the murderers:" others plucked up forms, tables, and stalls about the market-place, as they had done before at the funerals of Clodius, and having laid them all on a heap together, they set them on fire, and thereupon did put the body of Caesar, and burnt it in the midst of the most holy places. And furthermore, when the fire was thoroughly kindled, some here, some

[34] III.i. 227–251.

[35] III.ii. 78–264.

[36] Shakespeare, of course, makes remarkable use of this hint of Antony's eloquence.

there, took burning firebrands, and ran with them to the murderers' houses that killed him, to set them on fire. Howbeit the conspirators, foreseeing the danger before, had wisely provided for themselves and fled.

[37]But there was a poet called Cinna, who had been no partaker of the conspiracy, but was always one of Caesar's chiefest friends: he dreamed, the night before, that Caesar bade him to supper with him, and that, he refusing to go, Caesar was very importunate with him, and compelled him; so that at length he led him by the hand into a great dark place, where, being marvellously afraid, he was driven to follow him in spite of his heart. This dream put him all night into a fever; and yet notwithstanding, the next morning, when he heard that they carried Caesar's body to burial, being ashamed not to accompany his funerals, he went out of his house, and thrust himself into the press of the common people that were in a great uproar. And because some one called him by his name Cinna, the people, thinking he had been that Cinna who in an oration he made had spoken very evil of Caesar, they, falling upon him in their rage, slew him outright in the market-place. This made Brutus and his companions more afraid than any other thing, next unto the change of Antonius. Wherefore they got them out of Rome, and kept at the first in the city of Antium, hoping to return again to Rome, when the fury of the people was a little assuaged. The which they hoped would be quickly, considering that they had to deal with a fickle and inconstant multitude, easy to be carried, and that the Senate stood for them: who notwithstanding made no enquiry for them that had torn poor Cinna the poet in pieces, but caused them to be sought for and apprehended that went with firebrands to set fire on the conspirators' houses. [38]The people growing weary now of Antonius' pride and insolency, who ruled all things in a manner with absolute power, they desired that Brutus might return again; and it was also looked for that Brutus would come himself in person to play the plays which were due to the people, by reason of his office of praetorship. But Brutus, understanding that many of Caesar's soldiers which served under him in the wars, and that also had lands and houses given them in the cities where they lay, did lie in wait for him to kill him, and that they daily by small companies came by one and by one into Rome, he durst no more return thither: but yet the people had the pleasure and pastime in his absence, to see the games and sports he made them, which were sumptuously set forth and fur-

---

[37] III.iii. 1ff.

[38] Shakespeare omits all this and moves right on to the civil war (IV.i.), an approach that is more dramatic and that permits a more heroic picture of Antony.

nished with all things necessary, sparing for no cost. For he had brought a great number of strange beasts, of the which he would not give one of them to any friend he had, but that they should all be employed in his games: and went himself as far as Byzantium, to speak to some players of comedies and musicians that were there. And further he wrote unto his friends for one Canutius, an excellent player, that, whatsoever they did, they should entreat him to play in these plays. "For," said he, "it is no reason to compel any Grecian, unless he will come of his own good will." Moreover he wrote also unto Cicero, and earnestly prayed him in any case to be at these plays.

[39]Now the state of Rome standing in these terms, there fell out another change and alteration, when the young man Octavius Caesar came to Rome. He was the son of Julius Caesar's niece, whom he had adopted for his son, and made his heir, by his last will and testament. But when Julius Caesar, his adopted father, was slain, he was in the city of Apollonia (where he studied) tarrying for him, because he was determined to make war with the Parthians: but when he heard the news of his death, he returned again to Rome. Where, to begin to curry favour with the common people, he first of all took upon him his adopted father's name, and made distribution among them of the money which his father had bequeathed unto them. By this means he troubled Antonius sorely, and by force of money got a great number of his father's soldiers together, that had served in the wars with him. . . .

[*The city of Rome was soon divided into two factions — that of Antonius versus that of Octavius Caesar. Brutus in the meantime left Italy for Athens, while Porcia returned to Rome. Brutus raised a large army and was preparing to invade Asia when the news came to him of "the great change at Rome."*]

Octavius Caesar was in arms, by commandment and authority from the Senate, against Marcus Antonius. But after that he had driven Antonius out of Italy, the Senate began then to be afraid of him, because he sued to be Consul, which was contrary to the law; and kept a great army about him when the empire of Rome had no need of them. On the other side Octavius Caesar, perceiving the Senate stayed not there, but turned unto Brutus that was out of Italy, and that they appointed him the government of certain provinces: then he began to be afraid for his part, and sent unto Antonius to offer him his friendship. Then coming on with his army near to Rome, he made himself to be chosen Consul, whether the Senate would or not, when

---

[39] III.i. 276ff., for comparison and contrast.

he was yet but a stripling or springal[40] of twenty years old, as himself reports in his own Commentaries. So when he was Consul, he presently appointed judges, to accuse Brutus and his companions for killing of the noblest person in Rome and chiefest magistrate without law or judgment: and made L. Cornificius accuse Brutus, and M. Agrippa, Cassius. So the parties accused were condemned, because the judges were compelled to give such sentence. The voice went, that when the herald (according to the custom after sentence given) went up to the chair or pulpit for orations, and proclaimed 'Brutus' with a loud voice, summoning him to appear in person before the judges, the people that stood by sighed openly, and the noblemen that were present hung down their heads, and durst not speak a word. Among them the tears fell from Publius Silicius' eyes: who, shortly after, was one of the proscripts or outlaws appointed to be slain. [41]After that, these three, Octavius Caesar, Antonius, and Lepidus, made an agreement between themselves, and by those articles divided the provinces belonging to the empire of Rome among themselves, and did set up bills of proscription and outlawry, condemning two hundred of the noblest men of Rome to suffer death, and among that number Cicero was one. . . .

[Brutus transported his army into Asia and joined with Cassius's army at Smyrna.]

[42]Now whilst Brutus and Cassius were together in the city of Smyrna, Brutus prayed Cassius to let him have some part of his money whereof he had great store; because all that he could rape and rend of his side, he had bestowed it in making so great a number of ships, that by means of them they should keep all the sea at their commandment. Cassius' friends hindered this request and earnestly dissuaded him from it, persuading him, that it was no reason that Brutus should have the money which Cassius had gotten together by sparing and levied with great evil will of the people their subjects, for him to bestow liberally upon his soldiers, and by this means to win their good wills, by Cassius' charge. This notwithstanding, Cassius gave him the third part of this total sum. . . .

[Cassius and Brutus then separated for a while, each conquering and looting Asian cities, until]

---

[40] youngster.

[41] IV.i. 1–9.

[42] Shakespeare uses a variation of this incident as the cause of a later quarrel between Brutus and Cassius: IV.iii. 69–85.

[43]Brutus sent to pray Cassius to come to the city of Sardis, and so he did. Brutus, understanding of his coming, went to meet him with all his friends. There both their armies being armed, they called them both *Emperors*. Now as it commonly happened in great affairs between two persons, both of them having many friends and so many captains under them, there ran tales and complaints betwixt them. Therefore, before they fell in hand with any other matter, they went into a little chamber together, and bade every man avoid, and did shut the doors to them. Then they began to pour out their complaints one to the other, and grew hot and loud, earnestly accusing one another, and at length fell both a-weeping. Their friends that were without the chamber, hearing them loud within, and angry between themselves, they were both amazed and afraid also, lest it would grow to further matter: but yet they were commanded that no man should come to them. Notwithstanding, one Marcus Phaonius, that had been a friend and a follower of Cato while he lived, and took upon him to counterfeit a philosopher, not with wisdom and discretion, but with a certain bedlam and frantic motion: he would needs come into the chamber, though the men offered to keep him out. But it was no boot to let[44] Phaonius, when a mad mood or toy took him in the head: for he was a hot hasty man, and sudden in all his doings, and cared for never a senator of them all. Now, though he used this bold manner of speech after the profession of the Cynic philosophers (as who would say, *Dogs*) yet his boldness did no hurt many times, because they did but laugh at him to see him so mad. This Phaonius at that time, in despite of the door-keepers, came into the chamber, and with a certain scoffing and mocking gesture, which he counterfeited of purpose, he rehearsed the verses which old Nestor said in Homer:

> "My lords I pray you hearken both to me,
> For I have seen mo years than suchie three."

Cassius fell a-laughing at him: but Brutus thrust him out of the chamber, and called him dog, and counterfeit Cynic. Howbeit his coming in brake their strife at that time, and so they left each other. The self-same night Cassius prepared his supper in his chamber, and Brutus brought his friends with him. So when they were set at supper, Phaonius came to sit down after he had washed. Brutus told him aloud, 'no man sent for him,' and bade them set him at the *upper* end: meaning indeed, at the *lower* end of the bed. Phaonius made no ceremony, but thrust in amongst the middest of them, and made all

---

[43] IV.ii. 31ff.; IV.iii. 1–138.
[44] hinder.

the company laugh at him. So they were merry all supper-time, and full of their philosophy. The next day after, Brutus, upon complaint of the Sardians, did condemn and note Lucius Pella for a defamed person, that had been a Praetor of the Romans, and whom Brutus had given charge unto: for that he was accused and convicted of robbery and pilfery in his office. This judgment much misliked Cassius, because he himself had secretly (not many days before) warned two of his friends, attainted and convicted of the like offences, and openly had cleared them: but yet he did not therefore leave to employ them in any manner of service as he did before. And therefore he greatly reproved Brutus, for that he would shew himself so straight and severe, in such a time as was meeter to bear a little than to take things at the worst. Brutus in contrary manner answered, that he should remember the Ides of March, at which time they slew Julius Caesar, who neither pilled nor polled the country, but only was a favourer and suborner of all them that did rob and spoil, by his countenance and authority. And if there were any occasion whereby they might honestly set aside justice and equity, they should have had more reason to have suffered Caesar's friends to have robbed and done what wrong and injury they had wanted than to bear with their own men. "For then," said he, "they could but have said we had been cowards, but now they may accuse us of injustice, beside the pains we take, and the danger we put ourselves into." And thus may we see what Brutus' intent and purpose was.

But as they both prepared to pass over again out of Asia into Europe, there went a rumour that there appeared a wonderful sign unto him. Brutus was a careful man, and slept very little, both for that his diet was moderate, as also because he was continually occupied. He never slept in the day-time, and in the night no longer than the time he was driven to be alone, and when everybody else took their rest. But now whilst he was in war, and his head ever busily occupied to think of his affairs and what would happen, after he had slumbered a little after supper, he spent all the rest of the night in dispatching of his weightiest causes; and after he had taken order for them, if he had any leisure left him, he would read some book till the third watch of the night, at what time the captains, petty captains, and colonels, did use to come to him. [45]So, being ready to go into Europe, one night very late (when all the camp took quiet rest) as he was in his tent with a little light, thinking of weighty matters, he thought he heard one come in to him, and casting his eye towards the door of his tent, that he saw a wonderful strange and monstrous shape of a body coming towards him, and said never a word. So Brutus boldly asked what he was, a god

[45] IV.iii. 275–306.

or a man, and what cause brought him thither? The spirit answered him, "I am thy evil spirit, Brutus: and thou shalt see me by the city of Philippi." Brutus being no otherwise afraid, replied again unto it: "Well, then I shall see thee again." The spirit presently vanished away: and Brutus called his men unto him, who told him that they heard no noise, nor saw anything at all. Thereupon Brutus returned again to think on his matters as he did before: and when the day brake, he went unto Cassius, to tell him what vision had appeared unto him in the night. [46]Cassius being in opinion an Epicurean, and reasoning thereon with Brutus, spake to him touching the vision thus. "In our sect, Brutus, we have an opinion, that we do not always feel or see that which we suppose we do both see and feel, but that our senses being credulous and therefore easily abused (when they are idle and unoccupied in their own objects) are induced to imagine they see and conjecture that which in truth they do not. For our mind is quick and cunning to work (without either cause or matter) anything in the imagination whatsoever. And therefore the imagination is resembled to clay, and the mind to the potter: who, without any other cause than his fancy and pleasure, changeth it into what fashion and form he will. And this doth the diversity of our dreams shew unto us. For our imagination doth upon a small fancy grow from concept to concept, altering both in passions and forms of things imagined. For the mind of man is ever occupied, and that continual moving is nothing but an imagination. But yet there is a further cause of this in you. For you being by nature given to melancholic discoursing, and of late continually occupied, your wits and senses, having been over-laboured, do easilier yield to such imaginations. For, to say that there are spirits or angels; and if there were, that they had the shape of men, or such voices or any power at all to come unto us, it is a mockery. And for mine own part, I would there were such, because that we should not only have soldiers, horses, and ships, but also the aid of the gods, to guide and further our honest and honourable attempts." With these words Cassius did somewhat comfort and quiet Brutus. [47]When they raised their camp, there came two eagles that, flying with a marvellous force, lighted upon two of the foremost ensigns, and always followed the soldiers, which gave them meat and fed them, until they came near to the city of Philippi: and there, one day only before the battle, they both flew away.

Now Brutus had conquered the most part of all the people and nations of that country; but if there were any other city or captain to overcome, then they made all clear before them, and so drew towards

---

[46] I.ii. 140–141; V.i. 77–79.
[47] V.i. 80–84.

the coasts of Thassos. There Norbanus, lying in camp in a certain place called the straits, by another place called Symbolon (which is a port in the sea), Cassius and Brutus compassed him in in such sort, that he was driven to forsake the place, which was of great strength for him, and he was also in danger beside to have lost all his army. For Octavius Caesar could not follow him because of his sickness, and therefore stayed behind: whereupon they had taken his army, had not Antonius' aid been, which made such wonderful speed, that Brutus could scant believe it. [48]So Caesar came not thither for ten days after: and Antonius camped against Cassius, and Brutus on the other side, against Caesar. The Romans called the valley between both camps, the Philippian fields: and there were never seen two so great armies of the Romans, one before the other, ready to fight. In truth, Brutus' army was inferior to Octavius Caesar's in number of men; but for bravery and rich furniture, Brutus' army far excelled Caesar's. For the most part of their armours were silver and gilt, which Brutus had bountifully given them: although, in all other things, he taught his captains to live in order without excess. But for the bravery of armour and weapon, which soldiers should carry in their hands, or otherwise wear upon their backs, he thought that it was an encouragement unto them that by nature are greedy of honour, and that it maketh them also fight like devils that love to get, and to be afraid to lose: because they fight to keep their armour and weapon, as also their goods and lands. Now when they came to muster their armies, Octavius Caesar took the muster of his army within the trenches of his camp, and gave his men only a little corn, and five silver drachmas to every man to sacrifice to the gods, and to pray for victory. But Brutus, scorning this misery and niggardliness, first of all mustered his army, and did purify it in the fields, according to the manner of the Romans: and then he gave unto every band a number of wethers to sacrifice, and fifty silver drachmas to every soldier. So that Brutus' and Cassius' soldiers were better pleased, and more courageously bent to fight at the day of battle, than their enemies' soldiers were. Notwithstanding, being busily occupied about the ceremonies of this purification, it is reported that there chanced certain unlucky signs unto Cassius. For one of his sergeants that carried the rods before him, brought him the garland of flowers turned backward, the which he should have worn on his head in the time of sacrificing. Moreover it is reported also, that another time before, in certain sports and triumph where they carried an image of Cassius' victory, of clean gold, it fell by chance, the man stumbling that carried it. And yet further, there was seen a marvellous number of fowls of prey, that feed upon dead carcases:

---

[48] V.i. 1–6.

and bee-hives also were found, where bees were gathered together in a certain place within the trenches of the camp: the which place the soothsayers thought good to shut out of the precinct of the camp, for to take away the superstitious fear and mistrust men would have of it. [49]The which began somewhat to alter Cassius' mind from Epicurus' opinions, and had put the soldiers also in a marvellous fear. [50]Thereupon Cassius was of opinion not to try this war at one battle, but rather to delay time, and to draw it out in length, considering that they were the stronger in money, and the weaker in men and armour. But Brutus, in contrary manner, did alway before, and at that time also, desire nothing more than to put all to the hazard of battle, as soon as might be possible: to the end he might either quickly restore his country to her former liberty, or rid him forthwith of this miserable world, being still troubled in following and maintaining of such great armies together. But perceiving that, in the daily skirmishes and bickerings they made, his men were always the stronger and ever had the better, that yet quickened his spirits again, and did put him in better heart. And furthermore, because that some of their own men had already yielded themselves to their enemies, and that it was suspected moreover divers others would do the like, that made many of Cassius' friends which were of his mind before (when it came to be debated in council, whether the battle should be fought or not) that they were then of Brutus' mind. But yet was there one of Brutus' friends called Atellius, that was against it, and was of opinion that they should tarry to the next winter. Brutus asked him what he should get by tarrying a year longer? "If I get nothing else," quoth Atellius again, "yet have I lived so much longer." Cassius was very angry with this answer: and Atellius was maliced and esteemed the worse for it of all men. Thereupon it was presently determined they should fight battle the next day. So Brutus, all supper-time, looked with a cheerful countenance, like a man that had good hope, and talked very wisely of philosophy, and after supper went to bed. [51]But touching Cassius, Messala reporteth that he supped by himself in his tent with a few of his friends, and that all supper-time he looked very sadly, and was full of thoughts, although it was against his nature: and that after supper he took him by the hand, and holding him fast (in token of kindness, as his manner was) told him in Greek: "Messala, I protest unto thee, and make thee my witness, that I am compelled against my mind and will (as Pompey the Great was) to jeopard the liberty of our country to the hazard of a battle. And yet we must be lively, and of good

---

[49] V.i. 77–79.
[50] IV.iii. 196–225.
[51] V.i. 70–92.

courage, considering our good fortune, whom we should wrong too much to mistrust her, although we follow evil counsel." Messala writeth, that Cassius having spoken these last words unto him, he bade him farewell, and willed him to come to supper to him the next night following, because it was his birthday. The next morning, by break of day, the signal of battle was set out in Brutus' and Cassius' camp, which was an arming scarlet coat: and both the chieftains spake together in the midst of their armies. [52]There Cassius began to speak first, and said: "The gods grant us, O Brutus, that this day we may win the field, and ever after to live all the rest of our life quietly one with another. But since the gods have so ordained it, that the greatest and chiefest things amongst men are most uncertain, and that if the battle fall out otherwise to-day than we wish or look for, we shall hardly meet again, what art thou then determined to do, to fly, or die?" Brutus answered him, being yet but a young man, and not over greatly experienced in the world: "I trust (I know not how) a certain rule of philosophy, by the which I did greatly blame and reprove Cato for killing himself, as being no lawful nor godly act, touching the gods: nor concerning men, valiant; not to give place and yield to divine providence, and not constantly and patiently to take whatsoever it pleaseth him to send us, but to draw back and fly: but being now in the midst of the danger, I am of a contrary mind. For if it be not the will of God that this battle fall out fortunate for us, I will look no more for hope, neither seek to make any new supply for war again, but will rid me of this miserable world, and content me with my fortune. For I gave up my life for my country in the Ides of March, for the which I shall live in another more glorious world." Cassius fell a-laughing to hear what he said, and embracing him, "Come on then," said he, "let us go and charge our enemies with this mind. For either we shall conquer, or we shall not need to fear the conquerors." After this talk, they fell to consultation among their friends for the ordering of the battle. [53]Then Brutus prayed Cassius he might have the leading of the right wing, the which men thought was far meeter for Cassius, both because he was the elder man, and also for that he had the better experience. But yet Cassius gave it him, and willed that Messala (who had charge of one of the warlikest legions they had) should be also in that wing with Brutus. So Brutus presently sent out his horsemen, who were excellently well appointed, and his footmen also were as willing and ready to give charge.

Now Antonius' men did cast a trench from the marsh by the which they lay, to cut off Cassius' way to come to the sea: and Caesar, at

---

[52] V.i. 93ff.
[53] V.i. 16–20.

the least his army stirred not. As for Octavius Caesar himself, he was not in his camp because he was sick. And for his people, they little thought the enemies would have given them battle, but only have made some light skirmishes to hinder them that wrought in the trench, and with their darts and slings to have kept them from finishing of their work: but they, taking no heed to them that came full upon them to give them battle, marvelled much at the great noise they heard, that came from the place where they were casting their trench. In the meantime Brutus, that led the right wing, sent little bills to the colonels and captains of private bands, in the which he wrote the word of the battle; and he himself, riding a-horseback by all the troops, did speak to them, and encouraged them to stick to it like men. [54]So by this means very few of them understood what was the word of the battle, and besides, the most part of them never tarried to have it told them, but ran with great fury to assail the enemies; whereby, through this disorder, the legions were marvellously scattered and dispersed one from the other. For first of all Messala's legion, and then the next unto them, went beyond the left wing of the enemies, and did nothing, but glancing by them overthrew some as they went; and so going on further, fell right upon Caesar's camp, out of the which (as himself writeth in his Commentaries) he had been conveyed away a little before, through the counsel and advice of one of his friends called Marcus Artorius: who, dreaming in the night, had a vision appeared unto him, that commanded Octavius Caesar should be carried out of his camp. Insomuch as it was thought he was slain, because his litter (which had nothing in it) was thrust through and through with pikes and darts. There was great slaughter in this camp. For amongst others, there were slain two thousand Lacedaemonians, who were arrived but even a little before, coming to aid Caesar. The other also that had not glanced by, but had given a charge full upon Caesar's battle, they easily made them fly, because they were greatly troubled for the loss of their camp; and of them there were slain by hand three legions. Then, being very earnest to follow the chase of them that fled, they ran in amongst them hand over head into their camp, and Brutus among them. [55]But that which the conquerors thought not of, occasion shewed it unto them that they were overcome; and that was, the left wing of their enemies left naked and unguarded of them of the right wing, who were strayed too far off, in following of them that were overthrown. So they gave a hot charge upon them. But, notwithstanding all the force they made, they could not break into the midst of their battle, where they found them that received them and

---

[54] V.iii. 1–7.
[55] V.iii. 7–11.

valiantly made head against them. Howbeit they brake and overthrew the left wing where Cassius was, by reason of the great disorder among them, and also because they had no intelligence how the right wing had sped. So they chased them, beating them into their camp, the which they spoiled, none of both the chieftains being present there. For Antonius, as it is reported, to fly the fury of the first charge, was gotten into the next marsh and no man could tell what became of Octavius Caesar, after he was carried out of his camp. Insomuch that there were certain soldiers that shewed their swords bloodied, and said that they had slain him, and did describe his face and shewed what age he was of. Furthermore, the forward and the midst of Brutus' battle had already put all their enemies to flight that withstood them, with great slaughter: so that Brutus had conquered all on his side, and Cassius had lost all on the other side. For nothing undid them but that Brutus went not to help Cassius, thinking he had overcome them as himself had done; and Cassius on the other side tarried not for Brutus, thinking he had been overthrown as himself was. And to prove that the victory fell on Brutus' side, Messala confirmeth, that they won three eagles, and divers other ensigns of the enemies, and their enemies won never a one of theirs. Now Brutus returning from the chase, after he had slain and sacked Caesar's men, he wondered much that he could not see Cassius' tent standing up high as it was wont, neither the other tents of his camp standing as they were before, because all the whole camp had been spoiled, and the tents thrown down, at the first coming of their enemies. But they that were about Brutus, whose sight served them better, told them that they saw a great glistering of harness, and a number of silvered targes, that went and came into Cassius' camp, and were not (as they took it) the armours nor the number of men that they had left there to guard the camp; and yet that they saw not such a number of dead bodies and great overthrow as there should have been, if so many legions had been slain. This made Brutus at the first mistrust that which had happened. So he appointed a number of men to keep the camp of his enemy which he had taken, and caused his men to be sent for that yet followed the chase, and gathered them together, thinking to lead them to aid Cassius, who was in this state as you shall hear. First of all, he was marvellous angry to see how Brutus' men ran to give charge upon their enemies, and tarried not for the word of the battle, nor commandment to give charge: and it grieved him beside, that after he had overcome them, his men fell straight to spoil, and were not careful to compass in the rest of the enemies behind: but with tarrying too long also, more than through the valiantness or foresight of the captains his enemies, Cassius found himself compassed in with the right wing of his enemy's army. Whereupon his horsemen brake immediately, and fled for life towards the sea. Furthermore perceiving his footmen to give ground, he did what he could to keep them from flying, and took an ensign from one of the ensign-bearers that fled, and stuck it fast at his feet: although with much ado he could scant keep his own guard together.

[56]So Cassius himself was at length compelled to fly, with a few about him, unto a little hill, from whence they might easily see what was done in all the plain: howbeit Cassius himself saw nothing, for his sight was very bad, saving that he saw (and yet with much ado) how the enemies spoiled his camp before his eyes. He saw also a great troop of horsemen, whom Brutus sent to aid him, and thought that they were his enemies that followed him: but yet he sent Titinius, one of them that was with him, to go and know what they were. Brutus' horsemen saw him coming afar off, whom when they knew that he was one of Cassius' chiefest friends, they shouted out for joy; and they that were familiarly acquainted with him lighted from their horses, and went and embraced him. The rest compassed him in round about on horseback, with songs of victory and great rushing[57] of their harness, so that they made all the field ring again for joy. But this marred all. For Cassius, thinking indeed that Titinius was taken of the enemies, he then spake these words: "Desiring too much to live, I have lived to see one of my best friends taken, for my sake, before my face." After that, he got into a tent where nobody was, and took Pindarus with him, one of his bondsmen whom he reserved ever for such a pinch, since the cursed battle of the Parthians, where Crassus was slain, though he notwithstanding scaped from that overthrow: but then, casting his cloak over his head, and holding out his bare neck unto Pindarus, he gave him his head to be stricken off. So the head was found severed from the body: but after that time Pindarus was never seen more. Whereupon some took occasion to say that he had slain his master without his commandment. By and by they knew the horsemen that came towards them, and might see Titinius crowned with a garland of triumph, who came before with great speed unto Cassius. But when he perceived, by the cries and tears of his friends which tormented themselves, the misfortune that had chanced to his captain Cassius by mistaking, he drew out his sword, cursing himself a thousand times that he had tarried so long, and so slew himself presently in the field. [58]Brutus in the mean time came forward still, and understood also that Cassius had been overthrown: but he knew nothing of his death till he came very near to his camp. So when

---

[56] V.iii. 12–90.
[57] clashing.
[58] V.iii. 91ff.

he was come thither, after he had lamented the death of Cassius, calling him the last of all the Romans, being impossible that Rome should ever breed again so noble and valiant a man as he, he caused his body to be buried, and sent it to the city of Thassos, fearing lest his funerals within his camp should cause great disorder. Then he called his soldiers together, and did encourage them again. And when he saw that they had lost all their carriage, which they could not brook well, he promised every man of them two thousand drachmas in recompense. After his soldiers had heard his oration, they were all of them prettily cheered again, wondering much at his great liberality, and waited upon him with great cries when he went his way, praising him, for that he only of the four chieftains was not overcome in battle. And to speak the truth, his deeds shewed that he hoped not in vain to be conqueror. For with few legions he had slain and driven all them away that made head against him: and if all his people had fought, and that the most of them had not outgone their enemies to run to spoil their goods, surely it was like enough he had slain them all, and had left never a man of them alive. There were slain of Brutus' side about eight thousand men, counting the soldiers' slaves, whom Brutus called *Brigas:* and of the enemy's side, as Messala writeth, there were slain, as he supposeth, more than twice as many more. Wherefore they were more discouraged than Brutus, until that, very late at night, there was one of Cassius' men called Demetrius, who went unto Antonius, and carried his master's clothes, whereof he was stripped not long before, and his sword also. This encouraged Brutus' enemies, and made them so brave, that the next morning betimes they stood in battle array again before Brutus. . . .

[*Brutus's camp seethed with uneasiness. Cassius's leaderless soldiers proved difficult to manage, and Brutus's own soldiers began to desert. The bitter cold further lowered morale and discipline, and Brutus was not told until too late of an important victory won by his navy. (In fact, he was told twenty days too late, a time period which Shakespeare telescopes into the single battle scene that comprises Act V.) On the night before the final battle*]

[59]it is reported that the monstrous spirit which had appeared before unto Brutus in the city of Sardis, did now appear again unto him in the selfsame shape and form, and so vanished away, and said never a word. Now Publius Volumnius, a grave and wise philosopher, that had been with Brutus from the beginning of this war, doth make no mention of this spirit; but saith that the greatest eagle and ensign was

---

[59] V.v. 15–20.

covered over with a swarm of bees; and that there was one of the captains, whose arm suddenly fell a sweating, that it dropped oil of roses from him, and that they oftentimes went about to dry him, but all would do no good. And that, before the battle was fought, there were two eagles fought between both armies, and all the time they fought there was a marvellous great silence all the valley over, both the armies being one before the other, marking this fight between them; and that in the end, the eagle towards Brutus gave over and fled away. But this is certain, and a true tale, that when the gate of the camp was open, the first man the standard-bearer met that carried the eagle, was an Aethiopian, whom the soldiers, for ill luck, mangled with their swords.

Now after that Brutus had brought his army into the field, and had set them in battle array, directly against the forward of his enemy, he paused a long time before he gave the signal of battle. For Brutus riding up and down to view the bands and companies, it came in his head to mistrust some of them, besides that some came to tell him so much as he thought. Moreover, he saw his horsemen set forward but faintly, and did not go lustily to give charge, but still stayed to see what the footmen would do. Then suddenly, one of the chiefest knights he had in all his army, called Camulatius, and that was alway marvellously esteemed of for his valiantness, until that time: he came hard by Brutus on horseback, and rode before his face to yield himself unto his enemies. Brutus was marvellous sorry for it: wherefore, partly for anger, and partly for fear of greater treason and rebellion, he suddenly caused his army to march, being past three of the clock in the afternoon. So in that place where he himself fought in person, he had the better, and brake into the left wing of his enemies; which gave him way, through the help of his horsemen that gave charge with his footmen, when they saw the enemies in amaze and afraid. Howbeit, the other also on the right wing, when the captains would have had them to have marched, they were afraid to have been compassed in behind, because they were fewer in number than their enemies, and therefore did spread themselves, and leave the midst of the battle. Whereby they having weakened themselves, they could not withstand the force of their enemies, but turned tail straight and fled. And those that had put them to flight, came in straight upon it to compass Brutus behind, who, in the middest of the conflict, did all that was possible for a skilful captain and valiant soldier, both for his wisdom, as also his hardiness, for the obtaining of victory. But that which won him the victory at the first battle, did now lose it him at the second. For at the first time, the enemies that were broken and fled were straight cut in pieces: but at the second battle, of Cassius' men that were put to flight, there were few slain: and they that saved themselves by speed, being afraid because they had been overcome, did discourage the rest of the army when they came to join with them, and filled all the army with fear and disorder. [60]There was the son of Marcus Cato slain, valiantly fighting among the lusty youths. For notwithstanding that he was very weary and over-harried, yet would he not therefore fly; but manfully fighting and laying about him, telling aloud his name, and also his father's name, at length he was beaten down amongst many other dead bodies of his enemies, which he had slain round about him. [61]So there were slain in the field all the chiefest gentlemen and nobility that were in his army, who valiantly ran into any danger to save Brutus' life: amongst whom there was one of Brutus' friends called Lucilius, who seeing a troop of barbarous men making no reckoning of all men else they met in their way, but going all together right against Brutus, he determined to stay them with the hazard of his life; and being left behind, told them that he was Brutus: and because they should believe him, he prayed them to bring him to Antonius, for he said he was afraid of Caesar, and that he did trust Antonius better. These barbarous men, being very glad of this good hap, and thinking themselves happy men, they carried him in the night, and sent some before unto Antonius, to tell him of their coming. He was marvellous glad of it, and went out to meet them that brought him. Others also understanding of it, that they had brought Brutus prisoner, they came out of all parts of the camp to see him, some pitying his hard fortune, and others saying that it was not done like himself, so cowardly to be taken alive of the barbarous people for fear of death. When they came near together, Antonius stayed a while bethinking himself how he should use Brutus. In the meantime Lucilius was brought to him, who stoutly with a bold countenance said: "Antonius, I dare assure thee, that no enemy hath taken nor shall take Marcus Brutus alive, and I beseech God keep him from that fortune: for wheresoever he be found, alive or dead, he will be found like himself. And now for myself, I am come unto thee, having deceived these men of arms here, bearing them down that I was Brutus, and do not refuse to suffer any torment thou wilt put me to." Lucilius' words made them all amazed that heard him. Antonius on the other side, looking upon all them that had brought him, said unto them: "My companions, I think ye are sorry you have failed of your purpose, and that you think this man hath done you great wrong: but I assure you, you have taken a better booty than that you followed. For instead of an enemy you have brought me a friend: and for my part, if you had brought me Brutus alive, truly I cannot tell what I should have

[60] V.iv. 2–11.
[61] V.iv. 12ff.

done to him. For I had rather have such men my friends, as this man here, than mine enemies." Then he embraced Lucilius, and at that time delivered him to one of his friends in custody; and Lucilius ever after served him faithfully, even to his death. [62]Now Brutus having passed a little river, walled in on every side with high rocks and shadowed with great trees, being then dark night, he went no further, but stayed at the foot of a rock with certain of his captains and friends that followed him: and looking up to the firmament that was full of stars, sighing, he rehearsed two verses, of the which Volumnius wrote the one, to this effect:

> "Let not the wight from whom this mischief went,
> O Jove, escape without due punishment." —

and saith that he had forgotten the other. Within a little while after, naming his friends that he had seen slain in battle before his eyes, he fetched a greater sigh than before, specially when he came to name Labio and Flavius, of whom the one was his lieutenant, and the other captain of the pioneers of his camp. In the meantime one of the company being athirst, and seeing Brutus athirst also, he ran to the river for water, and brought it in his sallet.[63] At the same time they heard a noise on the other side of the river: whereupon Volumnius took Dardanus, Brutus' servant, with him, to see what it was: and returning straight again, asked if there were any water left. Brutus smiling, gently told him, "All is drunk, but they shall bring you some more." Thereupon he sent him again that went for water before, who was in great danger of being taken by the enemies, and hardly escaped, being sore hurt.

Furthermore, Brutus thought that there was no great number of men slain in battle: and to know the truth of it, there was one called Statilius, that promised to go through his enemies, for otherwise it was impossible to go see their camp: and from thence, if all were well, that he would lift up a torch-light in the air, and then return again with speed to him. The torchlight was lifted up as he had promised, for Statilius went thither. Now Brutus seeing Statilius tarry long after that, and that he came not again, he said: "If Statilius be alive, he will come again." But his evil fortune was such that, as he came back, he lighted in his enemies' hands and was slain. Now the night being far spent, Brutus as he sat bowed towards Clitus, one of his men, and told him somewhat in his ear: the other answered him not, but fell a-weeping. Thereupon he proved Dardanus, and said somewhat also

---

[62] V.v. 1–51.
[63] helmet.

to him: at length he came to Volumnius himself, and speaking to him in Greek, prayed him for the studies' sake which brought them acquainted together, that he would help him to put his hand to his sword, to thrust it in him to kill him. Volumnius denied his request, and so did many others: and amongst the rest, one of them said, there was no tarrying for them there, but that they must needs fly. Then Brutus, rising up, "We must fly indeed," said he, "but it must be with our hands, not with our feet." Then taking every man by the hand, he said these words unto them with a cheerful countenance: "It rejoiceth my heart, that not one of my friends hath failed me at my need, and I do not complain of my fortune, but only for my country's sake: for as for me, I think myself happier than they that have overcome, considering that I leave a perpetual fame of virtue and honesty, the which our enemies the conquerors shall never attain unto by force or money; neither can let their posterity to say that they, being naughty and unjust men, have slain good men, to usurp tyrannical power not pertaining to them." Having so said, he prayed every man to shift for himself, and then he went a little aside with two or three only, among the which Strato was one, with whom he came first acquainted by the study of rhetoric. He came as near to him as he could, and taking his sword by the hilt with both his hands, and falling down upon the point of it, ran himself through. Others say that not he, but Strato (at his request) held the sword in his hand, and turned his head aside, and that Brutus fell down upon it, and so ran himself through, and died presently. [64]Messala, that had been Brutus' great friend, became afterwards Octavius Caesar's friend: so, shortly after, Caesar being at good leisure, he brought Strato, Brutus' friend, unto him, and weeping said: "Caesar, behold, here is he that did the last service to my Brutus." Caesar welcomed him at that time, and afterwards he did him as faithful service in all his affairs as any Grecian else he had about him, until the battle of Actium. It is reported also that this Messala himself answered Caesar one day, when he gave him great praise before his face, that he had fought valiantly and with great affection for him at the battle of Actium (notwithstanding that he had been his cruel enemy before, at the battle of Philippi, for Brutus' sake): "I ever loved," said he, "to take the best and justest part." [65]Now Antonius having found Brutus' body, he caused it to be wrapped up in one of the richest coat-armours he had. Afterwards also, Antonius understanding that this coat-armour was stolen, he put the thief to death that had stolen it, and sent the ashes of his body unto

---

[64] V.v. 52–67.
[65] Compare Plutarch's history with Shakespeare's imagination in this episode: V.v. 68–75.

Servilia his mother. [66]And for Porcia, Brutus' wife, Nicolaus the Philosopher and Valerius Maximus do write, that she, determining to kill herself (her parents and friends carefully looking to her to keep her from it), took hot burning coals and cast them into her mouth, and kept her mouth so close that she choked herself. There was a letter of Brutus found written to his friends, complaining of their negligence, that, his wife being sick, would not help her, but suffered her to kill herself; choosing to die, rather than to languish in pain.

[*The Characters of Brutus and Cassius*]

Marcus Brutus came of that Junius Brutus, for whom the ancient Romans made his statue of brass to be set up in the Capitol, with the images of the kings, holding a naked sword in his hand: because he had valiantly put down the Tarquins from the kingdom of Rome. But that Junius Brutus, being of a sour stern nature not softened by reason, being like unto swordblades of too hard a temper, was so subject to his choler and malice he bare unto the tyrants, that for their sakes he caused his own sons to be executed. But this Marcus Brutus in contrary manner, whose life we presently write, having framed his manners of life by the rules of virtue and study of philosophy, and having employed his wit, which was gentle and constant, in attempting of great things, methinks he was rightly made and framed unto virtue. So that his very enemies which wish him most hurt, because of his conspiracy against Julius Caesar, if there were any noble attempt done in all this conspiracy, they refer it wholly unto Brutus; and all the cruel and violent acts unto Cassius, who was Brutus' familiar friend, but not so well given and conditioned as he. . . .

Now Cassius would have done Brutus much honour, as Brutus did unto him, but Brutus most commonly prevented him, and went first unto him, both because he was the elder man as also for that he was sickly of body. And men reputed him commonly to be very skilful in wars, but otherwise marvellous choleric and cruel, who sought to rule men by fear rather than with lenity: and on the other side, he was too familiar with his friends, and would jest too broadly with them. But Brutus, in contrary manner, for his virtue and valiantness, was well beloved of the people and his own, esteemed of noblemen, and hated of no man, not so much as of his enemies; because he was a marvellous lowly and gentle person, noble-minded, and would never be in any rage, nor carried away with pleasure and covetousness, but had ever an upright mind with him, and would never yield to any wrong or injustice;

---

[66] IV.iii. 147–157.

the which was the chiefest cause of his fame, of his rising, and of the goodwill that every man bare him: for they were all persuaded that his intent was good.

THE LIFE OF MARCUS ANTONIUS

[Marcus Antonius (83–30 B.C.) spent his youth savoring the corruptions of Rome. He left Rome to fight in Syria and Egypt, and when he returned was made a tribune through Caesar's influence. He was Caesar's second in command at Pharsalia, and when Caesar was made dictator he made Antonius "general of the horsemen," an office second in power and dignity only to that of dictator. Whereupon Antonius left his dissolute manner of life and married the widow Fulvia, a virago who, surmises Plutarch, taught Antonius "obedience to women."]

Now when Caesar was returned from his last war in Spain, all the chiefest nobility of the city rode many days journey from Rome to meet him, where Caesar made marvellous much of Antonius above all the men that came unto him. For he always took him into his coach with him throughout all Italy, and behind him Brutus Albinus and Octavius the son of his niece, who afterwards was called Caesar, and became Emperor of Rome long time after. So Caesar being afterwards chosen Consul the fifth time, he immediately chose Antonius his colleague and companion; and desired, by deposing himself of his consulship, to make Dolabella Consul in his room, and had already moved it to the senate. But Antonius did stoutly withstand it, and openly reviled Dolabella in the Senate, and Dolabella also spared him as little. Thereupon Caesar being ashamed of the matter, he let it alone. Another time also, when Caesar attempted again to substitute Dolabella Consul in his place, Antonius cried out, that the signs of the birds were against it: so that at length Caesar was compelled to give him place, and to let Dolabella alone, who was marvellously offended with him. Now in truth Caesar made no great reckoning of either of them both. For it is reported that Caesar answered one that did accuse Antonius and Dolabella unto him for some matter of conspiracy:[1] "Tush," said he, "they be not those fat fellows and fine combed men that I fear, but I mistrust rather these pale and lean men," meaning by Brutus and Cassius, who afterwards conspired his death and slew him. Antonius, unawares, afterwards gave Caesar's enemies just occasion and colour to do as they did: as you shall hear. [2]The Romans by chance

---

[1] I.ii. 190–210.
[2] I.ii. 1–11.

celebrated the feast called *Lupercalia*, and Caesar, being apparelled in his triumphing robe, was set in the Tribune where they use to make their orations to the people, and from thence did behold the sport of the runners. The manner of this running was thus. On that day there are many young men of noble house, and those specially that be chief officers for that year, who running naked up and down the city, anointed with the oil of olive, for pleasure do strike them they meet in their way with white leather thongs they have in their hands. Antonius, being one among the rest that was to run, leaving the ancient ceremonies and old customs of that solemnity, he ran to the tribune where Caesar was set, and carried a laurel crown in his hand, having a royal band or diadem wreathed about it, which in old time was the ancient mark and token of a king. [3]When he was come to Caesar, he made his fellow-runners with him lift him up, and so he did put his laurel crown upon his head, signifying thereby that he had deserved to be king. But Caesar, making as though he refused it, turned away his head. The people were so rejoiced at it, that they all clapped their hands for joy. Antonius again did put it on his head: Caesar again refused it; and thus they were striving off and on a great while together. As oft as Antonius did put this laurel crown unto him, a few of his followers rejoiced at it: and as oft also as Caesar refused it, all the people together clapped their hands. And this was a wonderful thing, that they suffered all things subjects should do by commandment of their kings: and yet they could not abide the name of a king, detesting it as the utter destruction of their liberty. Caesar, in a rage, arose out of his seat, and plucking down the collar of his gown from his neck, he shewed it naked, bidding any man strike off his head that would. This laurel crown was afterwards put upon the head of one of Caesar's statues or images, the which one of the tribunes plucked off. The people liked his doing therein so well, that they waited on him home to his house, with great clapping of hands. Howbeit Caesar did turn them out of their offices for it.

[4]This was a good encouragement for Brutus and Cassius to conspire his death, who fell into a consort with their trustiest friends, to execute their enterprise, but yet stood doubtful whether they should make Antonius privy to it or not. All the rest liked of it, saving Trebonius only. He told them that, when they rode to meet Caesar at his return out of Spain, Antonius and he always keeping company, and lying together by the way, he felt his mind afar off: but Antonius, finding his meaning, would hearken no more unto it, and yet notwithstanding never made Caesar acquainted with this talk, but had faithfully kept

---

[3] I.ii. 216–289.
[4] I.iii. 1ff.; II.i. 1–190.

it to himself. After that, they consulted whether they should kill
Antonius with Caesar. But Brutus would in no wise consent to it,
saying, that venturing on such an enterprise as that, for the maintenance of law and justice, it ought to be clear from all villany. ⁵Yet
they, fearing Antonius' power, and the authority of his office, appointed certain of the conspiracy, that when Caesar were gone into
the senate, and while others should execute their enterprise, they
should keep Antonius in a talk out of the senate-house. ⁶Even as they
had devised these matters, so were they executed: and Caesar was slain
in the midst of the senate. ⁷Antonius being put in a fear withal, cast
a slave's gown upon him, and hid himself. But afterwards when it was
told him that the murderers slew no man else, and that they went
only into the Capitol, he sent his son unto them for a pledge, and
bade them boldly come down upon his word. The selfsame day he
did bid Cassius to supper, and Lepidus also bade Brutus. The next
morning the senate was assembled, and Antonius himself proffered a
law, that all things past should be forgotten, and that they should
appoint provinces unto Cassius and Brutus: the which the senate
confirmed, and further ordained, that they should cancel none of
Caesar's laws. Thus went Antonius out of the senate more praised and
better esteemed than ever man was, because it seemed to every man
that he had cut off all occasion of civil wars, and that he had shewed
himself a marvellous wise governor of the commonwealth, for the
appeasing of these matters of so great weight and importance. ⁸But
now, the opinion he conceived of himself after he had a little felt the
good-will of the people towards him, hoping thereby to make himself
the chiefest man if he might overcome Brutus, did easily make him
alter his first mind. ⁹And therefore, when Caesar's body was brought
to the place where it should be buried, he made a funeral oration in
commendation of Caesar, according to the ancient custom of praising
noble men at their funerals. When he saw that the people were very
glad and desirous also to hear Caesar spoken of, and his praises uttered,
he mingled his oration with lamentable words; and by amplifying of
matters did greatly move their hearts and affections unto pity and
compassion. In fine, to conclude his oration, he unfolded before the
whole assembly the bloody garments of the dead, thrust through in
many places with their swords, and called the malefactors cruel and
cursed murderers. With these words he put the people into such a

---

⁵ III.i. 25–26.
⁶ III.i. 35–77.
⁷ III.i. 95–252.
⁸ Contrast Antonius's motives here with III.ii. 254–284.
⁹ III.ii. 78ff.

fury, that they presently took Caesar's body, and burnt it in the market-place, with such tables and forms as they could get together. Then when the fire was kindled, they took firebrands, and ran to the mur-derers' houses to set them on fire, and to make them come out to fight. Brutus therefore and his accomplices, for safety of their persons, were driven to fly the city. Then came all Caesar's friends unto Antonius, and specially his wife Calpurnia, putting her trust in him, she brought the most part of her money into his house, which amounted to the sum of 4000 talents; and furthermore brought him all Caesar's books and writings, in the which were his memorials of all that he had done and ordained. Antonius did daily mingle with them such as he thought good, and by that means he created new officers, made new senators, called home some that were banished, and delivered those that were prisoners: and then he said, that all those things were so appointed and ordained by Caesar. Therefore the Romans, mocking them that were so moved, they called them Charonites, because that, when they were overcome, they had no other help but to say, that thus they were found in Caesar's memorials, who had sailed in Charons' boat, and was departed. Thus Antonius ruled absolutely also in all other matters, because he was Consul, and Caius, one of his brethren, Praetor, and Lucius the other, Tribune.

[10]Now things remaining in this state at Rome, Octavius Caesar the younger came to Rome, who was the son of Julius Caesar's niece, as you have heard before, and was left his lawful heir by will, remaining, at the time of the death of his great uncle that was slain, in the city of Apollonia. This young man at his first arrival went to salute Antonius, as one of his late dead father Caesar's friends, who by his last will and testament had made him his heir; and withal, he was presently in hand with him for money and other things which were left of trust in his hands; because Caesar had by will bequeathed unto the people of Rome threescore and fifteen silver drachmas to be given to every man, the which he as heir stood charged withal. Antonius at the first made no reckoning of him, because he was very young, and said, he lacked wit and good friends to advise him, if he looked to take such a charge in hand, as to undertake to be Caesar's heir. But when Antonius saw that he could not shake him off with those words, and that he was still in hand[11] with him for his father's goods, but specially for the ready money, then he spake and did what he could against him. And first of all, it was he that did keep him from being Tribune of the people: and also, when Octavius Caesar began to meddle with the dedicating of the chair of gold, which was prepared by the senate to

---

[10] III.ii. 267ff.
[11] urgent.

honour Caesar with, he threatened to send him to prison, and moreover desisted not to put the people in an uproar. This young Caesar, seeing his doings, went unto Cicero and others, which were Antonius' enemies, and by them crept into favour with the senate: and he himself sought the people's good will every manner of way, gathering together the old soldiers of the late deceased Caesar, which were dispersed in divers cities and colonies. Antonius, being afraid of it, talked with Octavius in the Capitol, and became his friend. But the very same night Antonius had a strange dream, who thought that lightning fell upon him, and burnt his right hand. Shortly after word was brought him, that Caesar lay in wait to kill him. Caesar cleared himself unto him, and told him there was no such matter: but he could not make Antonius believe to the contrary. [12]Whereupon they became further enemies than ever they were: insomuch that both of them made friends of either side to gather together all the old soldiers through Italy, that were dispersed in divers towns: and made them large promises, and sought also to win the legions on their side, which were already in arms. Cicero on the other side, being at that time the chiefest man of authority and estimation in the city, he stirred up all men against Antonius: so that in the end he made the senate pronounce him an enemy to his country, and appointed young Caesar sergeants to carry axes before him, and such other signs as were incident to the dignity of a Consul or Praetor: and moreover, sent Hircius and Pansa, then Consuls, to drive Antonius out of Italy. These two Consuls, together with Caesar, who also had an army, went against Antonius that besieged the city of Modena, and there overthrew him in battle: but both the Consuls were slain there.

Antonius flying upon this overthrow, fell into great misery all at once: but the chiefest want of all other, and that pinched him most, was famine. Howbeit he was of such a strong nature, that by patience he would overcome any adversity: and the heavier fortune lay upon him, the more constant shewed he himself. Every man that feeleth want or adversity, knoweth by virtue and discretion what he should do: but when indeed they are overlaid with extremity, and be sore oppressed, few have the hearts to follow that which they praise and commend, and much less to avoid that they reprove and mislike: but rather to the contrary, they yield to their accustomed easy life, and through faint heart, and lack of courage, do change their first mind and purpose. [13]And therefore it was a wonderful example to the sol-

---

[12] Shakespeare shows us this hostility with swift dramatic compression. V.i. 16–20.

[13] *Antony and Cleopatra*: I.iv. 55–71.

diers, to see Antonius, that was brought up in all fineness and superfluity, so easily to drink puddle water, and to eat wild fruits and roots:
and moreover it is reported, that even as they passed the Alps, they
did eat the bark of trees, and such beasts as never man tasted of their
flesh before. Now their intent was to join with the legions that were
on the other side of the mountains, under Lepidus' charge: whom
Antonius took to be his friend, because he had holpen him to many
things at Caesar's hand, through his means. When he was come to
the place where Lepidus was, he camped hard by him: and when he
saw that no man came to him to put him in any hope, he determined to
venture himself, and to go unto Lepidus. Since the overthrow he had
at Modena, he suffered his beard to grow at length and never clipt it,
that it was marvellous long, and the hair of his head also without
combing: and besides all this, he went in a mourning gown, and after
this sort came hard to the trenches of Lepidus' camp. Then he began
to speak unto the soldiers, and many of them their hearts yearned for
pity to see him so poorly arrayed, and some also, through his words,
began to pity him: insomuch that Lepidus began to be afraid, and
therefore commanded all the trumpets to sound together to stop the
soldiers' ears, that they should not hearken to Antonius. This notwithstanding, the soldiers took the more pity of him, and spake secretly
with him in Clodius' and Laelius' means, whom they sent unto him
disguised in women's apparel, and gave him counsel that he should not
be afraid to enter into their camp, for there were a great number of
soldiers that would receive him, and kill Lepidus, if he would say the
word. Antonius would not suffer them to hurt him, but the next
morning he went with his army to wade a ford, at a little river that
ran between them: and himself was the foremost man that took the
river to get over, seeing a number of Lepidus' camp, that gave him
their hands, plucked up the stakes, and laid flat the bank of their
trench to let him into their camp. When he was come into their
camp, and that he had all the army at his commandment, he used
Lepidus very courteously, embraced him, and called him father: and
though indeed Antonius did all, and ruled the whole army, yet he
always gave Lepidus the name and honour of the captain. Munacius
Plancus, lying also in camp hard by with an army, understanding the
report of Antonius' courtesy, he also came and joined with him.

Thus Antonius being afoot again, and grown of great power, re-
passed over the Alps, leading into Italy with him seventeen legions,
and ten thousand horsemen, besides six legions he left in garrison
among the Gauls, under the charge of one Varius, a companion of his
that would drink lustily with him, and therefore in mockery was surnamed Cotylon, to wit, a bibber. So Octavius Caesar would not lean

to Cicero, when he saw that his whole travail and endeavour was only to restore the commonwealth to her former liberty. [14]Therefore he sent certain of his friends to Antonius, to make them friends again: and thereupon all three met together (to wit, Caesar, Antonius, and Lepidus) in an island environed round about with a little river, and there remained three days together. Now as touching all other matters they were easily agreed, and did divide all the empire of Rome between them, as if it had been their own inheritance. But yet they could hardly agree whom they would put to death: for every one of them would kill their enemies, and save their kinsmen and friends. Yet at length, giving place to their greedy desire to be revenged of their enemies, they spurned all reverence of blood and holiness of friendship at their feet. For Caesar left Cicero to Antonius' will, Antonius also forsook Lucius Caesar, who was his uncle by his mother: and both of them together suffered Lepidus to kill his own brother Paulus. Yet some writers affirm, that Caesar and Antonius requested Paulus might be slain, and that Lepidus was contented with it. In my opinion there was never a more horrible, unnatural, and crueller change than this was. For thus exchanging murder for murder, they did as well kill those whom they did forsake and leave unto others, as those also which others left unto them to kill: but so much more was their wickedness and cruelty great unto their friends, for that they put them to death being innocents, and having no cause to hate them. After this plot was agreed upon between them, the soldiers that were thereabouts would have his friendship and league betwixt them confirmed by marriage, and that Caesar should marry Claudia, the daughter of Fulvia, Antonius' wife. This marriage also being agreed upon, they condemned 300 of the chiefest citizens of Rome to be put to death by proscription. And Antonius also commanded them to whom he had given commission to kill Cicero, that they should strike off his head and right hand, with the which he had written the invective orations (called *Philippides*) against Antonius. So when the murderers brought him Cicero's head and hand cut off, he beheld them a long time with great joy, and laughed heartily, and that oftentimes, for the great joy he felt. Then when he had taken his pleasure of the sight of them, he caused them to be set up in an open place, over the pulpit for orations (where, when he was alive, he had often spoken to the people), as if he had done the dead man hurt, and not blemished his own fortune, shewing himself (to his great shame and infamy) a cruel man, and unworthy the office and authority he bare. His uncle Lucius

---

[14] Plutarch has the triumvirs meet on an island; Shakespeare implies they meet in a villa in Rome (IV.i). Note the real life Antonius's hatred of Cicero, which Shakespeare chooses to overlook.

Caesar also, as they sought for him to kill him and followed him hard, fled unto his sister. The murderers coming thither, forcing to break into her chamber, she stood at her chamber-door with her arms abroad, crying out still: "You shall not kill Lucius Caesar, before you first kill me, that bare your captain in my womb." By this means she saved her brother's life. [15]Now the government of these Triumviri grew odious and hateful to the Romans, for divers respects: but they most blamed Antonius, because he, being elder than Caesar, and of more power and force than Lepidus, gave himself again to his former riot and excess, when he left to deal in the affairs of the commonwealth. But setting aside the ill name he had for his insolency, he was yet much more hated in respect of the house he dwelt in, the which was the house of Pompey the great, a man as famous for his temperance, modesty, and civil life, as for his three triumphs. For it grieved them to see the gates commonly shut against the captains, magistrates of the city, and also ambassadors of strange nations, which were sometimes thrust from the gate with violence: and that the house within was full of tumblers, antic dancers, jugglers, players, jesters, and drunkards, quaffing and guzzling; and that on them he bestowed the most part of his money he got by all kind of possible extortions, bribery, and policy. For they did not only sell by the crier the goods of those whom they had outlawed and appointed to murder, slanderously deceived the poor widows and young orphans, and also raised all kinds of imposts, subsidies, and taxes, but understanding also that the holy Vestal nuns had certain goods and money put in their custody to keep, both of men's in the city and those also that were abroad, they went thither and took them away by force.

Octavius Caesar perceiving that no money would serve Antonius' turn, he prayed that they might divide the money between them;[16] and so did they also divide the army, for them both to go into Macedon to make war against Brutus and Cassius: and in the meantime they left the government of the city of Rome unto Lepidus. When they had passed over the seas, and that they began to make war, they being both camped by their enemies, to wit, Antonius against Cassius, and Caesar against Brutus, Caesar did no great matter, but Antonius had alway the upper hand, and did all. For at the first battle Caesar was overthrown by Brutus, and lost his camp, and very hardly saved himself by flying from them that followed him. Howbeit, he writeth himself in his Commentaries, that he fled before the charge was given, because of a dream one of his friends had. Antonius on the other side overthrew Cassius in battle, though some write that he was not there himself at

---

[15] A suggestion for Shakespeare of the riotous aspect of Antony's character.
[16] Acts IV, V.

the battle, but that he came after the overthrow, whilst his men had the enemies in chase. So Cassius, at his earnest request, was slain by a faithful servant of his own called Pindarus, whom he had enfranchised: because he knew not in time that Brutus had overcome Caesar. Shortly after they fought another battle again, in the which Brutus was overthrown, who afterwards also slew himself.

[The Character of Antonius]

He had a noble presence, and shewed a countenance of one of a noble house: he had a goodly thick beard, a broad forehead, crooked-nosed, and there appeared such a manly look in his countenance, as is commonly seen in Hercules' pictures, stamped or graven in metal. Now it had been a speech of old time, that the family of the Antonii were descended from one Anton the son of Hercules, whereof the family took name. This opinion did Antonius seek to confirm in all his doings: not only resembling him in the likeness of his body, as we have said before, but also in the wearing of his garments. For when he would openly shew himself abroad before many people, he would always wear his cassock girt down low upon his hips, with a great sword hanging by his side, and upon that, some ill-favoured cloak. Furthermore, things that seem intolerable in other men, as to boast commonly, to jest with one or other, to drink like a good fellow with everybody, to sit with the soldiers when they dine, and to eat and drink with them soldier-like, it is incredible what wonderful love it won him amongst them. And furthermore, being given to love, that made him the more desired, and by that means he brought many to love him.

⚔ APPIANUS ALEXANDRINUS

The Roman Civil Wars, c. 160 A.D.

translated by W.B.,[1] *1578*

From Book II*

Antonius and Lepidus (as I said) minded[2] to revenge Caesar's death, either for friendship's sake, or for a practise between them, or for desire of rule. . . . Having this fetch, Antony thus answered the messengers: "For private displeasure we will work nothing, but for offense and matter wherein we are all sworn to Caesar to be keepers of his body and defend it against violence, it is requisite by our oath to follow the fact[3] that is done and the rather to live with a few pure, than all to be in danger of these execrations. Yet for their honor that be of that opinion, we will debate with you in the Senate house and take the way for the city that by common consent shall seem good." Thus Antony answered safely.[4] They gave thanks and departed with sure hope that all should have gone well and that the Senate would have favored their cause thoroughly. . . . Caesar's money and the books of his doings were carried to Antony, either because Calphurnia for the danger of her house did send them to Antony, as more sure, or that Antony did so command it. This done, a decree was made by Antony that night to call the Senate before day at the Temple of the Goddess of the Earth, not far from his own house. For neither durst he go to the Senate house in the Capitol, because of the sword players gathered there, nor bring the army into the town for troubling of it; notwithstanding, Lepidus brought them in.

---

* text modernized.

[1] Ernest Schanzer, in his definitive *Shakespeare's Appian* (English Reprints Series, Liverpool, 1956) conjectures that W. B. is "likely" William Barker (fl. 1570).

[2] decided.

[3] deed: i.e., the assassination.

[4] Suggesting a guileful Antony. Compare with Shakespeare's Antony (in contrast to Plutarch's).

Day drawing nigh, other Senators came to the Temple of the Goddess of the Earth, and Cinna,[5] the praetor, having on again his
garment, which the day before he had thrown off as given him of a
tyrant, made haste thither; whom, when part of the uncorrupted people and part of Caesar's soldiers saw, being in a rage because the day
before he was the first that openly spoke evil of Caesar, being his
kinsman, they threw stones at him and drove him into an house, and
got wood to have burned it, had not Lepidus come with the army and
forbidden them. This was the first token whereby Caesar's friends
had confidence that the conspirators and the hired fellows were afraid.

[6]In the Senate house there were few that were pure from violence
and contention. The most part with divers device favored the man-
quellers,[7] and thought them most worthy of trust to be there for
common consultation, and of offenders to make them judges — the
which Antony did not let, because he knew they [the assassins] would
not come, as they did not indeed. Then in trial of the Senate, some
very earnestly and plainly praised the fact,[8] naming them tyrant-killers,
and willed they should be rewarded. Others denied the reward themselves [the assassins] not desiring it nor having done it for that intent,
but thought it just they should only be commended as well-doers.
Some would not allow that commendation, but only thought it enough
if they were forgiven. Thus did they devise and forecast at the first to
what the Senate would incline, that after by little and little they
might the easier obtain the rest. The uncorrupted company did abhor
the act as wicked, yet for the reverence of their great houses were not
against but that they [the assassins] should be saved. Yet that they
should be honored as well-doers, they could not abide. Others spoke
against this, that it was not convenient so to have them. . . . Antony
marking all things deceitfully[9] perceiving that ample and evident matter of speeches was offered, determined to turn their cogitation with a
private care and fear of themselves, and understanding that a great
part of these Senators were appointed to offices and priesthoods in
the city, and to governments of armies and provinces by Caesar, for
the time to come (for he should be long forth with his army, the space
of five years) commanding silence as Consul, thus said:

[10]"They that would have voices tried upon Caesar must know afore
that if he ruled as an officer lawfully chosen, then all his acts and de-

---

[5] The conspirator, not the poet Cinna whom the mob kills in the conspirator's place: III.iii. 1ff.

[6] Compare with III.ii. 1–56.

[7] murderers

[8] See footnote 3.

[9] See Shakespeare's Antony.

[10] Compare with III.ii. 78–264.

crees must stand in force; but if by violence we think he played the
tyrant, then must his body be cast out of the city unburied and all his
acts be revoked. . . ."

Thus Antony did kindle a fire, not for Caesar but for themselves,
and held his peace. Then they by and by in throngs with shouts,
started up, and denied that any other trial should be made by the
voices of the people, but that the things appointed should be assuredly
held.

The matter standing thus, Antony and Lepidus went out of the
Senate house, for certain [citizens] that came running from the multitude did call them, and as they were seen from above, and silence
hardly[11] put to them that made such noise, one cried unto them,
whether of his own mind, or that he was suborned, and bade them take
heed, lest they suffered the like. Then Antony loosing his gown, showed
his curet,[12] incensing the lookers on, as though now no man could be safe
unless he wore armor, no, not [even] the Consul. There were some cried
that the fact[13] might be punished, and more made request for peace. To
whom he thus said: "Of that we will consider, as shall be fit to be;
and what it is, that it may avail. But the surety of it is hard to be
found, since neither oath nor execration could profit Caesar." And
to them that called for revenge, he turned and commended them as
more careful of their oaths and honesty. "I would be," said he, "your
captain and cry as you do, but that I am a Consul, to whom belongs
rather to speak for profit than for justice. For so do they within persuade us. And so Caesar himself, for the profit of the city, sparing
them that he had taken in war, was of the same destroyed." Thus
wrought Antony artificially.[14] And they that thought the fact to be
punished required Lepidus that he would punish it. Lepidus intending
to speak, they that stood far off prayed him to go into the common
place that all might hear him indifferently.[15] He [Lepidus] went
straight forth with opinion that the people's minds were new turned,
and when he was come to the place of speech he lamented weeping
and thus said:[16] "Here I was yesterday with Caesar, and now am I
here to inquire of Caesar's death. What will you have done?" Many
cried that they should revenge Caesar. The hired men cried for peace
in the city, to whom he said, "We will so, but what peace speak you
of? With what oaths can it be sure? For all our country oaths we have
sworn to Caesar, and we that are compted the least of them that did

---

11 with difficulty.
12 cuirass.
13 See footnote 3.
14 See Shakespeare's Antony.
15 equally.
16 This speech by Lepidus too contains suggestions for III.ii. 78–264.

swear, have trodden all under the foot."[17] Then he turned to them
that cried for revenge. "Caesar," said he, "is gone from us, an holy
and honored man indeed. And we be afraid to hurt the city, and them
that be left. This does the Senate treat of, and many think it good."
Then they cried that he alone should take it in hand. "I will," said
he, "for it is a just oath to me alone. But it is not enough that I and
you alone do will it, or that we alone can fulfill it." Handling the
matter thus craftily, the hired men, knowing that he [Lepidus] was
ambitious, praised him and exhorted him to take the office of Caesar's
priesthood, of the which he being very glad, said, "You shall remember
me of this hereafter, if I shall be worthy of it" . . . Antony gathering
the people's humor, looked over them with a smiling countenance,
and finding them to dissent among themselves and the people to do
nothing earnestly, having beholden all sufficiently he determined to
save the men [in the Senate] hiding one necessity with another, that
both they should be saved by especial grace and that Caesar's acts
should be confirmed by decree, and the Senate's orders take effect.

☐ *Some Sources for Further Study*

1. MARCUS TULLIUS CICERO (106–43 B.C.) — *Correspondence.* His
   letters pertinent to the events in *Julius Caesar* supply Shakespeare's
   historical sources with their most incisive first hand material.
2. PLUTARCH (c. 46–120 A.D.) — *The Life of Cicero,* from *Parallel
   Lives.* The paragraph on Cicero's learning Greek hints at I.ii. 281–
   287.
3. JACQUES AMYOT — *Lives of Plutarch* (1559).
4. *A Mirror for Magistrates* — "Julius Caesar" (1587).
5. THOMAS KYD — *Cornelia* (c. 1594). A translation influenced by
   the Countess of Pembroke of *Cornelie,* 1574, a play by Robert
   Garnier, typical of that author's Senecan style but offering valid
   comments on the violence of the Roman Civil Wars that followed
   the assassination of Caesar.

---

[17] Lepidus probably means that "we" commoners too have foresworn our
oaths.

twelfth night

The principal source for the main plot of *Twelfth Night* is "Apolonius and Silla," a novella by Barnaby Riche from a collection of his entitled *Riche His Farewell to Military Profession*, 1581. Riche's story has an Italian source, a novella by Matteo Bandello subsequently translated by Francois de Belleforest and puffed out with his usual rhetoric — Riche's dialogue strongly resembles the language of Belleforest. Bandello in turn went back to an anonymous play, *The Deceived Ones (Gl' Ingannati)*, as his source and like the play uses *The Sack of Rome* to precipitate the action — Riche uses a shipwreck and Shakespeare follows him in this. Riche's story contains the following elements repeated in *Twelfth Night*: the shipwreck; the close resemblance between brother and sister (though they are not twins, as in Shakespeare); the heroine disguised as a man; her employment by the duke; the duke's love for another lady; the lady's love for the disguised heroine; the brother's arrival, which sets off the obvious complications; their happy resolution.

A second basal source for *Twelfth Night* is *The Deceived Ones*, 1531, also the source for Bandello's novella. It too contains the brother-sister resemblance, the sister as page, the master's haughty beloved, the brother's arrival and much the same complications as in "Apolonius and Silla." *The Deceived Ones*, however, contrasts with "Apolonius and Silla" from deep within. It is earthy and bawdy, like nature uninhibited, while Riche's story has an overlay of elegance that reaches toward the sublime courtliness of Shakespeare's main plot. The tone of *The Deceived Ones* sounds more like that of the Sir Toby-Maria-Aguecheek subplot of *Twelfth Night*, and given that clue we can go on to find other relationships between *The Deceived Ones* and the *Twelfth Night* subplot as well. Virginio's egging on Gherardo to woo his daughter suggests Sir Toby's prodding Aguecheek to woo Olivia; the servants' eavesdropping during Isabella's pursuit of Lelia has a faint counterpart in the eavesdropping during Feste's badgering of Malvolio in the cellar; and Virginio's timid attack on Gherardo suggests the Viola-Aguecheek duelling scene. Another possible link between this source and Shakespeare's play is the reference, twice made in *The Deceived Ones*, to "Twelfth Night," once in the prologue and once in Act I, scene ii. (Also, a certain Agnol Malevolti [evil faces] is cited in a preface to this play, but its connection with Shakespeare's Malvolio seems too tenuous to pursue.)

Riche's story is mainly concerned with plot and keeps character drawing at a sketchy minimum, while *The Deceived Ones* exudes a typical *commedia dell'arte* bluntness and practicality that confines character drawing to direct, physical thrusts. One looks in vain for early overtones of, say, the complex and idealistic motivations of Viola in Lelia, or even in Silla whose proper habitat is the Italian, not the London, stage. Modena and Constantinople are not Illyria, and Shakespeare's heroine partakes more of his own world of Julia, Juliet, Portia, and Rosalind. Duke Orsino too has few character traits in common with his source equivalents. With his inflated, amorous sentiments darkened by a base of melancholy he seems like a Proteus, Lysander, or Orlando suddenly brought up short by middle age. The subplot characters bear a somewhat closer relation to their dramatic source. Granting certain national differences — *The Deceived Ones* is rollicking Italian *Kitsch*; Shakespeare's British roisterers are more cavalier — Clemenzia bears a strong resemblance to Maria; Virginio and Gherardo suggest Sir Toby and Aguecheek; and the starchy pedant smacks faintly of Malvolio — though Malvolio seems more of an earthbound Cassius despoiled of the glory that was Rome.

Nothing in either source suggests the graceful and profound use that *Twelfth Night* will make of music. Music begins and ends the play, its loveliest scene (II.iv) is punctuated by it, and the play's noblest character bears its name. (Olivia, almost right for the duke, has a name that is *almost* an anagram for Viola.) The duke's opening speech, on music, does much to reveal his character, which must be grasped if the play is to have any meaning at all. The song "O Mistress Mine" summarizes the plot of the play in its first stanza, and the song that ends the play may well be telling us its central theme: that the rain — nature, the natural — rains down every day throughout the life of man. If this is so, then here dramatic source and Shakespeare play reflect a similar idea, for *The Deceived Ones* hotly pursues the natural throughout youth and age, and none of its characters is too old but that he still yearns, like Sir Toby, to "make the welkin dance."

"APOLONIUS AND SILLA"*

Apolonius Duke, having spent a year's service in the wars against the Turk, returning homeward with his company by sea, was driven by force of weather to the Isle of Cyprus, where he was well received by Pontus, governor of the same isle, with whom Silla, daughter to Pontus, fell so strangely in love, that after Apolonius was departed to Constantinople, Silla, with one man, followed, and coming to Constantinople, she served Apolonius in the habit of a man, and after many pretty accidents falling out, she was known to Apolonius, who, in requital of her love, married her.

There is no child that is born into this wretched world, but before it doth suck the mother's milk it takes first a sip of the cup of error, which makes us, when we come to riper years, not only to enter into actions of injury but many times to stray from that is right and reason. But in all other things, wherein we show ourselves to be most drunk with this poisoned cup, it is in our actions of love; for the lover is so estranged from that is right, and wanders so wide from the bounds of reason, that he is not able to deem white from black, good from bad, virtue from vice; but only led by the appetite of his own affections, and grounding them on the foolishness of his own fancies will so settle his liking on such a one as either by desert or unworthiness will merit rather to be loathed than loved.

If a question might be asked, what is the ground indeed of reasonable love, whereby the knot is knit of true and perfect friendship, I think those that be wise would answer — desert: that is, where the party beloved does requite us with the like; for otherwise, if the bare show of beauty or the comeliness of personage might be sufficient to confirm us in our love, those that be accustomed to go to fairs and

---

* text modernized.

markets might sometimes fall in love with twenty in a day; desert must then be (of force) the ground of reasonable love; for to love them that hate us, to follow them that flee from us, to fawn on them that frown on us, to curry favor with them that disdain us, to be glad to please them that care not how they offend us: who will not confess this to be an erroneous love, neither grounded upon wit nor reason? Wherefore, right courteous gentlewomen, if it please you with patience to peruse this history following, you shall see Dame Error so play her part with a leash[1] of lovers, a male and two females as shall work a wonder to your wise judgement in noting the effect of their amorous devices and conclusions of their actions: the first neglecting the love of a noble dame, young, beautiful, and fair; [the second] who only for his good will played the part of a serving man, contented to abide any manner of pain only to behold him. He again setting his love of a dame, that despising him (being a noble duke) gave herself to a serving man (as she had thought); but it otherwise fell out, as the substance of this tale shall better describe. And because I have been something tedious in my first discourse, offending your patient ears with the hearing of a circumstance overlong, from henceforth that which I mind to write shall be done with such celerity as the matter that I pretend to pen may in any wise permit me; and thus follows the history.

During the time that the famous city of Constantinople remained in the hands of Christians, amongst many other noblemen that kept their abiding in that flourishing city, there was one whose name was Apolonius, a worthy duke, who being but a very young man, and even then new come to his possessions, which were very great, levied a mighty band of men at his own proper charges, with whom he served against the Turk during the space of one whole year: in which time, although it were very short, this young duke so behaved himself, as well by prowess and valiance showed with his own hands, as otherwise by his wisdom and liberality used towards his soldiers, that all the world was filled with the fame of this noble duke. When he had thus spent one year's service, he caused his trumpet to sound a retreat, and gathering his company together, and embarking themselves, he set sail, holding his course towards Constantinople: but, being upon the sea, by the extremity of a tempest which suddenly fell, his fleet was desevered, some one way, and some another;[2] but he himself recovered the Isle of Cyprus, where he was worthily received by Pontus, duke and governor of the same isle, with whom he lodged while his ships were new repairing.

---

[1] gathering.
[2] I.ii. 28–29.

This Pontus, that was lord and governor of this famous isle, was an ancient duke, and had two children, a son and a daughter: his son was named Silvio, of whom hereafter we shall have further occasion to speak; but at this instant he was in the parts of Africa, serving in the wars.

The daughter her name was Silla, whose beauty was so peerless, that she had the sovereignty among all other dames, as well for her beauty as for the nobleness of her birth. This Silla, having heard of the worthiness of Apolonius, this young duke, who besides his beauty and good graces had a certain natural allurement, that being now in his company in her father's court, she was so strangely attached with the love of Apolonius, that there was nothing might content her but his presence and sweet sight; and although she saw no manner of hope to attain to that she most desired, knowing Apolonius to be but a guest, and ready to take the benefit of the next wind, and to depart into a strange country, whereby she was bereaved of all possibility ever to see him again, and therefore strived with herself to leave her fondness, but all in vain; it would not be, but like the fowl which is once limed, the more she strives, the faster she ties herself. So Silla was now constrained, perforce her will, to yield to love, wherefore, from time to time, she used so great familiarity with him as her honor might well permit, and fed him with such amorous bait as the modesty of a maid could reasonably afford; which when she perceived did take but small effect, feeling herself so much outraged[3] with the extremity of her passion, by the only countenance that she bestowed upon Apolonius, it might have been well perceived that the very eyes pleaded unto him for pity and remorse. But Apolonius, coming but lately from out the field from the chasing of his enemies, and his fury not yet thoroughly dissolved, not purged from his stomach, gave no regard to those amorous enticements, which, by reason of his youth, he had not been acquainted withal. But his mind ran more to hear his pilots bring news of a merry wind to serve his turn to Constantinople, which in the end came very prosperously; and giving Duke Pontus hearty thanks for his great entertainment, taking his leave of himself and the lady Silla, his daughter, departed with his company, and with a happy gale arrived at his desired port. Gentlewomen, according to my promise, I will here, for brevity's sake, omit to make repetition of the long and dolorous discourse recorded by Silla for this sudden departure of her Apolonius, knowing you to be as tenderly hearted as Silla herself, whereby you may the better conjecture the fury of her fever. But Silla, the further that she saw herself bereaved of all hope ever any more to see her beloved Apolonius, so much the more contagious were

[3] so frantic.

her passions, and made the greater speed to execute that she had premeditated in her mind, which was this. Amongst many servants that
did attend upon her, there was one whose name was Pedro, who had a
long time waited upon her in her chamber, whereby she was well assured of his fidelity and trust; to that Pedro therefore she betrayed
first the fervency of her love borne to Apolonius, conjuring him in the
name of the Goddess of Love herself, and binding him by the duty
that a servant ought to have, that tenders his mistress's safety and
good liking, and desiring him, with tears trickling down her cheeks,
that he would give his consent to aid and assist her in that she had
determined, which was for that she was fully resolved to go to Constantinople, where she might again take the view of her beloved
Apolonius, that he, according to the trust she had reposed in him,
would not refuse to give his consent, secretly to convey her from out
her father's court, according as she should give him direction, and
also to make himself partaker of her journey, and to wait upon her
till she had seen the end of her determination.

Pedro, perceiving with what vehemency his lady and mistress had
made request unto him, albeit he saw many perils and doubts depending in her pretence,[4] notwithstanding, gave his consent to be at her
disposition, promising her to further her with his best advice, and to
be ready to obey whatsoever she would please to command him. The
match being thus agreed upon, and all things prepared in a readiness
for their departure, it happened there was a galley of Constantinople
ready to depart, which Pedro understanding, came to the captain, desiring him to have passage for himself and for a poor maid that was
his sister, which were bound to Constantinople upon certain urgent
affairs: to which request the captain granted, willing him to prepare
aboard with all speed, because the wind served him presently to depart.

Pedro now coming to his mistress, and telling her how he had
handled the matter with the captain, she liking very well of the device,
disguising herself into very simple attire, stole away from out her
father's court, and came with Pedro whom now she calls brother,
aboard the galley, where all things being in readiness, and the wind
serving very well, they launched forth with their oars, and set sail.
When they were at the sea, the captain of the galley, taking the view
of Silla, perceiving her singular beauty, he was better pleased in beholding of her face than in taking the height either of the sun or stars, and
thinking her, by the homeliness of her apparel, to be but some simple
maiden, calling her into his cabin, he began to break with her, after the
sea fashion, desiring her to use his own cabin for her better ease, and

---

[4] purpose, intention.

during the time that she remained at the sea she should not want a bed; and then, whispering softly in her ear he said that for want of a bedfellow he himself would supply that room. Silla, not being acquainted with any such talk, blushed for shame, but made him no answer at all. My captain, feeling such a bickering within himself, the like whereof he had never endured upon the sea, was like to be taken prisoner aboard his own ship and forced to yield himself a captive without any cannon shot; wherefore, to salve all sores and thinking it the readiest way to speed, he began to break with Silla in the way of marriage, telling her how happy a voyage she had made to fall into the liking of such a one as himself was, who was able to keep and maintain her like a gentlewoman, and for her sake would likewise take her brother into his fellowship, whom he would by some means prefer in such sort that both of them should have good cause to think themselves thrice happy, she to light of[5] such a husband, and he to light of such a brother. But Silla, nothing pleased with these preferments, desired him to cease his talk for that she did think herself indeed to be too unworthy such a one as he was; neither was she minded yet to marry, and therefore desired him to fit his fancy upon some that were better worthy than herself was and that could better like of his courtesy than she could do. The captain, seeing himself thus refused, being in a great chafe he said as follows:

"Then seeing you make so little accompt[6] of my courtesy, proffered to one that is so far unworthy of it, from henceforth I will use the office of my authority. You shall know that I am the captain of this ship and have power to command and dispose of things at my pleasure; and seeing you have so scornfully rejected me to be your loyal husband, I will now take you by force and use you at my will, and so long as it shall please me will keep you for mine own store; there shall be no man able to defend you, nor yet to persuade me from that I have determined."

Silla, with these words being struck into a great fear, did think it now too late to rue her rash attempt, determined rather to die with her own hands than to suffer herself to be abused in such sort; therefore she most humbly desired the captain, so much as he could to save her credit, and saying that she must needs be at his will and disposition, that for that present he would depart, and suffer till night, when in the dark he might take his pleasure without any manner of suspicion to the residue of his company. The captain, thinking now the goal to be more than half won, was contented so far to satisfy her request, and departed out, leaving her alone in his cabin.

---

[5] on.

[6] account.

Silla, being alone by herself, drew out her knife, ready to strike herself to the heart, and, falling upon her knees, desired God to receive her soul as an acceptable sacrifice for her follies which she had so willfully committed, craving pardon for her sins and so forth, continuing a long and pitiful reconciliation to God, in the midst whereof there suddenly fell a wonderful storm, the terror whereof was such, that there was no man but did think the seas would presently have swallowed them: the billows so suddenly arose with the rage of the wind, that they were all glad to fall to heaving out of water, for otherwise their feeble galley had never been able to have brooked the seas. [7]This storm continued all that day and the next night; and they being driven to put romer[8] before the wind to keep the galley ahead the billow were driven upon the main shore, where the galley broke all to pieces: there was every man providing to save his own life; some got upon hatches, boards, and casks, and were driven with the waves to and fro; but the greatest number were drowned, amongst the which Pedro was one; but Silla herself being in the cabin, as you have heard, took hold of a chest that was the captain's, the which, by the only providence of God, brought her safe to the shore, the which when she had recovered, not knowing what was become of Pedro her man, she deemed that both he and all the rest had been drowned, for that she saw no body upon the shore but herself. Wherefore, when she had a while made great lamentations, complaining her mishaps, she began in the end to comfort herself with the hope that she had to see her Apolonius, and found such means that she broke open the chest that brought her to land, wherein she found good store of coin, and sundry suits of apparel that were the captain's. [9]And now, to prevent a number of injuries that might be proffered to a woman that was left in her case, she determined to leave her own apparel, and to sort herself into some of those suits, that, being taken for a man, she might pass through the country in the better safety; and, as she changed her apparel, she thought it likewise convenient to change her name; wherefore, not readily happening of any other, she called herself Silvio, by the name of her own brother, whom you have heard spoken of before.

In this manner she traveled to Constantinople, where she inquired out the palace of the Duke Apolonius; and thinking herself now to be both fit and able to play the servingman, she presented herself to the duke, craving his service. The duke, very willing to give succor unto strangers, perceiving him to be a proper smug[10] young man, gave him

---

[7] I.ii. 1–17.

[8] rome: obs. meaning stretch, so that romer is probably a sail rigged to swivel according to shifts in the wind.

[9] I.ii. 53–59.

[10] clean cut.

entertainment. Silla thought herself now more than satisfied for all the casualties that had happened unto her in her journey, that she might at her pleasure take but the view of the Duke Apolonius, and above the rest of his servants was very diligent and attendant upon him;[11] the which the duke perceiving, began likewise to grow into good liking with the diligence of his man, and therefore made him one of his chamber: who but Silvio then was most near about him, in helping of him to make him ready in a morning, in the setting of his ruffs, in the keeping of his chamber? Silvio pleased his master so well, that above all the rest of his servants about him he had the greatest credit, and the duke put him most in trust.

At this very instant there was remaining in the city a noble dame, a widow whose husband was but lately deceased, one of the noblest men that were in the parts of Grecia, who left his lady and wife large possessions and great livings. This lady's name was called Julina, who, besides the abundance of her wealth and the greatness of her revenues, had likewise the sovereignty of all the dames of Constantinople for her beauty. [12]To this Lady Julina Apolonius became an earnest suitor; and, according to the manner of wooers, besides fair words, sorrowful sighs, and piteous countenances, there must be sending of loving letters, chains, bracelets, broaches, rings, tablets, gems, jewels, and presents, I know not what. So my duke, who in the time that he remained in the Isle of Cyprus had no skill at all in the art of love, although it were more than half proffered unto him, was now become a scholar in love's school, and had already learned his first lesson; that is, to speak pitifully, to look ruthfully, to promise largely, to serve diligently, and to please carefully: now he was learning his second lesson; that is, to reward liberally, to give bountifully, to present willingly, and to write lovingly. Thus Apolonius was so busied in his new study, that I warrant you there was no man that could challenge him for playing the truant, he followed his profession with so good a will: [13]and who must be the messenger to carry the tokens and love letters to the Lady Julina, but Silvio, his man: in him the duke reposed his only confidence to go between him and his lady.

Now, gentlewomen, do you think there could have been a greater torment devised, wherewith to afflict the heart of Silla, than herself to be made the instrument to work her own mishap, and to play the attorney in a cause that made so much against herself? But Silla, altogether desirous to please her master, cared nothing at all to offend herself, followed his business with so good a will, as if it had been in her own preferment.

[11] I.iv. 1–8.
[12] I.i. 1–23.
[13] I.iv. 10ff.

[14]Julina, now having many times taken the gaze of this young youth, Silvio, perceiving him to be of such excellent perfect grace, was so entangled with the often sight of this sweet temptation, that she fell into as great a liking with the man as the master was with herself; and on a time, Silvio being sent from his master with a message to the Lady Julina, as he began very earnestly to solicit in his master's behalf, Julina, interrupting him in his tale, said: [15]"Silvio, it is enough that you have said for your master; from henceforth, either speak for yourself, or say nothing at all." Silla, abashed to hear these words, began in her mind to accuse the blindness of love, that Julina, neglecting the good will of so noble a duke, would prefer her love unto such a one, as nature itself had denied to recompense her liking.

[16]And now, for a time leaving matters depending as you have heard, it fell out that the right Silvio indeed (whom you have heard spoken of before, the brother of Silla) was come to his father's court into the Isle of Cyprus; where, understanding that his sister was departed in manner as you have heard, conjectured that the very occasion did proceed of some liking had between Pedro her man (that was missing with her) and herself: but Silvio, who loved his sister as dearly as his own life, and the rather for that, as she was his natural sister, both by father and mother, so the one of them was so like the other in countenance and favor that there was no man able to discern the one from the other by their faces, saving by their apparel, the one being a man, the other a woman.

Silvio, therefore, vowed to his father not only to seek out his sister Silla but also to revenge the villainy which he conceived in Pedro for the carrying away of his sister; and thus departing, having traveled through many cities and towns, without hearing any manner of news of those he went to seek for, at the last he arrived at Constantinople, whereas he was walking in an evening for his own recreation, on a pleasant green yard, without the walls of the city, he fortuned to meet with the Lady Julina, who likewise had been abroad to take the air;[17] and as she suddenly cast her eyes upon Silvio, thinking him to be her old acquaintance, by reason they were so like one another, as you have heard before, said unto him, "Sir Silvio, if your haste be not the greater, I pray you, let me have a little talk with you, seeing I have so luckily met you in this place."

---

[14] I.v. 273–317.
[15] III.i. 117–121.
[16] Contrast the motivation here with Shakespeare's Sebastian seeking Viola: II.i. 26–33.
[17] IV.i. 1ff.

Silvio, wondering to hear himself so rightly named, being but a stranger, not of above two days' continuance in the city, very courteously came towards her, desirous to hear what she would say.

Julina, commanding her train something to stand back, said as follows: "Seeing my good will and friendly love has been the only cause to make me so prodigal to offer that I see is so lightly rejected, it makes me to think that men be of this condition, rather to desire those things which they can not come by, than to esteem or value of that which both largely and liberally is offered unto them: but if the liberality of my proffer has made to seem less the value of the thing that I meant to present, it is but in your own conceit,[18] considering how many noble men there have been here before, and be yet at this present, which have both served, sued, and most humbly entreated, to attain to that, which to you of myself I have freely offered, and I perceive is despised, or at the least very lightly regarded."

Silvio, wondering at these words, but more amazed that she could so rightly call him by his name, could not tell what to make of her speeches, assuring himself that she was deceived and did mistake him, did think, notwithstanding, it had been a point of great simplicity, if he should forsake that which Fortune had so favorably proffered unto him, perceiving by her train that she was some lady of great honor, and viewing the perfection of her beauty and the excellency of her grace and countenance, did think it impossible that she should be despised, and therefore answered thus:

"Madame, if before this time I have seemed to forget myself, in neglecting your courtesy which so liberally you have meant unto me, please it you to pardon what is past, and from this day forward Silvio remains ready prest[19] to make such reasonable amends as his ability may any ways permit, or as it shall please you to command."

Julina, the gladdest woman that might be to hear these joyful news, said: "Then, my Silvio, see you fail not tomorrow at night to sup with me at my own house, where I will discourse farther with you what amends you shall make me." To which request Silvio gave his glad consent, and thus they departed, very well pleased. And as Julina did think the time very long till she had reaped the fruit of her desire, so Silvio he wished for harvest before corn could grow, thinking the time as long till he saw how matters would fall out; but, not knowing what lady she might be, he presently (before Julina was out of sight) demanded of one that was walking by, what she was, and how she was called, who satisfied Silvio in every point, and also in what part of the town her house did stand, whereby he might inquire it out.

---

[18] in the Renaissance sense of fanciful idea.
[19] ready, ready prest: quite ready.

Silvio, thus departing to his lodging, passed the night with very unquiet sleep, and the next morning his mind ran so much of his supper, that he never cared neither for his breakfast nor dinner; and the day, to his seeming, passed away so slowly, that he had thought the stately steeds had been tired that draw the chariot of the sun, or else some other Joshua had commanded them again to stand, and wished that Phaethon had been there with a whip.

[20]Julina, on the other side, she had thought the clock setter had played the knave, the day came no faster forward: but six o'clock being once struck, recovered comfort to both parties; and Silvio, hastening himself to the palace of Julina, where by her he was friendly welcomed, and a sumptuous supper being made ready, furnished with sundry sorts of delicate dishes, they sat them down, passing the supper time with amorous looks, loving countenances, and secret glances conveyed from the one to the other, which did better satisfy them than the feeding of their dainty dishes.

Supper time being thus spent, Julina did think it very unfitly[21] if she should turn Silvio to go seek his lodging in an evening, desired him therefore that he would take a bed in her house for that night; and, bringing him up into a fair chamber that was very richly furnished, she found such means, that when all the rest of her household servants were abed and quiet, she came herself to bear Silvio company, where, concluding upon conditions that were in question between them, they passed the night with such joy and contentation[22] as might in that convenient time be wished for. But only[23] that Julina, feeding too much of some one dish above the rest, received a surfeit whereof she could not be cured in forty weeks after — a natural inclination in all women which are subject to longing and want the reason to use a moderation in their diet. But the morning approaching, Julina took her leave, and conveyed herself into her own chamber; and when it was fair daylight, Silvio, making himself ready, departed likewise about his affairs in the town, debating with himself how things had happened, being well assured that Julina had mistaken him; and, therefore, for fear of further evils, determined to come no more there, but took his journey towards other places in the parts of Grecia, to see if he could learn any tidings of his sister Silla.

The Duke Apolonius, having made a long suit and never a whit the nearer of his purpose, came to Julina to crave her direct answer, either

---

[20] The following two paragraphs offer another contrast to the tone and mood of Shakespeare's main plot.

[21] improper.

[22] contentment.

[23] except.

to accept of him and such conditions as he proffered unto her, or else to give him his last farewell.

Julina, as you have heard, had taken an earnest penny[24] of another, whom she had thought had been Silvio, the Duke's man, was at a controversy in herself what she might do: one while she thought, seeing her[25] her occasion served so fit, to crave the duke's good will, for the marrying of his man; then again, she could not tell what displeasure the duke would conceive, in that she should seem to prefer his man before himself, did think it therefore best to conceal the matter, till she might speak with Silvio, to use his opinion how these matters should be handled: and hereupon resolving herself, desiring the duke to pardon her speeches, said as follows.

"Sir Duke, for that from this time forward I am no longer of myself, having given my full power and authority over to another, whose wife I now remain by faithful vow and promise: and albeit I know the world will wonder when they shall understand the fondness[26] of my choice, yet I trust you yourself will nothing dislike with me, since I have meant no other thing than the satisfying of mine own contentation and liking."

The duke, hearing these words, answered: "Madam, I must then content myself, although against my will, having the law in your own hands to like of whom you list, and to make choice where it pleases you."

Julina, giving the duke great thanks, that would content himself with such patience, desired him likewise to give his free consent, and good will to the party whom she had chosen to be her husband.

"Nay, surely, madam," (quoth the duke) "I will never give my consent that any other man shall enjoy you than myself: I have made too great accompt of you, than so lightly to pass you away with my good will. But seeing it lies not in me to let you, having (as you say) made your own choice, so from hence forwards I leave you to your own liking, always willing you well, and thus will take my leave."

The duke departed towards his own house, very sorrowful that Julina had thus served him: but in the mean space that the duke had remained in the house of Julina, some of his servants fell into talk and conference with the servants of Julina; where, debating between them of the likelihood of the marriage between the duke and the lady, one of the servants of Julina said, that he never saw his lady and mistress use so good countenance to the duke himself, as she had done to Silvio his man; and began to report with what familiarity and courtesy

---

[24] in the sense of down payment.
[25] to herself.
[26] foolishness.

she had received him, feasted him and lodged him, and that, in his opinion, Silvio was like to speed before the duke, or any others that were suitors.

This tale was quickly brought to the duke himself, who, making better inquiry in the matter, found it to be true that was reported; and, better considering of the words which Julina had used towards himself, was very well assured that it could be no other than his own man, that had thrust his nose so far out of joint: wherefore, without any further respect, caused him to be thrust into a dungeon, where he was kept prisoner in a very pitiful plight.[27]

Poor Silvio, having got intelligence by some of his fellows what was the cause that the duke his master did bear such displeasure unto him, devised all the means he could, as well by mediation by his fellows, as otherwise by petitions and supplications to the duke, that he would suspend his judgment till perfect proof were had in the matter, and then, if any manner of thing did fall out against him, whereby the duke had cause to take any grief, he would confess himself worthy not only of imprisonment, but also of most vile and shameful death. With these petitions he daily plied the duke, but all in vain; for the duke thought he had made so good proof, that he was thoroughly confirmed in his opinion against his man.

But the Lady Julina, wondering what made Silvio that he was so slack in his visitation, and why he absented himself so long from her presence, began to think that all was not well; but in the end, perceiving no decoction[28] of her former surfeit, received as you have heard, and finding herself an unwonted swelling in her belly, assuring herself to be with child, fearing to become quite bankrupt of her honor, did think it more than time to seek out a father, and made such secret search and diligent inquiry, that she learned the truth how Silvio was kept in prison by the duke his master; and minding to find a present remedy, as well for the love she bore to Silvio, as for the maintenance of her credit and estimation, she speedily hasted to the palace of the duke, to whom she said as follows.

"Sir Duke, it may be that you will think my coming to your house in this sort does something pass the limits of modesty, the which I protest before God, proceeds of this desire, that the world should know how justly I seek means to maintain my honor. But to the end I seem not tedious with prolixity of words, nor to use other than direct circumstances, know, sir, that the love I bear to my only beloved

---

[27] This situation and Silvio's petitions in the following paragraph suggest a source for Malvolio's imprisonment: IV.ii. 1ff. V.i. 285–319.
[28] relief.

Silvio, whom I do esteem more than all the jewels in the world, whose personage I regard more than my own life, is the only cause of my attempted journey, beseeching you, that all the whole displeasure, which I understand you have conceived against him, may be imputed unto my charge, and that it would please you lovingly to deal with him, whom of myself I have chosen, rather for the satisfaction of mine honest liking, than for the vain pre-eminences or honorable dignities looked after by ambitious minds."

[29]The duke, having heard this discourse, caused Silvio presently to be sent for, and to be brought before him, to whom he said: "Had it not been sufficient for thee, when I had reposed myself in thy fidelity and the trustiness of thy service that thou shouldst so traitorously deal with me, but since that time hast not spared still to abuse me with so many forgeries and perjured protestations, not only hateful unto me, whose simplicity thou thinkest to be such, that by the plot of thy pleasant tongue thou wouldst make me believe a manifest untruth: but most abominable be thy doings in the presence and sight of God, that hast not spared to blaspheme His holy name by calling Him to be a witness to maintain thy leasings,[30] and so detestably wouldst forswear thyself in a matter that is so openly known."

Poor Silvio, whose innocence was such that he might lawfully swear, seeing Julina to be there in place, answered thus.

"Most noble duke, well understanding your conceived grief, most humbly I beseech you patiently to hear my excuse, not minding thereby to aggravate or heap up your wrath and displeasure, protesting, before God, that there is nothing in the world which I regard so much, or do esteem so dear, as your good grace and favor; but desirous that your grace should know my innocence, and to clear myself of such impositions,[31] wherewith I know I am wrongfully accused, which, as I understand, should be in the practising of the Lady Julina, who stands here in place, whose acquittance for my better discharge now I most humbly crave, protesting, before the Almighty God, that neither in thought, word, or deed, I have not otherwise used myself than according to the bond and duty of a servant, that is both willing and desirous to further his master's suits; which if I have otherwise said than that is true, you, Madame Julina, who can very well decide the depths of all this doubt, I most humbly beseech you to certify a truth, if I have in any thing missaid, or have otherwise spoken than is right and just."

Julina, having heard this discourse which Silvio had made, perceiv-

---

[29] V.i. 104–148.
[30] lies.
[31] charges.

ing that he stood in great awe of the duke's displeasure, answered thus: "Think not, my Silvio, that my coming hither is to accuse you of any misdemeanor towards your master, so I do not deny but in all such embassages wherein towards me you have been employed, you have used the office of a faithful and trusty messenger; neither am I ashamed to confess that the first day that mine eyes did behold the singular behavior, the notable courtesy, and other innummerable gifts wherewith my Silvio is endowed, but that beyond all measure my heart was so inflamed, that impossible it was for me to quench the fervent love, or extinguish the least part of my conceived torment, before I had betrayed the same unto him, and of my own motion craved his promised faith and loyalty of marriage; and now is the time to manifest the same unto the world which has been done before God and between ourselves, knowing that it is not needful to keep secret that which is neither evil done nor hurtful to any person. Therefore (as I said before) Silvio is my husband by plighted faith, whom I hope to obtain without offence or displeasure of anyone, trusting that there is no man that will so far forget himself as to restrain that which God hath left at liberty for every wight, or that will seek by cruelty to force ladies to marry otherwise than according to their own liking. Fear not then, my Silvio, to keep your faith and promise which you have made unto me; and as for the rest, I doubt not things will so fall out as you shall have no manner of cause to complain."

Silvio, amazed to hear these words, for that Julina by her speech seemed to confirm that which he most of all desired to be quit of, said: "Who would have thought that a lady of so great honor and reputation would herself be the ambassador of a thing so prejudicial and uncomely for her state! What plighted promises be these which be spoken of? Altogether ignorant unto me, which if it be otherwise than I have said, you sacred goddess consume me straight with flashing flames of fire. But what words might I use to give credit to the truth and innocence of my cause? Ah, Madame Julina! I desire no other testimony than your own, I desire no other testimony than your own honesty and virtue, thinking that you will not so much blemish the brightness of your honor, knowing that a woman is, or should be, the image of courtesy, continence, and shamefastness, from the which so soon as she stoops, and leaves the office of her duty and modesty, besides the degradation of her honor, she thrusts herself into the pit of perpetual infamy. And as I cannot think you would so far forget yourself by the refusal of a noble duke, to dim the light of your renown and glory, which hitherto you have maintained amongst the best and noblest ladies, by such a one as I know myself to be, too far unworthy your degree and calling, so most humbly I beseech you to confess a truth, whereto tend those vows and promises you speak of, which speeches be so obscure unto me, as I know not for my life how I might understand them."

Julina, something nipped with these speeches, said: "And what is the matter, that now you make so little accompt of your Julina? That, being my husband in deed, have the face to deny me, to whom thou art contracted by so many solemn oaths? What! Art thou ashamed to have me to thy wife? How much ought'st thou rather to be ashamed to break thy promised faith, and to have despised the holy and dreadful name of God? but that time constrains me to lay open that which shame rather wills I should dissemble and keep secret; behold me then here, Silvio, whom thou has gotten with child; who, if thou be of such honesty, as I trust for all this I shall find, then the thing is done without prejudice, or any hurt to my conscience, considering that by the professed faith thou didst accompt me for thy wife, and I received thee for my spouse and loyal husband, swearing by the Almighty God that no other than you have made the conquest and triumph of my chastity, whereof I crave no other witness than yourself and mine own conscience."

I pray you, gentlewomen, was not this a foul oversight of Julina, that would so precisely swear so great an oath that she was gotten with child by one that was altogether unfurnished with implements for such a tourney? For God's love take heed, and let this be an example to you when you be with child how you swear who is the father before you have had good proof and knowledge of the party; for men be so subtle and full of sleight that, God knows, a woman may quickly be deceived.

But now to return to our Silvio who, hearing an oath sworn so divinely that he had gotten a woman with child, was like to believe that it had been true in very deed; but remembering his own impediment, thought it impossible that he should commit such an act, and therefore, half in a chafe he said:

"What law is able to restrain the foolish indiscretion of a woman that yields herself to her own desires? What shame is able to bridle or withdraw her from her mind and madness, or with what snaffle is it possible to hold her back from the execution of her filthiness? But what abomination is this, that a lady of such a house should so forget the greatness of her state, the alliance whereof she is descended, the nobility of her deceased husband, and makes no conscience to shame and slander herself with such a one as I am, being so far unfit and unseemly for her degree! But how horrible is it to hear the name of God so defaced, that we make no more accompt but for the maintenance of our mischiefs, we fear no whit at all to forswear His holy name, as though He were not in all His dealings most righteous, true, and just, and will not only lay open our leasings[32] to the world, but will likewise punish the same with most sharp and bitter scourges."

Julina, not able to endure him to proceed any farther in his sermon, was already surprised with a vehement grief, began bitterly to cry out, uttering these speeches following.

"Alas! is it possible that the sovereign justice of God can abide a mischief so great and cursed? Why may I not now suffer death, rather than the infamy which I see to wander before mine eyes? Oh, happy, and more than right happy, had I been, if inconstant fortune had not devised this treason, wherein I am surprised and caught! Am I thus become to be entangled with snares, and in the hands of him who enjoying the spoils of my honor will openly deprive me of my fame, by making me a common fable to all posterity in time to come? Ah, traitor, and discourteous wretch! Is this the recompense of the honest and firm amity which I have borne thee? Wherein have I deserved this discourtesy? By loving thee more than thou art able to deserve? Is it I, arrant thief! is it I, upon whom thou thinkest to work thy mischiefs? Dost thou think me no better worth, but that thou may'st prodigally waste my honor at thy pleasure? Didst thou dare to adventure upon me, having my conscience wounded with so deadly a treason? Ah, unhappy, and, above all others, most unhappy! that have so charely[33] preserved mine honor and now am made a prey to satisfy a young man's lust that has coveted nothing but the spoil of my chastity and good name!"

Herewithal her tears so gushed down her cheeks, that she was not able to open her mouth to use any farther speech.

The duke, who stood by all this while and heard this whole discourse, was wonderfully moved with compassion towards Julina, knowing that from her infancy she had ever so honorably used herself, that there was no man able to detect her of any misdemeanor, otherwise than beseemed a lady of her state: whereof, being fully resolved that Silvio, his man, had committed this villainy against her, in a great fury, drawing his rapier, he said unto Silvio:

"How canst thou, arrant thief! show thyself so cruel and careless to such as do thee honor? Hast thou so little regard of such a noble lady, as humbles herself to such a villain as thou art, who, without any respect either of her renown or noble state, canst be content to seek the wreck and utter ruin of her honor? But frame thyself to make such satisfaction as she requires, although I know, unworthy wretch, that thou art not able to make her the least part of amends, or I

---

[32] lies.
[33] carefully.

swear by God that thou shalt not escape the death which I will minister to thee with my own hands, and therefore advise thee well what thou dost."

Silvio, having heard this sharp sentence, fell down on his knees before the duke, craving for mercy, desiring that he might be suffered to speak with the Lady Julina apart, promising to satisfy her according to her own contentation.[34]

"Well," (quoth the duke) "I take thy word; and therewithal I advise thee that thou perform thy promise, or otherwise I protest, before God, I will make thee such an example to the world, that all traitors shall tremble for fear how they do seek the dishonoring of ladies."

But now Julina had conceived so great grief against Silvio, that there was much ado to persuade her to talk with him; but remembering her own case, desirous to hear what excuse he could make, in the end she agreed, and being brought into a place severally by themselves, Silvio began with a piteous voice to say as follows.

"I know not, madam, of whom I might make complaint, whether of you or of myself, or rather of Fortune, which has conducted and brought us both into so great adversity. I see that you receive great wrong, and I am condemned against all right; you in peril to abide the bruit of spiteful tongues, and I in danger to lose the thing that I most desire; and although I could allege many reasons to prove my sayings true, yet I refer myself to the experience and bounty of your mind." And herewithal loosing his garments down to his stomach, showed Julina his breasts and pretty teats surmounting far the whiteness of snow itself, saying: "Lo, madame! behold here the party whom you have challenged to be the father of your child. See, I am a woman, the daughter of a noble duke, who, only for the love of him whom you so lightly have shaken off have forsaken my father, abandoned my country, and, in manner as you see, am become a serving man, satisfying myself but with the only sight of my Apolonius. And now, madame, if my passion were not vehement, and my torments without comparison, I would wish that my feigned griefs might be laughed to scorn, and my dissembled pains to be rewarded with flouts: but my love being pure, my travail continual, and my griefs endless, I trust, madame, you will not only excuse me of crime, but also pity my distress, the which, I protest, I would still have kept secret, if my fortune would so have permitted."

Julina did now think herself to be in a worse case than ever she was before, for now she knew not whom to challenge to be the father of her child; wherefore, when she had told the duke the very certainty

---

[34] to her heart's content.

of the discourse which Silvio had made unto her, she departed to her own house, with such grief and sorrow, that she purposed never to come out of her own doors again alive, to be a wonder and mocking stock to the world.

[35]But the duke, more amazed to hear this strange discourse of Silvio, came unto him, whom when he had viewed with better consideration, perceived indeed that it was Silla, the daughter of Duke Pontus, and embracing her in his arms, he said.

"Oh, the branch of all virtue, and the flower of courtesy itself! Pardon me, I beseech you, of all such discourtesies as I have ignorantly committed towards you, desiring you that without further memory of ancient griefs you will accept of me, who is more joyful and better contented with your presence than if the whole world were at my commandment. Where has there ever been found such liberality in a lover, which having been trained up and nourished amongst the delicacies and banquets of the court, accompanied with trains of many fair and noble ladies, living in pleasure and in the midst of delights, would so prodigally adventure yourself, neither fearing mishaps, nor misliking to take such pains as I know you have not been accustomed unto? O, liberality never heard of before! O, fact that can never be sufficiently rewarded! O, true love most pure and unfeigned!" Herewithal sending for the most artificial[36] workmen, he provided for her sundry suits of sumptuous apparel, and the marriage day appointed, which was celebrated with great triumph through the whole city of Constantinople, everyone praising the nobleness of the duke; but so many as did behold the excellent beauty of Silla gave her the praise above all the rest of the ladies in the troop.

[37]The matter seemed so wonderful and strange that the bruit was spread throughout all the parts of Grecia, insomuch that it came to the hearing of Silvio; who, as you have heard, remained in those parts to inquire of his sister. He being the gladdest man in the world, hasted to Constantinople, where coming to his sister, he was joyfully received, and most lovingly welcomed, and entertained of the duke his brother-in-law. After he had remained there two or three days, the duke revealed unto Silvio the whole discourse how it happened between his sister and the Lady Julina, and how his sister was challenged for getting a woman with child. Silvio, blushing with these words, was stricken with great remorse to make Julina amends, understanding her to be a noble lady, and was left defamed to the world through his default. He therefore betrayed the whole circumstance to the duke,

---

[35] V.i. 223–284. Shakespeare manages the denouement much more skillfully.
[36] artful.
[37] V.i. 215–270.

whereof the duke being very joyful, immediately repaired with Silvio to the house of Julina, whom they found in her chamber in great lamentation and mourning. To whom the duke said: "Take courage, madame, for behold here a gentleman that will not stick both to father your child and to take you for his wife; no inferior person, but the son and heir of a noble duke, worthy of your estate and dignity."

Julina, seeing Silvio in place, did know very well that he was the father of her child, and was so ravished with joy that she knew not whether she were awake, or in some dream. Silvio, embracing her in his arms, craving forgiveness of all that was past, concluded with her the marriage day, which was presently accomplished with great joy and contentation to all parties. And thus, Silvio having attained a noble wife, and Silla, his sister, her desired husband, they passed the residue of their days with such delight as those that have accomplished the perfection of their felicities.

☿ ANONYMOUS, *1531*

(*Gl'Ingannati*) *The Deceived Ones**

CHARACTERS

GHERARDO FOIANI, father of Isabella
VIRGINIO BELLENZINI, father of Lelia and Fabrizio
FLAMMINIO DE' CARANDINI, in love with Isabella
FABRIZIO, son of Virginio
PIERO, a pedant
L'AGIATO ⎱ rival inn-keepers
FRULLA ⎰
GIGLIO, a Spaniard
SPELA, servant of Gherardo
SCATIZZA, servant of Virginio
CRIVELLO, servant of Flamminio
STRAGUALCIA, servant of Fabrizio
LELIA, daughter of Virginio (disguised as Fabio, a page)
ISABELLA, daughter of Gherardo
CLEMENZIA, nurse of Lelia
PASQUELLA, housekeeper of Gherardo
CITTINA, daughter of Clemenzia

The scene is Modena.

PROLOGUE

[*Addressed to* nobilissime donne (*most noble ladies*) *the Prologue first describes the love the Intronati has felt for them but urges the ladies to ignore the Intronati henceforth. As a peace offering to atone for past conduct*]

---

* translated by Joseph Satin. This play was written and presented by the *Intronati da Siena*, a social club that called itself "The Thunderstruck." Although acted in 1531, it was not published until 1537.

they [*Intronati*] have made a comedy in about three days. And today they want to present it to you, if you're willing. So you now know what these preparations mean, who I am and what I'm doing around here. As I understand it this comedy is called *The Deceived*, not because they were ever deceived by you; no, you never deceived them; they know you too well. (Still, you've always overwhelmed them and they couldn't protect themselves adequately.) It's called that because few characters appear in the plot who aren't deceived in the end. There are some deceits which I wish — God willing and for the feeling I have toward you — entrapped you often and that I were the deceiver. I wouldn't be cured of that deceit!

The plot is new and has no source other than their busy brains, which also control your fates on Twelfth Night.[1]

[*Then follow puns, praise of ladies' beauty, a statement that this play is laid in Modena, and the play begins.*]

ACT I

SCENE I.[2] A STREET IN FRONT OF VIRGINIO'S HOUSE.
GHERARDO and VIRGINIO, Old Men.

GHERARDO. Do this, Virginio. If as you've said you want to please me in this affair, let this blessed wedding take place as soon as possible. Once and for all, get me out of this tricky labyrinth I've run into stupidly without knowing why. If something holds you back, like not having money for gowns — I know you lost everything in that miserable Sack of Rome — and house furnishings — perhaps you're having trouble paying for the ceremony — tell me so straight out. I'll take care of everything. It's no effort. To get this thing over with a month earlier I'd spend ten *scudi* more to satisfy my desire and to know by the grace of God where I stand. You know, neither of us is green as grass any more; we're about like summer grass. The more delay, the more time is lost. So don't look puzzled, Virginio, that I push you so hard for this. Believe me, once I got this notion in my head I haven't slept half a night. Honestly, look what time I got up this morning. Before I came here I went to hear early mass at the Duomo so as not to wake you.

Now, if you've changed your mind perhaps and think your daughter too young for me — a man in middle age, maybe past —

---

[1] *la notte di beffana*: Epiphany; Twelfth Night.
[2] Contrast the earthiness and materialism of these first three scenes with ACT I, Scenes i, ii of Shakespeare's play.

tell me so frankly so that I can provide for myself elsewhere. 20
You'll be saving me a lot of trouble right away. For as you well
know, others think me quite a catch.

VIRGINIO. Gherardo, if I had the power, nothing could keep me
from marrying my daughter to you today. It happens that I lost
almost all my wealth in the Sack (together with Fabrizio, my beloved son) but by the grace of God I still have enough left to
count on a trousseau and wedding for my daughter without needing anyone's help. Don't think I'll back out on my promise to you,
as long as my daughter agrees to it. It's not fitting, as you know,
for merchants to renege on promises. 30

GHERARDO. That's something, Virginio, found more in words
than in deeds among merchants nowadays. But I believe you're
not one of those. Still, seeing myself led on day by day by day
makes me suspicious. And I'm not sure whether you couldn't, if
you wanted, make your daughter do what you told her to.

VIRGINIO. Listen to this. I had to go to Bologna, as you know
on some business with Buonaparte Ghisilieri, Cavalier of Casio.
Since I live in a villa alone, I didn't want to leave my daughter
with just the servants, so I sent her to the convent of San Crescenzio to her aunt, Sister Camilla, where she now is. I just got 40
back last night. You know that. And I've sent my servant to tell
her to return.

GHERARDO. Are you sure she's in the convent and nowhere else?

VIRGINIO. Sure? Where do you think she'd be? What kind of
a question is that?

GHERARDO. I'll tell you. I've been over that way on business
several times and asked for her. But I never got to see her. They
told me she wasn't there.

VIRGINIO. That's because those good sisters would like to make a
nun of her so as to inherit what little is left after my death. But 50
they won't succeed. I'm not so old that I can't have a few more
children, if I take another wife.

GHERARDO.[3] Old? I tell you my legs are as lusty now as when
I was twenty-five, especially mornings, before I piss. And if my
beard is white my tail is as green as the Tuscan poet's. I wouldn't
let any of these beardless boys who go around Modena nowadays
playing the dandy with their plumes straight up *alla Guelfa*,[4]
swords at their thighs, daggers at their hips, and their silk hats
beat me at anything except running away.

---

[3] There is more than slight resemblance between this scene and the first
scene between Sir Andrew and Sir Toby (I.iii. 47ff.).

[4] After the fashion of the Guelfs, a medieval political sect.

VIRGINIO. Your spirit is willing, but I don't know how your 60
flesh will make out.

GHERARDO. I'll want you to ask Lelia that after she's slept with
me the first night.

VIRGINIO. Now in the name of God, you'll have to be careful!
She's still just a girl. It isn't good to be a wild man right at the start.

GHERARDO. How old is she?

VIRGINIO. During the Sack of Rome, when she and I were put in
prison by those dogs, she was just finishing thirteen.

GHERARDO. She's just what I need. I wouldn't want her older
or younger. I have the most beautiful clothes, jewels, necklaces 70
and other adornments in Modena.

VIRGINIO. God willing, I delight in her good fortune and yours.

GHERARDO. Speed the day.

VIRGINIO. About the dowry, what is said is said.

GHERARDO. Do you think I'd change my mind? Goodbye for
now.

VIRGINIO. The best to you. (*Gherardo leaves.*) Here comes her
nurse. Now I won't have to send after her to bring Lelia here.

SCENE II. — CLEMENZIA, a Nurse, and VIRGINIO.

CLEMENZIA. I don't know what it means, but this morning all
my hens were cackling as though they wanted to start an earth- 80
quake, or make me rich from eggs. Something's going to happen
to me today. They never make this racket without something
special happening.

VIRGINIO. Look at her. She must have been talking with the
angels, or with the holy father at St. Francis.

CLEMENZIA. And something else happened to me that I don't
understand, although my confessor tells me that I do wrong to
think about things like these and to trust in prophecies.

VIRGINIO. What are you doing, talking that way to yourself?
Twelfth Night has already passed.[5] 90

CLEMENZIA. Oh! Good day, Virginio. God protect me, I was
coming to find you. You're up early. Welcome home.

VIRGINIO. What were you saying to yourself? Were you thinking maybe of snitching some bushels of grain or jars of oil or a
piece of lard the way you usually do?

---

[5] Perhaps Virginio is implying that Clemenzia's mutterings are only idle
words, not revelations; or perhaps, since the Twelfth Night sports and revelry
added up to festive and romantic occasions, that those days were over for
Clemenzia. The dialogue later in this scene strongly suggests the latter interpretation.

CLEMENZIA. Of course. Oh, how open handed he is! Perhaps he's making a dowry for his children.

VIRGINIO. What are you saying there?

CLEMENZIA. I was saying I didn't know what it means that my lovely kitten, which I lost fifteen days ago, came back this morning and caught a mouse in my closet and, playing with it, turned over a bottle of sweet wine which the priest at St. Francis gave me because I give him tidbits.

VIRGINIO. That's a marriage omen. Now, do you want me to give you another one, the true one?

CLEMENZIA. That is the true one.

VIRGINIO. Now, let's see what I can prophecy! But first what of your Lelia?

CLEMENZIA. Poor girl! Better she were never born.

VIRGINIO. Why?

CLEMENZIA. Why! Doesn't Gherardo Foiani go around everywhere saying she is his wife, that everything's arranged?

VIRGINIO. He's telling the truth. Doesn't it occur to you that she'll be well housed, honorably, with a rich man, supplied with the best of everything, mistress in her own home without having to fight like cats and dogs with any mother-in-law or sisters-in-law? He'll treat her like a daughter.

CLEMENZIA. That's the bad part. Young girls want to be treated like wives, not daughters. They want someone to push them around, to bite them, to warm them up on one side and then the other, not someone to treat them like daughters.

VIRGINIO. You think all women are like you? We two understand one another, but this isn't the same thing. Gherardo has a kind heart. He will treat her like a wife.

CLEMENZIA. How, being over fifty?

VIRGINIO. What does that matter? I'm almost the same age, and you know how I can wrestle.

CLEMENZIA. Oh, but very few can equal you. But if I thought you might give her to him, I'd choke her first.

VIRGINIO. Clemenzia, I have lost most of my fortune. Now I have to do the best I can. If Fabrizio is found one day and I've given her a dowry he would starve to death. I don't want that. I'm marrying her to Gherardo on the condition that if Fabrizio isn't found in four years she will have a thousand florins as dowry. If he returns she will have only two hundred.

CLEMENZIA. Poor girl! If it were up to me. . . .

VIRGINIO. What's to do? How long since you've seen her last?

CLEMENZIA. Fifteen days and more. I intended to go see her today.

VIRGINIO. I understand those nuns want to make a nun of her. 140
I guess they've put some bee in her bonnet the way they always do.
You go there and tell them from me that she's to come home.

CLEMENZIA. I wish you'd lend me two *carlini*[6] to buy some
wood. I haven't a scrap.

VIRGINIO. The devil take you! Get moving! Go, and I'll buy
it for you.

CLEMENZIA. First I want to go to Mass.

SCENE III. — STREET IN FRONT OF FLAMMINIO'S HOUSE.
LELIA, disguised as a boy and using the name of FABIO.

LELIA. This is awfully daring of me, when I think of it, leaving
the house at this hour alone, knowing as I do the crude customs
of these wild youths of Modena! Oh, what a fix I'd be in if one 150
of these scamps dragged me bodily into some house and tried to
find out whether I'm male or female! That would teach me not
to leave the house so early! But my reason is love, which I feel
for the cruel ingrate Flamminio. What a fate is mine! I love
someone who hates me, who scorns me. I serve someone who
doesn't know who I am. And to make things worse, I help him to
make love to someone else — if I told this to anybody he wouldn't
believe it — with no other hope than to satisfy my eyes with seeing
him all day long as I please. Up to now everything has gone well.
But what shall I do from here on? What course can I take? My 160
father has returned; Flamminio has moved to this city. I can't
stay here without being recognized, and if that happens, I'll be
slandered for life and made the butt of gossip for the whole city.
Therefore I've come out at this hour to consult with my nurse
whom I saw through my window coming this way. Together we'll
decide on the best course. But first I want to see if she recognizes
me in this costume. (*Clemenzia enters.*)

CLEMENZIA. In faith, Flamminio must have returned to Modena, for I see his door open. Oh! If Lelia knew this, the trip
home to her father would seem a thousand years long. But who's 170
this snip who keeps crossing my path this morning? Why are you
getting underfoot? Why don't you get out of my way? Why do
you keep circling me? What do you want of me? If you knew
how I felt about such types. . . .

LELIA. God grant you good day, Mother Chiseler.

CLEMENZIA. Go on. Give that stuff to people you say good
night to.

---

[6] about ten cents.

LELIA. If you've given others a good night, I'll give you a good day, if it please you.

CLEMENZIA. Don't give me a hard time, which you'd do this 180 morning . . . I know how to talk to you.

LELIA. Are you expected by the priest of St. Francis? Or are you going to find Brother Onion?

CLEMENZIA. A fever strike you! What business is it of yours where I go or where I am? What priest? What Brother Onion?

LELIA. Oh, don't get angry, Mother Live-it-up.

CLEMENZIA. Surely I know this one. I don't know where, but it seems to me I've seen him a thousand times. Tell me, lad, where do you know me from that you want to know all my business? Lift that cap off your face a little. 190

LELIA. Well! You pretend not to know me, eh?

CLEMENZIA. If you stay hidden neither I nor anyone else will recognize you.

LELIA. Come a little closer.

CLEMENZIA. Where?

LELIA. Over here a little. Now do you recognize me?

CLEMENZIA. Lelia, can it be you? Sorrow of my life! Bad luck to me! Yes, you are she! Oh! What does this mean, my child?

LELIA. Speak softly. You look as if you're losing your mind. I'll go away if you shout. 200

CLEMENZIA. Will you leave because of shame? Have you become a woman of the world?

LELIA. Yes, I am of the world. How many women have you seen out of the world? For my part, I was never there that I know about.

CLEMENZIA. Have you lost the name of virgin?

LELIA. The name, no, as far as I know, especially in this world. For the rest you'd better ask the Spaniards who kept me prisoner in Rome.

CLEMENZIA. Is this the honor you pay your father, your house, 210 yourself, and me who raised you? I'd like to choke you with these hands. Come indoors with me, go! I don't want you to be seen in this costume any more.

LELIA. Oh! Have a little patience, if you please.

CLEMENZIA. Aren't you ashamed to be seen this way?

LELIA. Am I the first? I've seen hundreds like this in Rome. And how many are there in this city who go about their affairs every night dressed this way?

CLEMENZIA. They are bawds!

LELIA. Mightn't there be one good girl among so many bawds? 220

CLEMENZIA. I want to know why you're going around that way and why you left the convent. Oh! If your father knew about this, wouldn't he kill you, you scalawag?

LELIA. Which would end my torment. Do you think I hold my life dear?

CLEMENZIA. Why are you doing this? Tell me.

LELIA. I'll tell you if you'll listen. That way you'll know how unhappy I am and why I go about in this costume outside the convent and what I want you to do. But come over here a bit so that passersby won't recognize me because I'm talking to you. 230

CLEMENZIA. I am burning with curiosity. Tell me quickly or I'll die!

LELIA. You know that after the terrible Sack of Rome my father lost everything, his property and my brother Fabrizio along with it. And so as not to be alone in his house he took me away from the service of the marchioness with whom he had placed me. We had to come back to our home in Modena to escape our evil fortune and to subsist on the little we had left. You also know that because my father was a friend of Count Guido Rangone, he was not well regarded by many people. 240

CLEMENZIA. Why tell me what I know better than you? I also know that was why you went out to your farm at Fontanile and that I went with you.

LELIA. True. And you also know how hard and bitter my life was at that time, not only far removed from any thoughts of love but from almost every human feeling, thinking that because I had been in the hands of soldiers everybody pointed a finger at me. I didn't believe I could live honorably enough to keep people from talking. You know how many times you scolded and cajoled me to live a happier life. 250

CLEMENZIA. Why tell me what I already know?

LELIA. So that you can understand what follows.[7] During those days it happened that Flamminio Carandini, being a member of our party, formed a close friendship with my father. He came to the house every day and sometimes watched me in secret, then sighing, would lower his gaze. And you were the cause of my encouraging him. I began to like his ways, his conversation and his manners more and more — but I still didn't think of love. But in the course of his visits to the house, an action here, a sign of love there, sighing, beseeching, watching me, it came to me 260 that he was deeply taken. So that I, who had never felt love, be-

---

[7] I.ii. 24–29.

lieved him worthy of thoughts of love, wanted nothing so passionately as the sight of him.

CLEMENZIA. I already knew all this.

LELIA. You know too that when the Spanish soldiers left Rome my father returned there to see whether anything of ours could be salvaged, and more important, whether there was any news of my brother. He sent me to my Aunt Giovanna at Mirandola to keep me from being alone until he returned. You well know how reluctantly I tore myself away from Flamminio. How many times you dried my tears! I stayed at Mirandola one year, and when my father returned you know that I went back to Modena more than ever in love with him who was my first love, whom I love so much, thinking that he would love me still as he first seemed to. 270

CLEMENZIA. Foolish girl! How many Modenese have you found who love one single girl for a year and who don't chase this one one month and another one the next month.

LELIA. I met him and found that he remembered me no better than if he had never seen me. Worse, his whole soul and desire were fixed on the love of Isabella, daughter of Gherardo Foiani, who besides being very beautiful is her father's only child — if that old lunatic doesn't take a wife and make others. 280

CLEMENZIA. He thinks he will surely get you, says that your father has promised you to him. But what you've told me still doesn't explain your going around dressed as a boy and why you left the convent.

LELIA. Let me talk and you will see this is to the point. (But to explain that previous point, I tell you the old man will never have me.) After my father returned from Rome he went to Bologna on some money matter and, not wanting me to return to Mirandola, put me in the Convent of San Crescenzio in the company of Sister Amabile, a relative, to await his speedy return, he thought. 290

CLEMENZIA. I know all that.

LELIA. There I stayed, and hearing nothing but love talked about by those reverend nuns, I gained confidence enough to reveal my love to Sister Amabile. She took pity on me, even to the point of having Flamminio come there several times to talk with her and with other nuns. That way I, hidden behind the drapes, could feast my eyes and ears upon him, which was my deepest desire. One day I heard among other things that he was deeply grieved by the death of his page and spoke in praise of his good service, adding that could he find an equal he would be the happiest man in the world and would keep the boy as close to him as possible. 300

CLEMENZIA.[8] Woe is me! I'm afraid this kid will make my life miserable.

LELIA. All at once I got the idea of seeing whether I could be this fortunate boy — when he left I talked it over with Sister Amabile — seeing whether Flamminio would take me along as a 310 servant, since he was not then living in Modena.

CLEMENZIA. Didn't I say this kid . . . I'm undone!

LELIA. She encouraged me, taught me what I would have to do and supplied me with clothes recently made for her to leave the house sometimes on her affairs, like the others did. Thus, early one morning I left the convent lively and in good spirits to meet him in the city in this costume. I went to Flamminio's palace which is not far from the convent and waited there until he came out. Here I can only praise my good fortune, for as soon as Flamminio saw me he asked me with great courtesy what I wanted 320 and where I was from.

CLEMENZIA. How is it possible you didn't die of shame?

LELIA. And so, prompted by love, I told him frankly that I was a Roman who, being poor, had gone to seek my fortune. He looked me up and down several times, making me afraid he might recognize me. Then he told me that if I wished to stay on with him he would gladly take me and would treat me like a gentleman. I consented, a little ashamed, though.

CLEMENZIA. Hearing you makes me sorry I was ever born. What value do you see in this madness? 330

LELIA. Value? Don't you imagine that a girl in love finds some small happiness in seeing her lord constantly, talking to him, touching him, hearing his secrets, observing his habits, chatting with him and being sure that if she doesn't enjoy him, at least no one else does.

CLEMENZIA. These are lunacies. It only adds wood to the fire if you do things like that without being sure that you're pleasing your sweetheart. What way do you serve him?

LELIA. At table, in his room. And I know that during these fifteen days I have come to him with so much pleasure that if 340 I could do the same in my proper clothing, what a blessing!

CLEMENZIA. Tell me, where do you sleep?

LELIA. In an ante-chamber, alone.

CLEMENZIA. If he were tempted by an evil desire one night and called you to sleep with him, what would you do?

LELIA. I don't want to think of evil until it comes. Should that happen I'll think about it and decide.

---

[8] I.ii. 53–59.

CLEMENZIA. What will people say when this is known, minx that you are?

LELIA. Who would talk about it if you say nothing? Now, 350 what I want you to do is this — for I saw my father return last night and suspect that he might send for me: arrange that he doesn't send for me for four or five days. Or make him believe I went to Roverino with Sister Amabile and will return soon.

CLEMENZIA. Why this?

LELIA.[9] I'll tell you. As I said a while ago Flamminio is in love with Isabella Foiani and sends me to her very often with letters and errands. She is so madly in love with me, thinking me a man, that she makes the most passionate advances. I pretend I am reluctant to love her until she makes Flamminio renounce his love. 360 I've already brought the affair to a head. I hope it will be concluded and he will leave her in three or four days.

CLEMENZIA. Your father told me to come for you. I want you to come into my house so that I can send for your clothes. I don't want you seen this way. Otherwise I'll tell your father everything.

LELIA. You'll drive me to where neither you nor he will ever see me again. Do it my way, please. I can't say any more — I hear Flamminio calling me. My lord! Wait for me at your home in an hour. I'll come to you. And be careful to call me Fabio degli Alberini, the name I use, if you ask about me — don't make a 370 mistake. I come, my lord! Goodbye.

CLEMENZIA. In faith, she's seen Gherardo coming. That's why she ran away. Now what will I do? This isn't a thing to tell her father, nor can I leave her there. I'll keep still till I talk to her again.

[SCENE IV. *Clemenzia flatters Gherardo by telling him Lelia is fond of him. His servant, Spela, comments bitterly on the way she is deceiving him.* SCENE V. *Scatizza returns from the convent unable to learn where Lelia is.*]

ACT II

SCENE I. STREET IN FRONT OF FLAMMINIO'S HOUSE.
LELIA, dressed as the boy FABIO, and FLAMMINIO.

FLAMMINIO. [10]It is a strange thing, Fabio, that up to now I haven't been able to extract one kind reply from that cruel, un-

---

[9] I.iv,v.

[10] This scene has several elements in common with II.iv.

grateful Isabella. Yet seeing you always granted a willing audience and received so gladly makes me believe she doesn't hate me. Indeed, I never did anything I know of to displease her. You can judge from her conversation what might annoy her about me. Tell me again, please, Fabio, what she told you last night when I sent you with that letter.

LELIA. I have already repeated it twenty times.

FLAMMINIO. Oh, tell me once again. Why should you mind?

LELIA. I do mind. I mind seeing you unhappy, which grieves me as much as you. Being your servant as I am I must seek only to please you. Perhaps her answers may make you angry at me.

FLAMMINIO. Don't believe it, my Fabio. I love you like a brother. I know you wish me well and therefore be sure that I will never part with you, as time will tell, God willing. But what did she say?

LELIA. Haven't I told you? The greatest pleasure you can give her in the world is to leave her alone and to not think of her any more, for she has turned her heart elsewhere. In sum, that she has no eyes for you and that you are wasting your time by pursuing her, since you'll find yourself empty handed in the end.

FLAMMINIO. Does it seem to you, Fabio, that she says these things from the heart or only because she has some complaint about me? She often used to show me favor a while back. I can't believe she hates me, accepting my letters and messages as she does. I'll pursue her to the end. I want to see what there is to see. What say you, Fabio, don't you agree?

LELIA. No, sir.

FLAMMINIO. Why?

LELIA. Because if I were you I should expect her to feel honored by my attentions. Aren't there enough women around for someone as noble, virtuous, gentle, and handsome as you? Do it my way, master. Leave her and attach yourself to someone else who loves you. Surely you will find her. Yes, perhaps as beautiful as the other. Tell me, have you no one who loves you in this country?

FLAMMINIO. Yes, there is one, among others, named Lelia who has features just like yours. I have thought so a thousand times. She is called the most beautiful, accomplished, and courtly young lady in this country — I'd like to show her to you one day. She would think herself blessed if I once showed her a little interest. She is rich and was at court and has been in love with me for nearly a year. She showed me a thousand favors, then went away to Mirandola and fate made me fall in love with this one who has been as rude to me as the other was courteous.

LELIA. Master, you deserve to suffer, for if you don't appreciate a girl who loves you, it is only fair that another won't appreciate you.

FLAMMINIO. What do you mean?

LELIA. If that poor girl was your first love and still loves you more than ever, why abandon her to pursue another? I don't know whether God can ever pardon such a sin. Ah, Signor Flamminio, you have surely done great harm.

FLAMMINIO. You are still a lad, Fabio, and cannot know the power of love. I am forced to love and adore this one. I cannot   430 know or think about anyone but her. Therefore go back to her, talk to her and see if you can draw skillfully from her lips what she has against me, why she doesn't want to see me.

LELIA. You are wasting your time.

FLAMMINIO. I like to waste my time this way.

LELIA. You won't get anywhere.

FLAMMINIO. Patience.

LELIA. Let her go.

FLAMMINIO. I can't. Go there, I pray you.

LELIA. I'll go, but . . .   440

FLAMMINIO. Come back soon with her answer. I'll go up to the church.

LELIA. If the time is right, I'll not fail.

FLAMMINIO. Fabio, if you do this thing it will be good for you too!   (*Flamminio leaves.*)

LELIA. He left just in time. Here is Pasquella coming to find me.

SCENE II. — PASQUELLA, housekeeper of GHERARDO, and LELIA.

PASQUELLA. [11]I don't think there's greater trouble or vexation in the world than to serve a young lady in love, like mine. Especially one who isn't afraid of a mother or sisters or anybody, like mine. A few days ago she fell into such a passion and frenzy of   450 love that she's had no rest day or night. She scratches, she rubs, now she runs to the *loggia*, now to the window, downstairs, upstairs, not stopping, as though she had quicksilver in her feet. Jesu! Oh, for my part I know what it is to be young and in love, and I've done the same things. But I rested too — sometimes. At least I loved a man who counted, who was mature, knew what to do. But that one dotes on a young squirt who can hardly tie his own laces without help. Every day she sends me after this charmer, as if I had no work to do at home. And does his master believe he's

---

[11] This scene might be compared with III.i. 1–75.

carrying messages for him? Here he comes now. What luck! 460
Good day, Fabio, I was coming to look for you, my charmer.

LELIA. And a thousand crowns to you, my Pasquella. What is
your beautiful mistress doing and what does she want of me?

PASQUELLA. What do you think she's doing? Weeping, wasting
away because you haven't passed by her house yet this morning.

LELIA. Does she want me to go there before daybreak?

PASQUELLA. I think she'd want you with her all night.

LELIA. I have other things to do. Serving my master is enough
for me, you understand, Pasquella?

PASQUELLA. I know your master wouldn't be unhappy to come 470
to her. Do you sleep with him perhaps?

LELIA. Please God that I might be so much in his good graces!
Then I would not be as unhappy as I am.

PASQUELLA. Wouldn't you rather sleep with Isabella?

LELIA. Not I.

PASQUELLA. Eh! You're lying.

LELIA. Would it were not so.

PASQUELLA. Let's go now. My mistress says to request you to
come to her soon. Her father isn't at home and she must talk to you
about something important. 480

LELIA. Tell her that if she doesn't first break off with Flamminio
she is wasting her time. She well knows I would be ruined.

PASQUELLA. Come tell her yourself.

LELIA. I have something else to do, I tell you. Can't you hear
me?

PASQUELLA. What do you have to do? Do it, and I'll come right
back.

LELIA. Oh! You're giving me a headache. Go, in God's name.

PASQUELLA. You don't want to come?

LELIA. No, I tell you. Don't you understand? 490

PASQUELLA. In truth, Fabio, you're too proud. Let me remind
you of something. You're young and don't know what's good for
you. Your appeal won't last forever. Your beard will come.
You won't always have those pink cheeks and red lips. You won't
always be chased after by everyone. Then you'll know how foolish
you were. You'll repent when it's too late. Tell me, how many in
this city could get Isabella to look at them graciously? Yet you
seem to be making a joke of it!

LELIA. Why doesn't she look at others then and leave me alone?
I don't care. 500

PASQUELLA. Oh, God! It's too true that young people don't
have all the brains they need.

LELIA. Go away, Pasquella, don't preach to me any more. You do it badly.

PASQUELLA. Proud brat, you'll soon be without these airs. Come, my dear Fabio, my heart, please come soon. If you don't she'll send me to look for you again and won't believe I gave you her message.

LELIA. Go, Pasquella. I'll come. I was only joking.

PASQUELLA. When, my joy?   510

LELIA. Soon.

PASQUELLA. How soon?

LELIA. Soon. Go.

PASQUELLA. I'll wait for you outside the house. All right?

LELIA. Yes, yes.

PASQUELLA. Er, you know, if you don't come I'll get angry.

[SCENE III. (*Before Gherardo's house. Nearby are two inns, the Looking Glass and the Madman.*) *Giglio, a Spaniard, who loves Isabella tries to get Pasquella to let him enter Isabella's house and offers her a rosary when he returns that evening. She agrees to let him enter, intending to trick him out of the rosary — which he does not intend to let her have.*]

SCENE IV. STREET IN FRONT OF FLAMMINIO'S HOUSE.
FLAMMINIO, CRIVELLO, his servant, SCATIZZA, servant of
VIRGINIO.

FLAMMINIO. You haven't gone to see if you can find Fabio. And he doesn't come. I don't know what to make of this delay.

CRIVELLO. I was going and you called me back. How is that my fault?   520

FLAMMINIO. Go now and if he is still in Isabella's house wait for him until he leaves and have him come at once.

CRIVELLO. How will I know whether he's coming or not? Would you rather I asked at her house?

FLAMMINIO. What a jackass! Does that seem a good idea to you? [12]It seems I have no servant in my house worth beans except Fabio. Please God I can treat him well. What are you mumbling? What are you saying?

CRIVELLO. What do you want me to say? I say yes. Fabio is good, Fabio is beautiful, Fabio serves you well, Fabio with you,   530 Fabio with the lady . . . Fabio is everything; Fabio does everything. But . . .

---

[12] I.iv. 1–8.

FLAMMINIO. What does "but . . ." mean?

CRIVELLO. It won't always be a good risk.

FLAMMINIO. What do you mean, risk?

CRIVELLO. That you shouldn't always take that risk. He's a stranger. One day he might rob you.

FLAMMINIO. Would that the rest of you were as reliable. Ask Scatizza, who's coming here, whether he's seen him. I'll go to Porrini's bank. . . .   540

> (*Flamminio leaves, enter Scatizza who leaves with
> Crivello to find Fabio.*)

[SCENE V. *Spela fumes at Gherardo who had sent him to buy perfume in a shop.*]

SCENE VI. STREET IN FRONT OF GHERARDO'S HOUSE.
CRIVELLO, SCATIZZA, LELIA, and ISABELLA.

CRIVELLO. [13]Now you get the idea. And if you want to come I'm willing to find another girl for you.

SCATIZZA. Make a little effort. If you find a servant girl I like I promise we'll have the best time in the world. I have the key to the granary, the cellar, the pantry, and the woodshed. If I had a way of unloading the goods secretly, we could live like lords. Anyway, you can't make out any other way with masters like these.

CRIVELLO. I've told you, I'll tell Bita to get a well stacked one for you so that the four of us can have a great time at the carnival.

SCATIZZA. But this is the last day.   550

CRIVELLO. We'll do it during Lent while our masters are flirting at church. Look, Gherardo's door is opening. Step back here a little.

SCATIZZA. Why?

CRIVELLO. Out of respect.

> (*Enter Lelia and Isabella. Crivello and
> Scatizza are hiding behind them.*)

LELIA. [14]Come, Isabella, do not forget what you promised me.

ISABELLA. And don't you forget to come and see me. Listen, one word.

CRIVELLO. If I had this deal I know how my master would for-   560
give *me!*

---

[13] Scenes like this one have much the same flavor as the subplot scenes in Shakespeare's play, especially such scenes as II.iii. and II.v.

[14] Compare with III.i. 105ff.

SCATIZZA. You'd hatch the chickens yourself, eh?

CRIVELLO. What do you think?

LELIA. What else?

ISABELLA. Listen a moment.

LELIA. I am.

ISABELLA. Is anyone outside?

LELIA. Not a living soul.

CRIVELLO. What the devil does she want?

SCATIZZA. This is too much.   570

CRIVELLO. Let's watch.

ISABELLA. Listen, one word.

CRIVELLO. They're very close to one another.

SCATIZZA. Indeed!

ISABELLA. You know? I'd like . . .

LELIA. What?

ISABELLA. I'd like . . . Come closer.

SCATIZZA. Come closer, wow!

ISABELLA. See whether anyone is around.

LELIA. Didn't I tell you? No one.   580

ISABELLA. I'd like you to come back after dinner when my father is out.

LELIA. I will do it. But as my master passes by here, please back away from the window and keep it locked.

ISABELLA. If I don't obey, you needn't love me.

SCATIZZA. Where the devil is she putting her hand?

CRIVELLO. Oh, my poor master! Yes, yes! I knew it all along!

LELIA. Goodbye.

ISABELLA. You wish to leave?

SCATIZZA. Kiss her, and a plague upon you!   590

CRIVELLO. She's afraid of being seen.

LELIA. Go back inside.

ISABELLA. I want a favor from you.

LELIA. What?

ISABELLA. Come inside the doorway a little.

SCATIZZA. They've done it.

ISABELLA. Oh, you're a brute!

LELIA. We'll be seen.

CRIVELLO. Ah, me! I'm burning up. One for me!

SCATIZZA. Didn't I tell you he'd kiss her?   600

CRIVELLO. And I tell you I'd rather have seen this kiss than earn a hundred *scudi*.

SCATIZZA. I saw it. As if it happened to me!

CRIVELLO. Oh! What'll the master do when he finds out!

SCATIZZA. The devil! Don't tell him.

ISABELLA. Forgive me. Your extreme beauty and the great love I have for you made me do what you might judge immoral. But God knows, I couldn't restrain myself.

LELIA. Do not excuse yourself to me, my lady. For I know what I am and what I have set about to do because of too much love. 610

ISABELLA. And what is that?

LELIA. What? To deceive my master, which is wrong.

ISABELLA. May God vex him!

CRIVELLO. Go to, you faithless baggage! No wonder the young sprout urged the master to give up this love.

SCATIZZA. Every hen makes its own nest. In the end all women are the same.

LELIA. It's late now and I must find my master. Peace be with you. 620

ISABELLA. Listen. (*She kisses him again.*)

CRIVELLO. Oh, twice! May you dry up! May evil come of this!

SCATIZZA. God's body, she's swollen one of my legs!

LELIA. Close the door. Goodbye.

ISABELLA. I am yours.

LELIA. And I am yours. (*Isabella leaves.*) On the one hand, I'm having the best sport in the world with her thinking I'm a man. On the other, I'd like to get out of this mess and don't know how to do so. She has already reached the kissing stage and will go farther the first chance she gets. And I'll have lost every- 630 thing, since she'll find out my secret. I want to find Clemenzia and get her advice — but here comes Flamminio.

CRIVELLO. Scatizza, my master said he'd wait for me at Porrini's bank. I want to bring him this good news. In case he doesn't believe me, you assure him I'm not lying.

SCATIZZA. I won't let you down. But if you did it my way you'd be quiet about this. You'd always have Fabio by the throat and make him do whatever you wanted.

CRIVELLO. I hate him, I tell you. He's ruined me.

SCATIZZA. Do as you please. 640

SCENE VII. OUTSIDE FLAMMINIO'S HOUSE.
FLAMMINIO and LELIA.

FLAMMINIO. Is is possible that I am so beside myself and think so little of myself that I want to love someone despite her wishes, to serve a tormenter who cares nothing about me, who won't waste a glance on me? Can I be so petty, so contemptible that I cannot lift this shame and torment off my back? But here is Fabio. Well now, what have you accomplished?

LELIA. Nothing.

FLAMMINIO. Why were you so long returning? Did you turn into a post?

LELIA. I delayed because I wanted to talk to Isabella.   650

FLAMMINIO. And did you?

LELIA. She wouldn't listen to me. If you did things my way, you would look elsewhere and thus settle this affair. From everything I can gather you're wasting your time. She certainly seems unwilling to show you the slightest favor.

FLAMMINIO. Name of God! Do you know, just now as I was passing her house she backed away from the window when she saw me with as much scorn and fury as if she had seen some foul and frightful thing!

LELIA. Let her go, I tell you. In this entire city can't someone   660
else possibly deserve your love as much as she? Haven't you ever loved another woman as much as she?

FLAMMINIO. Would it weren't so! That I fear is the cause of all my misfortune. For I passionately loved Lelia, that daughter of Virginio Bellenzini I told you about. I'm afraid Isabella suspects that love still lingers and for this reason doesn't want to see me. But I'll make her understand I don't love Lelia any more, rather that I hate her and can't even bear to remember her. I'll make her any kind of promise she wants never to see Lelia again. I want you to tell her this.   670

LELIA. [15]Ah, me!

FLAMMINIO. What's the matter with you?

LELIA. Ah me!

FLAMMINIO. Where does it hurt?

LELIA. Ah me! My heart.

FLAMMINIO. How long have you had it? Lean on me a bit. Does your body pain you?

LELIA. No, sir.

FLAMMINIO. Maybe your stomach is upset.

LELIA. I tell you the pain is in my heart.   680

FLAMMINIO. And perhaps a greater one in mine. You've gotten pale. Go home and make a warm poultice for your chest and have your back rubbed. That's it. I'll be there right away and call the doctor if necessary to take your pulse and find out what's wrong

---

[15] Contrast the remainder of this scene with the patience of Viola: II.iv. 110ff.

with you. Give me your arm. You're ice cold. Get going —
gently, gently. What strange things happen to a man! I wouldn't
want to lose him for anything I own. I don't know where there's
ever been a more courteous, well-mannered servant in the world
than this youth. Besides, he seems to love me so much that if he
were a woman I'd think he were sick because of me. Fabio, go 690
home I tell you and warm your feet a little. I'll be there right
away. Tell them to expect me. (*Flamminio leaves.*)

LELIA. Now, miserable one, you have heard with your own ears
and from his own mouth how much this ingrate loves you. Unhappy Lelia! Why waste more time serving this cruel master?
Neither your patience nor your prayers nor your service have done
you any good. No, nor your deceits. Unhappy me! Rejected,
spurned, avoided, hated! Why serve one who rejects me? Why
long for one who spurns me? Why chase after one who flees me?
Why love one who hates me? Ah, Flamminio! You love only 700
Isabella. You want only her. Have her, take her.

I'll leave him now or die. I'll not serve him in this costume any
more nor come between them, since he hates me so much. I'll go
to Clemenzia who is waiting for me at home and with her will
decide what to do with my life.

Scene VIII. CRIVELLO and FLAMMINIO.

CRIVELLO. If it isn't true hang me by the neck, cut out my
tongue. It's true, I tell you.

FLAMMINIO. When did it happen?

CRIVELLO. When you sent me to look for him.

FLAMMINIO. What happened? Tell me once again, because he 710
denies talking to her today.

CRIVELLO. It would be a good thing if you made *him* tell it!
While I was waiting to see whether he was in the house, I saw him
come out. And when he wanted to leave Isabella called him inside again. Seeing nobody around who might be watching, they
kissed.

FLAMMINIO. How is it they didn't see you?

CRIVELLO. Because I moved back into the doorway opposite so
they couldn't see me.

FLAMMINIO. How could you see them? 720

CRIVELLO. With my eyes. Do you think I saw them with my
elbows, perhaps?

FLAMMINIO. And he kissed her?

CRIVELLO. I don't know whether she kissed him or he her — I
think they were kissing one another.

FLAMMINIO. Were their faces close enough together for them to kiss?

CRIVELLO. Faces no, lips yes.

FLAMMINIO. Oh! Can lips touch without faces touching?

CRIVELLO. If a man had a mouth in his shoulders, maybe. 730
But lips being where they are, I doubt it.

FLAMMINIO. Be sure you saw it well and that you don't say later: it seemed to me. This is a grave thing you are telling me.

CRIVELLO. Being buried is graver.[16]

FLAMMINIO. How could you see them?

CRIVELLO. By looking with my eyes open. By being there to look and by having nothing else to do.

FLAMMINIO. If this is true then you have killed me.

CRIVELLO. It is true. She called him, she came up to him, hugged him and kissed him. Now if you want to die, die. 740

FLAMMINIO. Amazing how the traitor denied even being there! Now I know why the rascal advised me to leave her. To enjoy her himself! Call me no man if I don't take such revenge that it will be a warning to servants not to betray their masters as long as the earth endures. Still, finally, I don't want to believe it unless I have more proof. I know you're a malcontent and you don't like him. You're doing this to make me kick him out. But, by God, I'll make you tell the truth or kill you. Did you see it?

CRIVELLO. Yes.

FLAMMINIO. He kissed her? 750

CRIVELLO. They were kissing.

FLAMMINIO. How many times?

CRIVELLO. Two times.

FLAMMINIO. Where?

CRIVELLO. In her vestibule.

FLAMMINIO. You lie in your throat. A while ago you said in her doorway.

CRIVELLO. I meant near the doorway.

FLAMMINIO. Tell the truth! (*beats Crivello.*)

CRIVELLO. Oh! Oh! I regret having told it. 760

FLAMMINIO. Was it true?

CRIVELLO. Yes, sir. But I forgot to tell you I have a witness.

FLAMMINIO. Who?

---

[16] The original line is an in-joke that will not come across in English. It reads "*Mangia* on top of the Tower of Siena is graver." *Mangia* (for *Mangiaguadagni*) is a large bronze figure on top of the Municipal Palace that strikes the hours. The line *means* therefore: there are graver, more serious things than that kiss.

CRIVELLO. Virginio's Scatizza.

FLAMMINIO. Did he see it too?

CRIVELLO. As I did.

FLAMMINIO. And if he doesn't confirm this?

CRIVELLO. Kill me.

FLAMMINIO. That I'll do.

CRIVELLO. And if he confirms it?   770

FLAMMINIO. I'll kill two people!

CRIVELLO. Ah, me! But why?

FLAMMINIO. I don't mean you. Isabella and Fabio.

CRIVELLO. And burn down their house with Pasquella and anyone else that's inside.

FLAMMINIO. Let's find Scatizza. If I don't pay them back, if
they don't hear from me, if this whole world doesn't see . . . I'll
have such revenge! Oh, traitor! Come along.

ACT III

[SCENE I. (*Before Gherardo's house and the inns.*) *Piero, the
pedant points out the places of interest to Fabrizio, who left Modena
too early to remember it. Stragualcia is bored, being hungry.*

SCENE II. *Agiato and Frulla, inn-keepers of the Looking-Glass and
the Madman, quarrel over the new arrivals' patronage. A look at
Frulla's daughter persuades them to stay at his inn, the Madman.*]

SCENE III. OUTSIDE VIRGINIO'S HOUSE.
VIRGINIO and CLEMENZIA.

VIRGINIO. Are these the manners you've taught her? Is this the
honor she pays me? Oh, unlucky me! Have I escaped so many   780
perils for this? To see my property left without heir? To see my
home ruined, my daughter a whore? To become the talk of the
town? Not to be able to raise my head in public? To be pointed
at by youngsters, mocked by old men, put in a comedy by the
Intronati, used as an example in stories, my name on the lips of
the local ladies? And don't suppose there aren't gossips and that
people don't like to slander. I think everybody knows already,
for I'm certain that it takes only one woman to spread the story
over the city in three hours. Unhappy father! Miserable, sad
old man! What will I do? What must I think?   790

CLEMENZIA. You'd do better to make less noise and try to arrange the best possible way for her to come home without the
whole city finding out about it. May Sister Novellante Ciancini
have as much breath in her body as I believe her story that Lelia

goes around dressed as a man. Beware of their telling you this. They want to make a nun of her so you'll leave them all your property.

VIRGINIO. Why shouldn't she be telling the truth? She told me that Lelia is taken for a boy by a gentleman of this city who still doesn't know she's a girl. 800

CLEMENZIA. Anything is possible but, for me, I can't believe it.

VIRGINIO. And I can't believe that he doesn't know that she's a girl.

CLEMENZIA. That's not what I meant.

VIRGINIO. But I did, and it hurts. I myself am to blame, though, letting you bring her up and knowing what you are.

CLEMENZIA. No more talk, Virginio. If I'm a bawd, you made me one. You well know that before you turned up no one had me except my husband. Young girls want a different kind of treatment from that, let me tell you. Aren't you ashamed of wanting to 810 marry her to a windbag old enough to be her grandfather?

VIRGINIO. What's the matter with old men, bawd? They're a thousand times better than young ones.

CLEMENZIA. You've no feelings. One should overlook your ravings, I suppose, and just try to set you straight.

VIRGINIO. If I find her I'll drag her home by the hair.

CLEMENZIA. You'll be doing like the man did who took the horns concealed in his bosom and put them on his head.

VIRGINIO. I don't care. That'll be all right so long as I cut them off me. 820

CLEMENZIA. Be careful, don't lose your head.

VIRGINIO. I have a description of how she is dressed. I'll hunt till I find her. Then we'll see.

CLEMENZIA. Do what you wish. I'm leaving. I've wasted my time washing coal. But . . .

SCENE IV. OUTSIDE THE MADMAN INN; GHERARDO'S HOUSE
NEARBY.
FABRIZIO and FRULLA.

FABRIZIO. [17]While my two servants are sleeping I'll go about the city. When they wake up tell them I went toward the square.

FRULLA. Yes, sir. If I didn't see you wearing these clothes I'd swear you were the page of a gentleman of this city. He is dressed 830 in white like you and looks enough like you that you seem to be he.

---

[17] III.iii. 18–24.

FABRIZIO. Have I a twin brother perhaps?

FRULLA. It could be.

FABRIZIO. Tell my tutor to search for he knows who.

FRULLA. Depend on me. (*Frulla leaves.*)

SCENE V.
PASQUELLA and FABRIZIO.

PASQUELLA. [18]Faith, there he is. I was afraid I'd have to search the whole city for him. Well met, Fabio. I was looking for you. You've saved me a chore. My mistress says, sweetheart, you're to come to her right away for something important to both of you. I don't know what it could be. 840

FABRIZIO. Who is your mistress?

PASQUELLA. You know who she is well enough. Faith, you're really stuck on one another.

FABRIZIO. I'm not stuck. But if she wants we'll get stuck and in a hurry.

PASQUELLA. You two are something special. I wish I was young again and had a young body. I know if I were you I'd have put respect and hesitation aside by now. But you'll do it well, yes indeed.

FABRIZIO. Madonna! Go away. You don't know me. You've 850 got the wrong party.

PASQUELLA. Oh, don't be angry, Fabio mine. What I said was for your own good.

FABRIZIO. I'm not angry at all. But that isn't my name and I don't know who you think I am.

PASQUELLA. Pretend to be two people if you please. But you know, young fellow, there aren't many in this city as rich and beautiful as she. I wish you'd bring this business to a close. Going back and forth every day with messages makes people talk, which doesn't help you and is no honor to her. 860

FABRIZIO. What is this? I don't understand. Either she is crazy or mistakes me for someone else. I'm going to see where she wants to take me. Let's go.

PASQUELLA. Oh! I think I hear people in the house. Stay here in the doorway and I'll see whether Isabella's alone. I'll signal you to come in if no one's there.

FABRIZIO. I want to see how this fantasy ends. Maybe she's some courtesan's servant and thinks she can get money from me. She's badly mistaken, for I'm almost like the Spaniards and

---

[18] IV.i. 1ff.

would sooner take a crown of hers than give her a nickel of mine.   870
One of us won't be clipped here. Let me back away from the
house a little and see what kind of people go in and out so as to
know what kind of lady this is.

SCENE VI.
GHERARDO, VIRGINIO, and PASQUELLA.

GHERARDO. Pardon me. If this is so, I renounce her. And I
believe that if your daughter did that, it's because she doesn't
want me. And I think that she's taken on someone else, too.

VIRGINIO. Don't think that, Gherardo. Don't you trust me?
I beg you not to spoil the arrangements.

GHERARDO. I beg you not to talk to me.

VIRGINIO. Oh! You go back on your word?   880

GHERARDO. To someone who's gone back on me? Yes, I do.
Besides, you don't know whether I could get her back or not.
You're trying to sell me a bird in the bush. While you were talking
with Clemenzia I heard everything.

VIRGINIO. If I don't get her back, I can't give her to you. But
if I do get her, wouldn't you like the wedding to take place right
away?

GHERARDO. Virginio, my first wife was the most honorable
lady in this city and my daughter is as pure as a dove. How can
you ask me to take home a girl who runs away from her father   890
and goes from house to house dressed as a boy the way bawds do?
I'd never be able to marry off my daughter, don't you see?

VIRGINIO. After a few days people would stop talking. Who do
you think knows of it? Only you and I.

GHERARDO. And later the whole town will be full of it.

VIRGINIO. That's not so.

GHERARDO. When did she run away?

VIRGINIO. Either yesterday or this morning.

GHERARDO. God's will. But who knows whether she's in
Modena?   900

VIRGINIO. She is.

GHERARDO. Find her then, and we'll talk.

VIRGINIO. Do you promise to take her?

GHERARDO. I'll see.

VIRGINIO. Promise me.

GHERARDO. I won't promise, but . . .

VIRGINIO. Say it straight out.

GHERARDO. Hold on. (*Enter Pasquella.*) Pasquella, what are you doing? And where's Isabella?

PASQUELLA. Er, what? She's on her knees before the altar.   910

GHERARDO. Blessed girl! My daughter is always praying. That's the best thing in the world.

PASQUELLA. Well said! She fasts every fast day and says her prayers like a little saint.

GHERARDO. She makes me remember the blessed soul of her mother.

PASQUELLA. True. Oh, how much good that poor lady did! She gave herself more penance and more hairshirts than any ladies today. She spent her life giving alms. If it hadn't been for love of you, not a friar, priest or beggar would have stopped at her   930 doorway without getting everything she had.

VIRGINIO. Those were fine qualities.

PASQUELLA. Hundreds of times she got up hours before daylight to go to the first mass of the friars of St. Francis because she didn't want to be seen, or thought a pig like certain sinners I know.

GHERARDO. Pig? What do you mean?

PASQUELLA. Pig, that's it.

VIRGINIO. That's a bad word.

PASQUELLA. I'm sure I heard someone call her that.

GHERARDO. You mean prig.   940

PASQUELLA. Maybe. But I tell you your daughter will be more like that than she was.

GHERARDO. God willing.

VIRGINIO. Oh, Gherardo! There she is, the one you were talking about. Oh, unhappy father! Is she hiding or running away because she saw me? Let's catch her.

GHERARDO. See you don't make a mistake. Maybe that's not her.

VIRGINIO. Who wouldn't recognize her? She's just like Sister Novellante described her.   950

PASQUELLA. This affair is going badly. I'll get out of here.

Scene VII.
VIRGINIO, GHERARDO, and FABRIZIO.

VIRGINIO. [19]So, my fine girl. Do you think this costume suitable for you? Is this the honor you confer on your house? Is

---

[19] Elements of this scene resemble situations in IV.i. 26ff.

this the joy you give a poor old man? If only I had died when I conceived you! You were born only to dishonor me, to bury me alive. Oh, Gherardo! How does your bride look to you? Does she do us honor?

GHERARDO. I wouldn't say so. Bride, eh?

VIRGINIO. Bawd! Hussy! How well off would you be if this man didn't want you for a wife any more and you didn't find 960 another. But he'll ignore your madness. He still wants you.

GHERARDO. Go easy!

VIRGINIO. Get in the house, scum! Your mother's milk must have been cursed the day you were born.

FABRIZIO. My dear old fellow, have you children, relatives or friends in this city who take care of you?

VIRGINIO. Listen to that answer. Why do you say that?

FABRIZIO. I'm amazed they let you out needing medical care so badly. In another country you'd be in a straitjacket.

VIRGINIO. I ought to put you in a straitjacket! I'd like to cut 970 your throat! Bring me a knife.

FABRIZIO. You don't really know me, old fellow. Maybe you're insulting me thinking me a foreigner. I'm as good a Modenese as you, well born, of as good a house as yours.

GHERARDO. She's beautiful, though. If this is the only wrong she's done, I still want her.

VIRGINIO. Why did you run away from your father and from the place I sent you?

FABRIZIO. You never sent me anywhere that I know. My running away from here was necessary. 980

VIRGINIO. Necessary? Who made you?

FABRIZIO. The Spaniards.

VIRGINIO. And where are you coming from?

FABRIZIO. From the barracks.

VIRGINIO. The barracks?

FABRIZIO. Yes, the barracks.

GHERARDO. There's nothing can be done!

VIRGINIO. Shame on you!

FABRIZIO. The same to you.

VIRGINIO. Gherardo, please, let's put her in your house so she 990 won't be seen this way.

GHERARDO. I won't do it. Take her to yours.

VIRGINIO. If you love me, open your door a little.

GHERARDO. No, I tell you.

VIRGINIO. Listen. Be careful she doesn't go somewhere else.

FABRIZIO. I have known many crazy Modenese, more than I could count. But I never saw anyone so crazy as this old man

who isn't even straitjacketed or locked up. What a splendid sickness! As I make it out, his craziness makes young men seem women to him! This is a purer madness than the one Molza[20] 1000
tells us of the Sienese lady who thought she was a glazed pot. And it's more fitting for women to be short on brains than old men who for a thousand reasons ought to be very wise. I wouldn't have wanted to miss telling this crazy story on carnival evenings for a hundred crowns. Here they come now. Let's see what they say.

GHERARDO. I'll be frank with you. On the one hand, maybe; on the other, no. Question her a little more.

VIRGINIO. Come here.

FABRIZIO. What do you want, good old fellow. 1010

VIRGINIO. You're a real bawd, you are.

FABRIZIO. Don't insult me. I'll not put up with it.

VIRGINIO. Shameless!

FABRIZIO. Oh! Oh! Oh! Oh! Oh! Oh! Oh!

GHERARDO. Let her speak. Don't you see her rage. Humor her.

FABRIZIO. What does he want of me? What have I to do with you or him?

VIRGINIO. Still burning to talk? Whose child are you?

FABRIZIO. Virginio Bellenzini's. 1020

VIRGINIO. Would God you weren't! You'll kill me before my time.

FABRIZIO. How can a sixty year old man die before his time? Would everyone could live so long. It's your turn to die; you've lived too long.

VIRGINIO. That's your sin, bawd!

GHERARDO. Enough of these words. My daughter, my sister, don't answer your father that way.

FABRIZIO. Birds of a feather flock together. They both have the same sickness. What a house! Ha! Ha! Ha! Ha! Ha! 1030

VIRGINIO. Still laughing?

GHERARDO. That's a bad sign, making fun of your father.

FABRIZIO. What father? What mother? I never had any father but Virginio and any mother but Giovanna. You're a jackass. Do you think I am without friends here?

GHERARDO. Virginio, do you know what I think? That this poor girl's wits have turned melancholy.

---

[20] Francesco Maria Molza (1489–1544) a native of Modena, an elegant if licentious writer of pastorals, sonnets, and satires.

VIRGINIO. Woe's me! I should have recognized it right away when I saw how frenziedly she greeted me.

GHERARDO. No. This can come from something else. 1040

VIRGINIO. From what?

GHERARDO. When a woman has lost her honor she's lost to the world.

VIRGINIO. She has some craziness in her head, I tell you.

GHERARDO. Still, she remembers her parents' names. Yet seems not to know you.

VIRGINIO. Let's take her into your house, since it's nearby. I can't take her to mine without being seen by the whole city.

FABRIZIO. What are those codgers talking about, those brothers of Melchizedek? 1050

VIRGINIO. Let's first draw her inside as gently as we can. Then we'll lock her in a room with your daughter by force.

GHERARDO. All right.

VIRGINIO. Come, my daughter. I don't want to be angry with you any more. I forgive you for everything, provided you intend to behave.

FABRIZIO. Thank you.

GHERARDO. That's a good girl.

FABRIZIO. That's the other spring chicken.

GHERARDO. Come, it isn't proper to be arguing outside dressed 1060 like this. Come into the house. Pasquella, open the door.

VIRGINIO. Enter, my daughter.

FABRIZIO. I won't do it.

VIRGINIO. Why?

FABRIZIO. I don't want to enter somebody else's house.

GHERARDO. Bless me, a Penelope.

VIRGINIO. Didn't I say my daughter was good and beautiful.

GHERARDO. Her costume shows that.

VIRGINIO. I want to say just one word.

FABRIZIO. Say it out here. 1070

GHERARDO. What's wrong! This house is yours. You're to be my wife.

FABRIZIO. What wife? Old liar!

GHERARDO. Your father has promised you to me.

FABRIZIO. Do you think I am some baggage to be handled, eh?

VIRGINIO. Come, don't anger me! Listen, my daughter, I don't want anything that you don't want.

FABRIZIO. Old man, you don't know me.

VIRGINIO. Just come in here and listen to one word.

FABRIZIO. One word, ten. Do you think I'm afraid of you. 1080

(Enters the house.)

VIRGINIO. Gherardo, now that we have her in here let's arrange to lock her in the room with your daughter until we can have her clothes brought here.

GHERARDO. As you wish, Virginio. Pasquella, bring the key for the downstairs bedroom and call Isabella here.

ACT IV

[SCENE I. (*The Madman Inn*) (*Stragualcia and Piero insult one another, then the pedant goes off in search of Fabrizio.*]

SCENE II. OUTSIDE GHERARDO'S HOUSE, THE MADMAN INN
NEARBY.
GHERARDO, VIRGINIO, and PEDANT.

GHERARDO. About the dowry, what is said is said. I'll dower her as you wish and you add a thousand florins if your son is not found.

VIRGINIO. So be it.

PEDANT. If I am not mistaken I have seen this gentleman be- 1090 fore, but I don't remember where.

VIRGINIO. What are you looking at, good sir?

PEDANT. Certainly, this is my former master.

GHERARDO. Let him look as he pleases. He must be new to this city. In other places they don't mind people staring as we do here.

PEDANT. If I'm staring, it is not without reason. Tell me, do you know Sr. Virginio Bellenzini of this city?

VIRGINIO. Yes, I know him. No one's a better friend of mine than he. But what do you want of him? If you're thinking of 1100 staying with him let me tell you he has other affairs and can't accommodate you. Look for another host.

PEDANT. You are certainly he. *Salvete, patronorum optime.*[21]

VIRGINIO. Would you be Sr. Pietro de' Pagliaricci, my son's tutor?

PEDANT. Yes, I am.

VIRGINIO. Oh, my son! Unhappy me! What news of him? Where did you leave him? Where did he die? Why were you so long in letting me know? Did those traitors, those Jews, those dogs kill him? My son! The best thing I had in the world. Oh 1110 my dear tutor, quickly, tell me I beg you.

---

[21] Greetings, best of masters.

PEDANT. Do not weep, sir, if you please.

VIRGINIO. Oh Gherardo, my son-in-law! Here's the man who raised my poor son while he was alive. Oh, Oh! My son! Where are you buried? Do you know nothing? Tell me, why don't you? I'm dying with desire to know and with fear of hearing what I'll hear.

PEDANT. Oh master, do not weep. Why are you weeping?

VIRGINIO. Why shouldn't I weep for so gentle a son? So wise, so gifted, so well bred, killed by those traitors. 1120

PEDANT. May God keep you, you and he. Your son is alive and well.

GHERARDO. Bad for me if this is so. I've lost a thousand florins.

VIRGINIO. What? Alive and well? If this were so he'd be with you now.

GHERARDO. Virginio, do you know this man well? This isn't some trick?

PEDANT. *Parcius ista viris, tamen obiieienda memento.*[22]

VIRGINIO. Tell me some news, tutor.

PEDANT. During the Sack of Rome your son was the prisoner 1130 of one Captain Orteca.

GHERARDO. Get ready to listen: now the story begins.

PEDANT. And because Captain Orteca had two others in his company who were thinking of robbing him, he sent us to Siena secretly. He came there a few days later worried that the Sienese — who are friends of justice and reason and are very fond of our city and above all are good men — might arrest him and set us free. He took your son from Siena to a castle of the Lord of Piombino. *Per usque millies,*[23] he fixed our ransoms at a thousand ducats and made us write requesting it. 1140

VIRGINIO. My son! Did they torture him at all?

PEDANT. Assuredly not. They treated him like a gentleman.

GHERARDO. This is killing me.

PEDANT. We never got any replies to the letters we sent.

GHERARDO. You understand, he'll get you to hand over some money.

VIRGINIO. Continue.

PEDANT. Then, after conducting us to the Spanish camp at Corregia this captain was killed and the court took his property and set us free. 1150

---

[22] Yet I remember those orders of his more than the man himself. A garbled sentence; apparently the pedant uses a plural, *viris*, in place of a singular, *viro*.

[23] over and over.

VIRGINIO. Where is my son?

PEDANT. Nearer than you think.

VIRGINIO. In Modena perhaps?

PEDANT. If you promise me drink money, *quia omnis labor optat praemium*,[24] I'll tell you.

GHERARDO. So that's what you're after, swindler.

PEDANT. You are wrong. I, a swindler? *Absit*.[25]

VIRGINIO. I promise whatever you want. Where is he?

PEDANT. At the Madman Inn.

GHERARDO. It's over. A thousand florins lost. But what do I **1160** care? As long as I have her, that's enough. I'm rich enough.

VIRGINIO. Let's go, tutor. I still can't believe I'll see him, embrace him, kiss him and hug him.

PEDANT. Master, oh *quanto mutatur ab illo!*[26] He is no longer a child to be hugged. You will not know him. He has grown and I am certain that he will not recognize you, you have changed so. *Praeterea*,[27] you have this beard, which you did not use to wear. If I had not heard you speak I should never have recognized you. How is Lelia?

VIRGINIO. Well. She's gotten big and fat. **1170**

GHERARDO. What does he mean, fat? If she's that way, keep her, I don't want her.

VIRGINIO. I mean she's now a grown up lady. Oh tutor, I have not embraced you yet.

PEDANT. Master, I say this not to boast, but what I have done for your son . . . I well know. And I have ample reason for saying so, for I have never asked him to do anything that he did not agree to right away.

VIRGINIO. What has he learned?

PEDANT. He has wasted no time, *licuit per varios casus, per tot* **1180** *diserimina rerum*.[28]

VIRGINIO. Call him outside and tell him nothing. I want to see if he recognizes me.

PEDANT. He left the inn a brief while ago. Let us see if he has returned.

[SCENE III. — *They return to the inn but Fabrizio has not returned. Stragualcia greets them and greedily takes rewards from Virginio. As*

---

[24] Since all labor seeks reward.

[25] Let him stay lost.

[26] How much he is changed from that!

[27] Besides.

[28] It was possible through various misfortunes, through so many varieties of things.

Gherardo starts for home and his locked up Lelia, in she comes still dressed as Fabio.]

SCENE IV.
LELIA, CLEMENZIA, and GHERARDO.

LELIA. Does it seem to you, Clemenzia, that fate is making sport of me?

CLEMENZIA. Keep calm and leave things to me. I'll find some way to make you happy. Go and change those clothes. Don't be seen this way.   1190

GHERARDO. I'm going to greet her and find out how she escaped. God content you Lelia, my sweet bride. Who opened the door for you? The maid, eh? I'm pleased that you have come to your nurse's house, but to be seen in this costume does little honor to you or me.

LELIA. Oh, unhappy! He has recognized me. To whom are you speaking? What Lelia? I am not Lelia.

GHERARDO. Oh? A short while ago when we locked you up with my daughter Isabella didn't you admit to your father and me that you were Lelia? And didn't you think I'd know you, my   1200
bride? Go and change those clothes.

LELIA. May God help you as much as I would like you for a husband.

CLEMENZIA. Go home, Gherardo. All girls play hard to get, some in one way, some another. And you know how few, maybe none, don't get caught sometime. Still, these are things we don't talk about.

GHERARDO. For my part no one will ever know. But how did she escape from my house locked in with Isabella?

CLEMENZIA. Who? Her?   1210

GHERARDO. Her.

CLEMENZIA. You're mistaken. She hasn't left me all day. For a joke she just put on those clothes the way girls do and asked me to see whether they fitted.

GHERARDO. You want to trick me. I tell you we locked her in the house with Isabella.

CLEMENZIA. Where did you just come from?

GHERARDO. From the Madman Inn. I went there with Virginio.

CLEMENZIA. Were you drinking?

GHERARDO. Just one.   1220

CLEMENZIA. Then go to sleep. You need it.

GHERARDO. Let me see Lelia a moment before I leave. I want to give her some news.

CLEMENZIA. What news?

GHERARDO. Her brother has come back safe and well and her father's waiting for him at the inn.

CLEMENZIA. Who? Fabrizio?

GHERARDO. Fabrizio.

CLEMENZIA. If I believed that, I'd kiss you.

GHERARDO. How beautiful is happiness! Let's bring some to   1230
Lelia right away.

CLEMENZIA. I'll run to tell her. (*runs off.*)

GHERARDO. And I to give a swelling to the rascal who let her escape. (*runs off.*)

SCENE V. OUTSIDE GHERARDO'S HOUSE.
PASQUELLA.

PASQUELLA. Woe is me! I was so scared I had to leave the house. And ladies, I know if I didn't tell you what frightened me you'd never know. I want to tell you about this — but not you crude men who'd only burst into laughter. Those two old goats kept saying this lad was a girl and they locked him in the bedroom with my mistress, Isabella. And they gave me the key.   1240
I went in to see what they were doing and found them hugging and kissing. I thought I'd better make sure whether he was male or female. My mistress had him stretched out on the bed and called me to help her while she held his hands. He let himself be held. I undressed the front of him and suddenly felt myself jabbed in the hand by I don't know what kind of thing. I didn't know whether it was a pestle or a carrot or something else, but whatever it was I'd never felt one of its size before. When I saw it get that big, sisters, I ran out and locked the door! And I'm sure I wouldn't go back in there alone. But I'll lend the key to   1250
any of you who doesn't believe me and wants to find out for herself.

[*Giglio arrives and, Scene VI, Pasquella first gets his rosary then locks him out of the house.*]

SCENE VII.
GHERARDO and PASQUELLA.

GHERARDO. What were you doing at the doorway with that Spaniard? What's up between you and him?

PASQUELLA. He was asking for some rosary. Me, I didn't understand him.

GHERARDO. You've really carried out my orders well! I'd like to break your bones.

PASQUELLA. Why?

GHERARDO. Because you've let Lelia go. Didn't I tell you not to open the door for her?   1260

PASQUELLA. When did she go? Isn't she in the bedroom?

GHERARDO. May God curse you.

PASQUELLA. I know she's there.

. GHERARDO. I know she's not here. I just left her at her nurse Clemenzia's house.

PASQUELLA. Haven't I just left her in her bedroom, on her knees, saying her paternosters?

GHERARDO. Maybe she got back ahead of me.

PASQUELLA. I tell you she hasn't left. I'm sure. The bedroom's been locked.   1270

GHERARDO. Where's the key?

PASQUELLA. Here it is.

GHERARDO. Give it to me. If she isn't there I'll break your bones.

PASQUELLA. And if she's there will you get me a negligee?

GHERARDO. Agreed.

PASQUELLA. Let me open it.

GHERARDO. No, I want to. You'd find some reason why you couldn't.   (*Gherardo runs off to the bedroom.*)

PASQUELLA. Oh, I'm terribly afraid he'll find them still cook-   1280
ing. Still, I left them a good while ago.

SCENE VIII.
FLAMMINIO, PASQUELLA, and GHERARDO.

FLAMMINIO. Pasquella, how long has it been since my Fabio was here?

PASQUELLA. Why?

FLAMMINIO. Because he is a traitor and I shall punish him. Since Isabella has left me for him he'll get what he deserves. What a fine thing for a lady in her position, to fall in love with a page!

PASQUELLA. Oh, don't say that. The caresses she gives him are for the love of you.   1290

FLAMMINIO. [29]Tell her she'll be sorry some day. Tell him I'm carrying this dagger in my hand, and when I find him I'll cut off his tongue, his ears, and one eye, put them on a plate and send

---

[29] V.i. 132–134.

him off with them as a present to her. I'll make her sick from having kissed him.

PASQUELLA. Indeed! While the dog barks the wolf feasts.

FLAMMINIO. You'll see.

GHERARDO. Ah, me! Have I come to this? To this! Unhappy me! That traitor Virginio, that double crosser! He took me for a fool. He's slipped a stud in ahead of me. Oh, God! What'll I do?   1300

PASQUELLA. What's the matter, master?

GHERARDO. The matter? Who is that with my daughter?

PASQUELLA. Don't you know her? Isn't it Virginio's daughter?

GHERARDO. Daughter, eh? Daughter. What would my daughter do with daughters? Woe is me!

PASQUELLA. Don't say such bad things. What's the matter? Isn't that Lelia?

GHERARDO. It's a man, I tell you.

PASQUELLA. It can't be. How do you know?   1310

GHERARDO. I saw him with my own eyes.

PASQUELLA. Doing what?

GHERARDO. On top of my daughter, miserable me!

PASQUELLA. Oh, they must be playing.

GHERARDO. Some playing!

PASQUELLA. You saw it was a man?

GHERARDO. Yes, I tell you. I opened the door suddenly and he was in a dressing gown and had no time to close it.

PASQUELLA. If you saw everything then you saw it was a girl.

GHERARDO. I tell you it was a man, with enough to make two   1320
men.

PASQUELLA. What does Isabella say?

GHERARDO. What should she say? The shame of it!

PASQUELLA. You're not letting him go, are you? What are you going to do?

GHERARDO. To do? Denounce him to the governor and have him punished.

PASQUELLA. Maybe he'll run away.

GHERARDO. I've locked him in. But here's Virginio, just the one I want.   1330

SCENE IX.
PEDANT, VIRGINIO, and GHERARDO.

PEDANT. I am assuredly amazed that he hasn't returned to the inn by now. I do not know what to say.

VIRGINIO. Was he armed?

PEDANT. I believe so.

VIRGINIO. He must have been taken. We have a mayor who'd fleece bedbugs.

PEDANT. I do not think they would show such discourtesies to foreigners.

GHERARDO. Ho, Virginio. Was that a good deed? A friendly deed? Was that the family tie you wanted between us? Who did 1340 you think you were tricking? You think I'd put up with that? I'd like . . .

VIRGINIO. What are you complaining about, Gherardo, what did I do? I never tried to get you into the family. You pounded it into my head for a year. Now if you don't want it, don't go through with it.

GHERARDO. Do you still treat me like an innocent lamb? Double crosser, pander, cheat, traitor! The governor will hear of this.

VIRGINIO. Gherardo, those remarks aren't worthy of you, 1350 especially about me.

GHERARDO. And now this rascal doesn't want me to complain! You've become proud because you've found your son, eh?

VIRGINIO. You're not well.

GHERARDO. Oh God! Because I'm not as young as I was? I ought to tear you apart for what you did.

VIRGINIO. May I know what you're talking about?

GHERARDO. Shameless!

VIRGINIO. I've been too patient.

GHERARDO. Thief!   1360

VIRGINIO. Liar!

GHERARDO. You're lying in your throat, but wait!

VIRGINIO. I'm waiting.

PEDANT. Gentlemen, what madness is this?

GHERARDO. Don't hold me back.

PEDANT. And you, sir, put your coat back on.

VIRGINIO. Who does he think he's dealing with? Give me back my daughter.

GHERARDO. I'll cut your throat and ears.

PEDANT. What business does this gentleman have with you?   1370

VIRGINIO. I don't know. Except that a short while ago I sent my daughter Lelia to his house, whom he wanted to be his wife. Now look at him. I'm afraid he's done something to her.

(*Virginio rushes off.*
Gherardo starts after him drawing his dagger.)

PEDANT. Ah, sir! Not weapons!

GHERARDO. Let me go.

PEDANT. What is your complaint?

GHERARDO. This traitor's ruined me.

PEDANT. How so?

GHERARDO. If I don't tear him apart, if I don't quarter him with this dagger . . . 1380

PEDANT. Tell me, please, what the matter might be.

GHERARDO. Now that the traitor's run away come into the house and I'll tell you everything. Aren't you his son's tutor who came to the inn with us?

PEDANT. I am, yes.

GHERARDO. Enter.

PEDANT. Do you guarantee my safety?

GHERARDO. Of course!

ACT V

SCENE I. OUTSIDE GHERARDO'S HOUSE.
VIRGINIO, STRAGUALCIA, SCATIZZA, GHERARDO, and PEDANT.

VIRGINIO. [30]All of you come with me. Stragualcia, you too.

STRAGUALCIA. With arms or without? I'm not armed. 1390

VIRGINIO. Get some weapons from the inn.

SCATIZZA. Master, you'll need a lance with that shield.

VIRGINIO. I don't care about a lance. This is enough for me.

SCATIZZA. This buckler would suit you better since you're in your dressing gown.

VIRGINIO. No, this protects better. Oh, that innocent lamb has put me in a fury. He's killed that poor girl, I'm afraid.

STRAGUALCIA. Here's a good weapon, master. I can spit him like a bird with this pike.

SCATIZZA. Do you want to barbecue him? 1400

STRAGUALCIA. I've had combat experience, so I know that the first thing one must do is store up provisions.

SCATIZZA. Oh? What's this bottle for?

STRAGUALCIA. To refresh the soldiers in case they retreat after the first skirmish.

SCATIZZA. I like that, because it'll happen.

STRAGUALCIA. Let's spit the old man, the girl, the servants and everybody in the house all together like slices of liver! I'll stick the pike up the old man's butt and make it come out his eyes. And I'll pin the others across like thrushes. 1410

---

[30] This scene bears some resemblance to the Viola-Sir Andrew duelling scene (III.iv. 238ff.).

VIRGINIO. The house is open. They must have laid an ambush.

STRAGUALCIA. Ambush? That's bad. I'm more afraid of traps than swords. Here's the tutor coming out.

PEDANT. Leave things to me. I shall settle this matter for you, Master Gherardo.

STRAGUALCIA. Be careful, master, this teacher might be a traitor in cahoots with your enemies. You generally can't trust his kind. Do you want me to begin by spitting him, so's I rack one up?

PEDANT. Master Virginio, why these weapons?   1420

STRAGUALCIA. Ah, ha! Didn't I tell you?

VIRGINIO. What's happened to my daughter? Give her to me. I want to take her home. And have you found Fabrizio?

PEDANT. I have indeed.

VIRGINIO. Where is he?

PEDANT. In here. He has taken a most beautiful wife, if it please you.

VIRGINIO. Wife, eh? Who?

STRAGUALCIA. Quick work! This is rich!

PEDANT. The beautiful and gentle daughter of Gherardo.   1430

VIRGINIO. Oh? Gherardo wanted to kill me just now!

PEDANT. *Rem omnem a principio audies.*[31] Let us go toward the house and you will hear the entire story. Master Gherardo, come outside.

GHERARDO. Virginio, the strangest thing in the world! Come in!

STRAGUALCIA. Spit him? But he's just stewing meat!

GHERARDO. Lay down your arms. This is a laughing matter.

VIRGINIO. Can I do so safely?

PEDANT. Safely, upon my word.   1440

VIRGINIO. Very well. The rest of you lay down your arms, go home, and bring me my clothes.

PEDANT. Fabrizio, come and meet your father.

VIRGINIO. Isn't this Lelia?

PEDANT. No, this is Fabrizio.

VIRGINIO. My son!

FABRIZIO. My father, so long sought for!

VIRGINIO. My son, how many tears I've shed.

GHERARDO. Into the house, where you'll know everything. And let me mention that your daughter is at Clemenzia's house.   1450

VIRGINIO. Oh God, how I do thank Thee.

---

[31] You will hear the whole thing from the beginning.

Scene II. A street in front of clemenzia's house.
crivello, flamminio, and clemenzia.

CRIVELLO. I saw him with these eyes and heard him with these ears in Clemenzia's house.

FLAMMINIO. You're sure it was Fabio.

CRIVELLO. Do you think I don't know him?

FLAMMINIO. Let us go there. If I find him . . .

CRIVELLO. You'll spoil everything. Be patient until he comes out.

FLAMMINIO. God couldn't give me more patience.

CRIVELLO. You'll spoil the broth.   1460

FLAMMINIO. I'm spoiling myself! Tick, tock, tick.

CLEMENZIA. Who's there?

FLAMMINIO. A friend of yours. Come on down.

CLEMENZIA. What do you want, Master Flamminio?

FLAMMINIO. Open up, so I can tell you.

CLEMENZIA. Wait while I come down.

FLAMMINIO. When she opens the door, go inside. See if he is there and call me.

CRIVELLO. Leave it to me.

CLEMENZIA. What are you saying, Signor Flamminio?   1470

FLAMMINIO. What are you doing in the house with my page?

CLEMENZIA. What page? And you, busybody, where are you going? Are you trying to force your way into my house?

FLAMMINIO. Clemenzia, by all that's holy, if you don't give me back . . .

CLEMENZIA. What do you want back?

FLAMMINIO. My page who has run away to your house.

CLEMENZIA. There's no manservant of yours in my house. But there is a maid.

FLAMMINIO. Clemenzia, this is no time to quibble. We've   1480 always been friends. We've had good times together. But this is too important an affair.

CLEMENZIA. This must be the frenzy of love. Come, Flamminio, wait for your anger to cool.

FLAMMINIO. Give me back Fabio, I tell you.

CLEMENZIA. I'll give him back to you.

FLAMMINIO. Good. Have him come down.

CLEMENZIA. Not so wild, by my faith! If I were a young girl and liked you, I'd have nothing to do with you. And what about Isabella?   1490

FLAMMINIO. I wish she were quartered.

CLEMENZIA. Eh! You don't mean that.

FLAMMINIO. Don't mean that? I could tell you plenty about what I saw.

CLEMENZIA. Oh, yes! You young men are the most ungrateful people in the world and deserve everything that happens to you.

FLAMMINIO. That can't be said of me. I may have every other fault, but ungrateful, no. No man lives who hates ingratitude more than I.

CLEMENZIA. I didn't mean you. But in this city there's a 1500 young girl who, flirted with by a Modenese gentleman of your rank, fell so much in love with him that she couldn't see anybody else in the world.

FLAMMINIO. Blessed man! Happy man! I wish I could say the same for me.

CLEMENZIA. It happened that her father sent this poor, love-struck girl away from Modena. She wept endlessly upon leaving, afraid he might forget her. And he did take another girl right away, as though he'd never seen the first one.

FLAMMINIO. He can't be a gentleman. He's more of a traitor. 1510

CLEMENZIA. There's worse. Listen. After a few months the young girl returned here and found that her sweetheart loved another girl, who didn't love him. And she left her home and father and risked her honor in order to serve him. Dressed as a manservant she lived close to her sweetheart.

FLAMMINIO. Did this affair happen in Modena?

CLEMENZIA. You know both parties.

FLAMMINIO. I would rather be this happy man than the Duke of Milan.

CLEMENZIA. What's more, this sweetheart of hers, not recog- 1520 nizing her, used her as a messenger between his beloved and him. And the poor girl submitted to all that in order to please him.

FLAMMINIO. Oh virtuous lady! Oh steadfast love! Truly an example for future centuries! Why couldn't such a thing have happened to me.

CLEMENZIA. Eh? You wouldn't leave Isabella anyway.

FLAMMINIO. I would leave anyone for such a girl. I beg you, Clemenzia, tell me who she is.

CLEMENZIA. Gladly. But first I want to know on your word as a gentleman what you'd do to that poor young girl if such a 1530 thing happened to you. Whether you'd chase her away when you knew what she'd done, or kill her, or judge her worthy of reward.

FLAMMINIO. I swear to you by the sun in the heavens that I would never show myself among lords and gentlemen again if I didn't take such a girl for my wife — whether she were ugly, poor, humble, or the daughter of the Duke of Ferrara.

CLEMENZIA. That's a fine gesture. But do you swear to it?

FLAMMINIO. I swear it, and I'll do it.

CLEMENZIA. (to Crivello.) You be a witness.

CRIVELLO. I have heard, and I know he'll do it.   1540

CLEMENZIA. Now I want to show you who the lady is and who the cavalier. Fabio! Fabio! Come down to your master who's asking for you.

FLAMMINIO. What do you think, Crivello, should I kill the traitor or not? He's certainly a good servant.

CRIVELLO. I'm amazed! What I was thinking turns out to be true. Well then, pardon him. What's to do? That flirt Isabella never wanted you anyway.

FLAMMINIO. You are right.

SCENE III.
PASQUELLA, CLEMENZIA, FLAMMINIO, LELIA, and CRIVELLO.

PASQUELLA. [32]Leave it to me. I'll tell him what you've told   1550
me.

CLEMENZIA. Here, Master Flamminio, is your Fabio. Look at him closely. Do you recognize him? Are you amazed? This same girl is that faithful constant lovestruck young girl I told you about. Look at her closely and see whether you recognize her. Are you struck dumb, Flamminio? What does this mean? That you're the one who valued his lady's love so little. That's the truth. Now don't feel cheated. Admit what I told you is true. And keep your promise to me or I'll spread the word how faithless you are.   1560

FLAMMINIO. I don't believe there was ever a lovelier cheat in the whole world. Could I be so blind that I never recognized her?

CRIVELLO. Who was blinder than I? I could have figured it out a thousand times. A curse on it! Oh, I've been a fool!

PASQUELLA. Clemenzia, Virginio says you're to come to his house right away. He's given a bride to his son Fabrizio who returned today and needs you to set the house in order. As you know, no other women are there.

CLEMENZIA. Bride? Who is she?

PASQUELLA. Isabella, daughter of my master Gherardo.   1570

FLAMMINIO. Who? Gherardo Foiani's Isabella or another one?

PASQUELLA. Another one? I mean her. Flamminio, you'd better learn that the lazy pig never gets the softest fruit.

---

[32] V.i. 260–284.

FLAMMINIO. Are you sure?

PASQUELLA. Positive. I witnessed the whole affair. I saw him give her the ring, they embraced, they kissed and then a great celebration. And before he gave her the ring my mistress gave him . . . what I well know.

FLAMMINIO. When did this happen?

PASQUELLA. Just now. Then they sent me to run and tell Clemenzia and to summon her. 1580

CLEMENZIA. Tell them, Pasquella, that I'll come right away. Go.

LELIA. Oh God, how much good dost Thou give me all at once! I shall die of happiness.

PASQUELLA. Wait a bit. I still have much to do, alas. Now I'm off to buy certain ointments. Oh! I forgot to ask whether Lelia was here in your house. Gherardo's consented to marry her.

CLEMENZIA. You know she's here well enough. Do you want 1590 her to marry that old creep, your master? He ought to be ashamed.

PASQUELLA. You don't know my master well. If you knew how passionate he is you wouldn't talk that way.

CLEMENZIA. Yes, yes, I believe you. You must have found out for yourself.

PASQUELLA. The way you found out about yours. Well now, I'm leaving.

FLAMMINIO. Gherardo wants to marry her?

CLEMENZIA. Alas, yes. You see how unlucky the poor girl is.

FLAMMINIO. Before he marries her he dies. Clemenzia, I do 1600 believe that God has taken pity upon this virtuous girl and upon my soul, so that neither will be lost. Mistress Lelia, if it please you, I would wish no other wife but you. And on my honor as a gentleman I assure you that if I cannot have you I will never marry.

LELIA. Flamminio, you are my lord and well know what I have done and for whom. I have never wanted anything but this.

FLAMMINIO. You have proved it well. Forgive me if I caused you sorrow by not recognizing you. I deeply repent and admit I was wrong. 1610

LELIA. Master Flamminio, you could never do anything that didn't please me.

FLAMMINIO. Clemenzia, I don't want to wait any longer, lest some accident mar this good fortune. I want to marry her right away if she wishes.

LELIA. Most willingly.

CRIVELLO. Thanks be to God! Master Flamminio, are you willing? Know then that I'm a notary. Here are my credentials.

FLAMMINIO. More willing than I ever was to do anything else.

CRIVELLO. Marry her and take her right off to your bedroom. 1920 Oh! I didn't tell you to kiss her yet.

CLEMENZIA. You know what should be done now? You two wait in my house while I explain everything to Virginio — and give Gherardo a bad night!

FLAMMINIO. Please do. And tell Isabella too.

[SCENE IV. (*In front of Gherardo's house.*) *Giglio tries to retrieve his rosary, but Pasquella tricks him again and he leaves.*

SCENE V. *Cittina, Clemenzia's daughter, soliloquizes on what she hears in Lelia's and Flamminio's bedroom.*]

SCENE VI.
ISABELLA, FABRIZIO, and CLEMENZIA.

ISABELLA. I thought surely that you were the servant of a gentleman of this city. You look so much like him that he must be your brother.

FABRIZIO. Others have mistaken me for him today. I was almost beginning to think that the innkeeper had made me a 1630 changeling.

ISABELLA. Here is Clemenzia who wants to speak to you.

CLEMENZIA. It can't be anyone but he. He looks exactly like Lelia.[33] Oh, Fabrizio, my son, welcome home. How are you?

FABRIZIO. Well, my dear nurse. And Lelia?

CLEMENZIA. Very well. Let's go inside. I have much to tell both of you.

SCENE VII. IN FRONT OF CLEMENZIA'S HOUSE.
VIRGINIO and CLEMENZIA.

VIRGINIO. I am so delighted at finding my son that I agree to anything.

CLEMENZIA. This has all been God's will. It's much better this 1640 way than if she married that dry stick Gherardo. Let me go inside to see how things are coming. I left the couple very close together, and alone. Come, come. All is well.

---

[33] In this play, unlike Shakespeare's, brother and sister do not confront each other.

Scene VIII.
STRAGUALCIA, *to the audience.*

Spectators, don't wait for them to come out any more, for any longer would make the longest story ever. If you want to come to supper with us, I'll wait for you at the Madman. And bring money, because you won't be served gratis. But if you don't want to come (and it seems you don't), stay here and enjoy yourselves.

And you, *Intronati*, show us your pleasure.

□ *Some Sources for Further Study*

1. PLAUTUS (c. 250–184 B.C.) — *Casina.* Love pursuits involving a young girl and an older man. *Menaechmi.* Mistaken identity involving twins — more a source for *The Comedy of Errors,* though.
2. TERENCE — *Andria* (*The Girl from Andros,* 166 B.C.). Similarity of exposition between it and *The Deceived Ones.*
3. MATTEO BANDELLO —*Novelle* (1554). Book II, Novella 36.
4. GIOVANBATTISTA GIRALDI CINTHIO — *Hecatommithi* (1565). Decade V, Novella 8.
5. NICCOLO SECCHI — *Gl'Inganni* (*The Deceits,* 1562). A play that bears some resemblance to *The Deceived Ones:* disguises, a duel between cowards.
6. CURZIO GONZAGA — *Gl'Inganni* (1592). Little resemblance to the other Italian dramatic sources except that the heroine, disguised as a youth, calls herself Cesare (Viola calls herself Cesario).
7. *Commedia dell'Arte.* See source 6, p. 166.

hamlet

The main source for *Hamlet* is an earlier play, now lost, known as the source *Hamlet* or, more fashionably, *Ur-Hamlet*. It had been performed by 1589, because in that year Thomas Nash wrote in a prefatory epistle to Robert Greene's *Menaphon*: "yet English Seneca read by candle light yields many good sentences, as 'Blood is a beggar,' and so forth: and if you entreat him fair in a frosty morning he will afford you whole Hamlets, I should say handfulls of tragical speeches."

Other references to *Ur-Hamlet* include this entry from the *Diary* of Philip Henslowe:

"9. of June 1594. . . . R[eceive]d at hamlet. viijs [eight shillings]:" and his mention on June 11 that *Hamlet* was performed by the Lord Chamberlain's men, Shakespeare's company. And in 1596 Thomas Lodge, describing the personification Hate Virtue in his *Wit's Misery and the World's Madness* wrote that he "looks as pale as the vizard [mask] of the ghost which cried so miserably at the Theater like an oyster wife, 'Hamlet, Revenge.' "

The favorite choice for authorship of *Ur-Hamlet* is Thomas Kyd, whose *Spanish Tragedy*, c. 1586, in common with Shakespeare's *Hamlet*, contains a ghost, a revenge motif, simulated madness, a play within a play, and a "faithful" Horatio. Moreover, Nash's preface to *Menaphon* goes on after the lines quoted above to say: "The sea exhaled by drops will in continuance be dry, and Seneca, let blood line by line and page by page, at length must needs die to our stage; which makes his famished followers to imitate the Kidde in Aesop." a clue to the identity of English Seneca. And Robert Armin in his *Nest of Ninnies*, 1608, writes: "There are, as Hamlet says, things called whips in store." presumably alluding to these lines spoken by Hieronimo in *The Spanish Tragedy*:

> And there is Nemesis, and Furies,
> And things called whips,
> And they sometimes do meet with murderers.

If Kyd was not the author of Ur-Hamlet, then he was certainly that author's model.

While we do not have the Ur-Hamlet we do have its and Shakespeare's anterior sources and, equally important, a later play derived from it and from Shakespeare's Hamlet. Sources and derived play together furnish enough material on either side of Ur-Hamlet to help us reconstruct it in part and thereby to credit Shakespeare's earlier sources with their just measure of influence. The original source of all Hamlets is the mythical hero story by Saxo Grammaticus (the Lettered), a Danish historian whose Historica Danica, written in Latin around the close of the twelfth century, looks forward to the Scottish historian Hector Boece (see Macbeth, p. 533) in its mixture of fact and dramatic fiction. Saxo's story matches, at least in broadest outline, the entire plot of Shakespeare's play. Amleth's father, Horvendile, is killed by his wicked brother Feng, who afterwards marries Geruth, the widow of Horvendile. To save himself from Feng, Amleth pretends madness. As a test of his madness he is tempted by a courtesan; as another test he is placed in his mother's bedroom and spied upon, whereupon he kills the spy and upbraids his mother for her faithlessness. He is sent by Feng to England with two companions who carry a message to the King of England ordering his death, but he escapes by a ruse and his companions are killed instead. After becoming betrothed to the English princess he returns to Jutland where he kills Feng's henchmen and finally Feng himself. This ends the part of the story that was dramatized, although the lust and faithlessness of Hermentrude, the Scottish queen and second wife of Amleth, provide Shakespeare at least with additional suggestions for the character of Gertrude.

Shakespeare and the author of Ur-Hamlet possibly knew Saxo's version of the story of Amleth. They certainly knew and found most congenial the version adapted by François de Belleforest as one of his Histoires Tragiques, 1582. (An English translation was not made of Belleforest's Histoire until 1608, and that translation was clearly done with one eye on Shakespeare's play.) Belleforest's plot follows in the tracks of the Saxo story but changes its essence. Saxo presents a precise, reportorial account while Belleforest dramatizes, loosely and in poor proportion perhaps, but with a bustle that points toward the stage. He also adds these techniques and stylistic qualities of his own: moral and psychological observations, as in Feng's preparations for killing his brother; long spun character analyses, as in the early description of Geruth (which should be compared with the one by Saxo); inflated dialogue, like that between Amleth and Geruth in her chamber, reminiscent of Hamlet's "words, words, words"; and action-stopping asides, which point toward soliloquies. One of these asides, on Amleth's power of divination (pp. 407–408), provides a double point of contact with Shakespeare's play: it sets in motion overtones of the supernatural and it links Amleth's power to "the force of his melancholy" and to "the influence of Saturn," the planet symbolic of melancholy.

After the fact is Der Bestrafte Brudermord (Fratricide Punished), a pirated crisscross between Ur-Hamlet and Shakespeare's play, converted into German and first presented, so far as is known, in Dresden in 1626. It begins with a Prologue which presents Night "in a car covered with stars," recalling the melodramatic fancy of Thomas Kyd and, perhaps, Ur-Hamlet; there are some plot differences between this play and Shakespeare's which may also have come from Ur-Hamlet, but that is all conjectural. The essential difference between Hamlet and Der Bestrafte Brudermord is the hasty, stripped quality of the latter, reminiscent of The True Tragedy of Richard III and presumably an echo of the tenor and tone of Ur-Hamlet. Acts I and V presented in the text convey the flavor of the German adaptation and the over-all measure of its contrast with Hamlet. Of detailed interest, Polonius in this version is called Corambus (I.viii) — in a pirated quarto of Shakespeare's play he was called Corambis, perhaps from Ur-Hamlet; and Phantasmo (Act V) seems to be Osric inflated, perhaps a clue that Shakespeare deflated him.

Rich and detailed as Hamlet is, if we combine the elements of The Spanish Tragedy with those of Shakespeare's known sources we find that Shakespeare adds surprisingly little to the plot. Even the Fortinbras subplot may be discerned in the Viceroy-Alexandro-Villuppo subplot of The Spanish Tragedy with its parallel situation of betrayal and happy outcome. As in Henry IV, Part One Shakespeare was left especially free to pour the gold of his sensibility into a well shaped crucible, and the character of Hamlet, in contrast to the Amleth of his sources, gauges the scope of Shakespeare's unstoppered achievement. For Hamlet is a genius and a Renaissance Prince and he sums up the best that the richest period in Western Christian civilization has to offer. The other characters, great and small, are drawn with comparable fullness and their source counterparts can only furnish stick-drawing bases for contrast: Claudius with Fengon, Gertrude with Geruth, Ophelia with "the woman sent by [Amleth's] uncle," Horatio with his namesake in The Spanish Tragedy, and so forth.

The direct sources contribute little to the ideas in Hamlet. For these we must look to the total culture of the Renaissance, and the richness of interaction between Hamlet and Renaissance culture is almost infinite. In its Christian sense Hamlet is the story of a royal scapegoat who must sacrifice himself to save the many (the kingdom of Denmark); in a political sense Hamlet is the model Renaissance Prince and Claudius a usurper like Richard III. As for the other ideas scattered throughout the play, Kenneth Muir, in mentioning a few "examples out of many" finds sources for ideas in Lavater's *Of Ghosts and Spirits*, Nash's *Pierce Penniless*, Swinburne's *Treatise on Wills*, Lyly's *Euphues*, Marlowe's *Dido*, Montaigne's *Essays* and Guazzo's *Civil Conversation*; plus hints from Plutarch, Virgil, Ovid, and possibly Lucan.[1]

To these sources may be added the Platonic Doctrine of Ideas in Hamlet's first long speech; the Medieval concept of *contemptu mundi* in his first soliloquy; Horatio as Castiglione's *Courtier* and Hamlet as Elyot's *The Governour* and their friendship an echo of Tasso's *Manso*; Pico della Mirandola's *Oration on the Dignity of Man* in Hamlet's "What a piece of work is a man"; the Epicurean stoicism of Hamlet's "If it be now, 'tis not to come"; Augustine's *Confessions* and Petrarch's *Meum Secretum* in the gravediggers scene, to mention but a few more. Given the lean contributions of the direct sources, one can only stand back and marvel at how much Shakespeare owed to the Renaissance in general in this play — and at how much the Renaissance in general owed to him.

---

[1] Kenneth Muir, *Shakespeare's Sources* (London: Methuen & Co., 1961), pp. 121–122.

Historica Danica (*Danish History*), c. 1190[1]

translated by Oliver Elton[2]

BOOK III

[Rorik succeeded Hother as King of Denmark and established himself by putting down a revolt of the Kurlanders, Swedes, and Slavs, whom Hother had subjugated earlier. He then appointed two brothers, Horwendil and Feng, to govern Jutland in place of their deceased father, Gerwendil. Horwendil reigned in Jutland for three years, then took to the sea in search of adventure. Koll, King of Norway, pursued Horwendil's fleet for his own greater glory, and they met on an island and fought in single combat. Horwendil killed Koll and then "Pursued and slew Koll(er)'s sister Sela, who was a skilled warrior and experienced in roving."]

He had now passed three years in valiant deeds of war; and, in order to win higher rank in Rorik's favour, he assigned to him the best trophies and the pick of the plunder. His friendship with Rorik enabled him to woo and win in marriage his daughter Gerutha, who bore him a son Amleth.

Such great good fortune stung Feng with jealousy, so that he resolved treacherously to waylay his brother, thus showing that goodness is not safe even from those of a man's own house. [3]And behold, when a chance came to murder him, his bloody hand sated the deadly

---

[1] An arbitrary date based on the general agreement that the work was written during the latter part of the twelfth century and the assumption that it was done shortly after a similar work by Saxo's elder contemporary, Sueno Aggonis (Svend Aageson), whose brief annals, in Latin, were written c. 1185.

[2] Saxo Grammaticus, *The Danish History* (Books I–IX), trans. Oliver Elton (London: D. Nutt, 1894).

[3] I.v. 35–83.

passion of his soul. Then he took the wife of the brother he had butchered, capping unnatural murder with incest. For whoso yields to one iniquity, speedily falls an easier victim to the next, the first being an incentive to the second. Also the man veiled the monstrosity of his deed with such hardihood of cunning, that he made up a mock pretence of goodwill to excuse his crime, and glossed over fratricide with a show of righteousness. Gerutha, said he, though so gentle that she would do no man the slightest hurt, had been visited with her husband's extremest hate; and it was all to save her that he had slain his brother; for he thought it shameful that a lady so meek and unrancorous should suffer the heavy disdain of her husband. Nor did his smooth words fail in their intent; for at courts, where fools are sometimes favoured and backbiters preferred, a lie lacks not credit. Nor did Feng keep from shameful embraces the hands that had slain a brother; pursuing with equal guilt both of his wicked and impious deeds.

Amleth beheld all this, but feared lest too shrewd a behaviour might make his uncle suspect him. [4]So he chose to feign dulness, and pretend an utter lack of wits. This cunning course not only concealed his intelligence but ensured his safety. Every day he remained in his mother's house utterly listless and unclean, flinging himself on the ground and bespattering his person with foul and filthy dirt. His discoloured face and visage smutched with slime denoted foolish and grotesque madness. All he said was of a piece with these follies; all he did savoured of utter lethargy. In a word, you would not have thought him a man at all, but some absurd abortion due to a mad fit of destiny. He used at times to sit over the fire, and, raking up the embers with his hands, to fashion wooden crooks,[5] and harden them in the fire, shaping at their tips certain barbs, to make them hold more tightly to their fastenings. When asked what he was about, he said that he was preparing sharp javelins to avenge his father. This answer was not a little scoffed at, all men deriding his idle and ridiculous pursuit; but the thing helped his purpose afterwards. Now it was his craft in this matter that first awakened in the deeper observers a suspicion of his cunning. For his skill in a trifling art betokened the hidden talent of the craftsman; nor could they believe the spirit dull where the hand had acquired so cunning a workmanship. Lastly, he always watched with the most punctual care over his pile of stakes that he had pointed in the fire. Some people, therefore, declared that his mind was quick enough, and fancied that he only played the

---

[4] II.ii. 171–221; 393–398.
[5] The principal props in Amleth's revenge, though Shakespeare makes no use of them whatever.

simpleton in order to hide his understanding, and veiled some deep purpose under a cunning feint. [6]His wiliness (said these) would be most readily detected, if a fair woman were put in his way in some secluded place, who should provoke his mind to the temptations of love; all men's natural temper being too blindly amorous to be artfully dissembled, and this passion being also too impetuous to be checked by cunning. Therefore, if his lethargy were feigned, he would seize the opportunity, and yield straightway to violent delights. So men were commissioned to draw the young man in his rides into a remote part of the forest, and there assail him with a temptation of this nature. Among these chanced to be a foster-brother of Amleth, who had not ceased to have regard to their common nurture; and who esteemed his present orders less than the memory of their past fellowship. He attended Amleth among his appointed train, being anxious not to entrap, but to warn him; and was persuaded that he would suffer the worst if he showed the slightest glimpse of sound reason, and above all if he did the act of love openly. This was also plain enough to Amleth himself. For when he was bidden mount his horse, he deliberately set himself in such a fashion that he turned his back to the neck and faced about, fronting the tail; which he proceeded to encompass with the reins, just as if on that side he would check the horse in its furious pace. By this cunning thought he eluded the trick, and overcame the treachery of his uncle. The reinless steed galloping on, with the rider directing its tail, was ludicrous enough to behold.

Amleth went on, and a wolf crossed his path amid the thicket. When his companions told him that a young colt had met him, he retorted, that in Feng's stud there were too few of that kind fighting. This was a gentle but witty fashion of invoking a curse upon his uncle's riches. When they averred that he had given a cunning answer, he answered that he had spoken deliberately: for he was loth to be thought prone to lying about any matter, and wished to be held a stranger to falsehood; and accordingly he mingled craft and candour in such wise that, though his words did [not] lack truth, yet there was nothing to betoken the truth and betray how far his keenness went.

Again, as he passed along the beach, his companions found the rudder of a ship which had been wrecked, and said they had discovered a huge knife. "This," said he, "was the right thing to carve such a huge ham;" by which he really meant the sea, to whose infinitude, he thought, this enormous rudder matched. Also, as they passed the sandhills, and bade him look at the meal, meaning the sand, he replied that it had been ground small by the hoary tempests of the

---

[6] Compare with II.ii. 48–167.

ocean. His companions praising his answer, he said that he had spoken it wittingly. Then they purposely left him, that he might pluck up more courage to practise wantonness. [7]The woman whom his uncle had dispatched met him in a dark spot, as though she had crossed him by chance; and he took her and would have ravished her, had not his foster-brother, by a secret device, given him an inkling of the trap. For this man, while pondering the fittest way to play privily the prompter's part, and forestall the young man's hazardous lewdness, found a straw on the ground and fastened it underneath the tail of a gadfly that was flying past; which he then drove towards the particular quarter where he knew Amleth to be: an act which served the unwary prince exceedingly well. The token was interpreted as shrewdly as it had been sent. For Amleth saw the gadfly, espied with curiosity the straw which it wore embedded in its tail, and perceived that it was a secret warning to beware of treachery. Alarmed, scenting a trap, and fain to possess his desire in greater safety, he caught up the woman in his arms and dragged her off to a distant and impenetrable fen. Moreover, when they had lain together, he conjured her earnestly to disclose the matter to none, and the promise of silence was accorded as heartily as it was asked. For both of them had been under the same fostering in their childhood; and this early rearing in common had brought Amleth and the girl into great intimacy.

So, when he had returned home, they all jeeringly asked him whether he had given way to love, and he avowed that he had ravished the maid. When he was next asked where he did it, and what had been his pillow, he said that he had rested upon the hoof of a beast of burden, upon a cockscomb, and also upon a ceiling. For, when he was starting into temptation, he had gathered fragments of all these things, in order to avoid lying. And though his jest did not take aught of the truth out of the story, the answer was greeted with shouts of merriment from the bystanders. The maiden, too, when questioned on the matter, declared that he had done no such thing; and her denial was the more readily credited when it was found that the escort had not witnessed the deed. Then he who had marked the gadfly in order to give a hint, wishing to show Amleth that to his trick he owed his salvation, observed that latterly he had been singly devoted to Amleth. The young man's reply was apt. Not to seem forgetful of his informant's service, he said that he had seen a certain thing bearing a straw flit by suddenly, wearing a stalk of chaff fixed on its hinder parts. The cleverness of this speech, which made the rest split with laughter, rejoiced the heart of Amleth's friend.

---

[7] Compare with III.i. 88–157. The wanton woman in this passage by Saxo might be the source for the songs Ophelia sings: IV.v. 23–66.

Thus all were worsted, and none could open the secret lock of the young man's wisdom. But a friend of Feng, gifted more with assurance than judgment, declared that the unfathomable cunning of such a mind could not be detected by any vulgar plot, for the man's obstinacy was so great that it ought not to be assailed with any mild measures; there were many sides to his wiliness, and it ought not to be entrapped by any one method. Accordingly, said he, his own profounder acuteness had hit on a more delicate way, which was well fitted to be put in practice, and would effectually discover what they desired to know. Feng was purposely to absent himself, pretending affairs of great import. [8]Amleth should be closeted alone with his mother in her chamber; but a man should first be commissioned to place himself in a concealed part of the room and listen heedfully to what they talked about. For if the son had any wits at all he would not hesitate to speak out in the hearing of his mother, or fear to trust himself to the fidelity of her who bore him. The speaker, loth to seem readier to devise than to carry out the plot, zealously proffered himself as the agent of the eavesdropping. Feng rejoiced at the scheme, and departed on pretence of a long journey. [9]Now he who had given this counsel repaired privily to the room where Amleth was shut up with his mother, and lay down skulking in the straw. But Amleth had his antidote for the treachery. Afraid of being overheard by some eavesdropper, he at first resorted to his usual imbecile ways, and crowed like a noisy cock, beating his arms together to mimic the flapping of wings. Then he mounted the straw and began to swing his body and jump again and again, wishing to try if aught lurked there in hiding. Feeling a lump beneath his feet, he drove his sword into the spot, and impaled him who lay hid. Then he dragged him from his concealment and slew him. Then, cutting his body into morsels, he seethed it in boiling water, and flung it through the mouth of an open sewer for the swine to eat, bestrewing the stinking mire with his hapless limbs. Having in this wise eluded the snare, he went back to the room. [10]Then his mother set up a great wailing, and began to lament her son's folly to his face; but he said: "Most infamous of women! dost thou seek with such lying lamentations to hide thy most heavy guilt? Wantoning like a harlot, thou hast entered a wicked and abominable state of wedlock, embracing with incestuous bosom thy husband's slayer, and wheedling with filthy lures of blandishment him who had slain the father of thy son. This, forsooth, is the way that the mares couple with the vanquishers of their mates; for brute beasts are naturally incited to pair indiscrimi-

---

[8] III.i. 190–195.
[9] III.iv. 1–33; 211–216.
[10] III.iv. 34–199.

nately; and it would seem that thou, like them, hast clean forgot thy first husband. As for me, not idly do I wear the mask of folly; for I doubt not that he who destroyed his brother will riot as ruthlessly in the blood of his kindred. Therefore it is better to choose the garb of dulness than that of sense, and to borrow some protection from a show of utter frenzy. Yet the passion to avenge my father still burns in my heart; but I am watching the chances, I await the fitting hour. There is a place for all things; against so merciless and dark a spirit must be used the deeper devices of the mind. And thou, who hadst been better employed in lamenting thine own disgrace, know it is superfluity to bewail my witlessness; thou shouldst weep for the blemish in thine own mind, not for that in another's. On the rest see thou keep silence." With such reproaches he rent the heart of his mother and redeemed her to walk in the ways of virtue; teaching her to set the fires of the past above the seductions of the present.

When Feng returned, nowhere could he find the man who had suggested the treacherous espial; he searched for him long and carefully, but none said they had seen him anywhere. Amleth, among others, was asked in jest if he had come on any trace of him, and replied that the man had gone to the sewer, but had fallen through its bottom and been stifled by the floods of filth, and that he had then been devoured by the swine that came up all about that place. This speech was flouted by those who heard; for it seemed senseless, though really it expressly avowed the truth.

Feng now suspected that his stepson was certainly full of guile, and desired to make away with him, but durst not do the deed for fear of the displeasure, not only of Amleth's grandsire Rorik, but also of his own wife. [11]So he thought that the King of Britain should be employed to slay him, so that another could do the deed, and he be able to feign innocence. Thus, desirous to hide his cruelty, he chose rather to besmirch his friend than to bring disgrace on his own head. Amleth, on departing, gave secret orders to his mother to hang the hall with knotted tapestry, and to perform pretended obsequies for him a year thence; promising that he would then return. Two retainers of Feng then accompanied him, bearing a letter graven on a wood — a kind of writing material frequent in old times; this letter enjoined the king of the Britons to put to death the youth who was sent over to him. [12]While they were reposing, Amleth searched their coffers, found the letter, and read the instructions therein. Whereupon he erased all the writing on the surface, substituted fresh characters, and

---

[11] IV.iii. 42ff.
[12] V.ii. 12–53.

so, changing the purport of the instructions, shifted his own doom upon his companions. Nor was he satisfied with removing from himself the sentence of death and passing the peril on to others, but added an entreaty that the King of Britain would grant his daughter in marriage to a youth of great judgment whom he was sending to him. Under this was falsely marked the signature of Feng.

Now when they had reached Britain, the envoys went to the king, and proffered him the letter which they supposed was an implement of destruction to another, but which really betokened death to themselves. The king dissembled the truth, and entreated them hospitably and kindly. Then Amleth scouted all the splendour of the royal banquet like vulgar viands, and abstaining very strangely, rejected that plenteous feast, refraining from the drink even as from the banquet. All marvelled that a youth and a foreigner should disdain the carefully-cooked dainties of the royal board and the luxurious banquet provided, as if it were some peasant's relish. So, when the revel broke up, and the king was dismissing his friends to rest, he had a man sent into the sleeping-room to listen secretly, in order that he might hear the midnight conversation of his guests. Now, when Amleth's companions asked him why he had refrained from the feast of yestereve, as if it were poison, he answered that the bread was flecked with blood and tainted; that there was a tang of iron in the liquor; while the meats of the feast reeked of the stench of a human carcase, and were infected by a kind of smack of the odour of the charnel. He further said that the king had the eyes of a slave, and that the queen had in three ways shown the behaviour of a bondmaid. Thus he reviled with insulting invective not so much the feast as its givers. And presently his companions, taunting him with his old defect of wits, began to flout him with many saucy jeers, because he blamed and cavilled at seemly and worthy things, and because he attacked thus ignobly an illustrious king and a lady of so refined a behaviour, bespattering with the shamefullest abuse those who merited all praise.

All this the king heard from his retainer; and declared that he who could say such things had either more than mortal wisdom or more than mortal folly; in these few words fathoming the full depth of Amleth's penetration. Then he summoned his steward and asked him whence he had procured the bread. The steward declared that it had been made by the king's own baker. The king asked where the corn had grown of which it was made, and whether any sign was to be found there of human carnage? The other answered, that not far off was a field, covered with the ancient bones of slaughtered men, and still bearing plainly all the signs of ancient carnage; and that he had himself planted this field with grain in springtide, thinking it more fruitful than the rest, and hoping for plenteous abundance; and so, for aught he knew, the bread had caught some evil savour from this blood-shed. The king, on hearing this, surmised that Amleth had spoken truly, and took the pains to learn also what had been the source of the lard. The other declared that his hogs had, through negligence, strayed from keeping, and battened on the rotten carcase of a robber, and that perchance their pork had thus come to have something of a corrupt smack. The king, finding that Amleth's judgment was right in this thing also, asked of what liquor the steward had mixed the drink? Hearing that it had been brewed of water and meal, he had the spot of the spring pointed out to him, and set to digging deep down; and there he found, rusted away, several swords, the tang whereof it was thought had tainted the waters. Others relate that Amleth blamed the drink because, while quaffing it, he had detected some bees that had fed in the paunch of a dead man; and that the taint, which had formerly been imparted to the combs, had reappeared in the taste. The king, seeing that Amleth had rightly given the causes of the taste he had found so faulty, and learning that the ignoble eyes wherewith Amleth had reproached him concerned some stain upon his birth, had a secret interview with his mother, and asked her who his father had really been. She said she had submitted to no man but the king. But when he threatened that he would have the truth out of her by a trial, he was told that he was the offspring of a slave. By the evidence of the avowal thus extorted he understood the whole mystery of the reproach upon his origin. Abashed as he was with shame for his low estate, he was so ravished with the young man's cleverness, that he asked him why he had aspersed the queen with the reproach that she had demeaned herself like a slave? But while resenting that the courtliness of his wife had been accused in the midnight gossip of a guest, he found that her mother had been a bondmaid. For Amleth said he had noted in her three blemishes showing the demeanour of a slave; first, she had muffled her head in her mantle as bondmaids do; next, that she had gathered up her gown for walking; and thirdly, that she had first picked out with a splinter, and then chewed up, the remnant of food that stuck in the crevices between her teeth. Further, he mentioned that the king's mother had been brought into slavery from captivity, lest she should seem servile only in her habits, yet not in her birth.

Then the king adored the wisdom of Amleth as though it were in-spired, and gave him his daughter to wife; accepting his bare word as though it were a witness from the skies. Moreover, in order to fulfil the bidding of his friend, he hanged Amleth's companions on the morrow. Amleth, feigning offence, treated this piece of kindness as a grievance, and received from the king, as compensation, some gold, which he afterwards melted in the fire, and secretly caused to be poured into some hollowed sticks.

When he had passed a whole year with the king he obtained leave to make a journey, and returned to his own land, carrying away of all his princely wealth and state only the sticks which held the gold. On reaching Jutland, he exchanged his present attire for his ancient demeanour, which he had adopted for righteous ends, purposely assuming an aspect of absurdity. Covered with filth, he entered the banquet-room where his own obsequies were being held, and struck all men utterly aghast, rumour having falsely noised abroad his death. At last terror melted into mirth, and the guests jeered and taunted one another, that he whose last rites they were celebrating as though he were dead, should appear in the flesh. When he was asked concerning his comrades, he pointed to the sticks he was carrying, and said, "Here is both the one and the other." This he observed with equal truth and pleasantry; for his speech, though most thought it idle, yet departed not from the truth; for it pointed at the wergild[13] of the slain as though it were themselves. [14]Thereon, wishing to bring the company into a gayer mood, he joined the cupbearers, and diligently did the office of plying the drink. Then, to prevent his loose dress hampering his walk, he girded his sword upon his side, and purposely drawing it several times, pricked his fingers with its point. The bystanders accordingly had both sword and scabbard riveted across with an iron nail. Then, to smooth the way more safely to his plot, he went to the lords and plied them heavily with draught upon draught, and drenched them all so deep in wine, that their feet were made feeble with drunkenness, and they turned to rest within the palace, making their bed where they had revelled. Then he saw they were in a fit state for his plots, and thought that here was a chance offered to do his purpose. So he took out of his bosom the stakes he had long ago prepared, and went into the building, where the ground lay covered with the bodies of the nobles wheezing off their sleep and their debauch. Then, cutting away its supports, he brought down the hanging his mother had knitted, which covered the inner as well as the outer walls of the hall. This he flung upon the snorers, and then applying the crooked stakes, he knotted and bound them up in such insoluble intricacy, that not one of the men beneath, however hard he might struggle, could contrive to rise. After this he set fire to the palace. The flames spread, scattering the conflagration far and wide. It enveloped

---

[13] Fine paid for the murder.
[14] Compare with V.ii. 236–338.

the whole dwelling, destroyed the palace, and burnt them all while they were either buried in deep sleep or vainly striving to arise. Then he went to the chamber of Feng, who had before this been conducted by his train into his pavilion; plucked up a sword that chanced to be hanging to the bed, and planted his own in its place. Then, awakening his uncle, he told him that his nobles were perishing in the flames, and that Amleth was here, armed with his old crooks to help him, and thirsting to exact the vengeance, now long overdue, for his father's murder. Feng, on hearing this, leapt from his couch, but was cut down while, deprived of his own sword, he strove in vain to draw the strange one. O valiant Amleth, and worthy of immortal fame, who being shrewdly armed with a feint of folly, covered a wisdom too high for human wit under a marvellous disguise of silliness! and not only found in his subtlety means to protect his own safety, but also by its guidance found opportunity to avenge his father. By this skilful defence of himself, and strenuous revenge for his parent, he has left it doubtful whether we are to think more of his wit or his bravery.

[The death of Feng ends Book Three of Saxo's history-mythology. Book Four rounds out the life of Amleth. After the fire he hid for a while, fearing the wrath of the people. Then at an assembly of nobles and common people he appeared and revealed the whole story of his persecutions and revenge. The people were so moved that they appointed him King of Jutland.

After that he returned to Britain and his wife, but his murder of Feng had alienated his father-in-law, the king, who years ago had made a pact with Feng that either would avenge the other's death. Accordingly the king sent Amleth to Scotland as his emissary with a letter to the Scottish queen, Hermentrude, whom he said he desired to marry. Hermentrude was a debauched and ruthless woman who, the king believed, would assuredly make love to Amleth and then murder him. The king's letter was stolen from Amleth by one of Hermentrude's warriors, and she secretly altered it to request her to marry not the king but Amleth. Amleth, aware of her deception, nevertheless consented to the marriage. Smitten by the handsome youth, Hermentrude returned with him to Britain where his first wife patiently accepted her rival because "it would be unworthy for her to hate him as an adulterer more than she loved him as a husband." But her father declared war on his son-in-law, and his larger army soon cut down most of Amleth's troops. During the night, however, Amleth had all of his dead soldiers propped up on their horses so that "the wing composed of the dead was as thick as the troop of the living." The next day this ruse so terrified the king's army that — thinking that

Amleth had an unlimited supply of men — they ran away, and the Danes killed the King of Britain.

Meanwhile, Rorik had died and Wiglek, who succeeded him, so harassed Geruth that Amleth was forced to make war upon him. Hermentrude, whom Amleth had come to love deeply, insisted on going with him "and promised she would not forsake him even on the field." But when Amleth was slain by Wiglek "she yielded herself up unasked to be the conqueror's spoil and bride."[15]]

---

[15] A pattern of conduct imitated by Shakespeare's Gertrude.

FRANCOIS DE BELLEFOREST
Histoires Tragiques (Tragic Stories), 1582

VOLUME V, THIRD STORY*

The deception by which Amleth, afterwards King of Denmark, avenged the murder of his father Horvendile by Fengon, brother of Horvendile, along with other incidents in the life of Amleth.

[Rorique, King of Denmark, turned over the government of Jutland to Horvendile and Fengon, sons of the former governor, Gervendile. Horvendile was a peerless sea captain who enjoyed a series of brilliant victories. As a result he was challenged to single combat by Collere, King of Norway. Horvendile slew Collere and also his sister, a famous warrior, and taking all the treasure off the Norwegian ships sent the bulk of it to his sovereign, King Rorique.]

The king, pleased by these gifts and happy to have such a good man as his subject, tried to obligate him forever by means of a great favor and courtesy. He gave him his daughter, Geruth, as a wife, whom this good man loved dearly. The king himself conducted her to Jutland to further honor the marriage. The wedding was celebrated according to ancient custom. To be brief, Amleth was born of this marriage, the one around whom I have constructed this story.[1]

Fengon, brother of this royal son-in-law Horvendile, goaded by envy, felt his heart bursting with spite as much for jealousy as for Horvendile's great reputation as a soldier. He feared he would lose his share of the kingdom — rather, he wanted it all for himself in order to overshadow the memory of his brother's triumphs. Come what may, he planned to kill him.

He succeeded in this quite easily. No one suspected him, all thinking that only virtue and courtesy could come from such a tie

---

* translated by Joseph Satin.
[1] This is the first of many personal interjections. In contrast to Saxo's objective story telling, Belleforest speaks directly to the reader time and again.

of kinship and respectability. But as I have said, the wish to rule respects neither blood nor friendship and cares not for virtue. It is without respect, reverence for laws, or concern for the divine right of kings — for he who usurps another's benefits cannot possibly care about divine right. Wasn't this a subtle and crafty counsellor? But he should have known, later on, that the mother knowing her husband's plans would not put her son within the reach of death.

[2]Fengon, having secretly assembled a band of men, then felt he was strong enough to carry out his plan. He burst in upon his brother at a banquet and treacherously killed him. But first he carefully exonerated himself from so foul a murder. Before putting his bloody hand on his brother he incestuously soiled his brother's bed, thus abusing his wife whose honor he should have upheld with the vigor he debased it. Thus he corrupted her. It is quite true that a man who pursues one vice — and great and detestable sins are linked together — cares nothing about abandoning himself to a worse one. He covered his bold craftiness with the guise of such simplicity that it seemed he had punished his brother because of the honest love he bore his sister-in-law. His love for her excused his crime among the common people; the nobility found it an act of justice. Moreover, Geruth was as gentle and courteous a princess as there was among kingdoms of the North and had never offended a single one of her subjects, be they commoners or courtiers. This adulterer and murderer slandered the dead king, saying he had wanted to kill Geruth, that he was about to do so when he, Fengon, defended the lady and killed his brother, parrying blows struck at the innocent princess without reason or provocation.

He had no lack of witnesses to testify as the slanderer told them to. These were the men in his band, participants in the plot. And in conclusion, instead of pursuing him as an incestuous murderer each of these court followers applauded and flattered him on the prosperity of his fortune. The nobles paid more attention to those false witnesses, those slanderers, than to those who recalled the virtues of the murdered man and might have wanted to punish those villains, his assassins.

[3]Thereupon Fengon, emboldened by such treatment, dared enter into marriage with her whom he had treated violently during the life of the good Horvendile, soiled his name with a double vice while burdening his conscience with a double sin: of incestuous adulterer and murdering thief. And that unfortunate lady who had been wedded to one of the bravest and wisest princes of the North consented to lower herself so vilely as to betray his faith in her, and what is worse, to marry the murderer of her legitimate husband. This made many people

---

[2] I.v. 35–83.
[3] Compare with I.ii. 137–157.

think that perhaps she had instigated the murder because of adulterous pleasure. Where can one find a more shameless woman than a great lady who has abandoned honor? This princess, who earlier was honored by all for her rare virtues and courtesy, and loved by her husband, forgot rank and duty as soon as she lent ear to the ambitious tyrant Fengon. (I do not want to indulge myself against her sex. There are enough who work at exposing them, running down all women for the faults of some. I would say that nature should either have taken away man's desire to couple with them or else given him a spirit strong enough to endure the setbacks he receives from them without complaining so much — so strangely too, since it is his own beastliness that overcomes him. For if woman is the imperfect animal he claims, as unconquerable a beast as he knows so well and proclaims, why are all men mad enough to chase her and stupid and brutish enough to trust her caresses?)

Geruth having thus forgotten herself, Prince Amleth found himself in mortal danger. Abandoned by his mother, ignored by everyone, he felt sure that Fengon would not wait long to send him to Horvendile. [4]To deceive the tyrant, who suspected that when Amleth came of age he would not hesitate to avenge his father's death, Amleth counterfeited madness. By the subtle trick of pretending to have lost his mind, he veiled his plans and protected his life from the treacheries and ambitions of the tyrant. Because he had been at the school of the Roman Prince named Brutus,[5] because he too had pretended madness, Hamlet was able to imitate his ways and wisdom.[6] Since he went daily to the queen's palace, who took more pains to please her lover than care to avenge her husband or to safeguard her son's inheritance, he dirtied himself foully, rolling in the filth and muck around the palace. He rubbed his face with mud in the streets, running through them like a maniac, without a word. His loss of sense, his sheer frenzy, all his actions and gestures had the appearance of a man deprived of all reason and understanding, the kind who served only as a butt for the pages and fancy courtiers in the train of his uncle and stepfather. But meanwhile the young nobleman took note of them, so as to avenge himself one day in a way that would never be forgotten. This was a mark of great wisdom and spirit in a young prince, who was able, in spite of his handicap of indignity and scorn, to become one of the hap-

---

[4] II.ii. 171–221; 393–398.

[5] Lucius Junius Brutus (fl. 500 B.C.) who escaped death from Tarquin the Proud by feigning idiocy (Brutus: stupid) and who lived thereby to drive Tarquin from Rome. This reference dates for us the history of Amleth, at least according to Belleforest.

[6] Compare the narrative technique and analytic method of these next three paragraphs with Saxo, pp. 386–387.

piest kings of his age. (Too, no one was ever reputed wiser or more prudent than Brutus who pretended he had lost his mind. Note that his pretense of ruin came from good counsel and wise deliberation, so as to preserve his property and avoid the rage of his tyrant; also to find a means of deposing King Tarquin and of freeing a people oppressed under the yoke of a long, miserable servitude. To these two you may add King David who pretended madness among the kings of Palestine to save his life. Thus he taught a lesson to those who are unhappy with a king but lack sufficient strength to prevail against him or to gain revenge. Now when I talk of opposing a great man by whom one has been injured, you must understand that this in no way includes our own sovereign whom we may not resist nor plan treason against nor conspire against in any way.

He who wishes to follow this path of pretended madness must speak quite pleasantly to the man he wishes to deceive. He must praise his actions, seem to admire him above all others, and reverse everything in his own nature. To truly seem a fool and counterfeit madness he must dissemble and kiss the hand of someone he would like to bury one hundred feet below the earth. All that is far removed from Christian perfection, which disallows bitter pride or desire for vengeance.)

Amleth thus pretending extreme madness did some things full of high significance and spoke so aptly that a wise man would have soon known what kind of nature produced such special insights. For as he was standing near the fire and cutting blunt sticks in the shape of daggers, someone asked him laughing what those pegs were good for. "I am preparing," he said, "pointed darts to avenge the death of my father." The fools, as I have said, considered this a foolish remark, but clever men with a good sense of smell began to scent what was happening. They understood that this madness concealed a keen subtlety and that it might one day endanger their king; they decided that such rude simplicity veiled a crafty wisdom, that this subtle coloring obscured a brilliant spirit. Therefore they advised the king to try in whatever way he could to take away this coloring and reveal the young man's deception. They decided the best trick to trap him was this: they would put him with a beautiful woman in a secret place and she would try to win him with the most loving and alluring caresses possible. For it is natural that every young man, especially those reared in luxury, will be carried away by the pleasures of the flesh. He will throw himself with such fervor into the enjoyment of physical beauty, that it would be almost impossible to hide his passion or to conceal its grip or to run away from it, whatever trick he may use. If the occasion presents itself, secretly, for passionate excitement, the sensual appetite is forced to obey.

[7]Thus several courtiers were appointed to take the prince to an isolated place in the woods. There they offered him a woman, inciting him to enjoy her embraces and kisses. (These methods are common even to our own time and not only test whether men have lost their wits but also deprive men of strength, virtue, and judgement by means of sensual and infernal bonds forged by their servants, ministers of corruption.) The poor prince would have been in danger of succumbing to this assault, except that a certain gentleman was more loyal to Horvendile than to the tyrant who had set the trap to catch the son in the same way that the father had been caught. This gentleman accompanied the treacherous courtiers more to warn the prince than to ambush and betray him. He knew that the slightest sign Amleth gave of being sane would be enough to cost him his life. And he let Amleth know, by signs, what peril he would be in if he paid the slightest heed to the caresses and affections of the woman sent by his uncle. This amazed the prince, who was struck by the lady's beauty. But she too informed him of the plot, for she had loved him since childhood. She would have been grieved by his demise, and even more so to lose him without enjoying him whom she loved more than herself. Thus the young nobleman deceived the courtiers. And the woman affirmed that he had made no move to possess her, whatever he might say to the contrary. Everyone agreed that he was truly mad, that his brain had no power capable of reason or understanding.

Among the friends of Fengon was one who, unlike all the others, suspected the tricks and subtleties of this pretended madman. He said it was impossible for so clever a gallant and wit, counterfeiting madness, to be discovered by common or obvious devices. Therefore some cleverer and subtler method had to be invented where the trap would be so powerfully attractive that the gallant could not use his customary pretenses. He said he knew of a plan for surprising Amleth, for making him fall into the net and revealing what was in his soul. King Fengon was to pretend to embark on a voyage of great importance. [8]In the meanwhile Amleth would be closeted seemingly alone with his mother in a bedroom. But someone would be hidden in it behind them to hear the proposals, plans, and the schemes laid out by this shrewd and tricky madman. He assured the king that if there was any wisdom still left in the mind of the young man he would quickly reveal it to his mother without fear, out of loyalty to her who had borne and nurtured him.

[9]This friend even offered himself as spy and witness of the counsels between son and mother. Thus he could not be considered someone

---

[7] Compare with III.i. 88–157.

[8] III.i. 190–195.

[9] III.iv. 1–33.

who offered advice but refused to carry it out in the service of his king. The king was much pleased by this plot, deeming it the best way to cure the prince of his madness. And as though taking a long journey he left the palace and went hunting. His adviser secretly entered the queen's bedroom, hiding himself behind an arras a short time before the son was placed there with his mother. Amleth, being clever and cautious, suspected some treachery as soon as he entered the chamber. If he spoke to his mother seriously he might be overheard, so he continued his mad practices, began crowing like a cock and beating his arms the way a cock does his wings. He jumped onto the arras, and feeling someone hidden behind it immediately struck a blow with his broadsword. Then dragging the half dead courtier out he killed him and cut him to pieces. Then he boiled the body and threw the cooked pieces into the large moat full of garbage which served to feed the pigs.

Having found the ambush and punished its inventor, he came back to the queen. She wept in torment, seeing all her hopes destroyed, for whatever her crimes, she greatly grieved to see her only son an object of mockery. Everyone blamed her for his madness, evidence of which she had just seen with her own eyes. It was a great blow to her conscience, and she believed that God had sent this punishment to her because she had joined incestuously with the tyrant murderer of her husband who was now trying in every way to end his stepson's life. She accused herself of a natural indiscretion, a common companion of those who love the pleasures of the flesh too much. (That type of person blots out all reason and heeds only lightness and inconstancy.) [10] Her brief span of pleasure was enough to make her repent forever and to curse the hour when flighty desire had seized her spirit and blinded her eyes to the honor required of a lady of her rank. She had scorned the sacred tradition of noblewomen of breeding and virtue. She recalled the renown and praise given by the Danes to Rinde, daughter of King Rothere, the most chaste and modest lady of her time, who never consented to marry anyone, noble or even prince. She had surpassed all in virtue as she did in beauty, gentle conduct, and grace.

While the queen thus tormented herself, Amleth reentered. He searched all the recesses of the chamber, mistrusting his mother as well as the others. Finding himself alone with her he spoke to her wisely as follows: "What treachery is this, O most infamous of all prostitutes to the desires of a disgusting lecher? Beneath the most deceptive colors you hide the most wicked acts, the most hateful crimes that a person can imagine or commit. What faith can I have in you, who like a

---

[10] III.iv. 34–199. This passage in Belleforest furnishes an interesting intermediary step between Saxo and Shakespeare.

lascivious wanton abandoning all shame, runs into the outstretched arms of this criminal, this traitor tyrant who murdered my father? You caress incestuously the thief of your loyal husband's legitimate bed. You fondle shamelessly a man who calls himself the dear father of your unhappy son — who is now deprived of all comfort unless the gods let him soon escape from a captivity so unworthy of his rank, his noble race, and his illustrious lineage. Is it for a queen, a daughter of a king, to yield to the appetites of beasts, coupling like a mare with the one who overcomes her first husband? You obey the will of an abominable king who has killed a more valiant and better man than he, and who has dimmed, by murdering Horvendile, the glory and honor of the Danes. They are now reduced to nothing, lacking strength or courage since the luster of chivalry has been taken from them by the most cowardly, cruel villain on earth. I refuse to consider him my father, nor can I look upon him as my uncle any longer. Nor are you my beloved mother, for instead of respecting your royal birth, which should have joined us more closely together, you formed an alliance with another, and instead of reflecting honor, you reflect suspicion of having consented to the murder of your husband by marrying his cruel enemy. Ah, Queen Geruth! It is the business of bitches to mate with evil, to desire marriage with many males. Lechery, nothing more, has blotted out from your soul the memory of the worth and virtues of that good king, your husband, my father. Unbridled desire has led the daughter of Rorique to embrace the tyrant Fengon with no respect for the shade of Horvendile, so unworthy of this curious treatment. His brother murdered him treacherously and his wife betrays him like a coward — she whom he treated so well and for whose love he looted Norway of its riches to increase the treasures of the house of Rorique and to make Geruth the wife of the bravest prince in Europe. It is unwomanly and much less the act of a princess in whom gentleness, courtesy, compassion and love ought to glow, to leave her dear son thus abandoned by fortune and in the bloody, murderous clutch of a thief and criminal. Even savage beasts would not do this. Lions, tigers, panthers, and leopards fight to protect their young; birds protect their little ones with beak, claw, and wing. Yet instead of protecting me you expose me to death. Are you not betraying me, knowing the wickedness of the tyrant, whose plans call for the death of his brother's line, yet not even trying to save me by sending me to Switzerland or Norway, or even risking Britain, instead of leaving me the prey of your infamous adulterer. Forgive me, madam, I beg you, if overcome by grief I speak so sharply to you and respect you less than my duty. Having forgotten me and damned the memory of my dead father, you must not be surprised if I exceed the bounds of restraint. You see into what straits I have fallen and how misfortune has led me. Because of your lightness and lack of wisdom I am forced to play the madman and to imitate a madman's ways to save my life instead of taking up arms, following adventure, and trying in every way to gain fame as the true son of the valiant King Horvendile. My gestures, grimaces, and words suggest madness, but not without cause and purpose: I want everyone to think me devoid of sense and reason. I well know that he who had no qualms about killing his own brother, used to killing, eager to rule with his wickedness and treason unchecked, would hardly scruple to kill any descendant of his murdered brother with the same cruelty. It is better, therefore, to pretend madness than to follow my real nature, whose clear and holy light I hide under this shadow just as the sun hides its light behind some heavy cloud during the heat of summer. The face of a madman serves to conceal my gallantry. The gestures of a madman are right for me, so that I may wisely conserve my life for Denmark and for the memory of the former king, my father. For the desire for vengeance is so heavy in my heart that, if I live, I hope to have vengeance so terrible that it will be talked about forever in these lands. But I must wait for the time, the means, and the occasion so as not to rush matters and cause my own ruin before carrying out the scheme that is in my heart. Against an evil, treacherous, and savage man one must use the subtlest craft and devices possible to conceal one's plans. Not having strength on my side, reason must direct my plans, pretences, secrets. In conclusion, madame, do not weep at the sight of my madness. Rather lament the sin you have committed and suffer for that crime which has sullied the former fame and glory of Queen Geruth. For the vices of others need not trouble our consciences; we must repent instead our own misdeeds and follies. For the rest, do not, by all you hold dear, tell the king or anyone else about this. Leave me free to continue, for I hope to bring my plan to its conclusion."

Although the queen was touched to the quick and Amleth had touched sharply on her most sensitive feelings, she forgot pride and a great joy possessed her. For she perceived the noble nature of her son, and such great wisdom gave her hope. On the one hand she did not dare to lift her eyes to look at him, remembering her crime; on the other she would gladly have embraced him because of his wise counsel, forceful enough to quench at once the fires of lust within her which had made her Fengon's mistress. Too, his counsel stirred in her heart a memory of the virtues of her legitimate husband; and her heart lamented at seeing the living image of his virtue and wisdom in this son of hers. Overcome by honest emotion and bathed in tears she finally embraced him with the same love that a virtuous mother uses to kiss and caress her child. After feasting her eyes on Amleth for a long time, as though held by some deep contemplation and some great astonishment, she spoke to him as follows:

"I well know, my son, that I have wronged you in allowing this marriage to Fengon, the cruel tyrant and murderer of your father, my faithful husband. But when you consider my slight chance of resistance, the treachery of those in the palace, the slight trust we could place in the courtiers all committed to him, the army he had ready if I had refused the alliance, you would excuse me instead of accusing me of lechery and inconstancy. You would excuse rather than suspect that Geruth had consented to the murder of her husband. I swear to you that if it had been in my power to resist the tyrant, that the spilling of my blood had been able to save the life of my lord and husband, I would have done so with as willing a heart as has already prevented the shortening of your life, which being taken I would no longer want to live in this world. Now, since you are of sound mind, I see a greater chance of avenging your father. Nevertheless, my dear son, if you care for yourself and for the memory of your father — even if you wish to do nothing for her who does not, in your opinion, deserve the name of mother — I beg you to conduct this affair wisely. Do not be hasty nor too excitable in this undertaking. Do nothing more than what is reasonable to carry out your plan. You see that you can trust almost no one. And I have no woman to whom I might dare tell a single secret which would not be reported to your enemy who, no matter how much he pretends to love me in order to enjoy my caresses, nevertheless mistrusts and fears me because of you. Nor is he so stupid as to be easily convinced that you are mad. If you do anything that smacks of seriousness or wisdom, no matter how secretly, he will know of it at once. I fear that the demons might be showing him what is happening between us now — so contrary and unhappy is our fortune — or that this murder you have committed might cause our ruin. I shall pretend to know nothing about it and will also keep secret your wisdom and your brave undertaking. I pray that the gods guide your heart, my son, direct your counsel, and protect your undertaking. Would that I might see you enjoying the property that is yours and the crown of Denmark that the tyrant has stolen from you; would that I might rejoice in your prosperity; would that I might have the joy of seeing how bravely you take vengeance on the murderer of your father and those who favored and supported him."

"Madam," replied Amleth, "I will have faith in your words and will not inquire further into your affairs. I beg you, by the love you owe your son, no longer to respect this lecher, my enemy, whom I will kill although every demon watches over him. Nor can any of his courtiers help him. They will themselves depart this life when he dies, having been dishonest accomplices in the death of my father, companions in Fengon's treason, cruelty and murder. It is justice that all who traitorously killed their king pay justly for their crimes. You know, madame, how Hothere, your grandfather, father of the good King Rorique, conquered Guimon and burned him alive because that cruel villain had treated his lord Gevare the same way when he captured him treacherously at night. Who does not know that traitors and perjurers cannot be trusted at all and that treaties made with a murderer are like spider webs and have the same value as a thing not promised? But when I lay hands on Fengon, that will not be treason nor a crime, since he is not my king nor lord. I will punish him justly as a vassal who has acted disloyally against his lord, his prince. Since glory is the reward of the virtuous, and the honor and praise of those who serve their natural prince, why should not scorn and shameful death be the reward of traitors, those who dare lay violent hands on sacred and divine kings who represent the majesty and image of the gods? In sum, glory is the crowning virtue, the reward of constancy; it shuns meanness, cowardice, and base and vile natures. Thus, either I will die gloriously, or else sword in hand, flushed with victory and triumph, I will tear out the lives of those who make mine unhappy and who dim the luster of my birthright and the glorious memory of my ancestors. What is the use of living, when shame and infamy are executioners who torture our conscience, when cowardice turns the heart away from brave undertakings and diverts the spirit from its honest desire for lasting glory and praise? I know that it is foolish to pick a fruit before its time or to try to enjoy a good thing before it is earned. But I expect to do so well and hope for so much of Fortune which has guided my life until now, that I cannot die without revenging myself on my enemy — who will himself be the instrument of his own ruin. Fortune will help me to carry out what I could not dare to undertake alone."

After a time Fengon arrived at court, as though he had come from some far journey, and inquired about the courtier who had undertaken to spy out Amleth's pretended madness. To his astonishment Fengon could get no news or even rumors about him. [11]For this reason he asked the madman if he knew what could have become of this courtier.

The prince was incapable of lying. None of the answers he gave during his pretended madness ever departed from the truth, for every noble soul is the mortal enemy of falsehood. The prince answered therefore that the courtier Fengon was seeking had gone down to the privy where the pigs had found him choked by the filth of the place, and had filled their bellies with him.

---

[11] IV.iii. 17–41.

One would have suspected anything except that this murder was done by Amleth. Still, Fengon felt uneasy and kept imagining this madman was playing some evil trick upon him. He would have killed Amleth willingly but feared his grandfather, King Rorique. [12]Too, he hesitated to offend the madman's mother, who loved and caressed Amleth and seemed heartbroken to see him thus bereft of his senses.

However, wanting to dispose of him, he sought the aid of a foreigner and decided to make the King of Britain his minister of murder. For he preferred to sully his friend's reputation with this evil deed rather than commit so infamous a crime himself. [13]He resolved to send Amleth to the King of Britain and to ask the king by letter to end Amleth's life.[14] Amleth, learning that he was being sent to Britain, immediately suspected the purpose of this journey. Therefore he went to the queen and begged her not to seem unhappy at his departure, rather to pretend to be happy, as though free of the presence of someone who, although she loved him, was killing her with grief, seeing him deprived of all use of reason. He urged the queen to hang tapestries from nails in the main hall at his departure, and to keep his pegs for him, which he had sharpened when he said he was making arrows to avenge the death of his father. Finally he instructed her to stage his last rites and funeral at the end of one year, assuring her that at that time she would see him return and that she would be happy and more than satisfied because of his journey. [15]With him were sent two of Fengon's faithful ministers, carrying letters carved in wooden tablets telling the King of England to kill Amleth. But the clever Danish prince visited the hold while his companions were sleeping and learned of his uncle's treachery and the wickedness of those courtiers who were leading him to the slaughter. He effaced those words about his murder and in their place he carved an order to the British king to have his companions hung and strangled. And not content with shunting to them the death planned for him he added an order that the British king give his daughter in marriage to the nephew of Fengon.

When they arrived in Britain, the ambassadors presented themselves to the king and gave him their master's letters. When he saw the contents, he pretended that all was well and waited his chance to carry out the wishes of Fengon. In the meantime he treated the Danes very graciously and paid them the honor of dining with them. (For the kings in those days were not so supercilious as now and did not hold

---

[12] IV.vii. 5–12.
[13] IV.iii. 42ff.
[14] III.iv. 200–210.
[15] V.ii. 12–53.

their persons so dear, nor were so chary of their presence as one sees these days, when petty kings and nobles are as hard to approach as a monarch of Persia used to be, who covered his face with a veil and never allowed it to be seen.)

While his companions enjoyed themselves at table among the British, the subtle Amleth discourteously refused to touch any meat and drink served at the royal table. Everyone was astonished to see the young stranger show no respect for the finest food and drink offered at the king's table, to reject them as something filthy, bad tasting, and worse prepared.

The king, who concealed his thoughts at that time, had his guests taken to their chamber and ordered one of his servants to hide himself there in order to report to him the conversation of the strangers upon going to bed.

As soon as they were alone in the room, Amleth's companions asked him why he had scorned the food and drink presented to him at table and had failed to honor the great king's table with suitable courtesy and honor. They added that he had done wrong and brought dishonor to the king who had sent them, for it seemed as though Fengon were sending men to Britain forewarned about being poisoned by this honorable king. The prince, who had done none of this without a purpose, answered them bluntly: "Why should I want to eat bread dipped in human blood, to dirty my throat with the rust of iron, and to taste meat which has the stench and corruption of putrified human bodies and recalls the taste of carrion cast long ago into a charnel house? And why should I respect a king who has the look of a slave and a queen who has done three things worthy of a common woman, things more proper to a chambermaid than to one of great majesty." And he added several sharp, painful comments about the king and queen and also about others who had attended the reception for the ambassadors from Denmark.

[16]Amleth had said nothing that was not true — as you will learn hereafter — for at that time all of those Northern countries were under the rule of Satan, and an infinity of enchanters were there. There was no well raised son who did not know enough demonology to serve his turn, even as in Gothland and Biarmy. There were great numbers who knew more things than the sanctity of the Christian religion allows. You see this clearly if you read the histories of Norway and Gothland. Thus Amleth, while his father lived, was indoctrinated into that art whereby the evil spirits abuse mankind and inform princes of things already past.

---

[16] Compare the following six paragraphs with the concept in I.v. 166–167. They might also have been one source for the ghost of Hamlet, Sr.

I do not intend to discuss here the elements of divination, and whether this prince through the force of his melancholy[17] had received this power of divining things that he could not have known otherwise. Philosophers who comment on judgment attribute the power of divination to those who, under the influence of Saturn,[18] often blurt out things unconsciously, and then when their fervor ebbs cannot even remember who said them. That is why Plato says that many diviners and poets, after the power and impulse of their passion cools, can hardly understand what they have written — although during their transports they speak so well and in so orderly a fashion that authors and critics put them in the first rank and praise their discourses and subtle arguments.

I also do not care to speculate upon a belief held by several that a rational soul can become the domicile of lesser demons and by this means can learn the science and secrets of all natural and human things. And I give less credit to stories of governors supposedly helped in this world by magicians by whose means they claim to work miracles.

What Amleth divined would have seemed a miracle, for it will be found later to be perfectly true, if the devil had not perfect knowledge of past events. But I will not commit so great a sin or fall into so great an error as to tell you that the devil knows the future. You might wish to compare predictions made through conjecture with those made through the spirit of God and announced by the holy prophets, who alone have enjoyed the miraculous knowledge of the future and have recounted the miracles and secrets of the Almighty. Only frauds, who want to give God's enemy, that father of lies, divinity attribute to him the knowledge of what will come. They cite the conversation of Saul with the Witch, though that is the only example found in the Holy Scriptures and is especially put there for the contemplation of wicked men. It is not sufficient to support a universal truth. Indeed, magicians themselves confess that they cannot predict the future according to universal rule, but rather by signs borrowed from similar cases. By these conjectures, they claim, they can offer some opinions about coming events.

But all this is supported by as weak a prop of conjecture, and has as thin a basis, as any foolish recent experience that lends itself to fiction. And an intelligent man would be very foolish, especially one who would embrace the purity of Christian doctrine, to seek for truth among magicians or to rely on any of their appearances or fallacious writings.

---

[17] In Belleforest, *"pour la vehemence de la melancholie."* An anticipation, and perhaps suggestion, of the celebrated melancholy of Hamlet.

[18] Saturn, in astrology, the patron planet of melancholy.

As for the effects of magic, I will grant them some truth, seeing history full of such effects and that the Holy Bible bears witness to them and defends them. Consider how the laws of the Gentiles and commands of emperors have taken magic into account, and the heretic Mohammed, the friend of the devils, whose craft he used to tyrannize the Orient, has laid heavy penalties on those who practice these illicit and damnable arts.

Let us leave this subject and return to Amleth, brought up in these follies according to the manner of his country. When his companions heard his reply they reproached him and said he could not give greater evidence of his madness than by scorning what was praiseworthy and by rejecting what everyone else considered important. They added that he had grossly forgotten his position to thus accuse so excellent a man as the king and to slander the queen, one of the noblest and wisest princesses in this part of the world. They threatened to have him punished as his tactlessness deserved. But Amleth, continuing his pretended madness, made fun of them and said that he had done and suggested nothing more than the truth.

In time the king was informed of all this by the eavesdropper. He straightway judged that Amleth, in speaking so ambiguously, was either quite mad or else one of the wisest men of his time to be able to reply so pointedly to his companions. The better to know the truth, the king had the baker brought to him who had made the bread for his table. He asked the baker where the wheat had been cut for this bread, and whether that field had any sign or evidence of combat there to suggest human blood had spilled upon it. He was told that not far from there was a field laden with the bones of men killed there a while ago in some savage battle, that one could still see a piled up mound of them. Since that land was richer and more fertile because of the dead bodies, they reaped the finest wheat there every year that could be chosen for the king's table. The king, confirming the truth of the young prince's first words, then asked where the pigs fed which had been served at his table. And he learned that they had escaped from their sty and had fed upon the corpse of a thief who had been killed for his crimes. The king, astonished, then inquired where the water came from to make the beer served at his table. And he learned that just at the head of the stream used for this beer, excavations had uncovered swords and rusty armor which gave a bad taste to the beverage.

(I wish to tell you at this point of the prophecies of Merlin concerning Amleth, made before Amleth was one year old. However, if you have been following what has been said up to now, it is hardly difficult to perceive that the minister of Satan had been serving him here, giving those blunt answers to the young man. Yet such service is all

quite natural — to those who know what life is about and who do not
bother to dream about the future.)

When all these things were explained to him, the king was moved by
a curiosity to know why the Danish nobleman had said that he had the
look of a slave. He suspected that the Dane was accusing him of low
birth, that his father had not been a king. In order to clear up his
suspicion he sent for his mother. Bringing her secretly to a chamber
where they were all alone, he begged her to tell him on her honor
the circumstances of his birth. The good lady, certain that no one had
ever known of her affairs, swore to him that the king alone could boast
of having enjoyed her embraces. But he who had earlier been convinced of the truth of Amleth's statements threatened his mother with
force if she did not confess everything to him willingly. He then
learned that she had formerly given her body to a slave and thus made
the slave the father of the King of Britain. Thereupon the king was
astonished and ashamed.

(I leave this event for those people to think about who value themselves higher than other people, and to wonder whether there might
not be a skeleton in their closets. If they inquire more deeply than
they should, they might learn something that they do not wish to
know.)

The king concealed his shame and kept a tight rein on himself, not
wishing to make a public scandal of his mother's lasciviousness. He
preferred to leave the great sin unpunished rather than to seem contemptible to his subjects, who might have overthrown him, not wanting a bastard to reign over their fine kingdom.

Though the king was distressed to learn of his dilemma he was
highly pleased by the subtlety and noble nature of the prince. He
went to find him and asked him why he had blamed the queen for
three things more proper to a slave than to the dignity of a great lady.
The king was not content with just the pain of knowing himself a
bastard. He wanted to hear why Amleth accused the lady he loved
most in the world; he wanted to learn about things that distressed him
as much as his own misfortune. And thus he learned that his queen
was the daughter of a chambermaid. Amleth cited several foolish ex-
pressions of hers which not only revealed her peasant blood and low
condition but also how her humors reflected the low birth of her
parents. Her mother, he assured the king, was still in servitude.

The king, full of admiration for this young man whom he considered
far above the common run of men, gave him his daughter in marriage.
Thus the letters forged by the crafty Amleth were obeyed. And the
next day the British king had Fengon's two courtiers hanged, according
to the wishes of his dear friend. Although Amleth was delighted by
his trick, he pretended to be deeply upset and threatened to avenge

this insult. To appease him the king gave him a great heap of gold, which the prince ordered melted down and put into two hollowed staffs for a purpose you shall hear about later on.

Of all the royal wealth he carried none to Denmark except these staffs, making the journey to his homeland as soon as one year was ended. First, however, he got leave to do so from his future father-in-law, promising to return as soon as possible in order to marry the British princess.

When Amleth arrived at his uncle's palace he entered the hall just as they were celebrating his own funeral. The mourning ceased and everyone was greatly surprised. For they all thought him dead, for which most of them were glad, knowing the pleasure his death gave to Fengon. A few had been lamenting, remembering the glory of the late Horvendile whose victories could never be forgotten. These men, therefore, were delighted to learn that the rumor of Amleth's death was false, that the tyrant had not yet triumphed over the true heir of Denmark, that instead the gods had returned Amleth his sanity for the good of his kingdom.

Astonishment changed to laughter, and everyone at the funeral banquet made fun of his companion for having been so easily deceived about Amleth's death. They wondered whether the prince had recovered his sanity and asked him what had happened to the two who had journeyed to England with him. He answered them by showing them the two hollowed staffs filled with gold — given him by the King of Britain to appease him for the death of his companions — and said, "Here are the two who accompanied me."

Several there who already suspected his true nature were certain that he had played some masterful trick on those two and that he had saved himself by casting them into the grave dug for him. Fearing to follow the victims' fate or of courting evil fortune they left the palace — which was well for them, in view of the exploits of the prince on the day of his funeral. [19]That was the final day for those who gloated over his downfall. For those were quick to celebrate anything, and the arrival of Amleth offered them yet another chance to raise their goblets. The prince played the part of steward and gentleman-servant. He kept their bowls filled and served the courtiers in such a way that they all became besotted with wine and stuffed with food. They had to lie down right at the dinner table, so senseless and ill-mannered had they become from too much drinking — a vice well known in Germany and all the nations of the North. Amleth, seeing so great an opportunity to avenge himself on his enemies by a single coup, while at the same time protected by the actions, gestures, and customs of a

---

[19] Compare with V.ii. 236–338.

madman, seized opportunity by the forelock. Seeing those bodies sodden with wine lying on the ground like pigs, some sleeping, others vomiting the wine that they guzzled, he took the huge tapestry hung on the wall, dropped it on top of them and nailed it to the wooden floor. At each corner he hammered in the pegs which he had sharpened and which were spoken of before. These served as anchors, holding the men so that in spite of all their efforts they could not possibly break loose. Then he swiftly set fire to the four corners of the royal palace so that none of those in the hall could possibly escape. Each would purge his sins in a fire which would dry up all of the wine he had swigged; each would die blanketed in the heat of the flames.

Having seen to this the young man, knowing that his uncle had retired to his lodgings before the end of the banquet, went there and entered his uncle's chamber. He seized the sword of his father's murderer and left his own in its place, which someone had nailed to the scabbard during the banquet. Then, turning to Fengon he said, "I am amazed, corrupt king, at the way you sleep when your palace is on fire. Flames have consumed all the courtiers who helped with your cruelties and hateful tyrannies. I do not know how you can have such confidence in your fortune as to sleep seeing Amleth near you, armed with the shafts he sharpened a long time ago and now quite ready to avenge the crime and treachery done by you to his lord and father."

At last Fengon knew the truth about his nephew, hearing him speak thus sanely and seeing the naked sword in his hand. As Amleth lifted it to cut off his life, he jumped lightly from his bed and grasped his nephew's nailed sword. While he struggled to pull it from the scabbard Amleth gave him a terrible blow across the neck which toppled his head to the ground. "This is the reward of all your kind," said Amleth, "to die violently this way. And on your journey to Hell do not fail to tell your brother, whom you traitorously murdered, that his son sent you there as a messenger. Comforted by this deed his soul may rest content among the blessed spirits and may free me of the obligation which bound me to pursue this vengeance against my own kin. It was you, my uncle, who cut me off from the friendship and ties of blood."

(In truth a man who is courageous and worthy of eternal praise, if armed with crafty madness and pretending to have lost his mind, will deceive thereby the wisest, subtlest, and cleverest of men. Thus he may not only guard his life against a tyrant's traps and pressures but also uniquely and unexpectedly avenge the murder of his father. By conducting his affairs with prudence and carrying out his plans with great bravery and constancy he will cause men of good will to debate which is more worthy of him: his constancy and magnanimity, or his wisdom in designing, shaping, and putting his plans into perfect operation a long time after they were formulated.)[20]

[As in Saxo's version, Amleth tells the people his story and they make him King of Denmark (not Jutland, as in Saxo). In this version he kills the King of Britain for treachery and returns to Denmark with two wives, the second being Hermetrude, Queen of Scotland. Viglere, his uncle, makes war on him and kills him. Hermetrude marries the victor.]

---

[20] This moralizing paragraph matches the final lines of Saxo, Book III. Characteristically Belleforest continues in this vein for another page, which is here omitted.

ꙮ ANONYMOUS, C. 1626[1]

Fratricide Punished, or Prince Hamlet of Denmark*

translated by Horace Howard Furness, 1877

ACT I.

SCENE I. — TWO SOLDIERS.

FIRST SENTINEL. Who's there?

SECOND SENTINEL. A friend!

FIRST SENT. What friend?

SEC. SENT. Sentinel!

FIRST SENT. O ho, comrade! — if thou com'st to relieve me, I wish the time may not be so long to thee as it has been to me.

SEC. SENT. Eh! comrade, it is not so cold now.

FIRST SENT. Cold or not, I've had a hell's sweat here.

SEC. SENT. Why so frightened? — that's not right in a soldier He must fear neither friend nor foe; no, nor the devil himself.   10

FIRST SENT. Yes, but just let him grab thee behind, and thou'lt soon learn to pray *Miserere Domine*.

SEC. SENT. But what is it that has particularly frightened thee?

FIRST SENT. I'll tell thee. I've seen a ghost in the front of the castle, and he wanted twice to pitch me down from the bastion.

SEC. SENT. Then relieve guard, you fool! A dead dog doesn't bite. I'll see whether a ghost that has neither flesh nor blood can hurt me.

FIRST SENT. Just look out, if he shows himself to thee again, what he does to thee. I'm off to the watch-house. Adieu!   20

(Exit.)

---

* *Der Bestrafte Brudermord oder: Prinz Hamlet aus Dännemark*

[1] The date of its earliest authentic mention, when it was acted in Dresden. Some conjecture dates it as early as 1603, but without supporting evidence. The translation appears in the Variorum edition of *Hamlet*.

SEC. SENT. Only be off: perhaps you were born on a Sunday: they say such folks can see all kinds of ghosts. I'll now mount guard. (*Healths proclaimed within, to the sound of trumpets.*) Our new King makes merry. They are drinking healths.

SCENE II. — GHOST OF THE KING APPROACHES THE SENTINEL, AND FRIGHTENS HIM, AND THEN EXIT.

SEC. SENT. O holy Anthony of Padua, defend me! I see now what my comrade told me. O Saint Velten (*sic*)! if my first round were only over, I'd run away like any rogue. (*Sennet and drums within.*) If I only had a drink of wine from the king's table, to put out the fear and fire in my heart! (*Ghost from behind gives him a box on the ear, and makes him drop his musket,* 30 *and exit.*) The devil himself is after me. Oh, I'm so frightened, I can't stir!

SCENE III. — HORATIO AND SOLDIERS.

SEC. SENT. Who's there?

HOR. The watch!

SEC. SENT. Which one?

HOR. The first!

SEC. SENT. Stand, watch! Corporal, forward, to arms!
(*Francisco and Watch come forward,
and give the word from the other side.*)

HOR. Sentinel, look well to thy post; the Prince himself may perhaps go the rounds. Be caught sleeping, and it may cost thee the best head thou'st got.   40

SEC. SENT. Ah! if the whole company were here, not a man of them would go to sleep; and I must be relieved, or I'll run away, though I be hanged to-morrow on the highest gallows.

HOR. What for?

SEC. SENT. Oh, your worship, there's a ghost here which appears every quarter of an hour; it set upon me so that I fancy myself a live man in purgatory.

FRAN. Just what the sentinel last relieved told me.

SEC. SENT. Ay, ay; only just wait a bit. It won't keep away long.
(*Ghost goes across the stage.*)

HOR. On my life it is a ghost, and looks just like the late king of   50 Denmark.

FRAN. He bears himself sadly, and seems as if he wanted to say something.

HOR. There is some mystery in this.

SCENE IV. — HAMLET.

SEC. SENT. Who's there?

HAM. Hush!

SEC. SENT. Who's there?

HAM. Hush!

SEC. SENT. Answer, or I'll teach thee better manners.

HAM. A friend! 60

SEC. SENT. What friend?

HAM. Friend to the kingdom.

FRAN. By my life, it is the Prince.

HOR. Your highness, is it you or not?

HAM. What! are you here, Horatio? What brings you here?

HOR. Your highness, I have gone [*visitirt*] the rounds to see that every one is at his post.

HAM. That's like an honest soldier, for on you rests the safety of the king and kingdom.

HOR. Your highness, a strange thing has happened: regularly 70 every quarter of an hour a ghost appears; and, to my mind, he is very like the dead king, your father. He does much harm to the sentinels on this post.

HAM. I hope not; for the souls of the pious rest quietly till the time of their resurrection.

HOR. Yet so it is, your highness. I've seen it myself.

FRAN. And he frightened me very much, your highness.

SEC. SENT. And he gave me a sound box on the ear.

HAM. What time is it?

FRAN. It is just midnight. 80

HAM. Good! — just the time when ghosts, if they walk, show themselves. (*Healths again, and trumpets.*) Holloa! what is this?

HOR. I fancy that at court they are still jolly with their toasts.

HAM. Right, Horatio! My father and uncle makes himself bravely merry with his followers [*Adhoerenten*]. Alas, Horatio! I know not why it is that since my father's death I am all the time so sick at heart, while my royal mother has so soon forgotten him, and this King still sooner, for while I was in Germany he had himself quickly crowned king in Denmark, but with a show of right he has made over to me the crown of Norway, and appealed to the 90 election of the states.

SCENE V. — GHOST.

SEC. SENT. Oh dear! here's the ghost again!

HOR. Does your highness see now?

FRAN. Your highness, don't be frightened.

(*Ghost crosses the stage, and beckons to Hamlet.*)

HAM. The Ghost beckons me. Gentlemen, stand aside a little. — Horatio, do not go too far away. I will follow the ghost, and see what he wants.   (*Exit.*)

HOR. Gentlemen, let us follow him to see that he take no harm.
(*Exeunt.*)

Ghost beckons Hamlet to the middle of the stage,
and opens his jaws several times.

HAM. Tell who thou art, and say what thou desirest.

GHOST. Hamlet!

HAM. Sir!

GHOST. Hamlet!   100

HAM. What desirest thou?

GHOST. Hear me, Hamlet, for the time draws near when I must betake myself again to the place whence I have come; hear, and give heed to what I shall relate to thee.

HAM. Speak, thou sacred shade of my royal father!

GHOST. Then hear, my son Hamlet, what I have to tell thee of thy father's unnatural death.

HAM. What? unnatural death?   110

GHOST. Ay, unnatural death! Know that I had the habit, to which nature had accustomed me, of walking in my royal pleasure-garden every day after my noontide meal, and there to enjoy an hour's rest. One day when I did this, behold, my brother came, thirsting for my crown, and had with him the subtile [*subtilen*] juice of so-called Hebenon [*Ebeno*]. This oil, or juice, has this effect: that as soon as a few drops of it mix with the blood of man, they at once clog the veins and destroy life. This juice he poured, while I was sleeping, into my ear, and as soon as it entered my head I had to die instantly; whereupon it was given out that I had 120 had a violent apoplexy. So was I of my kingdom, my wife, and my life robbed by this tyrant.

HAM. Just Heaven! If this be true, I swear to revenge thee.

GHOST. I cannot rest until my unnatural murder be revenged.
(*Exit.*)

HAM. I swear not to rest until I have revenged myself on this fratricide.

SCENE VI. — HORATIO, HAMLET, FRANCISCO.

HOR. How is it with your highness? Why so terror-stricken? Mayhap you have been hurt [*alterirt*].

HAM. Yes, verily, and indeed beyond measure.

HOR. Has your highness seen the Ghost?   130

HAM. Ay! truly have I seen it, and also spoken to it.

HOR. O Heaven! this bodes something strange.

HAM. He revealed to me a horrible thing; therefore I pray you, gentlemen, stand by me in a matter that calls for vengeance.

HOR. Of my fidelity you are surely convinced: only disclose it to me.

FRAN. Your highness cannot doubt as to my help either.

HAM. Gentlemen, before I reveal the matter you must swear an oath on your honor and faith.

FRAN. Your highness knows the great love I bear you. I will willingly risk my life if you wish to avenge yourself.   140

HOR. Only just propose the oath to us: we will stand by you faithfully.

HAM. Then lay your finger on my sword: We swear!

HOR. AND FRAN. We swear!

GHOST (within). We swear!

HAM. Holla! what is this? Once more: We swear!

HOR. AND FRAN. We swear!

GHOST. We swear!

HAM. This must mean something strange. Come, once more,   150 and let us go to the other side. We swear!

HOR. AND FRAN. We swear!

GHOST. We swear!

HAM. What is this? Is it an echo which sends back our own words? Come, we will go to another spot. We swear!

GHOST. We swear!

HAM. Oh! I hear now what this means. It seems that the Ghost of my father is displeased at my making the matter known. Gentlemen, I pray you, leave me; to-morrow I will tell you all.

HOR. AND FRAN. Your highness, farewell.   160

(Exit Francisco.)

HAM. Horatio, come here.

HOR. What is your highness's will?

HAM. Has the other gone?

HOR. Yes, he has gone.

HAM. I know, Horatio, that thou hast been at all times true to me; to thee I will reveal what the Ghost told me, — namely, that my father died a violent death. My father, — he who is now my father, — murdered him.

HOR. O Heaven! what do I hear?

HAM. Thou knowest, O Horatio! that my departed father was   170 wont every day after his noontide meal to sleep an hour in his pleasure-garden. The villain, knowing this, comes to my father and pours into his ear, whilst he is asleep, the juice of Hebenon, from which powerful poison my father at once gave up the ghost. This the accursed dog did in order to obtain the crown; but from this moment I will begin a feigned madness, and, thus feigning, so cunningly will I play my part that I shall find an opportunity to avenge my father's death.

HOR. If so it stands, I pledge myself to be true to your highness.

HAM. Horatio, I will so avenge myself on this ambitious man   180 and adulterer and murderer that posterity shall talk of it for ever. I will now go, and, feigning madness, wait upon him until I find an opportunity to effect my revenge.   (*Exeunt.*)

SCENE VII. — KING, QUEEN, HAMLET, CORAMBUS, AND COURT.

KING. Although our brother's death is still fresh in the memory of us all, and it befits us to suspend all state-shows, we must nevertheless change our black mourning suits into crimson, purple, and scarlet, since my late departed brother's widow has now become our dearest consort. Let, then, every one show himself cheerful, and make himself a sharer of our pleasure. But you, Prince Hamlet, do you be content. See here, how your lady   190 mother is grieved and troubled at your melancholy. We have heard, too, that you have determined to go back to Wittenberg; do not do so for your mother's sake. Stay here, for we love you and like to see you, and would not that any harm should happen to you. Stay with us at court, or, if not, you can betake yourself to your kingdom, Norway.

QUEEN. Dearly-beloved son, Prince Hamlet, it greatly astonishes us that you have thought to go away from here, and to betake yourself to Wittenberg. You know well that your royal father has lately died, and if you leave us, the grief and melancholy which   200 now oppress our hearts will only be the greater. Then, dearest son, stay here, and every pleasure and delight, if so it please you, shall be freely yours.

HAM. Your command I will obey with all my heart, and will here remain and not depart.

KING. Do so, dearest Prince. But, Corambus, how is it with your son Leonhardo? Has he already set out for France?

COR. Ay, gracious lord and King, he has gone already.

KING. But is it with your consent [*Consens*]?

COR. Ay, with over-consent, with middle-consent, and with   210 under-consent. Oh, your majesty, he got an extraordinary, noble, excellent, and splendid consent from me.

KING. As he has your consent, it may go well with him, and may the gods bring him safe back again. But we have it now in mind to hold a carouse [*Carisell*], whereby our dearest spouse may forget her melancholy. But you, Prince Hamlet, with the other nobles, must show yourself mirthful. For the present, however, we will make an end of our festivities, for the day is dawning to put to flight black night. You, however, dearest consort, I shall accompany to your bed-chamber.　　　　　　　　　　　　　　　　**220**

Come, let us, arm in arm and hand in hand,
Enjoy the pledge that love and rest demand.

ACT V.

SCENE I. — HAMLET.

HAM. Unfortunate Prince! how much longer must thou live without peace. How long dost thou delay, O righteous Nemesis! before thou whettest thy righteous sword of vengeance for my uncle, the fratricide? Hither have I come once more, but cannot attain to my revenge, because the fratricide is surrounded all the time by so many people. But I swear that, before the sun has finished his journey from east to west, I will revenge myself on him.

SCENE II. — HORATIO.

HOR. Your highness, I am heartily glad to see you here again in **230** good health. But, I pray you, tell me why you have returned so soon.

HAM. Ah, Horatio, thou hast nearly missed never seeing me again alive; for my life was already at stake, had not the Almighty power specially protected me.

HOR. How? What says your highness? How did it happen?

HAM. Thou knowest that the King gave me two fellow-travellers as servants to accompany me. Now it happened that one day we had contrary [*contrairen*] winds, and we anchored at an island not far from Dover. I went on shore with my two companions to get **240** a little fresh air. Then came these cursed rascals, and would have taken my life, and said that the King had bribed them to it. I begged for my life, and promised to give them as great a reward, and that, if they reported me to the King as dead, I would never again go near the court. But there was no pity in them. At last the gods put something into my head; whereupon I begged them that,

before my death, I might offer a prayer, and that when I cried
'Shoot!' they were to fire at me. But just as I gave the word I fell
on the ground, and they shot each other. Thus have I this time
escaped with my life. My arrival, however, will not be agreeable 250
to the King.

HOR. Oh, unheard-of treachery!

SCENE III. — PHANTASMO.

HAM. Look, Horatio, this fool is far dearer to the King than my
person. Let us hear what he has to say.

PHAN. Welcome home, Prince Hamlet! Do you know the
news? The King has laid a wager on you and the young Leonhardus. You are to fight together with rapiers, and he who gives the
other the first two[sic] hits is to win a white Neapolitan horse.

HAM. Is this certain what thou sayest?

PHAN. Yes, it is precisely so.   260

HAM. Horatio, what can this mean? I and Leonhardus are to
fight one another. I fancy they have been quizzing this fool, for
you can make him believe what you choose. — See here, Signora
[sic] Phantasmo, it is terribly cold.

PHAN. Ay, ay, it is terribly cold.   (*His teeth chatter.*)

HAM. It is not so cold now as it was.

PHAN. Ay, ay, it is just the happy medium.

HAM. But now it is very hot.   (*Wipes his face.*)

PHAN. Oh, what a terrible heat! (*Also wipes away the perspiration.*)

HAM. And now it is neither really hot, nor really cold.   270

PHAN. Yes, it is now just temperate [*temperirt*].

HAM. There, thou seest, Horatio, one can quiz him as much
as one likes. — Phantasmo, go back to the King and say that I
will shortly wait on him. (*Exit Phantasmo.*) Come now, Horatio,
I will go at once and present myself to the King. But ah! what
means this? Blood flows from my nose, and my whole body
shakes. Oh, woe's me! what has happened?   (*Swoons.*)

HOR. Most noble prince! — O Heaven! what means this? —
Be yourself again, your highness. Most noble Prince, what's the
matter? What ails you?   280

HAM. I know not, Horatio. When I thought of returning to the
court, a sudden faintness came over me. What this may mean is
known to the gods.

HOR. Ah, Heaven grant that this omen [*Omen*] portends nothing bad!

HAM. Be it what it may, I'll none the less go to the court, even
though it cost me my life.   (*Exit.*)

SCENE IV. — KING, LEONHARDUS, PHANTASMO.

KING. Leonhardus, get thyself ready, for Prince Hamlet will soon be here too.

LEON. Your majesty, I am already prepared, and I will do my 290 best.

KING. Look well to it! Here comes the Prince —

SCENE V. — HAMLET, HORATIO.

HAM. All happiness and health to your majesty!

KING. We thank you, Prince. We are greatly rejoiced that melancholy has in some degree left you. Wherefore, we have arranged a friendly match between you and the young Leonhardus. You are to fight with rapiers, and the one who makes the first three [sic] hits shall win a white Neapolitan horse, with saddle and trappings.

HAM. Your majesty must pardon me, for I have had but little practice with rapiers. But Leonhardus has just come from France, 300 where, doubtless, he has had good practice. Therefore you must excuse me.

KING. Prince Hamlet, do it to gratify us, for we are desirous of knowing what sort of feints the Germans and French use.

SCENE VI. — QUEEN.

QUEEN. Gracious lord and King, I have to announce to you a great calamity!

KING. Heaven forbid! What is it?

QUEEN. Ophelia went up a high hill, and threw herself down, and killed herself.

LEON. Alas! Unfortunate Leonhardus! thou has lost within a 310 short space of time both a father and a sister! Whither will misfortune lead thee? I could for grief wish myself dead.

KING. Be comforted, Leonhardus. We are gracious to you; only begin the contest. — Phantasmo, bring the rapiers. — Horatio, you shall be umpire.

PHAN. Here is the warm beer.

HAM. Well, then, Leonhardus, come on, and let us see which of us is to fit the other with the fool's cap and bells. Should I, however, make a mistake [einen Exces begehen], pray excuse [excusiren] me, for it is long since I have fought. 320

LEON. I am your highness's servant: you are only jesting.

(During the first bout they fight fair. Leonhardus is hit.)

HAM. That was one, Leonhardus!

LEON. True, your highness! Now for revenge [Allo Revange]! (*He drops his rapier, and seizes the poisoned sword which lies ready [parat], and gives the Prince a thrust in carte [die Quarte] in the arm. Hamlet parries [pariret] on Leonhardus, so that they both drop their weapons. Each runs for his rapier. Hamlet gets the poisoned sword, and stabs Leonhardus mortally.*) Woe is me! I have a mortal thrust. I receive what I thought to pay another. Heaven have mercy on me!   330

HAM. What the devil is this, Leonhardus? Have I wounded you with the rapier? How does this happen?

KING. Go quick, and bring my beaker with wine, so that the combatants may refresh themselves a little. Go, Phantasmo, and fetch it. (*Descends from the throne. Aside.*) I hope that when they both drink of the wine they will then die, and no one will know of this trick.

HAM. Tell me, Leonhardus! how has this come about?

LEON. Alas, Prince! I have been seduced into this misfortune by the King. See what you have in your hand! It is a poisoned   340 sword.

HAM. O Heaven! what is this? Preserve me from it!

LEON. I was to have wounded you with it, for it is so strongly poisoned that who gets the least wound from it must straightway die.

KING. Ho, gentlemen! rest yourselves a little and drink. (*While the King is rising from his chair and speaking these words, the Queen takes the cup out of Phantasmo's hand and drinks, the King cries out.*) Ho! what keeps the goblet? — Alas, dearest wife! what are you doing? This wine is mixed with deadly poison! Oh   350 woe! what have you done?

QUEEN. Oh woe! I am dying!

(*The King stands in front of the Queen.*)

HAM. And thou, tyrant, shalt bear her company in death.

(*Hamlet stabs him from behind.*)

KING. Oh woe! I receive my evil reward!

LEON. Adieu [*sic*], Prince Hamlet — Adieu, world! I am dying also. — Ah, forgive me, Prince!

HAM. May Heaven receive thy soul! for thou art guiltless. But this tyrant, I hope he may wash off his black sins in hell. — Ah, Horatio, now is my soul at rest, now that I have revenged myself on my enemies! 'Tis true I have also received a hit on my arm,   360 but I hope it will signify nothing. I grieve that I have stabbed Leonhardus; but I know not how I got the accursed sword into my hand. But as is the labor, so is the reward; he has received his pay. Nothing afflicts me more than my lady mother. Still, she too has deserved this death for her sins. But tell me, who gave her the cup that has poisoned her?

PHAN. I, Prince. I too brought the poisoned sword; but the poisoned wine was to be drunk by you alone.

HAM. Hast thou also been an instrument in this misery? Lo, there! thou also hast thy reward!　　　　　　　　　　　　370

(*Stabs him dead.*)

PHAN. Stab away, till your sword is tired!　　[*dass euch die Klinge verlahme!*]

HAM. Alas, Horatio! I fear that my completed revenge will cost me my life, for I am sore wounded in the arm. I am growing very faint; my limbs grow weak; my legs will no longer stand; my voice fails me; I feel the poison in all my limbs. But I pray you, dear Horatio, carry the crown to Norway, to my cousin, the Duke Fortempras [*sic*], so that the kingdom may not fall into other hands. Alas! Oh woe! I die!

HOR. Alas, most noble Prince! still look for aid! — O Heaven! 380 he is dying in my arms! Alas! what has not this kingdom suffered for ever so long from hard wars? Scarcely is there peace but internal disturbance, ambition, faction, and murder fill the land anew. In no age of the world could such a lamentable tragedy ever have happened as has now, alas! been enacted at this court. With the help of the faithful councillors I will make all preparations that these high personages shall be interred according to their rank. Then will I at once [*cito*] betake myself to Norway with the crown, and hand it over as this unfortunate Prince commanded.　　　　　　　　　　　　390

So is it when a King with guile usurps the throne,
And afterward with treachery maintains it as his own.
With mockery and scorn he ends his days abhorred,
For as the labor is, so follows the reward.

☐ *Some Sources for Further Study*

Properly speaking, everything that contributed to Renaissance culture could be pertinent to this play. The following dramas are specifically suggested for those who might wish to trace the dramatic tradition of the royal scapegoat from its classical sources to its culmination in *Hamlet.*

1. AESCHYLUS (c. 525–455 B.C.) — The *Oresteia.* In this trilogy Orestes, Clytemnestra, Aegisthus, and Elektra bear comparison

with Hamlet, Gertrude, Claudius, and Ophelia, as do Aeschylus's interplay between vengeance and love.

2. SOPHOCLES (c. 497–407 B.C.) — *Oedipus Tyrannus*. The theme of the royal scapegoat in a classical setting.

3. SENECA (c. 1 B.C.–65 A.D.) — *Oedipus*. Here the ghost of Laus reveals the truth to Oedipus.

4. THOMAS KYD — *The Spanish Tragedy* (c. 1586).

Othello

From the standpoint of sources *Othello* is unique. Instead of a major central source ringed by a cluster of tangential ones, as in the English history plays, or a scatter gun barrage of peer sources as in *The Merchant of Venice*, it uses one brief central source — the rest is Shakespeare; so that by laying source and play side by side we may feel the full power of the transforming hand. The source is a novella by Giovanbattista Giraldi Cinthio, the seventh story of the third Decade of his *Hecatommithi*, no known translation of which existed in Shakespeare's day. In the absence of any contrary evidence we may assume that Shakespeare read the story in the original, for the same reasons canvassed in the headnote to *The Merchant of Venice*. Wisps of the Cinthio story have been traced to *The Arabian Nights* and to the *Gesta Romanorum*, but the core of the plot is his own, perhaps suggested by an actual event.

Shakespeare follows its basic situations but varies some details. Cinthio's Moor falls in love with Disdemona in Venice and despite parental objections marries her, as in Shakespeare. Disdemona accompanies the Moor to Cyprus, en route incurring the hatred of an ensign who determines to revenge himself on her and on the Moor; in Shakespeare Iago plots revenge for a varied patchwork of reasons. Cinthio's captain is demoted for drawing his sword on a soldier, and Disdemona's request to reinstate him gives the ensign the wedge he needs to separate Disdemona and the Moor; the ensign steals Disdemona's handkerchief, leaves it near the captain's bed, and he tries unsuccessfully to return it to her; Desdemona loses her handkerchief and Cassio gives it to his mistress to copy. The Moor and Othello both eavesdrop while the captain (Cassio) laughs and jokes too far off to be heard; both Othellos see the handkerchief in the hands of another lady and arrange for the murder of the captain, who receives a wound in the leg. At this juncture Shakespeare backs away from his source. In Cinthio the ensign kills Disdemona and makes it look like an accident, justice overtakes the Moor in Venice and the ensign later on in his homeland,

and for a different crime. In Shakespeare Othello kills Desdemona, confesses openly, and Iago is apprehended at once.

Besides a better knit plot and a more righteous ending, Shakespeare alters his source by means of characters. He adds a jealous suitor, Roderigo, and Montano, and Ludovico, that classic portrait of a Venetian diplomat, for whom "a lady in Venice would have walked barefoot to Palestine for a touch of his nether lip." He also fattens the roles of Brabantio and Emilia, to their marked advantage and that of the other characters around them.

Characterization in Othello plumbs deep into the kind of unconscious prodding Shakespeare had used in Julius Caesar. The prime example is the way Iago infects Othello with his own animal attitudes until Othello too uses animal images (III.iii. 270) and finally, during his interview with Ludovico, "Goats and monkeys!" explodes irrelevantly from the deepest recesses of his mind. All of the main characters provide brilliant contrast to the pale stereotypes of the source story. Cinthio's "virtuous" Disdemona is raised almost to the archetype of virtue; the "valiant" Moor takes on such noble stature that his toppling into chaos is titanic; the "handsome" ensign "with the most evil character in the world" becomes a boon companion, diabolic puppeteer, and petty sniper almost too complex for definition; his pallid wife is transformed into a contented compromiser who, however, instinctively hits upon the darkest truths; and even little touches like the "daily beauty" of Michael Cassio charge minor figures with sudden life.

If Cinthio's spare novella of domestic woe may be said to contain any idea, it is the insular one expressed by Disdemona: "I am very much afraid that I'll turn out to be an example to young people not to marry against their parents' wishes; and that Italian ladies will learn because of me not to go with a man who is segregated by nature, Heaven, and way of life from us." While Desdemona echoes no such sentiments, Othello does (III.iii. 263–265) and Iago rarely omits them. For the major ideas of Othello, however, Shakespeare again turned from his source to the world of the Renaissance, and from the Christian aspect of that world he drew the concept of a divine Desdemona versus a demon Iago with the cloudy soul of Othello hung in the balance. The play is thick with Christian imagery, and Cassio's first greeting to Desdemona:

> Hail to thee, lady! And the grace of Heaven,
> Before, behind thee, and on every hand,
> Enwheel thee round! (II.i. 85–87)

suggests her symbolic Christian role; similarly Othello's pact with Iago (III.iii. 460 ff.) patently caricatures a pact with the devil.

It is generally agreed that Shakespeare was somewhat indebted to Pliny's *Natural History* for the exotica of Othello's language, and one of the most pertinent Pliny passages has been included here to give the reader some idea of how it may have been reshaped by Shakespeare's sensibility. There is lively debate as to whether Shakespeare read Pliny in Latin or whether he might have known the translation done by Philemon Holland in 1601. Kenneth Muir in Appendix II of his *Shakespeare's Sources* presents some telling arguments, but in the absence of conclusive evidence a modern translation is presented here.

Much has been written about the language of *Othello*, and a final comparison between the language of Shakespeare and that of his source may at least serve as a showcase for Shakespeare's poetic achievement in this play. In describing the birth of love between the Moor and Disdemona Cinthio writes:

> A virtuous lady of marvelous beauty named Disdemona fell in love with him, attracted not by physical desire but rather by his virtue. And he, conquered by the lady's beauty and nobility of mind, fell equally in love with her.

And Shakespeare:

> She gave me for my pains a world of sighs.
> She swore, in faith, 'twas strange, 'twas passing strange,
> 'Twas pitiful, 'twas wondrous pitiful.
> She wished she had not heard it, yet she wished
> That Heaven had made her such a man. She thanked me
> And bade me, if I had a friend that loved her,
> I should but teach him how to tell my story
> And that would woo her. Upon this hint I spake.
> She loved me for the dangers I had passed,
> And I loved her that she did pity them.

(I.iii. 159–168)

☙ GIOVANBATTISTA GIRALDI CINTHIO

Hecatommithi[1] (One Hundred Stories), 1565

DECADE THREE, STORY SEVEN*

[2]There was once in Venice a most valiant Moor who for his personal bravery and great skill and judgment in warfare was highly regarded by those patricians whose Republic prized manly acts above all else. [3]A virtuous lady of marvelous beauty named Disdemona fell in love with him, attracted not by physical desire but rather by his virtue. And he, conquered by the lady's beauty and nobility of mind, fell equally in love with her. Their love was so ideal as to unite them in matrimony, although the lady's parents did what they could to get her to marry another. While they remained in Venice the couple lived together in such harmony and peace that they never exchanged a single harsh word.

[4]It happened that the Signory of Venice was sending replacement troops to the island of Cyprus, and it chose the Moor to captain the soldiers being sent. Although he was overjoyed at the offer — since so high an honor was generally given only to noble, brave, and faithful citizens of the highest merit — nevertheless his joy diminished when he considered the length and difficulty of the voyage ahead, fearing that it might make Disdemona ill. The lady, however, whose only happiness in the world was the Moor's happiness, was delighted by this testimony to her husband's ability from so powerful and noble a Republic. She could hardly wait for the time when her husband and his troops would set out and she would accompany them. But she noticed to her sorrow that the Moor was troubled, and not knowing the cause

---

* translated by Joseph Satin.

[1] The stories in this collection are divided into "decades" or groups of ten. Decade Three treats of the unfaithfulness of husbands and wives. Despite its title, the complete collection contains one hundred and thirteen stories.

[2] I.ii. 18–24.

[3] I.iii. 90–198.

[4] I.iii. 221–275. Note how Shakespeare distills the events of this paragraph into a single brief passage.

she asked him one day at dinner: "Why is it, my Moor, that since the Signory paid you so high an honor you have been so melancholy?" The Moor told her: "My delight in the honor," said the Moor, "is lessened by the love I bear you, for I am faced with one of two problems: either I take you with me on the perilous sea; or to spare you that, I leave you in Venice. The first choice would grieve me because every suffering and every danger you encounter would be a torment to me. The second choice, leaving you behind, would make me hateful to myself since, leaving you, I should be leaving my life."

"Come now, my husband," said Disdemona when she understood the situation, "what thoughts are these that come into your mind? I would want to come with you wherever you went, even if I had to pass through fire in my smock instead of merely sailing with you in a safe ship. If there is suffering and danger, I want to be at your side. And I would deem myself little loved by you if you thought of leaving me in Venice, safe rather than by your side when there is danger. I want you to prepare for our journey with all of the peace of mind befitting one of your rank." The Moor embraced her joyfully and with an affectionate kiss told her: "May God continue this love of ours for a long time, my blessed wife."

Shortly after, all the necessary gear was prepared and packed for the journey. He and his wife and his troops entered the galley and, sails to the wind, their journey to Cyprus began on a calm sea. [5]Among the troops there was an ensign, a handsome figure of a man but with the most evil character in the world. The Moor liked him very much, knowing nothing about his wickedness. For although he had the vilest soul, his appearance and his lofty, elegant language so masked the evil of his heart that on the surface he seemed a Hector or an Achilles. [6]He too was taking his wife with him to Cyprus. She was a lovely, honorable young girl, and since too she was Italian, became very dear to the Moor's wife who spent most of her time with her. In the same company was a captain dearly liked by the Moor. He used to go to the Moor's home often and dine with him and his wife. Therefore the wife, who knew how much her husband liked him, expressed a deep affection for him, which pleased the Moor very much. [7]The evil ensign, with no regard at all for the kindness shown his wife, nor for friendship, nor faith, nor for the debt he owed the Moor, fell passionately in love with Disdemona and turned all his thoughts to the problem of possessing her. He did not dare to reveal his passion for fear that if the Moor found out he would kill him straightway. Instead he

[5] I.i. 155–158.
[6] Compare with II.i. 85–167.
[7] Compare this motivation with I.i. 6–33; II.i. 297–308.

tried as subtly as he could to show the lady in various ways that he loved her. But she, who thought only of the Moor, paid no heed to the ensign nor to anyone else. Everything he did to make her aware of him went unnoticed. Whereupon he imagined that this was because she was in love with the captain, and decided to get rid of him. [8]Not only did he bend his mind in that direction, but his love for the lady changed into the bitterest hatred. He pondered deeply how he might kill the captain and also prevent the Moor from enjoying Disdemona. After turning various evil ideas over in his mind, he finally decided to accuse her of adultery letting her husband know that the captain was her lover. Knowing full how deeply the Moor loved Disdemona and felt friendship for the captain he realized that he could only achieve his aims through clever deception. And he set about to wait for the proper time and place to begin his evil undertaking.

[9]A short while later the Moor demoted his captain for having drawn his sword against a soldier on guard duty and wounding him. [10]The punishment grieved Disdemona and she tried to reconcile her husband and the captain time and again. [11]In the meantime the Moor confided to the evil ensign that his wife was pestering him so much about the captain that he feared he would finally give in to her. The villain used that incident to spin his web, saying: "Perhaps Disdemona has some reason for looking kindly on him." "Why so?" asked the Moor. "I don't want to interfere between husband and wife," replied the ensign, "but if you keep your eyes open you will see for yourself." And there was nothing the Moor could do to make the ensign explain any farther.

[12]His words so pierced the soul of the Moor that, worrying about what they might mean, he grew quite melancholy. One day when his wife tried to soften his anger against the captain, pleading with him not to throw away the service and friendship of so many years for a small fault — especially since the wounded soldier and the captain were friends again — the Moor turned upon her in a rage and said: "A fine thing, Disdemona, your deep concern for him. He is not your brother, in fact no relative at all, and yet your heart yearns for him." The lady said with courteous humility: "I do not want to make you angry with me. I only ask this because I grieve to see you deprived of so dear a friend — as you yourself told the captain he was. He has not committed a crime so serious as to deserve so much anger.

---

[8] II.i. 309ff.
[9] II.iii. 1–249.
[10] II.iii. 306–338.
[11] III.iii. 1–240.
[12] III.iv. 33–98.

But you, my Moor, are so passionate by nature that little things can move you to anger and revenge." The Moor replied still more angrily: "I can prove things that wouldn't be believed! I'll have such revenge that I'll be satisfied!" The lady was astonished by those words, and seeing her husband enraged at her as never before she said humbly: "I asked you for this with only good intentions. Since I do not want you angry at me any more I will not say another word about it."

[13]The Moor regarded this request as a sign of favor for the captain and supposed that what the ensign had told him must have meant that Disdemona loved the captain. Full of melancholy he went to that villain and tried to make him speak more openly. The ensign, resolved to harm this poor lady, after pretending not to want to speak for fear of displeasing seemed overcome by the Moor's pleading and said: "I must admit that it pains me beyond belief to have to tell you something that will hurt you more than anything else. But since you want me to, and out of concern for your honor, since you are my ruler, I am forced to speak out. I will do my duty now and answer you fully. Your lady wants your captain back in your good graces because of the pleasure she has with him whenever he comes to your house, since she has come to hate the color of your skin."

[14]These words cut to the roots of the Moor's heart, but to learn more (although he already believed the ensign because of the suspicion already bred in his soul) he said angrily: "I do not know what holds me back from tearing out your tongue, daring to slander my wife this way!" "Captain," said the ensign, "I told myself not to expect any other treatment for this well-meant deed. But because of everything I owe you, and my concern for your honor, I say again that this is how things stand. Your lady, with a show of loving you, has so shut your eyes to things that you haven't seen what you should — which is exactly why I am telling you the truth. What is more, the captain himself has told me about it, the way people do who are not completely happy unless others know about it. If I had not been afraid of your anger," he went on, "I should have done him the service of killing him, which he deserves. But since telling you what nobody has a better right to know brings me such injustice I wish I had kept silent and thus escaped your wrath." The Moor in total rage said: "If you don't make me see with my own eyes what you have told me, I'll make you wish you were born a mute!"

"It would have been easy to do," the villain suggested, "when he used to visit your house. But now that you have booted him out, not for what he deserves but rather for something trivial, it will be awk-

---

[13] III.iii. 258–277.
[14] III.iii. 359–405.

ward at best. I assume he still enjoys Disdemona, whenever you give him the opportunity. But he has to act much more cautiously now that you hate him than he did before. Still, I have some hope of being able to show you what you do not want to believe."

With these words they parted. The unhappy Moor as if pierced with the sharpest arrow went home to await the day when the ensign would show him what would torment him forever. No less troubled was the cursed ensign, for the lady's chastity — as he learned from observing her — made him wonder whether he would ever find a way to make the Moor believe his lies.

His mind explored various directions and came up with a new evil. [15]The Moor's wife often visited the ensign's wife, as already noted, and stayed with her a good part of the day. She wore a handkerchief that he knew the Moor had given her, worked upon with great skill in the Moorish manner. It was most precious to her and equally so to the Moor, and seeing this he resolved to steal it from her and thereby prepare a deadly trap for her. He had a three year old daughter who loved Disdemona dearly. One day when that unhappy lady was at this monster's home he took his daughter in his arms and held her out to the lady. She took the child and pressed her to her bosom while this traitor, with skillful sleight of hand, took the handkerchief from her sash so deftly that she did not notice. Then he went off full of joy.

Disdemona went home knowing nothing of this, and occupied with other thoughts forgot about the handkerchief. [16]For the next few days she looked for it without finding it and began to grow terrified that the Moor might ask her for it, as he often did. [17]The evil ensign waited a little while, then went to the captain's house and with wicked cunning left the handkerchief at the head of his bed. The captain would not have seen it if it had not fallen right underneath his foot while he was getting up the next morning. He could not imagine how it had come into his home, knowing it belonged to Disdemona. He decided to return it to her, and waiting until the Moor was out he went to his back door and knocked.

Fate seemed to be conspiring with the ensign to bring about the death of the unhappy lady. For just at that moment the Moor came home and hearing the knock went to the window and called out angrily: "Who is knocking there?" The captain, hearing the Moor's voice and afraid he would come down and punish him further, ran away without a word. The Moor descended the staircase, opened the door and ran out into the street but found no one. He reentered his

---

[15] Compare with III.iii. 282–320.
[16] III.iv. 23–29.
[17] III.iii. 321–322.

house in an evil mood and asked his wife who that was who was knocking. The lady answered truthfully enough that she did not know. "It looked like the captain," said the Moor. "I do not know," she said, "whether it was he or someone else." The Moor's rage returned and he trembled so with anger that he sought out the ensign, told him what had happened, and urged him to find out from the captain everything he could about this affair. The ensign, delighted with this turn of events, promised to do so.

[18]One day he spoke to the captain while the Moor was nearby and could see them talking together. The ensign talked of everything except the lady, meanwhile laughing as heartily as possible, showing signs of amazement and gesturing with his hands and head as though he were hearing remarkable stories. As soon as they parted, the Moor went to the ensign to find out what he had heard. After lengthy persuasions the ensign finally said: "He hid nothing from me. He has enjoyed your wife, he told me, as many times as you have. Whenever you left the house he had his chance. And the last time he was with her she gave him that handkerchief you gave her when you married her."

The Moor thanked the ensign and he came to the conclusion that if his wife did not have the handkerchief, what the ensign had told him would clearly be true. [19]Therefore one day after dinner, while conversing with his wife, he asked her for the handkerchief. The unhappy lady, who had greatly feared this request, blushed deeply. To try to hide her confusion, which the Moor had seen clearly, she ran to her chest and pretended to search for it. After searching for a long time she said: "I don't know why I can't find it. Do you have it perhaps?" "If I had it," he said, "why would I ask for it? Search again more carefully." [20]As he left the room he began thinking of ways to kill his wife, and the captain too, in such a way that he would not be blamed for her death.

[21]Because he now thought about this night and day he could not conceal his change in attitude. And his wife often said to him: "What is the matter? What is disturbing you? You who used to be the liveliest man in the world are now the most melancholy." The Moor offered various excuses but none of them rang true. And since she knew that she had done nothing to disturb him, she began to worry that her constant presence was making him tired of her. She talked about this with the ensign's wife: "I do not know what to say about the

[18] IV.i. 75–187.
[19] III.iv. 51–98.
[20] IV.i. 178–179.
[21] This paragraph contains at least the germs of III.iv. 122–164.

Moor. He used to be deeply in love with me, but for several days now, for no reason I can understand, he has completely changed. I am very much afraid that I'll turn out to be an example to young people not to marry against their parents' wishes; and that Italian ladies will learn because of me not to go with a man who is segregated by nature, Heaven, and a way of life from us.[22] Since I know that he feels free to tell your husband all about his affairs, I beg you to help me if you know anything that can clear this up." She said all this weeping ceaselessly. [23]The ensign's wife knew everything (her husband had wanted her help in destroying the lady but could not get her to consent — nevertheless, fearing her husband she did not dare to say a word) but only suggested: "Be careful not to make your husband suspect anything and do everything you can to appear loving and faithful." "I do," she said, "but nothing helps."

[24]In the meantime the Moor kept searching for more proof of what he did not want to discover. He asked the ensign if he could find a way to show him the handkerchief in the captain's possession. Though that was a difficult task for the villain he nevertheless promised to use all his skill to do so. The captain had a woman in his home who did marvelous embroidery work on cloth imported from Rheims. Seeing that handkerchief and knowing it belonged to the Moor's wife, she determined to make one just like it before returning it. While she was working at this, the ensign noted that she worked near a window and that she could be seen there by passersby. He therefore showed the Moor this scene, and the Moor was convinced that his perfect wife was in truth an adulteress. [25]He conferred with the ensign about killing her and the captain, and after some debate the Moor urged the ensign to kill the captain, promising he would be eternally in the ensign's debt. At first the ensign refused to do such an unwise and dangerous thing, for the captain was capable and brave. But the Moor after much pleading and a large sum of money persuaded him to try.

[26]One night the captain was leaving the house of a courtesan. The night was dark and the ensign slipped up to him, sword drawn, and struck him a blow across the legs to make him fall. He slashed his right thigh, dropping the unfortunate man. He leaped upon him to kill him off, but as the captain was brave and used to blood and death he drew his own sword and, wounded as he was, began defending himself and crying out loudly, "Murder!" Hearing people coming,

---

[22] Nor is Shakespeare's play free of this primitive bigotry.
[23] Compare with IV.ii. 130–133.
[24] Compare with IV.i. 183–212.
[25] IV.i. 224–225.
[26] V.i. 1–72.

among them soldiers who were stationed nearby, the ensign ran away to avoid being seen. Then he turned back and pretended that he too was running in the direction of the noise. Joining the others he saw that the captain's leg was cut off and judged that although he was still alive that blow would nevertheless kill him. Delighted as he was by this, he nonetheless grieved with the captain as though he were his brother.

The next morning the news went all over the city and reached the ear of Disdemona. Because she was kindhearted she showed great sorrow for what had happened, not realizing how unfortunate this would be for her. The Moor drew the worst possible conclusion from her sorrow and went to the ensign and told him: "Do you know, my fool wife is so sorry for the captain that she is about to lose her mind." "How could she behave otherwise, since he is her very soul?" the ensign said. "Her very soul?" the Moor replied. [27]"I'll tear that soul right out of her body! As I am a man, I'll rid the world of that monster." The two of them debated whether to kill the lady with knife or with poison, but disliked either method. The ensign said: "One method occurs to me that will satisfy you and leave no suspicion. It is this: your house is an old one and the ceiling of your bedroom has many cracks. Let's beat Disdemona to death with a sock full of sand, since that method will leave no marks. When she's dead, we will knock down a part of the ceiling and break her head, pretending that a rotten timber fell and killed her. That way nobody will suspect you, thinking her death an accident."

[28]This cruel advice pleased the Moor. He waited for the right moment, and one night he hid the ensign in his closet before going to bed with his wife. According to plan the ensign made a strange noise in the closet, and hearing it the Moor said to his wife: "Did you hear that noise?" "I did," said she. "Get up," suggested the Moor, "and see what it is." The luckless Disdemona rose and as soon as she approached the closet the ensign stepped out. With his sand-filled stocking held ready, strong and steady-nerved, he smashed her cruelly in the small of the back. She dropped to the floor, hardly able to breathe. With what little strength she had left she called upon the Moor to help her. He came off the bed and spoke to her: "Vilest of women, here is your reward for dishonesty. Here is what happens to women who cuckold their husbands while pretending to love them." The ensign struck her again and the unhappy lady, hearing her husband's words and feeling death near, called upon Divine Justice to witness her faithfulness, since earthly justice had failed her. As she

---

[27] IV.i. 211–225. The murder method in Shakespeare is far less elaborate.
[28] Compare with V.ii. 1–125.

called upon God to help her the impious ensign struck her a third time and killed her.[29] Then they put her in the bed, smashed her skull, and made the ceiling fall down as planned. The Moor began to call for help as though his house were falling. At his cries his neighbors came running in and lifted the roof and found the lady dead under the timbers. Because of her goodness everyone lamented, and she was buried the next day amid universal sorrow.

[30]But God, who judges the souls of men with justice, would not allow that great crime to go unpunished. Indeed the Moor, who loved his wife more than his own eyes, finding himself without her began to feel so great a desire for her that he went looking for her throughout the house like a person who has lost his mind. And deciding that the ensign was the cause of his losing all the sweetness of life, and that he himself was lost, he hated that villain so that he could not bear to look at him. If he had not feared the stern justice of the Venetian Signory he would have killed him outright. Since he could not do so in safety he stripped the ensign of his rank and then tried to get him out of his company. The bitterest hatred imaginable grew up between them.

Therefore the ensign, worst of all villains, turned all his thoughts to destroying the Moor. He sought out the captain, who by now had recovered and walked about with the aid of a wooden leg, and told him: "The time has come when you can get revenge for your missing leg. If you want it, come with me to Venice. I will tell you there who the guilty party is. I cannot tell you here for many reasons. But there I will supply you with legal testimony."

The captain, who had found himself gravely wounded without knowing the cause, thanked the ensign and went with him to Venice. When they arrived there the ensign told him that the Moor was the one who had cut off his leg because of the notion that arose in his mind that the captain was making love to Disdemona. And for this same reason he had killed his wife and then claimed that the falling roof had killed her.

The captain then accused the Moor before the Signory of maiming him and of killing his wife, and he presented the ensign as his witness. The latter said that both accusations were true; that the Moor had

---

[29] The death of Disdemona from the *third* blow — the number three so often symbolized the Holy Trinity in the Renaissance — in such close juxtaposition with Cinthio's reference to Divine Justice may be a foreshadowing of the religious allegory in *Othello*. The linking of love, death, and eternity frequently appears in the work of Dante, Petrarch, and Boccaccio, and Cinthio would surely be aware of the tradition.

[30] There are several points of comparison, but more of contrast, between the remainder of this story and V.ii. 168ff.

told him everything and had tried to induce him to commit both crimes; that after the Moor had killed his wife because of the bestial jealousy in his mind he had told the ensign how he had managed it. The Signory, hearing of the cruelty practiced by a barbarian on one of its citizens had him arraigned and brought in from Cyprus. Many tortures were used to find out the truth, but the Moor courageously withstood each one and denied everything so completely that no information could be dragged out of him. But although he escaped death through his steadfastness, he was condemned to perpetual exile after his siege in prison, where he was finally killed, as he deserved, by his wife's kinsmen.

The ensign went back to his homeland and, up to his old habits, accused one of his companions of trying to get him to kill an enemy who was a nobleman. The companion was arrested and put to torture, but denied everything he was accused of. The ensign was then put to the same torture and was lashed with knotted cords so that his insides burst. He was released from prison and brought home where he died miserably. Thus God avenged the innocence of Disdemona.

This whole story, as I have told it to you, was told by the ensign's wife shortly after his death.

PLINY THE ELDER
Natural History, c. 77 A.D.

FROM BOOK VII*

We have already spoken of the human race as a whole in our discussion of mankind. We will not go on to treat of their numberless
manners and customs, as various as the groups into which mankind
is divided. Yet some customs ought not to be omitted, especially concerning those peoples who live far from the sea. I have no doubt that
some of the facts about them will seem astounding and incredible to
many. Who, for instance, would believe there were Ethiopians[1] before
seeing them? Indeed, what does not seem a miracle when seen for
the first time? How many things are unbelievable until they have
actually happened? In truth, we constantly underestimate the power
and majesty of Nature if our minds, instead of grasping Nature in her
entirety, consider her only in detail. Let me just mention peacocks,
the spotted skins of tigers and panthers, and the rich colors of many
animals. And what might be termed a minor example, but is really of
immense importance, is the existence of so many languages among the
various nations, so many modes of speech, so great a variety of expres-
sions, that a man from another country seems almost no fellow creature
at all. Moreover, our features, although comprising some ten parts and
little more, are so constructed that among many thousands of men no
two look alike, a result no art could possibly produce when confined
to so limited a number of combinations. However, in most of the
following statements about the curious variations among men I shall
cite other authorities on all subjects that might inspire doubt. The
Greek writers, however, who have proven themselves the most careful
observers over a long period of time, must be trusted.

---

* Reprinted from Joseph Satin, *Ideas in Context,* © 1958, by permission
of Houghton Mifflin Company.
[1] A possible link, possibly an unconscious one, between Othello and his
echoes of this passage in I.iii. 128–145.

[2]We have already stated that there are certain tribes of Scythians, and others, who feed upon human flesh. This fact might seem unbelievable unless we remembered that in the very center of this world, in Italy and Sicily, were such monsters as the Cyclops and the Laestrygones. And on the other side of the Alps it used to be the custom to offer human sacrifices, which is only slightly different from eating people.

In the northern regions, not far from where the north wind rises, whose cave is called Geskleithron [earth's boundary] live the Arimaspi of whom we spoke before. They have only one eye, placed in the middle of their forehead. This race carries on a fierce warfare with the Griffins, a kind of monster with wings, for the gold which the Griffins mine and guard with a curious greediness, while the Arimaspi are equally greedy to get hold of it. Many authors have written of this, the most illustrious being Herodotus and Aristeas of Proconnesus. Beyond the Scythian[3] Anthropophagi lies a country called Abarimon, situated in a certain valley of Mount Imaus, in whose forests live a savage race whose feet are turned backwards. They have amazing speed and wander about with the wild beasts. They cannot breathe in any climate except their own, therefore could not be taken from their kingdom to Alexander the Great, as we learn from Beeton, his cartographer. According to Isigonus of Nicaea, the Anthropophagi mentioned before as dwelling ten days' journey beyond the Borysthenes drink out of human skulls and hang the scalps upon their breasts, like so many napkins. The same author states that in Albania dwells a race of men whose eyes are of a sea-green color and who have white hair from infancy, and that these people see better in the night than in the day. He states also that the Sauromatae, who dwell thirteen days' journey beyond the Borysthenes, eat only every third day. Crates Pergamenus states that near Parium, in the Hellespont, were a race of men called Ophiogenes who could cure anyone stung by serpents by extracting the poison with a touch of the hand. Varro states that a few people still remain in that region whose saliva cures the stings of serpents. Agatharchides wrote that these same powers belonged to the Psylli, in Africa. They were named after King Psyllus, whose tomb is in the district of the Greater Syrtes. These people had a poison in their bodies which was fatal to serpents and the mere odor of it made serpents drowsy. The Psylli used to expose their children immediately after birth to the fiercest serpents and in this manner made proof of the fidelity of their wives, the serpents not being repelled by

---

[2] I.iii. 143.
[3] I.iii. 144.

children who were the product of adultery. The Psylli were almost entirely wiped out by the Nasamones, who now occupy their territory. A few of them, however, still survive, the descendants of those who either took to flight or else were absent during the battle. The Marsi, too, in Italy, possess this curative power, owe it to their descent from the son of Circe.

All men, moreover, possess a poison which acts upon serpents. Human saliva makes serpents flee as though scalded with boiling water. Saliva destroys them the moment it touches their throats, especially the saliva of a man who is fasting.

Calliphanes informs us that north of the Nasamones and the Machlyae, who border upon them, are the Androgyni, a people who unite the two sexes in the same individual. Aristotle states that their right breast is that of a male, their left that of a female. Isigonus and Nymphodorus inform us that in Africa are certain families of enchanters who, by means of their charms, can cause trees to wither and infants to die. Isigonus adds that among the Triballi and the Illyrii are enchanters who can even kill those on whom they gaze for any length of time, especially if their gaze is angry. The age of puberty is especially vulnerable to their evil doings. Even more remarkable is the fact that they have two pupils in each eye. Apollonides states that there are females like this in Scythia, known as Bythiae. Phylarchus states that a tribe of Thibii in Pontus, and many other persons too, have a double pupil in one eye and the image of a horse in the other. He adds that their bodies will not drown, even though weighted down by their garments. Not unlike them is a race described by Damon, the Pharnaces of Ethiopia, whose perspiration putrifies whatever body it touches. Cicero, one of our writers, states that the glances of all women who have a double pupil is poisonous.

Thus has Nature compensated for giving some men, like wild beasts, a taste for human flesh. She has produced poisons in every part of their bodies and eyes, and every kind of evil possible to man.

Not far from Rome, in the land of the Falisci, dwell a few families known by the name of Hirpi. They perform a yearly sacrifice to Apollo, on Mount Soracte, by walking across a mound of burning wood without even being singed. On this account the senate exempts them from military service and from all other duties. Some people are born with parts of their bodies endowed with marvellous powers. Such a man was King Pyrrhus, whose big toe on his right foot cured diseases of the spleen with a mere touch. It is said that this toe would not burn to ashes together with the remainder of his body and was therefore preserved in a casket in a temple.

India and Ethiopia especially abound in wonders. India produces the largest animals. Its dogs, for example, are bigger than those of any other country.[4] Its trees, too, are said to be so high that it is impossible to shoot an arrow over them. Their height is caused by the fertility of the soil, the mild climate, and the abundance of water. If it can be believed, a single fig-tree there shelters a whole troop of cavalry. And the reeds there are of such enormous length that a single segment makes a navigable boat that can hold three men. Many of the people are more than eight feet tall. They never expectorate and never feel pain in their heads, teeth or eyes and rarely feel pain in the other parts of their bodies, so well does the sun toughen them. Their philosophers, called Gymnosophists, remain in one position and gaze at the sun from its rising to its setting. All day long they stand in the burning sands, first on one foot and then on the other. Megasthenes writes of a race of men who dwell upon a mountain called Nulo, who have their feet turned backwards, with eight toes on each foot. On several mountains live over 120 men who have the heads of dogs and who wear the skins of wild animals. They bark instead of speaking and, armed with claws, live by hunting animals and birds. Ctesias wrote of a certain tribe in India whose females become pregnant only once in their lives and whose children turn white the instant they are born. He tells of another race named Monocoli who have only one leg but can leap with surprising agility. These people are also called Sciapodae [shadow feet] because during times of extreme heat they lie on their backs and protect themselves from the sun by the shade of their foot. These people dwell not very far from the Troglodytae.[5] To the west of them is a tribe without necks and with eyes in their shoulders. Among the mountains of eastern India in what is called the country of the Catharcludi are the great apes, most agile animals that sometimes go on all fours, sometimes walk erect like men. Because of their speed they can never be caught, except when they are either aged or sickly. Tauron gives the name of Choromandae to a nation which dwell in the woods and have no voices, only a horrible screech. They have hairy bodies, sea-green eyes, and the teeth of a dog. Eudoxus tells us that in southern India the men have feet some twenty inches long. Their women, however, are named Struthopodes [sparrow-footed] because of the smallness of their feet. Megasthenes tells of a people called Scyritae belonging to the nomads of India who have holes in their faces instead of noses and have flexible feet like the body of a snake. At the eastern edge of India, near the source of the river Ganges, are the Astomi, a people without mouths. Their bodies

---

[4] Compare I.iii. 142.
[5] I.iii. 144–145.

are completely hairy and they wear a covering of leaves. They subsist on odors which they inhale through their nostrils. They need neither meat nor drink and on a long journey only carry with them various sweet-smelling roots, flowers and wild apples, in order to have something to smell at. A slightly more pungent odor kills them easily.

□ Some Sources for Further Study

For a fascinating, if unlikely, claim that Othello was in real life a Venetian named Christoforo Moro, consult the findings of Rawdon Brown in the Variorum Othello.

KING LEAR

King Lear is unique among the plays in this volume in that the direct sources of its plot and subplot are each clearly defined and richly detailed. Moreover, we may trace the main plot source in a precise line of development from its origin. Its final development, and Shakespeare's direct source, is an anonymous play, *The True Chronicle of King Leir*, not published until 1606, about the time of Shakespeare's play, but mentioned in Henslowe's *Diary* and in the Stationers' *Register* in 1594. *The True Chronicle* presents the same major characters as *King Lear* and up to the midpoint of its third act closely corresponds to Shakespeare's masterpiece. Leir divides his kingdom on the basis of his daughters' professed love; Cordella, unable to flatter her father is disowned, although the courtier Perillus objects, and subsequently weds the King of Gallia (France); Gonorill, offended by Leir's knights, pressures him to leave and go to Ragan; Ragan proves unkinder than her sister, and Leir and Perillus decide to leave her and to embark for France — and here the plot of the chronicle play and Shakespeare's diverge. They converge again two more times: when Ragan's messenger is stayed from killing Leir and Perillus by a storm which melts him with pity and fear, and when Leir and Cordella are reunited. For the rest, in contrast to Shakespeare's play Leir and Perillus cross the Channel into France (in Shakespeare Lear does not leave England), the King of France invades England (in Shakespeare he cannot come), is victorious, and Leir is restored to his throne.

The True Chronicle of King Leir may be likened to the Ur-Hamlet stripped of the glamor of the unattainable. It has merits of its own, dramatic and delightful, and it points toward Shakespeare's play in many places, but it is not an indispensable shadow image of *King Lear*, rather a working model from which Shakespeare borrowed some parts. He could have found those same parts in the very first version of the Leir story in the *Historia Regum Britanniae* of Geoffrey of Monmouth, c. 1135. In Geoffrey's version there is the same division of the king-

445

dom, Cordeilla's costly honesty, the two ungrateful daughters, the flight to France and eventual restoration of the throne. But the historian then goes on to chronicle Cordeilla's reign after the death of Leir, in which after five years her nephews revolt and imprison her where "overwhelmed with grief at the loss of her kingdom, she slew herself." In this sequel may be found the source for the ending of Shakespeare's play.

Shakespeare possibly read about Leir in Geoffrey; he certainly read Holinshed's account, which parallels Geoffrey's but is a tighter, less detailed version. The story outline is the same as in Geoffrey, but Holinshed deals more briefly with the conflict between Gonorilla and Leir's household knights, and with the meeting between Leir and Cordeilla. Since both of those incidents loom large in *The True Chronicle* and in *King Lear* it seems likely that one or both playwrights were familiar with Geoffrey's account.

Essentially the same version of the Leir story reappears in Book II, Canto 10 of *The Faerie Queene* by Edmund Spenser, 1590. Here the story is redacted into six lovely stanzas which not only furnish a model for poetry but also two variants important to Shakespeare's play. Spenser is the first to state that Cordelia dies by hanging, which is the way she dies in *King Lear*. And he is the first to spell her name as Shakespeare will, which in the light of his intricate, symbolic manner suggests that Spenser at least may have selected this variant because "Delia" was a popular Renaissance anagram for ideal — as in the *Delia* sonnet sequence by Samuel Daniel, 1592. (Two other poetic waystops en route to *King Lear* deserve mention: "Cordila" in *A Mirror for Magistrates*, 1574, and a ballad, "King Leir and His Three Daughters," which comes quite close to Shakespeare's play but whose date of composition is doubtful.)

The Gloucester-Edmund-Edgar subplot emerges from Book II, Chapter 10 — compare with Spenser — of the *Arcadia* of Sir Philip Sidney, 1590, full grown enough to be grafted right onto the main trunk of the Lear story. In fact it starts with an "extreme" storm that may have reinforced the fainter suggestion in *The True Chronicle* for the storm on the heath in Shakespeare's play, in which case it may also have suggested the nexus of both plots. The *Arcadia* episode contains the following elements in common with the Gloucester subplot: the Prince of Paphlagonia has two sons, one of them illegitimate; Plexirtus, the latter, tricks his father into trying to kill Leonatus, his legitimate son; Leonatus runs away, and aferward Plexirtus blinds his father and drives him out of the court; the prince wanders helpless and alone until Leonatus returns to lead him; he asks to be taken to a high rock in order to commit suicide, but Leonatus refuses; later on there is a war of revolt and the supporters of Leonatus win and crown him king — this in contrast to Shakespeare — while the prince of Paphlagonia dies, "his heart broken with unkindness and affliction, stretched so far beyond his limits with this excess of comfort as it was able no longer to keep safe his royal spirits." — lines hauntingly like Edgar's account of Gloucester's death:

> But his flawed heart —
> Alack, too weak the conflict to support! —
> 'Twixt two extremes of passion, joy and grief,
> Burst smilingly.
>   (V.iii. 196–199).

As in all the great tragedies the characters in *King Lear* owe most of their depth and stature to their creator, but *King Lear*'s sources offer simple character traits that Shakespeare will make sophisticated use of. Geoffrey and Holinshed portray Leir as a cranky, wrathful old man, "sluggish with age," who later turns repentent, the while retaining a certain dignity; *The True Chronicle* complicates the portrait by emphasizing his meekness and humility. Cordelia is ideal and forgiving in all of the sources, and her sisters come off especially well in *The True Chronicle* as a pair of envious and vicious vixens, with Ragan far the worse of the two (in Shakespeare it is Goneril). Perillus in the source play suggests a passive Kent, though Kent has drunk deeper of Horatio than of Perillus. And the source play's Skalliger and messenger foreshadow the more slippery evil of Oswald, while Cornwall and Cambria bear resemblances to Shakespeare's Albany and Cornwall. The subplot characters in Sidney are at least adumbrations of Gloucester, Edmund, and Edgar, and while the bitter fool is Shakespeare's own, *The True Chronicle* does provide witty comic contrast through Mumford.

King Lear offers probably the most profound spiritual experience in all of Shakespeare, and its idea of the ennoblement achieved through repentance finds slight basis in the direct sources. *The True Chronicle* uses some Christian images in referring to Cordella, and its reconciliation scene between Cordella and Leir is provocative, but the major cause of Lear's progress toward salvation is his madness, found nowhere in the sources. That madness, like one of the "heroic frenzies" of Giordano Bruno's *De gli eroici furori*, 1585, blots out mere appearances and leaves in its place an inner light so penetrating and benevolent that Lear on meeting the blinded Gloucester at Dover instantly pardons him his adultery. For plot, character, and idea *King Lear* makes wholesale use of two neat and tidy source packages, but raises them from a little world whose main journey is across the Channel and back again aloft to a spacious and spiritual universe.

ꙮ GEOFFREY OF MONMOUTH

Historia Regum Britanniae (*History of Britain*)
c. 1135

translated by A. Thompson[1]

FROM BOOK II

When Bladud was thus given over to the destinies, his son Leir assumed the kingdom and ruled the country in manly fashion for three-score years. It was he who built the city on the River Soar, which in British is called Kaerleir, but in Saxon, Leircestre [Leicester]. Male issue was denied to him, his only children being three daughters named Gonorilla, Regan, and Cordeilla. [2]When he reached the verge of old age he decided to divide his kingdom among them and to marry them unto husbands worthy of them and of their share of the kingdom. In order to know which of his daughters was worthy of the largest share, he went to them and inquired as to which of them did love him most. When he asked Gonorilla how much she loved him, she at once called all the gods of heaven to witness that her father was dearer to her heart than the very soul that dwelled within her body. And her father said, "Because thou hast set my old age before thy own life, my dearest daughter, I will marry thee to whatever youth thou choose, with one-third of Britain as dowry." Next Regan, who was anxious to follow her sister's example and to wheedle equal kindness from her father, answered with a solemn oath that she could express her love only by saying that she loved him better than the whole world. Thereupon the credulous father promised to see her married with the same pomp as her elder sister, with another third of the kingdom for her share. But the last, Cordeilla, seeing how her

---

[1] Geoffrey of Monmouth, *Historia Regum Britanniae*, trans. A. Thompson and revised by J. A. Giles (London: J. Bohn, 1842). Text revised and modernized for this volume.
[2] I.i.

father had been cajoled by her sisters' flatteries and desiring to test him differently, answered him thus: "Father mine, is there a daughter anywhere who presumes to love her father more than a father? I trust there is none willing to admit to that, unless she were joking to conceal some truth. For myself, I have ever loved thee as a father, nor will I ever be turned aside from that love. Although thou art bent on wringing more from me, yet hear the true measure of my love. Ask no more of me than this: [3]'So much as thou hast, so much art thou worth, and so much do I love thee.'" Thereupon her father, thinking that she had spoken thus out of the hardness[4] of her heart, grew quite angry and answered in haste: "Since thou hast so despised thy father's old age that thou hast disdained to love me even as well as these thy sisters, I also will disdain thee. Never in my realm shalt thou have a share with thy sisters. However, since thou art my daughter I will not refuse to marry thee, upon some kind of terms, to some stranger from another land, should Fortune offer such a one. Only be sure of this: I will never trouble to marry thee with such honor as thy sisters, although up to this time I have loved thee better than the others. But now it seems that thou lovest me less than they."

Straightaway with the counsel of the nobles of the realm he gave the two sisters unto two dukes, of Cornwall and Albany,[5] together with one half of the island so long as he should live. And he willed that after his death they should have the whole of the kingdom of Britain. About this time Aganippus, King of the Franks, hearing of Cordeilla's beauty, dispatched his envoys to the king requesting that Cordeilla be given into his charge as his bride, whom he would marry with due rite of the wedding-torch. Her father, persisting in his wrath, answered that he would give her willingly but it must be without land or fee, seeing that he had divided his kingdom along with all his gold and silver between Cordeilla's sisters, Gonorilla and Regan. When Aganippus learned this, because he was on fire with love of the damsel, he sent again to King Leir saying that he had enough of gold and silver and other possessions, for one-third of Gaul was his, and that he wished to marry the damsel only that he might have sons by her to inherit his land. So at last the bargain was struck, and Cordeilla was sent to Gaul to be married unto Aganippus.

A long time after, when Leir began to grow more sluggish by reason of age, the dukes with whom (and his daughters) he had divided Britain

---

[3] Compare I.i. 94–95.

[4] *abundantia*, literally, fullness, in the sense of heaviness, hardness. Shakespeare uses "untender" in the same sense: I.i. 106.

[5] In the original, *Cornubiae, Albaniae*.

rebelled against him and took the realm and power which he had held manfully and gloriously up to that time. [6]When peace was restored one of his sons-in-law, Maglaunus, Duke of Albany, agreed to maintain him with threescore knights, so that he should not be without some semblance of state. But after he had stayed with his son-in-law two years, Gonorilla became indignant at the large number of his knights, who insulted her servants because their rations were not more plentiful. Whereupon, after speaking to her husband, she ordered her father to be content with a service of thirty knights and to dismiss the other thirty that he had. The king, angry at this, left Maglaunus and went off to Henvin, Duke of Cornwall, husband of his other daughter. Here at first he was received with honor, but discord arose within a year between the king's household and the duke's. Whereupon Regan, growing indignant, ordered her father to dismiss all his company except five knights to do him service. Her father, grieved beyond measure by this, returned once more to his eldest daughter, thinking to move her to pity and to persuade her to maintain himself and his retinue. However she had not put aside her earlier anger and swore by all the gods of heaven that he should never reside with her unless he contented himself with the service of a single knight and got rid of all the rest. Moreover, she upbraided the old man for going about with such a retinue, since he had nothing of his own to give away. Finding that she would not give in at all to his wishes, he at last obeyed and remained with one knight only. But when the remembrance of his former dignity came back to him, bearing witness to the misery of his present state, he began to think of going to his youngest daughter overseas. He strongly doubted that she would do anything for him, seeing that he had married her, as I have said, with such little honor. [7]Nevertheless, unwilling to endure so poor a life any longer he crossed the Channel into Gaul. When he found that two other princes were making the passage at the same time and that he had been assigned the third place, he broke into tears and sobbed: "You destinies that pursue your inevitable ways, wherefore was it your will to raise me to a happiness so fleeting? For it is keener grief to call to mind lost happiness than to suffer present sorrow. The memory of those days when in the midst of hundreds of thousands of warriors I used to batter down the walls of cities and lay waste the provinces of my enemies is more painful to me than my present calamity, which has incited those who used to grovel at my feet to desert me in my weakness. O angry fortune! Will the day ever come when I may requite the

---

[6] I.iii,iv,v; II.i. In Shakespeare and in *The True Chronicle* Leir begins with one hundred knights.

[7] As in *The True Chronicle*. In Shakespeare he makes for Dover.

evil that has thus driven me out in poverty for the length of my days? O Cordeilla, my daughter, how true were the words thou answered me, when I asked of thee how much thou didst love me! For thou saidst, 'So much as thou hast, so much art thou worth, and so much do I love thee.' So long, therefore, as I had that which was mine own to give, so long seemed I of worth unto them that were the lovers, not of myself but of my gifts. They loved me at times, but better loved the presents I gave unto them. Now that there are no more presents to give, they too have gone their ways. But with what demeanor, O dearest of my children, shall I dare appear before thee? I who, angry at these thy words, married thee less honorably than thy sisters who after all the kindnesses I have conferred upon them have allowed me to become an outcast and a beggar?"

Landing at last, his mind filled with these reflections and others of a like kind, he came to Karitia, where his daughter lived. [8]He waited outside the city and sent a messenger to beseech her compassion because he had neither food nor clothing. Upon hearing these tidings Cordeilla was much moved and wept bitterly. When she asked how many armed men he had with him, the messenger told her that he had none except a single knight who was waiting with him outside the city. Then she took as much gold and silver as was necessary and gave them to the messenger, bidding him to take her father to another city where he should bathe him, clothe him, and take care of him as though he had been ill. She bade him to obtain after that a retinue of forty knights, well appointed and armed, and that then her father should duly announce his arrival to Aganippus and herself. The messenger accordingly brought King Leir into another city and hid him there in secret until he had fully accomplished all that Cordeilla had ordered him to do.

[9]As soon as Leir was properly arrayed in kingly apparel and clothed with the trappings of royalty and served by a train of retainers, he sent word to Aganippus and his daughter that he had been driven out of the realm of Britain by his sons-in-law and had come to them for assistance in recovering his kingdom. They came forth with their great counsellors and nobles to receive him with high honor, and placed in his hands the power over all of Gaul until such time as they had restored him to his former dignity.

[10]In the meanwhile, Aganippus sent envoys throughout the whole of Gaul to summon every knight to come and help him to recover the kingdom of Britain for his father-in-law, King Leir. When they had

---

[8] IV.iii. 39–49.
[9] IV.vii. 20–84.
[10] Compare V.ii,iii.

all made ready, Leir led the assembled host, together with Aganippus and his daughter, into Britain, fought a battle with his sons-in-law and won the victory, thus bringing them again all under his own dominion. Three years after, he died, and Aganippus died also, and Cordeilla, now queen of Britain, buried her father in a certain underground chamber which she had had made under the river Soar at Leircestre. This underground chamber was founded in honor of Janus, the two-faced god, and there, at the yearly celebration of his day, all the workmen of the city plied their regular tasks.

When Cordeilla had governed the kingdom in peace for five years, the two sons of her sisters began to harass her. They were Marganus and Cunedagius, sons of Duke Maglaunus and Henvin, both of them youths of notable prowess. After the deaths of their fathers they had succeeded them in their dukedoms and were greatly angered that Britain should be ruled by a woman. [11]Therefore they assembled their hosts and rebelled against the queen, and they did not cease until they had laid waste to a number of provinces, defeated her in several battles, and at last captured her and put her in prison. There, overwhelmed with grief at the loss of her kingdom, she slew herself.

---

[11] Compare V.iii. 1–33; 257ff.

✆ RAPHAEL HOLINSHED

The Chronicles of England, Scotland, and Ireland,* 1587

[c. 749–694 B.C.] Leir the son of Baldud was admitted ruler over the Britains in the year of the world 3105, at what time Joas reigned in Judea. This Leir was a prince of right noble demeanor, governing his land and subjects in great wealth. He made the town of Caerlier, now called Leicester, which stands upon the river of Soar. It is written that he had by his wife three daughters without other issue whose names were Gonorilla, Regan, and Cordeilla, which daughters he greatly loved, but specially Cordeilla the youngest far above the two elder. [1]When this Leir therefore was come to great years, and began to wax unwieldy through age, he thought to understand the affections of his daughters towards him and prefer[2] her whom he [him?] best loved to the succession over the kingdom. Whereupon he first asked Gonorilla, the eldest, how well she loved him: who calling her gods to record protested that she "loved him more than her own life, which by right and reason should be most dear unto her." With which answer the father being well pleased, turned to the second and demanded of her how well she loved him: who answered (confirming her sayings with great oaths) that she loved him "more than tongue could express, and far above all other creatures of the world."

Then called he his youngest daughter Cordeilla before him, and asked of her what account she made of him, unto whom she made this answer as follows: "Knowing the great love and fatherly zeal that you have always borne towards me (for the which I may not answer you otherwise than I think, and as my conscience leads me) I protest unto you that I have loved you ever and will continually (while I live) love you as my natural father. And if you would more under-

---

* text modernized.
[1] I.i.
[2] give preferment to.

stand of the love that I bear you, ascertain yourself that so much as you have, so much are you worth, and so much I love you, and no more." The father, being nothing content with this answer, married his two eldest daughters the one unto Henninus, the Duke of Cornwall, and the other unto Maglanus, the Duke of Albania, betwixt whom he willed and ordained that his land should be divided after his death, and the one half thereof immediately should be assigned to them in hand. But for the third daughter Cordeilla he reserved nothing.

Nevertheless it fortuned that one of the princes of Gallia (which now is called France) whose name was Aganippus, hearing of the beauty, womanhood, and good conditions of the said Cordeilla, desired to have her in marriage, and sent over to her father requiring that he might have her to wife. To whom answer was made that he might have his daughter, but as for any dowry, he could have none, for all was promised and assured to her other sisters already. Aganippus notwithstanding this answer of denial to receive anything by way of dowry with Cordeilla took her to wife, only moved thereto (I say) for respect of her person and amiable virtues. This Aganippus was one of the twelve knights that ruled Gallia in those days, as in the British History it is recorded — but to proceed.

[3]After that Leir was fallen into age, the two dukes that had married his two eldest daughters, thinking it long ere the government of the land did come to their hands, arose against him in armor and reft from him the governance of the land, upon conditions to be continued for term of life: by the which he was put to his portion, that is, to live after a rate assigned to him for the maintenance of his estate, which in process of time was diminished as well by Maglanus as by Henninus. But the greatest grief that Leir took was to see the unkindness of his daughters, which seemed to think that all was too much which their father had, the same being never so little: insomuch that going from the one to the other he was brought to that misery that scarcely they would allow him one servant to wait upon him.

In the end, such was the unkindness, or (as I may say) the unnaturalness which he found in his two daughters, notwithstanding their fair and pleasant words uttered in time past, that being constrained of necessity he fled the land and sailed into Gallia, there to seek some comfort of his youngest daughter, Cordeilla, whom before time he hated. The lady Cordeilla hearing that he was arrived in poor state, she first sent to him privily a certain sum of money to apparel himself withal, and to retain a certain number of servants that might attend upon him in honorable wise, as appertained to the

---

[3] I.iii,iv; II.iv.

estate which he had borne.[4] [5]And then so accompanied, she appointed him to come to the court; which he did and was so joyfully, honorably, and lovingly received, both by his son-in-law Aganippus and also by his daughter Cordeilla, that his heart was greatly comforted: for he was no less honored than if he had been king of the whole country himself.

Now when he had informed his son-in-law and his daughter in what sort he had been used by his other daughters, Aganippus caused a mighty army to be put in a readiness, and likewise a great navy of ships to be rigged to pass over into Britain with Leir, his father-in-law, to see him again restored to his kingdom. It was accorded[6] that Cordeilla should also go with him to take possession of the land, the which he [Leir] promised to leave unto her as the rightful inheritor after his decease, notwithstanding any former grant made to her sisters or to their husbands in any manner of wise.

[7]Hereupon, when this army and navy of ships were ready, Leir and his daughter Cordeilla with her husband took the sea, and arriving in Britain fought with their enemies and discomfited them in battle, in the which Maglanus and Henninus were slain. And then was Leir restored to his kingdom, which he ruled after this by the space of two years,[8] and then died forty years after he first begun to reign. His body was buried at Leicester in a vault under the channel of the river of Soar beneath the town.

Cordeilla, the youngest daughter of Leir, was admitted queen and supreme governess of Britain in the year of the world 3155, before the building of Rome 54,[9] Uzziah then reigning in Judea and Jeroboam over Israel. This Cordeilla after her father's decease ruled the land of Britain right worthily during the space of five years, in which meantime her husband died. And then about the end of those five years her two nephews, Margan and Cunedag, sons to her aforesaid sisters, disdaining to be under the government of a woman, levied war against her and destroyed a great part of the land and finally took her prisoner and laid her fast in ward;[10] wherewith she took such grief, being a woman of a manly courage, and despairing to recover liberty, there she slew herself when she had reigned (as before is mentioned) the term of five years.

---

[4] IV.vii.
[5] To which he had belonged.
[6] agreed.
[7] Compare V.ii,iii.
[8] In Geoffrey, three years.
[9] i.e., 54 years before the building of Rome in 753 B.C.
[10] prison.

  EDMUND SPENSER

The Faerie Queene, 1590

BOOK II, CANTO 10

Next him king *Leyr* in happie peace long raynd,
But had no issue male him to succeed,
But three faire daughters, which were well uptraind
In all that seemęd fitt for kingly seed:
Mongst whom his realme he equally decreed
To have divided. Tho, when feeble age
Nigh to his utmost date he saw proceed,
He cald his daughters, and with speeches sage
Inquyrd, which of them most did love her parentage.

The eldest, Gonorill, gan to protest
That she much more than her owne life him lov'd;
And Regan greater love to him profest
Then all the world, when ever it were proov'd;
But Cordeill said she lov'd him as behoov'd:
Whose simple answere, wanting colours fayre
To paint it forth, him to displeasaunce moov'd,
That in his crown he counted her no hayre,
But twixt the other twain his kingdom whole did shayre.

So wedded th' one to Maglan king of Scottes,
And thother to the king of Cambria,
And twixt them shayrd his realme by equall lottes;
But without dowre the wise Cordelia[1]
Was sent to Aggannip of Celtica.
Their aged Syre, thus eased of his crowne,
A private life ledd in Albania
With Gonorill, long had in great renowne,
That nought him griev'd to beene from rule deposed downe.

---

[1] The first spelling of the name as Shakespeare will spell it.

But true it is that, when the oyle is spent,
The light goes out, and weeke is throwne away:
So, when he had resignd his regiment,
His daughter gan despise his drouping day,
And wearie wax of his continuall stay.
Tho to his daughter Regan he repayrd,
Who him at first well used every way;
But when of his departure she despayrd,
Her bountie she abated, and his cheare empayrd.

The wretched man gan then avise too late,
That love is not where most it is profest;
Too truely tryde in his extremest state.
At last, resolv'd likewise to prove the rest,
He to Cordelia him selfe addrest,
Who with entyre affection him receav'd,
As for her Syre and king her seemed best;
And after all an army strong she leav'd,
To war on those which him had of his realme bereav'd.

So to his crowne she him restord againe;
In which he dyde, made ripe for death by eld,
And after wild it should to her remaine,
Who peaceably the same long time did weld,
And all mens harts in dew obedience held;
Till that her sisters children, woxen strong,
Through proud ambition against her rebeld,
And overcommen kept in prison long,
Till weary of that wretched life her selfe she hong.[2]

---

[2] The first version in which Cordelia dies by hanging.

ANONYMOUS, C. *1594*

The True Chronicle History of King Leir*

CHARACTERS

LEIR, King of Brittany.[1]
KING OF GALLIA.
KING OF CORNWALL.
KING OF CAMBRIA.
PERILLUS, a Nobleman.
MUMFORD, a Knight.
SKALLIGER, a Courtier.
A MESSENGER.
THE GALLIAN AMBASSADOR.

GONORILL,
RAGAN,   } Daughters to Leir.
CORDELLA.

Nobles of Brittany and Gallia; two Mariners; two Captains; two
Watchmen; Attendants and Servants; Soldiers and Citizens.
Scene: Brittany and Gallia.

ACT I

SCENE I.

Enter King Leir and nobles.
LEIR. Thus to our grief the obsequies performed
Of our (too late) deceased and dearest queen,
Whose soul I hope, possessed of heavenly joys
Doth ride in triumph 'mongst the cherubins;

---

* text modernized. (The full title is *The True Chronicle History of King
Leir and his three daughters, Gonorill, Ragan, and Cordella.*)
    [1] Assuredly Britain rather than France (Bretagne). This would be in keep-
ing with the other sources and with Shakespeare's play.

[2]Let us request your grave advice, my lords,
For the disposing of our princely daughters,
For whom our care is specially employed,
As nature binds to advance their states,
In royal marriage with some princely mates:
For wanting now their mother's good advice,   10
Under whose government they have received
A perfect pattern of a virtuous life:
Left as it were a ship without a stern,
Or silly sheep without a pastor's care;
Although ourselves do dearly tender them,
Yet are we ignorant of their affairs:
For fathers best do know to govern sons;
But daughters' steps the mother's counsel turns.
A son we want for to succeed our crown,
And course of time has cancelled the date   20
Of further issue from our withered loins:
One foot already hangs in the grave,
And age has made deep furrows in my face:
[3]The world of me, I of the world am weary,
And I would feign resign these earthy cares,
And think upon the welfare of my soul:
Which by no better means may be effected,
Than by resigning up the crown from me
In equal dowry to my daughters three.

SKALLIGER. A worthy care, my liege, which well declares,   30
The zeal you bore unto our *quondam*[4] queen:
And since your grace has licensed me to speak,
I censure thus; Your Majesty knowing well,
What several suitors your princely daughters have,
[5]To make them each a jointer more or less,
As is their worth, to them that love profess.

LEIR. No more, nor less, but even all alike,
My zeal is fixed, all fashioned in one mold:
Wherefore unpartial shall my censure be,
Both old and young shall have alike for me.   40

---

[2] In Geoffrey of Monmouth's history Leir also relies upon the counsel of his nobles in arranging his daughters' marriage.

[3] I.i. 38–42.

[4] former.

[5] I.i. 52–54. In Shakespeare and in Geoffrey of Monmouth, this is Lear's idea.

NOBLE. My gracious lord, I heartily do wish,
That God had lent you an heir indubitate,[6]
Which might have set upon your royal throne,
When fates should loose the prison of your life,
By whose succession all this doubt might cease;
And as by you, by him we might have peace.
But after-wishes ever come too late,
And nothing can revoke the course of fate:
Wherefore, my liege, my censure deems it best,
To match them with some of your neighbor kings,   50
Bordering within the bounds of Albion,
By whose united friendship, this our state
May be protected 'gainst all foreign hate.

LEIR. Herein, my lords, your wishes sort with mine,
And mine (I hope) do sort with heavenly powers:
For at this instant two near neighboring Kings
Of Cornwall and of Cambria,[7] motion love
To my two daughters, Gonorill and Ragan.
My youngest daughter, fair Cordella, vows
No liking to a monarch, unless love allows.   60
She is solicited by divers Peers;
But none of them her partial fancy hears.
Yet, if my policy may her beguile,
I'll match her to some king within this isle,
And so establish such a perfect peace,
As fortune's force shall ne'er prevail to cease.

PERILLUS. Of us and ours, your gracious care, my Lord,
Deserves an everlasting memory,
To be enrolled in chronicles of fame,
By never dying perpetuity: 70
Yet to become so provident a prince,
Lose not the title of a loving father:
Do not force love, where fancy cannot dwell,
Lest streams being stopped, above the banks do swell.

LEIR. I am resolv'd, and even now my mind
Doth meditate a sudden stratagem,
To try which of my daughters loves me best:
Which till I know, I cannot be in rest.
This granted, when they jointly shall contend,
Each to exceed the other in their love: 80

---

[6] indubitable.
[7] In Shakespeare, Albany.

[8]Then at the vantage will I take Cordella,
Even as she doth protest she loves me best,
I'll say, "Then, daughter, grant me one request,
To show thou lovest me as thy sisters do,
Accept a husband, whom myself will woo."
This said, she cannot well deny my suit,
Although (poor soul) her senses will be mute:
Then will I triumph in my policy,
And match her with a king of Brittany.

 SKALLIGER.[9] I'll to them before and betray your secrecy. 90
 PERILLUS. Thus fathers think their children to beguile,
And oftentimes themselves do first repent,
When heavenly powers do frustrate their intent. (*Exeunt.*)

SCENE II.

Enter Gonorill and Ragan.

 GONORILL.[10] I marvel, Ragan, how you can endure,
To see that proud pert peat,[11] our youngest sister,
So slightly to account of us, her elders,
As if we were no better than herself!
We cannot have a quaint device so soon,
Or new made fashion, of our choice invention;
But if she like it, she will have the same, 100
Or study newer to exceed us both.
Besides, she is so nice and so demure;
So sober, courteous, modest, and precise,
That all the court has work enough to do,
To talk how she exceeds me and you.

 RAGAN. What should I do? Would it were in my power,
To find a cure for this contagious ill:
Some desperate medicine must be soon applied,
To dim the glory of her mounting fame;
Else ere it be long, she'll have both prick and praise,[12] 110
And we must be set by for working days.
Do you not see what several choice of suitors

---

 [8] I.i. 84–87.
 [9] Skalliger is roughly equivalent to Shakespeare's Oswald, as ACT II. Scene i. below bears out.
 [10] Compare this explicit hostility of Cordella's sisters with Shakespeare's glancing treatment of it: I.i. 274–284.
 [11] A spoiled child.
 [12] Praise for excellence.

She daily has, and of the best degree?
Say, amongst all, she hap to fancy one,
And have a husband when we have none:
Why then, by right, to her we must give place,
Though it be ne'er so much to our disgrace.

GONORILL.[13] By my virginity, rather than she shall have
A husband before me,
I'll marry one or other in his shirt: 120
And yet I have made half a grant already
Of my good will unto the King of Cornwall.[14]

RAGAN. Swear not so deeply (sister) here comes my Lord
Skalliger.
Something his hasty coming doth import.

(Enter Skalliger.)

SKALLIGER. Sweet princesses, I am glad I met you here so luckily,
Having good news which doth concern you both,
And craves speedy expedition.

RAGAN. For God's sake tell us what it is, my Lord,
I am with child until you utter it.   130

SKALLIGER. Madam, to save your longing, this it is:
Your father in great secrecy today,
Told me, he means to marry you out of hand
Unto the noble Prince of Cambria;
You, Madam, to the King of Cornwall's Grace:
Your younger sister he would feign bestow
Upon the rich King of Hibernia:
But that he doubts, she hardly will consent;
For hitherto she ne'er could fancy him.
If she do yield, why then, between you three,   140
He will divide his kingdom for your dowries.
But yet there is further mystery,
Which, so you will conceal, I will disclose.

GONORILL. Whatever thou speakest to us, kind Skalliger,
Think that thou speakest it only to thyself.

SKALLIGER. He earnestly desires for to know,
Which of you three do bear most love to him,
And on your loves he so extremely dotes,
As never any did, I think, before.
He presently doth mean to send for you,   150
To be resolved of this tormenting doubt:

---

[13] Lines like this, and line 130 below, make the sisters especially crude and earthy in this play, a characterization borne out by their final speeches in this scene.

[14] In Shakespeare it is Regan who is married to Cornwall.

And look, whose answer pleases him the best,
They shall have most unto their marriages.

    RAGAN. O that I had some pleasing mermaid's voice,
For to enchant his senseless senses with!

    SKALLIGER. For he supposes that Cordella will
(Striving to go beyond you in her love)
Promise to do whatever he desires:
Then will he straight enjoin her for his sake,
The Hibernian king in marriage for to take.   160
This is the sum of all I have to say;
Which being done, I humbly take my leave,
Not doubting but your wisdoms will foresee,
What course will best unto your good agree.

    GONORILL. Thanks, gentle Skalliger, thy kindness undeserved,
Shall not be unrequited, if we live.   (*Exit Skalliger.*)

    RAGAN. Now have we fit occasion offered us,
To be revenged upon her unperceived.

    GONORILL. Nay, our revenge we will inflict on her,
Shall be accounted piety in us: 170
I will so flatter with my doting father,
As he was ne'er flattered in his life.
Nay, I will say, that if it be his pleasure,
To match me to a beggar, I will yield:
For why, I know whatever I do say,
He means to match me with the Cornwall king.

    RAGAN. I'll say the like: for I am well assured,
What e'er I say to please the old man's mind,
Who dotes, as if he were a child again,
I shall enjoy the noble Cambrian prince: 180
Only, to feed his humor, will suffice,
To say, I am content with anyone
Whom he'll appoint me; this will please him more,
Than e'er Apollo's music pleased Iove.

    GONORILL. I smile to think, in what a woeful plight
Cordella will be, when we answer thus:
For she will rather die, than give consent
To join in marriage with the Irish king:
So will our father think, she loves him not,
Because she will not grant to his desire,   190
Which we will aggravate in such bitter terms,
That he will soon convert his love to hate:
For he, you know, is always in extremes.

    RAGAN. Not all the world could lay a better plot,
I long till it be put in practice.   (*Exeunt.*)

SCENE III.

Enter Leir and Perillus.

LEIR. Perillus, go seek my daughters,
Will them immediately come and speak with me.

PERILLUS. I will, my gracious Lord.   (*Exit.*)

LEIR. Oh, what a combat feels my panting heart,
'Twixt children's love, and care of commonweal!   200
How dear my daughters are unto my soul,
None knows, but he, that knows my thoughts and secret deeds.
Ah, little do they know the dear regard,
Wherein I hold their future state to come:
When they securely sleep on beds of down,
These aged eyes do watch for their behalf:
¹⁵While they like wantons sport in youthful toys,
This throbbing heart is pierced with dire annoys.
As doth the sun exceed the smallest star,
So much the father's love exceeds the child's.   210
Yet my complaints are causeless: for the world
Affords not children more conformable:
And yet, methinks, my mind presages still
I know not what; and yet I fear some ill.
          (*Enter Perillus, with the three daughters.*)
¹⁶Well, here my daughters come: I have found out
A present means to rid me of this doubt.

GONORILL. Our royal Lord and father, in all duty,
We come to know the tenor of your will,
Why you so hastily have sent for us?

LEIR. Dear Gonorill, kind Ragan, sweet Cordella,   220
Ye flourishing branches of a kingly stock,
Sprung from a tree that once did flourish green,
Whose blossoms now are nipped with winter's frost,
And pale grim death doth wait upon my steps,
And summons me unto his next assizes.
Therefore, dear daughters, as ye tender the safety
Of him that was the cause of your first being,
Resolve a doubt which much molests my mind,
Which of you three to me would prove most kind;
Which loves me most, and which at my request   230
Will soonest yield unto their father's hest.

---

¹⁵ A hint here of Gloucester's lines: IV.i. 38–39.
¹⁶ I.i. 37–122.

GONORILL. I hope, my gracious father makes no doubt
Of any of his daughter's love to him:
Yet for my part, to show my zeal to you,
Which cannot be in windy words rehearsed,
I prize my love to you at such a rate,
I think my life inferior to my love.
Should you enjoin me for to tie a millstone
About my neck, and leap into the sea,
At your command I willingly would do it: 240
Yea, for to do you good, I would ascend
The highest turret in all Brittany,
And from the top leap headlong to the ground:
Nay, more, should you appoint me for to marry
The meanest vassal in the spacious world,
Without reply I would accomplish it:
In brief, command whatever you desire,
And if I fail, no favor I require.
    LEIR. O, how thy words revive my dying soul!
    CORDELLA. O, how I do abhor this flattery!   250
    LEIR. But what says Ragan to her father's will?
    RAGAN. O, that my simple utterance could suffice,
To tell the true intention of my heart,
Which burns in zeal of duty to your grace,
And never can be quenched, but by desire
To show the same in outward forwardness.
Oh, that there were some other maid that durst
But make a challenge of her love with me;
I'd make her soon confess she never loved
Her father half so well as I do you.   260
Aye, then my deeds should prove in plainer case,
How much my zeal abounds to your grace:
But for them all, let this one mean suffice,
To ratify my love before your eyes:
I have right noble suitors to my love,
No worse than kings, and happily I love one:
Yet, would you have me make my choice anew,
I'd bridle fancy, and be ruled by you.
    LEIR. Did never Philomel sing so sweet a note.
    CORDELLA. Did never flatterer tell so false a tale.
    LEIR. Speak now, Cordella, make my joys at full,   270
And drop down nectar from thy honey lips.
    CORDELLA. I cannot paint my duty forth in words,
I hope my deeds shall make report for me:

But look what love the child doth owe the father,
The same to you I bear, my gracious Lord.

GONORILL. Here is an answer answerless indeed:
Were you my daughter, I should scarcely brook it.

RAGAN. Dost thou not blush, proud peacock as thou art,
To make our father such a slight reply? 280

LEIR. Why how now, minion, are you grown so proud?
Doth our dear love make you thus peremptory?
What, is your love become so small to us,
As that you scorn to tell us what it is?
Do you love us, as every child doth love
Their father? True indeed, as some,
Who by disobedience short their father's days,
And so would you; some are so father-sick,
That they make means to rid them from the world;
And so would you: some are indifferent, 290
Whether their aged parents live or die;
And so are you. But, didst thou know, proud girl,
What care I had to foster thee to this,
Ah, then thou wouldst say as thy sisters do:
Our life is less, than love we owe to you.

CORDELLA. Dear father, do not so mistake my words,
Nor my plain meaning be misconstrued;
My tongue was never used to flattery.

GONORILL. You were not best say I flatter; if you do,
My deeds shall show, I flatter not with you. 300
I love my father better than thou canst.

CORDELLA. The praise were great, spoke from another's mouth:
But it should seem your neighbors dwell far off.

RAGAN. Nay, here is one, that will confirm as much
As she has said, both for myself and her.
I say, thou dost not wish my father's good.

CORDELLA. Dear father —

LEIR. Peace, bastard imp, no issue of King Leir,
I will not hear thee speak one tittle more.
Call not me father, if thou love thy life, 310
Nor these thy sisters once presume to name:
Look for no help henceforth from me nor mine;
Shift as thou will, and trust unto thyself:
My kingdom will I equally divide
'Twixt thy two sisters to their royal dower,
And will bestow them worthy their deserts:
This done, because thou shalt not have the hope,
To have a child's part in the time to come,

I presently will dispossess myself,
And set up these upon my princely throne.   320
    GONORILL. I ever thought that pride would have a fall.
    RAGAN. Plain dealing, sister: your beauty is so sheen,
You'd need no dowry, to make you be a queen.
                              (*Exeunt Leir, Gonorill, Ragan.*)
    CORDELLA. Now whither, poor forsaken, shall I go
When mine own sisters triumph in my woe?
But unto Him which doth protect the just,
In Him will poor Cordella put her trust.
These hands shall labor, for to get my spending;
And so I'll live until my days have ending.   (*Exit.*)
    PERILLUS.[17] Oh, how I grieve, to see my lord thus fond,[18]   330
To dote so much upon vain flattering words.
Ah, if he but with good advice had weighed,
The hidden tenor of her humble speech,
Reason to rage should not have given place,
Nor poor Cordella suffer such disgrace.   (*Exit.*)

SCENE IV.

Enter the Gallian[19] King with Mumford, and three nobles more.

    KING.[20] Dissuade me not, my lords, I am resolved,
This next fair wind to sail for Brittany,
In some disguise, to see if flying fame
Be not too prodigal in the wondrous praise
Of these three nymphs, the daughters of King Leir.   340
If present view do answer absent praise,
And eyes allow of what our ears have heard,
And Venus stand auspicious to my vows,
And fortune favor what I take in hand;
I will return seized of as rich a prize
As Jason, when he won the golden fleece.
    MUMFORD. Heavens grant you may; the match were full of honor,
And well beseeming the young Gallian king.
I would your Grace would favor me so much,   350

----

[17] I.i. 123–190. Contrast Perillus's passive role with the active and significant one Shakespeare assigns to Kent.

[18] foolish.

[19] i.e., of Gaul, Gallic.

[20] Shakespeare has nothing resembling these next two scenes. The closest parallel is in Geoffrey of Monmouth, where Aganippus dispatches envoys to King Leir requesting Cordeilla's hand.

As make me partner of your pilgrimage.
I long to see the gallant British dames,
And feed mine eyes upon their rare perfections:
For till I know the contrary, I'll say,
Our dames in France are far more fair than they.
 KING. Lord Mumford, you have saved me a labor,
In offering that which I did mean to ask,
And I most willingly accept your company.
Yet first I will enjoin you to observe
Some few conditions which I shall propose.   360
 MUMFORD. So that you do not tie mine eyes for looking
After the amorous glances of fair dames:
So that you do not tie my tongue from speaking,
My lips from kissing when occasion serves,
My hands from congies,[21] and my knees to bow
To gallant girls; which were a task more hard,
Than flesh and blood is able to endure:
Command what else you please, I rest content.
 KING. To bind thee from a thing thou canst not leave,
Were but a mean to make thee seek it more: 370
And therefore speak, look, kiss, salute for me;
In these myself am like to second thee.
Now hear thy task. I charge thee from the time
That first we set sail for the British shore,
To use no words of dignity to me,
But in the friendliest manner that thou canst,
Make use of me as thy companion:
For we will go disguised in palmers' weeds,
That no man shall mistrust us what we are.
 MUMFORD. If that be all, I'll fit your turn, I warrant you.   380
I am some kin to the Blunts, and I think, the bluntest of
All my kindred; therefore if I be too blunt with you,
Thank yourself for praying me to be so.
 KING. Thy pleasant company will make the way seem short.
It rests now, that in my absence hence,
I do commit the government to you
My trusty lords and faithful counsellors.
Time cuts off the rest I have to say:
The wind blows fair, and I must needs away.
 NOBLES. Heavens send your voyage to as good effect,   390
As we your land do purpose to protect.   (*Exeunt.*)

---

[21] Dismissals, formal leaves to depart.

Scene V.

Enter the King of Cornwall and his man booted and spurred, a riding
wand, and a letter in his hand.

CORNWALL. But how far distant are we from the court?

SERVITOR. Some twenty miles, my Lord, or thereabouts.

CORNWALL. It seems to me twenty thousand miles:
Yet hope I to be there within this hour.

SERVITOR. (*to himself.*) Then are you like to ride alone for
me.
I think my Lord is weary of his life.

CORNWALL. Sweet Gonorill, I long to see thy face,
Which hast so kindly gratified my love.   400
> (*Enter the King of Cambria booted and spurred,*
> *and his man with a wand and a letter.*)

CAMBRIA. Get a fresh horse: for by my soul I swear,
> (*He looks on the letter.*)
I am past patience, longer to forbear
The wished sight of my beloved mistress,
Dear Ragan, stay and comfort of my life.

SERVITOR. (*to himself.*) Now what in God's name doth my
Lord intend?
He thinks he ne'er shall come at journey's end.
I would he had old Dedalus's waxen wings,
That he might fly, so I might stay behind:
For ere we get to Troynovant, I see,   410
He quite will tire himself, his horse and me.
> [22](*Cornwall and Cambria look one upon another,*
> *and start to see each other there.*)

CORNWALL. Brother of Cambria, we greet you well,
As one whom here we little did expect.

CAMBRIA. Brother of Cornwall, met in happy time:
I thought as much to have met with the Sultan of Persia,
As to have met you in this place, my Lord.
No doubt, it is about some great affairs
That makes you here so slenderly accompanied.

CORNWALL. To say the truth, my Lord, it is no less,
And for your part some hasty wind of chance   420
Has blown you hither thus upon the sudden.

---

[22] Compare this scene with Shakespeare's early statement of Lear's prefer-
ence for Albany: I.i. 1–2.

CAMBRIA. My Lord, to break off further circumstances,
For at this time I cannot brook delays:
Tell you your reason, I will tell you mine.

CORNWALL. In faith content, and therefore to be brief,
For I am sure my haste's as great as yours:
I am sent for, to come unto King Leir,
Who by these present letters promises
His eldest daughter, lovely Gonorill,
To me in marriage, and for present dowry,   430
The moiety of half his regimen.
The lady's love I long ago possessed.
But until now I never had the father's.

CAMBRIA. You tell me wonders, yet I will relate
Strange news, and henceforth we must brothers call;
Witness these lines: his honorable age,
Being weary of the troubles of his crown,
His princely daughter Ragan will bestow
On me in marriage, with half his seigniories,
Whom I would gladly have accepted of,   440
With the third part, her complements are such.

CORNWALL. If I have one half, and you have the other,
Then between us we must needs have the whole.

CAMBRIA. The hole! How mean you that? Zblood, I hope,
We shall have two holes between us.

CORNWALL. Why, the whole kingdom.

CAMBRIA. Aye, that's very true.

CORNWALL. What then is left for his third daughter's dowry,
Lovely Cordella, whom the world admires?

CAMBRIA. 'Tis very strange, I know not what to think,   450
Unless they mean to make a nun of her.

CORNWALL. 'Twere pity such rare beauty should be hid
Within the compass of a cloister's wall:
But howsoever, if Leir's words prove true,
It will be good, my Lord, for me and you.

CAMBRIA. Then let us haste, all danger to prevent,
For fear delays do alter his intent.   (*Exeunt.*)

Scene VI.

Enter Gonorill and Ragan.

GONORILL. Sister, when did you see Cordella last,
That pretty piece, that thinks none good enough
To speak to her, because (sir-reverence)   460
She has a little beauty extraordinary?

RAGAN. Since time my father warned her from his presence,
I never saw her, that I can remember.
God give her joy of her surpassing beauty;
I think her dowry will be small enough.

GONORILL. I have incensed my father so against her,
As he will never be reclaimed again.

RAGAN. I was not much behind to do the like.

GONORILL. Faith, sister, what moves you to bear her such good
will?   **470**

RAGAN. [23]In truth, I think, the same that moves you;
Because she doth surpass us both in beauty.

GONORILL. Beshrew your fingers, how right you can guess:
I tell you true, it cuts me to the heart.

RAGAN. But we will keep her low enough, I warrant,
And clip her wings for mounting up too high.

GONORILL. Whoever has her, shall have a rich marriage of her.

RAGAN. She were right fit to make a parson's wife:
For they, men say, do love fair women well,
And many times do marry them with nothing.   **480**

GONORILL. With nothing! Marry, God forbid: why, are there
any such?

RAGAN. I mean, no money.

GONORILL. I cry you mercy, I mistook you much:
And she is far too stately for the church;
She'll lay her husband's benefice on her back,
Even in one gown, if she may have her will.

RAGAN. In faith, poor soul, I pity her a little.
Would she were less fair, or more fortunate.
Well, I think long until I see my Morgan,   **490**
The gallant Prince of Cambria here arrive.

GONORILL. And so do I, until the Cornwall king
Present himself, to consummate my joys.
Peace, here comes my father.

(Enter Leir, Perillus and others.)

LEIR. Cease, good my lords, and sue not to reverse
Our censure, which is now irrevocable.
We have dispatched letters of contract
Unto the Kings of Cambria and of Cornwall;
Our hand and seal will justify no less:
Then do not so dishonor me, my Lords,   **500**
As to make shipwreck of our kingly word.
I am as kind as is the pelican,

---

[23] The motivation here is childishly simple.

That kills itself, to save her young ones' lives:
And yet as jealous as the princely eagle,
That kills her young ones, if they do but dazzle
Upon the radiant splendor of the sun.
Within this two days I expect their coming.

(*Enter Kings of Cornwall and Cambria.*)

But in good time, they are arrived already.
This haste of yours, my Lords, doth testify
The fervent love you bear unto my daughters: 510
And think yourselves as welcome to King Leir,
As ever Priam's children were to him.

CORNWALL. My gracious Lord, and father too, I hope,
Pardon, for that I made no greater haste:
But were my horse as swift as was my will,
I long ere this had seen your Majesty.

CAMBRIA. No other excuse of absence can I frame
Than what my brother has informed your Grace:
For our undeserved welcome, we do vow
Perpetually to rest at your command.   520

CORNWALL. But you, sweet love, illustrious Gonorill,
The regent, and the sovereign of my soul,
Is Cornwall welcome to your Excellency?

GONORILL. As welcome, as Leander was to Hero,
Or brave Aeneas to the Carthage queen:
So and more welcome is your Grace to me.

CAMBRIA. O, may my fortune prove no worse than his,
Since heavens do know, my fancy is as much.
Dear Ragan, say, if welcome unto thee,
All welcomes else will little comfort me.   530

RAGAN. As gold is welcome to the covetous eye,
As sleep is welcome to the traveller,
As is fresh water to sea-beaten men,
Or moistened showers unto the parched ground,
Or anything more welcomer than this,
So and more welcome lovely Morgan is.

LEIR. What rests then, but that we consummate
The celebration of these nuptial rites?
[24]My kingdom I do equally divide.
Princes, draw lots, and take your chance as falls.   540

(*Then they draw lots.*)

These I resign as freely unto you,
As erst by true succession they were mine.

---

[24] I.i. 129–141.

And here I (do) freely dispossess myself,
And make you two my true adopted heirs:
Myself will sojourn with my son of Cornwall,
And take me to my prayers and my beads.
I know my daughter Ragan will be sorry
Because I do not spend my days with her:
Would I were able to be with both at once;
They are the kindest girls in Christendom.   550

   PERILLUS.[25] I have been silent all this while, my Lord,
To see if any worthier than myself,
Would once have spoke in poor Cordella's cause:
But love or fear ties silence to their tongues.
Oh, hear me speak for her, my gracious Lord,
Whose deeds have not deserved this ruthless doom
As thus to disinherit her of all.

   LEIR. Urge this no more, and if thou love thy life:
I say, she is no daughter, that doth scorn
To tell her father how she loves him.   560
Whoever speaks hereof to me again,
I will esteem him for my mortal foe.
Come, let us in, to celebrate with joy,
The happy nuptials of these lovely pairs.

                        (*Exeunt omnes, manet Perillus.*)
   PERILLUS. Ah, who so blind, as they that will not see
The near approach of their own misery?
Poor lady, I extremely pity her:
And whilest I live, each drop of my heart blood
Will I strain forth, to do her any good.   (*Exit.*)

Scene VII.

*Enter the Gallian King, and
Mumford, disguised like pilgrims.*

   MUMFORD. My Lord, how do you brook this British air?   570
   KING. My Lord? I told you of this foolish humor,
And bound you to the contrary, you know.
   MUMFORD. Pardon me for once, my Lord; I did forget.
   KING. My Lord again? Then let's have nothing else,
And so be taken for spies, and then 'tis well.
   MUMFORD. Swounds, I could bite my tongue in two for anger;
For God's sake name yourself some proper name.
   KING. Call me Tresillus; I'll call thee Denapoll.

---

[25] I.i. 141–190. Compare these passages for dramatic force.

MUMFORD. Might I be made Monarch of the World,
I could not hit upon these names, I swear.   580

KING. Then call me Will, I'll call thee Jack.

MUMFORD. Well, be it so, for I have well deserved to be called
Jack.

KING.[26] Stand close; for here a British lady comes.

(*Enter Cordella.*)

A fairer creature ne'er mine eyes beheld.

CORDELLA. This is a day of joy unto my sisters,
Wherein they both are married unto kings;
And I, by birth, as worthy as themselves,
Am turned into the world, to seek my fortune.
How may I blame the fickle Queen of Chance,   590
That makes me a pattern of her power?
Ah, poor weak maid, whose imbecility
Is far unable to endure these brunts.
Oh, father Leir, how dost thou wrong thy child,
Who always was obedient to thy will!
But why accuse I fortune and my father?
No, no, it is the pleasure of my God:
And I do willingly embrace the rod.

KING. It is no goddess: for she doth complain
On fortune, and the unkindness of her father.   600

CORDELLA. These costly robes ill fitting my estate,
I will exchange for other meaner habit.

MUMFORD. Now if I had a kingdom in my hands,
I would exchange it for a milkmaid's smock and petticoat
That she and I might shift our clothes together.

CORDELLA. I will betake me to my thread and needle,
And earn my living with my fingers' ends.

MUMFORD. O brave! God willing, thou shalt have my custom,
By sweet St. Denis, here I sadly swear,
For all the shirts and night-gear that I wear.   610

CORDELLA. I will profess and vow a maiden's life.

MUMFORD. Then I protest thou shalt not have my custom.

KING. I can forbear no longer for to speak:
For if I do, I think my heart will break.

MUMFORD. Sblood, Will, I hope you are not in love with my
seamstress.

KING. I am in such a labyrinth of love,
As that I know not which way to get out.

---

[26] The following highly romantic scene, reminiscent of the style of Thomas
Dekker, becomes, in Shakespeare: I.i. 216–264.

MUMFORD. You'll never get out unless you first get in.

KING. I prithee, lack, cross not my passions.   620

MUMFORD. Prithee, Will, to her, and try her patience.

KING. Thou fairest creature, whatsoe'er thou art,
That ever any mortal eyes beheld,
Vouchsafe to me, who have overheard thy woes,
To show the cause of these thy sad laments.

CORDELLA. Ah pilgrims, what avails to show the cause,
When there's no means to find a remedy?

KING. To utter grief, doth ease a heart o'ercharged.

CORDELLA. To touch a sore, doth aggravate the pain.

KING. The silly mouse, by virtue of her teeth,   630
Released the princely lion from the net.

CORDELLA. Kind palmer, which so much desirest to hear
The tragic tale of my unhappy youth;
Know this in brief, I am the hapless daughter
Of Leir, sometime King of Brittany.

KING. Why, who debars his honorable age,
From being still the King of Brittany?

CORDELLA. None but himself has dispossessed himself,
And given all his kingdom to the Kings
Of Cornwall and of Cambria, with my sisters.   640

KING. Has he given nothing to your lovely self?

CORDELLA. He loved me not, and therefore gave me nothing,
Only because I could not flatter him;
And in this day of triumph to my sisters,
Doth fortune triumph in my overthrow.

KING. Sweet lady, say there should come a king,
As good as either of your sisters' husbands,
To crave your love, would you accept him?

CORDELLA. Oh, do not mock with those in misery,
Nor do not think, though fortune have the power,   650
To spoil mine honor, and debase my state,
That she hath any interest in my mind:
For if the greatest monarch on the earth,
Should sue to me in this extremity,
Except my heart could love, and heart could like,
Better than any that I ever saw,
His great estate no more should move my mind,
Than mountains move by blast of every wind.

KING. Think not, sweet nymph, 'tis holy palmer's guise,
To grieved souls fresh torments to devise: 660
Therefore in witness of my true intent,
Let heaven and earth bear record of my words:

There is a young and lusty Gallian king,
So like to me, as I am to myself,
That earnestly doth crave to have thy love,
And join with thee in Hymen's sacred bonds.
   CORDELLA. The like to thee did ne'er these eyes behold;
Oh live to add new torments to my grief:
Why didst thou thus entrap me unawares?
Ah palmer, my estate doth not befit   670
A kingly marriage, as the case now stands.
Whilome[27] when as I lived in honor's height,
A prince perhaps might postulate my love:
Now misery, dishonor and disgrace,
Hath light on me, and quite reversed the case.
Thy king will hold thee wise, if thou surcease
The suit, whereas no dowry will ensue.
Then be advised, palmer, what to do:
Cease for thy king, seek for thyself to woo.
   KING. Your birth's too high for any, but a king.   680
   CORDELLA. My mind is low enough to love a palmer,
Rather than any king upon the earth.
   KING. O, but you never can endure their life,
Which is so straight and full of penury.
   CORDELLA. O yes, I can, and happy if I might:
I'll hold thy palmer's staff within my hand,
And think it is the scepter of a queen.
Sometimes I'll set thy bonnet on my head,
And think I wear a rich imperial crown.
Sometimes I'll help thee in thy holy prayers,   690
And think I am with thee in Paradise.
Thus I'll mock fortune, as she mocks me,
And never will my lovely choice repent;
For having thee, I shall have all content.
   KING. 'Twere sin to hold her longer in suspense,
Since that my soul hath vowed she shall be mine.
Ah, dear Cordella, cordial to my heart,
I am no palmer, as I seem to be,
But hither come in this unknown disguise,
To view the admired beauty of those eyes.   700
I am the King of Gallia, gentle maid,
(Although thus slenderly accompanied)
And yet thy vassal by imperious love,
And sworn to serve everlastingly.

---

[27] while.

CORDELLA. Whatever you be, of high or low descent,
All's one to me, I do request but this:
That as I am, you will accept of me,
And I will have you whatsoever you be:
Yet well I know, you come of royal race,
I see such sparks of honor in your face.   710

MUMFORD. Have palmer's weeds such power to win fair ladies?
Faith, then I hope the next that falls is mine:
Upon condition I no worse might speed,
I would forever wear a palmer's weed.
I like an honest and plain dealing wench,
That swears (without exceptions) I will have you.
These foppets,[28] that know not whether to love a man or no,
Except they first go ask their mothers' leave, by this hand,
I hate them ten times worse than poison.

KING. What rests then our happiness to procure?   720

MUMFORD. Faith, go to church to make the matter sure.

KING. It shall be so, because the world shall say,
King Leir's three daughters were wedded in one day:
The celebration of this happy chance,
We will defer, until we come to France.

MUMFORD. I like the wooing, that's not long a doing. Well,
for her sake, I know what I know; I'll never marry whilest I live,
except I have one of these British ladies. My humor is alienated
from the maids of France.   (*Exeunt.*)

ACT II

SCENE I.

Enter Perillus solus.

PERILLUS. The king hath dispossessed himself of all,   730
Those to advance, which scarce will give him thanks:
His youngest daughter he has turned away,
And no man knows what is become of her.
He sojourns now in Cornwall with the eldest,
Who flattered him until she did obtain
That at his hands, which now she doth possess:
And now she sees he has no more to give,
It grieves her heart to see her father live.
Oh, whom should man trust in this wicked age,
When children thus against their parents rage?   740

---

[28] petty fops.

But he, the mirror of mild patience,
Puts up all wrongs, and never gives reply:
Yet shames she not in most opprobrious sort,
To call him fool and dotard to his face,
And sets her parasites of purpose oft,
In scoffing wise to offer him disgrace.
Oh iron age! O times! O monstrous, vile,
When parents are contemned of the child!
[29]His pension she has half restrained from him,
And will, ere long, the other half, I fear: 750
For she thinks nothing is bestowed in vain,
But that which doth her father's life maintain.
Trust not alliance; but trust strangers rather,
Since daughters prove disloyal to the father.
Well, I will counsel him the best I can:
Would I were able to redress his wrong.
Yet what I can, unto my utmost power,
He shall be sure of to the latest hour.   (*Exit.*)

Scene II.

Enter Gonorill and Skalliger.

GONORILL.[30] I prithee, Skalliger, tell me what thou thinkest:
Could any woman of our dignity   760
Endure such quips and peremptory taunts,
As I do daily from my doting father?
Doth it not suffice that I him keep of alms,
Who is not able for to keep himself?
But as if he were our better, he should think
To check and snap me up at every word.
I cannot make me a new fashioned gown,
And set it forth with more than common cost;
But his old doting doltish withered wit,
Is sure to give a senseless check for it.   770
I cannot make a banquet extraordinary,
To grace myself, and spread my name abroad,
But he, old fool, is captious by and by,
And says, the cost would well suffice for twice.
Judge then, I pray, what reason is it, that I
Should stand alone charged with his vain expense,
And that my sister Ragan should go free,

---

[29] I.iv. 316–317.
[30] I.iii. 3–7.

To whom he gave as much, as unto me?
I prithee, Skalliger, tell me, if thou know,
By any means to rid me of this woe.   780

SKALLIGER. Your many favors still bestowed on me,
Bind me in duty to advise your Grace,
How you may soonest remedy this ill.
The large allowance which he has from you,
Is that which makes him to forget himself.
Therefore abridge it half, and you shall see,
That having less, he will more thankful be:
For why, abundance makes us forget
The fountains whence the benefits do spring.

GONORILL. Well, Skalliger, for thy kind advice herein,   790
I will not be ungrateful, if I live:
I have restrained half his portion already,
And I will presently restrain the other,
That having no means to relieve himself,
He may go seek elsewhere for better help.[31]   (*Exit.*)

SKALLIGER. Go, viperous woman, shame to all thy sex,
The heavens, no doubt, will punish thee for this:
And me a villain, that to curry favor,
Have given the daughter counsel 'gainst the father.
But us the world doth this experience give,   800
That he that cannot flatter, cannot live.   (*Exit.*)

SCENE III.

Enter King of Cornwall, Leir, Perillus, and nobles.

CORNWALL. Father, what ails you to be so sad?
Methinks, you frolic not as you were wont.

LEIR.[32] The nearer we do grow unto our graves,
The less we do delight in worldly joys.

CORNWALL. But if a man can frame himself to mirth,
It is a mean for to prolong his life.

LEIR. Then welcome sorrow, Leir's only friend,
Who doth desire his troubled days had end.

CORNWALL. Comfort yourself, father, here comes your daughter,   810
Who much will grieve, I know, to see you sad.

LEIR. But more doth grieve, I fear, to see me live.
                                                    (*Enter Gonorill.*)

_____

[31] So that in this play Leir is acted upon, while in Shakespeare he becomes,
with enlightenment, the doer.
[32] Contrast Leir's melancholy with his anger in: I.iii,iv.

CORNWALL.[33] My Gonorill, you come in wished time,
To put your father from these pensive dumps.
In faith, I fear that all things go not well.

GONORILL. What, do you fear, that I have angered him?
Has he complained of me unto my Lord?
I'll provide him a piece of bread and cheese;
For in a time he'll practise nothing else,
Than carry tales from one unto another.   820
'Tis all his practise for to kindle strife,
'Twixt you, my Lord, and me your loving wife:
But I will take an order, if I can,
To cease the effect, where first the cause began.

CORNWALL. Sweet, be not angry in a partial cause,
He ne'er complained of thee in all his life.
Father, you must not weigh a woman's words.

LEIR. Alas, not I; poor soul, she breeds young bones,
And that is it makes her so touchy sure.

GONORILL. What, breeds young bones already! you will make   830
An honest woman of me then, belike.
O vile old wretch! Whoever heard the like,
That seeks thus his own child to defame?

CORNWALL. I cannot stay to hear this discord sound.   (*Exit.*)

GONORILL. For anyone that loves your company,
You may go pack, and seek some other place,
To sow the seed of discord and disgrace.   (*Exit.*)

LEIR. Thus, say or do the best that e'er I can,
'Tis wrested straight into another sense:
This punishment my heavy sins deserve,   840
And more than this ten thousand thousand times:
Else aged Leir them could never find
Cruel to him, to whom he has been kind.
Why do I over-live myself, to see
The course of nature quite reversed in me?
Ah, gentle death, if ever any wight
Did wish thy presence with a perfect zeal:
Then come, I pray thee, even with all my heart,
And end my sorrows with thy fatal dart.   (*He weeps.*)

PERILLUS. [34]Ah, do not so disconsolate yourself,   850
Nor dew your aged cheeks with wasting tears.

LEIR. What man art thou that takes any pity
Upon the worthless state of old Leir?

---

[33] I.iv. 207–332.
[34] I.iv. 8–104.

PERILLUS. One, who doth bear as great a share of grief,
As if it were my dearest father's case.

LEIR. Ah, good my friend, how ill art thou advised:
For to consort with miserable men:
Go learn to flatter, where thou may in time
Get favor 'mongst the mighty, and so climb:
For now I am so poor and full of want,   860
As that I ne'er can recompense thy love.

PERILLUS. What's got by flattery, doth not long endure;
And men in favor live not most secure.
My conscience tells me, if I should forsake you,
I were the hatefulest excrement on the earth:
Which well do know, in course of former time,
How good my Lord has been to me and mine.

LEIR. Did I ere raise thee higher than the rest
Of all thy ancestors which were before?

PERILLUS. I ne'er did seek it; but by your good Grace   870
I still enjoyed my own with quietness.

LEIR. Did I ere give thee living, to increase
The due revenues which thy father left?

PERILLUS. I had enough, my Lord, and having that,
What should you need to give me any more?

LEIR. Oh, did I ever dispossess myself
And give thee half my kingdom in good will?

PERILLUS. Alas, my Lord, there were no reason, why
You should have such a thought, to give it me.

LEIR. Nay, if thou talk of reason, then be mute;   880
For with good reason I can thee confute.
If they, which first by nature's sacred law,
Do owe to me the tribute of their lives;
If they to whom I always have been kind
And bountiful beyond comparison;
If they, for whom I have undone myself,
And brought my age unto this extreme want,
Do now reject, contemn, despise, abhor me,
What reason moves thee to sorrow for me?

PERILLUS. Where reason fails, let tears confirm my love,   890
And speak how much your passions do me move.
Ah, good my Lord, condemn not all for one:
You have two daughters left, to whom I know
You shall be welcome, if you please to go.

LEIR. Oh, how thy words add sorrow to my soul.
To think of my unkindness to Cordella!
Whom causeless I did dispossess of all.

Upon the unkind suggestions of her sisters:
And for her sake, I think this heavy doom
Is fallen on me, and not without desert: 900
Yet unto Ragan was I always kind,
And gave to her the half of all I had:
It may be, if I should to her repair,
She would be kinder, and entreat me fair.

    PERILLUS. No doubt she would, and practise ere't be long,
By force of arms for to redress your wrong.

    LEIR. Well, since thou doest advise me for to go,
I am resolved to try the worst of woe.   (*Exeunt.*)

Scene IV.

Enter Ragan solus.

    RAGAN. How may I bless the hour of my nativity,
Which bodes unto me such happy stars!   910
How may I thank kind fortune, that vouchsafes
To all my actions, such desired event!
I rule the King of Cambria as I please:
The states are all obedient to my will;
And look what ere I say, it shall be so;
Not any one, that dares answer no.
My eldest sister lives in royal state,
And wants nothing fitting her degree:
Yet has she such a cooling card[35] withal,
As that her honey savors much of gall.   920
My father with her is quarter-master still,
And many times restrains her of her will:
But if he were with me, and served me so,
I'd send him packing somewhere else to go,
I'd entertain him with such slender cost,
That he should quickly wish to change his host.   (*Exit.*)

Scene V.

Enter Cornwall, Gonorill, and attendants.

    CORNWALL. [36]Ah, Gonorill, what dire unhappy chance
Has sequestered thy father from our presence,
That no report can yet be heard of him?
Some great unkindness has been offered him,   930

---

[35] something disconcerting.
[36] I.iv. 333–356.

Exceeding far the bounds of patience:
Else all the world shall never me persuade,
He would forsake us without notice made.

   GONORILL. Alas, my Lord, whom doth it touch so near,
Or who has interest in this grief, but I
Whom sorrow had brought to her longest home,
But that I know his qualities so well?
I know, he is but stolen upon my sister
At unawares, to see her how she fares,
And spend a little time with her, to note   **940**
How all things go, and how she likes her choice:
And when occasion serves, he'll steal from her,
And unawares return to us again.
Therefore, my Lord, be frolic, and resolve
To see my father here again ere long.

   CORNWALL. I hope so too; but yet to be more sure,
I'll send a post immediately to know
Whether he be arrived there or no.   (*Exit.*)

   GONORILL. [37]But I will intercept the messenger.
And temper him before he doth depart,   **950**
With sweet persuasions, and with sound rewards,
That his report shall ratify my speech,
And make my Lord cease further to inquire.
If he be not gone to my sister's court,
As sure my mind presages that he is,
He haply may, by travelling unknown ways,
Fall sick, and as a common passenger,
Be dead and buried: would God it were so well;
For then there were no more to do but this,
He went away, and none knows where he is.
But say he be in Cambria with the king,   **960**
And there exclaim against me, as he will:
I know he is as welcome to my sister,
As water is into a broken ship.
Well, after him I'll send such thunderclaps
Of slander, scandal, and invented tales,
That all the blame shall be removed from me,
And unperceived rebound upon himself.
Thus with one nail another I'll expel,
And make the world judge, that I used him well.   **970**

---

[37] I.iv. 357–363. Gonorill's business with the messenger and the two
letters suggests Regan's colloquy with Oswald: IV.v. 1ff.

(*Enter the messenger that should go to Cambria,
with a letter in his hand.*)

GONORILL. My honest friend, whither away so fast?

MESSENGER. To Cambria, Madam, with letters from the king.

GONORILL. To whom?

MESSENGER. Unto your father, if he be there.

GONORILL. Let me see them. (*She opens them.*)

MESSENGER. Madam, I hope your Grace will stand between me and my neck-verse,[38] if I be called in question, for opening the king's letters.

GONORILL. 'Twas I that opened them, it was not thou.

MESSENGER. Aye, but you need not care; and so must I. A   980
handsome man be quickly trussed up, and when a man's hanged, all the world cannot save him.

GONORILL. He that hangs thee, were better hang his father,
Or that but hurts thee in the least degree,
I tell thee, we make great account of thee.

MESSENGER. I am o'erjoyed, I surfeit of sweet words: kind Queen, had I a hundred lives, I would spend ninety nine of them for you, for that word.

GONORILL. Aye, but thou wouldst keep one life still,
And that's as many as thou art like to have.   990

MESSENGER. That one life is not too dear for my good Queen; this sword, this buckler, this head, this heart, these hands, arms, legs, tripes, bowels, and all the members else whatsoever, are at your dispose; use me, trust me, command me: if I fail in any thing, tie me to a dung cart, and make a scavenger's horse of me, and whip me, so long as I have any skin on my back.

GONORILL. In token of further employment, take that.

(*Flings him a purse.*)

MESSENGER. A strong bond, a firm obligation, good in law, good in law: if I keep not the condition, let my neck be the forfeiture of my negligence.   1000

GONORILL. I like thee well, thou hast a good tongue.

MESSENGER. And as bad a tongue if it be set on it, as any oysterwife at Billingsgate has: why, I have made many of my neighbors forsake their houses with railing upon them, and go dwell elsewhere; and so by my means houses have been good

---

[38] A verse (usually the first verse of the 51st Psalm, in Latin) the reading of which saved one's neck. By virtue of the Biblical text "Touch not mine anointed, and do my prophets no harm" any person in holy orders brought before a secular court (later, any one that could read — being thus potentially a cleric) could plead privilege of clergy.

cheap in our parish. My tongue being well whetted with choler, is more sharp than a razor of Palermo.

GONORILL. Oh, thou art a fit man for my purpose.

MESSENGER. Commend me not, sweet Queen, before you try me. As my deserts are, so do think of me.   1010

GONORILL. Well said, then this is thy trial: instead of carrying the king's letters to my father, carry thou these letters to my sister, which contain matter quite contrary to the other; there shall she be given to understand, that my father has detracted her, given out slanderous speeches against her; and that he has most intolerably abused me, set my Lord and me at variance, and made mutinies amongst the commons.
These things (although it be not so)
Yet thou must affirm them to be true,
With oaths and protestations as will serve   1020
To drive my sister out of love with him,
And cause my will accomplished to be.
This do, thou wins my favor forever,
And makest a highway of preferment to thee
And all thy friends.

MESSENGER. It suffices, conceit it is already done:
I will so tongue-whip him, that I will
Leave him as bare of credit, as a poulter
Leaves a cony,[39] when she pulls off his skin.

GONORILL. Yet there is a further matter.   1030

MESSENGER. I thirst to hear it.

GONORILL. If my sister thinks convenient, as my letters import, to make him away, hast thou the heart to effect it?

MESSENGER. Few words are best in so small a matter: these are but trifles. By this book I will. (*Kisses the paper.*)

GONORILL. About it presently, I long till it be done.

MESSENGER.[40] I fly, I fly.   (*Exeunt.*)

SCENE VI.

Enter Cordella solus.

CORDELLA. [41]I have been over-negligent today,
In going to the temple of my God,

---

[39] Poulterer leaves a rabbit.
[40] Now it is the messenger instead of Skalliger who functions like Shakespeare's Oswald.
[41] Compare the Christian connotations of so many of the words in this soliloquy with IV.iii. 27–34; IV.vii. 45–59.

To render thanks for all His benefits,   1040
Which He miraculously has bestowed on me,
In raising me out of my mean estate,
When as I was devoid of worldly friends,
And placing me in such a sweet content,
As far exceeds the reach of my deserts.
My kingly husband, mirror of his time,
For zeal, for justice, kindness, and for care
To God, his subjects, me, and commonweal,
By his appointment was ordained for me.
I cannot wish the thing that I do want;   1050
I cannot want the thing but I may have,
Save only this which I shall ne'er obtain,
My father's love, oh this I ne'er shall gain.
I would abstain from any nutriment,
And pine my body to the very bones;
Barefoot I would on pilgrimage set forth
Unto the furthest quarters of the earth,
And all my lifetime would I sackcloth wear,
And mourning-wise pour dust upon my head,
So he but to forgive me once would please,   1060
That his gray hairs might go to heaven in peace.
And yet I know not how I him offended,
Or wherein justly I have deserved blame.
Oh sisters! you are much to blame in this,
It was not he, but you that did me wrong.
Yet God forgive both him and you and me,
Even as I do in perfect charity.
I will to church, and pray unto my Savior,
That ere I die, I may obtain his favor.   (*Exit.*)

Scene VIII.

Enter Leir and Perillus faint.

PERILLUS. [42]Rest on me, my Lord, and stay yourself,   1070
The way seems tedious to your aged limbs.

LEIR. Nay, rest on me, kind friend, and stay thyself,
Thou art as old as I, but more kind.

PERILLUS. Ah, good my Lord, it ill befits that I
Should lean upon the person of a king.

---

[42] I.v. 1ff. This passage parallels Shakespeare's scene in plot structure, but
not in conflict, suspense, or psychology.

LEIR. But it fits worse, that I should bring thee forth, 1080
That had no cause to come along with me,
Through these uncouth paths, and tireful ways,
And never ease thy fainting limbs a whit.
Thou hast left all, aye, all to come with me.
And I, for all, have nought to guerdon thee.

PERILLUS. Cease, good my Lord, to aggravate my woes
With these kind words, which cuts my heart in two,
To think your will should want the power to do.

LEIR. Cease, good Perillus, for to call me Lord,
And think me both the shadow of myself.

PERILLUS. That honorable title will I give
Unto my Lord, so long as I do live.
Oh, be of comfort; for I see the place
Whereas your daughter keeps her residence. 1090
And lo, in happy time the Cambrian Prince
Is here arrived, to gratify our coming.

> (*Enter the Prince of Cambria, Ragan, and nobles:*
> *look upon them, and whisper together.*)

LEIR. [43]Were I best speak, or sit me down and die?
I am ashamed to tell this heavy tale.

PERILLUS. Then let me tell it. if you please, my Lord:
'Tis shame for them that were the cause thereof.

CAMBRIA. What two old men are those that seem so sad?
Methinks, I should remember well their looks.

RAGAN. No, I mistake not, sure it is my father:
I must dissemble kindness now of force. 1100

> (*She runs to him, and kneels down, saying:*)

Father, I bid you welcome, full of grief,
To see your Grace used thus unworthily,
And ill befitting for your reverend age,
To come on foot a journey so unendurable.
Oh, what disaster chance has been the cause,
To make your cheeks so hollow, spare and lean?
He cannot speak for weeping: for God's love, come,
Let us refresh him with some needful things,
And at more leisure we may better know,
Whence springs the ground of this unlooked for woe. 1110

CAMBRIA. Come, father, ere we any further talk,
You shall refresh you after this weary walk.   (*Exeunt, manet Ragan.*)

RAGAN. Comes he to me with finger in the eye,

---

[43] II.iv. 128–184.

To tell a tale against my sister here?
Whom I do know, he greatly has abused:
And now like a contentious crafty wretch,
He first begins for to complain himself,
When as himself is in the greatest fault.
I'll not be partial in my sister's cause,
Not yet believe his doting vain reports: **1120**
Who for a trifle (safely) I dare say,
Upon a spleen is stolen thence away:
And here (forsooth) he hopes to have harbor,
And to be moaned and made on like a child:
But ere't be long, his coming he shall curse,
And truly say, he came from bad to worse:
Yet will I make fair weather, to procure
Convenient means, and then I'll strike it sure.   (*Exit.*)

ACT III

Scene I.

Enter messenger solus.
MESSENGER. Now happily I am arrived here,
Before the stately Palace of the Cambrian King;   **1130**
If Leir be here safe-seated, and in rest,
To rouse him from it I will do my best.
                    (*Enter Ragan.*)
Now bags of gold, your virtue is (no doubt)
To make me in my message bold and stout.
The King of Heaven preserve your Majesty,
And send your Highness everlasting reign.
    RAGAN. Thanks, good my friend; but what imports thy message?
    MESSENGER. [44]Kind greetings from the Cornwall Queen:
The residue these letters will declare.
                    (*She opens the letters.*)
    RAGAN. How fares our royal sister?   **1140**
    MESSENGER. I did leave her at my parting, in good health.
                    (*She reads the letter, frowns and stamps.*)
See how her color comes and goes again,
Now red as scarlet, now as pale as ash;
See how she knits her brow and bites her lips,
And stamps, and makes a dumb show of disdain,

---

[44] II.i. 124–126.

Mixed with revenge and violent extremes.
Here will be more work and more crowns for me.

    RAGAN. Alas, poor soul, and has he used her thus?
And is he now come hither, with intent
To set divorce betwixt my Lord and me?   1150
Doth he give out, that he doth hear report,
That I do rule my husband as I list,
And therefore means to alter so the case,
That I shall know my Lord to be my head?
Well, it were best for him to take good heed,
Or I will make him hop without a head,
For his presumption, dotard that he is.
In Cornwall he has made such mutinies,
First, setting of the king against the queen;
Then stirring up the commons 'gainst the king;   1160
That had he there continued any longer,
He had been called in question for his fact.
So upon that occasion thence he fled,
And comes thus silly stealing unto us:
And now already since his coming hither,
My Lord and he are grown in such a league
Than I can have no conference with his Grace:
I fear, he doth already intimate
Some forged cavillations 'gainst my state:
'Tis therefore best to cut him off in time,   1170
Lest slanderous rumors once abroad dispersed,
It is too late for them to be reversed.
Friend, as the tenor of these letters shows,
My sister puts great confidence in thee.

    MESSENGER. She never yet committed trust to me,
But that (I hope) she found me always faithful:
So will I be to any friend of hers,
That has occasion to employ my help.

    RAGAN. Hast thou the heart to act a stratagem,
And give a stab or two, if need require?   1180

    MESSENGER. I have a heart compact of adamant,
Which never knew what melting pity meant.
I weigh no more the murdering of a man,
Than I respect the cracking of a flea,
When I do catch her biting on my skin.
If you will have your husband or your father,
Or both of them sent to another world,
Do but command me do it, it shall be done.

RAGAN. It is enough, we make no doubt of thee;
Meet us tomorrow here, at nine o'clock: 1190
Meanwhile, farewell, and drink that for my sake.   (*Exit.*)

    MESSENGER. Aye, this is it will make do the deed:
Oh, had I every day such customers,
This were the gainfullest trade in Christendom!
A purse of gold given for a paltry stab!
Why, here's a wench that longs to have a stab.
Well, I could give it her, and ne'er hurt her neither.

SCENE II.

Enter the Gallian king and Cordella.

    KING. When will these clouds of sorrow once disperse,
And smiling joy triumph upon thy brow?
When will this scene of sadness have an end,   1200
And pleasant acts ensue, to move delight?
When will my lovely queen cease to lament,
And take some comfort to her grieved thoughts?
If of thyself thou deignst to have no care,
Yet pity me, whom thy grief make despair.

    CORDELLA. O, grieve not you, my Lord, you have no cause;
Let not my passions move your mind a whit;
For I am bound by nature, to lament
For his ill will, that life to me first lent.
If so the stock be dried with disdain,   1210
Withered and sere the branch must needs remain.

    KING. But thou art now graft in another stock,
I am the stock, and thou the lovely branch:
And from my root continual sap shall flow,
To make thee flourish with perpetual spring.
Forget thy father and thy kindred now,
Since they forsake thee like inhumane beasts;
Think they are dead, since all their kindness dies,
And bury them, where black oblivion lies.
Think not thou art the daughter of old Leir,   1220
Who did unkindly disinherit thee:
But think thou art the noble Gallian Queen,
And wife to him that dearly loves thee:
Embrace the joys that present with thee dwell,
Let sorrow pack and hide herself in hell.

    CORDELLA. Not that I miss my country or my kin,
My old acquaintance or my ancient friends,
Doth any whit distemperate my mind,

Knowing you, which are more dear to me,
Than country, kin, and all things else can be.   1230
Yet pardon me, my gracious Lord, in this:
For what can stop the course of nature's power?
As easy it is for the blackamoor
To stay themselves upon the liquid air,
And mount aloft into the element,
And overstrip the feathered fowls in flight:
As easy is it for the blackamoor
To live and thrive without the help of water:
As easy is it for the blackamoor
To wash the tawny color from his skin,   1240
Which all oppose against the course of nature,
As I am able to forget my father.
    KING. Mirror of virtue, Phoenix of our age!
Too kind a daughter for an unkind father,
Be of good comfort; [45]for I will dispatch
Ambassadors immediately for Britain,
Unto the King of Cornwall's court, whereas
Your father keeps now his residence,
And in the kindest manner him entreat,
That, setting former grievances apart,   1250
He will be pleased to come and visit us.
If no entreaty will suffice the turn,
I'll offer him the half of all my crown;
If that moves not, we'll furnish out a fleet,
And sail to Cornwall for to visit him;
And there you shall be firmly reconciled
In perfect love, as erst you were before.
    CORDELLA. Where tongue cannot sufficient thanks afford,
The King of Heaven remunerate my Lord.
    KING. Only be blithe, and frolic (sweet) with me: 1260
This and much more I'll do to comfort thee.   (*Exeunt.*)

SCENE III.

Enter messenger solus.

    MESSENGER. It is a world to see now I am flush,
How many friends I purchase everywhere!
How many seek to creep into my favor,
And kiss their hands, and bend their knees to me!

---

[45] This benevolence contrasts with the opportunism of Shakespeare's France:
III.i. 19–34.

No more, here comes the queen, now shall I know her mind,
And hope for to derive more crowns from her.

(*Enter Ragan.*)

RAGAN. My friend, I see thou mind'st thy promise well,
And art before me here, methinks, today.

MESSENGER. I am a poor man, and it like your Grace;   **1270**
But yet I always love to keep my word.

RAGAN. It is a thing of right strange consequence,
And well I cannot utter it in words.

MESSENGER. It is more strange, that I am not by this
Beside myself, with longing for to hear it.
Were it to meet the devil in his den,
And try a bout with him for a scratched face,
I'd undertake it, if you would but bid me.

RAGAN. Ah, good my friend, that I should have thee do,
Is such a thing, as I do shame to speak;   **1280**
Yet it must needs be done.

MESSENGER. 46I'll speak it for thee, Queen: shall I kill thy
father?
I know 'tis that: and if it be so, say.

RAGAN. Aye.

MESSENGER. Why, that's enough.

RAGAN. And yet that is not all.

MESSENGER. What else?

RAGAN. Thou must kill that old man that came with him.

MESSENGER. Here are two hands, for each of them is one.   **1290**

RAGAN. And for each hand here is a recompense.

(*Gives him two purses.*)

MESSENGER. Oh, that I had ten hands by miracle!
I could tear ten in pieces with my teeth,
So in my mouth you'd put a purse of gold.
But in what manner must it be effected?

RAGAN. Tomorrow morning ere the break of day,
I by a wile will send them to the thicket,
That is about some two miles from the court,
And promise them to meet them there myself,
Because I must have private conference,   **1300**
About some news I have received from Cornwall.
This is enough, I know, they will not fail,
And then be ready for to play thy part:

---

46 Like Geoffrey and Holinshed, Shakespeare does not have Regan arrange
to kill Lear. But this scene and Scene v may have suggested the blinding
of Gloucester (III.vii. 28ff.) and the eventual order to kill him (IV.v. 9–13).

Which done, thou mayest right easily escape,
And no man once mistrust thee for the fact:
But yet, before thou prosecute the act,
Show him the letter which my sister sent,
There let him read his own indictment first,
And then proceed to execution:
But see thou faint not; for they will speak fair.   1310
    MESSENGER. Could he speak words as pleasing as the pipe
Of Mercury, which charmed the hundred eyes
Of watchful Argos, and enforced him sleep:
Yet here are words so pleasing to my thoughts, (*To the purse.*)
As quite shall take away the sound of his.   (*Exit.*)
    RAGAN. About it then, and when thou hast dispatched,
I'll find a means to send thee after him.   (*Exit.*)

SCENE IV.

Enter Cornwall and Gonorill.

    CORNWALL. I wonder that the messenger doth stay,
Whom we dispatched for Cambria so long since:
If that his answer do not please us well,   1320
And he do show good reason for delay,
I'll teach him how to dally with his king,
And to detain us in such long suspense.
    GONORILL. My Lord, I think the reason may be this:
My father means to come along with him;
And therefore 'tis his pleasure he shall stay,
For to attend upon him on the way.
    CORNWALL. It may be so, and therefore till I know
The truth thereof, I will suspend my judgment.
                    (*Enter servant.*)
    SERVANT. [47]And't like your Grace, there is an ambassador   1330
arrived from Gallia, and craves admittance to your Majesty.
    CORNWALL. From Gallia? what should his message
Hither import? is not your father happily
Gone thither? well, whatsoe'er it be,
Bid him come in, he shall have audience.
                    (*Enter ambassador.*)
What news from Gallia? speak, Ambassador.
    AMBASSADOR. The noble King and Queen of Gallia first salutes,
By me, their honorable father, my Lord Leir:
Next, they commend them kindly to your Graces,

---

[47] III.i. 19–34.

As those whose welfare they entirely wish.   1340
Letters I have to deliver to my Lord Leir,
And presents too, if I might speak with him.

GONORILL. If you might speak with him? why, do you think,
We are afraid that you should speak with him?

AMBASSADOR. Pardon me, Madam; for I think not so,
But say so only, cause he is not here.

CORNWALL. Indeed, my friend, upon some urgent cause,
He is at this time absent from the court.
But if a day or two you here repose,
'Tis very likely you shall have him here,   1350
Or else have certain notice where he is.

GONORILL. Are not we worthy to receive your message?

AMBASSADOR. I had in charge to do it to himself.

GONORILL. (To herself.) It may be then 'twill not be done in
haste.
How doth my sister brook the air of France?

AMBASSADOR. Exceeding well, and never sick one hour,
Since first she set her foot upon the shore.

GONORILL. I am the more sorry.

AMBASSADOR. I hope, not so, Madam.   1360

GONORILL. Didst thou not say, that she was ever sick,
Since the first hour that she arrived there?

AMBASSADOR. No, Madam, I said quite contrary.

GONORILL. Then I mistook thee.

CORNWALL. Then she is merry, if she have her health.

AMBASSADOR. Oh no, her grief exceeds, until the time,
That she be reconciled unto her father.

GONORILL. God continue it.

AMBASSADOR. What, Madam?

GONORILL. Why, her health.   1370

AMBASSADOR. Amen to that: but God release her grief,
And send her father in a better mind,
Than to continue always so unkind.

CORNWALL. I'll be a mediator in her cause,
And seek all means to expiate his wrath.

AMBASSADOR. Madam, I hope your Grace will do the like.

GONORILL. Should I be a mean to exasperate his wrath
Against my sister, whom I love so dear? no, no.

AMBASSADOR. To expiate or mitigate his wrath:
For he has misconceived without a cause.   1380

GONORILL. O, aye, what else?

AMBASSADOR. 'Tis a pity it should be so, would it were otherwise.

GONORILL. It were great pity it should be otherwise.

AMBASSADOR. Then how, Madam?

GONORILL. Then that they should be reconciled again.

AMBASSADOR. It shows you bear an honorable mind.

GONORILL. (*Speaks to herself.*) It shows thy understanding
to be blind,

And that thou hadst need of an interpreter.

Well, I will know thy message ere't be long, 1390

And find a mean to cross it, if I can.

CORNWALL. Come in, my friend, and frolic in our court,

Till certain notice of my father come. (*Exeunt.*)

SCENE V.

Enter Leir and Perillus.

PERILLUS. [48]My Lord, you are up today before your hour,

'Tis news to you to be abroad so rathe.[49]

LEIR. 'Tis news indeed, I am so extreme heavy,

That I can scarcely keep my eyelids open.

PERILLUS. And so am I, but I impute the cause

To rising sooner than we use to do.

LEIR. Hither my daughter means to come disguised: 1400

I'll sit me down, and read until she come. (*Pulls out a book, and
sits down.*)

PERILLUS. She'll not be long, I warrant you, my Lord:

But say, a couple of these they call good fellows,

Should step out of a hedge, and set upon us,

We were in good case for to answer them.

LEIR. 'Twere not for us to stand upon our hands.

PERILLUS. I fear, we scant should stand upon our legs.

But how should we do to defend ourselves?

LEIR. Even pray to God to bless us from their hands:

For fervent prayer much ill hap withstands. 1410

PERILLUS. I'll sit and pray with you for company;

Yet was I ne'er so heavy in my life. (*They fall both asleep.*)
(*Enter the messenger, or murderer,
with two daggers in his hands.*)

MESSENGER. Were it not a mad jest, if two or three of my profession should meet me, and lay me down in a ditch, and play

---

[48] Contrast the feebleness and meekness of Leir in this scene with Shakespeare's Lear in a comparable scene such as II.iv.

[49] early.

rob thief with me, and perforce take my gold away from me,
whilest I act this stratagem, and by this means the gray beards
should escape? Faith, when I were at liberty again, I would make
no more to do, but go to the next tree, and there hang myself.

(Sees them, and starts.)

But stay, methinks, my youths are here already,
And with pure zeal have prayed themselves asleep.   1420
I think they know to what intent they came,
And are provided for another world. *(He takes their books away.)*
Now could I stab them bravely, while they sleep.
And in a manner put them to no pain;
And doing so, I showed them mighty friendship:
For fear of death is worse than death itself.
But that my sweet queen willed me for to show
This letter to them, ere I did the deed.
Mass, they begin to stir: I'll stand aside;
So shall I come upon them unawares.   1430

(They wake and rise.)

LEIR. I marvel that my daughter stays so long.

PERILLUS. I fear we did mistake the place, my Lord.

LEIR. God grant we do not miscarry in the place;
I had a short nap, but so full of dread,
As much amazeth me to think thereof.

PERILLUS. Fear not, my Lord, dreams are but fantasies,
And slight imaginations of the brain.

MESSENGER. Persuade him so, but I'll make him and you
Confess, that dreams do often prove too true.

PERILLUS. I pray, my Lord, what was the effect of it?   1440
I may go near to guess what it pretends.

MESSENGER. Leave that to me, I will expound the dream.

LEIR. Methought my daughters, Gonorill and Ragan,
Stood both before me with such grim aspects,
Each brandishing a falchion in their hand,
Ready to lop a limb off where it fell,
And in their other hands a naked poignard,
Wherewith they stabbed me in a hundred places,
And to their thinking left me there for dead;
But then my youngest daughter, fair Cordella,   1450
Came with a box of balsam in her hand,
And poured it into my bleeding wounds;[50]
By whose good means I was recovered well,

---

[50] Another Christian connotation for Shakespeare to associate with Cordelia.

In perfect health, as erst I was before:
And with the fear of this I did awake,
And yet for fear my feeble joints do quake.

MESSENGER. I'll make you quake for something presently.
Stand, stand.

(They reel.)

LEIR. We do, my friend, although with much ado.

MESSENGER. Deliver, deliver. 1460

PERILLUS. Deliver us, good Lord, from such as he.

MESSENGER. You should have prayed before, while it was time,
And then perhaps, you might have 'scaped my hands:
But you, like faithful watchmen, fell asleep,
The whilst I came and took your halberds from you. *(Shows
their books.)*
And now you want your weapons of defense,
How have you any hope to be delivered?
This comes, because you have no better stay,
But fall asleep, when you should watch and pray. 1470

LEIR. My friend, thou seemst to be a proper man.

MESSENGER. 'Sblood, how the old slave claws me by the elbow?
He thinks, belike, to 'scape by scraping thus.

PERILLUS. And it may be, are in some need of money.

MESSENGER. That to be false, behold my evidence. *(Shows
his purses.)*

LEIR. If that I have will do thee any good,
I give it thee, even with a right good will. *(He takes it.)*

PERILLUS. Here, take mine too, and wish with all my heart,
To do thee pleasure, it were twice as much. *(Takes his, and* 1480
weighs them both in his hands.)

MESSENGER. I'll none of them, they are too light for me. *(Puts
them in his pocket.)*

LEIR. Why then farewell: and if thou have occasion
In any thing, to use me to the Queen,
'Tis like enough that I can pleasure thee. *(They proffer to go.)*

MESSENGER. Hear you sir, hear you? pray, a word with you.
Methinks, a comely honest ancient man
Should not dissemble with one for a vantage.
I know, when I shall come to try this gear, 1490
You will recant from all that you have said.

PERILLUS. Mistrust not him, but try him when thou wilt:
He is her father, therefore may do much.

MESSENGER. I know he is, and therefore mean to try him:
You are his friend too, I must try you both.

BOTH. Prithee do, prithee do. (*Proffer to go out.*)

MESSENGER. Stay graybeards then, and prove men of your
words:

The Queen has tied me by a solemn oath,

Here in this place to see you both dispatched: 1500

Now for the safeguard of my conscience,

Do me the pleasure for to kill yourselves:

So shall you save me labor for to do it,

And prove yourselves true old men of your words.

And here I vow in sight of all the world,

I ne'er will trouble you whilst I live again.

LEIR. Afright us not with terror, good my friend,

Nor strike such fear into our aged hearts.

Play not the cat, which dallies with the mouse;

And on a sudden makes her a prey: 1510

But if thou art marked for the man of death

To me and to my Damon, tell me plain,

That we may be prepared for the stroke,

And make ourselves fit for the world to come.

MESSENGER. I am the last of any mortal race,

That ere your eyes are likely to behold,

And hither sent of purpose to this place,

To give a final period to your days,

Which are so wicked, and have lived so long,

That your own children seek to short your life. 1520

LEIR. Cam'st thou from France, of purpose to do this?

MESSENGER. From France? Zounds, do I look like a Frenchman? Sure I have not mine own face on; somebody hath changed
faces with me, and I know not of it: but I am sure, my apparel
is all English. Sirrah, what meanest thou to ask that question?
I could spoil the fashion of this face for anger. A French face!

LEIR. Because my daughter, whom I have offended,

And at whose hands I have deserved as ill,

As ever any father did of child,

Is Queen of France, no thanks at all to me, 1530

But unto God, who my injustice see.

If it be so, that she doth seek revenge,

As with good reason she may justly do,

I will most willingly resign my life,

A sacrifice to mitigate her ire:

I never will entreat thee to forgive,

Because I am unworthy for to live.

Therefore speak soon, and I will soon make speed;

Whether Cordella willed thee do this deed?

MESSENGER. As I am a perfect gentleman, thou speakst French 1540
to me:
I never heard Cordella's name before,
Nor never was in France in all my life:
I never knew thou hadst a daughter there,
To whom thou didst prove so unkind a churl:
But thy own tongue declares that thou hast been
A vile old wretch, and full of heinous sin.

LEIR. Ah no, my friend, thou art deceived much:
For her except, whom I confess I wronged,
Through doting frenzy, and over-jealous love, 1550
There lives not any under heaven's bright eye,
That can convict me of impiety:
And therefore sure thou dost mistake the mark:
For I am in true peace with all the world.

MESSENGER. You are the fitter for the King of Heaven:
And therefore, for to rid thee of suspense,
Know thou, the Queens of Cambria and Cornwall,
Thy own two daughters, Gonorill and Ragan,
Appointed me to massacre thee here.
Why wouldst thou then persuade me, that thou art 1560
In charity with all the world? but now
When thy own issue hold thee in such hate,
That they have hired me to abridge thy fate,
Oh, fie upon such vile dissembling breath,
That would deceive, even at the point of death.

PERILLUS. Am I awake, or is it but a dream?

MESSENGER. Fear nothing, man, thou art but in a dream,
And thou shalt never wake until doomsday;
By then, I hope, thou wilt have slept enough.

LEIR. Yet, gentle friend, grant one thing ere I die. 1570

MESSENGER. I'll grant you any thing, except your lives.

LEIR. Oh, but assure me by some certain token,
That my two daughters hired thee to this deed:
If I were once resolved of that, then I
Would wish no longer life, but crave to die.

MESSENGER. That to be true, in sight of heaven I swear.

LEIR. Swear not by heaven, for fear of punishment:
The heavens are guiltless of such heinous acts.

MESSENGER. I swear by earth, the mother of us all.

LEIR. Swear not by earth, for she abhors to bear 1580
Such bastards, as are murderers of her sons.

MESSENGER. Why then, by hell, and all the devils I swear.

LEIR. Swear not by hell; for that stands gaping wide,
To swallow thee, and if thou do this deed.

(*Thunder and lightning.*)[52]

MESSENGER. I would that word were in his belly again,
It (hath) frighted me even to the very heart;
This old man is some strong magician:
His words have turned my mind from this exploit.
Then neither heaven, earth, nor hell be witness;
But let this paper witness for them all. (*Shows Gonorill's letter.*)   1590
Shall I relent, or shall I prosecute?
Shall I resolve, or were I best recant?
I will not crack my credit with two Queens,
To whom I have already passed my word.
Oh, but my conscience for this act doth tell,
I get heaven's hate, earth's scorn, and pains of hell.

(*They bless themselves.*)

PERILLUS. O just Jehovah, whose almighty power
Doth govern all things in this spacious world,
How canst thou suffer such outrageous acts
To be committed without just revenge?   1600
O viperous generation and accursed,
To seek his blood, whose blood did make them first!

LEIR. Ah, my true friend in all extremity,
Let us submit us to the will of God:
Things past all sense, let us know;
It is God's will, and therefore must be so.
My friend, I am prepared for the stroke:
Strike when thou wilt, and I forgive thee here,
Even from the bottom of my heart.

MESSENGER. But I am not prepared for to strike.   1610

LEIR. Farewell, Perillus, even the truest friend,
That ever lived in adversity:
The latest kindness I'll request of thee,
And carry her her father's latest blessing:
Withal desire her, that she will forgive me;
For I have wronged her without any cause.
Now, Lord, receive me, for I come to Thee,
And die, I hope, in perfect charity.

---

[52] As this storm breaks out the messenger begins to melt with pity, and ll. 1603–1664 parallel Lear's reactions during the storm on the heath: III.ii. 1–73.

Dispatch, I pray thee, I have lived too long.

MESSENGER. Aye, but you are unwise, to send an errand 1620
By him that never means to deliver it:
Why, he must go along with you to heaven:
It were not good you should go all alone.

LEIR. No doubt, he shall, when by the course of nature,
He must surrender up his due to death:
But that time shall not come, till God permit.

MESSENGER. Nay, presently, to bear you company.
I have a passport for him in my pocket,
Already sealed, and he must needs ride post. (*Shows a bag of money.*)

LEIR. The letter which I read imports not so, 1630
It only touches me, no word of him.

MESSENGER. Aye, but the Queen commands it must be so,
And I am paid for him, as well as you.

PERILLUS. I, who have borne your company in life,
Most willingly will bear a share in death,
It skills not for me, my friend, a whit,
Nor for a hundred such as thou and I.

MESSENGER. Marry, but it doth, sir, by your leave; your good
days are past: though it be no matter for you, 'tis a matter for
me, proper men are not so rife. 1640

PERILLUS. Oh, but beware, how thou dost lay thy hand
Upon the high anointed of the Lord:
O, be advised ere thou dost begin:
Dispatch me straight, but meddle not with him.

LEIR. Friend, thy commission is to deal with me,
And I am he that hath deserved all:
The plot was laid to take away my life:
And here it is, I do entreat thee take it:
Yet for my sake, and as thou art a man,
Spare this my friend, that hither with me came: 1650
I brought him forth, whereas he had not been,
But for good will to bear me company.
He left his friends, his country and his goods,
And came with me in most extremity.
Oh, if he should miscarry here and die,
Who is the cause of it, but only I?

MESSENGER. Why that am I, let that ne'er trouble thee.

LEIR. O no, 'tis I. O, had I now to give thee
The monarchy of all the spacious world
To save his life, I would bestow it on thee: 1660
But I have nothing but these tears and prayers,

And the submission of a bended knee. (*Kneels.*)
O, if all this to mercy move thy mind,
Spare him, in heaven thou shalt like mercy find.

MESSENGER. I am as hard to be moved as another, and yet
methinks the strength of their persuasions stirs me a little.

PERILLUS. My friend, if fear of the almighty power
Have power to move thee, we have said enough:
But if thy mind be movable with gold,
We have not presently to give it thee: 1670
Yet to thyself thou mayst do greater good,
To keep thy hands still undefiled from blood:
For do but well consider with thyself,
When thou hast finished this outrageous act,
What horror still will haunt thee for the deed:
Think this again, that they which would incense
Thee for to be the butcher of their father,
When it be done, for fear if should be known,
Will find a means to rid thee from the world:
Oh, then art thou forever tied in chains   1680
Of everlasting torments to endure,
Even in the hottest hole of grisly hell,
Such pains, as never mortal tongue can tell.
(*It thunders. He quakes, and lets fall the dagger next to Perillus.*)
LEIR. O, heavens be thanked, he will spare my friend.
Now, when thou wilt, come make an end of me.
                    (*He lets fall the other dagger.*)
PERILLUS. Oh, happy sight! he means to save my Lord.
The King of Heaven continue this good mind.
LEIR. Why stay'st thou to do execution?
MESSENGER. I am as willful as you for your life:
I will not do it, now you do entreat me.   1690
PERILLUS. Ah, now I see thou hast some spark of grace.
MESSENGER. Beshrew you for it, you have put it in me.
The parlosest[53] old men that ere I heard.
Well, to be flat, I'll not meddle with you.
Here I found you, and here I'll leave you:
If any ask you why the case so stands?
Say that your tongues were better than your hands. (*Exit messenger.*)
PERILLUS. Farewell. If ever we together meet,
It shall go hard, but I will thee regreet.
Courage, my Lord, the worst is overpassed;   1700
Let us give thanks to God, and hie us hence.

---

[53] most talkative.

LEIR. Thou art deceived; for I am past the best,
And know not whither for to go from hence:
Death had been better welcome unto me,
Than longer life to add more misery.

PERILLUS. It were not good to return from whence we came,
Unto your daughter Ragan back again.
[54]Now let us go to France, unto Cordella,
Your youngest daughter, doubtless she will succor you.

LEIR. Oh, how can I persuade myself of that,   1710
Since the other two are quite devoid of love;
To whom I was so kind, as that my gifts,
Might make them love me, if 'twere nothing else?

PERILLUS. No worldly gifts, but grace from God on high,
Doth nourish virtue and true charity.
Remember well what words Cordella spake,
What time you asked her, how she loved your Grace.
She said, her love unto you was as much,
As ought a child to bear unto her father.

LEIR. But she did find, my love was not to her,   1720
As should a father bear unto a child.

PERILLUS. That makes not her love to be any less,
If she do love you as a child should do:
You have tried two, try one more for my sake,
I'll ne'er entreat you further trial make.
Remember well the dream you had of late,
And think what comfort it foretells to us.

LEIR. Come, truest friend, that ever man possessed,
I know thou counsellest all things for the best:
If this third daughter play a kinder part,   1730
It comes of God, and not of my desert.   (*Exeunt.*)

ACT IV

SCENE I.

Enter the Gallian ambassador solus.

AMBASSADOR. There is of late news come unto the court,
That old Lord Leir remains in Cambria:
I'll hie me thither presently, to impart
My letters and my message unto him.
I never was less welcome to a place
In all my lifetime, than I have been hither,

---

[54] III.vi. 93–99.

Especially unto the stately Queen,
Who would not cast one gracious look on me,
But still with lowering and suspicious eyes,   1740
Would take exceptions at each word I spake,
And feign she would have undermined me,
To know what my ambassage did import;
But she is like to hop without her hope,
And in this matter for to want her will,
Though (by report) she'll have't in all things else.
Well, I will post away for Cambria;
Within these few days I hope to be there.   (*Exit.*)

SCENE II.

Enter the King and Queen of Gallia, and Mumford.

KING. By this, our father understands our mind,
And our kind greetings sent to him of late: 1750
Therefore my mind presages ere't be long
We shall receive from Britain happy news.

CORDELLA. I fear my sister will dissuade his mind:
For she to me hath always been unkind.

KING. Fear not, my love, since we know the worst,
The last means helps, if that we miss the first:
If he'll not come to Gallia unto us,
Then we will sail to Britain unto him.

MUMFORD. [55]Well, if I once see Britain again, I have sworn,
I'll ne'er come home without my wench. And I'll not be fore-   1760
sworn, I'll rather never come home while I live.

CORDELLA. Are you sure, Mumford, she is a maid still?

MUMFORD. Nay, I'll not swear she is a maid, but she goes for
one: I'll take her at all adventures, if I can get her.

CORDELLA. Aye, that's well put in.

MUMFORD. Well put in? Nay, it was ill put in; for had it been
as well put in as ere I put in, in my days, I would have made her
follow me to France.

CORDELLA. Nay, you'd have been so kind, as take her with you,
or else, were I as she, I would have been so loving, as I'd stay   1770
behind you: yet I must confess, you are a very proper man, and
able to make a wench do more than she would do.

MUMFORD. Well, I have a pair of slops for the nonce, will
hold all your mocks.

---

[55] This subplot and the subsequent business of disguises has no parallel in
the other sources or in Shakespeare.

KING. Aye, and of the newest fashion.

CORDELLA. Aye, and of the newest fashion.

MUMFORD. More bobs, more; put them in still, they'll serve instead of bombast, yet put not in too many, lest the seams crack, and they fly out amongst you again: you must not think to outface me so easily in my mistress quarrel, who if I see once again, ten   1780
team of horses shall not draw me away, till I have full and whole possession.

KING. Aye, but one team and cart will serve the turn.

CORDELLA. Not only for him, but also for his wench.

MUMFORD. Well, you are two to one, I'll give you over and since I see you so pleasantly disposed, which indeed is but seldom seen, I'll claim a promise of you, which you shall not deny me: for promise is debt, and by this hand you promised it me. Therefore you owe it me, and you shall pay it me, or I'll sue you upon an action of unkindness.   1790

KING. Prithee, Lord Mumford, what promise did I make thee?

MUMFORD. Faith, nothing but this, that the next fair weather, which is very now, you would go in progress down to the seaside, which is very near.

KING. Faith, in this motion I will join with thee,
And be a mediator to my Queen.
Prithee, my love, let this match go forward,
My mind foretells, 'twill be a lucky voyage.

CORDELLA. Entreaty needs not, where you may command,
So you be pleased, I am right well content: 1800
Yet, as the sea I much desire to see;
So am I most unwilling to be seen.

KING. We'll go disguised, all unknown to any.

CORDELLA. Howsoever you make one, I'll make another.

MUMFORD. And I the third: oh, I am overjoyed!
See what love is, which gets with a word,
What all the world besides could ne'er obtain:
But what disguises shall we have, my Lord?

KING. Faith thus; my queen and I will be disguised,
Like a plain country couple, and you shall be Roger   1810
Our man, and wait upon us: or if you will,
You shall go first, and we will wait on you.

MUMFORD. 'Twere more than time; this device is excellent:
Come let us about it.   (*Exeunt.*)

SCENE III.

Enter Cambria and Ragan, with nobles.

CAMBRIA. What strange mischance or unexpected hap

Hath thus deprived us of our father's presence?
Can no man tell us what's become of him,
With whom we did converse not two days since?
My Lords, let everywhere light-horse be sent,
To scour about through all our regimen.   1820
Dispatch a post immediately to Cornwall,
To see if any news be of him there;
Myself will make a strict enquiry here;
And all about our cities near at hand,
Till certain news of his abode be brought.

    RAGAN. All sorrow is but counterfeit to mine,
Whose lips are almost sealed up with grief;
Mine is the substance, whilst they do but seem
To weep the less, which tears cannot redeem.
O, ne'er was heard so strange a misadventure,   1830
A thing so far beyond the reach of sense,
Since no man's reason in the cause can enter.
What hath removed my father thus from hence?
O, I do fear some charm or invocation
Of wicked spirits, or infernal fiends,
Stirred by Cordella, moves this innovation,
And brings my father timeless to his end.
But might I know, that the detested witch
Were certain cause of this uncertain ill,
Myself to France would go in some disguise,   1840
And with these nails scratch out her hateful eyes:
For since I am deprived of my father,
I loath my life, and wish my death the rather.

    CAMBRIA. [56]The heavens are just, and hate impiety,
And will (no doubt) reveal such heinous crimes:
Censure not any, till you know the right:
Let Him be judge, that bringeth truth to light.

    RAGAN. O, but my grief, like to a swelling tide,
Exceeds the bounds of common patience:
Nor can I moderate my tongue so much,   1850
To conceal them, whom I hold in suspect.

    CAMBRIA. This matter shall be sifted: if it be she
A thousand Frances shall not harbor her.

                 (*Enter the Gallian ambassador.*)

    AMBASSADOR. All happiness unto the Cambrian king.

    CAMBRIA. Welcome, my friend, from whence is thy ambassage?

---

[56] A theme suggestive of Shakespeare's play.

AMBASSADOR. I came from Gallia, unto Cornwall sent,
With letters to your honorable father,
Whom there not finding, as I did expect,
I was directed hither to repair.

RAGAN. Frenchman, what is the message to my father? 1860

AMBASSADOR. My letters, Madam, will import the same,
Which my commission is for to deliver.

RAGAN. In his absence you may trust us with your letters.

AMBASSADOR. I must perform my charge in such a manner,
As I have strict commandment from the king.

RAGAN. There is good packing twixt your king and you;
You need not hither come to ask for him,
You know where he is better than ourselves.

AMBASSADOR. Madam, I hope, not far off.

RAGAN. [57]Hath the young murderess, your outrageous queen, 1870
No means to color her detested deeds,
In finishing my guiltless father's days,
(Because he gave her nothing to her dower)
But by the color of a feigned ambassage,
To send him letters hither to our court?
Go carry them to them that sent them hither,
And bid them keep their scrolls unto themselves:
They cannot blind us with such slight excuse,
To smother up so monstrous vile abuse.
And were it not, it is 'gainst law of arms, 1880
To offer violence to a messenger,
We would inflict such torments on thyself,
As should enforce thee to reveal the truth.

AMBASSADOR. Madam, your threats no whit appal my mind,
I know my conscience guiltless of this act;
My King and Queen, I dare be sworn, are free
From any thought of such impiety:
And therefore, Madam, you have done them wrong,
And ill beseeming with a sister's love,
Who in mere duty tender him as much, 1890
As ever you respected him for dower.
The king, your husband, will not say as much.

CAMBRIA. I will suspend my judgement for a time,
Till more appearance gives us further light:
Yet to be plain, your coming doth enforce
A great suspicion to our doubtful mind,

---

[57] Another turn of plot not in Shakespeare nor in the other sources.

And that you do resemble, to be brief,
Him that first robs, and then cries, "Stop the thief."
    AMBASSADOR. Pray God some near you have not done the like.
    RAGAN. Hence, saucy mate, reply no more to us;   1900
                               (*She strikes him.*)
For law of arms shall not protect thy tongue.
    AMBASSADOR. Ne'er was I offered such discourtesy;
God and my King, I trust, ere it be long,
Will find a mean to remedy this wrong.   (*Exit ambassador.*)
    RAGAN. How shall I live, to suffer this disgrace,
At every base and vulgar peasant's hands?
It ill befits my imperial state,
To be thus used, and no man take my part. (*She weeps.*)
    CAMBRIA. What should I do? infringe the law of arms,
Were to my everlasting obloquy: 1910
But I will take revenge upon his master,
Which sent him hither, to delude us thus.
    RAGAN. Nay, if you put up this, be sure, ere long,
Now that my father thus is made away;
She'll come and claim a third part of your crown,
As due unto her by inheritance.
    CAMBRIA. But I will prove her title to be nought
But shame, and the reward of parricide;
And make her an example to the world,
For after-ages to admire her penance.   1920
This will I do, as I am Cambrian King,
Or lose my life, to prosecute revenge.
Come, first let's learn what news is of our father,
And then proceed, as best occasion fits.   (*Exeunt.*)

SCENE IV.

Enter Leir, Perillus, and two mariners in sea-gowns and sea-caps.
    PERILLUS. [58]My honest friends, we are ashamed to show
The great extremity of our present state.
In that at this time we are brought so low,
That we want money for to pay our passage.
The truth is so, we met with some good fellows,
A little before we came aboard your ship,   1930
Which stripped us quite of all the coin we had,

---

[58] Again, not in Shakespeare, but compare with the circumstances of Leir's
crossing the Channel in Geoffrey of Monmouth.

And left us not a penny in our purses:
Yet wanting money, we will use the mean,
To see you satisfied to the uttermost.

1ST MARINER. (*Looks on Leir.*) Here's a good gown, 'twould become me passing well, I should be fine in it.

2ND MARINER. (*Looks on Perillus.*) Here's a good cloak, I marvel how I should look in it.

LEIR. Faith, had we others to supply their room, though ne'er so mean, you willingly should have them. 1940

1ST MARINER. Do you hear, sir? You look like an honest man; I'll not stand to do you a pleasure: here's a good strong motley gabardine, cost me fourteen good shillings at Billingsgate, give me your gown for it, and your cap for mine, and I'll forgive your passage.

LEIR. With all my heart, and twenty thanks.
(*Leir and he change.*)

2ND MARINER. Do you hear, sir? You shall have a better match than he, because you are my friend: here is a good sheep's russet sea-gown, will bide more stress, I warrant you, than two of his; yes, for you seem to be an honest gentleman, I am content to 1950 change it for your cloak, and ask you nothing for your passage more.

(*Pulls off Perillus's cloak.*)

PERILLUS. My own I willingly would change with thee,
And think myself indebted to thy kindness:
But would my friend might keep his garment still.
My friend, I'll give thee this new doublet, if thou wilt
Restore his gown unto him back again.

1ST MARINER. Nay, if I do, would I might ne'er eat powdered beef and mustard more, nor drink can of good liquor whilst I live. My friend, you have small reason to seek to hinder me of 1960 my bargain: but the best is, a bargain's a bargain.

LEIR. Kind friend, it is much better as it is.
(*Leir to Perillus.*) For by this means we may escape unknown,
Till time and opportunity do fit.

2ND MARINER. Hark, hark, they are laying their heads together, they'll repent them of their bargain anon, 'twere best for us to go while we are well.

1ST MARINER. God be with you, sir, for your passage back again, I'll use you as unreasonable as another.

LEIR. I know thou wilt; but we hope to bring ready money 1970 with us, when we come back again. (*Exeunt mariners.*)
Were ever men in this extremity,

In a strange country, and devoid of friends,
And not a penny for to help ourselves?
Kind friend, what think'st thou will become of us?

PERILLUS. Be of good cheer, my Lord, I have a doublet
Will yield us money enough to serve our turns,
Until we come unto your daughter's court:
And then, I hope, we shall find friends enough.

LEIR. Ah, kind Perillus, that it is I fear,   1980
And makes me faint, or ever I come there.
Can kindness spring out of ingratitude?
Or love be reaped where hatred hath been sown?
59Can henbane join in league with Mithridites?60
Or sugar grow in wormwood's bitter stalk?
It cannot be, they are too opposite:
And so am I to any kindness here.
I have thrown wormwood on the sugared youth,
And like to henbane poisoned the fount,
Whence flowed the Mithridites of a child's good will.   1990
I, like an envious thorn, have pricked the heart,
And turned sweet grapes to sour unrelished sloes:
The causeless ire of my respectless breast,
Hath soured the sweet milk of dame nature's paps:
My bitter words have galled her honey thoughts,
And weeds of rancor choked the flower of grace.
Then what remainder is of any hope,
But all our fortunes will go quite aslope?

PERILLUS. Fear not, my Lord, the perfect good indeed
Can never be corrupted by the bad: 2000
A new fresh vessel still retains the taste
Of that which first is powered into the same;
And therefore, though you name yourself the thorn,
The weed, the gall, the henbane, the wormwood;
Yet she'll continue in her former state,
The honey, milk, grape, sugar, Mithridite.

LEIR. Thou pleasing orator unto me in woe,
Cease to beguile me with thy hopeful speeches:
O join with me, and think of nought but crosses,
And then we'll one lament another's losses.   2010

---

59 Suggestive of Lear's entrance into Dover "fantastically dressed with wild flowers" — see stage direction after IV.vi. 80.

60 An Asian king who fought the Romans during the first century B.C. and eventually killed himself in 63 B.C. During his lifetime he took poison in small regular doses so as to cultivate an immunity to it.

PERILLUS. Why, say the worst, the worst can be but death,
And death is better than for to despair;
Then hazard death, which may convert to life;
Banish despair, which brings a thousand deaths.

LEIR. Overcome with thy strong arguments, I yield
To be directed by thee, as thou wilt:
As thou yieldst comfort to my crazed thoughts,
Would I could yield the like unto thy body,
Which is full weak, I know, and ill apayed,[61]
For want of fresh meat and due sustenance.   2020

PERILLUS. Alack, my Lord, my heart doth bleed, to think
That you should be in such extremity.

LEIR. Come, let us go, and see what God will send;
When all means fail, He is the surest friend.   (*Exeunt.*)

SCENE V.

Enter the Gallian King and Queen, and Mumford with a basket,
disguised like country folk.

KING. This tedious journey all on foot, sweet love,
Cannot be pleasing to your tender joints,
Which ne'er were used to these toilsome walks.

CORDELLA. I never in my life took more delight
In any journey than I do in this:
It did me good, when as we happed to light   2030
Amongst the merry crew of country folk,
To see what industry and pains they took,
To win them commendations 'mongst their friends.
Lord, how they labor to bestir themselves,
And in their quirks to go beyond the moon,
And so take on them with such antic fits,
That one would think they were beside their wits!
Come away, Roger, with your basket.

MUMFORD. Soft, Dame, here comes a couple of old youths,
I must needs make myself fat with jesting at them.   2040

(*Enter Leir and Perillus very faint.*)

CORDELLA. Nay, prithee do not, they do seem to be
Men much overgone with grief and misery.
Let's stand aside, and hearken what they say.

LEIR. Ah, my Perillus, now I see we both
Shall end our days in this unfruitful toil,
Oh, I do faint for want of sustenance:

---

[61] appeased.

And thou, I know, in little better case.
No gentle tree affords one taste of fruit,
To comfort us, until we meet with men:
No lucky path conducts our luckless steps   2050
Unto a place where any comfort dwells.
Sweet rest betide unto our happy souls;
For here I see our bodies must have end.

    PERILLUS. Ah, my dear Lord, how doth my heart lament,
To see you brought to this extremity!
O, if you love me, as you do profess,
Or ever thought well of me in my life; (*He strips up his arm.*)
Feed on this flesh, whose veins are not so dry,
But there is virtue left to comfort you.
O, feed on this, if this will do you good,   2060
I'll smile for joy, to see you suck my blood.

    LEIR. I am no cannibal that I should delight
To slake my hungry jaws with human flesh:
I am no devil, or ten times worse than so,
To suck the blood of such a peerless friend.
O, do not think that I respect my life
So dearly, as I do thy loyal love.
Ah, Britain, I shall never see thee more,
That hast unkindly banished thy king:
And yet not thou dost make me to complain,   2070
But they which were more near to me than thou.

    CORDELLA. [62]What do I hear? This lamentable voice,
Methinks, ere now I oftentimes have heard.

    LEIR. Ah, Gonorill, was half my kingdom's gift
The cause that thou didst seek to have my life?
Ah, cruel Ragan, did I give thee all,
And all could not suffice without my blood?
Ah, poor Cordella, did I give thee nought,
Nor never shall be able for to give?
O, let me warn all ages that ensueth,
How they trust flattery, and reject the truth.   2080
Well, unkind girls, I here forgive you both,
Yet the just heavens will hardly do the like;
And only crave forgiveness at the end
Of good Cordella, and of thee, my friend;
Of God, whose Majesty I have offended,

---

    [62] The remainder of this scene suggests elements of IV.vi. 192–207; IV.vii.
26–84.

By my transgressions many thousand ways:
Of her, dear heart, whom I for no occasion
Turned out of all, through flatterers' persuasion:
Of thee, kind friend, who but for me, I know, 2090
Hadst never come unto this place of woe.

CORDELLA. Alack, that ever I should live to see
My noble father in this misery.

KING. Sweet love, reveal not what thou art as yet,
Until we know the ground of all this ill.

CORDELLA. O, but some meat, some meat: do you not see,
How near they are to death for want of food?

PERILLUS. Lord, which didst help thy servants at their need,
Or now or never send us help with speed.
Oh comfort, comfort! Yonder is a banquet, 2100
And men and women, my Lord: be of good cheer:
For I see comfort coming very near.
O my Lord, a banquet, and men and women!

LEIR. O, let kind pity mollify their hearts,
That they may help us in our great extremes.

PERILLUS. God save you, friends; and if this blessed banquet
Affords any food or sustenance,
Even for His sake that saved us all from death,
Vouchsafe to save us from the grip of famine.

CORDELLA. (*She brings him to the table.*) Here, father, sit 2110
and eat; here sit and drink:
And would it were far better for your sakes!
             (*Perillus takes Leir by the hand to the table.*)

PERILLUS. I'll give you thanks anon: my friend doth faint,
And needs present comfort.
                    (*Leir drinks.*)

MUMFORD. I warrant, he ne'er stays to say grace:
O, there's no sauce to a good stomach.

PERILLUS. The blessed God of Heaven hath thought upon us.

LEIR. The thanks be His, and these kind courteous folk,
By whose humanity we are preserved.
             (*They eat hungrily. Leir drinks.*)

CORDELLA. And may that draught be unto him, as was 2120
That which old Aeson[63] drank, which did renew
His withered age, and made him young again,
And may that meat be unto him, as was
That which Elias ate, in strength whereof

---

[63] father of Jason.

He walked forty days, and never fainted.
Shall I conceal me longer from my father?
Or shall I manifest myself to him?

    KING. Forbear a while, until his strength return,
Lest being overjoyed with seeing thee,
His poor weak senses should forsake their office,   **2130**
And so our cause of joy be turned to sorrow.

    PERILLUS. What cheer, my Lord? How do you feel yourself?

    LEIR. Methinks, I never ate such savory meat:
It is as pleasant as the blessed manna,
That rained from heaven among the Israelites:
It hath recalled my spirits home again,
And made me fresh, as erst I was before.
But how shall we congratulate their kindness?

    PERILLUS. In faith, I know not how sufficiently;
But the best mean that I can think on, is this: **2140**
I'll offer them my doublet in requital;
For we have nothing else to spare.

    LEIR. Nay, stay, Perillus, for they shall have mine.

    PERILLUS. Pardon, my Lord, I swear they shall have mine.
        (*Perillus proffers his doublet; they will not take it.*)

    LEIR. Ah, who would think such kindness should remain
Among such strange and unacquainted men:
And that such hate should harbor in the breast
Of those, which have occasion to be best?

    CORDELLA. Ah, good old father, tell to me thy grief,
I'll sorrow with thee, if not add relief.   **2150**

    LEIR. Ah, good young daughter, I may call thee so;
For thou art like a daughter I did owe.

    CORDELLA. Do you not owe her still? What, is she dead?

    LEIR. No, God forbid; but all my interest's gone,
By showing myself too much unnatural:
So have I lost the title of a father,
And may be called a stranger to her rather.

    CORDELLA. Your title's good still; for 'tis always known,
A man may do as him list with his own.
But have you but one daughter then in all?   **2160**

    LEIR. Yes, I have more by two, than would I had.

    CORDELLA. Oh, say not so, but rather see the end;
They that are bad, may have the grace to mend;
But how have they offended you so much?

    LEIR. If from the first I should relate the cause,
'Twould make a heart of adamant to weep;

And thou, poor soul, kind-hearted as thou art,
Dost weep already, ere I do begin.

CORDELLA. For God's love, tell it; and when you have done,
I'll tell the reason why I weep so soon.　　　　　　　　2170

LEIR. Then know this first, I am a Britain born,
And had three daughters by one loving wife;
And though I say it, of beauty they were sped;
Especially the youngest of the three,
For her perfections hardly matched could be;
On these I doted with a jealous love,
And thought to try which of them loved me best,
By asking them, which would do most for me?
The first and second flattered me with words,
And vowed they loved me better than their lives;　　　2180
The youngest said she loved me as a child
Might do; her answer I esteemed most viled,
And presently in an outrageous mood,
I turned her from me to go sink or swim:
And all I had, even to the very clothes,
I gave in dowry with the other two:
And she that best deserved the greatest share,
I gave her nothing, but disgrace and care.
Now mark the sequel: When I had done thus,
I sojourned in my eldest daughter's house,　　　　　2190
Where for a time I was entreated well,
And lived in state sufficing my content:
But every day her kindness did grow cold,
Which I with patience put up well enough,
And seemed not to see the things I saw;
But at the last she grew so far incensed
With moody fury, and with causeless hate,
That in most vile and contumelious terms,
She bade me pack, and harbor somewhere else.
Then was I fain for refuge to repair　　　　　　　　2200
Unto my other daughter for relief;
Who gave me pleasing and most courteous words;
But in her actions showed herself so sore,
As never any daughter did before:
She prayed me in a morning out betime,
To go to a thicket two miles from court,
Pointing that there she would come talk with me:
There she had set a shag-haired murdering wretch,
To massacre my honest friend and me.

Then judge yourself, although my tale be brief,   2210
If ever man had greater cause of grief.

KING. Nor never like impiety was done,
Since the creation of the world begun.

LEIR. And now I am constrained to seek relief
Of her to whom I have been so unkind;
Whose censure, if it do award me death,
I must confess she pays me but my due;
But if she show a loving daughter's part,
It comes of God and her, not my desert.

CORDELLA. No doubt she will, I dare be sworn she will.   2220

LEIR. How know you that, not knowing what she is?

CORDELLA. Myself a father have a great way hence,
Used me as ill as ever you did her;
Yet, that his reverend age I once might see,
I'd creep along, to meet him on my knee.

LEIR. Oh, no men's children are unkind but mine.

CORDELLA. Condemn not all, because of others' crime:
But look, dear father, look, behold and see
Thy loving daughter speaketh unto thee. (*She kneels.*)

LEIR. O, stand thou up, it is my part to kneel,   2230
And ask forgiveness for my former faults. (*He kneels.*)

CORDELLA. O, if you wish I should enjoy my breath,
Dear father rise, or I receive my death.
                    (*He rises.*)

LEIR. Then I will rise, to satisfy your mind,
But kneel again, til pardon be resigned. (*He kneels.*)

CORDELLA. I pardon you: the word beseems not me:
But I do say so, for to ease your knee;
You gave me life, you were the cause that I
Am what I am, who else had never been.

LEIR. But you gave life to me and to my friend,   2240
Whose days had else had an untimely end.

CORDELLA. You brought me up, when as I was but young,
And far unable for to help myself.

LEIR. I cast thee forth, when as thou wast but young,
And far unable for to help thyself.

CORDELLA. God, world, and nature say I do you wrong,
That can endure to see you kneel so long.

KING. Let me break off this loving controversy,
Which doth rejoice my very soul to see.
Good father, rise, she is your loving daughter.   2250
                    (*He rises.*)

And honors you with as respective duty,
As if you were the monarch of the world.
    CORDELLA. But I will never rise from off my knee. (*She kneels.*)
Until I have your blessing, and your pardon
Of all my faults committed any way,
From my first birth unto this present day.
    LEIR. The blessing, which the God of Abraham gave
Unto the tribe of Judah, light on thee,
And multiply thy days, that thou mayest see
Thy children's children prosper after thee.   2260
Thy faults, which are just none that I do know,
God pardon on high, and I forgive below.
                (*She rises.*)
    CORDELLA. Now is my heart at quiet, and doth leap
Within my breast, for joy of this good hap:
And now (dear father) welcome to our court,
And welcome (kind Perillus) unto me,
Mirror of virtue and true honesty.
    LEIR. O, he hath been the kindest friend to me,
That ever man had in adversity.
    PERILLUS. My tongue doth fail to say what heart doth think,   2270
I am so ravished with exceeding joy.
    KING. All you have spoke: now let me speak my mind,
And in few words much matter here conclude: (*He kneels.*)
If ere my heart do harbor any joy,
Or true content repose within my breast,
Till I have rooted out this viperous sect,
And repossessed my father of his crown,
Let me be counted for the perjuredest man,
That ever spake word since the world began. (*Rises.*)
    MUMFORD. Let me pray too, that never prayed before;   2280
                (*He kneels.*)
If ere I resalute the British earth,
(As ere't be long I do presume I shall)
And do return from thence without my wench,
Let me be gelded for my recompense. (*Rises.*)
    KING. Come, let's to arms for to redress this wrong:
Till I am there, methinks the time seems long.   (*Exeunt.*)

ACT V

SCENE I.

Enter Ragan sola.

RAGAN. [64]I feel a hell of conscience in my breast,
Tormenting me with horror for my fact,
And makes me in agony of doubt,
For fear the world should find my dealing out.   2290
The slave whom I appointed for the act,
I ne'er set eye upon the peasant since:
O, could I get him for to make him sure,
My doubts would cease, and I should rest secure.
But if the old men, with persuasive words
Have saved their lives, and made him to relent;
Then they are fled unto the Court of France,
And like a trumpet manifest my shame.
A shame on these white-livered slaves, say I,
That with fair words so soon are overcome.   2300
O God, that I had been but made a man;
Or that my strength were equal with my will!
These foolish men are nothing but mere pity,
And melt as butter doth against the sun.
Why should they have preeminence over us,
Since we are creatures of more brave resolve?
I swear, I am quite out of charity
With all the heartless men in Christendom.
A pox upon them, when they are afraid
To give a stab, or slit a paltry windpipe,   2310
Which are so easy matters to be done.
Well, had I thought the slave would serve me so,
Myself would have been executioner:
'Tis now undone, and if that it be known,
I'll make as good shift as I can for one.
He that repines at me, howe'er it stands,
'Twere best for him to keep him from my hands.   (*Exit.*)

SCENE II.

*Sound drums and trumpets. Enter the Gallian King, Leir, Mumford
and the army.*

---

[64] Compare this soliloquy with Goneril's words in IV.ii. and with her letter
to Edmund, IV.vi. 267–276. Clearly Shakespeare's Goneril equates with the
Ragan of this play.

KING. [65]Thus have we brought our army to the sea,
Whereas our ships are ready to receive us:
The wind stands fair, and we in four hours sail, 2320
May easily arrive on British shore,
Where unexpected we may them surprise,
And gain a glorious victory with ease.
Wherefore, my loving countrymen, resolve,
Since truth and justice fights on our sides,
That we shall march with conquest where we go.
Myself will be as forward as the first,
And step by step march with the hardiest wight:
And not the meanest soldier in our camp
Shall be in danger, but I'll second him. 2330
To you, my Lord, we give the whole command
Of all the army, next unto ourself;
Not doubting of you, but you will extend
Your wonted valor in this needful case,
Encouraging the rest to do the like,
By your approved magnanimity.

MUMFORD. My liege, 'tis needless to spur a willing horse,
That's apt enough to run himself to death:
For here I swear by that sweet saint's bright eyes,
Which are the stars, which guide me to good hap, 2340
Either to see my old Lord crowned anew,
Or in his cause to bid the world adieu.

LEIR. Thanks, good Lord Mumford, 'tis more of your good will,
Than any merit or desert in me.

MUMFORD. And now to you, my worthy countrymen,
Ye valiant race of Genovesian Gauls,
Surnamed Red-shanks, for your chivalry,
Because you fight up to the shanks in blood:
Show yourselves now to be right Gauls indeed, 2350
And be so bitter on your enemies,
That they may say, you are as bitter as gall.
Gall them, brave shot, with your artillery:
Gall them, brave halberds, with your sharp-point bills,
Each in their 'pointed place, not one, but all,
Fight for the credit of yourselves and Gaul.

KING. Then what should more persuasion need to those,
That rather wish to deal, than hear of blows?

---

[65] Contrast this scene with the actions of Shakespeare's King of France: IV.iii. 1–9.

Let's to our ships, and if that God permit,
In four hours sail, I hope we shall be there.   2360
    MUMFORD. And in five hours more, I make no doubt,
But we shall bring our wish'd desires about.   (*Exeunt.*)

SCENE III.[66]

Enter a captain of the watch and two watchmen.

    CAPTAIN. My honest friends, it is your turn tonight,
To watch in this place; near about the beacon,
And vigilantly have regard,
If any fleet of ships pass hitherward:
Which if you do, your office is to fire
The beacon presently, and raise the town.   (*Exit.*)

    1ST WATCHMAN. Aye, aye, aye, fear nothing; we know our
charge, I warrant: I have been a watchman about this beacon   2370
this thirty year, and yet I ne'er see it stir, but stood as quietly as
might be.

    2ND WATCHMAN. Faith neighbor, and you'll follow my 'vice,
instead of watching the beacon, we'll go to goodman Gennings,
and watch a pot of ale and a rasher of bacon: and if we do not
drink ourselves drunk, then so; I warrant, the bacon will see us
when we come out again.

    1ST WATCHMAN. Aye, but how if somebody excuse us to the
captain?

    2ND WATCHMAN. 'Tis no matter, I'll prove by good reason   2380
that we watch the beacon; ass, for example.

    1ST WATCHMAN. I hope you do not call me ass by craft, neigh-
bor.

    2ND WATCHMAN. No, no, but for example: Say here stands the
pot of ale, that's the beacon.

    1ST WATCHMAN. Aye, aye, 'tis a very good beacon.

    2ND WATCHMAN. Well, say here stands your nose, that's the
fire.

    1ST WATCHMAN. Indeed I must confess, 'tis somewhat red.

    2ND WATCHMAN. I see come marching in a dish half a score   2390
pieces of salt bacon.

    1ST WATCHMAN. I understand your meaning, that's as much
to say, half a score ships.

    2ND WATCHMAN. True you conster[67] right; presently, like a
faithful watchman, I fire the beacon, and call up the town.

---

[66] Shakespeare seems to have used nothing of the following three scenes.
[67] construe.

1ST WATCHMAN. Aye, that's as much to say, you set your nose
to the pot, and drink up the drink.

2ND WATCHMAN. You are in the right; come, let's go fire the
beacon.   (*Exeunt.*)

SCENE IV.

Enter the King of Gallia with a still march, Mumford and soldiers.

KING. Now march our ensigns on the British earth,   2400
And we are near approaching to the town:
Then look about you, valiant countrymen,
And we shall finish the exploit with ease.
Th' inhabitants of this mistrustful place
Are dead asleep, as men that are secure;
Here shall we skirmish but with naked men,
Devoid of sense, new waked from a dream,
That know not what our coming doth pretend,
Till they do feel our meaning on their skins:
Therefore assail: God and our right for us.   2410
                                                              (*Exeunt.*)

SCENE V.

*Alarum, with men and women half naked. Enter two captains without
doublets, with swords.*

1ST CAPTAIN. Where are these villains that were set to watch,
And fire the beacon, if occasion served,
That thus have suffered us to be surprised,
And never given notice to the town?
We are betrayed, and quite devoid of hope,
By any means to fortify ourselves.

2ND CAPTAIN. Tis ten to one the peasants are o'ercome with
drink and sleep, and so neglect their charge.

1ST CAPTAIN. A whirlwind carry them quick to a whirlpool
That there the slaves may drink their bellies full.   2420

2ND CAPTAIN. This 'tis, to have the beacon so near the alehouse.
                (Enter the watchmen drunk, with each a pot.)

1ST CAPTAIN. Out on ye, villains, whither run ye now?

1ST WATCHMAN. To fire the town, and call up the beacon.

2ND WATCHMAN. No, no, sir, to fire the beacon. (*He drinks.*)

2ND CAPTAIN. What, with a pot of ale, you drunken rogues?

1ST CAPTAIN. You'll fire the beacon, when the town is lost:
I'll teach you how to tend your office better. (*Draws to stab them.*)

(*Enter Mumford, Captains run away.*)

MUMFORD. Yield, yield, yield. (*He kicks down their pots.*)

1ST WATCHMAN. Reel? no, we do not reel: you may lack a pot 2430
of ale ere you die.

MUMFORD. But in mean space, I answer, you want none, well,
there's no dealing with you, y'are tall men, and well weaponed;
I would there were no worse than you in the town.   (*Exit.*)

2ND WATCHMAN. A speaks like an honest man, my choler's
passed already; come, neighbor, let's go.

1ST WATCHMAN. Nay, first let's see and we can stand.   (*Exeunt.*)

SCENE VI.[68]

Alarum, excursions, Mumford after them, and some half naked.
Enter the Gallian King, Leir, Mumford, Cordella, Perillus, and
soldiers, with the chief of the town bound.

KING. Fear not, my friends, you shall receive no hurt,
If you'll subscribe unto your lawful king,
And quite revoke your fealty from Cambria,   2440
And from aspiring Cornwall too, whose wives
Have practised treason 'gainst their father's life,
We come in justice of your wronged king,
And do intend no harm at all to you,
So you submit unto your lawful king.

LEIR. Kind countrymen, it grieves me, that perforce,
I am constrained to use extremities.

NOBLES. Long have you here been looked for, good my Lord,
And wished for by a general consent:
And had we known your Highness had arrived,   2450
We had not made resistance to your Grace:
And now, my gracious Lord, you need not doubt,
But all the country will yield presently,
Which since your absence have been greatly taxed,
For to maintain their overswelling pride.
We'll presently send word to all our friends;
When they have notice, they will come apace.

LEIR. Thanks, loving subjects, and thanks, worthy son,
Thanks, my kind daughter, thanks to you, my Lord,
Who willingly adventured have your blood,   2460
(Without desert) to do me so much good.

---

[68] These final three scenes relate to Shakespeare only by contrast, but
several of those contrasts, the fate of Cordella and Leir especially, can provide
useful insights into the creation of Shakespeare's art.

MUMFORD. Oh, say not so:
I have been much beholden to your Grace:
I must confess, I have been in some skirmishes,
But I was never in the like to this:
For where I was wont to meet with armed men,
I was now encountered with naked women.

CORDELLA. We that are feeble, and want use of arms,
Will pray to God to shield you from all harms.

LEIR. The while your hands do manage ceaseless toil, 2470
Our hearts shall pray, the foes may have the foil.

PERILLUS. We'll fast and pray, whilst you for us do fight,
That victory may prosecute the right.

KING. Methinks, your words do amplify (my friends)
And add fresh vigor to my willing limbs.

(*Drum.*)

But hark, I hear the adverse drum approach.
God and our right, Saint Denis, and Saint George.

(*Enter Cornwall, Cambria, Gonorill, Ragan, and the army.*)

CORNWALL. Presumptuous King of Gauls, how darest thou
Presume to enter on our British shore?
And more than that, to take our towns perforce, 2480
And draw our subjects' hearts from their true king?
Be sure to buy it at as dear a price,
As ere you bought presumption in your lives.

KING. Over-daring Cornwall, know, we came in right,
And just revengement of the wronged king,
Whose daughters there, fell vipers as they are,
Have sought to murder and deprive of life:
But God protected him from all their spite,
And we are come in justice of his right.

CAMBRIA. Nor he nor thou have any interest here, 2490
But what you win and purchase with the sword.
Thy slanders to our noble virtuous queens,
We'll in the battle thrust them down thy throat,
Except for fear of our revenging hands,
Thou fly to sea, as not secure on lands.

MUMFORD. Welshman, I'll so ferret you ere night for that word,
That you shall have no mind to crack[69] so well this twelvemonth.

GONORILL. They lie, that say we sought our father's death.

RAGAN. 'Tis merely forged for a color's sake, 2500
To set a gloss on your invasion.

---

[69] brag.

Methinks, an old man ready for to die,
Should be ashamed to broach so foul a lie.

CORDELLA. Fly, shameless sister, so devoid of grace,
To call our father liar to his face.

GONORILL. Peace, Puritan,[70] dissembling hypocrite,
Which art so good, that thou wilt prove stark naught:
Anon, when as I have you in my fingers,
I'll make you wish yourself in purgatory.

PERILLUS. Nay, peace thou monster, shame unto thy sex;   2510
Thou fiend in likeness of a human creature.

RAGAN. I never heard a fouler spoken man.

LEIR. Out on thee, viper, scum, filthy parricide,
More odious to my sight than is a toad;
Knowest thou these letters?

(*She snatches them and tears them.*)

RAGAN. Think you to outface me with your paltry scrawls?
You come to drive my husband from his right,
Under the color of a forged letter.

LEIR. Whoever heard the like impiety?

PERILLUS. You are our debtor of more patience: 2520
We were more patient when we stayed for you,
Within the thicket two long hours and more.

RAGAN. What hours? What thicket?

PERILLUS. There, where you sent your servant with your letters,
Sealed with your hand, to send us both to heaven,
Where, as I think, you never mean to come.

RAGAN. Alas, you are grown a child again with age,
Or else your senses dote for want of sleep.

PERILLUS. Indeed you made us rise betimes, you know,
Yet had a care we should sleep where you bade us stay,   2530
But never wake more till the latter day.

GONORILL. Peace, peace, old fellow, thou art sleepy still.

MUMFORD. Faith, and if you reason till tomorrow, you get no
other answer at their hands. 'Tis pity two such good faces should
have so little grace between them.
Well, let us see if their husbands with their hands,
Can do as much, as they do with their tongues.

CAMBRIA. Aye, with their swords they'll make your tongue unsay
What they have said, or else they'll cut them out.

KING. To 't, gallants, to 't, let's not stand brawling thus.   2540

(*Exeunt both armies.*)

---

[70] an intriguing anachronism.

SCENE VII.

Sound alarums; excursions. Mumford must chase Cambria away:
then cease.
Enter Cornwall.

CORNWALL. The day is lost, our friends do all revolt,
And join against us with the adverse part:
There is no means of safety but by flight,
And therefore I'll to Cornwall with my queen. (*Exit.*)
(Enter Cambria.)

CAMBRIA. I think, there is a devil in the camp hath haunted
me today; he hath so tired me, that in a manner I can fight no
more.

(Enter Mumford.)

Zounds! here he comes, I'll take me to my horse. (*Exit.*)
(Mumford follows him to the door, and returns.)

MUMFORD. Farewell Welshman, I'll give thee but thy due,
Thou hast a light and nimble pair of legs:
Thou art more in debt to them than to thy hands: 2550
But if I meet thee once again today,
I'll cut them off, and set them to a better heart. (*Exit.*)

SCENE VIII.

Alarums and excursions, then sound victory.
Enter Leir, Perillus, King, Cordella, and Mumford.

KING. [71]Thanks be to God, your foes are overcome,
And you again possessed of your right.

LEIR. First to the heavens; next, thanks to you, my son,
By whose good means I repossess the same:
Which if it please you to accept yourself,
With all my heart I will resign to you:
For it is yours by right, and none of mine.
First have you raised, at your own charge, a power 2560
Of valiant soldiers (this comes all from you);
Next have you ventured your own person's scathe.
And lastly (worthy Gallia never stained),
My kingly title I by thee have gained.

---

[71] While Shakespeare eschews this kind of happy ending for his version,
Nahum Tate's revision of the Shakespeare play in 1681, *The History of King
Lear*, restores the "happy" ending and adds a bonus romance between Cordelia
and Edgar. Sad to say, the Tate revision remained the accepted version of
King Lear until 1823.

KING. Thank heavens, not me, my zeal to you is such,
Command my utmost, I will never grutch.[72]

CORDELLA. He that with all kind love entreats his queen,
Will not be to her father unkind seen.

LEIR. Ah, my Cordella, now I call to mind,
The modest answer, which I took unkind;   2570
But now I see, I am no whit beguiled,
Thou lovedst me dearly, and as ought a child.
And thou (Perillus) partner once in woe,
Thee to requite, the best I can, I'll do:
Yet all I can, aye, were it ne'er so much,
Were not sufficient, thy true love is such.
Thanks, worthy Mumford, to thee last of all,
Not greeted last, cause thy desert was small;
No, thou hast lion-like laid on today,
Chasing the Cornwall king and Cambria;   2580
Who with my daughters, daughters did I say?
To save their lives, the fugitives did play.
Come, son and daughter, who bid me advance,
Repose with me a while, and then for France.

(*Sound drums and trumpets. Exeunt.*)

---

[72] grudge.

SIR PHILIP SIDNEY

Arcadia, 1590

FROM BOOK II, CHAPTER 10*

It was in the kingdom of Galacia, the season being (as in the depth of winter) very cold, and as then suddenly grown to so extreme and foul a storm, that never any winter (I think) brought forth a fouler child: so that the princes[1] were even compelled by the hail, that the pride of the wind blew into their faces, to seek some shrouding place with a certain hollow rock offering it unto them, they made it their shield against the tempest's fury. And so staying there, till the violence thereof was passed, they heard the speech of a couple, who not perceiving them (being hid within that rude canopy) held a strange and pitiful disputation which made them step out; yet in such sort as they might see unseen. There they perceived an aged man, and a young, scarcely come to the age of a man, both poorly arrayed, extremely weather-beaten: the old man blind, the young man leading him: and yet through all those miseries, in both these seemed to appear a kind of nobleness not suitable to that affliction. But the first words they heard were these of the old man.[2] "Well Leonatus," said he, "since I cannot persuade thee to lead me to that which should end my grief, and thy trouble, let me now entreat thee to leave me; fear not, my misery cannot be greater than it is, and nothing does become me but misery: fear not the danger of my blind steps, I cannot fall worse than I am. And do not I pray thee, do not obstinately continue to infect thee with my wretchedness. But flee, flee from this region, only worthy of me." "Dear father," answered he, "do not take away from me the only remnant of my happiness: while I have power to do you service, I am not wholly miserable." "Ah my son," said he, and with that he groaned, as if sorrow strove to break his heart, "how evil

---

* text modernized.

[1] Pyrocles and Musidorus, heroes of the main plot of Sidney's epic, who will, after countless digressions like this one, win the love of Pamela and Philoclea, daughters of the King of Arcadia.

[2] A reference to IV.vi. 1–80, developed further in the next paragraph.

fits it me to have such a son, and how much does thy kindness upbraid my wickedness?" These doleful speeches, and some others to like purpose (well showing they had not been born to the fortune they were in) moved the princes to go out unto them and ask the younger what they were. "Sirs," answered he, with a good grace, and made the more agreeable by a certain noble kind of piteousness, "I see well you are strangers, that know not our misery so well here known, that no man dare know but that we must be miserable. Indeed our state is such as though nothing is so needful unto us as pity, yet nothing is more dangerous unto us than to make ourselves so known as may stir pity. But your presence promises that cruelty shall not overrun hate. And if it did, in truth our state is sunk below the degrees of fear.

"This old man (whom I lead) was lately rightful prince of this country of Paphlagonia, by the hardhearted ungratefulness of a son of his deprived, not only of his kingdom (whereof no foreign forces were ever able to spoil him) but of his sight, the riches which Nature grants to the poorest creatures. [3]Whereby, and by other his unnatural dealings, he has been driven to such grief, as even now he would have had me to have led him to the top of this rock, thence to cast himself headlong to death, and so would have made me, who received my life of him, to be the worker of destruction. But noble gentlemen," said he, "if either of you have a father, and feel what dutiful affection is engrafted in a son's heart, let me entreat you to convey this afflicted prince to some place of rest and security; amongst your worthy acts it shall be none of the least, that a king of such might and fame, and so unjustly oppressed, is in any sort by you relieved."

But before they could make him answer, his father began to speak. "Ah my son," said he, "how evil an historian are you, that leave out the chief knot of all the discourse? My wickedness, my wickedness. And if thou do it to spare my cares (the only sense now left me proper for knowledge) assure thyself thou do mistake me. And I take witness of that sun which you see" (with that he cast up his blind eyes, as if he would hunt for light) "and wish myself in worse case than I do wish myself, which is as evil as may be, if I speak untruly; that nothing is so welcome to my thoughts as the publishing of my shame. Therefore know you gentlemen (to whom from my heart I wish that it may not prove ominous foretoken of misfortune to have met with such a miser[4] as I am) that whatsoever my son — O God, that truth binds me to reproach him with the name of my son — has said, is

---

[3] IV.vi. 1–80.
[4] miserable wretch.

true. [5]But besides those truths, this also is true, that having had in lawful marriage, of a mother fit to bear royal children, this son (such one as partly you see, and better shall know by my short declaration) and so enjoyed the expections (so as I needed envy no father for the chief comfort of mortality, to leave another one's self after me) I was carried by a bastard son of mine (if at least I be bound to believe the words of that base woman, my concubine, his mother) first to mislike, then to hate, lastly to destroy, to do my best to destroy, this son (I think you think) undeserving destruction. What ways he used to bring me to it, if I should tell you, I should tediously trouble you with as much poisonous hypocrisy, desperate fraud, smooth malice, hidden ambition, and smiling envy, as in any living person could be harbored: but I list it not, no remembrance (no, of naughtiness[6]) delights me but mine own; and methinks the accusing his trains[7] might in some manner excuse my fault, which certainly I loathe to do. But the conclusion is that I gave order to some servants of mine, whom I thought as apt for such charities as myself, to lead him out into a forest and there to kill him.

[8]"But those thieves (better natured to my son than myself) spared his life, letting him go, to learn to live poorly: which he did, giving himself to be a private soldier in a country hereby. But as he was ready to be greatly advanced for some noble pieces of service which he did, he heard news of me: who (drunk in my affection to that unlawful and unnatural son of mine) suffered myself so to be governed by him that all favors and punishments [were] passed by him, all offices and places of importance distributed to his favorites; so that ere I was aware, I had left myself nothing but the name of a king:[9] which he shortly weary of too, with many indignities (if anything may be called an indignity which was laid upon me) threw me out of my seat, and put out my eyes; and then (proud of his tyranny) let me go, neither imprisoning nor killing me: but rather delighting to make me feel my misery, misery indeed, if ever there were any; full of wretchedness, fuller of disgrace, and fullest of guiltiness. And as he came to the crown by so unjust means, as unjustly he kept it by force of stranger soldiers in citadels, the nests of tyranny and murderers of liberty; disarming all his own countrymen that no man durst show himself a wellwiller of mine: to say the truth (I think) few of them being so (con-

---

[5] I.i 8–32; I.ii; II.i. 1–87.
[6] of any one else's wickedness.
[7] allurements, snares.
[8] Compare with Edgar's disguising himself as a beggar.
[9] III.vii. 28ff.

sidering my cruel folly to my good son, and so foolish kindness to my unkind bastard): but if there were any who fell to pity of so great a fall, and had yet any sparks of unstained duty left in them towards me, yet durst they not show it, scarcely with giving me alms at their doors; which yet was the only sustenance of my distressed life, nobody daring to show so much charity as to lend me a hand to guide my dark step. [10]Till this son of mine (God knows, worthy of a more virtuous and more fortunate father) forgetting my abominable wrongs, not recking[11] danger, and neglecting the present good way he was in of doing himself good, came hither to do this kind office you see him perform towards me, to my unspeakable grief; not only because his kindness is a glass even to my blind eyes, of my naughtiness, but that above all griefs it grieves me he should desperately adventure the loss of his soul-deserving life for mine, that yet owe more to fortune for my deserts, as if he would carry mud in a chest of crystal. For well I know, he that now reigns, how much soever (and with good reason) he despises me, of all men despised; yet he will not let slip any advantage to make away with him whose just title (ennobled by courage and goodness) may one day shake the seat of a never secure tyranny. And for this cause I craved of him to lead me to the top of this rock, indeed I must confess, with meaning to free him from so serpentine a companion as I am. But he finding what I purposed, only therein since he was born, showed himself disobedient unto me. And now, gentlemen, you have the true story, which I pray you publish to the world, that my mischievous proceedings may be the glory of his filial piety, the only reward now left for so great a merit. And if it may be, let me obtain that of you which my son denies me: for never was there more pity in saving any, than in ending me; both because therein my agonies shall end, and so shall you preserve this excellent young man who else wilfully follows his own ruin."

The matter in itself lamentable, lamentably expressed by the old prince (which needed not take to himself the gestures of pity, since his face could not put off the marks thereof) greatly moved the two princes to compassion, which could not stay in such hearts as theirs without seeking remedy. But by and by the occasion was presented: for Plexirtus (so was the bastard called) came thither with forty horse only of purpose to murder his brother; of whose coming he had soon advertisement, and thought no eyes of sufficient credit in such a matter but his own; and therefore came himself to be actor and spectator. And as soon as he came, not regarding the weak (as he thought) guard of but two men, commanded some of his followers to set their

---

[10] IV.i.
[11] caring about.

hands to his[12] in the killing of Leonatus. But the young prince (though not otherwise armed but with a sword) how falsely soever he was dealt with by others, would not betray himself, but bravely drawing it out, made the death of the first that assaulted him warn his fellows to come more warily after him. But then Pyrocles and Musidorus were quickly become parties (so just a defense deserving as much as old friendship) and so did behave them among that company (more injurious than valiant) that many of them lost their lives for their wicked master.

Yet perhaps had the number of them at last prevailed, if the King of Pontus (lately by them [Pyrocles and Musidorus] made so) had not come unlooked for to their succor. Who (having had a dream which had fixed his imagination vehemently upon some great danger, presently to follow those two princes whom he most dearly loved) was come in all haste, following as well as he could their track with a hundred horses in that country which he thought (considering who then reigned) a fit place enough to make the stage of any tragedy.

But then the match had been so ill made for Plexirtus, that his ill-led life and worse gotten honor should have tumbled together to destruction had there not come in [13]Tydeus and Telenor with forty or fifty in their suit to the defense of Plexirtus. These two were brothers, of the noblest house of that country, brought up from their infancy with Plexirtus: men of such prowess as not to know fear in themselves, and yet to teach it others that should deal with them: for they had often made their lives triumph over most terrible dangers; never dismayed, and ever fortunate; and truly no more settled in their valor than disposed to goodness and justice, if either they had lighted on a better friend, or could have learned to make friendship a child, and not the father of Virtue. But bringing up (rather than choice) having first knit their minds unto him (indeed crafty enough, either to hide his faults, or never to show them, but when they might pay home) they willingly held out the course[14] rather to satisfy him than all the world; and rather to be good friends than good men: so as, though they did not like the evil he did, yet they liked him that did the evil; and though not counsellors of the offence, yet protectors of the offender. Now they having heard of this sudden going out, with so small a company, in a country full of evil-wishing minds toward him (though they knew not the cause) followed him; till they found him in such case as they were to venture their lives, or else he to lose his: which they did with

---

[12] to assist him.

[13] whose conduct resembles, faintly, that of the Dukes of Albany and Cornwall and whose character analysis suggests the Duke of Albany.

[14] kept on the same path; i.e., of friendship to Plexirtus.

such force of mind and body that truly I may justly say Pyrocles and Musidorus had never till then found any that could make them so well repeat their hardest lesson in the feats of arms. And briefly so they [Tydeus and Telenor] did, that if they overcame not, yet were they not overcome but carried away that ungrateful master of theirs to a place of security, howsoever the princes labored to the contrary. But this matter being thus far begun, it became not the constancy of the princes so to leave it; but in all haste making forces both in Pontus and Phrygia, they had in few days left him [Plexirtus] but only that one strong place where he was. For fear having been the only knot that had fastened his people unto him, that once untied by a greater force they all scattered from him, like so many birds whose cage had been broken.

In which season the blind king (having in the chief city of his realm set the crown upon his son Leonatus's head) with many tears (both of joy and sorrow) setting forth to the whole people his own fault and his son's virtue, after he had kissed him and forced his son to accept honor of him (as of his new become subject) even in a moment died, as it should seem: [15]his heart broken with unkindness and affliction, stretched so far beyond his limits with this excess of comfort as it was able no longer to keep safe his royal spirits.

☐ *Some Sources for Further Study*

1. ROBERT FABYAN — *The New Chronicles of England and France* (1516). Another chronicle version of the Leir story.
2. *A Mirror for Magistrates* — "Cordila" (1574).
3. WILLIAM WARNER — *Albion's England* (1586). The Leir story.
4. SAMUEL HARSNETT — *Declaration of Egregious Popish Impostures* (1603). An attack on superstition that contains many germs of the language of this play, especially of the scenes during the storm on the heath.
5. "King Leir and His Three Daughters," available in Thomas Percy, *Reliques of Ancient English Poetry*.

---

[15] V.iii. 196–199 and 257ff.

macBeth

Like the English history plays, Macbeth finds in Holinshed its basal source, but here the differences in handling Holinshed are as broad as those that separate history from tragedy. Where the history plays range at most across a dozen years, Macbeth hurdles almost a century, from 968–1057; where the history plays follow chronology at least in rough parallel, Macbeth collapses its time period into a span of at most two months; and where the history plays use Holinshed as a source of facts, Macbeth turns to Holinshed for sensationalism and witchery. Holinshed's own prime source for his Macbeth material was the Scotorum Historia of Hector Boece, 1527, material which one critic aptly terms "a circumstantial romance composed by Hector Boece." Holinshed's text abounds in Boece-inspired inaccuracies, but for Shakespeare these probably add rather than detract in this play. For Shakespeare in Macbeth is creating a world more hellish than Scottish where it matters little who really killed Macbeth, and what he wants from his favorite source this time is not earth but fire and air.

To piece together the plot of Macbeth Shakespeare selects two discrete situations, the murder of Duff around 968 and the murder of Duncan nearly a century later. From "Duff" Shakespeare made use of Duff's witch-ridden illness, whose symptoms suggest those of Lady Macbeth during the sleep-walking episode; the witches of Forres, their spells and incantations; Donwald's murder — abetted by his wife — of Duff under roughly the same circumstances as Shakespeare's Macbeth murders Duncan; and the weird darkness and fearful signs in nature in the wake of that murder.

From the "Duncan" section (1054–1057) Shakespeare takes the revolt of Macdonwald and the invasion of Sueno, King of Norway, characteristically fusing them into a single event; Macbeth's and Banquo's meeting with the witches; Duncan's decision to have Malcolm succeed him as king; the "very ambitious" Lady Macbeth; the flight of Malcolm to England after Duncan's murder; the murder of Banquo;

the kingly line descended from Fleance; the murder of Macduff's family and his flight to Malcolm in England; his return with the elder Siward; the witches' prophecies concerning Birnam Wood and Macbeth's not needing to fear "any man that should be or was born of any woman"; and the slaying of Macbeth by Macduff.

From "Malcolm" Shakespeare got the detail that henceforth — after Macbeth's demise — thanes would be made earls; from "Edward the Confessor" the details of the death of young Siward and of the king's gift of prophecy and his healing touch. On top of all those correspondences Shakespeare superadds the porter scene, the presence of the third murderer, the appearance of Hecate (perhaps the work of Thomas Middleton, not Shakespeare), the return of Banquo's ghost, and the doctor's remarkable discussion with Macbeth about "a mind diseased."

The version of Duncan and Macbeth by George Buchanan in his Latin History of Scotland, 1582, confronts the colorful Holinshed-Boece account with the hard clarity of a charcoal drawing. Since it was not available in English at the time of Macbeth, Shakespeare must have read it in Latin and apparently superimposed its more realistic, historical, psychological approach upon the supernatural Holinshed account. Henry N. Paul[1] covers the impact of Buchanan's History upon Macbeth more than thoroughly. Suffice it to mention here Buchanan's more complex characterization of Macbeth, the psychological touches during Macbeth's preparations for killing Banquo, and the stricter realism of Buchanan's account, including the historical fact that Macbeth was not killed by Macduff (as Holinshed reports) during Malcolm's invasion, was in fact not even killed in that battle at all.

There is a strong possibility that Macbeth was written to order for presentation before King James I during the visit of the King of Denmark in 1606. King James was a firm believer in magic, witchcraft, and the king's healing touch, all of which elements appear in Macbeth, and was the author of Daemonology, 1597, a book written "to resolve the doubting hearts of many; both that such assaults of Satan are most certainly practised, and that the instruments thereof merit most severely to be punished." The book consists of three parts, on magic in general, on sorcery and witchcraft, and on spirits and specters that trouble mankind. It contains a number of phrases and superstitions echoed in Shakespeare's play, suggesting that Shakespeare may have read it in preparation for writing Macbeth. Two of the more likely source passages are presented in the text to illustrate that possibility.

---

[1] Henry N. Paul, The Royal Play of Macbeth (New York: The Macmillan Company, 1950) pp. 213–219.

There are only two really complex characters in *Macbeth*, and suggestions for each appear in the sources. Lady Macbeth derives from Holinshed's "malice" of Donwald's wife, from Holinshed's Lady Macbeth "burning in unquenchable desire to bear the name of a queen," and from Buchanan's Lady Macbeth who "daily excited" her husband's ambitions, although her fearsome stature and her fall from reason to imagination are purely Shakespeare's achievements. Macbeth, whom critics have called a good man in the grip of evil, an evil man projecting his unconscious desires onto a non-existent spirit world, a man too little for the crimes he commits, and a monster set loose upon innocence, owes much of this ambiguity of interpretation to his sources. In Holinshed he is at once a model king and an evil one, and his simpler portrait in Holinshed is blurred by the superimposition of Buchanan's more psychological one, though here too Shakespeare's creation exceeds all the implications of his sources.

Macbeth is a tour de force of dramatic construction, and it may be that its success as pure drama crowds out idea. The play does suggest several ideas, growing out of the character of Macbeth, about the nature of good and evil and about ambition; and Holinshed and Buchanan, juxtaposed, set up a conflict between the world of superstition and the world of cold reason. But coming after the wisdom of *Hamlet* and *King Lear* its freight of Renaissance idea is notably light. Perhaps in view of its thickly strewn images of blood and hell *Macbeth* is a cosmic metaphor of mankind's crime and punishment, or perhaps, to alter Archibald MacLeish's famous line, it does not mean, but simply is.

RAPHAEL HOLINSHED

The Chronicles of England, Scotland, and Ireland,* 1587

DUFF

[968] After the corpse of Indulph was removed unto Colmekill and there buried, Duff the son of King Malcolm was crowned king at Scone with all due solemnity. In the beginning of the reign, Culene the son of King Indulph was proclaimed Prince of Cumberland: immediately whereupon the king transported over into the Western Isles to set an order there for certain misdemeanors used by divers robbers and pillers[1] of the common people. At his arrival amongst them he called the thanes of the Isles afore him, commanding straightly as they would avoid his displeasure to purge their countries of such malefactors, whereby the husbandmen and other commons might live in quiet without vexation of such barrators and idle persons as sought to live only upon other men's goods.

The thanes upon this charge given them by the king, took no small number of the offenders, partly by public authority and partly by lying in wait for them where they supposed their haunt was to resort: the which being put to execution according to that they had merited, caused the residue of that kind of people either to get them over into Ireland, either else to learn some manual occupation wherewith to get their living — yea, though they were never so great gentlemen born. Howbeit the nobles, with this extreme rigor showed thus by the king against their lineage, were much offended therewith, accounting it a great dishonor for such as were descended of noble parentage to be constrained to get their living with the labor of their hands — which only appertained to plowmen and such others of the base degree as were born to travail for the maintenance of the

---

* text modernized. The "Duff," "Duncan," and "Malcolm" sections are taken from *The History of Scotland*. The "Edward the Confessor" section, like all of the other Holinshed selections in this volume, comes from *The Chronicles of England*.

[1] pillagers.

536

nobility and to serve at their commandment by order of their birth and in no wise after such sort to be made in manner equal with them in state and condition in life.

Furthermore, they murmured closely amongst themselves how the king was only become friend to the commons and clergy of his realm, having no respect to the nobility, but rather declared himself to be an utter enemy thereof; so that he was unworthy to have the rule of the nobles and gentlemen unless he knew better what belonged to their degree. This murmuring did spread not only among them in the Isles, but also through all the other parts of his realm, so that they ceased not to speak very evil of the government of things. [2]In the meantime the king fell into a languishing disease, not so grievous as strange, that none of his physicians could perceive what to make of it. For there was seen in him no token that either choler, melancholy, phlegm, or any other vicious humor did anything abound whereby his body should be brought into such decay and consumption (so as there remained unneath[3] anything upon him save skin and bone).

And since it appeared manifestly by all outward signs and tokens that natural moisture did nothing fail in the vital spirits, his color also was fresh and fair to behold, with such liveliness of looks, the more was not to be wished for; he had also a temperate desire and appetite to his meat and drink. But yet could he not sleep in the nighttime by any provocations that could be devised, but still fell into exceeding sweats, which by no means might be restrained. The physicians perceiving all their medicines to want due effect, yet to put him in some comfort of help declared him that they would send for some cunning physicians into foreign parts, who happily being inured with such kind of diseases should easily cure him: namely so soon as the spring of the year was once come, which of itself should help much thereunto.

Howbeit the king, though he had small hope of recovery, yet had he still a diligent care unto the due administration of his laws and good orders of his realm, devising oft with his Council about the same. But when it was understood into what a perilous sickness he was fallen, there were no small number, that, condemning the authority of the magistrates, began to practise a rebellion. And amongst the chiefest were those of Murray land, who slaying sundry of the king's officers began to rage in most cruel wise against all such as were not consenting to their misordered tumult. The king's physician forbade in any wise that the king should be advertised of such business, for doubt of

---

[2] Compare the symptoms in this paragraph and the next with V.i. 1ff; V.iii. 37–46.

[3] underneath.

increasing his sickness with trouble of mind about the same. But about that present time there was a murmuring amongst the people, how the king was vexed with no natural sickness, but by sorcery and magical art practised by a sort of witches dwelling in a town of Murray land, called Forres.[4]

Whereupon, albeit the author of this secret talk was not known, yet being brought to the king's ear it caused him to send forthwith certain witty persons thither to inquire of the truth. They that were thus sent, dissembling the cause of their journey, were received in the dark of the night into the castle of Forres by the lieutenant of the same, called Donwald, who continuing faithful to the king had kept that castle against the rebels to the king's use. Unto him therefore these messengers declared the cause of their coming, requiring his aid for the accomplishment of the king's pleasure.

The soldiers, which lay there in garrison, had an inkling that there was some such matter in hand as was talked of amongst the people; by reason that one of them kept as a concubine a young woman, which was daughter to one of the witches, as his paramour, who told him the whole manner used by her mother and other companions, with their intent also, which was to make away the king. The soldier, having learned this of his leman, told the same to his fellows, who made report to Donwald. And he showed it to the king's messengers and therewith sent for the young damsel which the soldier kept, as then being within the castle, and caused her upon strict examination[5] to confess the whole matter as she had seen and knew. [6]Whereupon learning by her confession in what house in the town it was where they wrought their mischievous mystery, he sent forth soldiers about the midst of the night, who breaking into the house found one of the witches roasting upon a wooden broch[7] an image of wax at the fire, resembling in each feature the king's person, made and devised (as is to be thought) by craft and art of the devil. Another of them sat reciting certain words of enchantment and still basted the image with certain liquor very busily.

The soldiers finding them occupied in this wise took them, together with the image, and led them into the castle, where being strictly examined for what purpose they went about such manner of enchant-

---

[4] It is on a heath near Forres that Shakespeare's Macbeth first meets the witches. (I.ii,iii).

[5] For a precise idea of the full cruelty of that "strict examination," see such a work as *News From Scotland, Declaring the Damnable Life and Death of Doctor Fian*, Anon., 1591, which describes the tortures used to extract confessions from witches.

[6] Compare with I.iii. 1–37; IV.i. 1–43.

[7] walled, circular castle: i.e., a miniature replica of Duff's castle.

ment, they answered to the end to make away the king. For as the image did waste afore the fire, so did the body of the king break forth in sweat. And as for the words of the enchantment, they served to keep him still waking from sleep, so that as the wax ever melted so did the king's flesh. By the which means it should have come to pass that when the wax was once clean consumed the death of the king should immediately follow. So were they taught by evil spirits, and hired to work the feat by the nobles of Murray land. The standers by, that heard such an abominable tale told by these witches, straightway broke the image and caused the witches (according as they had well deserved) to be burnt to death.

It was said that the king at the very same time that these things were adoing within the castle of Forres was delivered of his languor and slept that night without any sweat breaking forth upon him at all, and the next day being restored to his strength was able to do any manner of thing that lay in man to do, as though he had not been sick before anything at all. But howsoever it came to pass, truth it is that when he was restored to his perfect health he gathered a power of men and with the same went into Murray land against the rebels there. And chasing them from thence, he pursued them into Ross, and from Ross into Caithness, where apprehending them he brought them back unto Forres and there caused them to be hanged up on gallows and gibbets.

Amongst them there were also certain young gentlemen, right beautiful and goodly personages, being near of kin unto Donwald, captain of the castle, and had been persuaded to be partakers with the other rebels, more through the fraudulent counsel of divers wicked persons than of their own accord. Whereupon the foresaid Donwald, lamenting their case, made earnest labor and suit to the king to have begged their pardon. [8]But having a plain denial he conceived such an inward malice towards the king (though he showed it not outwardly at the first) that the same continued still boiling in his stomach, and ceased not till, through setting on of his wife and in revenge of such unthankfulness, he found means to murder the king within the foresaid castle of Forres where he used to sojourn. For the king, being in that country, was accustomed to lie most commonly within the same castle, having a special trust in Donwald as a man whom he never suspected.

But Donwald, not forgetting the reproach which his lineage had sustained by the execution of those his kinsmen whom the king for a spectacle to the people had caused to be hanged, could not but show manifest tokens of great grief at home amongst his family: which,

[8] I.v. 1–71.

his wife perceiving, ceased not to travail with him till she understood what the cause was of his displeasure. Which at length when she had learned by his own relation, she — as one that bore no less malice in her heart towards the king for the like cause on her behalf[9] than her husband did for his friends — counselled him (since the king oftentimes used to lodge in his house without any guard about him other than the garrison of the castle, which was wholly at his commandment) to make him away, and showed him the means whereby he might soonest accomplish it.

Donwald thus being the more kindled in wrath by the words of his wife, determined to follow her advice in the execution of so heinous an act. Whereupon devising with himself for a while which way he might best accomplish his cursed intent, at length got opportunity and sped his purpose as follows. It chanced that the king upon the day before he purposed to depart forth of the castle was long in his oratory at his prayers, and there continued till it was late in the night. [10]At the last, coming forth, he called such afore him as had faithfully served him in pursuit and apprehension of the rebels, and giving them hearty thanks he bestowed sundry honorable gifts amongst them, of the which number Donwald was one, as he that had been ever accounted a most faithful servant to the king.

[11]At length, having talked with them a long time, he got him into his privy chamber only with two of his chamberlains, who having brought him to bed came forth again and then fell to banqueting with Donwald and his wife, who had prepared divers delicate dishes and sundry sorts of drinks for their rear supper or collation. Wherat they sat up so long, till they had charged their stomachs with such full gorges, that their heads were no sooner got to the pillow but asleep they were so fast that a man might have removed the chamber over them, sooner than to have awakened them out of their drunken sleep.

[12]Then Donwald, though he abhorred the act greatly in heart, yet through instigation of his wife he called four of his servants unto him (whom he had made privy to his wicked intent before, and framed to his purpose with large gifts) and now declaring unto them after what sort they should work the feat, they gladly obeyed his instructions. And speedily going about the murder, they entered the chamber (in which the king lay) a little before cock's crow, where they secretly cut his throat as he lay sleeping, without any bustling at all. And

---

[9] Compare with the sheer ambition of Lady Macbeth.

[10] I.vii. 31–35.

[11] I.vii. 61–72.

[12] There are several points of similarity between this paragraph and II.ii. 1–50, although Shakespeare does not use servant murderers or move the king's corpse.

immediately by a postern gate they carried forth the dead body into the fields, and throwing it upon an horse there provided ready for that purpose, they conveyed it unto a place about two miles distant from the castle, where they stayed and got certain laborers to help them to turn the course of a little river running through the fields there. And digging a deep hole in the channel they buried the body in the same, ramming it up with stones and gravel so closely that, setting the water in the right course again, no man could perceive that anything had been newly digged there. This they did by order appointed them by Donwald, as is reported, for that the body should not be found, and by bleeding (when Donwald should be present) declare him to be guilty of the murder.

For such an opinion men have, that the dead corpse of any man being slain will bleed abundantly if the murderer be present. But for what consideration soever they buried him there, they had no sooner finished the work but that they slew them whose help they used herein, and straightways thereupon fled into Orkney.

[13]Donwald, about the time that the murder was in doing, got him amongst them that kept the watch and so continued in company with them all the residue of the night. But in the morning when the noise was raised in the king's chamber how the king was slain, his body conveyed away, and the bed all berayed[14] with blood, he with the watch ran thither as though he had known nothing of the matter. And breaking into the chamber, and finding cakes of blood in the bed and on the floor about the sides of it, he forthwith slew the chamberlains, as guilty of that heinous murder. And then like a madman running to and fro, he ransacked every corner within the castle as though it had been to have seen if he might have found either the body or any of the murderers hid in any privy place. But at length coming to the postern gate, and finding it open, he burdened the chamberlains whom he had slain with all the fault, they having the keys of the gates committed to their keeping all the night. And therefore it could not be otherwise (said he) but that they were of counsel in the committing of that most detestable murder.

[15]Finally, such was his overearnest diligence in the severe inquisition and trial of the offenders herein that some of the lords began to mislike the matter and to smell forth shrewd tokens that he had the whole rule, [16]what by reason of his friends and authority together. They doubted[17] to utter what they thought till time and place should

---

[13] II.iii. 48–124.
[14] stained.
[15] II.iv. 22–36.
[16] i.e., directed the murder.
[17] feared.

better serve thereunto, and hereupon got them away every man to his home. [18]For the space of six months together after this heinous murder thus committed there appeared no sun by day nor moon by night in any part of the realm, but still was the sky covered with continual clouds; and sometimes such outrageous winds arose, with lightnings and tempests, that the people were in great fear of present destruction.

DUNCAN

[1040–1057] After Malcolm succeeded his nephew Duncan, the son of his daughter Beatrice. For Malcolm had two daughters: the one which was this Beatrice being given in marriage unto one Abbanath Crinen, a man of great nobility and Thane of Isles and west parts of Scotland, bore of that marriage the foresaid Duncan; the other called Doada was married unto Sinell, the Thane of Glamis, by whom she had issue one Macbeth,[1] a valiant gentleman, and one that if he had not been somewhat cruel of nature might have been thought most worthy the government of a realm. [2]On the other part, Duncan was so soft and gentle of nature that the people wished the inclinations and manners of these two cousins to have been so tempered and interchangeably bestowed betwixt them, that where the one had too much of clemency, and the other of cruelty, the mean virtue betwixt these two extremities might have reigned by indifferent partition in them both. So should Duncan have proved a worthy king and Macbeth an excellent captain. The beginning of Duncan's reign was very quiet and peaceable, without any notable trouble. But after it was perceived how negligent he was in punishing offenders, many misruled persons took occasion thereof to trouble the peace and quiet state of the commonwealth, by seditious commotions which first had their beginnings in this wise.

Banquo the Thane of Lochaber — of whom the house of the Stewards[3] is descended, the which by order of lineage hath now for a long time enjoyed the crown of Scotland even till these our days[4] — as he gathered the finances due to the king, and further punished somewhat sharply such as were notorious offenders, being assailed by a number of rebels inhabiting in that country and spoiled of the money and all other things, had much ado to get away with life, after he had received

---

[18] II.iv. 1–10.

[1] In Holinshed, Makbeth and Mackbeth; for consistency and clarity Shakespeare's spelling will be used in this version.

[2] I.vii. 16–18.

[3] Stuarts.

[4] See pp. 551–552.

sundry grievous wounds amongst them. Yet escaping their hands, after he was somewhat recovered of his hurts and was able to ride, he repaired to the court; where making his complaint to the king in most earnest wise, he purchased at length that the offenders were sent for by a sergeant at arms, to appear to make answer unto such matters as should be laid to their charge. But they augmenting their mischievous act with a more wicked deed, after they had misused the messenger with sundry kinds of reproaches, they finally slew him also.

Then doubting not but for such contemptuous demeanor against the king's regal authority they should be invaded with all the power the king could make, Macdonwald,[5] one of great estimation among them, making first a confederacy with his nearest friends and kinsmen, took upon him to be chief captain of all such rebels as would stand against the king in maintenance of their grievous offenses lately committed against him.[6] Many slanderous words also and railing taunts this Macdonwald uttered against his prince, called him a faint-hearted milksop, more meet to govern a sort of idle monks in some cloister than to have the rule of such valiant and hardy men of war as the Scots were. He used also such subtle persuasions and forged allurements that in a small time he had gotten together a mighty power of men. For out of the Western Isles there came unto him a great multitude of people, offering themselves to assist him in that rebellious quarrel; and out of Ireland in hope of the spoil came no small number of Kernes and Galloglasses, offering gladly to serve under him, whither it should please him to lead them.

Macdonwald thus having a mighty puissance about him, encountered with such of the king's people as were sent against him in Lochaber, and discomfiting them by mere force took their captain Malcolm, and after the end of the battle smote off his head. This overthrow being notified to the king did put him in wonderful fear, by reason of his small skill in warlike affairs. Calling therefore his nobles to a council, he asked of them their best advice for the subduing of Macdonwald and other the rebels. Here in sundry heads (as ever it happens) were sundry opinions which they uttered according to every man his skill. [7]At length Macbeth speaking much against the king's softness and overmuch slackness in punishing offenders, whereby they had such time to assemble together, he promised notwithstanding if the charge were committed unto him and unto Banquo so to order the matter that the rebels should be shortly vanquished and quite put

---

[5] In Holinshed, Makdowald.

[6] The situation which precedes and precipitates the beginning of Shakespeare's play.

[7] I.ii. 9–41.

down; and that not so much as one of them should be found to make resistance within the country.

And even so it came to pass. For being sent forth with a new power, at his entering into Lochaber the fame of his coming put the enemies in such fear that a great number of them stole secretly away from the Captain Macdonwald, who nevertheless enforced thereto gave battle unto Macbeth with the residue which remained with him. But being overcome, and fleeing for refuge into a castle (within the which his wife and children were enclosed) at length when he saw how he could neither defend the hold any longer against his enemies, nor yet upon surrender be suffered to depart with life saved, he first slew his wife and children and lastly himself — lest if he had yielded simply he should have been executed in most cruel wise for an example to others. Macbeth entering into the castle by the gates, as then set open, found the carcass of Macdonwald lying dead there among the residue of the slain bodies; which when he beheld, remitting no piece of his cruel nature with that pitiful sight, he caused the head to be cut off and set upon a pole's end and so sent it as a present to the king, who as then lay at Bertha. The headless trunk he commanded to be hung up upon an high pair of gallows.

Them of the Western Isles suing for pardon, in that they had aided Macdonwald in his traitorous enterprise, he fined at great sums of money. And those whom he took in Lochaber, being come thither to bear armor against the king, he put to execution. Hereupon the Islandmen conceived a deadly grudge towards him, calling him a covenant-breaker, a bloody tyrant, and a cruel murderer of them whom the king's mercy had pardoned. With which reproachful words Macbeth being kindled in wrathful ire against them, had passed over with an army into the Isles to have taken revenge upon them for their liberal talk, had he not been otherwise persuaded by some of his friends and partly pacified by gifts presented unto him on the behalf of the Islandmen, seeking to avoid his displeasure. Thus was justice and law restored again to the old accustomed course, by the diligent means of Macbeth. [8]Immediately whereupon word came that Sueno, King of Norway was arrived in Fife with a puissant army to subdue the whole realm of Scotland. . . .

The cruelty of this Sueno was such, that he neither spared man, woman, nor child of what age, condition, or degree soever they were. Whereof when King Duncan was certified,[9] he set all slothful and lingering delays apart and began to assemble an army in most speedy

---

[8] I.ii. 31–33; 45–62. Shakespeare combines the two battles — with Macdonwald and Sueno — into a single scene. The first battle follows the source closely; the second differs widely from it.

[9] informed.

wise, like a very valiant captain. For oftentimes it happens that a dull coward and slothful person, constrained by necessity, becomes very hardy and active. Therefore when his whole power was come together, he divided the same into three battles. The first was led by Macbeth, the second by Banquo, and the king himself governed in the main battle or middle ward, wherein were appointed to attend and wait upon his person the most part of all the residue of the Scottish nobility.

The army of Scottishmen being thus ordered came unto Culross, where encountering with the enemies, after a sore and cruel fought battle Sueno remained victorious, and Malcolm with his Scots discomfited. Howbeit the Danes were so broken by this battle that they were not able to make long chase on their enemies, but kept themselves all night in order of battle for doubt lest the Scots, assembling together again, might have set upon them at some advantage. On the morrow, when the fields were discovered, and that it was perceived how no enemies were to be found abroad, they [the Danes] gathered the spoil which they divided amongst them, according to the law of arms. Then was it ordained by commandment of Sueno that no soldier should hurt either man, woman, or child, except such as were found with weapon in hand ready to make resistance; for he hoped now to conquer the realm without further bloodshed.

But when knowledge was given how Duncan was fled to the castle of Bertha, and that Macbeth was gathering a new power to withstand the incursions of the Danes, Sueno raised his tents and coming to the said castle laid a strong siege round about it. Duncan seeing himself thus environed by his enemies, sent a secret message by council of Banquo to Macbeth, commanding him to abode at Inchcuthill, till he [Macbeth] heard from him some other news. In the meantime Duncan fell in feigned communication with Sueno, as though he would have yielded up the castle into his hands under certain conditions. And this did he to derive time and put his enemies out of all suspicion of any enterprise meant against them, till all things were brought to pass that might serve for the purpose. At length, when they were fallen at a point for rendering up the hold, Duncan offered to send forth of the castle into the camp great provision of vittles to refresh the army: which offer was gladly accepted of the Danes, for that they had been in great penury of sustenance many days before.

The Scots hereupon took the juice of mekilwort[10] berries and mixed the same in their ale and bread, sending it thus spiced and confec-

---

[10] the deadly nightshade. It has been suggested that mekilwort might be the "insane root that takes the reason prisoner" (I.iii. 84–85). Holinshed got the story of its use from Boece, whose Latin history describes mekilwort as *solatium amentiale*: relief of madness.

tioned in great abundance unto their enemies. They rejoicing that they had got meat and drink sufficient to satisfy their bellies fell to eating and drinking after such greedy wise that it seemed they strove who might devour and swallow up most, till the operation of the berries spread in such sort through all the parts of their bodies that they were in the end brought into a fast dead sleep that in manner it was impossible to awake them. Then forthwith Duncan sent unto Macbeth, commanding him with all diligence to come and set upon the enemies, being in easy point to be overcome. Macbeth making no delay came with his people to the place where his enemies were lodged, and first killing the watch afterwards entered the camp and made such slaughter on all sides without any resistance that it was a wonderful matter to behold. For the Danes were so heavy of sleep that the most part of them were slain and never stirred. Others that were awakened either by the noise or other ways forth, were so amazed and dizzy-headed upon their awakening that they were not able to make any defense. So that of the whole number there escaped no more but only Sueno himself and ten other persons, by whose help he got to his ships lying at rode[11] in the mouth of Tay.

The most part of the mariners, when they heard what plenty of meat and drink the Scots had sent unto the camp, came from the sea thither to be partakers thereof, and so were slain amongst their fellows. By means whereof when Sueno perceived how through lack of mariners he should not be able to convey away his navy, he furnished one ship thoroughly with such as were left and in the same sailed back into Norway, cursing the time that he set forward on this unfortunate journey. The other ships which he left behind him, within three days after his departure from thence, were tossed so together by violence of an east wind that beating and rushing one against another they sunk there — and lie in the same place even unto these days, to the great danger of other such ships as come on that coast: for being covered with the flood when the tide comes, at the ebbing again of the same some part of them appear above water.

The place where the Danish vessels were thus lost is yet called Drownlow Sands. This overthrow received in manner aforesaid by Sueno was very displeasant to him and his people, as should appear, in that it was a custom many years after that no knights were made in Norway except they were first sworn to revenge the slaughter of their countrymen and friends thus slain in Scotland. The Scots having won so notable a victory, after they had gathered and divided the spoil of the field, caused solemn processions to be made in all places of the realm, and thanks to be given to Almighty God that had sent them so

---

[11] anchor. rode: literally, the rope attached to an anchor.

fair a day over their enemies. But whilst the people were thus at their processions, word was brought that a new fleet of Danes was arrived at Kinghorn, sent thither by Canute, King of England, in revenge of his brother Sueno's overthrow. To resist these enemies, which were already landed and busy in spoiling the country, Macbeth and Banquo were sent with the king's authority; who having with them a convenient power, encountered the enemies, slew part of them, and chased the others to their ships.[12] They that escaped and got once to their ships obtained of Macbeth for a great sum of gold that such of their friends as were slain at this last bickering might be buried in Saint Colme's inch.[13] In memory whereof, many old sepulchers are yet in the said inch, there to be seen graven with the arms of the Danes, as the manner of burying noblemen still is and heretofore has been used.

A peace was also concluded at the same time betwixt the Danes and Scottishmen, ratified (as some have written) in this wise: that from thenceforth the Danes should never come into Scotland to make any wars against the Scots by any manner of means. And these were the wars that Duncan had with foreign enemies in the seventh year of his reign. [14]Shortly after happened a strange and uncouth wonder, which afterward was the cause of much trouble in the realm of Scotland, as you shall after hear. It fortuned as Macbeth and Banquo journeyed towards Forres, where the king then lay, they went sporting by the way together without other company save only themselves, passing through the woods and fields. When suddenly in the midst of a land there met them three women in strange and wild apparel, resembling creatures of elder world, whom when they attentively beheld, wondering much at the sight. The first of them spake and said: "All hail Macbeth, Thane of Glamis" (for he had lately entered into that dignity and office by the death of his father, Sinell). The second of them said: "Hail Macbeth, Thane of Cawdor." But the third said, "All hail Macbeth, that hereafter shall be King of Scotland."

Then Banquo: "What manner of women," said he, "are you, that seem so little favorable unto me, whereas to my fellow here, besides high offices you assign also the kingdom, appointing forth nothing for me at all?" "Yes," said the first of them, "we promise greater benefits unto thee than unto him, for he shall reign in deed, but with an unlucky end. Neither shall he leave any issue behind him to succeed in his place. Where contrarily thou in deed shalt not reign at all,

---

[12] These invasions of Sueno and Canute are fictitious. Holinshed took them from Boece, and Shakespeare, copying Holinshed, perpetuates the inaccuracy.

[13] island.

[14] I.iii. 38–82. Compare especially ll. 48–50.

but of thee those shall be born which shall govern the Scottish kingdom by long order of continual descent." Herewith the foresaid
women vanished immediately out of their sight. [15]This was reputed at
the first but some vain fantastical illusion by Macbeth and Banquo,
insomuch that Banquo would call Macbeth in jest, King of Scotland;
and Macbeth again would call him in sport likewise the father of
many kings. But afterwards the common opinion was that these
women were either the wierd[16] sisters, that is (as you would say) the
goddesses of destiny, or else some nymphs or fairies endowed with
knowledge of prophecy by their necromantical science. Because everything came to pass as they had spoken. [17]For shortly after, the Thane
of Cawdor being condemned at Forres of treason against the king
committed, his lands, livings, and offices were given of the king's liberality to Macbeth.

[18]The same night after, at supper, Banquo jested with him and
said, "Now Macbeth thou hast obtained those things which the two
former sisters prophecied; there remains only for thee to purchase that
which the third said should come to pass." Whereupon Macbeth
revolving the thing in his mind began even then to devise how he
might attain to the kingdom. But yet he thought with himself that
he must tarry a time, which should advance him thereto (by the
Divine providence) as it had come to pass in his former preferment.
[19]But shortly after it chanced that King Duncan, having two sons by
his wife, which was the daughter of Siward, Earl of Northumberland,
he made the elder of them, called Malcolm, Prince of Cumberland, as
it were thereby to appoint him his successor in the kingdom immediately after his decease. Macbeth sore troubled herewith, for that he
saw by this means his hope sore hindered (where, by the old laws of
the realm, the ordinance was that if he that should succeed were not
of able age to take the charge upon himself, he that was next of blood
unto him should be admitted). He began to take council how he
might usurp the kingdom by force, having a just quarrel so to do (as
he took the matter) for that Duncan did what in him lay to defraud
him of all manner of title and claim which he might, in time to come,
pretend unto the crown.

[20]The words of the three wierd sisters also (of whom before you

---

[15] I.iii. 83–88.

[16] from O. E. wyrd: fate.

[17] I.ii. 63–65; I.iii. 89–107.

[18] I.iii. 117–144.

[19] I.iv. 35–53.

[20] I.v. 1ff. This paragraph is also a swift precis of the events of I.v,vii and
all of Act II.

have heard) greatly encouraged him hereunto. But specially his wife lay sore upon him to attempt the thing, as she that was very ambitious, burning in unquenchable desire to bear the name of a queen. At length therefore, communicating his proposed intent with his trusty friends, amongst whom Banquo was the chiefest, upon confidence of their promised aid he slew the king at Inverness, or (as some say) at Botgosvane, in the sixth year of his reign. Then having a company about him of such as he had made privy to his enterprise, he caused himself to be proclaimed king and forthwith went unto Scone where (by common consent) he received the investure of the kingdom according to the accustomed manner. The body of Duncan was first conveyed unto Elgin, and there buried in kingly wise. But afterwards it was removed and conveyed unto Colmekill and there laid in a sepulcher amongst his predecessors, in the year after the birth of Our Savior, 1046.[21]

[22]Malcolm Canmore and Donalbain,[23] the sons of King Duncan, for fear of their lives (which they might well know that Macbeth would seek to bring to end for his more sure confirmation in the estate) fled into Cumberland, where Malcolm remained till time that Saint Edward,[24] the son of Ethelred, recovered the dominion of England from the Danish power: the which Edward received Malcolm by way of most friendly entertainment. But Donald passed over into Ireland, where he was tenderly cherished by the king of that land. Macbeth, after the departure thus of Duncan's sons, used great liberality towards the nobles of the realm, thereby to win their favor. And when he saw that no man went about to trouble him, he set his whole intention to maintain justice and to punish all enormities and abuses which had chanced through the feeble and slothful administration of Duncan. And to bring his purpose the better to pass without any trouble or great business, he devised a subtle wile to bring all offenders and misdoers unto justice: soliciting sundry of his liege people with high rewards, to challenge and appeal such as most oppressed the commons to come at a day and place appointed to fight singular combats within barriers in trial of their accusations. When these thieves, barrators, and other oppressors of the innocent people were come to darren[25] battle in this wise (as is said) they were straightway apprehended by armed men and trussed up in halters on gibbets, according as they had

---

[21] Another inaccuracy from Boece. Duncan was actually slain in 1040.

[22] II.iii. 141–145.

[23] in Holinshed, Donald Bane.

[24] King Edward the Confessor.

[25] old variant of deraigne. To deraigne battle: to wage single combat to decide a claim.

justly deserved. The residue of misdoers that were left were punished and tamed in such sort that many years after all theft and raffings[26] were little heard of, the people enjoying the blissful benefit of good peace and tranquility. Macbeth, showing himself thus a most diligent punisher of all injuries and wrongs attempted by any disordered persons within his realm, was accounted the sure defense and buckler of innocent people. And hereto he also applied his whole endeavor: to cause young men to exercise themselves in virtuous manners, and men of the church to attend their divine service according to their vocation.[27] . . .

[Holinshed goes on to list a long series of "laws made by King Macbeth set forth according to Hector Boece." Most of them are good laws, provisions for the protection of churchmen, of daughters' inheritances, and of "ladies, virgins, widows, orphans, and the communality" by all sworn knights; but a few show signs of the tyrant that Macbeth will become: prohibition against marriage by neighboring nobles and confiscation of all arms worn when not in defence of the king.]

These and the like commendable laws Macbeth caused to be put as then in use, governing the realm for the space of ten years in equal justice. But this was but a counterfeit zeal of equity showed by him, partly against his natural inclination, to purchase thereby the favor of the people. Shortly after he began to show what he was, instead of equity practising cruelty. For the prick of conscience (as it chances ever in tyrants, and such as attain to any estate by unrighteous means) caused him ever to fear, lest he should be served of the same cup as he had ministered to his predecessor. [28]The words also of the three wierd sisters would not out of his mind, which as they promised him the kingdom so likewise did they promise it at the same time unto the posterity of Banquo. He willed therefore the same Banquo with his son named Fleance to come to a supper that he had prepared for them, which was indeed, as he had devised, present death at the hands of certain murderers: whom he hired to execute that deed, appointing them to meet with the same Banquo and his son without the palace as they returned to their lodgings, and there to slay them — so that he would not have his house slandered, but that in time to come he might clear himself, if anything were laid to his charge upon any suspicion that might arise.

---

[26] rioting.
[27] All this in startling contrast to Shakespeare's Macbeth.
[28] III.i. 1ff.

[29]It chanced yet by the benefit of the dark night, that though the father were slain the son yet, by the help of Almighty God reserving him to better fortune, escaped that danger; and afterwards having some inkling (by the admonition of some friends which he had in the court) how his life was sought no less than his father's, who was slain not by chance medley[30] (as by the handling of the matter Macbeth would have had it to appear) but even upon a prepensed[31] device. Whereupon to avoid further peril he fled into Wales.

[32]But here I think it shall not much make against my purpose if (according to the order which I find observed in the Scottish history) I shall in few words rehearse the original line of those kings which have descended from the foresaid Banquo: that they which have enjoyed the kingdom by so long continuance of descent from one to another, and that even unto these our days, may be known from whence they had their first beginning.

Fleance therefore (as before is said) fled into Wales, where shortly after by his courteous and amiable behavior he grew into such favor and estimation with the prince of that country, that he might unneath[33] have wish any greater. At length also he came into such familiar acquaintance with the said prince's daughter that she of courtesy in the end suffered him to get her with child: which being once understood, her father the prince conceived such hateful displeasure towards Fleance that he finally slew him and held his daughter in most vile estate of servitude, for that she had consented to be on this wise deflowered by a stranger. At the last yet, she was delivered of a son named Walter, who within few years proved a man of greater courage and valiancy than any others had commonly been found. . . . [After the vicissitudes of a number of generations the line of Fleance comes to Robert Steward (Stuart).] The first of the Stewards which wore the crown in Scotland . . . [more vicissitudes and then another king who] was called James the First, and married the Lady Jane, daughter to John Beauford, Earl of Somerset in England. He had by her two sons born at one birth, Alexander and James. The first died young; the second attained the crown, named James the Second. James the First had also six daughters, of the which the eldest was given in marriage

---

[29] III.iii. 1ff.

[30] combat.

[31] planned.

[32] Holinshed's processional account of the line of Fleance is in large part retained here because it strongly suggests the visual procession in IV.i. that follows line 111. In actual fact, the Stuart family did not descend from Fleance.

[33] underneath, in the sense of basically.

to the Dauphin of France, the second to the Duke of Britain, the third to the Lord of Feir, the fourth to the Lord of Dalkeith, the fifth to the Earl of Huntley, and the sixth had no succession. James the Second married Margaret, daughter to the Duke of Gelderland, and begot on her three sons and two daughters.

The first succeeded him in the kingdom, and was called James the Third. . . . James the third married Margaret, daughter to the King of Denmark, of the which marriage was born James the Fourth, Alexander, that was Bishop of Saint Andrews and Duke of Albany, and John Steward, Earl of Mar, but these two died without issue.

James the Fourth married Margaret, daughter to King Henry the Seventh of England, and begot on her James the Fifth, who marrying first the Lady Magdalen, daughter to Francis, the French king, has no issue by her, for that she died in the year next after her coming into Scotland. And then shortly after the said James the Fifth married the Lady Marie de Lorrain, Duchess of Lonvile, a widow, and by her had he issue Mary, Queen of Scotland, that took to husband Henry Steward, Lord Darnley, by whom she had issue Charles James, now king of Scotland.[34]

But to return unto Macbeth, in continuing the history and to begin where I left, you shall understand that after the contrived slaughter of Banquo nothing prospered with the foresaid Macbeth. [35]For in manner every man began to doubt his own life and durst [not] unneath[36] appear in the king's presence. And even as there were many that stood in fear of him, so likewise stood he in fear of many, in such sort that he began to make those away by one surmised cavillation[37] or other whom he thought most able to work him any displeasure.

[38]At length he found such sweetness by putting his nobles thus to death that his earnest thirst after blood in this behalf might in no wise be satisfied. For you must consider he won double profit (as he thought) hereby: for first they were rid out of the way whom he feared; and then again his coffers were enriched by their goods which were forfeited to his use, whereby he might better maintain a guard of armed men about him to defend his person from injury of them whom he had in any suspicion. Further, to the end he might the more cruelly oppress his subjects with all tyrantlike wrongs, he built a strong castle on the top of an high hill called Dunsinane, situated in Gowrie, ten miles from Perth on such a proud height that, standing there aloft, a man might

---

[34] who, at the time *Macbeth* was presented had become the first King of Great Britain and Ireland.

[35] III.vi. 7–10.

[36] underneath: used here in the sense of in truth.

[37] unfair objection.

[38] III.iv. 122.

behold well near all the countries of Angus, Fife, Stermond, and Ernedale, as it were lying underneath him. This castle then, being founded on the top of that high hill, put the realm to great charges before it was finished. For all the stuff necessary to the building could not be brought up without much toil and business. But Macbeth, being once determined to have the work go forward, caused the thanes of each shire within the realm to come and help towards that building, each man his course about.[39]

At the last, when the turn fell unto Macduff,[40] Thane of Fife, to build his part he sent workmen with all needful provision and commanded them to show diligence in every behalf, that no occasion might be given for the king to find fault with him, in that he came not himself as others had done — which he refused to do, for doubt lest the king bearing him (as he partly understood) no great good will would lay violent hands upon him, as he had done upon divers others. [41]Shortly after, Macbeth coming to behold how the work went forward, and because he found not Macduff there, he was sore offended and said, "I perceive this man will never obey my commandments till he be ridden with a snaffle. But I shall provide well enough for him." [42]Neither could he afterwards abide to look upon the said Macduff, either for that he thought his puissance over great, either else for that he had learned of certain wizards, in whose words he put great confidence (for that the prophecy had happened so right, which the three fairies or wierd sisters had declared unto him) how that he ought to take heed of Macduff, who in time to come should seek to destroy him.

And surely hereupon had he put Macduff to death but that a certain witch, whom he had in great trust, had told that he should never be slain with man born of any woman, nor vanquished till the wood of Birnam came to the castle of Dunsinane. By this prophecy Macbeth put all fear out of his heart, supposing he might do what he would without any fear to be punished for the same. For by the one prophecy he believed it was impossible for any man to vanquish him, and by the other impossible to slay him. This vain hope caused him to do many outrageous things, to the grievous oppression of his subjects. [43]At length Macduff, to avoid peril of life, purposed with himself to pass into England to procure Malcolm Canmore to claim the crown of Scotland. But this was not so secretly devised by Macduff but that Macbeth had knowledge given him thereof. For kings (as is said) have sharp sight like unto lynxes, and long ears like unto

---

[39] taking his turn.

[40] in Holinshed, Makduff.

[41] III.vi. 21–23.

[42] IV.i. 69–100. Shakespeare follows these next few sentences closely.

[43] III.vi. 24–43.

Midas.[44] For Macbeth had in every nobleman's house one sly fellow or other in fee with him, to reveal all that was said or done within the same, by which sleight he oppressed the most part of the nobles of his realm.

[45]Immediately then, being advertised whereabout Macduff went, he came hastily with a great power into Fife and forthwith besieged the castle where Macduff dwelled, trusting to have found him therein. They that kept the house without any resistance opened the gates and suffered him to enter, mistrusting no evil. But nevertheless Macbeth most cruelly caused the wife and children of Macduff, with all others whom he found in that castle, to be slain. Also he confiscated the goods of Macduff, proclaimed him traitor, and confined[46] him out of all the parts of his realm. But Macduff was already escaped out of danger and gotten into England unto Malcolm Canmore, to try what purchase he might make by means of his support to revenge the slaughter so cruelly executed on his wife, his children, and other friends. [47]At his coming unto Malcolm, he declared into what great misery the state of Scotland was brought by the detestable cruelties exercised by the tyrant Macbeth, having committed many horrible slaughters and murders both as well of the nobles as commons, for the which he was hated right mortally of all his liege people, desiring nothing more than to be delivered of that intolerable and most heavy yoke of thralldom which they sustained at such a caitiff's hands.

Malcolm, hearing Macduff's words which he uttered in very lamentable sort, for mere compassion and very ruth that pierced his sorrowful heart, bewailing the miserable state of his country, he fetched a deep sigh; which Macduff perceiving began to fall most earnestly in hand with him, to enterprise the delivering of the Scottish people out of the hands of so cruel and bloody a tyrant, as Macbeth by too many plain experiments did show himself to be. Which was an easy matter for him to bring to pass, considering not only the good title he had but also the earnest desire of the people to have some occasion ministered whereby they might be revenged of those notable injuries which they daily sustained by the outrageous cruelty of Macbeth's misgovernance. Though Malcolm was very sorrowful for the oppression of his countrymen, the Scots, in manner as Macduff had declared, yet doubting whether he were come as one that meant unfeignedly as he spoke, or else as sent from Macbeth to betray him, he thought to have

---

44 Midas, King of Lydia, who decided in favor of the pipe of Pan over the lyre of Apollo, whereupon Apollo made his ears grow long like those of a donkey.

45 IV.ii. 1ff.

46 banished.

47 IV.iii. 1–132.

some further trial. And thereupon dissembling his mind at the first he answered as follows:

"I am truly very sorry for the misery chanced to my country of Scotland, but though I have never[48] so great affection to relieve the same, yet by reason of certain incurable vices which reign in me I am nothing meet[49] thereto. First, such immoderate lust and voluptuous sensuality (the abominable fountain of all vices) follows me that if I were made king of Scots I should seek to deflower your maids and matrons in such wise that mine intemperancy should be more importable[50] unto you than the bloody tyranny of Macbeth now is." Hereunto Macduff answered: "This surely is a very evil fault, for many noble princes and kings have lost both lives and kingdoms for the same. Nevertheless there are women enough in Scotland, and therefore follow my council: make thyself king, and I shall convey the matter so wisely that thou shalt be so satisfied at thy pleasure in such secret wise that no man shall be aware thereof."

Then said Malcolm, "I am also the most avaricious creature on the earth; so that if I were king I should seek so many ways to get lands and goods that I would slay the most part of all the nobles of Scotland by surmised accusations, to the end I might enjoy their lands, goods, and possessions. And therefore to show you what mischief may ensue on you through mine insatiable covetousness, I will rehearse unto you a fable. There was a fox having a sore place on her overset with a swarm of flies that continually sucked out her blood. And when one that came by and saw this manner, demanded whether she would have the flies driven beside her she answered no. 'For if these flies that are already full, and by reason thereof suck not very eagerly, should be chased away, others that are empty and felly[51] and hungered should light in their places and suck out the residue of my blood far more to my grievance than these, which now being satisfied do not much annoy me.' Therefore," said Malcolm, "suffer me to remain where I am, lest if I attain to the regimen of your realm mine unquenchable avarice may prove such that you would think the displeasures which now grieve you should seem easy in respect of the unmeasurable outrage which might ensue through my coming amongst you."

Macduff to this made answer how it was a far worse fault than the other, for avarice is the root of all mischief. "And for that crime the most part of our kings have been slain and brought to their final end. Yet notwithstanding, follow my counsel and take upon thee the

---

[48] ever.
[49] fit, suitable.
[50] unbearable.
[51] cruel.

crown. There is gold and riches enough in Scotland to satisfy thy greedy desire." Then said Malcolm again, "I am furthermore inclined to dissimulation, telling of leasings,[52] and all other kinds of deceit, so that I naturally rejoice in nothing so much as to betray and deceive such as put any trust or confidence in my words. Then, since there is nothing that more becomes a prince than constancy, verity, truth, and justice, with the other laudable fellowship of those fair and noble virtues which are comprehended only in soothfastness,[53] and that lying utterly overthrows the same, you see how unable I am to govern any province or region. And therefore since you have remedies to cloak and hide all the rest of my other vices, I pray you find shift to cloak this vice amongst the residue."

Then said Macduff: "This yet is the worst of all. And there I leave thee and therefore say, oh ye unhappy and miserable Scotsmen, which are thus scourged with so many and sundry calamities, each one above other! You have one cursed and wicked tyrant that now reigns over you, without any right or title, oppressing you with his most bloody cruelty. This other that has the right to the crown is so replete with the inconstant behavior and manifest vices of Englishmen that he is nothing worthy to enjoy it. For by his own confession he is not only avaricious and given to insatiable lust, but so false a traitor withal that no trust is to be had unto any word he speaks. Adieu, Scotland, for now I account myself a banished man forever, without comfort or consolation." And with those words the brackish tears trickled down his cheeks very abundantly.

At the last, when he was ready to depart, Malcolm took him by the sleeve and said: "Be of good comfort, Macduff, for I have none of these vices before remembered, but have jested with thee in this manner only to prove thy mind. For divers times heretofore has Macbeth sought by this manner of means to bring me into his hands. But the more slow I have showed myself to condescend to thy motion and request, the more diligence shall I use in accomplishing the same." Incontinently hereupon they embraced each other, and promising to be faithful the one to the other they fell in consultation how they might best provide for all their business, to bring the same to good effect. Soon after, Macduff repairing to the borders of Scotland addressed his letters with secret dispatch[54] unto the nobles of the realm, declaring how Malcolm was confederate with him to come hastily into Scotland to claim the crown. And therefore he required them, since

---

[52] lies.
[53] truthfulness.
[54] speed.

he [Malcolm] was right inheritor thereto, to assist him with their powers to recover the same out of the hands of the wrongful usurper.

[55]In the meantime, Malcolm purchased such favor at King Edward's hands that old Siward, Earl of Northumberland, was appointed with ten thousand men to go with him into Scotland to support him in this enterprise for recovery of his right. After these news were spread abroad in Scotland, the nobles drew into two several factions, the one taking part with Macbeth and the other with Malcolm. Hereupon ensued oftentimes sundry bickerings and divers light skirmishes. For those that were of Malcolm's side would not jeopard[56] to join with their enemies in a pight[57] field till his coming out of England to their support. [58]But after that Macbeth perceived his enemies' power to increase by such aid as came to them forth of England with his adversary Malcolm, he recoiled back into Fife, there purposing to abide in camp fortified at the castle of Dunsinane and to fight with his enemies if they meant to pursue him. Howbeit some of his friends advised him that it should be best for him either to make some agreement with Malcolm, or else to flee with all speed into the Isles. And to take his treasure with him to the end he might wage sundry great princes of the realm to take his part, and retain strangers in whom he might better trust than in his own subjects which stole daily from him. [59]But he had such confidence in his prophecies that he believed he should never be vanquished till Birnam Wood were brought to Dunsinane, nor yet to be slain with any man that should be or was born of any woman.

[60]Malcolm following hastily after Macbeth came the night before the battle unto Birnam Wood. And when his army had rested a while there to refresh them, he commanded every man to get a bough of some tree or other of that wood in his hand, as big as he might bear, and to march forth therewith in such wise that on the morrow they might come closely and without sight in this manner within view of his enemies. [61]On the morrow when Macbeth beheld them coming in this sort, he first marvelled what the matter meant; but in the end remembered himself that the prophecy which he had heard long before that time, of the coming of Birnam Wood to Dunsinane Castle, was likely to be now fulfilled. Nevertheless he brought his men in order of

---

[55] IV.iii. 134–139.
[56] hazard.
[57] pitched.
[58] V.ii. 11–14.
[59] V.iii. 1–10.
[60] V.iv. 3–7.
[61] V.v. 29ff.

battle and exhorted them to do valiantly. [62]Howbeit his enemies had scarcely cast from them their boughs when Macbeth, perceiving their numbers, betook him straight to flight: whom Macduff pursued with great hatred even till he came unto Lunfannaine, where Macbeth perceiving that Macduff was hard at his back leapt beside his horse saying, "Thou traitor, what means it that thou shouldst thus in vain follow me that am not appointed to be slain by any creature that is born of a woman? Come on, therefore, and receive thy reward which thou hast deserved for thy pains." And therewithal he lifted up his sword thinking to have slain him.

But Macduff quickly avoiding from his horse, ere he came at him, answered (with his naked sword in his hand) saying: "It is true, Macbeth. And now shall thine insatiable cruelty have an end. For I am even he that thy wizards have told thee of, who was never born of my mother, but ripped out of her womb." Therewithal he stepped unto him and slew him in the place. Then cutting his head from his shoulders he set it upon a pole and brought it unto Malcolm. This was the end of Macbeth, after he had reigned seventeen years over the Scottishmen. In the beginning of his reign he accomplished many worthy acts, very profitable to the commonwealth (as you have heard), but afterward by illusion of the devil he defamed the same with most terrible cruelty. He was slain in the year of the Incarnation, 1057, and in the sixteenth year of King Edward's reign over the Englishmen.

MALCOLM

[1057] Malcolm Canmore thus recovering the realm (as you have heard) by support of King Edward, in the sixteenth year of the same Edward's reign, he was crowned at Scone the 25 day of April in the year of our Lord, 1057. Immediately after his coronation he called a parliament at Forfair in the which he rewarded them with lands and livings that had assisted him against Macbeth, advancing them to fees and offices as he saw cause, and commanded that specially those that bore the surname of any offices or lands should have and enjoy the same. He created many earls, lords, barons, and knights. [1]Many of them that before were thanes were at this time made earls: as Fife, Menteith, Atholl, Lennox, Murray, Caithness, Ross, and Angus. These were the first earls that have been heard of amongst the Scottishmen (as their histories do make mention).

---

[62] V.viii. 1–34; 54–59.
[1] V.viii. 62–64.

EDWARD THE CONFESSOR

[1054][1] About the thirteenth year of King Edward[2] his reign (as some write) or rather about the nineteenth or twentieth year, as should appear by the Scottish writers, Siward, the noble Earl of Northumberland with a great power of horsemen went into Scotland and in battle put to flight Macbeth that had usurped the crown of Scotland; and that done placed Malcolm, surnamed Canmor, the son of Duncan, sometime King of Scotland, in the government of that realm, who afterward slew the said Macbeth and then reigned in quiet. Some of our English writers say that this Malcolm was King of Cumberland, but others report him to be son to the King of Cumberland. But here is to be noted, that if Macbeth reigned till the year 1061, and was then slain by Malcolm, Earl Siward was not at that battle. For as our writers do testify he died in the year 1055, which was in the year next after (as the same writers affirm) that he vanquished Macbeth in fight and slew many thousands of Scots and all those Normans which (as you have heard) were withdrawn into Scotland when they were driven out of England.

[3]It is recorded also that in the foresaid battle, in which Earl Siward vanquished the Scots, one of Siward's sons chanced to be slain; whereof although the father had good cause to be sorrowful, yet when he heard that he died of a wound which he had received in fighting stoutly, in the forepart of his body, and that with his face towards the enemy, he greatly rejoiced thereat to hear that he died so manfully. But here is to be noted that not now, but a little before that Earl Siward went into Scotland himself in person, he sent his son with an army to conquer the land whose hap was there to be slain. And when his father heard the news he demanded whether he received the wound whereof he died in the forepart of the body or in the hind part. And when it was told him that he received in the forepart, "I rejoice," said he, "even with all my heart, for I would not wish either to my son nor to myself any other kind of death."[4]

---

[1] V.ii. 1–5.

[2] of whom Holinshed elsewhere makes the following mention, reminiscent of IV.iii. 140–159: "As hath been thought, he was inspired with the gift of prophecy and also to have had the gift of healing infirmities and diseases. He used to help those that were vexed with the disease commonly called the king's evil, and left that virtue, as it were, a portion of inheritance unto his successors, the kings of this realm."

[3] V.ii. 9–11; V.vii. 4–11; V.viii. 38–49.

[4] Holinshed records that the Elder Siward died of the flix (dysentery) in the fifteenth year of King Edward's reign.

GEORGE BUCHANAN

The History of Scotland,* 1582

translated by James Aikman[1]

From Book VII

. . . [King] Malcolm, who laboured so strenuously, that the law enacted by his father, almost by force, for substituting the children of
the king in the room of their deceased father, should be confirmed
by the universal suffrage of the people, left no male descendant. He
had, however, two daughters, one named Beatrix, whom he gave in
marriage to Crinus, a nobleman, thane of the western isles, and chief
of the thanes, who was in that age, called the abthane, the other
named Doaca, he married to the thane of Angus, whence was born
Macbeth, or Macbed, of whom I shall speak afterwards.

DUNCAN I.

Malcolm being slain, as has been related, his grandson, Duncan, by
his daughter Beatrix, succeeded him, a prince of amiable manners, but
more indulgent to his relations than became a king. He was of a gentle
disposition, and gave early indications of his great popularity; for, in
the most difficult times, when he had been appointed, by his grandfather, governor of Cumberland, and by reason of the Danish troops
spread everywhere, he could not obtain access to the king of England,
to take the legal oaths, yet he faithfully supported the English cause,
until the whole of that kingdom being subdued, Canute undertook
an expedition against him, and then, at last he swore fealty to the
Danes, upon the same conditions as he had formerly done homage to
the English. He was also popular in this — that he administered justice
with the greatest equity, and every year visited his provinces to hear the

---

* *Rerum Scoticarum Historia*
[1] George Buchanan, *The History of Scotland*, trans. James Aikman (Edin-
burgh: T. Ireland, 1829).

complaints of the poor, and, as far as he could prevent it, suffered none of them to be oppressed by the violence of the powerful. But as these virtues procured for him the affection of the good, so they weakened his authority among the lovers of turbulence; [2]and his clemency towards the peaceable, increased the audacity of the wicked.

A disposition to despise the king's authority, first displayed itself in Lochaber, in opposition to Bancho, the thane of that county, a strict distributor of justice, whose severity in punishing being insupportable to some offenders, they entered into a conspiracy against him, and having plundered his estate, they drove him away wounded and half dead. As soon as the state of his wounds enabled him to endure the journey, he laid his complaint before the king, who sent a public officer to bring the criminals to justice; but he, after suffering every species of indignity, was put to death, so much security did the lenity of this good prince, which they denominated indolence, give to these miscreants. The chief of the faction, who committed this outrage, Macdual,[3] despairing of pardon, prepared openly for war. He called to his assistance the Islanders, always prepared for disturbance, and allured the most daring of the Irish, by the hopes of plunder, whom he taught to be under no dread of punishment from a soft and indolent king, fitter to reign over monks than over brave men, but to indulge the highest expectations; for it could not be doubted, he added, but that the Scots, fettered as they had been by a long peace under the last king, would at once, upon the signal being given for war, vindicate their ancient liberty. These exhortations were enforced by some success at the beginning, which increased the courage of his followers. One Malcolm, chosen from among the principal of the nobles, was sent by the king with a body of troops immediately against the rebels, but his army being defeated, he was himself taken and beheaded.

The king, much distressed at this disaster, having called a council, consulted with them about repairing it. When the rest hesitated about delivering their opinions, Macbeth, the king's maternal cousin, attributed the blame of the miscarriage to the late indolent inaction which had destroyed the military habits of the people,[4] but if the command were given to him, along with Bancho, who was acquainted with the country, he promised, in a short time, to restore tranquillity. [5]Macbeth was a man of a penetrating genius, a high spirit, unbounded ambition, and, if he had possessed moderation, was worthy of any

---

[2] I.viii. 16–18.

[3] or Macdonwald.

[4] I.ii. 9–41.

[5] Compare this character analysis of Macbeth with the one in Holinshed, p. 542.

command however great; but in punishing crimes he exercised a severity, which, exceeding the bounds of the laws, appeared apt to degenerate into cruelty. When the chief command of the army was conferred upon this chieftain, many of the insurgents were so terrified, that, laying aside all the hopes which they had conceived from the indolence of the king, they fled in various directions in search of lurking places. The Islanders and Irish, however, having their flight cut off, and being reduced to the utmost desperation, died almost to a man, bravely fighting. Macdual, with a few followers, shut up in a neighbouring tower, and deprived of all hope of pardon, escaped by voluntary death from the insults of his enemies. Macbeth, not content with this punishment, cut off his head, which he sent to the king, at Perth, and exhibited his body as a spectacle in a conspicuous place. Those of the Islanders whom he took, he caused to be hanged.

[6]This domestic sedition being quelled, a new Danish invasion produced a far greater degree of alarm. Sueno, the most powerful king of the Danes, dying, left three kingdoms to his three sons, England to Harold, Norway to Sueno, and Denmark to Canute. On the death of Harold, which happened shortly after, Canute succeeded to the kingdom of England, and Sueno, king of Norway, emulous of his brother's fame, arrived in Fife with a great fleet. On the report of his arrival, Macbeth was sent to raise an army, Bancho being left in military command with the king, who, roused as it were from an ignoble sleep, was forced at last to march against the enemy. The combatants encountered each other near Culross, and maintained the battle with such obstinacy, that the one party was almost rendered incapable for flight, and the other equally unable to pursue. The Scots, who appeared to themselves to have been worsted, rather by the disadvantages of the ground, than the bravery of the enemy, retreated to Perth, and remained there watching his motions. Sueno, who thought that by a little exertion, Scotland in a short time would be wholly in his power, pushed on to Perth, to besiege Duncan, having sent round his fleet by the river Tay, to meet him at that place. Duncan, although Macbeth was approaching at no great distance with fresh re-enforcements, and was, from the aspect of affairs, confident of success, yet, yielding to Bancho, who advised that he should take advantage of stratagem, sent messengers, one to Macbeth, to desire him to halt, and one to Sueno, to propose a surrender. The king of the Scots demanded, that, upon the city being delivered up, he should be allowed to retire with his army in safety. Sueno, who thought the proposal proceeded from despair, would listen to nothing but unconditional surrender.

---

[6] I.ii. 31–33; 45–62.

Other messengers were, therefore, sent with ample powers, who were instructed to protract the time in writing out the conditions; and who, in order to make a greater show of kindness, promised that the king, while the articles of peace were arranging, would send into the Norwegian camp, a sufficient supply of those necessaries of which he understood they were in want; which gift was agreeable, not so much on account of the good will of the Scots, or the want of the Norwegians, as that they thought it a sign that the fierce spirits of the former were humbled and broken. A great quantity of bread was therefore sent, together with wine and ale, into which had been infused the juice of a poisonous herb, that grows abundantly in Scotland, commonly called sleepy nightshade.[7] The stem is more than two feet in height, and spreads into branches at the upper part; the leaves are somewhat broad, and pointed at the extremity, of a dull green colour: the berries, which are pretty large, and black when ripe, grow out from the stalk, under the root of the leaves; the taste of the juice is sweet, and almost insipid; the seed is small like the grains of a fig; the qualities of the berry, the root, but especially the seed, are somniferous, and if taken in large quantities, produce madness. All the provisions being infected with this herb, those who carried them to the enemies' camp, partook liberally of them, in order to prevent any suspicion of deceit, inviting the Danes to swallow copious draughts; and Sueno, himself, took a hearty "cup o' kindness," after the custom of his country.

Duncan, who knew what the consequence would be when the strength of the potion, together with sleep, should begin to operate, had already received Macbeth silently, with his army, into the city, at a gate opposite the side where the enemy lay; and on being informed, by his spies, that the Danes were stretched, completely overpowered by wine and sleep, he sent Bancho, who was well acquainted with the road and the passes of the enemies' camp, forward with the greater part of the army, placing the rest in ambush. On entering the camp, and raising a loud shout, he found every thing in a state of greater carelessness and confusion than he had imagined. A few, roused by the noise, when they began to run about hurriedly like madmen, were slain by the first who met them. To the rest, death was almost, in general, but a continuation of their sleep. The king, who was dead drunk, was seized by a few who were not quite so much intoxicated, and being not only deprived of strength, but of sensation, was thrown like a burden over a baggage horse, and carried to the fleet. But there the case was as bad as in the camp, for almost all the sailors were killed on shore, and it

---

[7] In Holinshed, mekilwort. See p. 545.

was with the utmost difficulty that as many could be collected as could manage one vessel. By their means, however, the king escaped home to his own country. The rest of the ships, in attempting to put to sea, were dashed against each other, by a furious tempest, and broken, and sunk, at the mouth of the Tay, where the sand collecting, together with other wreck in the river, has formed a dangerous bank for sailors, now known by the name of Drumlaw sands. While the Scots were rejoicing over this victory obtained without bloodshed, intelligence was brought them that a Danish fleet had arrived at Kinghorn, sent by Canute, to the assistance of Sueno, the sailors from which, having landed, spoiled Fife without resistance. Bancho was, upon this, immediately despatched against them with a body of men, and having attacked the most advanced, he defeated them with great slaughter. These consisted almost wholly of the chief men of the expedition, the rest were easily driven back to their ships. Bancho is reputed to have sold the right of sepulture for the slain, for a large sum, and their tombs are said to be yet seen in the island of Aemona [Inchcolm.] The Danes having so often, and with such wretched success, sent expeditions to Scotland, are reported to have taken a solemn oath, that they would never again return thither as enemies.

[8]After this tide of success, both at home and abroad, when peace was re-established throughout the whole of Scotland, Macbeth, who had always despised the inactivity of his cousin, cherished secretly the hope of seizing the throne, in which he is said to have been confirmed by a dream. On a certain night, when he was far distant from the king, three women appeared to him of more than human stature, of whom one hailed him thane of Angus, another, thane of Moray, and the third saluted him king. His ambition and hope being strongly excited by this vision, he revolved in his mind every way by which he might obtain the kingdom, when a justifiable occasion, as he thought, presented itself. — [9]Duncan had two sons, by the daughter of Sibard, governor of Northumberland, Malcolm Canmore [great head,] and Donald Bane [white]. Of these he made Malcolm, while yet a boy, governor of Cumberland. This appointment highly incensed Macbeth, who thought it an obstacle thrown in the way of his ambition, which — now that he had obtained the two first dignities promised by his nocturnal visitors — might retard, if not altogether prevent, his arriving at the third, as the command of Cumberland was always considered the next step to the crown. [10]His mind, already sufficiently ardent of itself, was daily excited by the importunities of his wife,

[8] I.iii. 38–82.
[9] I.iv. 35–53.
[10] I.v–viii; II.

who was the confidant of all his designs. Wherefore, having consulted with his most intimate friends, among whom was Bancho, and having found a convenient opportunity, he waylaid the king at Inverness, and killed him, in the seventh year of his reign; then, collecting a band together, he proceeded to Scoon, where, trusting to the favour of the people, he proclaimed himself king. The children of Duncan, amazed at this sudden misfortune, their father slain, and the author of the murder upon his throne, surrounded on every side by the snares of the tyrant, who sought, by their death, to confirm the kingdom to himself, for some time endeavoured to save themselves by flight, and shifting frequently the places of their concealment. But when they saw they could be no where safe, if within the reach of his power, and having no hope of mercy from a man of so barbarous a disposition, they fled in different directions, Malcolm into Cumberland, and Donald to his relations in the Aebudae.[11]

MACBETH

Macbeth, in order to establish himself on the throne he had so iniquitously acquired, won the favour of the nobles by large gifts. As he was secure of the king's children, on account of their age, and of the neighbouring kings, on account of their mutual animosities, having gained the more powerful, he determined to procure the affection of the people by his equity, and retain it by his strict administration of justice. Wherefore, he determined to punish the robbers, who had grown insolent through the lenity of Duncan. But when he saw that this could not be effected without raising a great commotion, he contrived, by men selected for the purpose, to scatter the seeds of dissension among them, and induce them to challenge each other to decide their disputes by battle, in small parties of equal numbers, in places widely distant, and upon the same day. On which day, when they assembled according to appointment, they were all seized by trusty officers, whom the king had stationed for apprehending them, and their execution struck terror into the rest. He, likewise, put to death the thanes of Caithness, Ross, Sutherland, and Nairn, together with some other powerful chieftains, by whose feuds the people were terribly harassed. He, afterwards, went to the Aebudae, where he executed severe justice, and returning thence, he summoned repeatedly Macgill, or Macgild, the most powerful chief of Galloway, to stand trial. But he — Macgill — more afraid of being charged with having belonged to the party of Malcolm, than dreading any crime of which he could have been accused — refused to obey; on which, Macbeth sent some

---

[11] An island off the northern coast of Ireland.

detachments against him, who, having vanquished him in battle, put him to death. By these means, perfect tranquillity being restored, he applied himself to frame laws, an object which had been much neglected by the preceding kings, and enacted very many and very useful statutes, which now, to the great detriment of the public, are allowed to remain unnoticed, and almost unknown. Thus, for ten years, he so governed the kingdom, that, if his obtaining it by violence were forgotten, he would be esteemed inferior to none of the kings who preceded him.

[12]But when he had strengthened himself by so many safeguards, and thus gained the favour of the people; the murder of the king — as is very credible — haunting his imagination, and distracting his mind, occasioned his converting the government, which he had obtained by perfidy, into a cruel tyranny. He first wreaked his unbounded rage on Bancho, his accomplice in the treason, instigated, as is reported, by the prophecy of some witches, who predicted that Bancho's posterity would enjoy the kingdom. Wherefore, fearing that so powerful and active a chief, who had already dipt his hands in royal blood, might imitate the example which he himself had set, he familiarly invited him, along with his son, to an entertainment, and caused him to be assassinated on his return, in such a manner, as if he had been accidentally killed in a sudden affray. Fleanchus, his son, being unknown, escaped in the dark, but, informed by his friends that his father had been killed by the treachery of the king, and that his own life was sought after, fled secretly to Wales. This murder, so cruelly and perfidiously committed, inspired the nobles with such dread, each for his own safety, that they all departed to their houses, few of them, and they but rarely, ever venturing to court; so that the cruelty of the king, being openly exercised upon some, and secretly suspected by all, mutual terror produced mutual hatred between him and his nobles, and then, when concealment became impossible, he began to exhibit an undisguised tyranny. He publicly executed the most powerful chieftains, upon the most frivolous pretences, and frequently upon fictitious accusations; and with the produce of their confiscations, he supported a band of ruffians, under the name of Royal Guards.

The king, however, not yet thinking his life sufficiently protected, commenced building a castle upon Dunsinnan hill, whence there is an extensive prospect upon every side; and when the building proceeded but slowly, on account of the difficulty of the carriage of the materials, he commanded all the thanes, throughout the whole kingdom, to provide by turns for the work labourers and carriages, and ordered that they should themselves superintend the operations, as

---

[12] III.i–iii.

inspectors. Macduff, thane of Fife, was then exceedingly powerful, but not daring to trust his life in the king's hands, frequently sent workmen thither, and, likewise, several of his most intimate friends to urge their labour. The king, either desirous to see how the work proceeded, as he pretended, or, as Macduff feared, to apprehend him, came to view the building, when, by chance, a yoke of oxen, unequal to the task, could not drag a load over a steep ascent. [13]The king eagerly seized the occasion to vent his indignation, threatening that he would subdue the contumacious spirit of the thane, which was already well known to him, and place the yoke on his own neck, which speech being reported to Macduff, he commended his family to his wife, and, without delay, passed over to Lothian, in a little vessel hastily rigged out for the occasion, and thence proceeded to England. [14]Macbeth, having heard of his intended flight, proceeded immediately with a strong force to Fife, if possible to prevent him. At his arrival, he was immediately admitted into Macduff's castle, but not finding the thane, he wreaked his vengeance upon his wife, and his children who remained. He confiscated also his estate, proclaimed himself a rebel, and threatened to inflict a severe punishment on any one who dared to hold any communication with him. He likewise behaved with great cruelty towards the rest of the rich and the powerful, without distinction; and, in contempt of his nobility, administered the internal affairs of the kingdom, by the advice of his household, without ever deigning to consult them.

[15]In the meantime, Macduff, having arrived in England, found Malcolm living in a royal style, at the court of king Edward; for Edward having been recalled from exile to the throne, when the power of the Danes was broken in England, was for many reasons interested in behalf of Malcolm, who had been presented to him by his maternal grandfather, Sibard, either because his father and grandfather, when they commanded in Cumberland, were always attached to his ancestors, or, because a similarity of circumstances, and a recollection of their mutual dangers, had produced a mutual friendship, for both kings had been driven into exile unjustly, by tyrants, or, because the misfortunes of kings easily interest the minds of the greatest strangers. The thane, therefore, as soon as he could find a proper opportunity, addressed Malcolm in a long speech, in which he lamented the unhappy necessity of his flight, represented the cruelty of Macbeth towards all ranks, and the universal hatred of all ranks towards him, and strongly urged Malcolm to attempt the recovery of his paternal throne, especially,

---

[13] IV.ii. 1ff.

[14] III.vi. 24–31.

[15] IV.iii. 1–139.

as he could not without the greatest guilt, leave the impious murder of his father unpunished, neglect the miseries of a people committed to him by God himself, or turn a deaf ear to the just petitions of his friends. Besides, he might rely on the assistance of his ally, the excellent king Edward, and on the affections of the people, who hated the tyrant, nor would the favour of the Deity, to aid a just cause against the wicked, be withheld. In fine, nothing would be wanting, if he were not wanting to himself. Malcolm, who had often before been solicited to return, by spies, sent from Macbeth to draw him into a snare, determined, before he should commit himself to fortune in so great an affair, to prove the fidelity of Macduff. He therefore replied, I am not indeed ignorant of what you tell me, but I am afraid that you are wholly unacquainted with me, whom you invite to assume the crown; for the same vices which have destroyed many kings, lust and avarice, exist in me also, and although now hid in a private station, would break forth in the licence of a regal state. Beware then, lest you do not rather invite me to destruction, than to a kingdom. Macduff answered, that licentious desires after variety, might be counteracted by a lawful marriage, and avarice removed, by being placed above the fear of penury. Malcolm rejoined, that he now rather chose to confess to him ingenuously as a friend, than hereafter to be caught in faults, which might prove dangerous to both; that he did not believe in the existence, either of truth or sincerity; that he confided in no man; that he was apt to change his designs with every breath of suspicion, and, that from the inconstancy of his own disposition, he formed his judgment of every other person. On which, Macduff exclaimed, away! dishonour of thy royal blood and name, more fit to dwell in a desert, than to reign; and was about to retire in anger, when Malcolm taking him by the hand, explained to him the reason of his simulation, that he had so often been deceived by the emissaries of Macbeth, that he dared not rashly trust himself to every body, but with regard to Macduff, his lineage, his manners, his character, and his circumstances, claimed his confidence. Then mutually plighting their faith, they proceeded to consult on the means for accomplishing the destruction of the tyrant. Having, by secret messengers, sent previous information of their design to their friends, they received from king Edward, ten thousand soldiers, under the command of Sibard, Malcolm's maternal grandfather.

[16]The report of this army's march, excited a great commotion in Scotland, and many daily flocked to the new king. Macbeth, being almost wholly deserted, when in this so sudden defection he saw no better alternative, shut himself up in the castle of Dunsinnan, and

---

[16] V.ii–vi.

sent his friends with money into the Aebudae, and Ireland, to procure soldiers. Malcolm hearing of his intentions, marched directly against him, accompanied, wherever he went, by the acclamations of the people, and their prayers for his success. The soldiers joyfully seized this as an omen of victory, and placing green boughs in their helmets, represented an army rather returning in triumph, than marching to battle. Astonished at this confidence of the enemy, Macbeth immediately fled[17] and the soldiers, deserted by their leader, surrendered to Malcolm. Macduff having followed the tyrant, overtook him, and slew him. Here some of our writers relate a number of fables, more adapted for theatrical representation, or Milesian romance, than history, I therefore omit them. Macbeth reigned seventeen years over Scotland, during the first ten of which he performed the duty of the best of kings, but in the seven last, he equalled the cruelty of the most barbarous tyrants.

MALCOLM III, SURNAMED CANMORE

Malcolm having thus recovered his paternal kingdom, was proclaimed king at Scoon, on the fifth day of April, A. D. 1057. Immediately on entering upon the government, he summoned a convention at Forfar, in which his first act was to restore their estates to the children of those, whose fathers Macbeth had murdered. [18]By some he is thought to have introduced new and foreign titles of distinction, by which the degrees of honour are discriminated, adopted from our neighbours, but not less barbarous than those formerly in use — such as dukes, marquisses, earls, barons, ridaros, or knights. Macduff, thane of Fife, was the first who was created an earl, but many others were honoured with new titles, according to their various degrees of merit.

---

[17] a development quite different from that in Holinshed and Shakespeare. Buchanan's version is the historically accurate one. Macbeth was defeated by Siward on July 27, 1054, but escaped and was not killed until August, 1057. Holinshed reports the correct date of Macbeth's death, but under circumstances pertaining to events of 1054.

[18] V.viii. 62–64.

❧ KING JAMES THE FIRST

Daemonology, 1597

From the Second Book[1]

CHAPTER III*

PHILOMATHES. You have said now enough of their [witches] initiating in that order. It rests then that you discourse upon their practices, from [when] they be past apprentices. For I would fain hear what is possible to them to perform in very deed. Although they serve a common master with the necromancers, (as I have before said) yet serve they him in another form. For as the means are divers, which allure them to these unlawful arts of serving of the devil, so by divers ways use they their practices, answering to these means which first the devil used as instruments in them — though all tending to one end: to wit, the enlarging of Satan's tyranny and crossing of the propagation of the kingdom of Christ, so far as lies in the possibility, either of the one or other sort, or of the devil their master. [2]For where the magicians, as allured by curiosity in the most part of their practices, seek principally the satisfying of the same, and to win to themselves a popular honor and estimation, these witches on the other part, being enticed either for the desire of revenge or of worldly riches, their whole practices are either to hurt men and their gods or what they possess, for satisfying of their cruel minds in the former, or else by the wreck in whatsoever sort of any whom God will permit them to have power of to satisfy their greedy desire in the last point.

EPISTEMON. In two parts their actions may be divided: the actions of their own persons, and the actions proceeding from them towards any other. And this division being well understood will easily resolve you what is possible to them to do. For although all that they confess

---

* text modernized (for the Chap. V excerpt as well).
[1] entitled "The Description of Sorcery and Witchcraft in Special."
[2] I.iii. 1–29. It must be remembered that all of these possibilities in common between *Macbeth* and *Demonology* would have as their basal source the whole corpus of folk superstition.

is no lie upon their part, yet doubtlessly, in my opinion, a part of it is not in deed according as they take it to be. And in this I mean by the actions of their own persons. [3]For as I said before, speaking of Magi, that the devil illudes[4] the senses of these scholars of his in many things, so say I, the like of these witches. . . .

CHAPTER V

. . . PHILOMATHES. But before you go further, permit me I pray you to interrupt you one word, which you have put me in memory of, by speaking of women. What can be the cause that there are twenty women given to that craft [witchcraft] where there is one man?

EPISTEMON. The reason is easy, for as that sex is frailer than man is, so is it easier to be entrapped in these gross snares of the devil, as was over well proved to be true by the serpent's deceiving of Eve at the beginning, which makes him the homelier[5] with that sex since [then].

PHILOMATHES. Return now where you left.

EPISTEMON. To some others at these times he [the devil] teaches how to make pictures of wax or clay: that by the roasting thereof, the persons that they bear the name of may be continually melted or dried away by continual sickness.[6] [7]To some he gives such stones or poultices as will help to cure or cast on diseases. And to some he teaches kinds of uncouth poisons which mediciners understand not (for he is far cunninger than man in the knowledge of all the occult properties of nature); not that any of these means which he teaches them (except the poisons which are composed of things natural) can of themselves help anything to these turns[8] that they are employed in, but only being God's ape, as well in that as in all other things . . . leaving all the small trifles among wives, and to speak of the principal points of their craft: for the common trifles thereof they can do without converting well enough by themselves. These principal points I say are these: they can make men or women to love or hate others — which may be very possible to the devil to effectuate, seeing he being a subtle spirit knows well enough how to persuade the corrupted affection of them whom God will permit him so to deal with. [9]They can lay the sickness of one upon another, which likewise is very possible unto him [the devil]; for since by God's permission he laid

---

[3] III.v. 1–14.
[4] deceives.
[5] more at home.
[6] See the witches' persecution of Duff, pp. 537–539.
[7] IV.i. 1–38.
[8] charms, spells.
[9] I.iii. 18–26.

sickness upon Job, why may he not far easier lay it upon any other? For as an old practician, he knows well enough what humor dominates in any of us. And as a spirit he can subtly wake up the same, making it peccant or to abound as he thinks meet for troubling of us, when God will so permit him. And for the taking off of it, no doubt he will be glad to relieve such of present pain as he may think by these means to persuade to be caught in his everlasting snares and fetters. They [witches] can bewitch and take the life of men or women by roasting of the pictures. . . . [10]They can raise storms and tempests in the air, either upon sea or land, though not universally; but in such a particular place and prescribed bounds as God will permit them so to trouble. Which likewise is very easy to be discerned from any other natural tempests that are meteors, in respect of the sudden and violent raising thereof, together with the short enduring of the same. And this is likewise very possible to their master to do, he having such affinity with the air as being a spirit, and having such power of the forming and moving thereof, as you have heard me already declare. For in the Scripture, that style of the Prince of the air is given unto him. They can make folks to become frenetic or maniacal, which likewise is very possible to their master to do, since they are but natural sicknesses. And so he may lay on these kinds, as well as any others. They can make spirits either to follow and trouble persons, or haunt certain houses and affray[11] oftentimes the inhabitants — as has been known to be done by our witches at this time. And likewise they can make some to be possessed with spirits, and so to become very demoniacs. And this last sort is very possible likewise to the devil their master to do, since he may easily send his own angels to trouble in what form he pleases, any whom God will permit him so to use. . . .

□ *Some Sources for Further Study*

1. SENECA (1 B.C.–65 A.D.) — *Agamemnon*. Clytemnestra and Cassandra contribute hints for the character of Lady Macbeth.
2. JOHN LESLIE — *De Origine, Oribus, et Rebus Gestis Scotorum* (1578). For a different perspective on Banquo.
3. KING JAMES I — *A Fruitful Meditation* (1603). More on superstition, this time in the guise of a commentary on the book of *Revelation*.
4. WILLIAM STEWART, "Buik of the Chronicles of Scotland." A long poem not published until 1858. Shakespeare possibly knew it and derived some suggestions from it for Lady Macbeth.

---

[10] I.iii. 11–17.
[11] frighten.

antony and cleopatra

As in all the Roman history plays the central source is North's
Plutarch followed this time in as close detail as anywhere in
Shakespeare's canon. Unlike *Julius Caesar* the focus here is on a single
Life, that of Marcus Antonius, and covers his last eleven years, from
41–30 B.C. Shakespeare typically cuts through intervals of tangential
importance, such as Antonius's campaign against the Parthians and the
year's delay of the Roman-Egyptian war after the Battle of Actium,
but he still weights this play with a sense of the slow passage of time.
He manages this in part by a spread out canvas — his scenes shuttle
between Rome, Alexandria, Messina, Syria, Athens, Actium — in part
by a piling up of small incidents almost all from Plutarch: Cleopatra's early memories of Caesar and of Pompey; eight wild boars
roasted whole at a breakfast; Antony's cheating at fishing; the embassy
of Thyreus; Antony's personal challenge to Octavius; Seleucus's spiteful betrayal; Cleopatra's experiments with poison. Even an item from
Antonius's early days, his soldierly behavior in the face of hardship,
is used here, although it belongs chronologically to the *Julius Caesar*
period (see p. 307). By unfurling the four corners of the world and
by sowing small incidents densely among them Shakespeare makes
space as vast as time in this play, converting his source material into a
massive structure.

He also makes close use of the wording of North-Plutarch, notably
in his account of Antony's first meeting with Cleopatra (II.ii. 191–245)
and of Antony's suicide (IV.xiv. 27ff.), but for the vaulting diction of
the lovers he seems more indebted to a later source, the Countess of
Pembroke's *Antonie*, 1592. A translation in blank verse of Robert
Garnier's drama, M. *Antoine*, 1578, *Antonie* is composed of sluggish
Senecan monologues, yet its diction at times approaches the language
of Shakespeare's lovers. The excerpts in the text, bridged by sum-
maries of the intervening parts, include the content closest to *Antony
and Cleopatra* and also two of the better poetic passages, Cleopatra's

promise to follow Antonie even to death (Act II) and her final speech, whose closing quatrain reads:

> A thousand kisses, thousand thousand more
> Let you my mouth for honor's farewell give:
> That in this office weak my limbs may grow,
> Fainting on you, and forth my soul may flow.

Plutarch offers a number of suggestions, through incident and analysis, for the characters of Antony and Cleopatra, and while Shakespeare uses these in rough outline he goes on to idealize his hero and heroine and to set them in a near perfect balance of tension more sublime and vital than Plutarch ever suggests. Shakespeare owes a greater debt to Plutarch's characterization of Octavius Caesar, which concludes the Plutarch selection in the text and which suggests the broad outlines of Shakespeare's character. For the character of Enobarbus he owes to Plutarch a name and a single incident — Enobarbus's desertion — nothing more. Enobarbus as all-too-human human being hung between polar forces beyond his grasp is Shakespeare's own, indebted, if anywhere, to Kent and to Horatio.

In this Life, as in those dealing with Julius Caesar, Plutarch gives examples of the truth of omens, and Shakespeare again takes up this idea, retelling Plutarch's account of swallows building their nests in Cleopatra's ship (IV.xii. 3–9) and of the mysterious "marvellous sweet harmony" heard shortly before the final defeat of Antony (IV.iii. 1ff.). The dominant idea of this play, however, is vaster in scope than the truth of omens — although that truth forms a part of it — and belongs at once to the Renaissance itself and, provocatively, to Plutarch's Life of Antonius. The love of Antony and Cleopatra "needs find out new heaven, new earth" Antony tells us early in the play, and in time it becomes apparent that each finds the perfect universe in the other's love and that their deaths destroy that universe, which may well symbolize the passing of the Renaissance — certainly the cold scientism of Octavius suggests the manner of a later age. Their kind of love is the culmination of a Renaissance tradition that began with Dante's idealism of Beatrice and developed by stages into the mutual idealization of lovers in Spenser's The Faerie Queene (Britomart and Artegall, Arthur and Gloriana). Shakespeare could have found the concept in Spenser, or Tasso or Ariosto among other sources, but he at least finds reinforcement of it in Plutarch's Amimetobion (p. 578) defined as "no life comparable and matchable with it," and suggesting why Cleopatra can say after the death of Antony

> The odds is gone
> And there is nothing left remarkable
> Beneath the visiting moon.

✴ PLUTARCH (C. 46–120 A.D.)

Parallel Lives

translated by Sir Thomas North, 1579[1]

THE LIFE OF MARCUS ANTONIUS

[*The historical interval between* Julius Caesar *and* Antony and Cleopatra *is only one year, from 42 to 41 B.C. After the defeat of Brutus and Cassius, Antonius marched to Athens and from there to Asia. In Cilicia he ordered Cleopatra, queen of Egypt, to come to him and explain why she had favored Brutus and Cassius against the triumvirate. When she appeared he fell in love with her and followed her to Alexandria.*

Plutarch prefaces this segment of his Life of Marcus Antonius *with a brief character analysis, which does much to set the stage for coming events; it also forms an interesting contrast with his analysis of the "immature" Antony in the* Julius Caesar *sources (see above).*]

[Marcus Antonius] had a noble mind, as well to punish offenders as to reward well-doers: and yet he did exceed more in giving than in punishing. Now for his outrageous manner of railing he commonly used, mocking and flouting of every man, that was remedied by itself; for a man might as boldly exchange a mock with him, and he was as well contented to be mocked as to mock others: but yet it oftentimes marred all. For he thought that those which told him so plainly and truly in mirth, would never flatter him in good earnest in any matters of weight. But thus he was easily abused by the praises they gave him, not finding how these flatterers mingled their flattery under this familiar and plain manner of speech unto him, as a fine device to make difference of meats with sharp and tart sauce; and also to keep him

---

[1] The modernized version used here (with slight emendations by the present editor) is by the Rev. Walter W. Skeat, *Shakespeare's Plutarch* (London: Macmillan and Co., 1875).

by this frantic jesting and bourding[2] with him at the table, that their common flattery should not be troublesome unto him, as men do easily mislike to have too much of one thing: and that they handled him finely thereby, when they would give him place in any matter of weight and follow his counsel, that it might not appear to him they did it so much to please him, but because they were ignorant, and understood not so much as he did.

[3]Antonius being thus inclined, the last and extremest mischief of all other (to wit, the love of Cleopatra) lighted on him, who did waken and stir up many vices yet hidden in him, and were never seen to any: and if any spark of goodness or hope of rising were left him, Cleopatra quenched it straight, and made it worse than before. The manner how he fell in love with her was this. Antonius, going to make war with the Parthians, sent to command Cleopatra to appear personally before him when he came into Cilicia, to answer unto such accusations as were laid against her, being this: that she had aided Cassius and Brutus in their war against him. The messenger sent unto Cleopatra, to make this summons unto her, was called Dellius; who when he had throughly considered her beauty, the excellent grace and sweetness of her tongue, he nothing mistrusted that Antonius would do any hurt to so noble a lady, but rather assured himself, that within few days she should be in great favour with him. Thereupon he did her great honour, and persuaded her to come into Cilicia, as honourably furnished as she could possible; and made her not to be afraid at all of Antonius, for he was a more courteous lord than any that she had ever seen. Cleopatra on the other side, believing Dellius' words, and guessing by the former access and credit she had with Julius Caesar and C. Pompey (the son of Pompey the Great) only for her beauty, she began to have good hope that she might more easily win Antonius. [4]For Caesar and Pompey knew her when she was but a young thing, and knew not then what the world meant: but now she went to Antonius at the age when a woman's beauty is at the prime, and she also of best judgment. So she furnished herself with a world of gifts, store of gold and silver, and of riches and other sumptuous ornaments, as is credible enough she might bring from so great a house, and from so wealthy and rich a realm as Egypt was. But yet she carried nothing with her wherein she trusted more than in herself, and in the charms and enchantment of her surpassing beauty and grace. [5]Therefore, when

---

[2] joking.
[3] I.i. 1–13.
[4] I.v. 29ff. (see especially ll. 73–74).
[5] II.ii. 191–245. There is an exceptionally close parallel between Shakespeare's lines and the rest of this paragraph.

she was sent unto by divers letters, both from Antonius himself and also from his friends, she made so light of it, and mocked Antonius so much, that she disdained to set forward otherwise, but to take her barge in the river of Cydnus; the poop whereof was of gold, the sails of purple, and the oars of silver, which kept stroke in rowing after the sound of the music of flutes, hautboys, citterns, viols, and such other instruments as they played upon in the barge. And now for the person of her self, she was laid under a pavilion of cloth of gold of tissue, apparelled and attired like the goddess Venus, commonly drawn in picture: and hard by her, on either hand of her, pretty fair boys apparelled as painters do set forth god Cupid, with little fans in their hands, with the which they fanned wind upon her. Her ladies and gentlewomen also, the fairest of them, were apparelled like the nymphs Nereids (which are the mermaids of the waters) and like the Graces; some steering the helm, others tending the tackle and ropes of the barge, out of the which there came a wonderful surpassing sweet savour of perfumes, that perfumed the wharf's side, pestered with innumerable multitudes of people. Some of them followed the barge all along the river-side: others also ran out of the city to see her coming in. So that in the end, there ran such multitudes of people one after another to see her, that Antonius was left posted alone in the market-place, in his imperial seat, to give audience: and there went a rumour in the people's mouths, that the goddess Venus was come to play with the god Bacchus, for the general good of all Asia. When Cleopatra landed, Antonius sent to invite her to supper to him. But she sent him word again, he should do better rather to come and sup with her. Antonius therefore, to shew himself courteous unto her at her arrival, was contented to obey her, and went to supper to her: where he found such surpassing sumptuous fare, that no tongue can express it. But amongst all other things, he most wondered at the infinite number of lights and torches hanged on the top of the house, giving light in every place, so artificially set and ordered by devices, some round, some square: that it was the rarest thing to behold that eye could discern, or that ever books could mention. The next night Antonius, feasting her, contended to surpass her in magnificence and fineness: but she overcame him in both. So that he himself began to scorn the gross service of his house, in respect of Cleopatra's sumptuousness and fineness. And when Cleopatra found Antonius' jests and slants to be but gross and soldier-like, in plain manner, she gave it him finely, and without fear taunted him throughly. Now her beauty (as it is reported) was not so surpassing as unmatchable of other women, nor yet such as upon present view did enamour men with her: but so sweet was her company and conversation, that a man could not possibly but be taken. And besides her beauty, the good grace she had to talk and discourse, her courteous nature that tempered her words and deeds, was a spur that pricked to the quick. Furthermore, besides all these, her voice and words were marvellous pleasant: for her tongue was an instrument of music to divers sports and pastimes, the which she easily turned into any language that pleased her. She spake unto few barbarous people by interpreter, but made them answer her self, or at the least the most part of them: as the Aethiopians, the Arabians, the Troglodytes, the Hebrews, the Syrians, the Medes, and the Parthians, and to many others also, whose languages she had learned. Whereas divers of her progenitors, the kings of Egypt, could scarce learn the Egyptian tongue only, and many of them forgot to speak the Macedonian.

⁶Now Antonius was so ravished with the love of Cleopatra, that though his wife Fulvia had great wars, and much ado with Caesar for his affairs, and that the army of the Parthians (the which the king's lieutenants had given to the only leading of Labienus) was now assembled in Mesopotamia, ready to invade Syria; yet (as though all this had nothing touched him) he yielded himself to go with Cleopatra unto Alexandria, where he spent and lost in childish sports (as a man might say) and idle pastimes, the most precious thing a man can spend (as Antiphon saith), and that is, time. ⁷For they made an order between them, which they called *Amimetobion* (as much to say, no life comparable and matchable with it) one feasting each other by turns, and in cost exceeding all measure and reason. And for proof hereof, I have heard my grandfather Lampryas report, that one Philotas, a physician, born in the city of Amphissa, told him that he was at that present time in Alexandria, and studied physic; and that having acquaintance with one of Antonius' cooks, he took him with him to Antonius' house (being a young man desirous to see things), to shew him the wonderful sumptuous charge and preparation of the one only supper. ⁸When he was in the kitchen, and saw a world of diversities of meats, and amongst others eight wild boars roasted whole, he began to wonder at it, and said: "Sure you have a great number of guests to supper." The cook fell a-laughing, and answered him: "No," quoth he, "not many guests, nor above twelve in all: but yet all that is boiled or roasted must be served in whole, or else it would be marred straight: for Antonius peradventure will sup presently, or it may be a pretty while hence, or likely enough he will defer it longer, for that he hath drunk well today, or else hath had some other great matters in hand:

---

⁶ I.ii. 83–115.

⁷ I.i. 33–40. The theme of this speech pervades the entire play, so that in a sense this passage in Plutarch provides a source for one of Shakespeare's main ideas in this play.

⁸ II.ii. 184–185.

and therefore we do not dress one supper only, but many suppers, because we are uncertain of the hour he will sup in." Philotas the physician told my grandfather this tale, and said moreover, that it was his chance shortly after to serve the eldest son of the said Antonius, whom he had by his wife Fulvia; and that he sat commonly at his table with his other friends, when he did not dine nor sup with his father. It chanced one day there came a physician that was so full of words, that he made every man weary of him at the board: but Philotas, to stop his mouth, put out this subtle proposition to him: "It is good in some sort to let a man drink cold water that hath an ague: but every man that hath an ague, hath it in some sort: *ergo*, it is good for every man that hath an ague to drink cold water." The physician was so gravelled[9] and amated[10] withal, that he had not a word more to say. Young Antonius burst out into such a laughing at him, and was so glad of it, that he said unto him: "Philotas, take all that, I give it thee;" shewing him his cupboard full of plate, with great pots of gold and silver. Philotas thanked him, and told him he thought himself greatly bound to him for this liberality, but he would never have thought that he had had power to have given so many things, and of so great value. But much more he marvelled, when shortly after one of young Antonius' men brought him home all the pots in a basket, bidding him set his mark and stamp upon them, and to lock them up. Philotas returned the bringer of them, fearing to be reproved if he took them. Then the young gentleman Antonius said unto him: "Alas, poor man, why doest thou make it nice to take them? knowest thou not that it is the son of Antonius that gives them thee, and is able to do it? if thou wilt not believe me, take rather the ready money they come to: because my father peradventure may ask for some of the plate, for the antique and excellent workmanship of them." This I have heard my grandfather tell oftentimes.

But now again to Cleopatra. Plato writes that there are four kinds of flattery: but Cleopatra divided it into many kinds. [11]For she (were it in sport, or in matters of earnest) still devised sundry new delights to have Antonius at commandment, never leaving him night nor day, nor once letting him go out of her sight. For she would play at dice with him, drink with him, and hunt commonly with him, and also be with him when he went to any exercise or activity of body. And sometime also, when he would go up and down the city disguised like a slave in the night, and would peer into poor men's windows and their shops, and scold and brawl with them within the house, Cleopatra

---

9 puzzled.
10 disconcerted.
11 I.i. 47–54.

would be also in a chamber-maid's array, and amble up and down the streets with him, so that oftentimes Antonius bare away both mocks and blows. Now though most men misliked this manner, yet the Alexandrians were commonly glad of this jollity, and liked it well, saying very gallantly and wisely: 'that Antonius shewed them a comical face, to wit, a merry countenance: and the Romans a tragical face, to say, a grim look.' But to reckon up all the foolish sports they made, revelling in this sort, it were too fond[12] a part of me, and therefore I will only tell you one among the rest. [13]On a time he went to angle for fish, and when he could take none, he was as angry as could be, because Cleopatra stood by. Wherefore he secretly commanded the fishermen, that when he cast in his line, they should straight dive under the water, and put a fish on his hook which they had taken before: and so snatched up his angling-rod, and brought up a fish twice or thrice. Cleopatra found it straight, yet she seemed not to see it, but wondered at his excellent fishing: but when she was alone by herself among her own people, she told them how it was, and bade them the next morning to be on the water to see the fishing. A number of people came to the haven, and got into the fisher-boats to see this fishing. Antonius then threw in his line, and Cleopatra straight commanded one of her men to dive under water before Antonius' men, and to put some old salt-fish upon his bait, like unto those that are brought out of the country of Pont. When he had hung the fish on his hook, Antonius, thinking he had taken a fish indeed, snatched up his line presently. Then they all fell a-laughing. Cleopatra laughing also, said unto him: "Leave us, my lord, Egyptians (which dwell in the country of Pharus and Canobus) your angling-rod: this is not thy profession, thou must hunt after conquering of realms and countries."

[14]Now Antonius delighting in these fond and childish pastimes, very ill news were brought him from two places. The first from Rome, that his brother Lucius and Fulvia his wife fell out first between themselves[15] and afterwards fell to open war with Caesar, and had brought all to nought, that they were both driven to fly out of Italy. The second news, as bad as the first: that Labienus conquered all Asia with the army of the Parthians, from the river of Euphrates and from Syria

---

12 foolish.

13 II.v. 15–18.

14 I.ii. 92–134.

15 Fulvia was bitterly incensed over Cleopatra's rivalry and tried to incite Octavius Caesar to make war on Antonius. When that failed she joined with Antonius's brother, Lucius, against Octavius. Lucius's motives for warfare were idealistic: he opposed the rule by the triumvirate in favor of democracy. Fulvia's motives were urgently personal: Antony, whom she had taught "obedience to women," was her third husband. A falling out between Fulvia and Lucius was inevitable.

unto the country of Lydia and Ionia. Then began Antonius with much ado a little to rouse himself, as if he had been wakened out of a deep sleep, and, as a man may say, coming out of a great drunkenness. So, first of all he bent himself against the Parthians, and went as far as the country of Phoenicia: but there he received lamentable letters from his wife Fulvia. Whereupon he straight returned towards Italy, with two hundred sail: and as he went, took up his friends by the way that fled out of Italy to come to him. By them he was informed, that his wife Fulvia was the only cause of this war: who being of a peevish, crooked, and troublesome nature, had purposely raised this uproar in Italy, in hope thereby to withdraw him from Cleopatra. But by good fortune his wife Fulvia, going to meet with Antonius, sickened by the way, and died in the city of Sicyon:[16] and therefore Octavius Caesar and he were the easier made friends again. [17]For when Antonius landed in Italy, and that men saw Caesar asked nothing of him, and that Antonius on the other side laid all the fault and burden on his wife Fulvia; the friends of both parties would not suffer them to unrip any old matters, and to prove or defend who had the wrong or right, and who was the first procurer of this war, fearing to make matters worse between them: but they made them friends together, and divided the empire of Rome between them, making the sea Ionium the bounds of their division. For they gave all the provinces eastward unto Antonius, and the countries westward unto Caesar, and left Africa unto Lepidus: and made a law, that they three, one after another, should make their friends Consuls, when they would not be themselves. This seemed to be a sound counsel, but yet it was to be confirmed with a straiter bond, which fortune offered thus. There was Octavia, the eldest sister of Caesar, not by one mother, for she came of Ancharia, and Caesar himself afterwards of Accia. It is reported, that he dearly loved his sister Octavia, for indeed she was a noble lady, and left the widow of her first husband Caius Marcellus, who died not long before: and it seemed also that Antonius had been widower ever since the death of his wife Fulvia. For he denied not that he kept Cleopatra, neither did he confess that he had her as his wife: and so with reason he did defend the love he bare unto this Egyptian Cleopatra. Thereupon every man did set forward this marriage, hoping thereby that this lady Octavia, having an excellent grace, wisdom, and honesty, joined unto so rare a beauty, when she were with Antonius (he loving her as so worthy a lady deserveth) she should be a good means to keep good love and amity betwixt her brother and him. So

---

[16] of a broken heart, it is generally believed. For dramatic economy Shakespeare has Antony learn of Fulvia's death in Alexandria (I.ii. 122).

[17] II.ii. 28–155; 168–171.

when Caesar and he had made the match between them, they both
went to Rome about this marriage, although it was against the law
that a widow should be married within ten months after her husband's
death. Howbeit the senate dispensed with the law, and so the marriage
proceeded accordingly.

[18]Sextus Pompeius at that time kept in Sicilia, and so made many
an inroad into Italy with a great number of pinnaces and other pirates'
ships, of the which were captains two notable pirates, Menas and
Menecrates, who so scoured all the sea thereabouts, that none durst
peep out with a sail. Furthermore, Sextus Pompeius had dealt very
friendly with Antonius, for he had courteously received his mother
when she fled out of Italy with Fulvia, and therefore they thought
good to make peace with him. So they met all three together by the
mount of Misena, upon a hill that runneth far into the sea: Pompey
having his ships riding hard by at anchor, and Antonius and Caesar
their armies upon the shore-side, directly over against him. Now,
after they had agreed that Sextus Pompeius should have Sicily and
Sardinia, with this condition, that he should rid the sea of all thieves
and pirates, and make it safe for passengers, and withal, that he should
send a certain of wheat to Rome, one of them did feast another, and
drew cuts who should begin. It was Pompeius' chance to invite them
first. Whereupon Antonius asked him: "And where shall we sup?"
"There," said Pompey; and shewed him his admiral galley which had
six banks of oars: "that," said he, "is my father's house they have left
me." He spake it to taunt Antonius, because he had his father's house,
that was Pompey the Great. So he cast anchors enough into the sea,
to make his galley fast, and then built a bridge of wood to convey them
to his galley, from the head of mount Misena:[19] and there he welcomed
them, and made them great cheer. Now in the midst of the feast,
when they fell to be merry with Antonius' love unto Cleopatra, Menas
the pirate came to Pompey, and whispering in his ear, said unto him:
"Shall I cut the cables of the anchors, and make thee lord not only of
Sicily and Sardinia, but of the whole empire of Rome besides?" Pompey, having paused a while upon it, at length answered him: "Thou
shouldest have done it, and never have told it me; but now we must
content us with that we have: as for myself, I was never taught to
break my faith, nor to be counted a traitor." The other two also did
likewise feast him in their camp, and then he returned into Sicily.

Antonius, after this agreement made, sent Ventidius before into Asia
to stay the Parthians, and to keep them they should come no further:

---

[18] I.iv. 47–55; II.ii. 156–166; II.vi. 1ff. Sextus was a son of Pompey the
Great who with Marcus Crassus and Julius Caesar had formed the first
triumvirate.

[19] II.vii. 1ff.

and he himself in the mean time, to gratify Caesar, was contented to be chosen Julius Caesar's priest and sacrificer, and so they jointly together dispatched all great matters concerning the state of the empire. [20]But in all other manner of sports and exercises, wherein they passed the time away the one with the other, Antonius was ever inferior unto Caesar, and always lost, which grieved him much. With Antonius there was a soothsayer or astronomer of Egypt, that could cast a figure, and judge of men's nativities, to tell them what should happen to them. He, either to please Cleopatra, or else for that he found it so by his art, told Antonius plainly, that his fortune (which of itself was excellent good, and very great) was altogether blemished and obscured by Caesar's fortune: and therefore he counselled him utterly to leave his company, and to get him as far from him as he could. "For thy demon," said he, (that is to say, the good angel and spirit that keepeth thee) "is afraid of his: and being courageous and high when he is alone, becometh fearful and timorous when he cometh near unto the other." Howsoever it was, the events ensuing proved the Egyptian's words true: for it is said, that as often as they two drew cuts for pastime, who should have anything, or whether they played at dice, Antonius always lost. Oftentimes when they were disposed to see cock-fight, or quails that were taught to fight one with another, Caesar's cocks or quails did ever overcome. The which spited Antonius in his mind, although he made no outward shew of it: and therefore he believed the Egyptian the better. [21]In fine, he recommended the affairs of his house unto Caesar, and went out of Italy with Octavia his wife, whom he carried into Greece after he had had a daughter by her.

So Antonius lying all the winter at Athens, news came unto him of the victories of Ventidius, who had overcome the Parthians in battle, in the which also were slain Labienus and Pharnabates, the chiefest captains king Orodes had. For these good news he feasted all Athens, and kept open house for all the Grecians, and many games of price were played at Athens, of the which he himself would be judge. Wherefore leaving his guard, his axes, and tokens of his empire at his house, he came into the shew-place or lists (where these games were played) in a long gown and slippers after the Grecian fashion, and they carried tipstaves before him, as marshals' men do carry before the judges, to make place: and he himself in person was a stickler to part the young men, when they had fought enough. After that, preparing to go to the wars, he made him a garland of the holy olive, and carried a vessel with him of the water of the fountain Clepsydra, because of an

[20] II.iii. 10–38.
[21] III.ii. 23ff.

oracle he had received, that so commanded him. [22]In the meantime, Ventidius once again overcame Pacorus (Orodes' son, king of Parthia) in a battle fought in the country of Cyrrestica, he being come again with a great army to invade Syria: at which battle was slain a great number of the Parthians, and among them Pacorus, the king's own son. This noble exploit, as famous as ever any was, was a full revenge to the Romans of the shame and loss they had received before by the death of Marcus Crassus:[23] and he made the Parthians fly, and glad to keep themselves within the confines and territories of Mesopotamia and Media, after they had thrice together been overcome in several battles. Howbeit Ventidius durst not undertake to follow them any farther, fearing lest he should have gotten Antonius' displeasure by it. Notwithstanding, he led his army against them that had rebelled, and conquered them again: amongst whom he besieged Antiochus king of Commagena, who offered him to give a thousand talents to be pardoned his rebellion, and promised ever after to be at Antonius' commandment. But Ventidius made him answer, that he should send unto Antonius; who was not far off, and would not suffer Ventidius to make any peace with Antiochus, to the end that yet this little exploit should pass in his name, and that they should not think he did anything but by his lieutenant Ventidius. The siege grew very long, because they that were in the town, seeing they could not be received upon no reasonable composition, determined valiantly to defend themselves to the last man. Thus Antonius did nothing, and yet received great shame, repenting him much that he took not their first offer. And yet at the last he was glad to make truce with Antiochus, and to take three hundred talents for composition. Thus after he had set order for the state and affairs of Syria, he returned again to Athens: and having given Ventidius such honours as he deserved, he sent him to Rome, to triumph for the Parthians. Ventidius was the only man that ever triumphed of the Parthians until this present day, a mean man born, and of no noble house or family: who only came to that he attained unto, through Antonius' friendship, the which delivered him happy occasion to achieve great matters. And yet to say truly, he did so well quit himself in all his enterprises, that he confirmed that which was spoken of Antonius and Caesar, to wit, that they were alway more fortunate when they made war by their lieutenants than by themselves. For Sossius, one of Antonius' lieutenants in Syria, did

---

[22] III.i. 1ff.

[23] A member of the First Triumvirate, Crassus had ruled the province of Syria until the Parthians under Orodes routed his army, took Crassus prisoner and executed him.

notable good service: and Canidius, whom he had also left his lieutenant in the borders of Armenia, did conquer it all. So did he also
overcome the kings of the Iberians and Albanians, and went on with his
conquests unto mount Caucasus. By these conquests the fame of
Antonius' power increased more and more, and grew dreadful unto all
the barbarous nations.

[24]But Antonius, notwithstanding, grew to be marvellously offended
with Caesar, upon certain reports that had been brought unto him,
and so took sea to go towards Italy with three hundred sail. And because those of Brundusium would not receive his army into their haven,
he went farther unto Tarentum. There his wife Octavia, that came
out of Greece with him, besought him to send her unto her brother,
the which he did. [25]Octavia at that time was great with child, and
moreover had a second daughter by him, and yet she put herself in
journey, and met with her brother Octavius Caesar by the way, who
brought his two chief friends, Maecenas and Agrippa, with him. She
took them aside, and with all the instance she could possible, entreated
them they would not suffer her, that was the happiest woman of the
world[26] to become now the most wretched and unfortunatest creature
of all others. "For now," said she, "every man's eyes do gaze on me,
that am the sister of one of the emperors, and wife of the other. And
if the worst counsel take place (which the gods forbid) and that they
grow to wars: for yourselves, it is uncertain to which of them two the
gods have assigned the victory or overthrow. But for me, on which
side soever the victory fall, my state can be but most miserable still."
These words of Octavia so softened Caesar's heart, that he went
quickly unto Tarentum. But it was a noble sight for them that were
present, to see so great an army by land not to stir; and so many ships
afloat in the road quietly and safe: and furthermore, the meeting and
kindness of friends, lovingly embracing one another. First, Antonius
feasted Caesar, which he granted unto for his sister's sake. Afterwards
they agreed together, that Caesar should give Antonius two legions to
go against the Parthians, and that Antonius should let Caesar have
an hundred galleys armed with brazen spurs at the prows. Besides all
this, Octavia obtained of her husband twenty brigantines for her
brother, and of her brother, for her husband, a thousand armed men.
After they had taken leave of each other, Caesar went immediately to
make war with Sextus Pompeius, to get Sicilia into his hands. Antonius
also, leaving his wife Octavia and little children begotten of her, with

---

[24] III.iv. 1ff.
[25] III.vi. 39ff.
[26] III.iv. 12–20.

Caesar, and his other children which he had by Fulvia, went directly into Asia.

Then began this pestilent plague and mischief of Cleopatra's love (which had slept a long time, and seemed to have been utterly forgotten, and that Antonius had given place to better counsel) again to kindle, and to be in force, so soon as Antonius came near unto Syria. And in the end, the horse of the mind, as Plato termeth it, that is so hard of rein (I mean the unreined lust of concupiscence) did put out of Antonius' head all honest and commendable thoughts; for he sent Fonteius Capito to bring Cleopatra into Syria: unto whom, to welcome her, he gave no trifling things: but unto that she had already, he added the provinces of Phoenicia, those of the nethermost Syria, the isle of Cyprus, and a great part of Cilicia, and that country of Jewry where the true balm is, and that part of Arabia where the Nabathaeans do dwell, which stretches out toward the ocean. These great gifts much misliked the Romans. But now, though Antonius did easily give away great seigniories, realms, and mighty nations unto some private men, and that also he took from other kings their lawful realms (as from Antigonus, king of the Jews, whom he openly beheaded, where never king before had suffered like death): yet all this did not so much offend the Romans, as the unmeasurable honours which he did unto Cleopatra. But yet he did much more aggravate their malice and ill-will towards him, because that Cleopatra having brought him two twins, a son and a daughter, he named his son Alexander, and his daughter Cleopatra; and gave them, to their surnames, the *Sun* to the one, and the *Moon* to the other. . . .

[Sending Cleopatra back to Egypt, Antonius marched into Arabia and Armenia at the head of a large army. Because he moved too fast, being eager to return to Cleopatra as soon as possible, his lines of supply grew dangerously thin. At this point the Parthians under King Phraortes, son of Orodes, began a merciless campaign of guerilla warfare which devastated and demoralized Antonius's army. Forced to retreat, Antonius did not have the heart to announce it to his army: "being ashamed for respects, he would not speak unto them at his removing, but willed Domitius Aenobarbus[27] to do it." After long and bitter running battles with the Parthians, on top of which came famine and disease, the remains of Antonius's army finally crossed the river of Araxes into Armenia. "There Antonius mustering his whole army, found that he had lost twenty thousand footmen, and four thousand

---

[27] Here is Plutarch's only mention in this *Life* of Domitius's full name, from whom Shakespeare got the name if not the character of Enobarbus and also one important incident (see p. 596).

horsemen, which had not all been slain by their enemies: for the most part of them died of sickness, making seven and twenty days' journey coming from the city of Phraata into Armenia. . . ."

Howbeit then, the great haste he made to return unto Cleopatra caused him to put his men to so great pains, forcing them to lie in the field all winter long when it snowed unreasonably, that by the way he lost eight thousand of his men, and so came down to the sea-side with a small company, unto a certain place called Blancbourg: which standeth betwixt the cities of Berytus and Sidon, and there tarried for Cleopatra. And because she tarried longer than he would have had her, he pined away for love and sorrow: so that he was at such a strait, that he wist not what to do, and therefore, to wear it out, he gave himself to quaffing and feasting. But he was so drowned with the love of her, that he could not abide to sit at the table till the feast was ended: but many times, while others banqueted, he ran to the sea-side to see if she were coming. At length she came, and brought with her a world of apparel and money to give unto the soldiers. But some say notwithstanding that she brought apparel and no money, and that she took of Antonius' money, and caused it to be given amongst the soldiers in her own name, as if she had given it them.

In the meantime it chanced that the king of the Medes and Phraortes, king of the Parthians, fell at great wars together, the which began (as it is reported) for the spoils of the Romans: and grew to be so hot between them that the king of Medes was no less afraid than also in danger to lose his whole realm. Thereupon he sent unto Antonius, to pray him to come and make war with the Parthians, promising him that he would aid him to his uttermost power. This put Antonius again in good comfort, considering that, unlooked for, the only thing he lacked (which made him he could not overcome the Parthians, meaning that he had not brought horsemen, and men with darts and slings enough) was offered him in that sort, that it did him more pleasure to accept it than it was pleasure to the other to offer it. Hereupon, after he had spoken with the king of Medes at the river of Araxes, he prepared himself once more to go through Armenia, and to make more cruel war with the Parthians than he had done before.

Now whilst Antonius was busy in this preparation, Octavia his wife, whom he had left at Rome, would needs take sea to come unto him. Her brother Octavius Caesar was willing to it, not for his respect at all (as most authors do report) as for that he might have an honest colour to make war with Antonius, if he did misuse her, and not esteem of her as she ought to be. But when she was come to Athens, she received letters from Antonius, willing her to stay there until his coming, and did advertise her of his journey and determination. The which thought it grieved her much, and that she knew it was but an excuse: yet by her letters to him of answer, she asked him whether he would have those things sent unto him which she had brought him, being great store of apparel for soldiers, a great number of horse, sums of money and gifts, to bestow on his friends and captains he had about him: and besides all those, she had 2000 soldiers, chosen men, all well armed like unto the Praetor's bands. When Niger, one of Antonius' friends whom he had sent unto Athens, had brought these news from his wife Octavia, and withal did greatly praise her, as she was worthy and well deserved, Cleopatra, knowing that Octavia would have Antonius from her, and fearing also that if with her virtue and honest behaviour (besides the great power of her brother Caesar) she did add thereunto her modest kind love to please her husband, that she would then be too strong for her, and in the end win him away: she subtly seemed to languish for the love of Antonius, pining her body for lack of meat. Furthermore, she every way so framed her countenance, that when Antonius came to see her, she cast her eyes upon him, like a woman ravished for joy. Straight again when he went from her, she fell a-weeping and blubbering, looking ruefully on the matter, and still found the means that Antonius should oftentimes find her weeping: and then when he came suddenly upon her, she made as though she dried her eyes, and turned her face away, as if she were unwilling that he should see her weep. All these tricks she used, Antonius being in readiness to go into Syria, to speak with the king of Medes. Then the flatterers that furthered Cleopatra's mind blamed Antonius, and told him that he was a hard-natured man, and that he had small love in him, that would see a poor lady in such torment for his sake, whose life depended only upon him alone. "For Octavia," said they, "that was married unto him as it were of necessity, because her brother Caesar's affairs so required it, hath the honour to be called Antonius' lawful spouse and wife: and Cleopatra, being born a queen of so many thousands of men, is only named Antonius' leman; and yet that she disdained not so to be called, if it might please him she might enjoy his company, and live with him: but if he once leave her, that then it is impossible she should live." To be short, by these their flatteries and enticements, they so wrought Antonius' effeminate mind that, fearing lest she would make herself away, he returned again unto Alexandria, and deferred the king of Medes to the next year following, although he received news that the Parthians at that time were at civil wars among themselves. This notwithstanding, he went afterwards and made peace with him. For he married his daughter, which was very young, unto one of the sons that Cleopatra had by him: and then returned, being fully bent to make war with Caesar.

When Octavia was returned to Rome from Athens, Caesar commanded her to go out of Antonius' house, and to dwell by herself, because he had abused her. Octavia answered him again, that she would not forsake her husband's house, and that if he had no other occasion to make war with him, she prayed him then to take no thought for her: "For," said she, "it were too shameful a thing, that two so famous captains should bring in civil wars among the Romans, the one for the love of a woman, and the other for the jealousy betwixt one another." Now as she spake the word, so did she also perform the deed: for she kept still in Antonius' house, as if he had been there, and very honestly and honourably kept his children, not only those she had by him, but the other which her husband had by Fulvia. Furthermore, when Antonius sent any of his men to Rome, to sue for any office in the commonwealth, she received them very courteously, and so used herself unto her brother, that she obtained the things she requested. Howbeit thereby, thinking no hurt, she did Antonius great hurt. For her honest love and regard to her husband made every man hate him, when they saw he did so unkindly use so noble a lady: but the greatest cause of their malice unto him was for the division of lands he made among his children in the city of Alexandria. And, to confess a truth, it was too arrogant and insolent a part, and done (as a man would say) in derision and contempt of the Romans.[28] For he assembled all the people in the show-place, where young men do exercise themselves, and there, upon a high tribunal silvered, he set two chairs of gold, the one for himself, and the other for Cleopatra, and lower chairs for his children; then he openly published before the assembly, that first of all he did establish Cleopatra queen of Egypt, of Cyprus, of Lydia, and of the lower Syria; and at that time also Caesarion king of the same realms. This Caesarion was supposed to be the son of Julius Caesar, who had left Cleopatra great with child. Secondly, he called the sons he had by her the kings of kings, and gave Alexander for his portion Armenia, Media, and Parthia, when he had conquered the country; and unto Ptolemy for his portion Phoenicia, Syria, and Cilicia. And therewithal he brought out Alexander in a long gown after the fashion of the Medes with a high cop-tank[29] hat on his head, narrow in the top, as the kings of the Medes and Armenians do use to wear them: and Ptolemy apparelled in a cloak after the Macedonian manner, with slippers on his feet and a broad hat, with a royal band or diadem. Such was the apparel and old attire of the ancient kings and successors of Alexander the Great. So after his sons had done their humble duties,

---

[28] III.vi. 1–19.
[29] conical.

and kissed their father and mother, presently a company of Armenian soldiers, set there of purpose, compassed the one about, and a like company of Macedonians the other. Now for Cleopatra, she did not only wear at that time (but at all other times else when she came abroad) the apparel of the goddess Isis, and so gave audience unto all her subjects, as a new Isis.

[30]Octavius Caesar reporting all these things unto the Senate, and oftentimes accusing him to the whole people and assembly in Rome, he thereby stirred up all the Romans against him. [31]Antonius on the other side sent to Rome likewise to accuse him, and the chiefest points of his accusations he charged him with, were these. First, that having spoiled Sextus Pompeius in Sicily, he did not give him his part of the isle. Secondly, that he did detain in his hands the ships he lent him to make that war. Thirdly, that having put Lepidus their companion and triumvir out of his part of the empire, and having deprived him of all honours, he retained for himself the lands and revenues thereof, which had been assigned unto him for his part. And last of all, that he had in manner divided all Italy amongst his own soldiers, and had left no part of it for his soldiers. Octavius Caesar answered him again: that for Lepidus, he had indeed deposed him, and taken his part of the empire from him, because he did over cruelly use his authority. And secondly, for the conquests he had made by force of arms, he was contented Antonius should have his part of them, so that he would likewise let him have his part of Armenia. And thirdly, that, for his soldiers, they should seek for nothing in Italy, because they possessed Media and Parthia, the which provinces they had added to the empire of Rome, valiantly fighting with their emperor and captain. [32]Antonius hearing these news, being yet in Armenia, commanded Canidius[33] to go presently to the sea-side with his sixteen legions he had: and he himself, with Cleopatra, went unto the city of Ephesus, and there gathered together his galleys and ships out of all parts, which came to the number of eight hundred, reckoning the great ships of burthen: and of those, Cleopatra furnished him with two hundred and twenty thousand talents besides, and provision of victuals also to maintain all the whole army in this war. So Antonius, through the persuasion of Domitius, commanded Cleopatra to return again into Egypt, and there to understand the success of this war. [34]But Cleopatra, fearing lest Antonius should again be made friends with Octavius Caesar by the

---

[30] III.vi. 19–21.

[31] III.vi. 22–38.

[32] III.vii. 58–60. Shakespeare makes it nineteen legions.

[33] Antonius's lieutenant general.

[34] Shakespeare has Canidius react quite otherwise (III.vii. 68–71) and Shakespeare's Cleopatra herself overrides all objections (III.vii. 1–19).

means of his wife Octavia, she so plied Canidius with money and filled his purse, that he became her spokesman unto Antonius, and told him there was no reason to send her from this war, who defrayed so great a charge: neither that it was for his profit, because thereby the Egyptians would then be utterly discouraged, which were the chiefest strength of the army by sea: considering that he could see no king of all the kings their confederates that Cleopatra was inferior unto, either for wisdom or judgment, seeing that long before she had wisely governed so great a realm as Egypt; and besides that, she had been so long acquainted with him, by whom she had learned to manage great affairs. These fair persuasions won him: for it was predestinated that the government of all the world should fall into Octavius Caesar's hands.

Thus, all their forces being joined together, they hoisted sail towards the isle of Samos, and there gave themselves to feasts and solace. For as all the kings, princes, and commonalties, people, and cities, from Syria unto the marshes Maeotis; and from the Armenians to the Illyrians, were sent unto, to send and bring all munition and warlike preparation they could: even so all players, minstrels, tumblers, fools, and jesters, were commanded to assemble in the isle of Samos. So that, where in manner all the world in every place was full of lamentations, sighs, and tears, only in this isle of Samos there was nothing for many days' space but singing and piping, and all the theatre full of these common players, minstrels, and singing-men. Besides all this, every city sent an ox thither to sacrifice, and kings did strive one with another who should make the noblest feasts, and give the richest gifts. So that every man said, "What can they do more for joy of victory, if they win the battle, when they make already such sumptuous feasts at the beginning of the war?" When this was done, he gave the whole rabble of these minstrels, and such kind of people, the city of Priene to keep them withal during this war. Then he went unto the city of Athens, and there gave himself again to see plays and pastimes, and to keep the theatres. Cleopatra, on the other side, being jealous of the honours which Octavia had received in this city, where indeed she was marvellously honoured and beloved of the Athenians; to win the people's goodwill also at Athens, she gave them great gifts: and they likewise gave her many great honours, and appointed certain ambassadors to carry the decree to her house, among the which Antonius was one, who (as a citizen of Athens) reported the matter unto her, and made an oration in the behalf of the city. Afterwards he sent to Rome to put his wife Octavia out of his house, who (as it is reported) went out of his house with all Antonius' children, saving the eldest of them he had by Fulvia, who was with his father: bewailing and lamenting her cursed hap, that had brought her to this, that she was accounted one of the chiefest causes of this civil war. The Romans did pity her, but much more Antonius, and those specially that had seen Cleopatra: who neither excelled Octavia in beauty, nor yet in young years.

Octavius Caesar understanding the sudden and wonderful great preparation of Antonius, he was not a little astonished at it (fearing he should be driven to fight that summer) because he wanted many things, and the great and grievous exactions of money did sore oppress the people. For all manner of men else were driven to pay the fourth part of their goods and revenue, but the libertines (to wit, those whose fathers or other predecessors had sometime been bondmen) were seissed[35] to pay the eighth part of all their goods at one payment. Hereupon there arose a wonderful exclamation and great uproar all Italy over, so that, amongst the greatest faults that ever Antonius committed, they blamed him most for that he delayed to give Caesar battle. For he gave Caesar leisure to make his preparations, and also to appease the complaints of the people. When such a great sum of money was demanded of them, they grudged at it, and grew to mutiny upon it: but when they had once paid it, they remembered it no more. Furthermore, Titius and Plancus (two of Antonius' chiefest friends, and that had been both of them consuls) for the great injuries Cleopatra did them, because they hindered all they could that she should not come to this war, they went and yielded themselves unto Caesar, and told him where the testament was that Antonius had made, knowing perfectly what was in it. The will was in the custody of the Vestal nuns: of whom Caesar demanded it. They answered him, that they would not give it him: but if he would go and take it, they would not hinder him. Thereupon Caesar went thither, and having read it first to himself, he noted certain places worthy of reproach: so assembling all the Senate, he read it before them all. Whereupon divers were marvellously offended, and thought it a strange matter that he, being alive, should be punished for that he had appointed by his will to be done after his death. Caesar chiefly took hold of this that he ordained touching his burial: for he willed that his body, though he died at Rome, should be brought in funeral pomp through the midst of the market-place, and that it should be sent into Alexandria unto Cleopatra. Furthermore, among divers other faults wherewith Antonius was to be charged for Cleopatra's sake, Calvisius, one of Caesar's friends, reproved him, because he had frankly given Cleopatra all the libraries of the royal city of Pergamum, in the which she had above two hundred thousand several books. Again also, that being on a time set at the table, he suddenly rose from the board and trod upon Cleopatra's foot, which was a sign given between them, of which they were agreed on. That he had also suffered the Ephesians in his presence to

---

[35] assessed.

call Cleopatra their sovereign lady. That divers times, sitting in his tribunal and chair of state, giving audience to all kings and princes, he had received love-letters from Cleopatra, written in tablets of onyx or crystal; and that he had read them sitting in his imperial seat. That one day when Furnius, a man of great account, and the eloquentest man of all the Romans, pleaded a matter before him, Cleopatra by chance coming through the market-place in her litter where Furnius was a-pleading, Antonius straight rose out of his seat, and left his audience to follow her litter. This notwithstanding, it was thought Calvisius devised the most part of all these accusations of his own head. Nevertheless they that loved Antonius were intercessors to the people for him, and amongst them they sent one Geminius unto Antonius, to pray him he would take heed that through his negligence his empire were not taken from him, and that he should be counted an enemy to the people of Rome. This Geminius, being arrived in Greece, made Cleopatra jealous straight of his coming, because she surmised that he came not but to speak for Octavia. Therefore she spared not to taunt him all supper-time; and moreover, to spite him the more, she made him to be set lowest of all at the board: the which he took patiently, expecting occasion to speak with Antonius. Now Antonius commanding him at the table to tell him what wind brought him thither, he answered, 'That it was no table-talk, and that he would tell him to-morrow morning fasting: but drunk or fasting, howsoever it were, he was sure of one thing, that all would not go well on his side, unless Cleopatra were sent back into Egypt.' Antonius took these words in very ill part. Cleopatra on the other side answered him, "Thou doest well, Geminius," said she, "to tell the truth before thou be compelled by torments:" but within few days after, Geminius stole away, and fled to Rome. The flatterers also, to please Cleopatra, did make her drive many others of Antonius' faithful servants and friends from him, who could not abide the injuries done unto them: among the which these two were chief, Marcus Syllanus, and Dellius the historiographer, who wrote that he fled because her physician Glaucus told him that Cleopatra had set some secretly to kill him. Furthermore, he had Cleopatra's displeasure, because he said one night at supper, that they made them drink sour wine, where Sarmentus at Rome drank good wine of Falerna. This Sarmentus was a pleasant young boy, such as the lords of Rome are wont to have about them to make them pastime, which they call their joys, and he was Octavius Caesar's boy. Now after that Caesar had made sufficient preparation, he proclaimed open war against Cleopatra, and made the people to abolish the power and empire of Antonius, because he had before given it up unto a woman. And Caesar said furthermore, that Antonius was not master of himself, but that Cleopatra had brought him beside himself by her charms and amorous [36]poisons: and that they, that should make war with them, should be Mardian the eunuch, Photinus, and Iras (a woman of Cleopatra's bed-chamber, that frizzled her hair, and dressed her head) and Charmion, the which were those that ruled all the affairs of Antonius' empire.

Before this war, as it is reported, many signs and wonders fell out. First of all, the city of Pisaurum, which was made a colony to Rome, and replenished with people by Antonius, standing upon the shore-side of the sea Adriatic, was by a terrible earthquake sunk into the ground. One of the images of stone, which was set up in honour of Antonius in the city of Alba, did sweat many days together: and though some wiped it away, yet it left not sweating still. In the city of Patras, whilst Antonius was there, the temple of Hercules was burnt with lightning. And at the city of Athens also, in a place where the war of the giants against the gods is set out in imagery, the statue of Bacchus with a terrible wind was thrown down in the theatre. It was said that Antonius came of the race of Hercules (as you have heard before), and in the manner of his life he followed Bacchus, and therefore he was called the new Bacchus. Furthermore, the same blustering storm of wind overthrew the great monstrous images at Athens that were made in the honour of Eumenes and Attalus, the which men had named and entitled 'the Antonians': and yet did they hurt none of the other images, which were many besides. [37]The admiral-galley of Cleopatra was called *Antoniad*, in the which there chanced a marvellous ill sign: swallows had bred under the poop of her ship, and there came others after them that drave away the first, and plucked down their nests.

Now when all things were ready, and that they drew near to fight, it was found, that Antonius had no less than 500 good ships of war, among which there were many galleys that had eight and ten banks of oars, the which were sumptuously furnished, not so meet for fight as for triumph: an hundred thousand footmen, and 12,000 horsemen; and had with him to aid him these kings and subjects following: Bocchus king of Lybia, Tarcondemus king of high Cilicia, Archelaus king of Cappadocia, Philadelphus king of Paphlagonia, Mithridates king of Comagena, and Adallas king of Thracia. All which were there, every man in person. The residue that were absent, sent their armies: as Polemon king of Pont, Manchus king of Arabia, Herodes king of Jewry;[38] and furthermore Amyntas king of Lycaonia and of the Galatians: and besides all these, he had all the aid the king of Medes sent unto him. Now for Caesar, he had 250 ships of war, 80,000 footmen,

[36] III.vii. 13–16.
[37] IV.xii. 3–9.
[38] Judaea.

and well near as many horsemen as his enemy Antonius. Antonius for his part had all under his dominion from Armenia and the river of Euphrates, unto the sea Ionium and Illyricum. Octavius Caesar had also, for his part, all that which was in our hemisphere or half-part of the world, from Illyria unto the ocean sea upon the west: then all from the ocean unto *mare Siculum:* and from Africa, all that which is against Italy, as Gaul and Spain. Furthermore, all, from the province of Cyrenia to Ethiopia, was subject unto Antonius. [39]Now Antonius was made so subject to a woman's will, that though he was a great deal the stronger by land, yet for Cleopatra's sake he would needs have this battle tried by sea: though he saw before his eyes, that for lack of water-men his captains did press by force all sorts of men out of Greece that they could take up in the field, as travellers, muleteers, reapers, harvest-men, and young boys; and yet could they not sufficiently furnish his galleys: so that the most part of them were empty, and could scant row, because they lacked water-men enough. But on the contrary side, Caesar's ships were not built for pomp, high and great only for a sight and bravery, but they were light of yarage[40] armed and furnished with water-men as many as they needed, and had them all in readiness in the havens of [41]Tarentum and Brundusium. So Octavius Caesar sent unto Antonius, to will him to delay no more time, but to come on with his army into Italy: and that for his own part he would give him safe harbour to land without any trouble; and that he would withdraw his army from the sea, as far as one horse could run, until he had put his army ashore, and had lodged his men. [42]Antonius on the other side bravely sent him word again and challenged the combat of him, man for man, though he were the elder; and that if he refused him so, he would then fight a battle with him in the fields of Pharsalia, as Julius Caesar and Pompey had done before. [43]Now whilst Antonius rode at anchor, lying idly in harbour at the head of Actium, in the place where the city of Nicopolis standeth at this present, Caesar had quickly passed the sea *Ionium*, and taken a place called Toryne, before Antonius understood that he had taken ship. Then began his men to be afraid, because his army by land was left behind. But Cleopatra making light of it, "And what danger, I pray you," said she, "if Caesar keep at Toryne."[44] The next morning by break of day, his enemies coming with full force of oars in battle against

---

[39] III.vii. 28–49.

[40] easy management. See III.vii. 39.

[41] III.vii. 22.

[42] III.xiii. 25–28.

[43] III.vii. 21–24, 55–57.

[44] a pun, Toryne being a city in Albania and also a ladle for stirring a pot (W.W.S.).

him, Antonius was afraid that if they came to join, they would take and carry away his ships that had no men of war in them. [45]So he armed all his water-men, and set them in order of battle upon the forecastle of their ships, and then lifted up all his ranks of oars towards the element, as well on the one side as on the other, with the prows against the enemies, at the entry and mouth of the gulf which beginneth at the point of Actium: and so kept them in order of battle, as if they had been armed and furnished with water-men and soldiers. Thus Octavius Caesar, being finely deceived by this stratagem, retired presently, and therewithal Antonius very wisely and suddenly did cut him off from fresh water. For, understanding that the places where Octavius Caesar landed had very little store of water, and yet very bad, he shut them in with strong ditches and trenches he cast, to keep them from sailing out at their pleasure, and so to go seek water farther off. [46]Furthermore, he dealt very friendly and courteously with Domitius, and against Cleopatra's mind. For he being sick of an ague when he went and took a little boat to go unto Caesar's camp, Antonius was very sorry for it, but yet he sent after him all his carriage, train, and men: and the same Domitius, as though he gave him to understand that he repented his open treason, died immediately after. [47]There were certain kings also that forsook him, and turned on Caesar's side, as Amyntas and Deiotarus. Furthermore, his fleet and navy that was unfortunate in all things, and unready for service, compelled him to change his mind, and to hazard battle by land. [48]And Canidius also, who had charge of his army by land, when time came to follow Antonius' determination, he turned him clean contrary, and counselled him to send Cleopatra back again, and himself to retire into Macedon, to fight there on the main land. And furthermore told him, that Dicomes king of the Getes promised to aid him with a great power: and that it should be no shame nor dishonour to him to let Caesar have the sea, because himself and his men both had been well practised and exercised in battles by sea, in the war of Sicilia against Sextus Pompeius: but rather that he should do against all reason (he having so great skill and experience of battles by land as he had), if he should not employ the force and valiantness of so many lusty armed footmen as he had ready, but would weaken his army by dividing them into ships. [49]But now, notwithstanding all these good persuasions, Cleopatra forced him to put all to the hazard of battle by sea: considering

[45] III.vii. 51–54.

[46] IV.v. 4ff.; IV.vi. 12ff.; IV.ix. 6–23.

[47] Although the real Domitius deserts before the Battle of Actium, Shakespeare's Enobarbus does not leave Antony until considerably after.

[48] III.vii. 29–34.

[49] III.x. 10–15.

with herself how she might fly and provide for her safety, not to help him to win the victory, but to fly more easily after the battle lost. Betwixt Antonius' camp and his fleet of ships, there was a great high point of firm land that ran a good way into the sea, the which Antonius used often for a walk, without mistrust of fear or danger. One of Caesar's men perceived it, and told his master that he would laugh if they could take up Antonius in the midst of his walk. Thereupon Caesar sent some of his men to lie in ambush for him, and they missed not much of taking him (for they took him that came before him) because they discovered too soon, and so Antonius escaped very hardly. [50] So when Antonius had determined to fight by sea, he set all the other ships on fire but three score ships of Egypt, and reserved only the best and greatest galleys, from three banks unto ten banks of oars. Into them he put two and twenty thousand fighting men, with two thousand darters and slingers. Now as he was setting his men in order of battle, there was a captain, a valiant man, that had served Antonius in many battles and conflicts, and had all his body hacked and cut: who, as Antonius passed by him, cried out unto him, and said: "O noble emperor, how cometh it to pass that you trust to these vile brittle ships? What, do you mistrust these wounds of mine, and this sword? Let the Egyptians and Phoenicians fight by sea, and set us on the main land, where we use to conquer or to be slain on our feet." Antonius passed by him and said never a word, but only beckoned to him with his hand and head, as though he willed him to be of good courage, although indeed he had no great courage himself. For when the masters of the galleys and pilots would have let their sails alone, he made them clap them on; saying, to colour the matter withal, that not one of his enemies should scape. All that day and the three days following, the sea rose so high and was so boisterous, that the battle was put off. [51] The fifth day the storm ceased, and the sea calmed again, and then they rowed with force of oars in battle one against the other: Antonius leading the right wing with Publicola, and Caelius the left, and Marcus Octavius and Marcus Justeius the midst. Octavius Caesar, on the other side, had placed Agrippa in the left wing of his army, and had kept the right wing for himself. For the armies by land, Canidius was general of Antonius' side, and Taurus of Caesar's side: who kept their men in battle ray, the one before the other, upon the sea-side, without stirring one against the other. Further, touching both the chieftains: Antonius, being in a swift pinnace, was carried up and down by force of oars through his army, and spake to his people to encourage them to fight valiantly, as if they were on main land,

---

[50] III.vii. 51.
[51] III.viii,ix.

because of the steadiness and heaviness of their ships: and commanded the pilots and masters of the galleys, that they should not stir, none otherwise than if they were at anchor, and so to receive the first charge of their enemies, and that they should not go out of the strait of the gulf. Caesar betimes in the morning going out of his tent, to see his ships throughout, met a man by chance that drave an ass before him: Caesar asked the man what his name was. The poor man told him that his name was Eutychus, to say, *Fortunate:* and his ass's name Nicon, to say, *Conqueror.* Therefore Caesar, after he had won the battle, setting out the market-place with the spurs of the galleys he had taken, for a sign of his victory, he caused also the man and his ass to be set up in brass. When he had visited the order of his army throughout, he took a little pinnace, and went to the right wing and wondered when he saw his enemies lie still in the strait, and stirred not. For discerning them afar off, men would have thought they had been ships riding at anchor: and a good while he was so persuaded. So he kept his galleys eight furlongs from his enemies. About noon there arose a little gale of wind from the sea, and then Antonius' men, waxing angry with tarrying so long, and trusting to the greatness and height of their ships, as if they had been invincible, they began to march forward with their left wing. Caesar, seeing that, was a glad man, and began a little to give back from the right wing, to allure them to come farther out of the strait and gulf, to the end that he might with his light ships, well manned with water-men, turn and environ the galleys of the enemies, the which were heavy of yarage, both for their bigness, as also for lack of water-men to row them. When the skirmish began, and that they came to join, there was no great hurt at the first meeting, neither did the ships vehemently hit one against the other, as they do commonly in fight by sea. For on the other side Antonius' ships, for their heaviness, could not have the strength and swiftness to make their blows of any force: and Caesar's ships on the other side took great heed not to rush and shock with the forecastles of Antonius' ships, whose prows were armed with great brazen spurs. Furthermore they durst not flank them, because their points were easily broken, which way soever they came to set upon his ships, that were made of great main square pieces of timber, bound together with great iron pins: so that the battle was much like unto a battle by land, or to speak more properly, to the assault of a city. For there were always three or four of Caesar's ships about one of Antonius' ships, and the soldiers fought with their pikes, halberds and darts, and threw halberds and darts with fire. Antonius' ships on the other side bestowed among them, with their crossbows and engines of battery, great store of shot from their high towers of wood that were set upon their ships. Now Publicola seeing Agrippa put forth his left wing of

Caesar's army, to compass in Antonius' ships that fought, he was driven also to luff off to have more room, and to go a little at one side, to put those farther off that were afraid, and in the midst of the battle; for they were sore distressed by Arruntius.

52 Howbeit the battle was yet of even hand, and the victory doubtful, being indifferent to both: when suddenly they saw the threescore ships of Cleopatra busily about their yard-masts, and hoisting sail to fly. So they fled through the midst of them that were in fight, for they had been placed behind the great ships, and did marvellously disorder the other ships. For the enemies themselves wondered much to see them sail in that sort, with full sail towards Peloponnesus. There Antonius shewed plainly, that he had not only lost the courage and heart of an emperor, but also of a valiant man; and that he was not his own man (proving that true which an old man spake in mirth, that the soul of a lover lived in another body, and not in his own); he was so carried away with the vain love of this woman, as if he had been glued unto her, and that she could not have removed without moving of him also. For when he saw Cleopatra's ship under sail, he forgot, forsook, and betrayed them that fought for him, and embarked upon a galley with five banks of oars, to follow her that had already begun to overthrow him, and would in the end be his utter destruction. When she knew his galley afar off, she lifted up a sign in the poop of her ship; and so Antonius, coming to it, was plucked up where Cleopatra was: howbeit he saw her not at his first coming, nor she him, but went and sat down alone in the prow of his ship, and said never a word, clapping his head between both his hands. In the meantime came certain light brigantines of Caesar's, that followed him hard. So Antonius straight turned the prow of his ship, and presently put the rest to flight, saving one Eurycles a Lacedaemonian, that followed him near, and pressed upon him with great courage, shaking a dart in his hand over the prow, as though he would have thrown it unto Antonius. Antonius seeing him, came to the forecastle of his ship, and asked him what it was that durst follow Antonius so near? "I am," answered he, "Eurycles the son of Lachares, who through Caesar's good fortune seeketh to revenge the death of my father." This Lachares was condemned of felony, and beheaded by Antonius. But yet Eurycles durst not venture upon Antonius' ship, but set upon the other admiral galley (for there were two), and fell upon him with such a blow of his brazen spur that was so heavy and big, that he turned her round, and took her, with another that was laden with very rich stuff and carriage. After Eurycles had left Antonius, he turned again to his place, and sat down, speaking never a word, as he did before: and so lived three days alone, without

speaking to any man. But when he arrived at the head of Taenarus, there Cleopatra's women first brought Antonius and Cleopatra to speak together, and afterwards to sup and lie together. [53]Then began there again a great number of merchants' ships to gather about them, and some of their friends that had escaped from this overthrow, who brought news, that his army by sea was overthrown, but that they thought the army by land was yet whole. [54]Then Antonius sent unto Canidius, to return with his army into Asia by Macedon. . . .

[A now remorseful Antony urged his friends to desert him, and he himself settled "very solitary" in Libya. Finding his lieutenant governor there also gone over to Caesar, he returned to Alexandria where Cleopatra was trying without success to salvage her sunken treasure ships. Embittered, "he forsook the city and company of his friends, and built him a house in the sea by the Isle of Pharos." Here follows a digression on Timon Misanthropos, Timon of Athens.]

But now to return to Antonius again. Canidius himself came to bring him news, that he had lost all his army by land at Actium: on the other side he was advertised also, that Herodes king of Jewry, who had also certain legions and bands with him, was revolted unto Caesar, and all the other kings in like manner: so that, saving those that were about him, he had none left him. All this notwithstanding did nothing trouble him: and it seemed that he was contented[55] to forego all his hope, and so to be rid of all his cares and troubles. Thereupon he left his solitary house he had built by the sea, which he called Timoneon, and Cleopatra received him into her royal palace. He was no sooner come thither, but he straight set all the city on rioting and banqueting again, and himself to liberality and gifts. He caused the son of Julius Caesar and Cleopatra to be enrolled (according to the manner of the Romans) amongst the number of young men: and gave Antyllus, his eldest son he had by Fulvia, the man's gown, the which was a plain gown without guard or embroidery, of purple. For these things, there was kept great feasting, banqueting and dancing in Alexandria many days together. Indeed they did break their first order they had set down, which they called Amimetobion (as much to say, 'no life comparable'), and did set up another, which they called Synapothanumenon (signifying the order and agreement of those that will die together), the which in exceeding sumptuousness and cost was not inferior to the first. For their friends made themselves to be enrolled

---

[53] III.xiii. 169–171.
[54] In Shakespeare Canidius deserts to Caesar: III.x. 33–35.
[55] III.xiii. 182–185.

in this order of those that would die together, and so made great feasts one to another: for every man, when it came to his turn, feasted their whole company and fraternity. [56]Cleopatra in the meantime was very careful in gathering all sorts of poisons together, to destroy men. Now to make proof of those poisons which made men die with least pain, she tried it upon condemned men in prison. For when she saw the poisons that were sudden and vehement, and brought speedy death with grievous torments; and in contrary manner, that such as were more mild and gentle had not that quick speed and force to make one die suddenly: she afterwards went about to prove the stinging of snakes and adders, and made some to be applied unto men in her sight, some in one sort, some in another. So when she had daily made divers and sundry proofs, she found none of them all she had proved so fit as the biting of an aspick,[57] the which causeth only a heaviness of the head, without swooning or complaining, and bringeth a great desire also to sleep, with a little sweat in the face; and so by little and little taketh away the senses and vital powers, no living creature perceiving that the patients feel any pain. For they are so sorry when any body awaketh them and taketh them up, as those that be taken out of a sound sleep are very heavy and desirous to sleep.

[58]This notwithstanding, they sent ambassadors unto Octavius Caesar in Asia, Cleopatra requesting the realm of Egypt for their children, and Antonius praying that he might be suffered to live at Athens like a private man, if Caesar would not let him remain in Egypt. And because they had no other men of estimation about them, for that some were fled, and those that remained they did not greatly trust, they were enforced to send Euphronius, the schoolmaster of their children. For Alexas Laodicean, who was brought into Antonius' house and favour by means of Timagenes, and afterwards was in greater credit with him than any other Grecian (for that he had ever been one of Cleopatra's ministers to win Antonius, and to overthrow all his good determinations to use his wife Octavia well): him Antonius had sent unto Herodes king of Jewry, hoping still to keep him his friend, that he should not revolt from him. But he remained there, and betrayed Antonius. For where he should have kept Herodes from revolting from him, he persuaded him to turn to Caesar: and trusting king Herodes, he presumed to come in Caesar's presence. Howbeit Herodes did him no pleasure, for he was presently taken prisoner, and sent in chains to his own country, and there by Caesar's commandment put to death. Thus was Alexas, in Antonius' life-time, put to death for betraying

---

[56] V.ii. 348–359.
[57] asp.
[58] III.xii. 1–25; IV.vi. 12–18.

of him. Furthermore, Caesar would not grant unto Antonius' requests:
but for Cleopatra, he made her answer, that he would deny her nothing
reasonable, so that she would either put Antonius to death, or drive
him out of her country. Therewithal he sent Thyreus[59] one of his men
unto her, a very wise and discreet man: who bringing letters of credit
from a young lord unto a noble lady, and that besides greatly liked her
beauty, might easily by his eloquence have persuaded her. He was
longer in talk with her than any man else was, and the queen herself
also did him great honour: insomuch as he made Antonius jealous of
him. Whereupon Antonius caused him to be taken and well-favouredly
whipped, and so sent him unto Caesar: and bade him tell him, that
he made him angry with him, because he shewed himself proud and
disdainful towards him; and now specially, when he was easy to be
angered, by reason of his present misery. "To be short, if this mislike
thee," said he, "thou hast Hipparchus, one of my enfranchised bondmen, with thee: hang him if thou wilt, or whip him at thy pleasure,
that we may cry quittance." [60]From henceforth Cleopatra, to clear herself of the suspicion he had of her, made more of him than ever she
did. For first of all, where she did solemnize the day of her birth very
meanly and sparingly, fit for her present misfortune, she now in contrary manner did keep it with such solemnity, that she exceeded all
measure of sumptuousness and magnificence: so that the guests that
were bidden to the feasts, and came poor, went away rich. [61]Now
things passing thus, Agrippa by divers letters sent one after another
unto Caesar, prayed him to return to Rome, because the affairs there
did of necessity require his person and presence. Thereupon he did
defer the war till the next year following: but when winter was done,
he returned again through Syria by the coast of Africa, to make wars
against Antonius and his other captains. [62]When the city of Pelusium
was taken, there ran a rumour in the city, that Seleucus (by Cleopatra's consent) had surrendered the same. But to clear herself that
she did not, Cleopatra brought Seleucus' wife and children unto
Antonius, to be revenged of them at his pleasure. Furthermore, Cleopatra had long before made many sumptuous tombs and monuments,
as well for excellency of workmanship, as for height and greatness of
building, joining hard to the temple of Isis. Thither she caused to be
brought all the treasure and precious things she had of the ancient
kings her predecessors: as gold, silver, emeralds, pearls, ebony, ivory,

---

59 III.xii. 26ff.; III.xiii. 46–152.

60 III.xiii. 185–187.

61 Shakespeare understandably omits this year's delay of the war which
Plutarch now relates.

62 The motivation for Seleucus's telling Caesar about Cleopatra's hidden
treasure, p. 609 (in Shakespeare V.ii. 137–190).

and cinnamon, and besides all that, a marvellous number of torches, faggots, and flax. So Octavius Caesar, being afraid to lose such a treasure and mass of riches, and that this woman for spite would set it on fire and burn it every whit, he always sent some one or other unto her from him, to put her in good comfort, whilst he in the mean-time drew near the city with his army. So Caesar came and pitched his camp hard by the city, in the place where they run and manage their horses. Antonius made a sally upon him, and fought very valiantly, so that he drove Caesar's horsemen back, fighting with his men even into their camp. Then he came again to the palace, greatly boasting of this victory, and sweetly kissed Cleopatra, armed as he was when he came from the fight, recommending one of his men of arms unto her, that had valiantly fought in this skirmish. Cleopatra, to reward his manliness, gave him an armour and headpiece of clean gold: howbeit the man-at-arms, when he had received this rich gift, stole away by night and went to Caesar. [63]Antonius sent again to challenge Caesar to fight with him hand to hand. Caesar answered him, "That he had many other ways to die than so." Then Antonius, seeing there was no way more honourable for him to die than fighting valiantly, he determined to set up his rest, both by sea and land. [64]So being at supper (as it is reported) he commanded his officers and household servants that waited on him at his board, that they should fill his cups full, and make as much of him as they could: "For," said he, "you know not whether you shall do so much for me tomorrow or not, or whether you shall serve another master: and it may be you shall see me no more, but a dead body." This notwithstanding, per-ceiving that his friends and men fell a-weeping to hear him say so, to salve that he had spoken, he added this more unto it, 'that he would not lead them to battle, where he thought not rather safely to return with victory, than valiantly to die with honour.' [65]Furthermore, the selfsame night, within a little of midnight, when all the city was quiet, full of fear and sorrow, thinking what would be the issue and end of this war, it is said that suddenly they heard a marvellous sweet harmony of sundry sorts of instruments of music, with the cry of a multitude of people, as they had been dancing, and had sung as they use in Bacchus' feasts, with movings and turnings after the manner of the Satyrs: and it seemed, that this dance went through the city unto the gate that opened to the enemies, and that all the troop, that made this noise they heard, went out of the city at that gate. Now such as in reason sought the depth of the interpretation of this wonder,

---

[63] IV.i. 1–6.
[64] IV.ii. 8ff.
[65] IV.iii. 1ff.

thought that it was the god unto whom Antonius bare singular devotion to counterfeit and resemble him, that did forsake them. The next morning by break of day, he went to set those few footmen he had in order upon the hills adjoining unto the city: and there he stood to behold his galleys which departed from the haven, and rowed against the galleys of the enemies, and so stood still, looking what exploits his soldiers in them would do. [66]But when by force of rowing they were come near unto them, they first saluted Caesar's men; and then Caesar's men resaluted them also, and of two armies made but one: and then did all together row toward the city.

When Antonius saw that his men did forsake him, and yielded unto Caesar, and that his footmen were broken and overthrown, he then fled into the city, crying out that Cleopatra had betrayed him unto them with whom he had made war for her sake. [67]Then she, being afraid of his fury, fled into the tomb which he had caused to be made, and there she locked the doors unto her, and shut all the springs of the locks with great bolts, and in the meantime sent unto Antonius to tell him that she was dead. [68]Antonius believing it, said unto himself: "What doest thou look for further, Antonius, sith spiteful fortune hath taken from thee the only joy thou hadst, for whom thou yet reservedst thy life?" When he had said these words, he went into a chamber and unarmed himself, and being naked, said thus: "O Cleopatra, it grieveth me not that I have lost thy company, for I will not be long from thee: but I am sorry that, having been so great a captain and emperor, I am indeed condemned to be judged of less courage and noble mind than a woman." Now he had a man of his called Eros, whom he loved and trusted much, and whom he had long before caused to swear unto him, that he should kill him when he did command him: and then he willed him to keep his promise. His man, drawing his sword, lifted it up as though he had meant to have stricken his master: but turning his head at one side, he thrust his sword into himself, and fell down dead at his master's foot. Then said Antonius: "O noble Eros, I thank thee for this, and it is valiantly done of thee, to shew me what I should do to myself, which thou couldest not do for me." Therewithal he took his sword, and thrust it into his belly, and so fell down upon a little bed. The wound he had killed him not presently, for the blood stinted a little when he was laid: and when he came somewhat to himself again, he prayed them that were about him to despatch him. But they all fled out of the chamber, and left him

---

[66] IV.xii. 9–29.

[67] IV.xiii. 1ff.

[68] IV.xiv. 27ff. An especially close parallel between Shakespeare and his source.

crying out, tormenting himself: until at last there came a secretary
unto him (called Diomedes) who was commanded to bring him into
the tomb or monument where Cleopatra was. When he heard that
she was alive, he very earnestly prayed his men to carry his body
thither, and so he was carried in his men's arms into the entry of the
monument. [69]Notwithstanding, Cleopatra would not open the gates,
but came to the high windows, and cast out certain chains and ropes,
in the which Antonius was trussed: and Cleopatra her own self, with
two women only, which she had suffered to come with her into these
monuments, trised[70] Antonius up. They that were present to behold
it said they never saw so pitiful a sight. For they plucked up poor
Antonius, all bloody as he was, and drawing on with pangs of death:
who holding up his hands to Cleopatra, raised up himself as well as he
could. It was a hard thing for these women to do, to lift him up: but
Cleopatra, stooping down with her head, putting to all her strength
to her uttermost power, did lift him up with much ado, and never let
go her hold, with the help of the women beneath that bade her be of
good courage, and were as sorry to see her labour so as she herself. So
when she had gotten him in after that sort, and laid him on a bed,
she rent her garments upon him, clapping her breast, and scratching
her face and stomach. Then she dried up his blood that had berayed
his face, and called him her lord, her husband, and emperor, forgetting
her own misery and calamity for the pity and compassion she took of
him. Antonius made her cease her lamenting, and called for wine,
either because he was athirst, or else for that he thought thereby to
hasten his death. When he had drunk, he earnestly prayed her, and
persuaded her, that she would seek to save her life, if she could possible,
without reproach and dishonour: and that chiefly she should trust
Proculeius above any man else about Caesar. And as for himself, that
she should not lament nor sorrow for the miserable change of his
fortune at the end of his days: but rather that she should think him
the more fortunate, for the former triumphs and honours he had received; considering that while he lived, he was the noblest and greatest
prince of the world; and that now he was overcome, not cowardly, but
valiantly, a Roman by another Roman. As Antonius gave the last gasp,
Proculeius came that was sent from Caesar. [71]For after Antonius had
thrust his sword in himself, as they carried him into the tombs and
monuments of Cleopatra, one of his guard (called Dercetaeus) took
his sword with which he had stricken himself, and hid it: then he
secretly stole away, and brought Octavius Caesar the first news of his

---

[69] IV.xv. 1ff. Another close parallel, but compare diction.
[70] drew.
[71] V.i. 4–48.

death, and shewed him his sword that was bloodied. Caesar hearing this news, straight withdrew himself into a secret place of his tent, and there burst out with tears, lamenting his hard and miserable fortune, that had been his friend and brother-in-law, his equal in the empire, and companion with him in sundry great exploits and battles. Then he called for all his friends and shewed them the letters Antonius had written to him, and his answers also sent him again, during their quarrel and strife: and how fiercely and proudly the other answered him, to all just and reasonable matters he wrote unto him.

[72]After this, he sent Proculeius, and commanded him to do what he could possible to get Cleopatra alive, fearing lest otherwise all the treasure would be lost: and furthermore, he thought that if he could take Cleopatra, and bring her alive to Rome, she would marvellously beautify and set out his triumph. But Cleopatra would never put herself into Proculeius' hands, although they spake together. For Proculeius came to the gates that were thick and strong, and surely barred, but yet there were some crannies through the which her voice might be heard; and so they without understood, that Cleopatra demanded the kingdom of Egypt for her sons: and that Proculeius answered her that she should be of good cheer, and not be afraid to refer all unto Caesar. After he had viewed the place very well, he came and reported her answer unto Caesar: who immediately sent Gallus to speak once again with her, and bade him purposely hold her in talk, whilst Proculeius did set up a ladder against that high window by the which Antonius was trised[73] up, and came down into the monument with two of his men, hard by the gate where Cleopatra stood to hear what Gallus said unto her. One of her women which was shut up in her monuments with her, saw Proculeius by chance as he came down, and shrieked out: "O poor Cleopatra, thou art taken." Then when she saw Proculeius behind her as she came from the gate, she thought to have stabbed herself in with a short dagger she wore of purpose by her side. But Proculeius came suddenly upon her, and taking her by both the hands, said unto her: "Cleopatra, first thou shalt do thyself great wrong, and secondly unto Caesar, to deprive him of the occasion and opportunity openly to shew his bounty and mercy, and to give his enemies cause to accuse the most courteous and noble prince that ever was, and to impeach him, as though he were a cruel and merciless man, that were not to be trusted." So even as he spake the word, he took her dagger from her, and shook her clothes for fear of any poison hidden about her. Afterwards, Caesar sent one of his

---

[72] V.i. 61ff.; V.ii. 9–64.
[73] drawn.

infranchised men called Epaphroditus, whom he straitly charged to look
well unto her, and to beware in any case that she made not herself
away: and for the rest, to use her with all the courtesy possible. And
for himself, he in the meantime entered the city of Alexandria, and
(as he went) talked with the philosopher Arrius, and held him by the
hand, to the end that his countrymen should reverence him the more,
because they saw Caesar so highly esteem and honour him. Then he
went into the show-place of exercises, and so up to his chair of state
which was prepared for him of a great height: and there, according
to his commandment, all the people of Alexandria were assembled,
who, quaking for fear, fell down on their knees before him and craved
mercy. Caesar bade them all stand up, and told them openly that he
forgave the people, and pardoned the felonies and offences they had
committed against him in this war: first, for the founder's sake of the
same city, which was Alexander the Great: secondly, for the beauty
of the city, which he much esteemed and wondered at: thirdly, for the
love he bare unto his very friend Arrius. Thus did Caesar honour
Arrius, who craved pardon for himself and many others, and specially
for Philostratus, the eloquentest man of all the sophists and orators of
his time, for present and sudden speech: howbeit, he falsely named
himself an Academic philosopher. Therefore Caesar, that hated his
nature and conditions, would not hear his suit. Thereupon he let his
grey beard grow long, and followed Arrius step by step in a long
mourning gown, still buzzing in his ears this Greek verse:

> A wise man, if that he be wise indeed,
> May by a wise man have the better speed.

Caesar understanding this, not for the desire he had to deliver Philostratus of his fear, but to rid Arrius of malice and envy that might have
fallen out against him, he pardoned him. Now touching Antonius'
sons, Antyllus, his eldest son by Fulvia, was slain, because his schoolmaster Theodorus did betray him unto the soldiers, who struck off his
head. And the villain took a precious stone of great value from his
neck, the which he did sew in his girdle, and afterwards denied that
he had it: but it was found about him, and so Caesar trussed him up[74]
for it. For Cleopatra's children, they were very honourably kept, with
their governors and train that waited on them. But for Caesarion, who
was said to be Julius Caesar's son, his mother Cleopatra had sent him
unto the Indians through Ethiopia, with a great sum of money. But
one of his governors also, called Rhodon, even such another as

---

[74] hung him.

Theodorus, persuaded him to return into his country, and told him that Caesar sent for him to give him his mother's kingdom. So, as Caesar was determining with himself what he should do, Arrius said unto him:

Too many Caesars is not good,

alluding unto a certain verse of Homer, that saith:

Too many lords doth not well.

Therefore Caesar did put Caesarion to death, after the death of his mother Cleopatra.

Many princes, great kings, and captains, did crave Antonius' body of Octavius Caesar, to give him honourable burial: but Caesar would never take it from Cleopatra, who did sumptuously and royally bury him with her own hands, whom Caesar suffered to take as much as she would to bestow upon his funerals. Now was she altogether overcome with sorrow and passion of mind, for she had knocked her breast so pitifully, that she had martyred it, and in divers places had raised ulcers and inflammations, so that she fell into a fever withal: whereof she was very glad, hoping thereby to have good colour to abstain from meat, and that so she might have died easily without any trouble. She had a physician called Olympus, whom she made privy to her intent, to the end he should help to rid her out of her life: as Olympus writeth himself, who wrote a book of all these things. [75]But Caesar mistrusted the matter by many conjectures he had, and therefore did put her in fear, and threatened her to put her children to shameful death. With these threats, Cleopatra for fear yielded straight, as she would have yielded unto strokes: and afterwards suffered herself to be cured and dieted as they listed.

Shortly after, Caesar came himself in person to see her, and to comfort her. Cleopatra, being laid upon a little low bed in poor estate (when she saw Caesar come into her chamber), suddenly rose up, naked in her smock, and fell down at his feet marvellously disfigured: both for that she had plucked her hair from her head, as also for that she had martyred all her face with her nails; and besides, her voice was small and trembling, her eyes sunk into her head with continual blubbering; and moreover, they might see the most part of her stomach torn in sunder. To be short, her body was not much better than her mind: yet her good grace and comeliness and the force of her beauty was not altogether defaced. But notwithstanding this ugly and pitiful state of hers, yet she shewed herself within, by her outward looks and

---

[75] V.ii. 128–133.

countenance. When Caesar had made her lie down again, and sat by her bedside, Cleopatra began to clear and excuse herself for that she had done, laying all to the fear she had of Antonius: Caesar, in contrary manner, reproved her in every point. Then she suddenly altered her speech, and prayed him to pardon her, as though she were afraid to die, and desirous to live. [76]At length, she gave him a brief and memorial of all the ready money and treasure she had. But by chance there stood one Seleucus by, one of her treasurers, who, to seem a good servant, came straight to Caesar to disprove Cleopatra, that she had not set in all, but kept many things back of purpose. Cleopatra was in such a rage with him, that she flew upon him, and took him by the hair of the head, and boxed him well-favouredly. Caesar fell a-laughing and parted the fray. "Alas," said she, "O Caesar: is not this a great shame and reproach, that thou having vouchsafed to take the pains to come unto me, and done me this honour, poor wretch and caitiff creature, brought into this pitiful and miserable state: and that mine own servants should come now to accuse me? though it may be I have reserved some jewels and trifles meet for women, but not for me (poor soul) to set out myself withal, but meaning to give some pretty presents and gifts unto Octavia and Livia, that they, making means and intercession for me to thee, thou mightest yet extend thy favour and mercy upon me." Caesar was glad to hear her say so, persuading himself thereby that she had yet a desire to save her life. [77]So he made her answer, that he did not only give her that to dispose of at her pleasure which she had kept back, but further promised to use her more honourably and bountifully than she would think for: and so he took his leave of her, supposing he had deceived her, but indeed he was deceived himself. [78]There was a young gentleman, Cornelius Dolabella, that was one of Caesar's very great familiars, and besides did bear no ill will unto Cleopatra. He sent her word secretly (as she had requested him) that Caesar determined to take his journey through Syria, and that within three days he would send her away before with her children. When this was told Cleopatra, she requested Caesar that it would please him to suffer her to offer the last oblations of the dead unto the soul of Antonius. This being granted her, she was carried to the place where his tomb was, and there falling down on her knees, embracing the tomb with her women, the tears running down her cheeks, she began to speak in this sort: "O my dear lord Antonius, it is not long since I buried thee here, being a free woman: and now I

---

[76] V.ii. 137–190.

[77] In the light of subsequent events perhaps that speech by Cleopatra was a subterfuge to get Caesar to relax his guard. If so it was successful.

[78] V.ii. 100–110; 197–207.

offer unto thee the funeral sprinklings and oblations, being a captive and prisoner; and yet I am forbidden and kept from tearing and murdering this captive body of mine with blows, which they carefully guard and keep only to triumph of thee: look therefore henceforth for no other honours, offerings, nor sacrifices from me: for these are the last which Cleopatra can give thee, sith now they carry her away. Whilst we lived together, nothing could sever our companies: but now, at our death, I fear me they will make us change our countries. For as thou, being a Roman, hast been buried in Egypt: even so, wretched creature, I, an Egyptian, shall be buried in Italy, which shall be all the good that I have received by thy country. If therefore the gods where thou art now have any power and authority, sith our gods here have forsaken us, suffer not thy true friend and lover to be carried away alive, that in me they triumph of thee: but receive me with thee, and let me be buried in one self tomb with thee. For though my griefs and miseries be infinite, yet none hath grieved me more, nor that I could less bear withal, than this small time which I have been driven to live alone without thee."

Then having ended these doleful plaints, and crowned the tomb with garlands and sundry nosegays, and marvellous lovingly embraced the same, she commanded they should prepare her bath; and when she had bathed and washed herself, she fell to her meat, and was sumptuously served. [79]Now whilst she was at dinner, there came a countryman and brought her a basket. The soldiers that warded at the gates, asked him straight what he had in his basket. He opened his basket, and took out the leaves that covered the figs, and shewed them that they were figs he brought. They all of them marvelled to see so goodly figs. The countryman laughed to hear them, and bade them take some if they would. They believed he told them truly, and so bade him carry them in. After Cleopatra had dined, she sent a certain tablet written and sealed unto Caesar, and commanded them all to go out of the tombs where she was, but the two women; then she shut the doors to her. Caesar, when he had received this tablet, and began to read her lamentation and petition, requesting him that he would let her be buried with Antonius, found straight what she meant, and thought to have gone thither himself: howbeit, he sent one before in all haste that might be, to see what it was. Her death was very sudden: for those whom Caesar sent unto her ran thither in all haste possible, and found the soldiers standing at the gate, mistrusting nothing, nor understanding of her death. But when they had opened the doors, they found Cleopatra stark-dead, laid upon a bed of gold, attired and

[79] V.ii. 241–331.

arrayed in her royal robes, and one of her two women, which was called Iras, dead at her feet: and her other woman (called Charmion) half dead, and trembling, trimming the diadem which Cleopatra wore upon her head. One of the soldiers seeing her, angrily said unto her: "Is that well done, Charmion?" "Very well," said she again, "and meet for a princess descended from the race of so many noble kings:" she said no more, but fell down dead hard by the bed. Some report that this aspick was brought unto her in the basket with figs, and that she had commanded them to hide it under the fig-leaves, that when she should see her: howbeit, that when she would have taken away she should think to take out the figs, the aspick should bite her before the leaves for the figs, she perceived it, and said, "Art thou here, then?" And so, her arm being naked, she put it to the aspick to be bitten. Others say again, she kept it in a box, and that she did prick and thrust it with a spindle of gold, so that the aspick, being angered withal, leapt out with great fury, and bit her in the arm. Howbeit few can tell the truth. For they report also, that she had hidden poison in a hollow razor which she carried in the hair of her head; and yet was there no mark seen on her body, or any sign discerned that she was poisoned, neither also did they find this serpent in her tomb: but it was reported only, that there was seen certain fresh steps or tracks where it had gone, on the tomb-side toward the sea, and specially by the door-side. Some say also that they found two little pretty bitings in her arm, scant to be discerned: the which it seemeth Caesar himself gave credit unto, because in his triumph he carried Cleopatra's image, with an aspick biting of her arm. And thus goeth the report of her death. [80]Now Caesar, though he was marvellous sorry for the death of Cleopatra, yet he wondered at her noble mind and courage, and therefore commanded she should be nobly buried, and laid by Antonius: and willed also that her two women should have honourable burial.

Cleopatra died being eight and thirty years old, after she had reigned two and twenty years, and governed about fourteen of them with Antonius.

[Character of Octavius Caesar]

[Plutarch offers ample character analysis of Antonius and Cleopatra in this Life but says little about the character of Octavius Caesar. The following passage, from Plutarch's Life of Octavius Caesar, will aid in understanding Octavius Caesar's actions and will throw fresh light upon the concepts he is made to represent in Shakespeare's play:]

---

[80] V.ii. 359–361.

[Octavius Caesar] was very modest and continent in all the parts of his life, saving that he was somewhat given to women and play: for the rest, he liked not great palaces, but was contented with mean lodgings: and if there were any ornament, it was in porches and parks. His household-stuff and apparel was nothing sumptuous nor costly. It pleased him well to make feasts; he very carefully made choice of his guests, and oftentimes he sat down at the table a long time after everybody, and would rise before others, which remained after he was up. In his ordinary diet he banished superfluity of meats, he delighted to be merry and pleasant among his friends, or to bring in pleasant players of comedies to pass the time away. And he did not tie himself to any certain hours to eat his meat, but when his stomach served him he took something. So that sometimes he supped not at all, and then, when every man was gone, he made them bring him meat, neither dainty nor delicate. Also he drunk very little wine; he slept in the day, and by times in the night, talking with some or reading: so that oftentimes he slept not till the break of day, and, for that he took no rest in the night, he might chance to sleep in his litter as they carried him in the streets in the daytime up and down Rome. He was a goodly prince, and that kept himself in good state from the beginning of his life to the latter end: not curious to set himself out, as little caring to be shaven as to wear long hair: and instead of a looking-glass, reading in his book or writing, even whilst the barber was trimming of him. Whether he spake or held his peace, he had so comely a face, that many of his enemies, bent to do him hurt, their hearts would not serve them so soon as ever they looked on him. He had very clear and lively eyes, but with time he was subject to many diseases and infirmities, the which he remedied with great care. As for his exercises, he left arms and horses immediately after the civil wars: for he was never any great soldier. He would play at tennis, at *pallone*, he would go abroad in his coach to walk and stir himself. Sometimes he would go a-fishing, or play at the bones, or at nuts, with young children of the Moors and Syrians that had some pretty manner and behaviour with them, and always spake words to move laughter. He was learned in the liberal sciences, very eloquent, and desirous to learn: insomuch that during the war of Mutina, in the midst of all his infinite affairs, he did read, he wrote, and made orations amongst his familiars. He never spake unto the Senate nor people, nor to his soldiers, but he had first written and premeditated that he would say unto them, although he had speech at commandment, to propound or answer to anything in the field. And because he would not deceive his memory, or lose time in superfluous speech, he determined ever to write all that he would say: and he was the first inventor of it. If he had to confer with any man, or with his wife in any matters of importance, he would put that down in his writing-tables, because he would speak neither more nor less. And he took pleasure to pronounce his words with a sweet voice and good grace, having continually about him for this purpose a fine man to frame his voice. But one day having a pain in his mouth, he made his oration to the people by an herald. He made many books and verses of divers sorts; but all is dead with the time. His speech was as the rest of his life, eloquent, well couched together, and sententious. He delighted to read good authors, but he gathered nothing other than the sentences teaching good manners: and having written them out word by word, he gave out a copy of them to his familiars: and sent them about to the governors of provinces, and to the magistrates of Rome and of other cities. He was somewhat, and too much, given to divinations,[1] he was marvellously afraid of thunder and lightning; he had a great confidence in dreams, and in such like vanities.

---

[1] A facet which Shakespeare ignores.

THE COUNTESS OF PEMBROKE

Antonie, 1592 *

ACT I

ANTONIUS.[1] Since cruel heaven is against me obstinate,
Since all mishaps of the round engine do
Conspire my harm: since men, since powers divine,
Air, earth, and sea are all injurious:
And that my Queen herself, in whom I lived,
The idol of my heart does me pursue:
It's meet I die. For her have I foregone
My country, Caesar unto war provoked
(For just revenge of sister's wrong, my wife,
Who moved my Queen (aye me!) to jealousy).   10
For love of her, in her allurements caught,
Abandoned life, I honor have despised,
Disdained my friends, and of the stately Rome
Despoiled the Empire of her best attire,
Contemned that power that made me so much feared,
A slave become unto her feeble face.[2]

O cruel, traitress, woman most unkind,
Thou dost, forsworn, my love and life betray;
And givst me up to rageful enemy,
Which soon (o fool!) will plague thy perjury.   20
Yielded Pelusium on this country's shore.
Yielded thou hast my ships and men of war,

---

* text modernized. *Antonie* is a translation of the French play *M. Antoine*
by Robert Garnier, 1578, and is apparently based on the 1585 revised edition
of Garnier's play.

[1] The spelling used here in the original text.
This first soliloquy is a summary of Shakespeare's Acts I–III.

[2] *Visage feint:* dissembling face. The Countess must have confused *feint*
with faint, or feeble.

That naught remains (so destitute am I)
But these same arms which on my back I wear.
Thou shouldst have had them too, and me unarmed
Yielded to Caesar naked of defense.
Which while I bear let Caesar never think
Triumph of me shall his proud chariot grace:
Not think with me his glory to adorn,
On me alive to use his victory.   30
    Thou only Cleopatra triumph hast,
Thou only hast my freedom servile made,
Thou only hast me vanquished: not by force
(for forced I cannot be) but by sweet baits
Of thy eyes' graces, which did gain so fast
Upon my liberty, that naught remained.
None else henceforth, but thou my dearest Queen,
Shall glory in commanding Antonie . . .

[*He goes on to recount how the force of her love drew him away
from the Parthian wars and back again to her.*]

    Returned low, dishonored, despised,
In wanton love a woman thee misleads   40
Sunk in foul sink. Meanwhile respecting naught[3]
Thy wife Octavia and her tender babes,
Of whom the long contempt against thee whets
The sword of Caesar, now thy lord become.
    Lost thy great Empire, all those goodly towns [that]
Reverenced thy name, as rebels now thee leave:
Rise against thee, and to the ensigns flock
Of conquering Caesar who enwalls thee round
Caged in thy hold, scarce master of thyself,
Late master of so many nations.   50
    Yet, yet, which is of grief extremest grief?
Which is yet of mischief highest mischief,
It's Cleopatra, alas! it's she,
It's she augments the torment of thy pain,
Betrays thy love, thy life (alas!) betrays,
Caesar to please, whose grace she seeks to gain:
With thought her crown to save, and fortune make
Only *thy* foe, which common ought have been.
    If her I always loved, and the first flame

---

[3] not at all.

Of her (heart-) killing love shall burn me last, 60
Justly complain I she disloyal is;
Nor constant is, even as I constant am,
To comfort my mishap; despising me
No more than when the heavens favored me.[4]
But ah! by nature women wavering are,
Each moment changing and rechanging minds.
Unwise, who blind in them, thinks loyalty
Ever to find in beauty's company.

[*The chorus concludes this act by observing that as long as man remains on earth he will have misfortune and griefs.*]

[ACT II. *Philostratus, a philosopher, laments the war and suffering that love — of Antony and Cleopatra — has brought to Egypt. The chorus takes up this same lament, after which Cleopatra enters.*]

CLEOPATRA.[5] That I have thee betrayed, dear Antonie,
My life, my soul, my sun? I had such thought? 70
That I have thee betrayed my lord, my king?
That I would break my vowed faith to thee?
Leave thee? deceive thee? yield thee to the rage
Of mighty foe? I ever had that heart?
Rather sharp lightning lighten on my head:
Rather may I to deepest mischief fall:
Rather the opened earth devour me:
Rather fierce tigers feed them on my flesh:
Rather, o rather let our Nilus send,
To swallow me quick, some weeping crocodile. 80
And didst thou then suppose my royal heart
Had ~~hatched~~, thee to ensnare, a faithless love?
And changing mind as fortune changed cheer,
I would weaken, thee (to win the stronger) lose?
O wretch! O captive! O too cruel hap!
And did not I sufficient loss sustain
Losing my realm, losing my liberty,
My tender offspring, and the joyful light

---

[4] i.e., despising me as much as the heavens once favored me.
[5] This self-justification by Cleopatra culminates in a speech of some poetic merit, the last eight lines of which contain the same profound idea of love that irradiates Shakespeare's play.

Of beamy sun, and yet, yet losing more.
Thee Antony[6] my care, if I lost not,   90
What yet remained? thy love, alas! thy love,
More dear than scepter, children, freedom, light.
    So ready I to row in Charon's barge,
Shall lease[7] the joy of dying in thy love,
So the sole comfort of my misery
To have one tomb with thee is me bereft.
So I in shady plains shall plain[8] alone,
Not (as I hoped) companion of thy moan.
O height of grief!
    ERAS. Why with continual cries   100
Your grief-full harms do you exasperate?
Torment yourself with murdering complaints?
Strain your weak breast so oft, so vehemently?
Water with tears this fair alabaster?
With sorrow's sting so many beauties wound?
Come, of so many kings want[9] you the heart
Bravely, stoutly, this tempest to resist?
    CLEOPATRA. My evils are wholly unsupportable,
No human force can them withstand, but death.
    ERAS. To him that strives naught is impossible.   110
    CLEOPATRA. In striving lies no hope of my mishaps.
    ERAS. All things do yield to force of lovely face.
    CLEOPATRA. My face too lovely caused my wretched case.
My face has so entrapped, so cast us down,
That for his conquest Caesar may it thank,
Causing that Antony [*sic*] one army lost,
The other wholly did to Caesar yield,
For not enduring (so his amorous sprite
Was with my beauty fired) my shameful flight.
Soon as he saw, from rank wherein he stood,   120
In hottest fight my galleys making sail:
Forgetful of his charge (as if his soul
Unto his lady's soul had been enchained)
He left his men, who so courageously
Did leave their lives to gain him victory. . . .

---

[6] The original uses this spelling in this instance. The spelling varies throughout the play and the variants are followed in this version.
[7] gather in.
[8] complain.
[9] lack.

CHAIRMIAN. Then, madame, help yourself, leave off in time
Antony's wrack,[10] lest it your wrack procure:
Retire you from him: save from wrathful rage
Of angry Caesar both your realm and you.
You see him lost, so as[11] your amity   130
Unto his evils can yield no more relief.
You see him ruined, so as your support
No more henceforth can him with comfort raise.
Withdraw you from the storm; persist not still
To lose yourself; this royal diadem
Regain of Caesar.
    CLEOPATRA. Sooner shining light
Shall leave the day, and darkness leave the night:
Sooner moist currents of tempestuous seas
Shall wave in heaven, and the nightly troops   140
Of stars shall shine within the foaming waves,
Than I thee, Antonie, leave in deep distress.
I am with thee, be it thy worthy soul
Lodge in thy breast, or from that lodging part
Crossing the joyless lake to take her place
[12]In place prepared for men demi-gods.
    Live, if thee please; if life be loathsome, die;
Dead and alive, Antonie, thou shalt see
Thy Princess follow thee, follow, and lament
Thy wrack, no less her own than was thy weal.   150

[*Cleopatra continues for a while in this repentent vein and then
the chorus describes the decline and present servitude of Egypt.*]

[ACT III. *Antony bitterly scores the faithlessness of Cleopatra, re-
counts the history of his past triumphs and glories and decides to die.
The chorus welcomes the "healthful succor" of death.*]

[ACT IV. *Dircetus, the messenger, announces to Caesar the death
of Antony. Caesar orders Proculeius to go to Cleopatra to "feed with
hope her soul disconsolate" while the chorus of Roman soldiers praises
Caesar and hopes that the end of the war has come.*]

---

[10] wreck, destruction.
[11] therefore.
[12] Compare with V.ii. 76–100.

ACT V[13]

Cleopatra, Euphron [tutor of Cleopatra's children].
Children of Cleopatra. Charmion. Eras.

CLEOPATRA. O cruel fortune! O accursed lot!
O plaguey love! O most detested brand!
O wretched joys! O beauties miserable!
O deadly state! O deadly royalty!
O hateful life! O queen most lamentable!
O Antony by my fault buriable!
O hellish work of heaven! alas! the wrath
Of all the gods at once on us is fallen.
Unhappy queen! O would I in this world
The wandering light of day had never seen!   160
Alas! of mine the plague and poison[14] I
The crown have lost my ancestors me left,
This realm I have to strangers subject made,
And robbed my children of their heritage.
    Yet this is naught (alas!) unto the price
[15]Of you dear husband, whom my snares entrapped:
Of you, whom I have plagued, whom I have made
With bloody hand a guest of mouldy tomb:
Of you, whom I destroyed, of you dear lord,
Whom I of empire, honor, life have spoiled.   170
    O hurtful woman! and can I yet live,
Yet longer live in this ghost-haunted tomb?
Can I yet breathe! can yet in such annoy,
Yet can my soul within this body dwell?
O Sisters, you that spin the threads of death!
O Styx! O Phlegethon! you brooks of hell!
O imps of night!
    EUPHRON.   Live for your children's sake:
Let not your death of kingdom them deprive.
Alas, what shall they do? Who will have care?   180
Who will preserve this royal race of yours?
Who pity take? Even now meseems I see

---

[13] Compare with Act V of Shakespeare's play. Garnier's Cleopatra does not commit suicide — it would be indecorous in this type of play — and Shakespeare does not bring Cleopatra's children or their tutor onstage, but there is a strong underlying similarity in the rhapsodic quality of the speeches of both Cleopatras.

[14] By my plaguing and poison.

[15] A suggestion here of V.ii. 342-346.

These little souls to servile bondage fallen,
And borne in triumph.
    CLEOPATRA.   Ah most miserable!
    EUPHRON. Their tender arms with cursed cord fast bound
At their weak backs.
    CLEOPATRA. Ah gods what pity mo[v]e!
    EUPHRON. Their sealy[16] necks to ground with weakness bend.
    CLEOPATRA. Never on us, good gods, such mischief send.   190
    EUPHRON. And pointed at with fingers as they go.
    CLEOPATRA. Rather a thousand deaths.
    EUPHRON. Lastly his knife
Some cruel caitiff in their blood imbrue.
    CLEOPATRA. Ah my heart breaks. By shady banks of hell,
By fields whereon the lonely ghosts do tread,
By my soul, and the soul of Antonie
I you beseech, Euphron, of them have care.
Be their good father, let your wisdom let
That they fall not into this tyrant's hands.   200
Rather conduct them where their friezed locks
Black Ethiopes to neighbor sun do show:
On wavy ocean at the water's will;
On barren cliffs of snowy Caucasus;
To tigers swift, to lions, and to bears:
And rather, rather unto every coast,
To every land and sea: for naught I fear
As rage of him, whose thirst no blood can quench.
Adieu, dear children, children dear, adieu . . .
    EUPHRON. Come children.   210
    CHILDREN.   We come.
    EUPHRON.   Follow we our chance.
The gods shall guide us.
    CHARMION.   O too cruel lot!
O too hard chance! Sister, what shall we do,
What shall we do, alas! if murdering dart
Of death arrive while that in slumbering swoon
Half dead she lie with anguish overgone?
    ERAS. Her face is frozen.
    CHARMION.   Madame for God's love   220
Leave us not thus: bid us yet first farewell.
Alas! weep over Antonie: let not
His body be without due rites entombed.

---

[16] innocent.

CLEOPATRA. Ah, ah.

CHARMION.   Madame.

CLEOPATRA.   Ay me!

ERAS.   How faint
she is?

 CLEOPATRA. My sisters, hold me up. How wretched I,
How cursed am! . . .   230
O goddess, thou whom Cyprus does adore,
Venus of Paphos, bent to work us harm
For old Julius' brood; if thou take care
Of Caesar, why of us takest thou no care?
Antonie did descend, as well as he,
From thine own son by long enchained line:
And might have ruled by one and selfsame fate,
True Trojan blood, the stately Roman state.
Antonie, poor Antonie, my dear soul,
Now but a block, the booty of a tomb.   240
Thy life, thy heat is lost, thy color gone,
And hideous paleness on thy face has seized.
Thy eyes, two suns, the lodging place of love,
Which yet for tents to warlike Mars did serve,
Locked up in lids (as fair day's cheerful light
Which darkness flies) do winking hide in night.
 Antonie by our true loves I thee beseech,
And by our hearts [that] sweet sparks have set on fire,
Our holy marriage, and the tender ruth
Of our dear babes, knot of our amity: 250
My doleful voice thy ear let entertain,
And take me with thee to the hellish plain.
Thy wife, thy friend: hear Antony, O hear
My sobbing sighs, if here thou be, or there.
[I] lived thus long, the winged race of years
Ended I have as destiny decreed,
Flourished and reigned, and taken just revenge
Of him who me both hated and despised.
Happy, alas too happy! if of Rome
Only the fleet had hither never come.   260
And now of me an image great shall go
Under the earth to bury there my woe.
What say I? where am I? O Cleopatra,
Poor Cleopatra, grief thy reason reaves.[17]

---

[17] robs.

No, no, most happy in this hapless case,
To die with thee, and dying thee embrace:
My body joined with thine, my mouth with thine,
My mouth, whose moisture burning sighs have dried:
To be in one self tomb, and one self chest,
And wrapt with thee in one self sheet to rest.   270
The sharpest torment in my heart I feel
Is that I stay from thee, my heart, this while.
Die will I straight now, now straight will I die,
And straight with thee a wandering shade will be,
Under the Cypress trees thou hauntst alone,
Where brooks of hell do falling seem to moan.
But yet I stay, and yet thee overlive,
That ere I die due rites I may thee give.
  A thousand sobs I from my breast will tear,
With thousand plaints thy funerals adorn: 280
My hair shall serve for thy oblations,
My boiling tears for thy effusions,
Mine eyes thy fire: for out of them the flame
(Which burned thy heart on me enamored) came.
  Weep, my companions, weep, and from your eyes
Rain down on him of tears a brinish stream.
Mine can no more, consumed by the coals
Which from my breast, as from a furnace, rise.
Martyr your breasts with multiplied blows,
With violent hands tear off your hanging hair,   290
Outrage your face: alas! why should we seek
(Since now we die) our beauties more to keep?
  I spent in tears, not able more to spend,
But kiss him now, what rests me more to do?
Then let me kiss you, you fair eyes, my light,
Front seat of honor, face most fierce, most fair!
O neck, O arms, O hands, O breast where death
(Oh mischief) comes to choke up vital breath.
[18]A thousand kisses, thousand thousand more
Let you my mouth for honor's farewell give: 300
That in this office weak my limbs may grow,
Fainting on you, and forth my soul may flow.[19]

---

[18] IV.xv. 20–21. Reminiscent too of *Othello*: V.ii. 358–359.
[19] The translation closes with the notation: "At Ramsbury. 26. of November, 1590." However the play was first printed in 1592.

☐ *Some Sources for Further Study*

1. ETIENNE JODELLE — *Cléopâtra Captive* (1552). The first regular French tragedy, along with Amyot's *Plutarch* the source for Garnier's *M. Antoine;* has the same static Senecan quality as Garnier's play but lacks its intensity of diction.
2. SAMUEL DANIEL — *Cleopatra* (1594). A sequel to the Countess of Pembroke's *Antonie,* similar to hers in style and in static quality.
3. ERNEST SCHANZER (ed.) — *Shakespeare's Appian* (1956). Less influential than in *Julius Caesar,* but contains possible hints for Sextus Pompeius and for Shakespeare's references to Lucius Antonius.
4. JEFFERSON BUTLER FLETCHER — *The Religion of Beauty in Woman* (1911). Essays on the concept of *Amimetobion* in the Italian Renaissance.